On Their Own

On Their Own

WOMEN JOURNALISTS
AND THE AMERICAN
EXPERIENCE IN VIETNAM

Joyce Hoffmann

DA CAPO PRESS

A Member of the Perseus Books Group

Designed by Pauline Brown
Set in 10.5 point Caslon by The Perseus Books Group

Library of Congress Cataloging-in-Publication Data

Hoffmann, Joyce.
  On their own : women journalists and the American experience in Vietnam / by Joyce Hoffmann. — 1st ed.
     p.   cm.
  Includes bibliographical references and index.
  ISBN 978-0-306-81059-6 (alk. paper)
  1. Vietnam War, 1961–1975—Journalists. 2. Women war correspondents—United States—Biography. 3. Women war correspondents—Vietnam—Biography. I. Title.
  DS559.46.H64 2008
  070.4'4995970430922—dc22

                                                          2008006495

Published by Da Capo Press
A Member of the Perseus Books Group
www.dacapopress.com

Da Capo Press books are available at special discounts for bulk purchases in the U.S. by corporations, institutions, and other organizations. For more information, please contact the Special Markets Department at the Perseus Books Group, 2300 Chestnut Street, Suite 200, Philadelphia, PA 19103, or call (800) 810-4145, extension 5000, or e-mail special.markets@perseusbooks.com.

10 9 8 7 6 5 4 3 2 1

FOR DAN

Contents

Introduction

I knew I had met my destiny.
—BARBARA GLUCK

SOUTH VIETNAM WAS no place for a woman. Or so thought the legions of male editors who were at the top of newsroom hierarchies in the mainstream media in the 1950s and 1960s. In fact, many of those men believed that a newsroom was no place for a woman, either. Women, nonetheless, established their ability to cover war in South Vietnam, both on and off the battlefield. Their acts of self-invention evolved in two definable and overlapping waves. Freelance writers in the vanguard were women determined to take for themselves the assignment that male editors were unlikely to give them. The second, later, group was populated by staffers at major news organizations who demanded—often without the gentle touch then still expected of women—a role in covering their generation's biggest story. Although women were slowly becoming more visible in print and broadcast news by the late 1960s, women who wanted to cover the war still had to "fight like hell to get the assignment in Vietnam."

A one-way ticket to Saigon gave would-be war correspondents access to the not-so-secret war being waged in Southeast Asia in the late 1950s and early 1960s. War correspondence was a specialized branch of journalism that was almost exclusively populated by men. That women would attempt to appoint themselves to this mythic male pursuit, in an era that prized conformity—especially for women—above all else was nothing short of astonishing. Beyond the newspaper editors who believed war was a man's business, the military brass blanched at the thought of the female correspondent

1

setting foot in the vicinity of a battlefield. The same mantra that military leaders intoned during World Wars I and II and Korea echoed again during the early years of Vietnam: "You realize we have no facilities for women, ma'am." Worse yet, many of the women's own male colleagues in Vietnam shared the military's dismay at the prospect of women covering war. They appeared to think that women had no place on the battlefield, a place where the twining of courage, fear, hate, and ecstasy created a singular brotherhood in which women had no place. In most American news organizations, women reported on women, and because the lives of women were so circumscribed, they were seldom the subject of serious news coverage. In a memoir of her life as a television journalist, Nancy Dickerson explained how society's conventions pared down women's aspirations. When she was hired as a producer at CBS News in 1954, Dickerson's real aspiration was to be a correspondent, "but this possibility was so far-fetched that I never even asked."

So why, in this white-glove era when women urged their daughters to "be like Jackie," would young women dare think they could cover a war? That so many did augured a generational change that dramatically altered the expectations of American women.

A confluence of shifting social values began to embolden women, and a few did pursue large ambitions. That atmosphere of widening expectations, combined with the singular circumstances of America's advisory role in Vietnam, opened unprecedented opportunities in journalism. The absence of censorship and the American military's liberal media accreditation rules gave women a chance to create their own identities as war correspondents. Staffers in a news organization were required to provide a letter from their employer requesting accreditation. A freelancer needed letters from two news organizations affirming their intention to publish or broadcast the individual's reports. A few surprisingly obscure news operations provided women with the necessary letters, *Goddard College News*, *Iron Age*, and the *Sebine Index* among them. One woman who was accredited on the basis of letters from a small wire service, the *Lithuanian Daily Worker*, and *Maryknoll Magazine* was flabbergasted. "Can you imagine," she said. "With this, I became an accredited war correspondent." A MACV (Military Assistance Command Vietnam) card was a ticket to ride, quite literally. It entitled its holder to free ground and air transportation, free food and shelter on any foray outside Saigon, the use of military press center facilities, and Post Exchange (PX) privileges. The number of women who seized the opportunity to cover their generation's war was astonishing. The fragmentary accreditation files that still exist indicate that 467 women were accredited by the MACV. More than half of that number either worked as secretaries and interpreters or were married to male correspondents assigned to Vietnam. Two hundred and sixty-seven of them were Americans, many of whom made only brief visits to the country. From those accreditation files, scholars have identified approximately 70 women whose print or broadcast stories or newspaper and magazine photographs established them as working journalists in Southeast Asia from the early 1960s until the mid-1970s.

Although women had certainly covered wars as far back as the mid-nineteenth century, their numbers could sometimes be counted in the single digits. In 1846, Margaret Fuller is believed to have become the first American woman to become a foreign correspondent when the *New York Tribune* sent her to Europe. She was an early advocate of women's rights and an intellectual who enjoyed close friendships with the likes of Henry David Thoreau. Together with Ralph Waldo Emerson, an ancestor of the Vietnam-era reporter Gloria Emerson, Fuller had edited the *Dial*, a renowned literary magazine first published in 1840. Fuller wrote from England, France, and finally from Italy, where she covered the Italian revolution until 1849, when all foreigners were ordered out of the country.

Teresa Dean discovered, after being assigned to cover the Dakota Sioux uprisings during the Battle of Wounded Knee in 1891, that her male colleagues were an inhospitable bunch. One historian concluded that the men assigned to cover the Sioux story so resented Dean that they excluded her from a group photograph of correspondents, presumably because they feared that the presence of a woman might raise questions among their editors about just how dangerous this assignment really was.

At the close of the nineteenth century, Anna N. Benjamin was one of several women who covered the Spanish-American War. She vowed to follow American troops to Cuba, "and not all the old generals in the army are going to stop me." The idea that her gender should exclude her from covering the story infuriated Benjamin. "You think it ridiculous my being here; you are laughing at me wanting to go. That's the worst of being a woman," she told a colleague. Working as a freelance writer, she later covered the Philippine Insurrection and the Boxer Rebellion in China for some of America's most prestigious publications: *Frank Leslie's Illustrated Weekly, Outlook,* the *Atlantic Monthly,* and the *New York Tribune.*

Peggy Hull, who had grown up on a farm in Kansas, was the first woman accredited by the War Department to cover the American Expeditionary

Forces in London and Paris. When America later entered World War I, she beseeched editors to send her to France on assignment. When they refused, she paid her own way to Europe where she discovered, just as Teresa Dean had twenty years before, that some colleagues resented her presence. Martha Gellhorn made her reputation as a war correspondent reporting the Spanish Civil War for *Collier's* in the 1930s. Later, she became one of the 127 women who were accredited to cover World War II. Military rules required them to pledge that they would cover "the woman's angle," a promise many of them never kept. Because military regulations placed all battlefield operations strictly off-limits to them, women were also excluded from press briefings until late in the war. But many were undeterred by these rules. Margaret Bourke-White, a *Time-Life* photographer, was the first woman to fly with a U.S. combat mission over enemy territory, on a bombing run over North Africa in 1943. Marguerite Higgins reported on the liberation of Dachau in 1945. In the Pacific, Dickey Chapelle was the first woman to land on Okinawa, to the enormous discomfort of the military and several male correspondents.

Late in that war, many women did get to the front despite the rules. Their collective successes should have opened new opportunities; however, in aftermath of World War II, all but a few women found that the gains they had made were all too quickly reversed. Just as the legions of Rosies, who had spent the war years riveting the machinery of combat, were largely banished from the nation's factories after the war, women journalists were similarly left without a place in the nation's newsrooms. As soldiers returned to their civilian lives, newspapers stopped hiring women. The number of foreign assignments dwindled; some women were fired to accommodate the flood of returning veterans to their respective professions. Many newspaper women who kept their jobs were once again relegated to fashion and society coverage. Even in broadcasting, where growth exploded after the war, women were consigned to the lowliest jobs—at least in the mainstream white press. Some women who had kept America's industrial machine running at peak speed while men were fighting in Europe and the Pacific wanted to keep their jobs. Although they received marginal support from the War Manpower Commission, and even from the occasional editorial, "women were laid off at a rate 75 percent higher than men." Worse still, those who resisted the call to resume their roles as housewives were portrayed as abnormal.

During the Korean War, an era of "massive inequality between the sexes" in America, the number of female reporters was so minuscule that, in fact, their mere presence near the battle lines became a story, as was the case when

Higgins covered the landing of American troops at Inchon in November 1950. The ranks of female war correspondents remained thin through much of the 1960s, and even into the 1970s, in large measure because "they were either flat out denied the opportunity or were so conditioned that they never even thought of going after the big stories of the day." The exception to this general rule—that premier newsroom beats and sometimes even the newsroom itself were off limits to women—was in America's black press. Although society news was a significant component of black newspapers and indeed was considered a choice assignment in some quarters, opportunities open to women ran the full range of newsroom jobs. Ethel Payne was unabashed when an interviewer asked years later why she, rather than a male reporter, was sent to Vietnam by the (male) publisher of the *Chicago Defender:* "Because I was the best writer they had."

If the Vietnam War, as David Halberstam once said, was a war in which the journalists made their reputations and the generals lost theirs, it was also a conflict in which women finally broke the barriers that had kept all but a few of them in women's news. In a parallel observation about journalists in Vietnam, one woman who covered the war said that "Vietnam was a place where men became stars and women got work." In Vietnam, women established that their skills, courage, and fortitude entitled them to be considered for any newsroom assignment. What distinguishes these Vietnam-era journalists from their predecessors who covered earlier wars are their numbers and their success in creating a widespread acceptance of the female war correspondent— both by the military and by newsroom bosses. In the field, however, women had to fight for it. Even when reluctant bosses, some under pressure of lawsuits or official discrimination complaints filed by women, belatedly agreed to assign women to Saigon, they issued specific directives to avoid combat and focus instead only on the human interest side of the war. Among the military, the general rule appeared to be that a willingness to accept women in combat situations was inversely proportional to military rank. Although average GIs generally seemed to welcome women reporters into their midst, the higher their rank the more averse military men were to allow women to join combat operations. One female journalist was refused permission to enter a combat area by an officer who told her that she reminded him of his daughter. Even as late as 1967, when more than a dozen women had been accredited to cover the war, General William C. Westmoreland tried to ban overnight stays by women with the troops during field operations. A group of women reporters banded together to resist that order, arguing that it would so limit their ability to cover the action that it effectively made them useless to their employers. They could not, after all, expect a "special taxi service in and out of the war," they argued. Their fight for access to any story anywhere was one of the major successes women in Vietnam scored for their profession, one that stayed in place long after the war ended.

Remarkably, changing the culture of the military was an easier victory than changing the tradition-bound thinking of the men who oversaw world affairs and the men in charge of America's newsrooms. It was a time when those who made foreign policy "thought women had no place in the world of diplomacy," a view apparently shared by the men in charge of newsrooms. In the post–World War II era, editors took the view that most female correspondents would never earn the confidence of European government officials. By 1968, fewer women worked as foreign correspondents on American newspapers than in the 1930s. In the Vietnam War, the longest holdouts appear to have been the men who ran the country's two major wire services, Associated Press (AP) and United Press International (UPI). Although both organizations routinely purchased the work of female freelancers who had made their own way to Vietnam, they resisted assigning their own female staffers to their Saigon bureaus until late in the war. UPI was the first to send a woman to Vietnam for a long-term assignment in 1970. AP finally made a similar move late in 1972. Women who wished for executive roles in journalism found the old rules remained even more firmly in place. In a declaration made in 1972, the Associated Press Managing Editors Association maintained that women had no aptitude for executive roles.

For the men and women who covered it, the Vietnam War became a new kind of war from which a new kind of war correspondent emerged. Beverly Deepe observed years later that "no U.S. textbooks had been written—in journalism, history, political science or military affairs—to teach anyone how to cover a war such as Vietnam." The strategy textbooks from World War II and Korea were obsolete. The nature of the enemy never had the clarity it had had in Germany and Japan during World War II or in Korea. It was a war without a front, but often fought by the American military as if there were one. Instead, the conflict had all the layered intricacies of the underground bunkers from which the enemy often waged war: hidden entrances, winding passageways, secret purposes, and an amazing capacity for accommodating the most harsh or unexpected circumstance. At any moment, the front might be in South Vietnam's cities, hamlets, hills, or jungles. Battles in South Vietnam could be—and were—portrayed simultaneously as victories and defeats, as with the battle at Ap Bac in 1963 and the 1968 Tet Offensive. American propaganda further confused perceptions of victories and defeats. Contradictory reports in the media muddled the situation. It seemed to Elizabeth Pond, who wrote for the *Christian Science Monitor,* that "correspondents who went to Vietnam with a point of view could always find evidence to support that point of view. Besides, you could write a better story if you had your mind made up." Making sense of Vietnam was far more difficult for those, like Pond, who arrived with an open mind. Margaret Kilgore, sent to Saigon by UPI in 1970, aptly described the complexity of the assignment shortly after her two-year posting ended: "The correspondent assigned to this war must be a political reporter, an expert on tactics, more familiar than many soldiers with a vast assortment of weaponry, a linguist, diplomat, administrator, daredevil and one of the most suspicious, cautious people on earth." No less than their male colleagues, many women wrote the truth as they saw it, even when that reporting contradicted the statements of American's political and military leaders. Journalists who reported what they witnessed endured the displeasure of America's political and military leaders, who often let their views be known to the bosses of those who transgressed. In a stark contrast to the standards of World War II, in Vietnam some journalists questioned the optimistic predictions they heard from American diplomats. In turn, those diplomats and officers made outcasts of the Saigon reporters who asked such questions. South Vietnam's autocratic leaders expelled a number of reporters as well.

Ideologically, the women reporters straddled both sides of the political divide. Indeed, a few resided at the extremes—as did their male counterparts. The hawkish, anti-Communist, bomb-them-back-to-the-Stone-Age mindset of the veteran photojournalist Dickey Chapelle and the arch ideologue Marguerite Higgins stood as a stark counterpoint to the dovish and decidedly antiwar America-is-evil perspectives that developed in Gloria Emerson, who first went to South Vietnam as a freelance writer in 1956 and returned as a resident correspondent for the *New York Times* in 1970. Martha Gellhorn was equally shrill in expressing her antiwar views. For Ethel Payne, an overarching commitment to the civil rights movement made objectivity a distant second in the order of her priorities not only in the stories she wrote about the experiences of America's black soldiers in Vietnam but also in every story she wrote during her long career at the *Chicago Defender.* Other reporters, notably Beverly Deepe, Kate Webb, and Elizabeth Pond, worked diligently to leave no ideological fingerprints in their stories.

Two women who covered the war—Pond and Webb—were captured and held by North Vietnamese forces. Two others—Jurate Kazickas and

Catherine Leroy—were wounded while covering combat. In 1966, Higgins died of a tropical disease she had contracted during a trip to South Vietnam. Dickey Chapelle was the first and today remains the only American woman covering a war to die during a combat operation.[1] Women who went to Vietnam won some of the profession's most coveted prizes: a Pulitzer, several George Polk awards and Overseas Press Club awards, a National Book Award, a Bancroft Prize for History.

These achievements notwithstanding, women who covered the war appear to be overlooked with some regularity, sometimes by fellow journalists and often by historians. During the many years I have spent researching and writing this book, those who asked about the nature of my project responded with what became a familiar refrain: "Oh, were there any women journalists in Vietnam?" or "I didn't know there were any women reporters in Vietnam." Not only did women report on the Vietnam War, but they did so in defiance of the constraints their culture imposed on them; in the process, they helped change journalism. Their numbers, their ability to cover the conflict's bewildering permutations, and their perspectives served to widen America's understanding of the conflict, sometimes in ways that men's reporting had not. Indeed, a book reviewer for the *Los Angeles Times* once wondered in print, "Will the Vietnam conflict be the first war recorded better by women than by men?"

Yet if one looks at each of the thousands of Vietnam-era books as a vast tapestry of the long war, few female journalists—indeed sometimes not one—are woven into the scene. When such women do capture the attention of authors, those references are likely to demonstrate the bemusement or dismay with which some male journalists beheld their presence in Vietnam. For example, Beverly Deepe's "more generous curves of the Western world" appear to be of greater interest to Richard Tregaskis than the quality of her work. Michael Herr's celebrated book *Dispatches* described the "girl reporters" who watched the war from a downtown Saigon rooftop bar and declared that Western women, if left too long in Southeast Asia, invariably grew "bored, distracted, frightened, unhappy." Even later in the war, when assigning a woman to Vietnam became more commonplace, the North Vietnamese and Viet Cong, who, under the terms of the Paris Peace Accords, established an official base in Saigon, welcomed the "lovely female journalists" who sought to interview them. One male war correspondent appears to have only

---

1. Elizabeth Neuffer of the *Boston Globe* died in Iraq in 2003 in a car accident on a drive from Tikrit to Baghdad.

a minimal memory of his female colleagues. "Who was there besides Frankie and Gloria?" asked Stanley Karnow, a correspondent in South Vietnam first for *Time* and *Life* magazines, then for the *Saturday Evening Post,* and later, the author of one of the widely read histories of the war.

In the early years of the war, women entered the press corps' all-male redoubt in Vietnam "at the risk of being humiliated and patronized," according to Peter Arnett. They were often dismissed as husband hunters, war groupies, or thrill seekers who created difficulty for "real" (male) journalists who had a job to do. One male photojournalist dismissed all but a few of these would-be war correspondents as "donut dollies and do-gooders." Only later did Arnett and many of his colleagues acknowledge, a few of them grudgingly, the skill and courage of women who reported on the war.

A touch of irony surrounds the way in which Vietnamese culture was considerably more open to women than American culture was at the time. Vietnamese men appear to have had fewer qualms than some American men harbored about working with women, even though the societal norms, grounded as they are in Confucian values, afforded men a higher status than women. Despite that embrace of these Asian notions of male superiority, women have traditionally assumed a near-equal role in making family decisions, most notably as they relate to household finances. One of the country's most enduring legends is that of the Trung Sisters, and their success, short-lived though it was, in deposing the country's Chinese occupiers in A.D. 39. The sisters reigned for just three years, but the memory of their achievement lingers. In North Vietnam, women played significant roles in the pursuit of independence. Some of the Vietnamese men who worked with American female journalists apparently held them in considerable esteem. Gloria Emerson prized her friendship with Nguyen Ngoc Luong, and he appears to have prized hers. As captives in Cambodia with their bureau chief, UPI's Cambodian employees in Phnom Penh could easily have turned on Kate Webb and secured their own freedom at her expense by labeling her a spy. And perhaps most remarkable of all was Pham Xuan An, who risked exposure and almost certain death to ensure the safe return of Elizabeth Pond after she was captured by the North Vietnamese in Cambodia in 1970. An, who in the aftermath of the war was revealed to have been a North Vietnamese agent, perhaps for the first time reached into his network of connections to secure the release of an American prisoner.

In proving their ability to work on men's turf, women discovered what men had long known—that war can be magnificent and spellbinding. On the battlefields, many women experienced for the first time the alchemy that binds terror, comradeship, and eroticism. For as the Greeks so long ago intuited, there is a peculiar kinship between love and war—passion is a soul mate to violence. That is no doubt why, in Greek mythology, Aphrodite becomes the mistress of Ares, the Olympian god of war. Some women were intoxicated by their battlefield experience and found themselves drawn again and again to the overwhelming fear that combat begets and the shared ecstasy that surviving it creates. For the men and many of the women who spent time in Vietnam, sex was entwined into the experience. The nature of war and the relative youth of so many Americans who went there would, all by itself, have created a sexually supercharged environment. Ernest Hemingway once observed that war takes one to the edge of life itself. For many women who covered the war, Vietnam was both a professional triumph and a love story.

The women who went to South Vietnam were, in many ways, revolutionaries before the feminist revolution of the 1960s formally began. They were part of what one sociologist called "a barely visible cultural rebellion of white, middle-class girls and young women in the 1950s." They pursued a lifestyle that was well outside all the better-worn social grooves. The women who dared, especially in the war's early years, made their individual journeys well before their contemporaries began pursuing equal rights, before activists began demonstrating across America, before women began filing discrimination suits when their demands for equal pay were ignored. The publication of Betty Friedan's bestseller, *The Feminine Mystique,* was still seven years away when Gloria Emerson went to Vietnam in 1956, ten years before the National Organization for Women was established in 1966. Beverly Deepe's arrival in 1962 came a decade before Gloria Steinem cofounded *Ms. Magazine* and women at the *New York Times* organized the Women's Caucus.

Women who went to Vietnam in search of a wider world certainly had a few examples of political activism and professional achievement in 1940s and 1950s America to look to. Margaret Chase Smith, a onetime journalist, was elected to the U.S. Senate in 1949, an office she held for twenty-four years. Anne Morrow Lindbergh had made a mark on aviation history and became a successful writer. Janet Flanner's "Letter from Paris," published in the *New Yorker* for five decades, made her one of America's best-known journalists. Few demonstrations of courage matched that of Rosa Parks in 1955 when she quietly refused to give up her seat on a bus in Montgomery, Alabama. Several women had examples in their own families: Frances FitzGerald's mother was a force in New York City's Democratic politics and became a member of the

U.S. delegation to the United Nations during the Kennedy administration. Dickey Chapelle's aunt was a Manhattan career woman in the 1940s. Emerson's grandmother was an activist in the women's suffrage movement. Martha Gellhorn's mother and grandmother were life-long social activists.

However, the norms of the white middle-class society in which most of these Vietnam correspondents came of age demanded conventional behavior. That meant marriage, children, and a home in the suburbs. It was an era when, as Friedan wrote in her book, "women were still expected to measure their self-worth according to the shine of their kitchen floors and the taste of their tuna casseroles." American society not only undervalued the majority of women who became wives and mothers but also devalued the minority who did not. The social standards of the 1950s, when these women were either growing up or finding their first jobs in journalism, held that any woman who harbored serious professional aspirations was aberrant, even deviant. At least one feminist scholar argues that the strategy of containment American leaders pursued in the face of Communism's perceived threats to democracy had a domestic parallel. The containment of women and minorities existed side by side with an American foreign policy designed to thwart the USSR's visions of world domination.

So how did so many renegades emerge from this consensus-driven, homogenized white world of the 1950s, a world in which the single woman was so often derided as an "old maid" or a "spinster," and score such successes? How did this generation of women, raised as many of them were by mothers who saw a daughter's future in the only endeavor society countenanced—marriage—did so many successfully flout the limits placed on them? Naturally, independent-minded people will chafe at restraints. But also, the culture of affluence, the same culture that worked to keep these women straitjacketed, unwittingly helped foster larger ambitions. Thanks to advertising's depiction of lives in which every wish could be realized, girls and young women received the contradictory message of a limitless horizon, a sense that they deserved fulfillment. Television, with its sense of immediacy, heightened that message and enlarged those desires. An obvious chasm separated a woman's position in society from what some women perceived as their potential. But it is improbable that any of the women who reported on the Vietnam War ever sorted out these forces that shaped their lives.

It is noteworthy that the women in this Vietnam narrative did not think of themselves as feminists and had little to do with the women's movement. Indeed, a few vehemently rejected women's liberation. Emerson, for example, said that although she understood "the immense value of the movement," which she had first known in England, she "could not bear the poster SAVE OUR SISTERS IN DA NANG." On the scale of values that she developed during the years she spent covering the war, the preoccupations of feminist leaders ultimately struck her as trivial. Whatever excitement she had perceived in the movement ended in 1971 after she spent an evening in the company of Germaine Greer in Saigon. "She was witty, wonderfully bright, very talkative," Emerson recalled. But her patience ran dry when Greer expressed consternation about a sign she had seen near a group of Vietnamese women filling sandbags in Long Binh. "Men at Work" it read. The war Emerson witnessed every day made it difficult for her to muster sympathy for those "oppressed" sisters in the movement. Oppression for her had a different order of magnitude, one reflected in her encounter with a young GI who tried to hand her a .45 revolver during a North Vietnamese ground attack in Khe Sanh. "In that lonely moment I became more equal with men than I have ever cared to be. I would have gladly shared the horror of it with the fiercely fashionable advocates of women's lib," Emerson wrote.

The story of women who covered America's war in Vietnam with pads and pens or microphones and cameras is essentially a story of how the female war correspondent was transformed from a novelty into the norm. Each of the women whose story is told in the chapters that follow wrote her own script, and in so doing invented a path for others to follow.

Collectively, they established the ability of female journalists to leap beyond the human interest side of war, the one side of war they were routinely allowed to cover when they were allowed to cover war at all. Vietnam, unlike the American wars that had preceded it, provided the opportunity for any woman to demonstrate that she could bring the necessary imagination and professional skill to the gamut of stories that war correspondence required. On the pages that follow, the history of how women demonstrated their ability to report on every side of the conflict, from the savagery and spectacle of battlefield engagements to the subtlest nuances of peace negotiations, is told in the connected and overlapping biographies of women who helped to shape perceptions of the longest war in American history.

In fiction, characters meet circumstance and reveal their inner nature in how they face that circumstance. This Vietnam story, too, is a story about characters and circumstance, how characters aggressively sought out circumstance and were transformed by it. Each of the biographies that unfolds in these pages tells a story of war and a story of society in transformation. Because women, sometimes in substantial numbers, covered every phase of the war, this book uses the chronology of the conflict to establish their place on the landscape of its history.

No one book can properly honor the dozens of women who went to Vietnam to report on the war, nor does this book presume to be the definitive work on this subject. The choice of women whose stories are told here is a product of subjective judgments based on my appraisal of the extent to which the women helped to shape American perceptions of the conflict and put their own stamp on the telling of events. Collectively, they incorporate a broad range of news outlets and represent a cross section of the ambitions and impulses that took women to Vietnam. In addition, each woman embodies a larger dimension or deeper truth about American culture and history in the narrative of the Vietnam experience. Although a claim might be made that certain omissions are a disservice to noteworthy women, the depth with which these stories are told required a measure of selectivity.

Each of the women who is the primary focus of a chapter in this book tells a rich and unique story about the American experience in Vietnam. Gloria Emerson, who went to South Vietnam in 1956 determined to establish herself as a freelance writer, came away with an apparent sense of responsibility for what she perceived as the country's backward people. Her first trip to Southeast Asia apparently convinced her that the Vietnamese could and should be enlightened and uplifted by the West. That conclusion, of course, mirrored her own government's post–World War II notion that America knew what was best for the rest of the world. The photojournalist Dickey Chapelle is a prototype of American hubris writ small: proud, unwavering in her rigid patriotism, convinced that America had a right, indeed a responsibility, to define the world order in the face of Communist threats. The war and the American fighting man were her exclusive focus. The only Vietnamese who interested her were those who embraced the fight against Communism. Her end came in 1965 when she died on maneuvers with the U.S. Marines. In the decade between her death and America's graceless exit from Southeast Asia, the nation's hubris was sorely wounded, too. Frances FitzGerald is a portrait of the intellectual rebellion that gripped many men and women of her generation. She rebuffed not only the systems that her family had valued and nurtured for generations but also questioned the uses to which American leaders put her father's work as a top official in the Central Intelligence Agency.

In some instances, women declined to be interviewed for this book. Gloria Emerson, for one, who died in 2004, said in 1997 that she was loath to revisit this time in her life, most particularly the two years she spent in Vietnam as a resident correspondent for the *New York Times*. She did not give interviews, she said, and insisted that she seldom spoke of the war. She described those years as "such a dark and powerful and terrible thing in my life." She had buried those memories, she said in a letter, and was emphatic in her wish not to have them recalled by anyone. In an early effort to discourage this project, she wrote of her "hope [that] you will turn to a different time, perhaps women correspondents in later wars (Bosnia comes to mind)." In a later letter, she declared, "There isn't any way for you to understand those years in Vietnam." Yet because her Vietnam experiences stand like a set of bookends around the story of America in Southeast Asia, any book about female correspondents in Vietnam would be incomplete without her. Thus, the biographical information and material about her 1956 trip to Vietnam in chapter 1 and her work for the *New York Times* in Chapter 7 were assembled from primary-source research and extensive reading. FitzGerald, another key character for anyone who aspires to tell the story of women and journalism in Vietnam, is, like Emerson, in a league of her own. For both women, Vietnam sometimes bordered on an obsession, one that absorbed their lives and forever defined their intellectual personas. Emerson and FitzGerald both became shapers of America's accepted wisdom on the war through their award-winning books. FitzGerald's *Fire in the Lake* and Emerson's *Winners & Losers* are considered essential reading for students of the Vietnam conflict.

The other women whose work is celebrated here may be less well known, but nonetheless left an important mark on journalism history. Chapelle and Liz Trotta of NBC News made the battlefield their specialty. Beverly Deepe, who covered the war from 1962 to 1969, first as a freelancer for *Newsweek* and later for the *New York Herald Tribune* and the *Christian Science Monitor,* was as adept at unraveling the political intrigues in Saigon as she was at covering battle. To my regret, Deepe also declined to be interviewed, saying that she intends someday to write her own memoir. Kate Webb's gripping reports of the Tet Offensive and its aftermath for United Press International made her one of the war's most respected correspondents. Later, she covered Cambodia with equal distinction. Laura Palmer, who became a radio news reporter in Saigon and was one of the last Americans to leave in April 1975, made her most lasting imprint on the Vietnam experience in her 1987 book about the people behind the mementos left at the Vietnam War memorial.

Some women, particularly Marguerite Higgins, played a large role in the context of Vietnam, but because both she and others have told her story before, she receives limited attention here. Still another group of noteworthy women become part of this story because their lives and their work intersected with those of the main characters. Although they appear here in what can be construed as cameo roles, this in no way diminishes the significance of women such as Peggy Durdin, Jill Krementz, Martha Gellhorn, Catherine Leroy, Ethel Payne, Pamela Sanders, Elizabeth Pond, Flora Lewis, Edith Lederer, and Tad Bartimus.

Inside their profession in the 1960s, these women and others were sometimes demeaned as "newshens." However, each woman had a sense of self that transcended those affronts. The worlds in which these women came of age, their diverse family history and backgrounds, their childhoods, their education, their professional lives, and yes, their romances, too, tell us something about the war and about America. Collectively, they demonstrated a keen sense of women's dignity, freedom, and ambition. These women were intuitive and restless, originals in an era that supplied few high-profile role models. They were iconoclastic in the roles they chose for themselves.

For many of them, Vietnam was a defining event that forever framed their lives. The experience stood as an affirmation of their ability to conquer fear, to achieve professional success, and to claim a place in what had until then been a man's world. Their decisions to go to Vietnam sometimes startled family and friends, and sometimes themselves as well. Some of these women look back on the lives they led with a touch of wonder: "I rather marvel at it myself now," Pamela Sanders once said of the decision to make her way to Indochina and work as a journalist. "I don't know what possessed me." Not only did the war demarcate events that had gone before from everything that came after in each of their lives, but, for many of them, it also became the foundation on which their intellectual and emotional existence rested. Perhaps the best description of Vietnam's impact on so many of the women who reported on the war comes from Barbara Gluck, who went to South Vietnam in May 1968 on what she expected to be a three-week vacation with her beau, the *New York Times* correspondent Joseph Treaster (whom she later married). The next step in her life became clear in a matter of hours. Gluck decided to abandon her career in advertising and telephoned New York's Young & Rubicam agency to say she was canceling her return flight. Saigon had quickly trumped the appeal of her job as a special assistant to Y&R's president and the glamour of spearheading its "I Love New York" advertising campaign. Recalling that moment years later, Gluck explained her resolve: "I knew I had met my destiny."

1

Staring Back
into Another Time

The whole thing was quite remarkable.
—JOHN MONTEITH GATES JR.

S HE HAD ALL the manners of a Vassar girl. Nearly a half century later, that
was how John Monteith Gates Jr., a handsome Harvard-educated spy, remembered his first encounter with Gloria Emerson, a fashion writer and
sometime model, at a Manhattan cocktail party late in 1955. She was an alluring presence, and, as Gates recalled, "the chemistry must have been fairly
instantaneous." Although many details were lost on the blurry edges of his
memory, Demi, as he was known among family and friends, conjectured that
one of Emerson's outrageous quips had drawn his eyes to hers that night. He
soon learned that cheeky and spontaneous asides were a trademark of her often brittle character. That air of spontaneity, however, was probably contrived.
Glo-Glo, as Gates soon nicknamed her, was an ever-restless spirit who invariably used a strategy. It is unlikely that she imagined her casual banter with
this Social Register sophisticate would soon lead her to Southeast Asia, or
that South Vietnam would not only become her center of gravity but would
also remain so for the rest of her life.

Emerson, who loved mischief, met Gates, an incorrigible flirt, just weeks before he departed for some vaguely defined mission in Southeast Asia. They soon became a highly combustible couple. She was a dramatic presence: She wore her glossy, black shoulder-length hair in a pageboy and she painted her manicured fingernails a carmine red. She was comfortable in her lanky, six-foot frame. In her blue eyes, Gates found mystery. And Emerson was equally beguiled by him. He could make her laugh. In keeping with the traditions of his social class, he had followed his father to St. Paul's and Harvard. His humor and his bravado caught and held her for years. Both were in their mid-twenties then, back when few Americans had even heard of a country named Vietnam, back when the war to come was still distant and largely unforeseen.

In Gates, friends say, Emerson found romance in just the kind of WASP-ish, Groton-Yale type to which she was unfailingly attracted. As a member of New York's young society set, he played a role that in an earlier decade might have been scripted by F. Scott Fitzgerald. He was tall, his eyes were blue, and and his voice was a baritone as mellow as a sip of oak-aged port. He spoke French and Spanish, and he had spent two years working for the CIA in Spain. Encouraged by little more than their evanescent acquaintance in New York and what Gates called one or two of his benign "hello-how-are-you letters" written after his return to South Vietnam, Emerson grabbed at the opportunity to chase her professional ambitions, to slake her lust for adventure and, yes, to follow her heart. Like so many journalists—both male and female—who later covered the war, for Emerson, South Vietnam was also a love story.

As a matter of record, Gates served as a lieutenant in the U.S. Marine Corps and was later assigned to a Central Intelligence Agency operation in South Vietnam. During his brief leave in 1955, when he met Emerson, Gates was demobilized by the Marines and was preparing to return to South Vietnam as a civilian. There he was to continue the clandestine operations he had started in March of that year. The demobilization subterfuge was linked to America's apparent determination to obey the letter, though not the spirit, of the Geneva Accords, which limited the number of U.S. military personnel stationed in South Vietnam. Gates and his work embodied all the murky convolutions that flourished in so many of America's cold war undertakings in Third World countries during the 1950s—the combination of which doubtless made him all the more attractive to Emerson. But Gates, who was still enlivened by the memory of Emerson's magnetism decades later, had perceived the affair as something of a fling, a passion-filled but fleeting romance that had occupied his days before he went off to serve his country in a new kind of war. Never, ever, did Gates imagine that this glamorous young woman would, in the coming months, forsake her job at the New York *Journal-American* and arrive unannounced on his doorstep in Saigon. In doing so, she was the first of many aspiring journalists who landed in Vietnam on the wings of ambition and romance.

Other young female writers had preceded her, to be sure. The author Mona Gardner had written fiction and nonfiction accounts of her travels in Asia during the late 1930s, including a 1939 book about Vietnam, *The Menacing Sun*. The journalist Charlotte Ebener arrived in Hanoi in December 1946 just after a guerrilla uprising in which the Vietnamese had "massacred every French citizen in sight." When she arrived, the city was virtually under siege despite the assurances from a French official who insisted, "Hanoi is completely safe now." Renewed Viet Minh attacks began on the evening Ebener went to dinner at the home of the American vice-counsel. They took shelter in the basement. In her 1955 memoir, *No Facilities for Women*, Ebener recalled that fifty-six hours passed before the shelling subsided and she felt it was safe to return to her hotel. Another gifted writer, Peggy Durdin, wrote about Vietnam in the late 1940s and 1950s for the *New York Times*, the *New Yorker*, and the *Nation*. But unlike those women, who were veteran travelers and accomplished writers, Emerson went to South Vietnam, as she later wrote, "wanting to be a journalist and not knowing how you do it." Demi Gates gave her the chance to try.

In later years, Emerson described her decision to flee the women's pages and set off for South Vietnam as "the most significant choice" she had ever made. She and the dozens of women who followed her found the stock stories assigned to female journalists in the 1950s and 1960s unfulfilling. The all-male hierarchy in American newsrooms functioned as a firewall to close off access to the profession's most challenging beats. Covering the New York City fashion scene as a fledgling young writer at the *Journal-American*, her first serious job in journalism, promised to stifle rather than stoke her aspirations. Stories about the latest trend in ladies' pumps written—according to the dictates of *Journal* policy—under a pseudonym, would surely suffocate her talents and deaden her dreams. The fifth-floor newsroom, with its spittoons, cigar-chomping rewrite men, and foul fish odors wafting in from the nearby Fulton Fish Market, was a highly unlikely milieu for this gifted and well-bred young descendant of Ralph Waldo Emerson. For Emerson, and for so many of her colleagues, the charms of the *Journal*'s raucous atmosphere in the mid-1950s were doubtless far sweeter in memory than they were in reality. The New York flagship of William Randolph Hearst's publishing empire, housed in an imposing yellow sandstone building amid the decaying tenements on Manhattan's South Street waterfront, was considered by many of its newsroom employees "a great place to leave."

In abandoning the Hearst society pages for all the unknowns of Saigon, Emerson thumbed her nose at the fundamental message newspaper society pages across the country had framed for their readers in the 1950s: A woman's greatest fulfillment came from her roles as wife and mother, and smart women, one society wag said, "don't go off the deep end about world affairs." But Emerson did. Just as Dorothy Thompson had set off for Paris in 1919 with little more than her talent and ambition, Emerson ventured east to a little-known city then considered "the Paris of the Orient." Thompson established herself as the first lady of American journalism and was heralded as one of the country's most influential women by *Time* in 1939. A long-time colleague who worked with Emerson in those years recalled, "She could not have known how exciting it would be."

The circumstances of Emerson's first journey to Southeast Asia, the conditions under which she labored as a would-be journalist once she got there, and her limited success in interesting editors in her work are a measure of the resistance that women of talent encountered in their efforts to establish themselves as foreign correspondents, and, later, as war correspondents. Emerson lacked credentials, to be sure, but news organization culture in the 1950s withheld from women the opportunities that qualified male reporters for those jobs. Emerson's first Vietnam adventure made a barely traceable mark on her profession—several agate lines in the 1956 and 1957 editions of *Reader's Guide to Periodical Literature* provide the only vestiges. Her first article, about a public health enterprise called Operation Brotherhood, appeared in the *Rotarian* and the *Reader's Digest*. The other, an article in *Mademoiselle*, described the lives young Americans led in Saigon. When she returned to Saigon in 1970, this time as a resident correspondent for the *New York Times*, she brought along all those memories that, together with her intuition and talent, produced some of the war's most memorable stories.

No less than America itself, Gloria Emerson became a casualty of the country's longest war. She once insisted that she declined requests for interviews about the war because "the prospect appalls me." Her impressions and memories from those years, she insisted, were now "so deeply embedded or erased to save myself that I would be of no help at all." In a parallel with America's own seduction in South Vietnam, Emerson discovered a place that would first enchant her and then, for decades, vex her. The enchantment came in 1956, when she found a people and a country that could be enriched by her own generosity of spirit and by America's beneficence. Back then, she still believed that the American model could and should be exported around the world. The vexation came in 1970, when she returned to find that the wider war America was waging in the name of democracy had inflicted enormous suffering on the people who had once so charmed her. The fighting not only had transformed Vietnam's bucolic landscape but also had sundered its social order. For Emerson, South Vietnam in the early 1970s, with its tableau of injustice and torment, was a land that perfectly matched her often melancholy temperament. David Halberstam thought she seemed more at ease during those years than at any other time in their acquaintance. With her high-strung temperament and supercharged RPM, Halberstam said, Emerson's work in Vietnam appeared to give her a purpose. "I think she seemed healthier when she was covering Vietnam [in the 1970s]. Everything fused together into a real cause."

But in 1956, through her association with Demi Gates, Emerson stood on the sidelines during some of the earliest and most secret American operations in Southeast Asia. She cemented friendships with the men whose names are etched in the history of America's fate in South Vietnam. The war she witnessed in 1956 was so secretive and furtive that, from the outside, it hardly looked like a war—at least not the kind Dickey Chapelle had witnessed during World War II and Marguerite Higgins had seen in Korea. Although occasional street violence in the mid- to late 1950s, most often alleged to be the handiwork of Viet Cong insurgents, foretold the future, the real war was being fought behind the scenes by Demi Gates and his CIA associates.

Gates joined the CIA soon after graduating from Harvard, where he had been a member of ROTC. He wanted action and chose the CIA rather than the Marines because he thought the agency offered him more effective ways to fight communism than traditional military service. It had pained him in the mid-1940s, just as it had so many other young men, that he had been too young to enlist and see action before World War II ended. "Just my awful luck," he fumed years later. Moreover, he had just the kind of Ivy League, old-money pedigree the agency then sought in its recruits. His mother, Ellen Crenshaw Houghton, was a friend of the journalist Joseph Alsop, a man who shared Eleanor's devotion to good manners and family bloodlines. Alsop was a frequent visitor through much of Gates's childhood. Ellen Gates was, according to her son, "a rabid [Francisco] Franco supporter" who gave the generalissimo money to buy ambulances in the late 1930s during the Spanish Civil War. Through his mother's Spanish friends, Gates successfully camouflaged his first CIA assignment when he was dispatched to Spain under deep cover. With great elan, Gates played the role of an irresponsible dilettante from the New World who was indulging himself in Europe's Old World enchantments. He had a Spanish tailor make him twenty suits; he partied at the city's fashionable nightclubs. In Madrid, he set up a small printing company that published anti-Communist Spanish-language comic books for readers in South America. After the CIA pulled the financial plug on his comic book operation late in 1954, Gates joined America's growing commitment to South Vietnam in the spring, when he was assigned to the Saigon Military Mission. By year's end, he was reassigned to the U.S. Department of Defense in yet another cover for the secret work he would continue to perform in Saigon.

Emerson, like so many other friends and associates, soon learned—or at least suspected—that Gates's military rank, like his new Defense Department post, veiled certain secrets. Although the general nature of his job was clear to friends and family, the rules of the game in that cold war era required that the only acknowledgment of his work be communicated through a knowing wink or a passing nod. As his younger brother, Peter Gates, recalled many years later: "He was very close-mouthed. We basically didn't discuss what he was doing. But I knew he was in the company." All of which made Gates an incomparably dashing and romantic figure. And Emerson, according to friends, was smitten. "He was the great love of her life," according to more than one friend. In her memoir, Emerson explained Gates's appeal: "An original and romantic man of a certain impeccable Eastern background."

But beyond Gates's magnetism, Emerson's own ambition and daring propelled her to Vietnam. Family models surely influenced her also: Emerson wrote in her memoir that her trip to Vietnam was inspired by her widely traveled grandmother, Bessie Benson Emerson, whose global adventures were noted on the society pages of her hometown newspaper in western Pennsylvania. The *Titusville Herald* described Mrs. Emerson as "a woman of exceptional cultural attainments." She was an early leader in the women's suffrage movement and a member of the Titusville Political Equality Club, associations that reflected a tradition of political activism stretching back to ancestors who emigrated from England in the seventeenth century. An expansive family genealogy compiled by one of Gloria Emerson's nephews establishes that her Benson and Emerson forebears had left England in the 1600s and established themselves in New England through the acquisition of substantial land grants. Erudition and truculence were also part of Emerson's heritage. Her distant cousin, four generations removed, the poet and philosopher Ralph Waldo Emerson, was described by one social historian as a man who "both typified and defined the cultured person for mid-nineteenth-century Americans." Her great-grandfather was another, lesser known, nineteenth-century man of distinction. After America's first oil well was drilled in Titusville in 1859, Byron D. Benson ranked among the wiliest characters involved in early oil explorations. His daring schemes and his dumpy stature led contemporaries to call him "the Napoleon of the oil region." The title was hardly an overstatement; after all, he dared to get the best of John D. Rockefeller Sr. Defying the many predictions of failure, Benson led a group of businessmen who built a 109-mile pipeline to carry oil to a distribution point beyond Rockefeller's control. Thus, in one brazen move, Benson broke Rockefeller's stranglehold on the distribution of Pennsylvania crude. It was a breathtaking triumph over America's first oil titan, a man whose unsavory business practices had bankrupted many a lesser man. In 1883, after fighting Rockefeller's every move to thwart his pipeline project, Benson accepted Standard Oil's offer of $5.5 million for a controlling interest in the Tide Water Pipeline Company. The deal, which gave Standard Oil 88.5 percent of the pipeline's capacity, established the Benson family fortune.

A combination of the refinement and deep thinking of Ralph Waldo Emerson together with the tenacity and daring so evident in Byron Benson came to life in Gloria Emerson, who was born on May 29, 1929. She once wrote that she was never quite sure to which social class she belonged. "It was a great jumble," Emerson later said. Ruth Shaw, her mother, was an "Irish chorus girl" who performed among the anonymous dancers in vaudeville spectaculars, a career she abandoned in the mid-1920s when she married William B. Emerson, the grandson of Byron Benson and the youngest of Charles and Bessie Emerson's five sons. In a conversation with her friend Charlotte Salisbury, Emerson characterized her father as "a rich man who inherited lots of Tide Water shares." Writing about men and their fears in a 1973 *Esquire* article, Emerson revealed that her father told her he liked wearing blue shirts on his daily treks to Wall Street during the early months of the

Great Depression. "He must have thought that Tide Water shares would not sink as long as he did," she commented.

Demi Gates remembers William Emerson as an unattractive "stage-door Johnny" who wasted his life on alcohol. Indeed, both of Emerson's parents appear to have become hopeless alcoholics as she grew up. More than once she told Gates that her mother and father occasionally soaked their corn flakes in gin at breakfast time. He believed her. When Ruth Emerson died of liver disease, Emerson told a confidant that it was "quite a relief." In response to a questionnaire Barbaralee Diamonstein sent to dozens of prominent American women in 1970 in connection with her book *Open Secrets,* Emerson said that her mother, as an alcoholic, "was oppressed—by herself."

One of Emerson's longtime friends drew a parallel between her and the young Jacqueline Bouvier in that both their fathers were self-indulgent wastrels whose daughters paid a considerable price for their fathers' deeply flawed characters. Bouvier, who in later years became Emerson's friend, ultimately derived her status through her mother's second marriage to Hugh D. Auchincloss, a man of wealth and social standing. But no altruistic stepfather entered Emerson's life. Her mother died in 1951, when Emerson was twenty-two. And her father, described by the same friend who drew the Jackie parallel as "the bent twig" in an old-line family, remarried—twice.

The Emersons lived on East 85th Street in Manhattan during Emerson's childhood. Unlike many other girls whose families had inherited wealth, Emerson attended Manhattan's public schools—P.S. 86 on Manhattan's Upper West Side and, later, Washington Irving High School, an all-girls public school. During Emerson's high school years, Washington Irving's curriculum in fashion design, nursing, music, and theater drew girls from all of New York City's five boroughs, including the daughters of immigrants who lived in the tenements of the Lower East Side. The school's alumnae rolls include the doll maker Madame Alexander, the fashion designer Norma Kamali, and the actresses Claudette Colbert and Sylvia Sydney.

Emerson's gifts as a writer are apparent in the poetry and prose she wrote for the *Sketchbook,* the high school's literary journal. In it she revealed an unquiet spirit. In poetry, she was drawn to the same images and ideas that have transfixed poets throughout the ages—the "long cold fingers of the November wind" and the "smiling crescent moon." In a brief verse she titled "Rebellion" she wrote of wanting to climb where the gulls fly, "And scoop a cloud up in my pocket / And beat my fists against the sky." Her prose, more fanciful than her poems, revealed an early gift for storytelling. Her ability to bind elements of character, scene, and narrative are obvious in a whimsical tale she titled "I Am Introduced to Noel Coward." As the autobiographical narrative unfolds, Gloria portrays herself as a twelve-year-old with distinct likes and dislikes. "I hated prunes, starched middies, and lavender handkerchiefs. On the other hand I adored Franchot Tone, green hair ribbons, and rice pudding." To instruct her in the subtleties of prose and elocution, her parents hired a drama coach, Miss Zaggora, a shrill and melodramatic crone who insinuated herself into the freckle-faced girl's life and removed her from a preoccupation with comic books and a passion for the Lone Ranger. On visits to the Emerson household, Miss Zaggora peered down Gloria's throat as she recited the Girl Scout oath. "My childish instincts told me Miss Zaggora was a ham," Gloria wrote. When this ham discovered, to her great horror, that GLA-(pause)RIA, as she called her pupil, had never heard of America's leading dramatist, Noel Coward, Miss Zaggora declared that this appalling void had to be remedied forthwith. Miss Zaggora, who worshiped Coward, initiated a ritual of reciting his plays. With William Emerson at the office, Ruth Emerson never home, and Lillian, the maid, deaf, Emerson lamented that she alone was left to endure the torture of her drama coach's recitations.

Demonstrating that even as a youthful writer she had a keen eye for the dramatic, Gloria's story reaches its climax with the unexpected arrival of Ruth Emerson at the very moment Miss Zaggora recited the line "Darling, you know I am living with . . ." Horrified that her daughter was being exposed to such an unsavory side of life, Ruth Emerson tore the script from Miss Zaggora's hand and banished her on the spot. Joyfully, Gloria returned to the company of the Lone Ranger, but she maintained an enduring affection for Noel Coward, whose raciness had delivered her from the clutches of her drama coach. Coward became her secret idol: "I felt like writing him and thanking him for freeing me of Miss Zaggora. But, somehow, I never did," her essay concludes.

Classmates remember Emerson as bright, highly opinionated, and daring enough to argue with the teachers. A few were awed that she could claim Ralph Waldo Emerson as an ancestor. She was popular, sometimes witty, but she also showed an intensity that her classmates recalled more than half a century later. Frances Burnett remembered Emerson as rebellious and politically involved. "She was never that friendly or happy-go-lucky," said another friend who followed her career. "I remember her as serious." Her classmates cannot remember seeing her at the senior prom, where they all danced the jitterbug or the swing. Nor did she join the long lines of girls outside the Paramount The-

ater, where her star-struck contemporaries waited for hours to see Frank Sina-
tra. To them, Emerson seemed like a type who would rather spend Saturday
afternoons in Greenwich Village's storefront political clubs where the ideological gamut ran from the Young Republicans to the Trotskyites. Emerson and
her classmate Maybelle Lum twice competed for positions on the student
council. "We used to get up and make speeches and campaign and all that
stuff," Lum recalled. By the time she graduated in 1946, Emerson had been
president of her senior class, an editor of the school's literary magazine, and
had earned membership in the school's honor society by virtue of her solid
B-plus average. That Emerson later quit her job and set off, a decade after
graduation, for a little-known Asian country on the basis of a tenuous acquaintance with a young spy hardly surprised Frances Burnett or Josephine Rey.

Hints of Emerson's capacity for brooding and of her outsized ambitions
are evident in her yearbook. She looks utterly downcast in her photograph, an
image that was accompanied by a brief text that set her far apart from almost
all her 675 classmates. Compared to the tightly corseted futures her peers envisioned, Emerson's goal sounded almost egomaniacal. There were, to be sure,
a few seniors who anticipated careers as accountants, bacteriologists, or even
doctors, but most of her classmates foresaw more prosaic lives as telephone
operators, salesgirls, and housewives. Alone among these hundreds of young
women, Gloria Emerson declared in 1946 that she wanted to become a senator. That was two years before Margaret Chase Smith, the Maine Republican
who had become a member of the U.S. House of Representatives in 1940,
won election to the U.S. Senate.[1] World War II had been over for less than a
year when Emerson graduated from Washington Irving High. She and her
classmates were entering a "world free from the ravages of air raids and naval
battles," according to the message Mary E. Meade, the school's principal,
wrote in the opening pages of the school's 1946 yearbook. Yet pessimism
seemed to abound, she added, and America's ideals were widely questioned.
Her expectation, Meade said, was that the young women of Washington Irving "will bring to this confused and cynical world the optimism of youth and
the certainty of your faith in our country and its history."

Despite Emerson's large ambitions, her notable academic achievements,
and a yearbook note that indicates she planned to attend Beloit College in
Wisconsin, Emerson's formal education ended when she graduated from

---

1. Although Smith was not the first woman to serve in the U.S. Senate, she was the first woman
elected to both houses of Congress.

Washington Irving. Although some friends and associates declare with certainty that Emerson went to Vassar College—where she is said to have been a classmate of Jacqueline Bouvier—she did not, according to Vassar's registrar's office. Nor did she attend Beloit College, the registrar's office there said. Although her grades would certainly have assured her admission to Smith, Vassar, or Wellesley, the kind of school young women in her Upper East Side neighborhood typically attended, a friend familiar with Emerson's family background conjectured that her father probably could not afford to pay for college.

Journalism, Emerson later claimed, was an accidental profession, one that began when she was twenty-one. She desperately needed a job, she explained in her response to Barbaralee Diamonstein's questionnaire. An opening at *Promenade,* a give-away magazine distributed in certain New York City hotels, marked the beginning of her career in 1951. Her baptism in daily journalism came in 1954 when she joined the women's staff of the *Journal-American.* Curiously, she mentioned the former but ignored the latter in an obituary she wrote about herself in 2004 when, fearing that her emerging symptoms of Parkinson's disease would stifle her ability to write, she made plans to commit suicide.

It's doubtful that the *Journal,* with its "splashy, almost unsightly" appearance, its preoccupation with celebrities, crime, and conservative causes—all of which appealed to its largely Catholic, blue-collar readership—was ever a newspaper of choice in the Emerson household. On its society pages, the *Journal* fed female readers daily doses of what one editor of the day labeled "the dismal arts." Emerson and her colleagues occupied a small, grimy room overlooking the tenements of Lower Manhattan. After a brief turn as an office gofer, Emerson was allowed to cover fashion shows, where she met a fellow fashion writer, Nan Robertson of the *New York Times,* who later became her colleague and long-time friend. Robertson was drawn to Emerson by her wry comments about the clothing paraded before them during fashion shows. "She was such a wildly imaginative person, full of exaggeration and fantasy. She convulsed me," Robertson recalled. Emerson quickly grasped the culture and sociology of fashion: "She understood that fashion was all about illusion and rapid obsolescence. It was about pretense, mystique, and flash," Robertson noted. Paris was the alpha and the omega of the fashion universe, and whether hems were up or down mattered a great deal to certain women in whose social circles, Robertson noted, it was essential never to sail against the fashion winds.

After all the laughs at the fashion shows, Emerson returned to South Street and, using her two-fingered typing system, pecked out the brief texts that accompanied photo layouts of dresses, slacks, coats, sweaters, and gowns. Unlike Robertson's, however, her byline apparently never accompanied those articles. The few *Journal* fashion writers who received bylines were socialites, former models, or the stylish girlfriends of key editors. According to Marylin Bender, management reasoned that *Journal* fashion writers who received bylines might be lured into better-paying jobs in the industry they covered. As a result, most society page staffers never saw their real names in print. Instead, if Emerson wrote about clothing, she was Barbara Bruce; if the subject was beauty, she became Karen March. A reporter who wrote about home furnishings did so as Dorris Morelle.

When her work days ended, Emerson and two other colleagues, Bender and Pat Lewis, hailed a cab and headed to their more genteel Midtown and Uptown neighborhoods. Their male colleagues often made their way to Moochies, a newsroom hangout with sawdust-covered floors and forty-cent boiler makers immortalized by Jimmy Breslin. Dave Anderson, a former *Journal-American* sports writer, summed up its ambiance: "You would never take your mother there." In fact, few of the *Journal*'s women staffers were ever seen in the waterfront dive.

Emerson's friends say her job at the *Journal* marked a time of starting over. She had been working at the newspaper for about six weeks when her husband, Andrew Alexander Znamiecki, whom she had married on May 1, 1954, committed suicide. "They had met somewhere in New York," Demi Gates recalled. "He was a charming man, very social. But he didn't make a go of it in business. She was the breadwinner." Marylin Bender still has a vivid memory of September 10, 1954. As had become their custom, she and Emerson had shared a cab after work. Bender's telephone rang just twenty minutes after she reached home. An editor on the *Journal*'s city desk was calling with the news that Emerson had just found her husband dead on the kitchen floor. In an apparent state of depression, Andrew Znamiecki had put his head in the gas oven.

During the months that followed, her job and the grubby room where the *Journal* women's pages were put together became something of a haven for Emerson, or so it appeared to her friends. There she could amass the experience that might eventually free her from society-page bondage, or at least bring her the same job on a better newspaper. For some staffers, the *Journal*'s meager pay scale was sufficient reason to circulate one's resume. For others, the *Journal*'s judgments about news and its presentation were an added incentive to make a move.

An editorial lust for crime and mobsters was conspicuous on the *Journal*'s pages. Gossip was a coveted commodity, and an adoration for high society leapt from its inside pages. A corral full of conservative columnists served up daily doses of cold war ideology. Otherwise, the *Journal*'s attention to foreign affairs was uneven at best. Its focus on international affairs often amounted to questions such as the one that bedeviled the British monarchy in 1955: "Should Meg Marry Peter?" The *Journal* devoted dozens of column inches to the royal quandary that arose when Princess Margaret, Queen Elizabeth II's sister, sought to marry the divorced Royal Air Force captain Peter Townsend, a desire that placed her heart at odds with her duty to the Crown. The *Journal* offered its readers prizes of $175 for 250-word solutions to the lovers' dilemma.

Beyond the Meg and Peter story, the *Journal*'s nonchalance about foreign affairs was set aside occasionally for William Randolph Hearst Jr.'s anti-Communist editorial rants—often displayed on the front page. International affairs also rated the front page when Hearst the Younger took one of his periodic junkets to distant lands, such as the one that won him a Pulitzer Prize in 1956, the year that Emerson set off for South Vietnam. Perhaps Bill Jr. really believed that his tabloid "kicked the hell out of every other newspaper in the city on a regular basis," as he claimed in his 1991 autobiography. He saw in the *Journal* newsroom a scene from an old-time movie, a place filled with folks who knew "they'd never change the world" and wanted only "to make New York laugh and cry." Hearst wrote that he had never met a *Journal* reporter who wanted to work for the *New York Times*. It's highly doubtful that he ever met Gloria Emerson.

Bender, Emerson's colleague at the *Journal* and later at the *Times,* recalled that before she set off on her trip to South Vietnam in 1956, Emerson tried mightily to interest her editors in buying the freelance stories she hoped to write from Saigon. No evidence exists either in the *Journal* files or in the rec-ollections of her colleagues that she succeeded in having an article from South Vietnam published in that newspaper. The *Journal*'s news editors, all of whom were men, rarely entrusted women with such important beats as politics, crime, and business. Moreover, South Vietnam was receiving little public notice in the 1950s. Even as late as 1964, Americans were paying scant attention to Southeast Asia. A Gallup poll in April of that year asked, "Have you given any attention to the developments in South Vietnam?" The results established that 63 percent of Americans had paid little heed to what by then had become a not-so-secret war. Among the 37 percent who were paying at-tention, there was an indifference and detachment that is perhaps best expressed by a U.S. senator from North Carolina whose own large dairy farms were located near a small mill town called Haw River. During a 1954 debate about American intervention to assist the French at Dien Bien Phu, Senator Kerr Scott declared, "Indochina is a long way from Haw River."

Indeed it was. It was a long way from Manhattan, too. But with few apparent misgivings, Gloria Emerson left New York in 1956; she had a one-way ticket, a few dollars, nowhere to live, and no real understanding of the primitive conditions she would encounter. Like so many of the women who followed her, Emerson audaciously hung her future on a slender thread. Demi Gates had no inkling of her plans. As he insisted decades later, his letters, almost identical to the ones he said he wrote to other women after reaching South Vietnam, had offered her nothing in the way of an invitation. And if she had signaled her intent to join him in Saigon, he surely would have told her, "Don't come." Instead, he woke up one morning and found her sitting on the terrace of the colonial villa where he lived with several CIA associates. As he stood there, flabbergasted, he wondered how she had reached Saigon and whether there were commercial flights into the country. He had flown in twice, and each time he had traveled aboard a military transport.[2]

"She took a real chance," Gates said, still seemingly awestruck decades later. "With no money, no job, and what reliability could she put on some guy like me? The whole thing was quite remarkable." Although America was hardly considered the enemy in those days, all Westerners faced danger in South Vietnam. Remnants of the Viet Minh, soon to be reconstituted and renamed the Viet Cong, routinely staged random attacks on French officials who remained in Vietnam, and Americans were occasionally caught in the crossfire. Anne Westerfield, the wife of a young American diplomat assigned to Saigon, recalled how a hand grenade exploded on the tarmac as she and her husband took their first steps on South Vietnamese soil in 1955. She dropped her four-week-old infant, asleep in a baby carrier, on his head. Yet Westerfield remained undaunted. Although coups, countercoups, and assorted uprisings were commonplace, the attacks targeted only the French who were easily distinguished by their footwear, she recalled. "The French always wore sandals; the Americans always wore white buck shoes." That distinction, and perhaps the naivete of her youth, allowed Anne Westerfield to live without fear.

Danger, however, was hardly the country's only discomfort. To describe the climate as inhospitable is an understatement. The torrential rains of the

---

2. At the time, both Pan American Airlines and Air France made flights to Saigon and Hanoi.

May-to-December monsoon season, averaging from twelve to fourteen inches a month, were interspersed with a heat of such intensity that it felt, as Emerson described it in one of her later stories, as if it had been "painted on." Living conditions in much of the country were harsh. Filth was ubiquitous. The lineup of home-grown Southeast Asian diseases included dysentery and a forbidding assortment of worms—hookworm, tapeworm, roundworm, flatworm—all of which played havoc with Western gastrointestinal systems. Potentially fatal maladies, among them tuberculosis and malaria, were ever present, too. Demi Gates and a few of his CIA cohorts suffered debilitating bouts of hepatitis.

Despite all the torments, Emerson appears to have thrived in South Vietnam. The ideological convictions she took with her, in her own telling, cast her as a believer in America's nobility, a political moderate who said she embraced the nation's strategy of containing Communism. Like Anne Wester-field, she thought America was saving the world. In Emerson's memory, the early 1950s had been a "malignant and frightening" time. "I can still hear the loud, crashing voice of Senator Joseph McCarthy from Wisconsin, as he punched out accusation after accusation against people he claimed were Reds, traitors, dupes and saboteurs," she recalled in her memoir. Although she was never personally touched by the excesses of McCarthyism, the pall it left on the national psyche engendered fears about her own vulnerability. Re-calling those years, Emerson wondered whether her casual friendship with a classmate at Washington Irving High School, a young woman whose parents had been members of the Communist Party in the 1930s, would ensnare her in the same horrors that were destroying so many lives.

Emerson's own opinions on foreign policy and the military were shaped by the World War II newsreels she had watched as a teenager. She had accepted without question America's never-flinch cold war policy. She once said she thought America had a responsibility to "tidy up the world." Why indeed would lesser, developing nations not want to be remade in America's image? She would have had no argument with the thinking that led Senator John F. Kennedy to declare in a 1956 speech, "South Vietnam represents the corner-stone of the Free World in Southeast Asia. It is our offspring. We cannot abandon it, we cannot ignore its needs."

So the work—or at least what she knew of the work—that engaged Demi Gates and his fellow CIA operatives appeared to her to be necessary and noble. Gates was part of a team created by U.S. Air Force Colonel Ed-ward G. Lansdale, a larger-than-life figure who had already shaped the destiny of the Philippines and had come to South Vietnam in 1954 to shape its future in the name of democracy. Lansdale, the former advertising executive who became America's leading authority on counterinsurgency in the 1950s and 1960s, is credited by some historians of the war as having created the nation of South Vietnam. He was dispatched with orders from the Departments of State and Defense "to assist the South Vietnamese in counter guerrilla training and to advise as necessary on governmental measures for resistance to Communist actions." Lansdale's personality blended hubris and naivete with strains of cultural chauvinism about America. His ego convinced him that his will could vanquish Communism in South Vietnam. Once the Geneva Accords had sanctioned the temporary division of the country at the 17th Parallel in 1954, Ngo Dinh Diem was named prime minister under circumstances that still remain obscure. The emperor, Bao Dai, who spent most of his time in France, remained the titular head of the South Vietnamese government. Lansdale quickly ingratiated himself with Diem, the first step in fulfilling his mission. It was a measure of his charisma that Demi Gates and his cohorts behaved as Lansdale's handmaidens in that mission and devoted themselves to him.

Membership on Lansdale's elite team gave a man swaggering rights in those days. Gates and his teammates called themselves the Rover Boys; some of their exploits appeared to combine James Bond–style daring and intrigue with the prankish shenanigans of frat house initiation rites. That some of the Saigon Military Mission's undertakings occasionally had severe and sometimes deadly consequences was later revealed in the Pentagon Papers.

As for the loyalty the group's members felt toward their boss, "if Lansdale had said, 'I want you guys to walk across South Vietnam,' we all would have walked," Gates recalled. Four decades later, Gates still spoke with wide-eyed awe about his first impressions of Saigon in 1955. He had arrived on a flight from Manila with Lansdale's aide, Charles Bohannan. Downtown Saigon was smoldering in the aftermath of an attack on the presidential palace by the Binh Xuyen sect, a crime syndicate that controlled Saigon's gambling and prostitution industries with its own 40,000-member militia. Sections of the city had been destroyed by mortar and artillery fire; civilian and military casualties had climbed into the hundreds, and thousands were left homeless in the house-to-house combat that ensued. Bullet holes pocked the buildings around the presidential palace. The Binh Xuyen militia and South Vietnamese army troops were still exchanging mortar fire around the city when Bohannan and Gates strode into Lansdale's Saigon villa, located about eight blocks from the palace.

Lansdale's "dynamic, piercing eyes" lingered in Gates's memory: "I was shaking like a leaf. I was twenty-five going on thirteen that day. I didn't know what I was supposed to do there." In his customary take-charge manner, Lansdale, who never acknowledged Gates's obvious fear and disorientation, packed Bohannan and Gates off to his staff house at 24 Rue Tabard, where most of his team lived.

All the anxiety Gates had felt during that first encounter with Lansdale quickly turned to adoration. Drawn by Lansdale's magnetism, Gates saw in him a man of high principle and conviction, one who, in different circumstances, "would have been a hero." Lansdale's team of young CIA operatives carried out an assortment of terrorism and sabotage campaigns, trained the South Vietnamese army in paramilitary tactics, nation-building, and psychological warfare. Gates recalled working with Putney Westerfield, William Mellor, Arthur Arundel, Victor Hugo, and Rufus Phillips III, all of whom lionized Lansdale. Emerson soon became a Lansdale admirer, too. He called her Glo-Glo. She called him Ed.

In "Mlle Readers in Saigon," an article published in *Mademoiselle* magazine in March 1957, Emerson wrote what might be the best description of the work of Demi Gates and other Americans in Vietnam in the mid-1950s. Among the Americans featured in Emerson's story were Gene and Ann Gregory, a couple who later became a subject of mystery and controversy. The Gregorys first went to Vietnam in 1952 with the U.S. Information Service and returned several years later on a fellowship from the Ford Foundation to conduct research on Vietnam's village administration. Gene took almost one hundred field trips to the country's remotest reaches; he hoped, according to Emerson, that his studies would shed light on the "intricate social, political and economic structure of a country that [was] just beginning to emerge from feudalism." In the years after Emerson left Vietnam, the Gregorys officially left government service and became part-owners and editors of the *Times of Vietnam,* an English language daily published in Saigon. Considerable speculation surrounded them in the early 1960s when it became clear that their newspaper's meager daily circulation of 3,000 copies could hardly support their increasingly lavish lifestyle. In 1963, *Newsweek* explained to its readers that although Gregory had for years been perceived as "a flabby James Bond, sent to spy on the Nhus," in reality he had been serving their cause and "building a tidy financial empire" in the process. Front page columns in his newspaper were frequently filled with diatribes authored by Ngo Dinh Nhu, the shrill pronouncements of his wife, Madame Nhu, or the criticisms of American newspapermen by American generals. The Gregorys created something of an international tempest in September 1963 when, in a front-page story, the newspaper claimed that "a Nazi-like band of cynical young men" in the CIA was plotting to overthrow the Diem regime. Barely two months later, on the same day that Diem was overthrown and assassinated, the *Times of Vietnam* published its final edition. Its offices were burned shortly after the coup.

Emerson's *Mademoiselle* story about the lives of Americans in Saigon in the mid-1950s also described the work of Putney Westerfield, a Yale man and member of the embassy staff "who is in frequent touch with Vietnamese politicians, journalists and members of the government as well as some foreign correspondents." In his work, Emerson wrote, Westerfield "studies and records the personalities, backgrounds and platforms of Vietnam's political organization. . . . Once a month he goes on field trips to the provinces to make reports or talk to local political leaders." That is precisely what Gates did in his work as a civilian advisor to South Vietnam's Dai Viet Party, which involved "civic action, political warfare, and paramilitary-type training," Gates explained. Emerson's *Mademoiselle* article also depicted how a small group of well-bred, well-educated, and well-married Americans in government service blended their private lives with their official responsibilities. For example, Westerfield and his wife, Anne, "a Vassar girl," lived in a partially air-conditioned "two-terraced house" owned by the U.S. government. Relaxation for the Westerfields was "a vigorous doubles game" played with friends on the tennis courts at the French-built Cercle Sportif, a pillar of French privilege that attracted the Westerfields in the 1950s and, in a later decade, Ambassador Henry Cabot Lodge. At the Westerfield home, three Chinese servants schooled by Anne in Western expectations tended to the family's assorted needs. At their frequent dinner parties, the Chinese cook served salads that "looked positively landscaped," Emerson wrote. Putney poured after-dinner brandy carried in from Hong Kong, and they played the Noel Coward records that had been packed in the thirty-two hundred pounds of possessions U.S. government employees were allowed to bring from home.

During those cloudless years in the late 1950s, it was still possible for the Lansdales, the Westerfields, the Gregorys, Emerson, Gates, and countless others to imagine themselves as guardians and protectors of Vietnam. "We were saving the world," recalled Anne Westerfield about the attitudes of most Americans in Vietnam. "It was all so simple then. We thought we were doing great things." The Rover Boys were but one small initiative in the vast American effort to re-create South Vietnam in its own image. In the countryside, a team of political scientists from Michigan State University taught the South Vietnamese the techniques of public administration; International Voluntary Services workers, a few of whom had actually learned the language that the French had concluded was too difficult to be mastered by the average European adult, were digging wells and building bridges, schools, and hospitals. Workers with the Agency for International Development were teaching farmers crop rotation techniques and advising them on the use of high-productivity seeds. America was lavishing $1 million a day on South Vietnam. The Eisenhower administration expected that money could buy a government in Saigon that would be loyal to America and fulfill its wishes, a government that suited the U.S. need for a stable, democratic foothold in Southeast Asia.

Gloria Emerson began contributing to the establishment of that foothold soon after her arrival. Gates arranged for her to live and work with members of Operation Brotherhood, a Lansdale-inspired, Filipino-run public health organization established with financial support from the CIA. Gates often "scrounged" penicillin and other drugs for the program from the departing French army and gave it to OB doctors. Having discerned a "synergy" between the mission of Operation Brotherhood and Emerson's talents as a writer, Gates suggested she become a volunteer and earn her keep by writing press releases and publicity material trumpeting OB's services. Lansdale, the eternal public relations man, understood the value of the publicity a good writer might garner for the program. So Emerson took up residence with the OB team at 25 Rue Chasseloup-Laubat, a scene she once described as "a cheerful stew." She quickly became a part of the mix that one American visitor likened to "a baby U.N. session" populated, in addition to its Filipino doctors, nurses, and nutritionists, with staff members from France, Japan, Nationalist China, Thailand, Malaya, and the United States. "Because she was my girlfriend," Gates recalled, "they took her in. She became their mascot." OB was billed as the brainchild of Oscar J. Arellano, a Filipino architect and the Asian vice president of the International Junior Chamber of Commerce. Gates remembers him as something of a "charming con artist, who probably skimmed some money from the OB treasury," but who also effectively organized a response to the public health crisis that arose in South Vietnam following the flight of nearly 1 million North Vietnamese to the South after the country was partitioned in 1954.

The Catholic exodus from the North was portrayed in the American media as evidence of how the Vietnamese would, when given the choice, "vote with their feet" and head for freedom in the South. That mass migration from the North, however, was anything but spontaneous. The refugees were spurred by promises of land and livelihoods and by Lansdale-inspired leaflets that proclaimed, "Christ is going South." Civil Air Transport planes, later revealed to be owned and operated by CIA, carried hundreds of the refugees. American naval vessels also ferried thousands of them to newly established camps below the 17th Parallel. Anne Westerfield remembers how she and other embassy wives volunteered in the Saigon orphanages, where babies from North Vietnam were housed.

Predictably, public health issues plagued the refugees who arrived in numbers that no one, save perhaps Lansdale, anticipated. South Vietnam, with its population of 11 million, had only 130 doctors and no viable public health system. In his autobiography, Lansdale, perhaps a bit disingenuously, described how his friend Arellano jumped into the breach; he recalled that "Arellano caught fire as he listened" to descriptions of the anticipated public health dilemma associated with this refugee movement. Several weeks later, the first brigade of medical volunteers arrived in South Vietnam. Emma Valeriano, a Filipino aristocrat married to Arellano at the time, helped establish Operation Brotherhood and brought the first doctors and nurses to South Vietnam. She called the program "a very idealistic crusade, a very Girl-Scout-type of operation at the beginning."

In Emerson's telling, 25 Rue Chasseloup-Laubat was "the noisiest building in the city, and the friendliest." By early 1956, seven OB teams had treated some 700,000 patients in six hospitals, six outpatient clinics and seven mobile units. As a part of what *Time* magazine dubbed a team of "health commandos," Emerson traveled with the medical missionaries to the South's remote villages; there they set up first-aid clinics and provided rudimentary public health services for the peasant population. In the lower reaches of the Mekong Delta, some patients reached the OB's aid stations by sampan; in the Central Highlands, by oxcart. The incapacitated were carried in hammocks slung to bamboo poles or carried on the shoulders of relatives. Besides an occasional bullet wound, the most common conditions and illnesses OB's doctors treated were malnutrition, malaria, intestinal parasites, and tuberculosis. Threats of smallpox, typhoid, and cholera epidemics were also urgent concerns in the refugee population.

Recalling how Emerson joined in the organization's work in 1956, Valeriano said the American woman was accepted in the circle of OB staffers because she was a friend of Demi Gates's. The Filipinos all "looked up to these young men." Soon it became clear that "Emerson was so sincere and thorough. She was always on the team, she rode in broken-down vehicles. She was willing to put herself in physical danger and get soiled in the name of the cause." Everyone in OB thought of Emerson as "a thoroughbred," Valeriano said. "Gloria stands tall in all our recollections."

"Gloria loved being in Operation Brotherhood," Gates recalled many years later. All the Filipino doctors and nurses admired her, and she thrived on their adulation. Out in the field, the diminutive South Vietnamese peasants were amazed by her six-foot frame. "She was a queen bee," Gates recalled. Her own enthusiasm and willingness to participate in all the dirty work endeared her to OB's organizers. To Arthur Arundel, one of Gates's colleagues on Lansdale's team, Emerson was "a dynamo." He recalled: "Everything she touched just lit up. Just moving around, she seemed to brighten the atmosphere around her."

Judging by an article she wrote about Operation Brotherhood that appeared in both the *Rotarian* and *Reader's Digest* in November of 1956, Emerson was mightily impressed by the effort. She applauded the Filipinos who worked to control South Vietnam's major public health problems. She quoted Arellano describing the participants as "a group of amateurs ready to dare the impossible. We rolled up our sleeves and plunged in." Indeed, she did.

Emerson's story described a trip she took to La Nga with a doctor, two nurses, an interpreter, and a social worker in response to an urgent call from the village priest. They set off at 4:00 A.M. for the four-hour trip through the jungle on roads that barely deserved the name. When they arrived in the settlement of 4,500 refugees, the priest rang the church bell and scores of sick people lined up outside the small hut that would serve as a dispensary. Emerson's story described a harrowing, late-night operation performed on Ngo Van Thai, a sobbing eighteen-year-old South Vietnamese youth whose right hand and arm had been mashed in the rollers of a sugar-cane mill. He had been carried from his village four miles away. Working by flashlight and a kerosene lamp, three Filipino doctors amputated the young man's arm above the elbow. After a ten-day convalescence, during which he lay on a strip of canvas in the little dispensary, Ngo departed. He soon returned bearing a gift for the medical team. Holding out a scrawny chicken in his remaining hand, he said, *"Bac-si, Cam-on."* In the translation of those four monosyllabic words, "Doctors, thank you," editors of *Reader's Digest* and the *Rotarian* found a headline for Emerson's story. The *Digest's* editors billed Operation Brotherhood as "an outstanding example of action people-to-people." Although a few members of Lansdale's team, Rufus Phillips, for example, knew that Operation Brotherhood received CIA funding, Gates thinks it is doubtful that Emerson knew that OB was, as Lansdale wrote in a report that later surfaced in the Pentagon Papers, under "a measure of CIA control." She did, however, note that "there seemed to be constant quarrels and difficulties between the Diem government and the leaders of OB."

Those revelations were still years away when Emerson wrote about how Arellano's team recruited scores of South Vietnamese youngsters into the country's first 4-H Club. They were taught to plant and harvest vegetables that would supplement the refugees' rice-based diet. OB teams were also teaching the villagers rudimentary sanitation lessons, such as digging deep-pit latrines, burning garbage, and laundering clothing to prevent the spread of disease. Yet years later, Arellano, the "gifted and inexhaustible man" whose efforts Emerson had so heartily applauded on the pages of *Reader's Digest,* became the object of her disdain. When she met him quite by chance in Hong Kong in 1970, he once again recited what she by then considered pro-American propaganda—"the same mush I had heard so eagerly in 1956"—she dismissed him as "either pitiful or capable of immense self-deceit."

For many Americans who lived there in 1956, South Vietnam seemed to be a country of promise, enchantment, and peace. Though the century-old colonial empire France had built from Vietnam, Laos, and Cambodia had ceased to exist after Dien Bien Phu, remnants of its grandeur endured. Saigon was elegant and graceful. The French had left behind a widespread use of their language, a lasting imprint on the country's architecture, an unmistakable stamp on the design of its cities, and the names of dead French generals on the city's café-lined streets. And even without the presence of French rule, a taste of France lingered in the country's cuisine. The magnetism of Vietnam for many Americans probably had more to do with the overlay of Western culture that the French had grafted onto an ancient Asian civilization than the civilization itself. Savoring all the European trappings imported by the French, men like Demi Gates found use for their prep school and college French courses, and they never had to master the cacophonous and sometimes shrill sounds of Vietnam's tonal language. After all, most of the Vietnamese with whom they dealt had long since learned French. "The whole thing was just elegant and romantic as hell. It was a dream country if you left it alone," recalled Ogden Williams, a CIA employee who was Lansdale's assistant. "My life in South Vietnam was life in Technicolor, as opposed to black and white. It was always an enormous letdown to come back to the States."

That America's first combat deaths in Vietnam were still three years away during the months Emerson spent in Vietnam doubtless helped to sustain that enchantment.[3] In 1956, Saigon remained a gem the French had created in what had been, before their arrival in 1859, an area of forest and swamps. On that reclaimed land, the French built the neo-Romanesque-style Notre Dame Cathedral designed by Antoine Bouvard. The nearby General Post Office, widely considered an architectural masterpiece, was the work of Gustav Eiffel. Lycee Chasseloup-Laubat, immortalized in the film version of Marguerite Duras's novel *The Lover*, was located on the street that was home to OB, and Emerson's apartment was on the Rue Catinat, where the French had built the Municipal Theater in 1899. Later, when Emerson returned to Saigon in 1970, the nearby Continental Palace Hotel, resplendent with rich wood, polished brass, and lush red velvet drapes, became her first residence.

Saigon's cultural life in the mid-1950s was enchanting. The renowned cellist Gregor Piatigorsky came to play at the city's Dainam Theater; the opera star Eleanor Sterber gave two concerts at the old Majestic Theater. Americans met friends for drinks at the Majestic Hotel, which anchored the northern end of the Rue Catinat to the banks of the Saigon River. They gathered at black-tie embassy parties, dined in fine restaurants, and patronized the city's cabarets. Elyette Conein, whose husband Lucien Conein was a man of considerable mystery and a member of the Lansdale team, recalls seeing "Gloria and Demi" in the city's fashionable restaurants—Le Mirale, La Caba, and Le Majestic. "Gloria was a stunning and beautiful young girl," Elyette Conein recalled. "She was charming, and totally in love with John." And, she added, Emerson seemed "very, very innocent." Emerson found it all elegant and romantic. Her only fear in 1956, she wrote years later, was Saigon's huge bat population. Nothing foretold that by 1970 the city would have more in common with an urban skid row in America than with the French-inspired jewel it was in the 1950s.

To Emerson and many others, South Vietnam appeared to be thriving in 1956. Indeed, an economic boom had begun that year: Rice and rubber were being exported and foreign corporations were beginning to establish a foothold. A measure of prosperity was taking root. But in the background, behind the economic successes President Ngo Dinh Diem took credit for in South Vietnam, and the political successes Ho Chi Minh claimed were his in the North,

---

3. The first two deaths occurred on July 8, 1959, during a Viet Cong attack in Bien Hoa, when an explosive was tossed into an army tent where American servicemen were watching a movie.

both countries were in turmoil. Seeking to rid the South of Viet Minh militants and sympathizers, Diem had unleashed a campaign of terror that started with the enactment in August 1956 of the so-called Ordinance 47, a law that made being a Communist or working with a Communist a capital offense. By year's end, his henchmen had tortured and executed nearly 90 percent of the enemy cells in his country's rich agricultural Mekong Delta. In the North, Ho Chi Minh's agricultural reform, efforts begun in 1955, paralleled what Diem was doing in the South. By 1956, the Agricultural Reform Tribunals in the North established to eradicate the country's landlords had ordered the torture and execution of from 3,000 to 5,000 farmers who owned small tracts of land.

In 1956, however, events in Southeast Asia seldom aroused excitement in American newsrooms. Stories about South Vietnam were as likely to originate in Washington, D.C., as in Saigon, as if to reflect the view of America's leaders that they were in control of that distant country. Although the Associated Press opened its Saigon bureau in 1950, not until January 1962 did an American newspaper open a bureau in Vietnam, when the *New York Times* assigned Homer Bigart, one of its leading reporters, to the post. Before that, the *Times* intermittently ran magazine articles written by Peggy Durdin, the brilliant writer whose husband, F. Tillman Durdin, was the newspaper's longtime Asia correspondent.

Durdin, the daughter of American missionaries, was born and raised in China. She spoke fluent Mandarin, had taught school in Shanghai, and had a thorough grasp of the history and politics in the region. She made a series of visits to French Indochina during the 1950s, and wrote insightful analyses of the French missteps that would eventually lead to their defeat at Dien Bien Phu, the disappearance of privilege and power of the colonizers in Asia, and the reasons Ho Chi Minh could win. In one story, Durdin described Saigon in 1951 as a city with an extraordinary capacity for self-delusion and denial. In the face of the barely concealed terror and violence all around them, the Saigonaise somehow maintained a veneer of calm and normalcy. Three years later, Durdin's assessment was even more dire. She wrote that "while the fire approache[d]" the city was mindlessly fiddling: "This great port city has a smell of doom about it, unmistakable to anyone who watched China go and Shanghai approach its end. Saigon is one of Asia's last great European-dominated cities, outdated like the rickshaw, nearing the end of an era."

Peggy Durdin was a peculiar product of the *New York Times,* one that reveals not only the culture of a great newspaper but also the value system that defined the role of American women. Aside from her intelligence as a writer and political thinker, Peggy Durdin was also a *New York Times* wife. In that role, like other women of her generation, she was destined to work in her husband's shadow. When Tillman Durdin was hired by the *Times* in 1937 to cover Asia, his wife lost any hope she might have had to become a *Times* staffer herself. Despite the near-epidemic nepotism so visible in its own upper ranks, the brass in the *New York Times* newsroom had a longstanding policy that precluded the hiring of any *Times* man's wife. Turner Catledge became such an enforcer of the policy during his tenure as executive editor that the practice became known as "Catledge's Rule."

Beyond Peggy Durdin's magazine articles, the *Times* also had given the region considerable attention in 1954 when the French were defeated at Dien Bien Phu. A year later, in the spring of 1955, the newspaper dispatched A. M. Rosenthal, then one of its rising stars, to cover the Binh Xuyen uprising, the last throes of which were underway when Gates arrived in Saigon. Later that year, the *Times* covered the comically rigged referendum that President Diem arranged at Lansdale's urging. Voters in the South were asked to approve or disapprove of a proposal to depose the emperor Bao Dai and to establish South Vietnam as a republic with Ngo Dinh Diem as president. Although Lansdale had urged moderation in the vote tallies, Diem apparently wanted to help himself to a landslide. His astonishing victory— 98.2 percent of the vote nationwide—included 605,025 votes in Saigon, where the number of registered voters totaled 450,000.

In early July, a *Times* reporter accompanied Richard M. Nixon, then vice president, on a state visit to South Vietnam. Several days before the trip, a *Times* editorial had applauded the decision to include South Vietnam on the itinerary. The editorial also voiced approval for President Diem's decision to ignore the Geneva Accords and reject its call for open elections. "There can be no free election in the Communist-controlled North," the *Times* concluded. Nixon, whose trip to South Vietnam was intended to assure the country's leaders of America's continuing economic and moral support, became the first guest speaker to address the South Vietnamese National Constituent Assembly.

Other stories with a Saigon dateline in 1956 ranged from Bernard Kalb's description of the passage of the constitution by the country's National Assembly to a brief item noting that the South Vietnamese government had banned the publication or circulation of "biased news or comment favoring Communist or anti-national activities." In October, Kalb revisited Saigon on the first anniversary of the founding of the Republic of South Vietnam to report on the National Assembly's vote on the constitution. The document, written by assembly members elected in March 1956, provided for a three-way division of governmental authority; however, it endowed the executive branch with the bulk of the power, a step perceived in some quarters as an act of faith in President Diem's leadership. With the approval of that constitution, the *Times* editorially welcomed the "new democracy" to the international family. Although the editorial expressed mild hesitation about the extraordinary presidential powers provided for in the constitution, it praised the country's great strides and declared that the South Vietnamese leaders "have given the world an object lesson in how to meet Communist subversion at the rice roots level." Other press outlets, most notably *Time* magazine, were similarly effusive in their praise of Diem and the republic over whose birth he had presided. Of lesser note was a new item in the *Times* about a government decree aimed at wiping out vestiges of French influence. It required South Vietnamese citizens with French first names, such as Jean, Henri, or Marcel, to change them to Vietnames names, such as Nguyen, Tran, or Trinh. The move meant that members of the country's once privileged Eurasian population would have to adjust to an environment in which they would join the ranks of more ordinary citizens.

Emerson's view of the French in Vietnam, at least as presented in her memoir, appears to have been one of skepticism mixed with hints of disdain. She wrote of how French women she encountered in Saigon in 1956 called to one another in voices that were too high and sharp. She wrote, too, of the "short" soldiers—soon to be shipped back to Marseilles—soldiers who left their shirts unbuttoned in Saigon's cafes. And she wrote of the fierce, small blond Frenchwoman, the proprietor of a beauty shop on the Rue Catinat, who was irritated by the sight of American men in the city. "They will never understand this country," she would sigh, "they will never change the Viets, they will not be happy here."

The same year that the South Vietnamese refashioned their country into a republic, the last of the French soldiers marched down the Rue Catinat and boarded boats for Marseille. With their departure, the remnants of French rule slowly began to vanish. Ceiling fans gave way to boxy air conditioners, Renaults were replaced by Chevrolets, the popularity of LaRue beer waned and Budweiser soon became the brand of choice in Saigon's bars.

Above all, attempts to impose American managerial efficiencies on the South Vietnamese democracy began to replace the system of French governance. Lansdale, Ogden Williams, and the Rover Boys all shared the dislike that most American leaders had felt since the 1930s for the way France had exploited Indochina during its decades of colonial rule. They perceived flaws in the French transportation, tariff, and taxation systems. The rail and road systems were ill-conceived and poorly maintained. Tariffs were designed to give France exclusive control of trade with South Vietnam. Land and head taxes levied on the South Vietnamese were arbitrary and high. Similarly, in American eyes, the French education system throughout South Vietnam was inadequate, as was the health care system France had created. In Vietnam, Laos, and Cambodia, France had exploited the region's abundant natural resources without regard for the needs of its people.

The Rover Boys, with their Pearl-Buck-Good-Earth view of Asia, believed that South Vietnam's backward society and primitive people could and should be remade in America's image. Emerson, Lansdale, and the Rover Boys were not imperialists in the same sense that France had been with its shameless abuse of the region's resources and people. They were, like so many Americans in 1956, compassionate imperialists. They would never disparage the South Vietnamese as "the Yellows" as the French had done.

But in American diplomatic circles at mid-century, the South Vietnamese and other Third World populations were perceived as childlike, guileless, incapable of self-governance, and defenseless in the face of external forces— such as the Communists. That sweeping judgment, which overlooked the nation's long history of rebellion against domination by the Chinese and later against the French, led seamlessly to the conclusion that after the defeat at Dien Bien Phu, Ho Chi Minh would quickly surrender to the mandates of Moscow.

Like so many other Americans in 1956, Emerson and Gates thought that "the American way of life" was the envy of other, poorer societies and that Uncle Sam's good will and bounty would be welcomed as gifts from a generous uncle. In the eyes of the Vietnamese, however, America's efforts to install a non-Communist government in South Vietnam were simply an extension of the recently ended century of French rule. For Ho Chi Minh, ideological imperialism was every bit as repugnant as France's brand of economic imperialism. A government forced on the nation from the outside was no less onerous than filling the landscape with rubber trees to produce Michelin tires for the Western world. Self-determination was Ho Chi Minh's and the National Liberation Front's Holy Grail, just as it had been for their ancestors, who had spent nearly 1,000 years ridding themselves of their Chinese occupiers. Nearly half a century after he left South Vietnam, Demi Gates could still fume about how the French had destroyed Vietnamese culture and were on their way to destroying its sense of identity. Yet so many of the qualities that he and Emerson came to love and cherish during their Asian idyll were manifestations of the culture France had imprinted upon Vietnam.

In time, Emerson moved away from the crowded quarters at 25 Rue Chasseloup-Laubat into what Gates later called a "rather grungy room" on the Rue Catinat, once Saigon's equivalent of New York's Fifth Avenue. Her fifth-floor walk-up was near the Caravelle Hotel, later a favorite of the many American journalists who either made it their home or shared drinks with friends in its famous rooftop bar. She called Rue Catinat, a 1.1-kilometer thoroughfare, "a pretty ribbon of a street." There she could find French bakeries featuring warm baguettes, sidewalk cafes that sold croissants and crepes, *epiceries* that sold specialty vegetables, and *maisons de coiffeur* where she had her hair done. In her memoir, she recalled the street's elegant shops, with their dwindling supplies of Christian Dior brassieres and Guerlain perfumes, as lingering reminders of France's long presence in Southeast Asia. To Emerson, Saigon was "a soft, plump, clean place"; a city calm and lush with trees— tamarind, mango, flame, and even a few rubber trees. Years later, she wrote of how the leafy canopy above Saigon's streets created a refuge from the often oppressive heat. Those same trees darkened in the rains, held the water, cooled the air; and "a few flashed silver underneath when the wind tickled or rubbed them."

Emerson also marveled at the Vietnamese people. She discerned in Vietnamese women a weightless quality. They looked so tiny and beautiful in their traditional long-sleeved, high-collared *ao dai,* described in one guidebook as a garment that "covers everything but hides nothing." The women who wore these fitted, knee-length gowns that were split at the waist and worn over trousers were graceful and unselfconscious. The fashion sense Emerson perceived in their matching blue and violet or rose and white parasols delighted her.

This was the stage on which she continued to hone her talents as a journalist. With Lansdale's help, according to Gates, Emerson interviewed President Diem, a session in the presidential palace that she described many years later as a surrealistic encounter with a character who appeared to have some mental disorder that bordered on madness. Dressed in his trademark white sharkskin suit, Diem spoke slowly, in French, and chain-smoked through what became an hours-long, meandering diatribe. A round dumpling of a man, he seemed to fancy himself a twentieth-century philosopher king. His long monologue, part sermon, part rant, was filled with the philosophical mumbo-jumbo that he routinely spewed on all his listeners, no matter whether he was speaking to a janitor, an ambassador, or, in later years, to selected members of the Saigon press corps. Recognizing perhaps that Emerson was unable to follow either his esoteric ideas or his serpentine line of thinking, Diem obligingly summarized his essential points on a small white card. "South Vietnam is conscious of representing the aspirations of non-Communist Asia," he wrote. "It is a grand responsibility and it is also a test for Southeast Asia." For decades, that card had a place among Emerson's mementos of South Vietnam. Demi Gates remembers that Emerson seemed contemptuous of Diem after that interview; he speculated that what she had found so distasteful was the intensity of the president's Catholicism.

On another occasion, she traveled with Diem on a Lansdale-inspired junket to the Plain of Jars, near the Cambodian border, and to Long Xuyen Province, where the president's American handlers hoped he would engage the nation's peasant population. With an assortment of American diplomats, experts, and military advisors in tow, Diem visited one of the huge refugee settlements populated by Catholics who had fled their homes in North Vietnam. Looking like a potentate who had never laid eyes on a peasant, Diem appeared stiff and unsmiling as he floated down a canal on a gunboat past the scores of refugees lining the river bank. Emerson remained unimpressed.

Away from the country's political life, Emerson took delight in South Vietnam's diverse geography. In a scrapbook she assembled and later described in her memoir, one photograph in particular recalls her trip to the demilitarized zone, a line that split the country in two along the Ben Hai River at the 17th Parallel. In that photo, Emerson stood beside a sign near a wooden bridge spanning the river that by all accounts was supposed to be the dividing line between freedom and tyranny. The sign read *Ligne de Demarcation Militaire Provisoire* (Provisional Military Demarcation Line). The bridge was mystifying in its simplicity. Neither the armed soldier patrolling on the opposite river bank nor the garrison behind him hinted that this bridge—at least in the depiction by America's leaders—was the place where good stood on one side and evil on the other. Emerson had expected to find some visual manifestation of Communism's dark and malevolent qualities here. Instead, all she could discern was an austere and artlessly constructed bridge.

She also traveled to Da Nang that year, when it was still called Tourane, and she found a breathtaking beauty in its gracefully curving waterfront. The white sand beaches and aquamarine waters of the South China Sea at Qui

Nohn and Nha Trang charmed her. In South Vietnam's interior, the country-side left its mark on her memory: Canals divided the rice fields into a patch-work of pristine blue-green squares inside of which stoop-shouldered figures wearing conical hats toiled at the same labors that had occupied their ances-tors for centuries. The sense of eternity lent majesty to those scenes. Emerson was spellbound by the country, from the tea plantations of Blao in the north-ern mountains to the flat, jungle terrain of Camau at the country's southern-most tip. She thought it was the most beautiful place she had ever seen. This, of course, was long before American military advisors dissevered the land into four military zones, giving them names that sounded like "Eye Corps"; it was before Buddhists began immolating themselves in Saigon's public squares to protest the government repression of religion, before pizza parlors opened all over the city to please GI palates, before brothels and bars replaced the side-walk cafes along the Rue Catinat—which by then was renamed Tu Do Street.

Just as she would years later when she returned to Saigon as a *New York Times* correspondent, Emerson befriended a South Vietnamese man who worked from time to time as her interpreter. His name was Mr. Luoc, and he was to have an enormous influence on her. Years later, she remembered him as an angry and complicated man with "strange, sad and astringent" qualities. He hated President Diem and seldom remained quiet about his sentiments. He frightened Emerson with his declarations that perhaps Diem, whose gov-ernment had imprisoned one of his relatives, "should be shot." Mr. Luoc also puzzled Emerson with his claims that Diem, like all people who came from Hue, was suspect. Diem was not realistic, he was a mystic, Mr. Luoc said. In Saigon, he explained, the president was feared rather than admired.

In the mid-1950s, Mr. Luoc, like Emerson, was in his mid-twenties. He hungered for an education but was too poor to attend the university. He wanted to improve his English, he told her with what she later thought was a sense of foreboding. It was important for the future, he said. The bond that grew between Emerson and Mr. Luoc led her, before she left South Vietnam in 1956, to give him the expensive man's wristwatch she wore. Because he had no address, there was no way for her to stay in touch with him after she returned to America. But his memory remained alive; when she returned to South Vietnam in 1970, she looked for him everywhere among the soldiers, casualties, and prisoners she encountered in her pursuit of stories. She looked not only at the men's faces but also at their wrists. She never found him and was left to wonder exactly what he had been trying to tell her in 1956, and what it was that had kept her from interpreting his message.

Gates and Emerson both read *The Quiet American*, Graham Greene's new and much-talked-about novel, during their months together in South Vietnam. She said she read it three times, "lying at night under mosquito netting." The book, she said, "told us too much and upset some of the younger CIA men," Gates among them. Indeed, he hated it. Decades later he still described it as "that dreadful book" and "a deliberate attempt to make the Americans look like meatheads and bad guys." In those early readings, Emerson said she found Greene's story "brilliant but cynical." She repeatedly returned to the story to savor what she perceived as Greene's sagacity. Speaking of the book many years after its publication, Emerson said, "It came back to haunt me more than I ever thought such a small, light book ever could." Graham Greene himself appears to have later captured Emerson's imagination. She once described to a friend how, just before she interviewed Greene in 1978, almost like a giddy high-schooler on a first date, she took special care in applying her mascara and selecting her wardrobe. During her interview at Greene's home in Antibes, he told her it was important "to be a piece of grit in the state machinery." Their conversation stretched over many hours, after which Emerson described herself as "besotted" with the famous British author, who died in 1991. "How could you not love him?" she gushed to an interviewer years later. She kept a framed photograph of him in her bedroom, placed on a shelf so that he was "smiling down at me." For years, the two writers exchanged letters, the contents of which are incorporated into the one novel Emerson wrote, *Loving Graham Greene*, published in 2000. A friend once described Emerson's story of Mollie Benson, the book's main character, and her pursuit of justice as "just one layer removed from biography." Mollie, Emerson told an audience at a New York City book signing, was something of a metaphorical first cousin to Fowler in *The Quiet American*, someone who "did not want to be a pointless person."

The Quiet American is largely based on Greene's experiences in Vietnam during three trips he made to Hanoi and Saigon between 1951 and 1954 as a journalist for a London newspaper. Like Emerson, he found himself mesmerized by the country's charms. On the second of those trips, the idea for a novel emerged after Greene had a long conversation with a young American economic aide, a man whose ideas about the need for a Third Force to counter the threat of communism became the political theme of the novel. Saigon in the mid-1950s was populated with people like Fowler, Greene's fictional British journalist who watched with arched eyebrows the arrival of all those well-meaning but blundering Americans. They would soon lie beneath the imaginary whitened tombstone of Rudyard Kipling's sage verse, Fowler was certain, the one with the epitaph that identified the Westerner who lay in the soil beneath as "a fool who tried to hustle the East." Saigon was also populated with those characters whom Fowler despised: idealistic young Americans like Alden Pyle, Graham Greene's quiet American, "an innocent abroad" in Southeast Asia. Generations of American missionaries and merchants had preceded Pyle to Asia, and, like them, he was intent on doing well by doing good. Although it was widely claimed in the late 1950s that Edward Lansdale was Greene's model for Pyle, Greene insisted the claim was mistaken. "Just for the record," he wrote the *British Sunday Telegraph* in 1966, "your correspondent is completely wrong in thinking that I took General Lansdale as the model for *The Quiet American.* Pyle was a younger, more innocent, and more idealistic member of the CIA." Pyle, it seems, had more in common with the men who called themselves the Rover Boys, men like Demi Gates.

Back in the 1950s, perhaps Emerson, and certainly Gates, preferred the Hollywood version of Greene's tale. Emerson, after all, still approved of America's efforts to "tidy up the world." If Greene's original story amounted to a political preachment against America's miscalculations, the film version of the novel overflowed with the Red menace and intimations that empires on which the sun had never set were now irrelevant in the world order. In keeping with the notion, Fowler is portrayed not as the prescient hero of Greene's novel but as an opium-addled, dissolute remnant of the British empire whose glory days had long passed. When the director Joseph Mankiewicz visited Saigon early in 1956 on a scouting mission for locations and insights, Gates was his tour guide. "We had long conversations about how to portray the Vietnamese capacity for trickery and the two-faced side of the Vietnamese personality," Gates recalled. Mankiewicz wanted to know how they could be friends by day and enemies by night. Lansdale instructed Gates to guide Mankiewicz in devising ways to make Americans look less dangerous in the film than they did in Greene's novel. Gates scored a wild success on that front: In the Mankiewicz film, the American good guys become the embodiment of righteousness.

That is precisely how Gates perceived his role in South Vietnam. The sense of nobility attached itself to the American effort, as if democracy might be spread like some hybrid seed that could, and surely would, take root in any soil. That is what made Gates's work attractive to so many people who viewed it from the outside—his younger brother among them. Peter Gates arrived in Saigon soon after Harvard University's 1956 commencement ceremony. His plan for a post-graduate global tour took him first to Japan and Hong Kong; he arrived in South Vietnam at the end of June. For six weeks, he watched from the sidelines as his brother went about the Rover Boys' daily routines. Because Gates was always so tight-lipped, Peter knew almost nothing about his brother's work. The furtive nature of Gates's work, too, endowed it with an aura of intrigue, especially when Peter perceived that his brother's life might be in danger. The Viet Minh, Peter was certain, were hardly fooled for a minute about what the Rover Boys were really up to. Although the danger seemed tantalizing at times, those glimpses of his brother's escapades were enough to persuade Peter to set aside his thoughts about joining the CIA. The threats he witnessed in Saigon were far too real; better to settle into a comfortable sinecure in a Manhattan law firm.

Beyond those insights into his brother's life as a spy, Peter also caught glimpses of Demi's ever-stormy relationship with Emerson, who, in Peter Gates's memory, "burned with a bright blue flame." He sensed that even then "a special sense of outrage always seemed to hang close to Gloria." She had cinematic qualities; her huge eyes, he said, seemed "designed for weeping." He saw her as always spoiling for a good fight. And on the day of his arrival, he witnessed a dramatic quarrel between the two lovers. Emerson joined Demi and Peter for a celebratory dinner at a French-Chinese restaurant in Cholon. But the brothers' joyful reunion, filled as it was with conversations about family, gossipy exchanges about acquaintances, and an assortment of jokes, largely excluded Emerson. Ignoring her, as Peter quickly learned, "is something you do at your own peril." After dinner, as they made their way back to her apartment on the Rue Catinat, her foul temper was rising like leavened bread in a warm oven. Demi and Peter, still absorbed in their own fraternal joy, were largely oblivious to her mood. The brothers diverted their attention from each other only long enough to bid Emerson a perfunctory good night at her doorstep. But as they ambled up the Rue Catinat, Gates sensed a need to acknowledge Emerson's conspicuous displeasure. He bought a potted plant from a street vendor, turned to Peter, and said, "I'll give her this and tell her I love her." With that, he made his way to her fifth-floor room carrying his peace offering. He muttered a brief apology for his inattention and handed it to her. Back outside, Demi told Peter, "I think I made it up to her." He was unaware that his gift had only further fueled her rage. The Gates brothers had no sooner resumed their conversation when the sounds of crockery crashing on pavement brought everyone on the street to a halt. To their disbelief, Gates's peace offering lay in smithereens near their feet. Gates turned volcanic and

stormed back up the stairs, his anger mounting with the thought that the pot
Emerson had just hurled out the window might have killed someone. Her
aim was so bad that the brothers had been in no danger, but he kept thinking
that she could have hit a cyclo driver. His fury erupted as he reached her door,
which she opened before he knocked. He slapped her face. Demi Gates said
this was the only time he had ever hit a woman. Emerson sometimes had that
effect on people. In a later decade, her long-distance exchanges with staffers
on the *New York Times* foreign desk occasionally took on a similar intensity,
but distance served to insulate them from much of her wrath. Friends, too,
invariably became acquainted with her capacity to exasperate.

Peter Gates was certain that his brother loved Emerson, but failed to understand why. That she would later become a figure of passionate and strident
antiwar views came as no surprise to either of the Gates brothers. Peter's recollection of Emerson's politics is at odds with those earlier, more moderate
views she ascribed to herself in her memoir. Indeed, he often wondered
whether Emerson's left-leaning associations had made Gates's CIA bosses
uncomfortable. Even though she had yet to make up her mind that "Ho Chi
Minh was the second coming of Christ and Americans were the Antichrist,"
Peter Gates nonetheless recalled that, at the time, "there wasn't a fringe organization she didn't love." Despite Gates's many assurances to the contrary, Peter continued to believe that Emerson's involvement in organizations that the
FBI considered pinko made her an "embarrassment" to the agency.[4] Politics
aside, however, Peter found Emerson delightful company. She frequently accompanied him and the Filipino medical teams on location during the shooting of a documentary about Operation Brotherhood, a job his brother had
found for him. Together they filmed a surgical procedure on a South Vietnamese child afflicted with a cleft palate. Gates recalled that the day was boiling hot and that flies buzzed around the medical team during the ninety
minutes it took to complete the operation.

As for Demi Gates and Emerson, most of their spats revolved around politics. Her liberal ideas always enraged him. Indeed, like his brother, he remembers none of those earlier conservative sentiments that she, at least in her
memoir, professed to embrace. He was certain she had been poisoned by "that
Eleanor Roosevelt" and the suspicious "front organizations" that her detractors

---

4. In response to Freedom of Information Act requests, the Central Intelligence Agency and the
Federal Bureau of Investigation said records indicate that neither agency ever opened a file on Gloria
Emerson.

were certain the former first lady led. They "argued endlessly" about Roosevelt, who, Demi Gates recalled, lured so many young ladies into the Socialist realm. "Gloria thought of her as some sort of goddess." She was not alone. Through much of the 1950s, Gallup polls repeatedly identified Eleanor Roosevelt as the "most admired" woman in America.

When Demi Gates's assignment in South Vietnam ended in the late summer of 1956, he and Emerson left South Vietnam together. He was returning to the United States ostensibly to receive his next assignment from the CIA. But he knew his years in government service were over. Making money, much more of it than a job with the CIA would ever pay, had become Demi Gates's goal. Besides, the CIA was run by bureaucrats, the same kind that run the business world, "but at least in business you can make money," he concluded. He was headed for Wall Street. He and Emerson traveled back to the United States via India, the Middle East, Greece, Italy, and France. Accompanied by Peter Gates at the outset, they stopped in New Delhi, Bombay, and Calcutta, where Gates's brother again saw demonstrations of Emerson's iron will and stubbornness. The threesome had scheduled a brief day trip to some long forgotten destination in India only to discover that their flight had been canceled. When they attempted to get a refund for their tickets at Air India's main office, Peter recalled, they were told, "Not to be giving refunds today." He remembers he and his brother were "really pissed off" but decided to forget it and enjoy the day. However, Emerson was not one to let go of $84 lightly, Peter recalled. Money appeared to mean far more to her than it did to the Gates brothers; indeed, she described money as "very" important in her answers to Barbaralee Diamonstein's questionnaire in 1970. "Plato said poverty makes men emotional. It makes me very emotional," she once said. So she dug in her heels and vowed to remain in the Air India office until she had her refund. Late that evening, she returned to their hotel in triumph—with cash in hand.

Gates and Emerson later traveled to Lebanon, where Emerson's sister, Patricia, lived with her husband, David Owen. As they continued their trip, Emerson and Gates toured Greece, Italy, and France, images of which she later assembled for him in a leather-bound album. In the black-and-white photos, she stands amidst the columns of the temple of Theseus; he takes the same pose at the temple of Athena Parthenos. They visited the Acropolis, the Odeum, and Delphi. They left Greece from Piraeus and sailed to Italy, where they wandered through the piazzas in Rome and struck romantic poses in Tivoli, near Hadrian's villa. They rode a motor scooter from Naples along the Amalfi Drive to Sorrento, Positano, and Ravello, and took a boat to the

Isle of Capri. "Ah, love," Gates sighed as he paged through the album much later in his life. In Paris, they posed amorously at the Tuileries, the Arc de Triomphe, and the Rue de la Paix. The last two photographs she pasted to the black, plastic-covered pages show Emerson preparing to board the SS *United States* for the journey back to America on October 18, 1956.

Although they maintained casual contact after their return from Vietnam, it was clear to Gates that "Gloria was never going to be Mrs. John Monteith Gates Jr." Her volatile personality had begun to irk him; her politics grew more offensive. Her temper seemed uncontrolled, especially when she yanked the telephone cord from a wall of his apartment because he was talking to another woman. Then, too, he admits, he was an unrepentant social climber—he was looking for a partner with greater social status, and yes, a woman with a lot more in the way of family money. Gates planned to acquire a lot of money in a short time. He would line his pockets with the losses of lesser men, he promised Emerson. Someday, he vowed, his picture would appear on the cover of *Time* magazine.

After her return to the States, among Emerson's first stories was an article about a fictional "New York Career Girl" that appeared in *Holiday*. She continued her series for *Mademoiselle* on those "young couples coping with life here and abroad." A few eerie autobiographical echoes threaded their way through her career-girl article about Priscilla Denton, who worked in an advertising agency, and managed to place a client's jewelry collection on the fashion pages of the *Journal-American*. Priscilla's sometime boyfriend, Peter, she said, "might end up on the cover of *Time* magazine."

In 1957, Emerson joined the staff of "the women's page" at the *New York Times*. Nan Robertson, the *Times* fashion writer whose acquaintance Emerson had made before she left the *Journal-American*, had urged her boss to hire her bright, witty friend. Emerson became part of the elite dozen or so women who worked for the legendary Elizabeth Penrose Howkins. Mrs. Howkins—no one ever, ever, called her Elizabeth—had been the editor of *Glamour* magazine and the British edition of *Vogue*. Like other fashion editors of the era, Mrs. Howkins often wore a hat indoors. Her nearly all-female staff occupied a corner of the ninth floor, six floors above the *Times*' block-long newsroom on West 43rd Street, which had yet to be integrated in any significant way by either gender or race. "The women's department," recalled *Times* staffer Sydney Schanberg, "was a different planet." He remembers that an invisible veil of perfume lingered in the hallway leading to Mrs. Howkins's redoubt, "so you knew you were walking into a different place."

Emerson's developing talents as a writer, her flawless fashion sense, her great humor, and her daring all worked to secure her place among such budding talents as Charlotte Curtis, who would soon inherit Mrs. Howkins's job; Marylin Bender, who was later named the Sunday business editor; Betsy Wade, who became a copyeditor on the foreign desk (and later a key player in the discrimination suit brought against the *New York Times* by its female employees); and Robertson, who wrote a book about the lawsuit and the *Times* women's fight for equality. Together, these women helped to produce the pages that for years bore the title "Food Fashions Family Furnishings." Staples of the section were the semiannual Paris showings of Balmain and Balenciaga collections, society balls where the aristocracy raised funds for respectable charities, and the Junior League's debutante cotillions. The real test, according to Bender, was covering the James Galanos collection. By all accounts, she aced it.

Wade remembers Emerson as "a ferociously hard worker" in those days. She thought of "Gloria's flighty personality" as "a trademark item . . . she would raise those long fingers in the air and sort of flap them at the top of her hair and say, 'Oh, I just can't think about that now. I can't do it. Can't think about it.' But she got the work done although she was constantly at the brink of disintegration or appeared to be at the brink of disintegration." In securing a job at the *Times,* Emerson believed then, she had gained admission to "the kingdom." It was the pinnacle of her professional aspirations. For a time, she loved the life that her work afforded her. But "Food Fashions Family Furnishings" would not fulfill her for long. In the "Four Fs" section, women of talent and ambition thought they were in "some kind of a ghetto," Robertson recalled. "Every one of us wanted a wider world. We all grew sick of writing about family, food, fashions, and the domestic concerns of women."

The fearless streak that had propelled Emerson to South Vietnam apparently remained intact, but she was left to channel it to endeavors beyond the *New York Times'* Four Fs. On a May morning in 1959, long before weekend skydiving by novices became commonplace, she jumped from a plane in the skies over Orange, Massachusetts. Robertson, whose desk adjoined Emerson's, remembers her growing terror as the day approached. Demi Gates had invited her to join him and his friend, Peter Gimbel, on the jump. She wrote of the experience, first in the *New York Times* in a news story about the recently opened sport parachute center that was attracting Ivy League collegians. Although the *Times* article included a photo of Emerson rigged up for her first jump, it made no mention of the actual jump. But first-person accounts of her feat appeared in the *Reader's Digest* in 1963, and in *Esquire* in 1976. Confessing that she was neither graceful, daring, athletic, nor self-possessed, Emerson wrote that she was the unlikeliest of characters to rig forty pounds of gear on her back and jump out of a single-engine airplane at twenty-four hundred feet. She wanted, she explained, "to be brave about something, not just about love, or a root canal, or writing that the shoes at Arnold Constable looked strangely sad." After take-off, fear paralyzed her, but escape was impossible. She was hooked to the static line. To her everlasting puzzlement, she did manage to jump out when her instructor shouted "Go!" even though every impulse resisted obedience to the command. In just a few seconds, joy and calm suffused her: "It was as if I had always longed to be a bird and had just learned how." In those moments, she could have scooped the clouds into her pocket, just as she had wished to do all those years ago in the lines of her high school poem.

Her description of that two-minute-and-two-second plunge included a fashion statement that surely would have won Mrs. Howkins's approbation. Along with the steel helmet, bulky jumpsuit, and "absurd" black boots that seemed to have a will of their own, on this first dive of her life Emerson wore a pair of white gloves that were once an accessory to her summer dresses— "old ones from Saks Fifth Avenue"—on which she wiped her leaking nose and tearing eyes as she fell earthward at sixteen feet per second. Later that day, she was introduced to General James Gavin, leader of the 82nd Airborne on D-Day at Normandy. She conjectured that the introduction was made as a way of demonstrating to him that even the gawkiest and least promising student could be taught to jump from an airplane.

Her parachuting escapade embodied the kind of determination and courage common to all the women who later made their way to South Vietnam as would-be journalists. Although female reporters had long since established their talent and mettle, for Emerson and those who followed her to South Vietnam, it was as if Margaret Bourke-White, Maggie Higgins, and Martha Gellhorn had never existed. The high school honor student who aspired to be a senator could hardly reach her potential by writing about sad-looking shoes. Although one must search hard to unearth her work from that South Vietnam sojourn in 1956, Emerson stands as a forerunner of the foreign correspondent she—and those who followed her—would later become. Her achievements both during and after the two years she spent as a resident correspondent for the *New York Times* in Saigon, in the words of one colleague, established her as "One of the great figures of 20th-century war correspondence."

In many of her observations about South Vietnam after her trip in 1956, colleagues discerned a subtext of unintended condescension, as if the backwardness and innocence she had perceived were conditions that could and should be treated and healed, rather like the dysentery and parasites she saw Operation Brotherhood doctors treat in the refugee enclaves. Driven perhaps by the same combination of obligation and sentimentality that led her to give Mr. Luoc her expensive wristwatch—believing, no doubt, that time, and knowledge of the time, had the same importance for Vietnamese people as it had for Americans—she personified the very attitudes that blinded America's leaders to the calamity their good intentions would create in Southeast Asia. For all the understanding she would bring to the war in her later reporting for the *Times,* during that first visit she appears to have been entrapped by the same logic that led America into what David Halberstam would later famously call the "quagmire."

Friends such as Nan Robertson squirmed in silent discomfort whenever Emerson spoke of the South Vietnamese people and her attachment to them. It all sounded so paternalistic; Emerson seemed to think of them as her "little brown brothers," Robertson recalled. Although Emerson appeared to friends to have only a passing interest in the struggle of black America's struggle for civil rights, her notion of responsibility for the South Vietnamese never seemed to wane. That realization astonished Robertson. The people on whom Emerson lavished so much admiration and affection were never, it seemed, perceived as her equals. Instead, she appeared, in the late 1950s, to have adopted the Vietnamese as her own personal white man's burden.

As a scene in the mural of the South Vietnam experience, Emerson's adventure as a would-be journalist during those earlier innocent years and her later role as a *New York Times* correspondent in the 1970s remain both a piece of journalism history and a story of America's self-delusion writ small. We did not necessarily know what was best for our "little brown brothers." The Vietnamese, we painfully discovered, preferred their independence to America's largesse, and they fought until 1975 to achieve it.

In the beginning, like Emerson, many of the women who followed her to Saigon wanted to be journalists but did not know how to do it. They were left to teach themselves. Like her, they flew to Saigon equipped only with one-way tickets and their ambitions. Together, these women proved that they did know how to do it. South Vietnam became the place where war, that archetypal male endeavor, became women's business, too. South Vietnam remained an incomparably exotic memory and became a magnetic force in Emerson's life. The country, she told Robertson and other friends, was her "destiny." In that scrapbook she assembled after her first trip to South Vietnam, Emerson could look back at the images of young schoolchildren seated at their desks, of villagers washing clothes in a river, and of a spit-polished soldier smiling as he was photographed for the first time in his life. They were all so charming in their apparent backwardness, so endearing in their apparent innocence. Fourteen years passed before she landed for the second time at Tan Son Nhut Airport. When she did, the place she had known, the country that lived for so long in her imagination and in all those photographs on the black pages of her scrapbook, was gone.

2

Called to
the Colors

She was one of us and we will miss her.
—WALLACE M. GREENE JR., COMMANDANT, USMC

GEORGETTE LOUISE MEYER Chapelle was a living emblem of America's discordant impulses. Her political ideology during the 1960s paralleled that of the national leaders she esteemed: War—hot or cold—was a necessary, and even noble, undertaking. America had a right to impose its will on other nations, Chapelle believed, even if doing so meant nuclear confrontation. But her humanitarian instincts tended to neutralize her fervor. In her belief that the nation should share its bounty, she embodied America's charitable disposition. Bombs and food bundles framed Chapelle's notions about American foreign policy. Her life, like her death, was as simple and as complex as the country she cherished. She was killed by a land mine on November 4, 1965, on a search-and-clear mission with the U.S. Marines during her fifth trip to South Vietnam.

Everybody always knew what would happen to Chapelle someday, wrote her colleague Richard Starnes a week after she died. But no one, perhaps not even Dickey herself, knew "whether she was a very brave person or whether she was just a woman hag-ridden with some dark compulsion to prove she was as good as any man on earth." Being around her was a strain because her fate was so obvious, Starnes noted. He added that she was "always full of an unbelievable zest for living, and always rushing headlong toward her own private appointment in Samarra."

Unlike so many female journalists for whom the war was a professional baptism, the Vietnam War came at the denouement of Chapelle's career. War and its consequences had marked the mileposts of her adult life. She first tasted combat during World War II and came away wanting more—and she found it. The humanitarian aid she brought to World War II Europe illuminated her understanding of war's cursed side. The Hungarian Revolution in 1956 fueled her hatred of Communism. Later, in Algeria in 1957, she was the first American photojournalist to write about the war from the perspective of the rebels who were fighting French colonial rule. And Fidel Castro's revolution in Cuba deepened her insights into the intricacies of leadership and power. In Vietnam, she was the first journalist to photograph the totality of the country and its war from an American viewpoint. Her images, published in a thirty-one-page spread in *National Geographic* in November 1962, were so widely copied that they became part of the war's iconography. She covered the Indochina conflict in the traditions of World War II: She was firmly on the team, generous in every interpretation of American motives, ready always to help vanquish Communism, and willing to subject herself to censorship for what she believed was the national interest.

Since her childhood in Milwaukee in the 1920s, Chapelle had searched for heroes. Her first was the polar explorer Admiral Richard E. Byrd, the aviator and adventurer who flew across the North Pole in 1926, and later led five expeditions to the Antarctic. Byrd was living proof of her belief that "you can go out and change the world," as she once told an interviewer. "If you don't, someone else will." In her career as a journalist, her stories invariably featured the heroics of men at war, men who were trying to change the world by defending democracy. She found the last of them in Vietnam. In photo essays and magazine articles, she glorified an anti-Communist priest whose armed congregation fought the Viet Cong, and she lionized a courageous helicopter pilot who flew the machines that were altering the equation of war in Vietnam. She celebrated the courage of the U.S. naval officer who led river boat patrols in the Mekong Delta. In those stories and others, Chapelle's view of the conflict in Southeast Asia was as stark as the black-and-white photograph that captured the last moments of her life in South Vietnam's coastal highlands. She was the third member of the press killed in the Vietnam War. She was the first—and still the only—American woman working as a journalist to die during a combat operation in wartime.

The Associated Press photographer Henri Huet took a photograph of Chapelle as she lay dying, a picture that captured the same life-and-death drama that she herself had hoped to find on her last mission with the U.S. Marines. When an explosion hurled her off her feet, a piece of shrapnel slit her carotid artery. In Huet's photo, a chaplain squatting in the underbrush is making the sign of the cross over Chapelle's crumpled body. In the background, an American Marine and a South Vietnamese soldier, both carrying M-14 rifles slung over their left shoulders, hesitate, appearing to resist the magnetic force of their curiosity. Blood is puddled in the dirt near her head. A small pearl earring is visible in her left lobe.

Just seconds before, as she made her way out of a bivouac area where she had spent the night, she had shouted to NBC newsman Dean Brelis, "Hey Dean, are you coming?" Brelis, who indicated he'd be along in a moment, noticed the tiny bouquet of pink flowers Chapelle had tucked in the band of what he called the "floppy, go-to-hell kind of hat" she was wearing. That Australian bush hat had become Chapelle's trademark. It was a gift from a fellow photographer, one who is said in a Chapelle biography to have been her lover. He had placed it on her head one day in Laos several years before, and she wore it on every military operation she covered during the five trips she made to Southeast Asia from 1961 to 1965. Moments after Chapelle passed him, Brelis heard an explosion. A Marine just ahead of her had tripped a nylon line tied to a hand grenade and wired to an 81 mm mortar. "It was almost as if they [the Viet Cong] had known the night before what our route was going to be," Brelis recalled, "and that's where they placed the bloody mines." He dashed to her, crouched down, and implored, "Dickey, Dickey. It's Dean. Can you hear me?" Chapelle was silent. Brelis, whose work as a war correspondent had begun in World War II, had seen enough dead people to know that Chapelle's wounds were mortal. But his experiences of death had always been with soldiers. He had never seen a colleague die. Nor had he watched a woman die. It was "so unseemly," Brelis recalled thinking. Her hat, blown off her head by the blast, lay nearby. Once again, the pink flowers caught his eye. How could this dainty woman with these pretty flowers in her hat die on this pleasant, innocent morning, he wondered. The flowers, he decided, were a symbol of her effusive spirit; they were "a sort of valentine."

The antiseptic language of the U.S. Marines' "Combat After Action Report" explained how, at 7:58 A.M., newswoman Dickey Chapelle was fatally wounded by "a booby trap consisting of an M-26 grenade coupled with a mortar shell and rigged with a fishline trip wire." A Marine walking just a few steps ahead of her tripped the line, and the explosion that followed killed her and injured five Marines and a corpsman. "Med Evac of the three most serious casualties occurred at 0822." One of those injured Marines later died.

Chapelle and four other journalists had joined Operation Black Ferret on November 3, just the day before. As always, she asked for no special treatment—even in middle age with her weakened knees sometimes balking during jungle marches. In Marine parlance, she "humped" her own gear—all forty pounds the soldiers carried as well as several cameras and, on this mission, a tape recorder. Being in the company of the Marines had given Chapelle a sanctuary during these later years of her life. She found comfort in their familiar routines. That night, she dug her own foxhole and called it her "Hilltop Hilton." Later, she joined the Marines around her, some of them young enough to be her sons, and broke open a can of C-rations. When she had finished eating, Chapelle pulled a Pall Mall from the pack she kept tucked in the top of her sock, the same place the Marines stowed theirs. She was, in the words of a fellow correspondent, an "old war dog." However, notwithstanding her gravelly voice, leathery skin, and the apparent ease with which she wore military boots, she was an old war dog with a singular style: She lit her Pall Malls with a gold Dunhill lighter and wore a gold Cartier watch—and those pearl earrings.

On the night before Chapelle's final mission, Captain Philip J. Fehlen offered the war correspondent a flak jacket to wear on the operation that was to begin shortly after dawn. Like the many other journalists to whom he had made the same offer, she declined. She'd rather not be burdened with the extra seven pounds, she told Fehlen. "I know to keep my head down," she said. Then, Chapelle slept. When a slight drizzle awakened her around midnight, she chatted with Ernest Zaugg, who occupied a nearby patch of ground. Zaugg was a freelancer who regularly sent stories to the *Milwaukee Journal*. The day before, they had marched together on dirt paths along the Songtra Bong River where "nothing revealed the hatred, murder and blood that seethed like a live volcano under the peaceful facade," Zaugg recalled in an article he wrote shortly after Chapelle's death. Reverting to the language her German grandmother had taught her during her childhood, Chapelle called their trek through the sugar cane fields and bamboo groves *ein idyllischer Spaziergang,* an idyllic walk. The war, they agreed during their conversation, "seemed like a dream; hardly a war at all, so quiet, so beautifully quiet." Chapelle told Zaugg that she hoped he would mention her in one of his stories for the *Journal:* "It would please my aunt."

At daybreak, a rainbow arced over the mountains to the northwest. Chapelle and Henri Huet breakfasted together on cans of C-rations. She had lost the bet they made the day before when they wagered on whose unit would receive enemy fire first. She had to pay Huet ten cents. Today, she hoped to reclaim that dime. After breakfast, she fell in line just behind the point man with the 2nd Platoon of Foxtrot Company in the Second Battalion of the Third Marine Regiment. Because Chapelle ranked as a minor celebrity, Huet had taken pictures of her arrival in Saigon six weeks earlier. And because of her reputation in journalism circles as a reporter who unfailingly found action, Horst Faas, AP's lead photographer in Saigon, assigned Huet to track her movements and hook up with whatever operation she covered.

"Dickey," the nickname she had adopted in high school as a tribute to Richard Byrd, always wanted to be in a forward position. Marching with "my" Marines, as she liked to call them, was both familiar and soothing; it made her a member of a large family and part of an important purpose as well. It made her feel whole, she once wrote to her mother back in Milwaukee. "It wasn't that she was a Marine Corps mascot or anything like that," a colleague observed in the days after her death. "She was a Marine." After the land mine exploded, Staff Sergeant Albert P. Miville, who had been knocked down by the blast, crawled to where Chapelle lay. "The blood was squirting out of her. I remember because I put my thumb over it [her neck wound] to try to stop the bleeding," he recalled. A corpsman rushed to her, but there was little he could do. Huet, who had followed the agitated shouts for a medic, took his photograph of Chapelle just before she was lifted onto a stretcher and loaded aboard a med-evac helicopter for transport to a field hospital. She died sprawled on the metal floor of the Huey with three wounded Marines lying nearby. Her last words, someone told her Aunt Louise in Milwaukee, were: "I guess it was bound to happen."

Dickey Chapelle's life occasionally had a film noir quality, but it often played out in Day-Glo and neon. Paradoxes defined her character. She wore combat garb and kid gloves with equal ease. Her vocabulary of expletives could test that of any Marine, yet she also loved poetry, especially the verses of Heinrich Heine, the nineteenth-century German Romantic poet whose work she recited in German. She was the bright, lively daughter of Midwestern Quakers who taught her to abhor violence and embrace pacifism, yet she still developed an enduring lust for war. She finished high school in three years, was her class valedictorian, and accepted the offer of a full scholarship from Massachusetts Institute of Technology. But her dreams of designing airplanes ended after just three semesters, when she flunked out. Notwithstanding her devotion to her country and her near-idol worship of the military, she rebuked the Kennedy administration for banning reporters from military maneuvers in the Bay of Pigs invasion and the Cuban Missile Crisis. The military, she argued, could not be trusted to report on its own activities.

Chapelle's life and death straddled a social revolution in America. Born in 1918, she had a political consciousness that developed during the waning years of the Great Depression. In her 1962 memoir titled *What's a Woman Doing Here?* Chapelle presented her life as a series of dangerous escapades—like the stories she occasionally wrote for *Argosy,* a men's adventure magazine. The book idealized her childhood, sanitized her marriage, and glamorized her achievements. She ignored her insecurities, whitewashed her health problems, and left unexplained her affiliation with some questionable characters. The story of her life bounces from Iwo Jima to Okinawa, from Hungary to Algeria, from Lebanon to Cuba to Southeast Asia, a travelogue of sorts in which she established herself as a footnote to the historic events of her time.

In 1935, when she was seventeen, Chapelle told her first editor, Earl N. Findley, that above all she wanted to be an original. That wish defined her for the rest of her life. Just as many of her grammar school classmates had considered her a source of amusement, so did some of her adult associates. Her colleagues doubtless rolled their eyes at her dramatic claims about how the Communists were determining the location of her next assignment. Her work, she liked to say, took her to the "bayonet borders of the world." When Vietnam became one of those bayonet borders, she saw the war there as a simple fight between the defenders of democracy and the godless Communists who threatened America's way of life. She saw none of the complexities that troubled so many Americans, including some of her colleagues in the press. Despite her insistence that she deplored war and went into combat not to celebrate war but to widen the understanding of its horrors, Chapelle's denunciations of the enemy were laced with strains of demagoguery. The same need for an enemy that she once discerned in Fidel Castro seemed to be her need as well. And her strategy for winning the war was equally simple: "It depends on whether the Viet Cong . . . are killing more of us or we are killing more of them," she once said.

Gloria Emerson had first gone to Southeast Asia in 1956 brimming with a youthful sense of possibility and promise, but a twinge of desperation appears to have driven Chapelle on her first trip to the region in 1961. Government news management efforts had interfered with her repeated attempts to cover Cuban rebels in Florida. In addition, signs of physical frailties had left her frustrated. Keeping up with Marines who were less than half her age was beginning to deplete her energy. The parachute jumps she had started making with the 101st Airborne Division in 1959 were taking their toll, and all those Pall Malls had left her with a hacking cough. Yet she remained steadfast and proud. When a colleague once tried to help her carry her gear, Chapelle was incensed. "Get your damned hands off that," she snapped. "I lug my own stuff and I take no favors from you or anybody. Leave it alone."

In some circles, Chapelle was perceived as a middle-aged has-been, too ready to recall the oft-told tales of her World War II glory days back on "Iwo" and Okinawa. The articles she wrote to accompany her photos only on occasion revealed a larger truth about the war in the way that Emerson's reports in the *New York Times* were to do in the early 1970s. Yes, hang a Leica around her neck and she'd come back with usable material, but she never would be a Robert Capa, the *Life* photographer who died in 1954, killed, like Chapelle, by a land mine in Vietnam. Her photographs never became enduring symbols of the Vietnam War in the way Larry Burrows's pictures in *Life* did before his death in a 1971 helicopter crash in Vietnam.[1] Nor did her photos embody the eloquence of the images the French photojournalist Catherine Leroy took later in the 1960s, or the pathos that Jill Krementz so often captured in her pictures of Vietnamese children. In Vietnam, Chapelle's work seldom transcended the moment in the way it occasionally had earlier in her career. The really great Vietnam era photographers "worked with good ideas," explained Wilber E. Garrett, her editor at *National Geographic*. "What Dickey did was shoot what was right in front of her. The reason that she was good was that she was in the right place."

For all the satisfaction she drew from witnessing the hot wars of the mid-twentieth century, the time she spent in Vietnam in the early to mid-1960s could hardly have been the most fulfilling in her life. The enthusiasm *Reader's Digest* and *National Geographic* had shown for her Vietnam reportage waned at times in the early 1960s. Those same editors, once so eager to underwrite

---

1. Henri Huet, the AP photographer who photographed Chapelle in her dying moments, was killed with Burrows in the crash.

her story ideas, had apparently tired of her work. Editors at *Reader's Digest*, for example, asked her to avoid the melodramatic "I-was-there" style and began to reject her story ideas. *National Geographic* also rejected at least two of her completed stories because, she was told, the quality of her photographs fell short of its standard. Even then, Chapelle's anti-Communist zealotry was beginning to lose its hold on the vital center of America's political thinking, where it had been firmly cemented in the post–World War II years. Chapelle had grown so enamored of the men who fought wars, so convinced that America had a right to mold the world to its liking, and so sure that South Vietnam was a piece of American real estate to be defended against Communist meddling that she began to lose credibility with the editors on whom she depended for assignments. When, during an interview on the *Tonight* show in 1962, Chapelle told Jack Paar that Vietnam was American real estate, "our last piece of real estate on the Asian continent," he took offense. "Aren't these sovereign people?" Paar asked Chapelle. Yet for all her jingoism, Dickey Chapelle was also much more than the cardboard cutout of a Commie-hating, Marine-loving warmonger that colleagues occasionally perceived. She was also a smart, courageous woman who left a mark on twentieth-century journalism.

The patriotic fervor Chapelle carried to Vietnam was nurtured in her childhood by the story of her family's first immigrant, her great-grandfather, who left Germany after being exiled for protesting the Duke of Wurttemberg's draft laws in 1848. America's promise loomed large in the family tale of how he had pursued liberty and freedom in the New World. In conversations about their own pilgrim, Georgie Lou, as she was known in the family, learned that the country and its constitution had to be defended. Perhaps that is why, on her daily walks to Atwater Elementary School, childhood friends saw her stop outside Shorewood Village Hall and salute the American flag as it fluttered in the Midwestern breeze.

Young Georgette was surrounded by adoring and permissive grandparents, aunts, and uncles. Her Aunt Georgette was an attractive New York divorcee who made a career as a labor relations specialist. Aunt Louise, known as Aunt Lutie, was married and ranked as something of a fixture in Milwaukee society. Grandfather George Engelhardt, a retired tobacco importer whose mustache sometimes emitted an aroma of Limburger cheese, taught his grandchildren how to fish. And Georgie Lou had a special kinship with her grandmother, Martha Engelhardt, who, before she emigrated to Wisconsin from Munich, aspired to be a circus performer, maybe a trapeze artist or a bareback rider. Martha taught her granddaughter German and introduced her to the poetry and fiction of Germany's literary giants. Grandmother Engelhardt also taught her to sew doll's clothes. But whatever charm Georgie Lou found in dolls was short-lived: Airplanes and the men who flew them began to enthrall her when she reached her teen years.

The large and loving family Chapelle described in her autobiography embodied so many of mainstream America's illusions about itself. In reality, the environment in which Chapelle grew up had something of a schizophrenic quality. Mary Holgate Dohmen, a school chum, recalls that Chapelle's father, Paul Meyer, was a "quiet, sweet man." Her mother, Edna Engelhardt Meyer, on the other hand, "pushed Georgie Lou ahead all the time." Like her daughter, Edna Meyer, in Dohmen's recollections, "was a different kind of person." On the few occasions Mary Dohmen went to Georgie Lou's house to play, Edna Meyer struck her as someone who was "a little scary to younger kids." She could be highly emotional and overly protective of Georgie Lou and her younger brother, Robert. Dohmen also remembers how Mrs. Meyer created embarrassing scenes in grade school, scenes that she thought must have mortified her classmate. In fourth or fifth grade, on the day after some boys had teased Georgie Lou on her walk home from school, the tall, stern Mrs. Meyer, looking rather like an extra in a Wagnerian opera, stalked into her daughter's classroom carrying a batch of freshly baked fudge. She talked to the children about the importance of being kind to others and, before passing out her home-made treat, she added, "I hope that you boys who have been mean to Georgie Lou will get the biggest pieces."

Georgie Lou was "extremely bright, even in grade school, but off on a plane of her own," Dohmen recalled. At an age when many girls absorbed themselves in Nancy Drew mysteries, Georgie Lou chose William Shakespeare's *Julius Caesar* as her topic for an oral book report she gave in fifth grade. Although she sometimes played with her classmates, Georgie Lou didn't quite fit in. "I probably knew her about best of all, but I didn't know her all that well," Dohmen said. Florence Vallencourt Lindsay, another of Chapelle's classmates, echoed that sentiment. "She wasn't concerned about what all the other kids were doing," she added. "She went her own way pretty much. Boys were a little intimidated because she was so bright. Girls didn't include her in things because she didn't care about putting her hair up in curlers."

A similar pattern of social interaction followed Chapelle to high school. Her growing preoccupation with flying created tensions at home and made her something of an oddball among her peers. And no wonder. Who among her classmates would have shared Georgie Lou's joy in finding books such as

Yancy's Aerial Navigation and Meteorology and *Simple Aerodynamics* under the Christmas tree? Her contemporaries decorated their rooms with photos of Hollywood stars—Claudette Colbert or Jean Harlow—but it was Richard Byrd's photograph, along with that of Baron Manfred von Richthofen—the Red Baron—that claimed space on Dickey's bedroom walls. After meeting Byrd backstage after a fund-raising appearance at the Milwaukee Auditorium in the early 1930s, she re-christened herself in his honor. Margaret Harrigan, a high school classmate, recalled how the yearbook staffers went overboard in writing the description of Georgie that appeared next to her senior photograph: "Georgie has evident appetency towards the profession of aeronautical engineering. As an avocation, GL reverts to literary composition as a solace, reporting for the *Ripples,* promulgating admonitions to hall offenders and serving as vice president of the Radio Club." The pomposity was deliberate "because she was so far beyond the rest of us, they used the biggest words in the dictionary to describe her," Harrigan explained. "They knew she wouldn't be happy if they used ordinary English. No other senior in Shorewood High School's Class of 1935 had a yearbook entry quite like hers."

As a teenager, Georgie Lou announced to her family that her future was in aviation. Edna Meyer turned apoplectic. It was far too dangerous. Instead, she declared, the written word would shape her daughter's career, one that would eventually be eclipsed by domesticity. Her overly protective nature was counterbalanced by Paul Meyer's determination to instill in his children a taste for adventure and daring. From their father, Georgie Lou and her brother, Robert, learned how to conquer fear. He gently encouraged them to walk the highest I-beams of still-skeletal buildings at construction sites around the Milwaukee suburbs. The trick, he told them, was never to look down. Although she had learned to pilot an airplane by the time she was eighteen, all her yearnings to become a professional pilot were stymied by her poor eye sight. That passion for flight, and doubtless the memories of her father's admonition never to look down, helped her earn her paratrooper's wings in July 1959—at the age of forty. She made her qualifying jump with the 1st Special Forces of the Army's 82nd Airborne Division and later received her wings from the 101st Airborne. Her paratroop certificate was signed by Major General William C. Westmoreland. Two years later, she earned her second set of paratrooper's wings from the South Vietnamese air force.

Chapelle's writing life began when she was fourteen, when she wrote an article about flying. The national magazine *United States Air Services* published her first story in September 1933. In writing about "Why We Want to

Fly: By One of Us, Age Fourteen," G. L. Meyer undertook to explain to mystified parents why 1 million of her contemporaries yearned to fly. "The aviation world, partly, no doubt, because it is unexplored by most of us, seems to be a place where dreams come true overnight, courage is tried and proved, heroes plentifully abound and there is no dearth of Glory—capitalized—in our minds," she wrote. In what might have been a reference to her own mother, G. L. Meyer further argued that a youthful fascination with flight served the interests of progress; she also urged parents to be less dismissive of their children's recurring plea, "Dad, can't we go to the airport?" Earl Findley, the editor, had no idea that his new and youngest writer had hoodwinked him. It never crossed his mind that G. L. Meyer, whom he paid $7.50 for her story, was a girl.

More than three decades later, in "Searching for Victor Charlie," the last article she wrote, Chapelle again made herself a group spokesperson. The story, published in the *National Observer* four days after her death, is her personal narrative of a search-and-clear mission, the offensive operation that had become a basic Marine strategy in Vietnam. There was a fifty-fifty chance that "we'll get us some Victor Charlies," a sergeant told her. Once again, Chapelle savored the sense of purpose and oneness that always washed over her during night patrols with the Marines. The fifty soldiers and one reporter were no longer individuals marching in the dark. "We are something more," Chapelle wrote. "It is an entity committed to the steady movement across space . . . we have become as inexorable as an organism on one course with one will." Chapelle's story heaped praise on the platoon's leader, Staff Sergeant Anthony Benz, and described the four-day mission in almost microscopic detail: the color of the hills and the sky, the agonizing hours spent maneuvering a rock-covered mountain so steep in places that they crawled on their hands and knees, the frigid water in a river they had to ford, the discomfort of sleeping in the rain, the fear evoked by the sound of a "cooing pigeon" in a place where she knew there were no such birds. Like so many of her stories, "Searching Vietnam for Victor Charlie" celebrated the deeds of individual Marines, an approach that put her in league with Ernie Pyle, the World War II journalist who gave a voice to the average GI. The mission, however, ended in disappointment. Sergeant Benz complained to Chapelle about the elusive enemy: "I just can't figure myself how Victor Charlie [the Viet Cong] thinks to win if he won't come out and fight us here." As in the scores of articles she wrote between 1933 and 1965, the first person singular figured prominently in the first and last articles of her thirty-two-year career.

Chapelle's work as a photographer began in the late 1930s, several years after she flunked out of MIT, years during which she wandered through several jobs linked to her love of flying. Shorewood High School's valedictorian had been admitted to MIT on a full scholarship and was one of only seven women accepted by the school in 1935. Findley, who became something of a pen pal after he published her article, had urged her to apply, and he wrote a letter in which he endorsed her as worthy of a scholarship. So, when she was sixteen, Georgie Lou had set off for Cambridge to begin her career as a "Tech woman." MIT, she hoped, would teach her how to design airplanes. She appears to have thrived on the freedom that the distance from Shorewood afforded her. On her first visit home for Christmas, her former classmates found her more flamboyant than ever. At the annual Christmas party Florence Vallencourt Lindsay's family held for their returning college-aged children and their friends, her old chum Mary Dohmen witnessed Dickey's still-healthy flair for the outlandish. At a time when it was scandalous for women to smoke, Dickey, with a cigarette in hand, sidled up to one of her former teachers and announced that the boys she encountered at MIT "preferred black lingerie." By the beginning of her sophomore year, however, the distractions of her outside interests became her undoing. Learning from machinists at the Boston Navy Yard how to assemble turbines was more enticing than class. Rather than take a chemistry exam, for which she was unprepared, she maneuvered her way aboard a flight bound for Worcester, a city that had been isolated by floods and whose residents were in desperate need of food. Freelance stories she wrote for the *Boston Traveler* took still more time away from her studies. By the end of her third semester, to Edna Meyer's consternation, her daughter's career as a "Tech woman" was over.

Back in Milwaukee, a series of jobs, most of them related to flying, followed, and so did her marriage. She typed for a flying circus in exchange for flying lessons. Later in Florida and in New York City, she worked in the publicity bureau of Transcontinental and Western Air (later Trans World Airlines). That's where Dickey met the man she would marry, Anthony Chapelle, a debonair, philandering pilot and World War I–era U.S. Navy photographer who was Transcontinental's director of photography. He was twenty years her senior. They met when she signed up for his photography class.

"An inveterate prevaricator," declared an FBI report on Chapelle, who first attracted the bureau's attention in 1942 when he "aroused suspicion due to his unusual curiosity concerning matters of a secret nature, and which were no concern to him." Another report in Anthony and Dickey Chapelle's heavily redacted FBI files describes him as a man who was "deceitful, unethical, who accepts fraudulent techniques, who would do anything for money." In the more prosaic words of one of his five wives (Dickey was his third), Chapelle could "charm the tits off a brass monkey." He captivated Dickey. In her, he found a woman who asked for a camera rather than a diamond ring to mark their engagement. He bought her an eight-pound Speed Graphic.

By the time they married in October 1940, in the garden of her parents' Shorewood home, Tony had transformed his young bride from a plump and gawky Wisconsin milkmaid into a woman few of her high school classmates later recognized. Dickey had dyed her lusterless brown hair blond, lost weight, traded her shapeless woolen suits for velvets and silk, and taken to wearing lipstick. Saks Fifth Avenue became her favorite store.

Chapelle's brother Robert, who was fifteen on his sister's wedding day, remembered Tony as an incomparably dashing figure. He was handsome and exuded strength; he seemed so worldly and wise. Along with the rest of the family, Robert was charmed by the man who arrived at the Meyer doorstep in his dark suit and black fedora, looking rather like a New York gangster. When Tony tendered advice, Robert once observed, he did so "in a voice that sounded halfway between God's and Humphrey Bogart's."

In the fifteen-year marriage that followed, Tony heaped expensive gifts on Dickey, among them the gold Cartier watch, the Dunhill lighter—and the pearl earrings she was wearing on the day she died. But their union frayed under the strains of his womanizing and her growing sense of independence. In her work as a photographer, the student ultimately eclipsed her teacher.

Early on, however, Tony was her guru and Dickey's career in photojournalism began with considerable promise. *Look,* a popular large-format news magazine that featured photojournalism, bought her story and photographs of a woman working in a New Jersey aircraft plant sewing fabric on the wings of the British Royal Air Force fighter planes. Following that success, *Look's* editors sent her to photograph the gun crews that traveled aboard freighters running the blockade of Panama in 1942—crews that were necessary because German submarines were an ever present threat in the waters of the Gulf of Mexico. She had pitched the story to *Look* editors as a way to join Tony at Coco Solo Naval Air Station in Panama, where he was sent after volunteering to teach sailors aerial photography.

That Central American adventure seemed foredoomed from the outset. To her dismay, the USS *Marta,* an aging United Fruit freight ship to which the navy had assigned her, unarmed and without an escort, never once came under attack during its two-week journey through dangerous waters. So much for the story about gun crews aboard blockade-running ships. Neither the story she wrote about the trip nor two others about a regiment of American soldiers training in the jungles of Panama were accepted by *Look*'s editors. Then camera problems abruptly ended her Central American assignment. What seemed like the sound of gunfire accompanied the malfunction of her flash attachment as she photographed Secretary of the Navy Frank Knox during his inspection trip in the Canal Zone. Secret Service men in the secretary's entourage all reached for their guns. That little melodrama called attention to the presence of a wife in a war zone. When Tony's commanding officer suggested that he send his wife back to New York, he countered that Dickey took her orders not from him but from the War Department. Within twenty-four hours, Tony received orders to return to New York. Days later, Dickey followed.

Later that year, as Tony began making arrangements to be ordered to Asia, Dickey started maneuvering for her own assignment with the U.S. Pacific Fleet. His assignment never materialized, but her accreditation came through in record time. Ralph Daigh, editor of *Life Story* magazine, sent her off to cover World War II with one command: "I want you to be sure you'll be the first woman somewhere. . . . Any of those islands will do." The echo of that directive probably shaped her response to the question military men invariably ask reporters. Whenever someone in uniform wanted to know, "Where do you want to go?" Chapelle answered, "As far forward as possible." That is where she was on the day she died. On occasion, she went "far forward" without permission, as she did not long after she arrived in the Pacific theater. Initially, assigned to the U.S. Navy hospital ship USS *Samaritan*, she photographed doctors and nurses treating soldiers wounded in the battle for Iwo Jima during February and March 1945. One set of her pictures, "The Dying Marine," was used by the Red Cross for the next decade in blood drives across America. The first of the two photos showed an injured U.S. Marine whose wounds had severely disfigured his face. The second, taken twenty-four hours later, showed a spirited young private who, after receiving fourteen pints of blood, bore almost no resemblance to the ravaged young man whom she had first photographed.

Stories with happy endings, however, were far outnumbered by those of sorrow. Along with the 6,000 Marines who died in the four weeks of fighting, there was the man with no face, the delirious soldier whose skin had been roasted in a Japanese attack on his tank, the men whose minds "had broken rather than believe the horrors they saw," and the canvas-wrapped bodies of the dead who were buried at sea. Even in her twenties, Chapelle seemed to blend in with the soldiers. When a young medic asked her to console a soldier who had just received a Dear John letter, she flinched. Surely talking to a woman would be of little comfort to him, she insisted. The medic was unmoved: "You see ma'am, you don't look like a woman. You look like another damn Marine."

At the suggestion of a colleague with Reuters News Agency, Chapelle asked for an assignment on Iwo Jima even as the fighting continued where Americans had established operations. Her assigned destination was a field hospital at Motoyama Airfield One, where her orders were to photograph the use of whole blood, but Chapelle longed to see combat. Through a combination of luck, subterfuge, and the help of a bored Marine, she finally reached "the front" near Mount Suribachi, where the Marines had raised an American flag twelve days before. The island's hilly, volcanic landscape was an indistinguishable series of sandy ridges devoid of landmarks to delineate any battle lines. Nothing she could see indicated that armies were at war. After climbing to a hilltop vantage point, she wasn't sure which way to point her camera but was too embarrassed to ask the Marine who had agreed to drive her. Thinking she could sort out the battle lines later, she photographed each compass point. She thought she heard wasps buzzing around her head as she clicked the shutter.

When she left the hilltop and returned to her Jeep, her driver roared, "That was the goddamfooldest thing I ever saw anybody do in my life! Do you realize that every sniper and half the artillery on both sides of this unmentionable battle had about ten minutes to make up their minds about you? My God, if you'd got shot, I'd have spent the rest of the unmentionable war filling out papers!" His anger baffled Chapelle. But back on Guam, her Reuters colleague gave her an explanation. Those wasps were bullets. Snipers had been firing at her. Chapelle was ecstatic. She remembered Winston Churchill's words about the thrills of battle: "It was like no other feeling in the world." She wrote a dramatic opening to the notes she took of the trip: FROM THE FRONT AT IWO JIMA MARCH 5 UNDER FIRE. For the rest of her life, Chapelle searched out opportunities to re-experience that exhilaration.

The next chance came a few weeks later when the Marines began their drive on Okinawa. In her impatience to go as far forward as possible, Chapelle was unwilling to wait until Rear Admiral H. B. Miller, the ranking public relations officer of the Pacific Fleet, okayed the movement of women to the island. Her pleas notwithstanding, Miller stood firm. When military nurses were ordered ashore, he said, she could join them. "I'm not going to have 100,000 soldiers and Marines pulling up their pants because you are ashore." End of discussion. On Landing Day plus three, Chapelle received permission to make an afternoon visit to the island field hospitals from an officer who knew nothing of Admiral Miller's ban on visits by women. When rough seas made her planned evening return from Okinawa too risky, she spent the next three days seeking permission to travel to a forward area hospital. Once there, however, she discovered she was hardly a welcome sight. "How the hell did you get here?" fumed a doctor when she arrived. "I could see that his outfit needed an unarmed photographer about as badly as an epidemic," Chapelle recalled in her autobiography. She redeemed herself early the next morning after four Marines were brought in by Jeep. Two of the soldiers had broken bones, one was already dead, and the fourth appeared to have a mortal chest wound. While the doctor operated for two hours, Chapelle held a heavy, military-issue flashlight for illumination. The Marine lived. The doctor's fury eased. He helped her get her photos the following day.

Ironically, Chapelle's own colleagues, rather than the Marine brass, were her undoing. Like many of his fellow war correspondents, John Lardner, who wrote for the North American Newspaper Alliance and the *New Yorker*, considered Chapelle's presence on the island offensive. After she had spent one night in Okinawa's Marine Corps press headquarters tent, Lardner wrote in a dispatch, "The nerves of the boys in our tent section were somewhat demoralized by the presence of the first American woman to go ashore on Okinawa, Miss Dickey Chapelle." When the report reached Admiral Kelly Turner of the Pacific Fleet, his order was unequivocal: "Get that woman out of here." One Marine told Chapelle that the order to find her and remove her from Okinawa said that she should be shot on sight. In unseemly haste, she was hustled off the island and shipped back stateside. Her behavior was denounced as a demonstration of recklessness and irresponsibility. The War Department revoked her press accreditation to the Pacific Fleet. She worried that she might never be re-accredited by the U.S. military again. Admiral Miller cold-shouldered all her pleas and ignored those editors whom she enlisted to plead with him on her behalf. Ralph Daigh, her editor at *Life Story*, argued in a letter to Miller that "the decision to discipline Mrs. Chapelle was made largely because of her sex." Later, when Chapelle herself pleaded with Miller, telling him that because her professional life was tainted she would be unemployed, he stood firm. "An excellent time for you to have given this thought would have been at Okinawa prior to the disembarkation following our many talks on the subject of women going ashore."

Worse still, in a foretaste of the rejection she later faced in Vietnam, her editors refused to run the photographs that had cost her so dearly, the photos she hoped would be her salvation. They were gripping but gory. "You ought to have known better than to make these, Dickey," a well-dressed young *Life Story* editor told her. "You know we can't use them. The wounded look too— too dirty." Chapelle was indignant. "Whatever suffering men could undergo in the name of the folks back home, surely anyone could endure to merely look at!" When Chapelle explained her position—having said "everything that needed saying and perhaps a few things that did not"—she was no longer a contributing editor at *Life Story*. That was in July 1945. Ultimately, *Cosmopolitan* published what she called her "unprettied pictures of the wounded."

She managed to land a well-paying but unfulfilling job as a photographer and editor at *Seventeen* magazine, but she traded the position in November 1947 for a chance to do humanitarian work in Europe. By the fall of that year, Dickey and Tony Chapelle had signed on as a team of unpaid photographers working for the American Friends Service Committee. Their job was to take pictures of the Quakers' food and clothing distribution program in Germany and behind the Iron Curtain in Poland, Czechoslovakia, and Hungary. The Chapelles' original six-week assignment lasted two years. In the bombed-out cities of Germany and Eastern Europe, Dickey and Tony photographed starving, homeless people living in rubble. Personal comforts mattered little to Dickey as long as their work produced in her fellow Americans the kind of generosity it would take to relieve the suffering. Tony, whose endurance and idealism hardly matched Dickey's, carried on even though the hardships affected his health. They established a nonprofit news agency called the American Voluntary Information Services Overseas. According to an IRS form they filed in 1950, the Chapelles declared that their purpose was "to spread perpetual peace." The lofty and unattainable nature of her goal, combined with a growing homesickness evidenced in letters to her family, began eroding Dickey's enthusiasm. By the end of 1949, with both their spirits and their cash depleted, Dickey and Tony left Europe.

By 1952, the Chapelles landed a government-sponsored assignment to document the distribution of economic aid and technical assistance in underdeveloped countries. Contrasted with their work in Europe, this was a cushy deal. Tony savored the luxury hotels and chauffeured limousines that came with the job. For seven months, he and Dickey took photographs of

American technicians building schoolhouses and bridges in remote villages of India, Iraq, and Iran. But their enviable posting ended abruptly when they failed to get the security clearance required to continue their work. Nothing in the Chapelles' CIA or FBI files hints at the reasons.

By the mid-1950s, Dickey Chapelle found a way back into photojournalism, still her passion. Her growing disquiet with the constraints of married life and Tony's continued womanizing had finally resulted in a separation, and her new need for economic self-sufficiency led her to a job at CARE. But photojournalism remained her passion, and without her press accreditation her career had stalled. In desperation, she devised a scheme she hoped would be irresistible to the Marines. She proposed spending two months in boot camp so that she could write a story about how a recruit is transformed into a U.S. Marine. In exchange, she would be re-accredited. The bargain was struck and, in November 1955, Chapelle, on a leave of absence from CARE, reported to Camp Pendleton, California; there she participated in the 4:00 A.M. marches, the drills, the push-ups, the weapons training, and the indoctrination sessions, training that doubtless helped her endure her many jungle marches in Vietnam. Searching for the secret of how an eight-week physical and mental ordeal remade these men into soldiers, she discovered an esprit de corps that bound them and transformed them into a single, determined fighting force. The experience, she later wrote, "taught me the bone-deep difference between a war correspondent and a girl reporter, even one willing to say she wants to go forward because the remark rings like a bell." She left Camp Pendleton believing she had become one of "The Old Corps." It was a belief she held until her dying day in Vietnam.

Soon after she returned to New York from California, Chapelle landed a high-paying job as director for public information at the Research Institute of America, a business advisory organization, where she was in charge of circulating the institute's economic surveys and forecasts. Still, war and the threat of war continued to beckon. In 1956, she jumped at the chance to document the anti-Communist uprising in Hungary. In a model of Soviet-style cold war overreaction, what had begun as peaceful demonstrations by students in Budapest quickly escalated into a full-scale military crackdown by the USSR. Thousands of Hungarians died and thousands of refugees fled. Chapelle made arrangements with the International Rescue Committee to deliver antibiotics to Hungary's freedom fighters and with *Life* magazine to cover the movement of refugees escaping into Austria. At least that's the story she told in her autobiography. Since Leo Cherne, her boss at the Research Institute of

America, also led the IRC's effort in getting humanitarian aid to the Hungarian refugees, the scenario seemed plausible.

Other accounts of the trip suggest she had a different purpose. In an interview years later, Cherne insisted that Chapelle did not go to Austria at his behest. She was, he noted, "carrying a substantial amount of money with her," perhaps as much as $10,000. Speculation has it that the real purpose of the trip, which Chapelle herself called "a suicide mission," was to get someone important to the IRC, and perhaps even to the American intelligence community, out of Hungary. When she left the United States, she carried an expensive Minox camera that was no bigger than a package of chewing gum. Whatever her purpose, the trip was pure Chapelle: It was filled with contradiction and courage; it not only hinted of furtive purpose but also suggested that good intentions had gone awry. The trip also underscored a ubiquitous riddle about her character: How could such an intelligent woman make such ill-advised judgments?

In Vienna, Chapelle stayed in the four-star Hotel Bristol, where she befriended James A. Michener, who was documenting the exodus of Hungarians for *Reader's Digest*, and his wife, Mari Michener. Chapelle planned to spend ten days in Andau, the Austrian frontier town thirty miles south of Vienna where Hungarian refugees crossed by way of a remote, planked footbridge. In Michener's description, it wasn't much of a bridge at all. No roads led to it. Journalists, Chapelle among them, routinely used the route to cross the border into Hungary. In his book *The Bridge at Andau*, Michener estimated that Chapelle probably guided "hundreds" of refugees to freedom in Austria.

On the night of December 4, 1956, Chapelle slipped into Hungary with two young freedom fighters on a mission that one contemporary declared "was not her finest hour." Chapelle's memoir claims implausibly that delivering ten pounds of penicillin to a hospital was her only purpose. And with that Minox camera, loaded with infrared film and taped beneath her brassiere, "I expected to make pictures to prove the penicillin had been delivered to a freedom-fighter doctor." Several hours after they crossed the border, a burst of machine-gun fire above their heads halted the trio in a cornfield. Within minutes, Dickey Chapelle was arrested by Soviet soldiers.

On the way to Budapest the following day, Chapelle expected her captors to deliver her to the U.S. embassy. Instead, she landed in Fo Street prison, an infamous Communist detention center. She successfully jettisoned her "most compromising bit of evidence," that tiny Minox, by tossing it out the car window along with the butt of a cigarette she had just smoked. The fellow with the machine gun in the front seat was none the wiser. Chapelle spent fifty-two days in a tiny, frigid prison cell, thirty-eight of them in solitary confinement. Interrogated, harassed, starved, and occasionally threatened with hanging, she was left by most of her countrymen, in a phrase that emerged decades later, "to dangle slowly, slowly in the wind." Her freelance status apparently made her easy to ignore. Michener praised Chapelle's exploits in his book, but because she was still in prison when it was published, he used a fictitious name and changed her gender "so that this book could not be used as evidence against her by the communist authorities." In Michener's telling, "a brave and daring photographer whose pictures helped tell the story of Hungary's mass flight to freedom . . . would go anywhere, and for the next several nights we patrolled the border together, bringing in hundreds of Hungarians. Sometimes we went well into Hungary, occasionally up to the bridge."

Neither Chapelle's employer nor the American government appeared interested in her whereabouts. Professional associates seemed similarly unconcerned. A fellow foreign correspondent who criticized her behavior, Julia Edwards, explained the dilemma. The U.S. embassy in Vienna took a hands-off position to safeguard its own policies. The American government, after all, retained the right to hang foreigners caught making an unauthorized entry into the United States in wartime, even if they claimed to be news photographers. At the International Rescue Committee, Cherne disassociated himself and his organization from Chapelle. He was said to have feared compromising his organization's larger goals. *Life* editors were apparently afraid of jeopardizing a new arrangement under which a staff correspondent was accredited to Budapest. Although *Life* used two of her photographs in its special issue about Hungary in early December, a spokesman denied that she worked for the magazine. Finally, her news media colleagues offered little sympathy. Edward Clarke, *Time* magazine's Vienna bureau chief, irritably declared that Chapelle "got what she deserved." Rumors circulated that Chapelle had entered Hungary with the hope of being arrested so that she could write about it—a charge that echoed decades later in connection with journalists who vanished after venturing into Cambodia.

Stories circulated by the Associated Press in late December brought attention to Chapelle's imprisonment and apparently led the U.S. Department of State to confront Hungarian authorities. In late January 1957, Chapelle was put on trial; the charge was illegal border crossing, a crime that carried a maximum five-year sentence. The judge, however, ruled that the fifty-plus days she had already served would suffice, and she was expelled from Hungary.

Before she walked out of Fo Street prison on January 27, 1957, Chapelle put on her pearl earrings with shaking hands. Richard Selby, the U.S. consul in Budapest, escorted Chapelle to the Austrian border. The only explanation she provided at a press conference was characteristically cryptic. She had slipped into Hungary to deliver "a token gift of medicines to the Hungarian people." Although "prison life was rough," she said the guards had given her German and English poetry books. One poem became her favorite: Thomas Gray's "Ode to Adversity." News of her release made the front page of the *New York Times*. Later she said that imprisonment had taught her something: "If you fought hard enough, whatever was left of you afterward would not be found stripped of honor."

Questions about her real purpose in Hungary were never satisfactorily answered. A memo in Dickey Chapelle's FBI file indicates that Tony Chapelle alleged that the State Department was aware of his former wife's trip to Hungary and that to secure her release he had made efforts to bribe Hungarian officials. In a letter to her brother, Robert, by that time a geology professor at the University of Wisconsin in Madison, Chapelle explained that she was no longer associated with *Life*, the International Rescue Committee, or the Research Institute of America. "Please feel free to draw your own conclusions, as long as they are unflattering to all three outfits." Then again, a few unflattering conclusions could be drawn about her, she conceded to Robert, "for not suspecting there was a Russian patrol in that damn Hungarian cornfield in the first place."

From the time she returned from Hungary until she died in 1965, combat and revolution were Chapelle's specialty. "Her travel itinerary," in the words of one observer, "could have been a spider's web draped over the globe." A familiar sight wherever men were at war, she took to calling herself "an interpreter of violence." That fascination with combat, she claimed in her autobiography, reached back into her childhood. At home she was taught by her Quaker parents that "violence in any form is unthinkable, [so] unthinkable that it became as attractive a mystery to me as sex seemed to be to other teenagers." Her brother's ideological leanings, however, differed sharply from Chapelle's; he embraced his parents' pacifist views.

The first major story Chapelle covered after the debacle in Hungary ranks as her most daring assignment. At a time when the American media reported on France's war in Algeria exclusively from the official French perspective, Chapelle spent nearly five weeks with the Algerian rebels. In the 1950s, the idea that a journalist might look at a war from the enemy's viewpoint, as Harrison Salisbury later did in North Vietnam in December 1966, tended to be seen as borderline treason. That Chapelle, still in disgrace among her colleagues for her escapade in Hungary, was the only American journalist whom an Algerian army officer could recruit to tell the rebels' story spoke volumes about how the American media followed their government's lead on matters associated with the colonial interests of its allies, and this was three years after the fall of Dien Bien Phu. For months, Abdel Kadar Chanderli, the rebels' United Nations representative, had looked in vain for an American reporter willing to follow along. Chapelle, however, was willing, indeed even eager, for the assignment. An exclusive story about war, especially one that involved ample measures of secrecy and intrigue, always left her salivating. French propaganda operations placed tight controls on news of the Algerian war, a conflict that marked one of the great press failures of the second half of the twentieth century. The American press never questioned France's claim that the uprising was a minor "internal difficulty" staged by barbaric, Communist-led Algerian outlaws who had no popular support. A British documentary about the rebellion was released in America in late 1956, but it had done little to awaken mainstream media interest. The *New York Times* continued to echo the official French view as it did in a 1957 editorial that declared, "The French are acting with dignity." France, the editorial concluded, had a responsibility to safeguard the 1.2 million citizens of French descent who then lived in Algeria. Chapelle was about to tell a very different story.

She flew from New York to Madrid where she was, as arranged, "kidnapped" by Algerian soldiers and flown to Rabat. She dressed in a burka to avoid detection by the French; at the border, she was spirited into Algeria by rebel soldiers. Covering this war, she quickly realized, would be vastly more strenuous than basic training with the Marines at Camp Pendleton. The rebel soldiers nicknamed her "Squirrel" and made her safety their highest concern. Why, Chapelle wondered, would they expend so much energy to keep her safe? America was France's ally; surely the French would not harm an American reporter. That was precisely the problem, explained a rebel leader. "They'll cut your throat. But first they'll face you toward Mecca, and then they'll say we did it."

She called the fight in Algeria a "bitter war, [a] rough war even by the unspeakable standards I had learned when I covered the battles for Iwo Jima and Okinawa." Leaders of the rebel unit Chapelle accompanied were especially anxious to show her that France was killing Algerians with NATO bombs supplied by the United States. "You know, your country really is my country's chief enemy," Ben Chafa, a ranking officer in the Scorpion Battalion, told her. "Not France, for we can bleed France white. But always, America revives her with arms and money when she would faint without them." That same dynamic would have a parallel in Vietnam—for nearly twenty years, the succession of governments in South Vietnam would have collapsed without American aid.

Of the twelve hundred photographs she took on that Algerian foray, the most startling were of a young Algerian spy who was captured and put to death for aiding the French. She was invited to witness his execution by firing squad. Hoping to prolong the young man's life, she agreed, but said she wanted to watch his trial first. The rebels hastily organized a proceeding during which the defendant, named Banamar, confessed that he had "killed more women and children of our people than [he could] count."

Chapelle's story of Banamar's execution echoed with the same drama and pathos that Richard Harding Davis had woven into his story, "The Death of Rodriguez," about the execution Davis witnessed in Cuba during the Spanish-American War. Adolfo Rodriguez, a nineteen-year-old farm boy in Cuba in 1897, marched to his death with heroic self-control, determined that the firing squad recognize him as a "man who meets his punishment fearlessly and who will let his enemies see that they can kill but cannot frighten him." In Banamar, Chapelle saw "the face of a poet and the grace of a ballet dancer." His composure never faltered. With the setting sun at his back, Banamar faced east, toward Mecca, when his executioners opened fire. "He fell backward as if the wind had pushed him. His eyes remained wide; the shock of the bullets might have been harder than he expected," Chapelle wrote. Banamar's execution symbolized a larger truth about war: It embodied "the tragic way that war twists young lives and yet, at the final moment, gives a man the courage to face death unafraid."

After thirty-two days, Chapelle's "kidnappers" delivered her and her photographs to a Madrid hotel. "Bon courage," they told her. Spadea, a little-known news distribution agency, sold her story to fifty clients. *Life* bought her execution photos, but decided, just as *Life Story* had with her Okinawa photos a decade earlier, that they were too brutal to publish. *Pageant*, a *Reader's Digest* look-alike, ran her story without the photos. Finally, in October 1958, *Argosy* published her story and her photos in a layout titled "The Executioners."

The Algerian assignment helped erase the stigma of Hungary. Julia Edwards, the fellow foreign correspondent who had criticized her in Hungary, praised her stories about Algeria: "Her success as the first American to cover the Algerian fighters' side of that war inspired several newsmen to follow in her footsteps." Edwards also asked why the French were dropping bombs from the NATO stockpiles on Algeria, the same question raised in Chapelle's reportage. Weren't those bombs designated for the protection of Western Europe rather than for use in this colonial war in Africa? Edwards's observations about Chapelle also noted that "after Algeria, wherever a gun was fired, Dickey was there."

Chapelle's experiences in Cuba between 1959 and 1961 became the catalyst for her first trip to Vietnam. Castro and his revolution captivated Chapelle in 1959. Like Herbert L. Matthews, a *New York Times* reporter who had interviewed Castro and several of his cohorts in 1957, Chapelle was enchanted by the thirty-two-year-old revolutionary. She witnessed Castro's triumphant arrival in Havana, where he installed himself in the presidential palace on January 8, 1959. "Waking up in a country that overnight has purged itself of a terrorist dictator," she enthused, "is an excellent way to comprehend why our own forebears fought and died for their liberty." She was certain that Castro, the man who called her "the polite little American with all that tiger blood in her veins," would follow an American model in his reconstruction of Cuba. "There is hope of democracy in the air," she wrote. In a ceremony in Washington four months later, when Castro awarded medals to a dozen American journalists for their coverage of his revolution that year, Chapelle, along with Homer Bigart and Matthews, received the honor.

A year later, however, Chapelle reassessed Castro because events had established that he was no Robin Hood. "The trouble is that Castro has not changed while his problems have. The overwhelming fault of his [Castro's] character was plain to see even then," she wrote. "This was his inability to tolerate the absence of an enemy, he had to stand—or better, rant and shout—against some challenge every waking moment." In 1961, Chapelle learned of U.S. plans to invade Cuba from her contacts in the exile community. That the CIA was playing an important role in the planned invasion became clear to her in Miami, where she arrived a day before thirteen hundred members of Brigade 2506 landed at the Bay of Pigs. She had hoped to reach the troops' staging area in Cuba even if she had to go in by parachute. But Chapelle discovered that her efforts were obstructed by the well-cloaked but unmistakable hand of the CIA.

It was her first taste of news management and she resented it. In frustration, she asked her *Reader's Digest* editor, Hobart Lewis, to whom she had been introduced by James Michener after her return from Hungary, to send her to Southeast Asia. In requesting an assignment in South Vietnam, Chapelle observed that maybe the American government wasn't working quite so hard at masking its presence there. She soon discovered that it was.

Chapelle was the first American woman in journalism to go to Southeast Asia for an extended stay after Gloria Emerson's 1956 trip. Unlike Emerson and so many of the other women who later ventured off to cover the war, Chapelle left the States on each of her five trips with assignments from magazines, among them *Reader's Digest, National Geographic, Argosy,* and the *National Observer.*

Change had overtaken South Vietnam in the years between Emerson's departure and Chapelle's arrival in May 1961. The Second Indochina War, as the Vietnamese called it, had begun in 1960. By mid-1961, the Viet Cong were blowing up the railroad lines and had undertaken an assassination campaign that resulted in the deaths of 4,000 low-ranking South Vietnamese officials. War had also spread to Laos and, to a lesser extent, to Cambodia. By this time, America's official policy involved providing South Vietnam's army with advisors who would teach them tactics to defeat the Communist guerrilla forces. In reality, as Chapelle would soon discover, the U.S. military stationed in the hills of Laos and in South Vietnam were engaged in armed combat. However, the extent of America's role in the politics of both countries remained largely hidden from the American people. Although Chapelle was willing to keep any secret that advanced America's cause, her impulse to celebrate the heroism of America's military men in the fight against Communism soon created a quandary for her.

The looking-glass environment that characterized so much of the American experience in Southeast Asia was inimical to the simplicity that defined Chapelle's understanding of America's preeminence in the world. Her efforts to impose upon the situation in Southeast Asia the same moral absolutes that structured her understanding of World War II exposed her as an ideologue. Her depictions of the conflict illustrated her inability to acknowledge the illusory quality of America's omnipotence and exceptionalism. In those arctic days of the cold war, both Chapelle and America's leaders judged any crisis in the world—major or minor—by its impact on the balance of power between the Soviet Union and the United States. From that perspective, events in some small Southeast Asian backwater that might otherwise have been interpreted as inconsequential to American interests loomed as a serious threat.

Laos appeared to be the most likely first domino. This tiny landlocked country of 2 million–plus people created far more immediate worries during the early months of John F. Kennedy's presidency than the situation in Vietnam. In April, just a month before Chapelle went to Southeast Asia, the U.S. Joint Chiefs of Staff were suggesting that a commitment of American troops might be needed to quell the growing insurgency in Laos because it was destabilizing the country's American-backed government. Kennedy demurred. The Bay of Pigs fiasco had left him suspicious of advice from his military advisors. Moreover, how could he convince the American public that a troop commitment in Laos was necessary when he had refused to intervene to save the Bay of Pigs operation? He understood that the decision might have long-term consequences in Vietnam. Realizing that a negotiated settlement in Laos was the best of his unsatisfactory options, Kennedy agreed to participate in peace talks in Geneva. At the same time, fears that his apparent reluctance to stand firm in Laos and Cuba might be interpreted in Moscow as weakness forced him to ratchet up America's commitment to Vietnam.

Reader's Digest asked Chapelle to investigate the situation in Laos, the place President Dwight D. Eisenhower had once called "the cork in the bottle." A triangular conflict underway there involved the neutralist government of Prince Souvanna Phouma, the allegedly neutralist but American-supported Royal Lao Army led by General Phoumi Nosavan, and the Communist Pathet Lao forces supported by North Vietnam and the Soviet Union.

When Chapelle arrived in Laos soon after the cease-fire was declared in May 1961, she quickly realized that it was a pretense. She spent five days watching the comings and goings at the capital's Wattay Airport, where she witnessed dozens of U.S. aircraft carrying hundreds of tons of rice and ammunition. Since no U.S. military planes were permitted on Laotian airbases, the CIA-operated Air America made most of those flights. From early May until late June, Chapelle traveled the country in the air, on the ground, and on water. She spent weeks with the Royal Lao troops and their U.S. advisors as they searched out Pathet Lao troops in the country's remote villages. When she saw a succession of cease-fire violations "by the Reds" along the way, she realized the obvious: These Green Berets were not short-term civilian technicians whose mission was limited to training Laotian troops; they were exchanging heavy artillery fire with the enemy deep in the mountains. "This," she wrote to Selma Blick, her secretary in New York, "is the noisiest goddamn cease-fire I've ever covered."

Chapelle wasn't one to ask questions about the CIA's clandestine operations, but she could see that Laos was being lost despite the Green Berets' sacrifices. The contradictions between what the government was saying and what she was seeing plagued her—but not in the same way those contradictions were to plague other journalists. She wrote to her Aunt Louise in Milwaukee about how "privileged and pleased" she felt to have witnessed the military action in Laos. However, she was also "terrifyingly challenged since what I have seen isn't exactly the way it's been told in the newspapers by less privileged reporters, and I am puzzled at how to reconcile what they've made their readers believe with what my own eyes have taught me." Although she had glimpsed the contradictions, Chapelle never pressed the point. In a letter to Lewis, her *Reader's Digest* editor, written from Vientiane on June 29, 1961, Chapelle outlined her conclusions about the war and her nation's participation in it. The men who were fighting were a "little handful of Americans—a few hundred alive and at least nineteen dead, wounded, missing, captured—who I've seen daily risk their lives to carry out U.S. policy in Laos." America, she added, had to stop hedging. It was time to declare that intervention is "leadership of the free world."

The story she wrote about the weeks she spent with a team of Green Berets was suffused with admiration and praise for their success in training Laotian troops. She defended what she characterized as the "much-maligned Lao soldier" because his ability to win the fight depended on how well trained and well led he was, a conclusion that foreshadowed the one she later reached about the ability of the South Vietnamese army. "The Men Who Did Not Give Up on Laos" was a celebratory portrait of the Green Berets' fight against Communism. Although she had seen enough to know better, Chapelle's story noted how the Green Berets rigidly adhered to their role as advisors. She described how Captain Frederick Gordon, in the middle of an enemy attack, tried to decide whether his soldiers should accompany Laotian troops as they delivered mortar hits against the enemy. What was training and what was fighting, Gordon appeared to ask himself. That story, however, languished for months with censors at the U.S. Department of Defense. Worse still, nearly eight hundred of the 1,000 photographs she had taken were lost somewhere in the Pentagon. Whether her editor, Lewis, joined the government's connivance in maintaining the secret of its role in Laos is unknown. In the end, he refused to run her story. Chapelle never learned why.

That decision, however, was still months away in the summer of 1961, when she took up residence in a "plush-lined foxhole" in Saigon's Majestic

Hotel. She wrote captions for her soon-to-be-published autobiography and concluded work on a supplementary chapter that was to run when *Reader's Digest* condensed the book in its February 1962 edition. As final editing proceeded, Chapelle grew increasingly agitated about the significance her editors at William Morrow were giving to her gender. Like so many of the women who went to Vietnam, Chapelle kept the feminist movement at arms' length even though she bristled at the constraints that denied women opportunities. Like Gloria Emerson, she hated being distinguished by gender. The title she chose for her book, *The Trouble I've Seen,* depicted far more accurately the spirit of her work than the one the publishing house had conjured up: *What's a Woman Doing Here?* Right up until the publication date, she argued against it because it implied that she was some kind of freak-show character. Writing from Saigon, she railed at Lawrence Hughes, her editor at William Morrow, telling him he "seems to have feminized the hell out of" her story. The overemphasis on what she called "the woman bit" would jeopardize her credibility as a combat reporter, she argued. The belief that the book's best sales prospects lay with an emphasis on her "being a broad rather than being a story-teller of integrity" was, she insisted, a serious misjudgment.

By August 1961, she had pitched still another story to *Reader's Digest,* this one about a Catholic priest leading a group of "brave anti-Reds successfully making a place for themselves in Asia." Father Augustine Nguyen Lac Hoa invited her to live with his people in Binh Hung, a Mekong Delta village in southern Vietnam. This "rugged man of God," as Chapelle called Father Hoa, had fled his native China for Haiphong when Mao Tse-Tung seized power in 1949. At the urging of a bishop, he returned to his parish in China, certain that he was marked for death. Instead, the Chinese imprisoned him but later released him hoping that he would help unite China's many Catholics in a church that would function without Vatican oversight. Although armed guards are said to have monitored his movements, Father Hoa escaped to Indochina; he then set out to help more than two hundred families in his parish do the same. By 1951, the group had been ferried in junks across the South China Sea. As the war with France grew tense in the early 1950s, Father Hoa led his flock to Cambodia—the distance equivalent to a trip from Miami to New York. After the fall of Dien Bien Phu in 1954, and as Communist infiltration of Cambodia increased, Father Hoa appealed to Ngo Dinh Diem, the South Vietnamese president, to give his parishioners a place to settle. In Binh Hung, Father Hoa and the settlers raised land from the mud and built two hundred bamboo houses. Using fishing knives for weapons and, later, six old French rifles, they created a village militia. President Diem himself named the group the Army of the Sea Swallow. The new army appears to have quickly become a darling of the Central Intelligence Agency.

In Binh Hung, Chapelle found the kind of moral clarity that nourished her spirit. Good and evil were sharply accentuated here. In Father Hoa, she found a character whom she transformed into a flesh-and-blood demonstration of God's unmistakable liking for democracy. She accompanied the Sea Swallows on nine patrols through mosquito-infested jungles—in daylight and in darkness—as the troops repeatedly engaged the enemy and most often, according to Chapelle, bested him. With glee, she wrote about a moonlight raid in which the Sea Swallows surprised an enemy raiding party that fled under fire, carrying four of their dead. Nothing, it seemed, was sweeter to her than killing Communists. Before she left Binh Hung, Father Hoa gave her the Sea Swallows patch and told her that she was the first non-Asian to be so honored.

In an apparent effort to endear Father Hoa to her readers, she transformed him from the tough-talking, take-no-prisoners drill sergeant his soldiers knew into a more palatable man of the cloth who addressed his flock with affection and kindness. Bernard Yoh, a onetime intelligence advisor to President Diem from whom Chapelle had sought advice on the story, wrote to her about his amusement: "I can imagine what Father Hoa will think when he reads the soft words you put in his mouth. The only words I have ever heard him address to his men were: 'You pig head,' 'Son of a dog.' . . . But I guess the 'my son and my daughter' stuff goes over better with American readers." The Sea Swallows were "expanding freedom in the world," Chapelle wrote in her *Reader's Digest* story. "Who can serve a greater cause?"

To say that American military leaders embraced Chapelle is an understatement. Several accepted her offer to share with them her insights on the war after her first trip to Southeast Asia. She was debriefed by, among others, U.S. Marine Commandant Wallace M. Greene Jr.; after that talk, she wrote a lengthy memo outlining a "Course of Action, Laos and Vietnam." The Departments of State and Defense had conflicting aims and hence undermined each other, she declared in her report. In Laos, she claimed, the State Department wanted to "compromise with Reds," but Defense sought to "kill Reds." America must "decide to start winning NOW," she wrote, devising a ruse that would allow the United States to send more troops to Vietnam without appearing to have compromised the country's noninterventionist policies.

President Diem should ask for U.S. troops, she counseled. Although Kennedy would refuse the request, he would use it as grounds to beef up the U.S. Military Assistance Advisory Group. Chapelle suggested an additional fifteen hundred men, a recommendation that revealed her ignorance of the magnitude of American plans for Southeast Asia. During 1962, the number of American "advisors" in South Vietnam jumped to 9,000—an increase of nearly 6,000 from December 1961.

Colonel Edward G. Lansdale, Demi Gates's onetime boss in the CIA who became one of President Kennedy's key advisors on guerrilla war, found Chapelle's ideology appealing. Just as he had appreciated the value of a gifted writer in Gloria Emerson in 1956, so, too, did he understand the value of a journalist who shared his views on Southeast Asia, especially one whose stories occasionally amounted to recruiting posters for the military. For her part, Chapelle—like Emerson—appears to have enjoyed the "Dear Ed" friendship with this presidential aide who wrote her occasional notes on White House stationery. Each heaped flattery on the other in a correspondence that spanned several years. He called her "a good girl guerrilla and fighter of the good fight." Soon after her return from South Vietnam in November 1961, Chapelle volunteered to brief Lansdale on her experiences in Southeast Asia. Later, she sent him her eyewitness report on events she had seen. She also sent him the draft of her story on the U.S. Special Forces in Laos, copies of which she had asked members of his staff and other military officials to read and approve. He said the story that *Reader's Digest* later declined to print was "a grand bit of writing" that "certainly captured the spirit of something which had eluded others." He added: "Sure did like it!"

Lansdale, always attuned to the public relations game that was his first career, once urged U.S. Air Force General Curtis LeMay to exploit the publicity potential Chapelle offered. Lansdale told LeMay that he should "give some help in getting her in with the Air Force activities which support some of the ground actions she knows so well." She understood guerrilla warfare from having covered so much of it, Lansdale explained to LeMay, the general who once suggested that North Vietnam should be bombed "back to the Stone Age." In a note to LeMay, Lansdale described Chapelle's understanding of counterinsurgency as equal to Ernie Pyle's understanding of the ground war in World War II.

Chapelle's ties to these high-level officials, particularly Lansdale, and her still-murky mission to Hungary raised suspicions about her possible association with America's intelligence operations. Memories of that misadventure led colleagues in Saigon—the AP photographer Horst Faas among them—to conclude that she had CIA connections. As a matter of policy, the agency declines to confirm or deny that any individual was used as a confidential and covert source. Information about intelligence connections is classified, and the agency says it has a "legal responsibility and obligation to protect [the information] from unauthorized disclosure." However, it was hardly unusual in those cold war years for leading journalists to report to and cooperate with the CIA. Indeed, the likes of Joseph Alsop, the Washington aristocrat and influential columnist who took a hard line on the war, welcomed the opportunity to serve their government. In a declaration that could surely have reflected Chapelle's sentiments, Alsop said in the 1970s: "The notion that a newspaperman doesn't have a duty to his country is perfect balls. I call it doing my duty as a citizen."

Whether the CIA would pursue an association with an incessant talker like Chapelle seems improbable. She was a veritable gusher, an unstoppable, 78-rpm spew of words that sometimes exhausted her listeners. With her life-long penchant for self-promotion, how could the agency trust her to keep its secrets? And her gravelly, almost belly-deep voice sometimes approached decibel levels in the noise pollution range. Indeed, she often joked that her career in radio began because WOR's Barry Farber said she had the only voice that could be heard above artillery fire and chopper blades. The whisper often required in espionage activities seemed well beneath her tonal range. The opposite conclusion, however, might also be drawn. Certainly the CIA might have provided her with the James Bond technology embodied in the tiny Minox camera she tossed out the car window on the way to Budapest in 1956. Its reputation for making lousy pictures hardly qualified it as equipment for the professional photojournalist.

Moreover, the curious relationship between some key *Reader's Digest* executives and government agencies also raises questions. For example, Hobart Lewis, the magazine's editor-in-chief and president of the Reader's Digest Association in the 1960s, was also chairman of the U.S. Advisory Commission on Information and a member of the Blue Ribbon Defense Committee on Vietnam. And when Lewis cabled Chapelle in May 1961—"Want you to cover all aspects of the guerrilla war, theirs and ours"—what exactly what did he mean? Although the *Digest* spent thousands of dollars to finance travels in Southeast Asia for ten months during 1961, the magazine published only one of the stories she wrote. Later, the *Digest* also spent considerable sums to finance her questionable escapades with anti-Castro Cuban exiles in Florida.

When she finally returned to the States in November 1961, her frustrations far outweighed whatever satisfaction her Vietnam sojourn had brought her. Her fortunes, however, turned the following year. Chapelle had never before savored the triumphs she enjoyed in 1962—nor would she again. Her memoir was praised in newspaper reviews across the country, including highly favorable comments in the *New York Times,* where Charles Poore urged readers to "put it on your reading list now." Women, he observed, "are decidedly men's equals" and "many, many women are much equaler than others." Almost by way of underscoring Poore's observation, that same year Chapelle became the second woman to receive the Overseas Press Club's George Polk Memorial Award for her reporting from Vietnam and for her autobiography. For years, she had coveted this accolade, named for the CBS correspondent killed in Greece in 1948.[2]

For Chapelle, the April 1962 awards ceremony at New York's Waldorf Astoria Hotel was the night when her peers, some of whom had been ambivalent—if not downright disrespectful—of her, would at long last acknowledge the value of her work. Her stock would soar, she hoped. Assignments from prominent and well-paying magazines would come her way. *Reader's Digest* and *National Geographic* would renew their interest in her work. Now, those editors at *Life* magazine, the ones who had been rejecting her photos for two decades and who had disassociated themselves from her Hungarian venture, would be forced to acknowledge that her work indeed had merit. Chapelle's agent, Nancy Palmer, was bewildered by the reluctance, particularly of editors at *Life,* to buy Chapelle's photographs. In a letter to Chapelle early in 1962, she bemoaned the repeated rejections. Palmer said she once showed a photo editor at *Life* a portfolio of Chapelle's pictures without mentioning who had taken them. What she initially took for enthusiasm quickly dried up after she named the photographer, Palmer explained in that letter to Chapelle. In her response, written two months before she won the Overseas Press Club honor, Chapelle said that neither *Life* nor *Look* had ever put much faith in her competence. "If someday I do win some recognition from my colleagues, say an Overseas Press Club award, we may get the stupid problem solved."

Chapelle's meticulous preparations for the awards ceremony bespoke the gravity she attached to it. Stuck in the Minnesota outback on a lecture tour

---

2. Marguerite Higgins, the *Herald Tribune* reporter who had landed with the U.S. Marines at Inchon during the Korean War, was the first woman to win the Polk Award in 1951.

when she learned of the award, she turned to Selma Blick, her part-time secretary in New York City, asking her to check out Saks Fifth Avenue for elbow-length, "dead-white" doeskin gloves. She also needed a solid-colored envelope bag on which she planned to pin her two pairs of military parachutist wings. Those wings, she told Blick, "had so much to do with my getting the award."

As Chapelle had hoped, the award apparently did catch the attention of at least one of those coveted "biggies," *National Geographic.* Not long after the awards ceremony, she was back in Vietnam with a *Geographic* assignment to write about how the use of helicopters was changing the face of war. Her piece was the cover story in the magazine's November 1962 issue. Helicopters, in the words of President Kennedy, were a necessity in a "war by guerrillas, subversives, insurgents, assassins; war by ambush instead of by combat." For Chapelle, the helicopter war story represented yet another opportunity to report from the "real front of the Free World."

To get the story, Chapelle spent seventeen days riding U.S. Army and Marine helicopters, experienced hostile fire on four occasions, and watched a variety of operations that engaged the enemy. She saw the evacuation of wounded Vietnamese, the capture of suspected Communists, and the airlifting of ammunition and food to remote mountain outposts. Years later, retired Lieutenant Colonel Archie Clapp remembered Chapelle riding aboard his helicopter on a mission with sixty Vietnamese infantrymen near Vinh Loi, a Mekong Delta village. "She liked to ride in my helicopter because I was always the first to land," Clapp recalled. As the helicopter neared the ground, "she jumped out the door and was charging toward the enemy so she could turn around and take pictures of the Marines" as they ran out to engage the Viet Cong. "I bawled her out every day about the risks she was taking. I'd tell her she was going to get hurt. She'd say yes, she understood, but then she'd go out and do it again the next day."

Clapp had never worked with a female reporter before. He was leery when she arrived, but soon put those doubts to rest. She was a "true professional," he concluded. Clapp also thought highly of Bigart, of the *New York Times,* with whom he had had several conversations. He had become acquainted with Burrows, the *Life* magazine photographer whose work he admired. Neither man, however, ranked as high in his esteem as Chapelle. Her story for *National Geographic* brimmed with admiration for the brass and the ordinary soldier. The caption accompanying a photograph of Lieutenant Colonel Clapp, for example, described him as the squadron commander who "has developed bold new helicopter tactics." Also on display was Chapelle's own daring. She wrote of how she had accompanied thirteen American-armed Vietnamese infantrymen and their American advisor on a mission to Ap My Thanh, a village "believed again to be infested with Communist guerrillas." Gunfire started moments after she jumped from the helicopter. Making her anti-Communist sentiments clear, Chapelle told readers she was writing from a place "where the fate of millions of people was being decided in blood, the blood of the men around me." She added: "If their battles were won, Southeast Asia might remain free; if the battles continued to be lost, the Communists would surely dominate all Viet Nam."

The photographs that accompanied the helicopter story are among the most dramatic images she took of the war. In one, a sobbing young Vietnamese woman cradled an infant in one arm as her fingers delicately touched her husband's corpse. In another, a collection of Vietnamese children gazed skyward with amazement at what the caption explained was mortar fire from above. Still other photos were aerial shots of South Vietnamese troops chasing suspected Viet Cong. There were pictures, too, of trussed or blindfolded prisoners. The photographs on that thirty-one-page spread, said Horst Faas, were "the most important thing she left behind." Faas, the AP combat photographer who covered the war from 1963 until 1972, studied the images on those pages when he was assigned to his agency's Saigon bureau. No other photographer had ever compiled as complete a photographic survey of South Vietnam's people, its army, its countryside, its war, and the role Americans were playing in it, Faas explained. "Nobody had ever photographed the place with the same depth and showed it in its full reality." Part of that "full reality" was the presence of an armed American serviceman ready to do battle with the South Vietnamese troops he was accompanying. Although President Kennedy had announced earlier in 1962 that military advisors would return fire if fired upon, the administration was still maintaining the fiction that American servicemen were not themselves engaged in combat but were "advising" South Vietnamese troops. Before its publication, the Department of State, according to *Geographic* editor Wilbur Garrett, asked that the magazine eliminate one of Chapelle's pictures. The editors refused.

When Faas was choosing photographs for *Requiem,* the volume he and Tim Page compiled in 1996 as a tribute to the many photojournalists who were killed covering the war, the Chapelle photo he selected was also one taken in 1962, that of a Viet Cong suspect who is about to be executed by a uniformed member of the Army of the Republic of Vietnam. Although the photo lacks the drama of the famous Eddie Adams picture taken on a Saigon street during the Tet Offensive, its aura of imminent death shocked the photo editor of *Life* at the time and he refused to use it. Although Banamar's execution in Algeria in 1957 had shaken Chapelle, there is no indication that she ever questioned the morality of summary justice in Vietnam. The French in Algeria, of course, were not her own personal enemy. The Communists were.

By the fall of 1962, at about the time her helicopter war story ran in *National Geographic,* the magazine asked her to return to Southeast Asia, this time to write a story on Cambodia. She refused what would have been the lucrative assignment because she had been invited to join friends in the U.S. Special Forces in South Vietnam during the same months, December 1962 until March 1963. She found the prospect of writing about Americans involved in heavy fighting more enticing than the Cambodia overview. In the end, the Special Forces story fell through and, try though she did, Chapelle never succeeded in snaring an assignment in Vietnam that year, the same year in which several young American journalists, including Beverly Deepe, reported on a series of momentous events, none of which Chapelle covered. Just two days into the year, South Vietnamese army units suffered a disastrous defeat by Viet Cong forces—who were outnumbered ten to one—in the battle at Ap Bac. Nor did Chapelle witness the Buddhist uprisings that resulted in a series of self-immolations by priests, grisly acts of protest that shook America's faith in the Diem regime's ability to rule. Finally, the year ended with the overthrow and assassination of President Diem in November.

Instead, Chapelle spent much of 1963 involved in yet another of her inglorious escapades, and yet again her colleagues were left shaking their heads in disbelief. In a scheme that seemed perhaps even more foolish than her exploits in Hungary, Chapelle joined a brigade of anti-Castro rebels intent on overthrowing Cuba's government. The mission and the secrecy surrounding it must have appealed to Chapelle's lust for danger. In the group's leader, Tony Cuesta, Chapelle found another hero. Cuesta and his fellow rebel, Ramon Font, had once traveled by boat from Florida to Caibarien, a seaport in northern Cuba, where they attacked and sank the Soviet freighter *Baku.* A *Life* magazine photographer had accompanied them, and the subsequent story hailed the men for their "derring-do." The CIA was said to have grounded the two raiders in Miami. But Cuesta, whom Chapelle once likened to George Washington, was not about to have his so-called Commandos L team restricted to American soil. He wanted to continue his attacks on Cuba, and Chapelle wanted to go along.

Lewis, at *Reader's Digest,* apparently sensed that Chapelle was becoming too involved in her story and would once again train a spotlight on her own participation in it. He wanted none of it in this story: "We hope you will write it as a military reporter and correspondent, reporting on the outfit. In this case, we do not want you to participate. We want complete unanimity, top objective reporting and no first person, 'I was there' material." But even in the face of those apparent reservations, Lewis continued to bless her work by financing it. He advanced her $1,000 for her expenses, money she used to rent a new headquarters for Cuesta. In another letter written in early June, Lewis told Chapelle that although the freedom fighters' bid to liberate Cuba was a futile gesture, it was nonetheless "a little candle of freedom flickering."

At their headquarters house in Hialeah, Chapelle joined the Cubans in their daily exercise regimes, survival classes, and meals of rice and beans. She kept the nitroglycerine in the refrigerator and spent her afternoons making bombs. Although Robert Meyer disapproved of his sister's activities, he sent her two books on handling explosives. "I thought if she was going to be fooling with the stuff, she should know what she was doing," he once said. The *Miami News* reported on a raid at the house by U.S. Customs agents and Miami police in which a cache of black powder, dynamite, liquid fuels, and blasting caps along with a 20 mm cannon and an arsenal of small arms were found and confiscated. The story noted that one occupant of the house was identified as "the American freelance writer, Dickey Capelle [*sic*]." Despite the size of the weapons arsenal, neither Chapelle nor her Cuban colleagues were arrested.

Her name appeared in print on two subsequent occasions as she tried to make her way to Cuba aboard small boats with her band of anti-Communist exiles. Each time she was thwarted by the U.S. Customs, although she suspected the CIA was behind these interventions. In October, Chapelle joined the Commandos L exiles as they headed to Cuba to stage another hit-and-run, *Baku*-style attack. Customs officials in Miami rounded up the three boats at sea and a fourth moored along the Miami River. Aboard the "mother boat," according to a brief article in the *New York Herald Tribune,* was a fatigue-clad woman identified as Dickey Chapelle.

In January 1964, Chapelle set off once again with a group of exiles, this time, she claimed, to rescue Cubans fleeing Castro. This escapade not only ended her eight-month association with Miami's anti-Castro Cubans, it also nearly ended her life. Aboard the cabin cruiser *Four Jays,* a gas explosion aborted the mission just twenty-five miles southeast of Miami. Chapelle and her Cuban cohorts jumped overboard before the boat sank and were rescued by a Cuban refugee. Chapelle's face and hands were badly burned. In an interview with the *Milwaukee Sentinel* on the following day, Chapelle said the explosion had been the "blast" of her life. "There was a gigantic column of black smoke . . . and my cameras [valued at $1,650] were in the bow," she said. She seemed to revel in the danger. Her recklessness, however, worried friends. Even Lansdale, the man who called her a "good girl guerrilla," warned her about the Cuban company she was keeping. Whether Chapelle knew that Lansdale was directing the Kennedy administration's efforts to overthrow and assassinate Castro, an undertaking known as Operation Mongoose, is unlikely. What is likely, however, is that Lansdale probably knew about some of her moves—especially since memoranda in Chapelle's FBI file indicate that the bureau was monitoring her activities in Miami.

There appear to be no exchanges of chummy letters between Lansdale and Chapelle in 1963, perhaps because she preferred not to heed his words of caution. He had "warned her about selecting her company among Cuban raiders," Lansdale explained in a letter written to a graduate student who was writing a master's thesis about Chapelle in 1968. "This was typical of Dickey, when she was going to stick her neck way out," he told Frederick Ellis. "The next I heard was when the U.S. Navy fished her out of the briny, badly hurt from the fire, explosion, and sinking of the boat of some Cuban adventurers en route to a raiding attack. She hadn't wanted me to stop her, thus the silence." Similarly, Lansdale added, two years later Chapelle maintained her silence before she took off on her last trip to Vietnam.

Devoted though she was to America and its military men, government meddling in her work as a journalist taxed even Chapelle's loyalty to the nation's leaders. Her 1963 Cuban adventures were neither the first nor the last time she perceived the unseen hand of the CIA at work to thwart her. Chapelle thought the Kennedy administration's determination to manage news was an intolerable attack on the First Amendment. The exclusion of reporters from military operations in the Bay of Pigs and later in the Cuban Missile Crisis left the government and the people at the mercy of military sources; these, in her estimation, were unreliable sources. Chapelle also railed at the Kennedy administration for preventing media coverage of an American arms airlift to India, whose government claimed that Chinese forces had attacked Indian troops along the nations' common border. Although nineteen members of the press—including Chapelle—were invited to cover the airlift, the reporters aboard the military transport flight to Calcutta never saw the weapons destined for India, and they were not allowed to witness fighting between Chinese and Indian troops. Chapelle, who had joined the press entourage on behalf of *Reader's Digest,* slammed the trip as a "press junket."

Without the press, Chapelle insisted, the military would become the sole guarantors of the integrity of history, even though they were "the least objective observers around." The administration's refusal to allow any media representatives to observe the Cuban blockade left the president and the people too dependent on the observations of military men, "the very men whose egos were most deeply bound up in the outcome." In attempting to spoon-feed reporters information about these and other critical events in Cuba, members of the Kennedy team were attempting to transform reporters into propagandists, Chapelle charged. Substituting government press releases for eyewitness observation, she added, "has all the authenticity of a patent medicine ad." Even in Vietnam, she questioned the government's news management efforts. "In 1961 and part of 1962, most press stories on Vietnam were releases or 'leaks' from a New York public relations firm hired indirectly with American aid funds by the Viet Nam government," she wrote, referring to the efforts by the so-called Vietnam Lobby to shape public opinion about America's involvement in Vietnam.

Chapelle joined the Overseas Press Club's protest against the Kennedy administration's heavy-handed effort to shape the news. Hanson W. Baldwin, the *New York Times* military affairs correspondent, brought attention to the problem of managed news in an *Atlantic* article in which he charged that the administration's practice of sending FBI agents to reporters' homes to uncover the sources of stories unfavorable to the president "smacked of totalitarianism rather than of democratic government." Chapelle shared Baldwin's views that "an aura of propaganda has surrounded the government's public presentation of the Cuban situation from the beginning." She believed, as Baldwin did, that the administration's news management policies posed a "potential danger to our form of democratic and representative government." In an unpublished "open letter" to President Kennedy, Chapelle said she had asked herself the famous question that he had asked all Americans. What she and all journalists could and should do for their country, she told the president, was "to carry on the tradition that belongs uniquely to us, to be the guarantors of integrity in print." Anything less endangered democracy.

By mid-1964, Chapelle had sold *National Geographic*'s editors on a story proposal that would take her back to Vietnam. She would write about the Ho Chi Minh Trail, the 1,300-mile collection of dirt roads and foot paths that was the lifeline for North Vietnamese army regulars fighting in South Vietnam, the route by which they kept their ranks replenished and re-supplied. She arrived in Vietnam in October 1964 and made her way to Vientiane. The Royal Lao Air Force was to provide Chapelle transportation to give her a glimpse of the trail, which led from the southern reaches of North Vietnam through Laos and Cambodia to various porous border points in western South Vietnam. Chapelle laced letters to her editors in Washington with optimism and predictions of historic firsts. But to her great disappointment, the promise of an airborne look at the trail was mysteriously withdrawn after she had spent weeks seeking approvals from Leonard Unger, the U.S. ambassador to Laos; the American High Command; from General Westmoreland's chief of staff; and from Laotian military officials. The Laotian general who had first approved her proposal had a sudden change of heart. Once again, Chapelle sensed the unseen hand of the CIA at work.

As a substitute, she took on a story later titled "Water War in Vietnam," the last article she wrote for *National Geographic*. In it, she detailed her observations of River Assault Group 23, one of the Vietnamese navy's "daring gunboat forces," in whose American leader, Harold Dale Meyerkord, she once again found a hero. He directed nineteen gunboats engaged in patrolling the thousands of miles of waterways that veined the country's agriculturally rich Mekong Delta. The water war story was formulaic Chapelle. A naval patrol team sought out Communists in armor-plated junks equipped with machine guns. Viet Cong mines planted in the shallow river bottoms were a danger, as were the armed guerrillas who hid in the jungle growth along the riverbanks, American advisors their favored targets. Chapelle's narrative described the staccato sounds of gunfire in the darkness and the sense of panic that comes with the proximity of death. Punctuating these dramatic scenes are large, philosophical questions, for which Chapelle provided rather timeworn answers:

> Why was it that humans still got along so badly that conflicts were settled like this, by young men betting their lives at hide-and-seek? Did I truly think I could, with the camera around my neck, help end the need for the carbine on my shoulder? [Americans] had brought all their expertise and dedication and raw nerve from the security of their home towns to the ultimate insecurity of guerrilla warfare as far from home as it was possible to go. Was that the American idea of global leadership? I knew it was at least one American's idea—mine.

The manuscript and photographs Chapelle submitted in February 1965, for which she was paid $5,800, "didn't make the grade," she was told in August by Herbert Wilburn, the *Geographic*'s illustrations editor. After her death, however, the editors had a change of heart. The story ran in February 1966.

Despite the many rejections during those later years, Chapelle succeeded in finding outlets for her stories—on the lecture circuit, where she first thrilled audiences after her release from Hungary's Fo Street prison in 1957. Early on, most of her appearances were in the Midwest, but later she began to draw crowds in Delaware, Kentucky, and Virginia, as well. In 1958, she talked about Algeria and the Middle East. In the 1960s, her remarks addressed Cuba and Southeast Asia. She always spoke without notes and occasionally appeared sporting a military camouflage helmet worn by the Vietnamese soldiers she so admired. Sometimes she wrapped herself in a Viet Cong flag that had been captured during a combat operation. "I've been at the scene in recent years to write about it when the free world lost to the Communists nine times," she explained during one appearance. "And I'm unalterably prejudiced in favor of our winning." In discussing the inadequacy of America's military training, she said that the demands of America's mothers to reduce the rigors of basic training had turned recruits into milquetoasts. She also denounced student protesters who opposed the war: "Hanoi just loves that kind of thing, you know. They love to point at our people back home who are undermining everything we're trying to do." She was routinely asked during these talks whether her style of journalism and domestic bliss could coexist. She always told young women that marriage was probably incompatible with a career as a war correspondent.

Chapelle made one of her periodic visits to her brother and his family in Madison, Wisconsin, early in April 1965, during the same week a teach-in was staged at University of Wisconsin. The program, conducted by the Faculty-Student Committee to End the War in Vietnam, incensed Chapelle. Convinced that the antiwar nature of the ten-hour marathon of lectures and panel discussions was one-sided, Chapelle helped to organize a counterforum. She wanted students to understand the "real story" in Southeast Asia, the story of the Communist horrors she had witnessed there. The war had to be fought, she declared. "The danger is that I will lose the freedom to sit here and talk to you without wondering which of you is the CIA man who will throw me in prison tomorrow for what I say." Students in the antiwar movement, she later said, "stick bayonets in the backs of our men serving in Vietnam."

Although her brother, Robert Meyer, and his wife, Marion, opposed American policy in Vietnam, these ideological differences were seldom discussed. "We really didn't agree with her view of the war," recalled Marion Meyer decades later. Yet Robert and Dickey "were brother and sister in every sense of the word," he told a reporter on the day after her death. Whenever Chapelle visited her brother in Madison, their conversations focused on family memories, on recollections of her childhood in Shorewood, and on Robert and Marion's three children. Chapelle would put on the old records of John Phillip Sousa marches and gaily lead her niece and nephews on a procession around the house. "It was all such fun," recounted Marion Meyer of her sister-in-law's visits. The family saw Chapelle for the last time in September 1965; this was when she spoke to a professional journalism sorority in Madison, a talk in which she mentioned her plans to return to Vietnam.

That month, she left on her last trip to South Vietnam. She had a twelve-week contract with the *National Observer,* the news weekly whose politics Chapelle described as "right of center." She had started freelancing for the publication during the 1965 crisis in the Dominican Republic when the prospect of a democratic social revolution gave rise, at least in the minds of American leaders, to fears of a second Cuba. The *Observer* soon became her bread-and-butter employer. While she was in Washington during the weeks before her departure, Chapelle paid a visit to General Wallace M. Greene Jr., the U.S. Marine Corps commandant. They chatted about why she was going back: to cover the U.S. Marines, she told him. During that visit, Greene paid her one of the most extraordinary gestures of respect any high-ranking service member can offer a civilian. When he noticed that no Marine insignia was among the emblems sewn on her Australian bush hat, he asked why. "Aren't they tough enough for you?" he wanted to know. With that, he tore his own eagle, globe, and anchor insignia from his lapel and handed it to her. Chapelle was speechless. By the time her visa to enter South Vietnam was approved in October, Greene's insignia had taken its place near the hat band where, less than four weeks later, her colleague, Dean Brelis, spied that incongruous sprig of pink flowers.

As a prelude to her own departure, Chapelle watched a group of newly trained recruits ship out for South Vietnam from the Marine Corps Air Station in El Toro, California. In the October 11, 1965, issue of the *National Observer,* Chapelle wrote about each individual leave taking and its impact on family members who were left behind. "The men were going to do a dirty job in a dirty place. . . . Wars always meant young men going out with wills and weapons honed and young women waiting with impatience but not without understanding for them to come back," she wrote. In Vietnam, Chapelle planned to write stories about the progress of America's Strategic Hamlet Program and to revisit Father Hoa in the village of Binh Hung. Her first priority, however, was to catch up with the U.S. Marines. Fittingly perhaps, they were the subject of her last article.

Most of the Dickey Chapelle's obituaries were kinder to her in death than some of her colleagues had been to her in life. *Newsweek* magazine praised her as a "highly talented journalist and a skilled photographer" whose male colleagues became her admirers because she never sought any of the privileges of her sex. The Associated Press quoted Assistant Secretary of Defense Arthur Sylvester, one of the government officials whose efforts at news management had provoked Chapelle's ire. He said of Chapelle that "her magnificent photographs and action-packed stories helped to keep the American public informed about the fight for freedom." In a sentiment her own brother endorsed, more than one obituary noted that Chapelle herself might have chosen to die just as she had—in battle with her beloved Marines. On the day of his sister's death, Robert Meyer gave a statement to the *Milwaukee Sentinel:* "If she had to choose between a short and exciting life or a long, less exciting one, I'm very sure that many years ago she had decided on the former."

The most glowing and forthright commentary about Chapelle came from a ranking military official. Retired Brigadier General S.L.A. Marshall, a military affairs analyst for the *Los Angeles Times,* challenged the idea that she died as she would have wished. Obituaries written by colleagues, Marshall wrote, amounted to little more than belated attempts to do justice to her unique career. He dismissed them as "faint praise." He noted that she was the first American woman ever to be killed in action, a point overlooked in most of the stories about her death. Chapelle had died, he said, in the most futile way possible for a field soldier—"blasted to kingdom come by an enemy booby trap triggered by a comrade." Had she been cut down by machine-gun fire during a charge across a paddy, Marshall explained, "there would have been reason to say, 'That's how she always wanted it.'" In a recitation of her achievements, Marshall noted that she had covered seven wars, revolutions, and revolts in countries around the world, and that in addition to being a seasoned paratrooper, she was skilled in handling every infantry weapon. "No male war correspondent in our time has a comparable record." Yet somehow the men "got the glory and the bylines while she was doing things the hard way."

The U.S. Marines held a memorial service for Chapelle in Da Nang on the morning after her death. Days later, at a memorial service in Saigon attended by about twenty of her colleagues, Chapelle was eulogized by a Lutheran chaplain, Colonel Theodore V. Koepke, as "capable, fearless, a faithful reporter; she exemplified the highest standards of the newspaper profession." Koepke also told her colleagues—Dean Brelis, Horst Faas, Peter Arnett, Jill Krementz, and Beverly Deepe among them—that "in the light of draft-card burnings, sit-ins, teach-ins and other negative attitudes of a small minority of Americans, she stood out as a monument to a cause." In New York, flags outside the Overseas Press Club building were lowered to half staff. In a letter to the editor written days after her death, Rear Admiral Miller, the top public information official for the Pacific Fleet, described Chapelle as "a hard worker with a tenaciousness beyond all belief, she was always pressuring to get into the center of any upcoming action." In Washington, General Greene, the Marine commandant who had given her his insignia just weeks before, said, "She was one of us and we will miss her."

In a rare display of its esteem for a civilian, Chapelle was buried with U.S. Marine Corps honors in the Meyer family plot near Milwaukee. Staff Sergeant Albert P. Miville, leader of the platoon she had accompanied on Operation Black Ferret, brought her ashes home to Shorewood and was an honorary pallbearer at her funeral service. John W. Cyrus, the Unitarian minister who officiated at her funeral, noted that the Marine Corps had become something of a second family to Chapelle: "In a sense she died at home." A Marine bugler sounded taps as the bronze urn containing her ashes was buried.

On the first anniversary of Chapelle's death, the U.S. Marines dedicated the Dickey Chapelle Memorial Dispensary near Chu Lai, a forty-four-bed medical facility built to serve the district's Vietnamese population by Marine engineers with funds from CARE and Chapelle's friends. A plaque unveiled outside the dispensary bore this inscription: "To the memory of Dickey Chapelle, war correspondent, killed in action near here on 4 November 1965. She was one of us and we will miss her." The plaque was signed by General Greene. Nearly four decades later, Chapelle's name was added to Shorewood High School's Wall of Fame, where she joined the school's first alumnus— Chief Justice William Rehnquist—to be so honored. At a ceremony to mark the occasion in May 2003, Chapelle was remembered by her grammar school classmate, Mary Dohmen, as a photojournalist who "captured the truth in words and pictures as she saw it for all Americans."

As much as and perhaps even more than most other reporters and photographers who covered the Vietnam War, Dickey Chapelle thrived on personal involvement in combat. One of the few hints she left to explain the abiding appeal of the battlefield is a copy of "Over the Parapet," a poem about war written by Robert W. Service, a banker who grew rich writing poetry. Mixed in with drafts of Chapelle's published and unpublished manuscripts is a typed copy of the eighty-line verse that romanticizes war in the way many of Chapelle's stories did. When and why she apparently rolled a sheet of paper into her typewriter and began copying Service's poem are a mystery. Perhaps he became her muse. Or maybe she thought his words expressed better than her own a fundamental truth about her spirit. Service's lines suggest how, amidst the horrors of war, one could also find romance, splendor, awe, and joy. War transported Service's narrator into a kind of ecstasy. Perhaps Chapelle saw herself in that anonymous character who dreams of war and declares:

> *All day long when the shells sail over*
> *I stand at the sandbags and take my chance;*

Or perhaps the poem's description of the primal attraction of war had a familiar echo:

> *But if there's horror, there's beauty, wonder;*
> *The trench lights gleam and the rockets play.*
> *That flood of magnificent orange yonder*
> *Is a battery blazing miles away.*
> *With a rush and a singing a great shell passes;*
> *The rifles resentfully bicker and brawl,*
> *And here I crouch in the dew-drenched grasses,*
> *And look and listen and love it all.*

Chapelle covered war for two decades of her life and she, too, looked and listened and probably loved it all.

3

Going Against the Grain

Those ladies were so tough and courageous.
—Pham Xuan An

W HEN MALCOLM BROWNE caught his first glimpse of Beverly Deepe in Saigon in March 1962, his first thought was, "What a sweet, corn-fed, innocent girl she is, and what a place for her to be in." She was twenty-six years old, a recent graduate of Columbia University's Graduate School of Journalism, and a lifelong high achiever who was about to invent herself as America's first female resident correspondent in Vietnam. She had arrived in Saigon on February 28 for what was to have been a two-week stop on a trip around the world. Soon, however, her itinerary changed. South Vietnam and her generation's war held Deepe for nearly seven years. "It was a story that just grew and grew," she said decades later.

On the surface, at least, she appeared confident that her scant experience would launch her career as a war correspondent. Never mind that her thin clip file bore little evidence of that promise. She had written stories for the *Daily Nebraskan* as an undergraduate at the University of Nebraska. She had interned at the Omaha bureau of the Associated Press during her college years. And she had written a handful of travelogues about her trips—first to Russia as an exchange student and, later, to Borneo and China—stories that were distributed by Associated Press Newsfeatures. Except for Dickey Chapelle's extended visits to Southeast Asia, which began in 1961, Deepe was the key—and sometimes the only—woman on the Vietnam beat until 1965.

From early 1962 until the end of 1968, Deepe wrote hundreds of stories about Vietnam. She covered the country's people, politics, economics, and social values as well as the role Americans were playing in Vietnam's war—from its ambassadors and generals to the foot soldiers who patrolled the jungles and mountains. One of America's best respected news magazines and later two of the country's leading newspapers depended on her reports of the war's most critical moments: Buddhist uprisings, the overthrow and assassination of President Ngo Dinh Diem, the country's ever-shifting cast of political leaders, the Tet Offensive, the battle of Hue, and the siege at Khe Sanh. Beyond those critical news events, she was also a keen analyst of South Vietnam's politics. She was a central figure in a 1964 diplomatic donnybrook between the American ambassador, Maxwell Taylor, and Vietnam's strongman, Lieutenant General Nguyen Khanh, who became president in January 1964 when he overthrew the military junta that had overthrown President Diem. Along with Browne, David Halberstam, Neil Sheehan, Peter Arnett, and other reporters who followed them to Vietnam, Deepe was also a player in the contretemps that placed journalists at odds with the governments of America and South Vietnam. She covered the war continuously for seven years, longer than most other Western correspondents.

Remarkably, she has preserved carbon copies of all her Vietnam-era articles and correspondence, twenty-nine bound volumes in all. Because Deepe plans to write her own memoir, she routinely declines requests for interviews. However, public statements she has made about the war show that, in addition to those paper-and-ink artifacts of her writing life, the Vietnam experience has left her with memories of death and horror that will never go away. She is, in short, a noteworthy but seldom-celebrated figure in the history of Vietnam War reportage.

Deepe was one of two women who established themselves as freelance correspondents in Southeast Asia in 1962. The other, Pamela Sanders, who lived in the Philippines in the early 1960s, was inspired in part by the sight of Deepe's byline on a newspaper story datelined Saigon. Like so many of the women who would follow them as the story progressed, Sanders reached the country with only the vaguest idea of how to cover war. Both women stepped well beyond the widely accepted boundaries of women's lives in deciding to take on the Vietnam assignment at a time when few American editors would ever have handed it to them. Sanders and Deepe had widely disparate views about a woman's role in society and about how to conduct their public and private lives. In many ways, the two personified the past and future of American womanhood in the early 1960s. Deepe embraced the more straitlaced demeanor of her mother's generation, but Sanders tossed off the straitjacket of tradition. Professionally, their successes created a model that other women followed.

Like Gloria Emerson and Dickey Chapelle, Beverly Deepe began writing as a teenager. "Beverly knew from day one" that she wanted to write, according to her mother. Like Chapelle, Deepe was her high school class valedictorian. Yet she grew up in an environment that was decidedly different from the urban and suburban settings in which Emerson and Chapelle had come of age: William Emerson went to Wall Street every day; Paul Meyer, except during the lean and jobless years of the Great Depression, was a salesman; Martin Deepe grew winter wheat on the Great Plains.

Carleton, Nebraska, Deepe's hometown, is a neatly squared, featureless Midwestern hamlet where the Union Pacific was once the lifeline to the world beyond its boundaries and grain elevators broke the horizon the way skyscrapers do in urban America. Life revolved around the soil that had for decades sustained Deepe's grandparents and, later, her parents, Martin and Doris Widler Deepe. This environment, in which few external forces beyond the weather really mattered, shaped in one of its children a desire to cross oceans and tell her stories to the world. Farm life, with all its demands and uncertainties, was the boot camp that prepared her for the crucible of Southeast Asia. "Growing up on a farm showed me the need for hard work, the discipline to perform that work when it needed to be done, the unpredictability of nature, and the rewards of taking well-calculated risks," she once told a group of journalism students at the University of Nebraska. But the corn-fed innocence Malcolm Browne had seen masked an extraordinary determination. She was as willful as Gloria Emerson without Emerson's mercurial temperament. She was as hard-hitting as Dickey Chapelle without the ideological baggage. Her high school English teacher recollected that Beverly "always tended to business." The "sweet" quality that Browne perceived grew no doubt out of Deepe's unpretentious nature, which is just what society demanded of a proper young lady who had come of age in the early 1950s.

Beverly Ann Deepe was born on June 1, 1935. Her corner of America's heartland began attracting Easterners and immigrants in 1862, when the passage of the Homestead Act enticed farmers to the Midwest with the promise of free land. With few restrictions, the law allowed homesteaders to claim a so-called quarter section—160 acres. Deepe's father was one of ten children, the son of Europeans who emigrated to Nebraska around the turn of the century and farmed the land. That their son Martin would begin farming in the late 1920s on land that adjoined theirs was entirely in keeping with southeastern Nebraska lifestyles. Martin Deepe was a tenant farmer until 1953, when, according to Thayer County property records, he bought the quarter section he had farmed for nearly twenty-five years. By 1962, when his daughter went to Vietnam, he owned nearly five hundred acres.

By Nebraska standards, Martin Deepe was a small farmer. James Hudson, who in 2002 operated the town's only remaining grain elevator, explained that in the 1940s, farms like Deepe's probably had a four-horse team to plow his fields, a couple of cows for milk, and a few chickens to stock the family larder. Like his neighbors, he placed an annual bet with nature when he hitched that team to the plow and furrowed the earth before sowing winter wheat. And each year, he hoped—sometimes in vain—for the right mixture of rain to freshen the earth, snow to cover the wheat's fragile roots, and a gentle wind to dry the wheat berries just before the late spring harvest. In late June, Martin Deepe and his neighbors shared the cost of renting a coal-fired thrasher to separate the berries from the chaff. Working together, the men moved from farm to farm, cutting the crop and feeding it into the towering black machine. Meanwhile, back at the homestead, "the ladies would fix meals at whatever farm was being harvested," Hudson explained.

The unseen hand of the Almighty was widely believed to order life's fundamentals—the weather chief among them. "The Gods Still Smile Upon Us," the *Hebron Journal Register* declared on page one after a half-inch rainfall salvaged a corn crop that had been threatened by drought and heat. School teachers occasionally turned to the Bible for guidance in resolving nettlesome disciplinary problems. In most farm families, church was a must on Sundays; the Deepes attended the Congregational United Church of Christ in Belvidere.

During Deepe's childhood, the *Journal Register,* a local weekly, captured in its columns the monumental and mundane character of agrarian life. Except for the big weather stories, such as the tornado that killed four residents and destroyed thirty homes on its way through in 1953, the *Journal Register's* front page usually featured auto accidents, marriages, and Red Cross blood drives. On its inside pages, the newspaper recorded the more prosaic side of life; church announcements and obituaries were a weekly standard, as were the community notes that kept folks apprised of their neighbors' comings and goings: "The Ladies Aid met Thursday P.M., at the Christian Church with a very good attendance," or "Mr. and Mrs. Martin Deepe and daughters, Mr. and Mrs. Don Widler and sons were Sunday P.M. visitors at the M. J. Widler home." Thayer County's farm families seldom strayed far from life's fundamentals. Beyond school and church, a child's life tended to be centered on chores. Most youngsters earned spending money by milking the cows and feeding the chickens. "When you live on a farm, you don't do a lot of social stuff. You are separated from other people," recalled Deepe's classmate Elizabeth Beechner. "You didn't do sleepovers." However, holidays were occasions for huge family gatherings. The annual county fair seemed to draw most of the population. The town's team baseball games were summertime favorites. Friends remember Beverly as a devoted New York Yankees fan; indeed, she idolized Joe DiMaggio.

During the 1940s, Beverly attended the one-room Coon-Ridge Country School, a clapboard building equipped with a matching outhouse, located at the intersection of two dirt roads. Good grades earned her and her sister, Barbara Joan, supplements to their weekly allowance. Like Chapelle's mother, Doris Deepe had high expectations and demanded academic excellence from her daughters. To ensure that they would grow up loving to read, Doris Deepe brought books home whenever she went to town; this early reading took her daughters to places well beyond the wheat fields that scrolled out to the edge of their horizon. Pearl S. Buck's *The Good Earth* left Beverly fascinated with China, the same imprint that it left on millions of Americans in the years after its publication in 1931. When Beverly and Barbara Joan reached Belvidere High School, the school newspaper's honor roll reports show, the sisters ran neck-and-neck for the most A grades nearly every marking period. Her classmates in Belvidere's Class of 1953 remembered Beverly as the smartest girl in town, and they made her class president in their senior year. Her oratories won prizes, and she earned a Nebraska State Regent Scholarship. The *Journal Register* ran her photo on its front page after her "Friends of the Land" essay on soil conservation won the $15 first prize in the Thayer County Soil Conservation District's High School Essay Contest.

Nearly a half-century after Beverly graduated, two of the school's four teachers remember her as exceptional, still ranking among the most gifted and energetic students they had ever taught. Grace Lake, Belvidere High's English and history teacher, had little difficulty singling out Beverly from the hundreds of other students she taught in her long career. "She was not a nonsensical person, she was serious about her work," Lake recalled. Roger Hanson, the math teacher, recalled Beverly as "one of the best students I ever had in forty-eight years of teaching."

Deepe's aspiration to be a journalist was well known among her nine classmates in the Class of 1953. Those aspirations, Deepe has said, grew in part from a *Life* magazine article about the seemingly enviable career of a "Girl War Correspondent" who had, in 1950, joined the U.S. Marines in the amphibious landing at Inchon on the west coast of Korea. Marguerite Higgins, as detailed by photojournalist Carl Mydans, gave war correspondence great allure. The six-page photo spread and accompanying text described how the *New York Herald Tribune* war correspondent was "winning the battle of the sexes on the Korean front." Higgins's life was presented as challenging, electrifying, and great fun. The caption under one photo—in which Higgins appeared as a smiling, fatigue-clad figure with a notebook bulging out of her shirt pocket—marveled at how, even covering a war, "Higgins still manages to look attractive." Mydans explained that she had become a "GI heroine" for her efforts to administer blood plasma to soldiers wounded in a surprise attack. He also repeated the observation of another admirer: "Maggie wears mud much like other women wear make-up." Higgins's work in Korea, the article concluded, demonstrated that "women are just as brave and sometimes braver than men and that they frequently have more stamina than their male opposites." Just a dozen years after she read Mydans's article about Higgins, Deepe herself was living in South Vietnam and by 1964, she was writing for the *Herald Tribune,* Higgins's newspaper.

Deepe's success as a journalist made her a star in Thayer County. She became a glittering light in the constellation of aunts, uncles, nieces, nephews, and assorted cousins who populated the extended Deepe and Widler clans. On trips home during her years in South Vietnam and after, folks in town wanted to hear her stories. She often told them to the women's club, to the Rotary Club, and to students at the University of Nebraska in Lincoln. Of course, family custom dictated that Beverly remain modest about her accomplishments even though many of her neighbors appeared to embrace her as their own celebrity. After all, no one they knew had ever had her photograph taken with South Vietnam's Premier Tran Van Huong, an image that ran in the weekly *Lincoln Journal.* No one they knew had ever enraged a U.S. ambassador by quoting his off-the-record remarks as she had done with comments made by Maxwell Taylor at a briefing from which Deepe had been excluded. No one they knew had snared exclusive interviews with a foreign leader like Lieutenant General Nguyen Khanh, as Deepe had in December 1964. *Time* magazine characterized that interview as a "singular achievement." Closer to home, the *Lincoln Journal* called it her "first spectacular news writing coup."

Her path away from Carleton took Deepe first to the University of Nebraska, where she majored in journalism and political science. Dreaming that she "could and would someday cover the Paris fashion shows," she took French. By December of her freshman year, she was listed on the masthead of the student newspaper, the *Daily Nebraskan*. In her sophomore year, Deepe was one of nineteen students in the journalism school honored for outstanding scholastic achievement. She participated in student government, involved herself in the local YMCA's Hungarian Student Project, which brought Hungarian refugees to campus, and was a leader of the Nebraska Committee on World Affairs. She belonged to the honorary journalism sorority and won the university's prestigious J. C. Seacrest Scholarship as well as the Nebraska Press Women's Award as the university's outstanding senior female journalist. She graduated in the Class of 1957 with a Phi Beta Kappa key.

Deepe worked at the *Lincoln Journal* during her early college years doing the kind of drudge work reserved for student labor—writing weather stories and obituaries, or recording the stock market's closing numbers at a nearby brokerage house. Neale Copple, then the managing editor, remembers Deepe as "a charming, good-looking woman who was very, very bright." He also recognized a mile-wide stubborn streak in Deepe. "When Beverly digs her heels in," he said, "there is no way to change her mind." During her later college years, she spent summers in the Associated Press Omaha bureau, work she described as her "flunky, vacation-fill-in job."

Just as Maggie Higgins had in 1941 and Liz Trotta would do in the following decade, Deepe enrolled in Columbia's Graduate School of Journalism. The New York Newspaper Women's Club awarded Deepe its annual Anne O'Hare McCormick scholarship, a $500 stipend named for the distinguished *New York Times* foreign affairs columnist who, in 1937, was the first woman to win a Pulitzer Prize.

The Columbia Journalism School curriculum hardly taught Deepe the adversarial pose she eventually brought to her work as a correspondent in Vietnam, the kind of approach that so profoundly altered the relationship between America's political and military leaders and the press. In the 1950s,

Columbia's journalism courses, like those in other American journalism schools, "seemed grounded in the premise that America's newspapers operated on a level that was close to perfection." As a consequence, Columbia students were taught standard journalistic practice. The Columbia program, described by one graduate as a "finishing school," focused on such textbook fundamentals as the unquestioning acceptance of official sources and the principles of objectivity. That holy grail of American journalism requires that journalists pursue fairness and balance by stripping their reporting of personal opinions and distortions. Little thought was given to the notion that objectivity without perspective and context might be misleading. No one imagined that political and military leaders might use the paradigms of objectivity to manipulate the truth, as a succession of presidents would do for more than a decade in Vietnam. Deepe and her classmates, according to James Boylan, who taught at Columbia in the late 1950s, never made an acquaintance with Ida Tarbell, an early twentieth-century muckraker who revealed the inner workings of John D. Rockefeller and his Standard Oil Company. Tarbell's *History of Standard Oil* (1904), had been a model of investigative reporting for half a century when Deepe was at Columbia. Nor did Columbia grad students learn about the legendary Horace Greeley, the one-time tramp printer who established the *New York Tribune* in 1841. Greeley became one of the most influential editors in the history of American journalism—and the publisher who seemed least averse to hiring women. A journalism education at Columbia appears to have had more in common with the way Dickey Chapelle practiced the craft—supporting the government without question—rather than challenging official pronouncements, as Deepe and many of her fellow correspondents were soon to do in South Vietnam.

During her three-semester program at Columbia, and after she graduated in 1958, Deepe worked for the famous pollster Samuel Lubell, whose identification and analysis of bellwether precincts to predict election outcomes continues to shape news media polling techniques. Before the 1958 congressional elections and the 1960 presidential race, Deepe did the kind of door-to-door interviews with voters for which Lubell was famous. The job required travel and provided an expense account. With all that money and so little time to spend it, Deepe's savings allowed her to hatch plans for a trip around the world. Her fervor for the trip, which would place heavy emphasis on Asia, was such that even after the two friends with whom she had planned to travel had a change of heart, she decided to go alone. "If I didn't go by myself, I'd probably fritter the money away," she recalled.

Deepe boarded an Asia-bound Polish freighter on the West Coast in the fall of 1961, at about the same time Dickey Chapelle was winding up her first journey to Southeast Asia. After stops in Shanghai and Borneo, Deepe made her way to Vietnam just as the country was about to command increasing attention in America. On February 9, as Deepe's ship steamed toward Southeast Asia, America passed the inconspicuous yet important milestone in the war that would soon give the Vietnam story growing significance: America announced its intention to appoint a four-star general to direct the U.S. mission in Vietnam, thus shifting the focus of its cold war strategy from Europe to Asia. The selection of U.S. Army General Paul D. Harkins to lead the Military Assistance Command Vietnam marked the first time since the U.S. intervention in Greece in 1947 that a four-star had been placed in such a post. A Pentagon spokesman characterized the administration's decision to replace its Military Assistance Advisory Group with this beefed-up command organization led by a top military man as a deliberate message: "We're drawing the line here. . . . This is a war we can't afford to lose." To underscore the depth of America's commitment, Attorney General Robert F. Kennedy declared that U. S. troops would stay in South Vietnam until Communist aggression was defeated. Fifty-two Americans died in Vietnam in service of that goal in 1962, up from sixteen the previous year. Beverly Deepe arrived in Vietnam just as her country was committing its prestige—and its blood—to the struggle.

At the time, Saigon was on its way to becoming what an article in *Paris Match* later called "a dustbin, bordello, and garrison all in one." With nearly 2 million people crammed into its twenty square miles, it ranked as one of the most crowded cities on earth. The central market, brimming as it did every day with fish, fruit, and freshly slaughtered chickens and pigs, seemed oblivious to the chaos around it.

But Saigon had a riptide of terror and intrigue. A bomb might explode in a crowded movie theater at any moment, even as barefoot worshipers lit red candles at the altars of exquisitely peaceful Buddhist temples. No longer were Americans immune from those attacks, as they had been when Anne Westerfield arrived in 1956. With the sandal-wearing French gone and nearly 12,000 Americans assigned to Vietnam by 1962, they were now a target.

Deepe soon became one of a core group of correspondents whose work— especially in 1962–1963—is considered by critics and defenders to have been the first step in the "domestic polarization that eventually led to U.S. disengagement from Vietnam."

In a move that underscored just how important Indochina was becoming, the *New York Times* opened a bureau in January 1962, the first American newspaper to do so. That Homer Bigart, its highly respected, two-time Pulitzer Prize–winning war correspondent, was assigned to the post attached special weight to the *Times*' new commitment. Two months earlier, Malcolm Browne had been dispatched by the Associated Press to run its Saigon bureau, then a single-reporter, store-front operation at 158 Rue Pasteur, near the Gia Long presidential palace. In April 1962, Neil Sheehan took over the United Press International bureau, another one-man enterprise, then located at 19 Ngo Duc Ke. Peter Arnett joined the AP operation late in June, on the same day that the combat photographer Horst Faas arrived in Saigon's AP bureau from Laos. The most contentious correspondent of them all, David Halberstam, arrived to replace Bigart in September.

Bigart, Browne, Sheehan, Arnett, Halberstam, and Faas had already covered intense and dangerous assignments: Bigart in World War II and Korea; Browne with *Stars and Stripes* in Korea; Arnett, a New Zealander, with the Associated Press in Laos and Indonesia; Faas and Halberstam during the brutal colonial war in the Congo. In the company of these seasoned journalists, Deepe's own experience was almost laughable. Stories about her life as an exchange student in the Soviet Union in 1958 amounted to wide-eyed glimpses of America's archenemy. The gee-whiz tone of her travel pieces about lifestyles in Borneo and the sights of China was just fine for the inside pages of *Omaha World Herald.* Writing about her two-day stop in Shanghai, for example, where she was confined to her ship because she had no visa, her story was a porthole view of the city. "Shanghai is an energetic city of junks, Russian-made jets, United States–made warships and an industrial mass that is overpowering to an American visitor," she wrote. "My first sight from the porthole was the muddy Whangpoo [river] boiling like a gigantic chocolate pudding as the early morning sunlight accented a solitary junk." Amidst the major leaguers who were beginning to populate the Saigon press corps, Beverly Deepe was still on the farm team. Nevertheless, she cobbled together a livelihood, just as Gloria Emerson had attempted to do in 1956. At the outset, in addition to the occasional assignments she received from Browne at AP, Deepe freelanced for an assortment of publications—the flashy tabloids *London Daily Express* and *London Sunday Express,* and, later, the light-hearted *Parade* weekly magazine and the occasionally frivolous *Cosmopolitan.*

That she had landed in a journalists' paradise must have been apparent to Deepe from the moment she arrived in Saigon. On February 27, one day before her arrival, the presidential palace had been bombed by two renegade, American-trained Vietnamese pilots who hoped to kill President Diem. Flying AD-6 Skyraiders, the pilots dropped bombs and napalm, and then strafed the building with machine-gun fire. The attack demolished a wing of the palace and, according to a *New York Times* report, "had come close to wiping out the country's leadership." With the exception of Madame Ngo Dinh Nhu—the president's sister-in-law, who fractured an arm when she fell from the second floor to the basement through a hole made by the bomb—no one in the president's collection of relatives was injured. Capitalizing on the miracle of his family's survival, Diem claimed that the airborne assassination attempt had failed because of "divine protection."

Hints of the press corps' disquiet with the military's seeming resistance to meeting its needs surfaced in May 1962, when Secretary of Defense Robert S. McNamara arrived on the first of his many tours. After just forty-eight hours in the country, the man who trusted numbers vastly more than he trusted human instinct, the man who saw in those numbers signs of victory, declared that he was "tremendously encouraged by developments" and had found "nothing but progress and hope for the future." America, he announced, had no plans to bring U.S. combat forces to Vietnam. When reporters questioned McNamara about their limited access to American operations in South Vietnam, and, in particular, challenged efforts by the South Vietnamese military to prevent them from riding on U.S. helicopters taking combat units to battle, McNamara left the impression that the Kennedy administration believed "reporters are magnifying incidents where servicemen find themselves in combat situations and are writing too much about American casualties."

Within several months, Deepe became one of the reporters whose dispatches displeased American officials. Thanks to the Associated Press, her one-time summer employer, Deepe had landed in Saigon with a letter of introduction to the chief of the AP's Saigon bureau, who, at the time, was Malcolm Browne. Having no apparent qualms about her gender, Browne invited Deepe to tag along with him on assignments. Although she never encountered combat on those excursions, "there was still some danger because the Viet Cong were always trying to ambush people, especially Americans, on the roads outside the city," Browne recalled. Since she was interested in the women of South Vietnam, Browne also took Deepe along when he visited Madame Nhu, the president's high-strung, often uncontrollable sister-in-law whose antics sometimes gave the American embassy more reason for hand-wringing than did the Viet Cong.

Much of the early story was not in Saigon but in the provinces, where Deepe spent most of her time during her first months in Vietnam. That her gender made her different there was instantly apparent. On her first visit to a U.S. Marine Corps squadron in the Mekong Delta in 1962, a commander barked out the procedures he wanted her to follow. In the best Marine tradition, he was curt and unequivocal: "You'll wear fatigues here all the time. We don't want women with legs down here." Concerns among military men for her safety created different issues. A Marine captain explained the problem succinctly: Soldiers were being killed all the time, but the death of a woman was considered a big insult and would result in too many uncomfortable questions. "They are ultra protective and super chivalrous in ruling on whether women may accompany their units into battle," she once told an interviewer. On Deepe's first helicopter combat mission that year, she flew in an old H-21 Shawnee, a Korean-era machine that its pilots called the Flying Banana. The pilot told Deepe that he used the helicopter, which he called the "Gray Ghost," to hunt tigers and chase butterflies. She also made trips to what she called the "revolutionary" strategic hamlets, and she drove without an escort along Route 19 in South Vietnam's northern provinces.

Deepe was the first woman to become a permanent member of the Saigon press corps. She had entered a man's world but, apparently by her preference and their choice, she never became "one of the boys." Just as John Lardner had taken exception to Dickey Chapelle's presence on Okinawa in 1945, just days after the U.S. Marines landed, some members of the Saigon press corps were inhospitable. They held the view that "the war was being fought by men against men and that women had no place being there," as Peter Arnett said. Arnett, assigned to Saigon four months after Deepe arrived, described the general attitude in his memoir, *Live From the Battlefield:* "We reporters tended to disparage the abilities of the women and gossip about them and their relationships, and were uninterested in helping them out with the authorities."

A passing mention of Deepe in *Vietnam Diary* by Richard Tregaskis underscores the novelty of her presence. In October 1962, on a helicopter ride from Quang Ngai to Da Nang, Tregaskis remarked that "a well-shaped correspondent of *Newsweek* magazine, Beverly Deepe" was among the passengers. Tregaskis, who wrote six books about his World War II experiences, was as sympathetic to America's cause in Vietnam as Joseph Alsop and Marguerite Higgins were. *Vietnam Diary,* his on-the-scene account of Vietnam in 1963, described Deepe as "a visiting correspondent of the more interesting sex, especially a glamorous one with the more generous curves of the Western world and the round eyes which are also such a novelty, and therefore so much in demand in this part of the world." Certain that an encounter with Deepe would be especially pleasing to his friends in the Marines, Tregaskis invited her to inspect the Marine Officer's Club at the helicopter base in Da Nang. Concocting a lie to make the invitation sound tempting, Tregaskis told Deepe that Colonel Julius W. Ireland, the commanding officer, had authorized him to issue the invitation. Although she declined the invitation for that evening, Deepe graciously agreed to visit the club two days hence. In what Tregaskis characterized as a "big event" at the officer's club, he noted in his diary, "Beverly Deepe, the glamorous correspondent, honored her promise to show up as the guest of Col. Ireland and was on hand with round eyes, curves in the right places, and wearing a dress!"

Deepe appears to have ignored the snubs, taken in stride the occasional silliness of her male colleagues, and remained "all about business," just as she had back in Nebraska. One of her earliest dispatches distributed by the Associated Press described four American women—a doctor and three nurses—who were sent to Vietnam by a Catholic women's organization in 1960. In a story reminiscent of the magazine articles on Operation Brotherhood that Gloria Emerson had written several years earlier, Deepe traveled to Kontum with Dr. Patricia Smith and looked on as she treated members of Vietnam's Montagnards—mountain tribes of ethnic minorities—for everything from the common cold to malaria and tuberculosis. Dr. Smith estimated that 75 percent of the children born into these mountain tribes died before they reached adulthood. The article was laced with the same awe that characterized Emerson's story about O.B.

Although these earliest articles offered little to suggest the successful future as a war correspondent that was awaiting Deepe in Vietnam, one piece definitely provided instant inspiration for another young woman. Her name was Pamela Sanders, and she was the restless daughter of an Englishman, Eric Sanders, who had worked as an accountant in Manila, and Margaret Greenfield, an American whose family had been part of the Philippine Islands' sugar trade for three generations. Sanders was in bed with the flu in her Manila apartment on May 15, 1962, when she heard President John F. Kennedy tell Americans that he was about to draw the line in Southeast Asia. In an address broadcast from Washington, D.C., Kennedy said that "because of recent attacks in Laos by Communist forces, and the subsequent movement of Communist military units toward the border of Thailand," he was dispatching additional American ground and air forces to Thailand to prevent further Communist aggression in Laos. "Where the hell is Laos?" Sanders wondered. In one of Manila's five English-language newspapers that same day, she caught sight of Deepe's byline on a wire service story out of Vietnam describing an American innovation in that country, something called "strategic hamlets." When she looked at the byline, Sanders wondered, "What the devil was a woman doing there? I thought, 'Wow! I can do that.'" She "shot out" of her sick bed, lunged for the atlas, and looked for Southeast Asia. Vietnam was there, but she had trouble finding Laos and Cambodia. Only after she found Vientiane did she get some idea of the country's location. The map people had consolidated the two countries into a place called Indochina. Sanders quickly dressed, packed a suitcase, and headed for Bangkok. "I didn't know whether I'd be back or not," she recalled. "My father was dubious, as he was about many of my enterprises."

Adventure had long been Sanders's companion. In 1941, as foreigners, Sanders and her family were interned by the Japanese in the Philippines during World War II. They were imprisoned, along with 3,000 others, mostly American and British citizens, on the campus of the University of Santo Tomas in Manila. Sanders left the Philippines when she was eighteen and lived for a time in New York City, where she studied theater. Later, she moved to San Francisco, where she befriended Herb Caen, whose column in the *San Francisco Chronicle* inspired her to try writing one of her own. When she returned to Manila in the early 1960s, Louis Stein, the editor of an English-language newspaper in Manila, hired her to write a breezy gossip column about the country's aristocrats. She was soon lured away by a rival newspaper, but the demands of writing a column five days a week, and her increasingly troubled personal life, undid her. After too many missed deadlines, Sanders lost her job as a columnist. Although the editor agreed to run anything she wrote in the newspaper's feature columns, she found the arrangement unsuitable. She wanted out.

So in April of 1962, Sanders had settled on a plan to sail around the world on the *Allegra*, "a ratty old schooner" from Boston then berthed in Manila Bay. The *Philippine Herald* had agreed to pay her for stories about her adventures along the way. But, just as she boarded ship, a Japanese photographer who claimed to have exclusive rights to take pictures of the ship balked at her presence. Sanders was left ashore. "I was crushed," she recalled. Then she caught the flu.

Even as she left Manila, precise details of her plan remained vague. Laos seemed to be where the action was, so she made it her destination. Her editor at the *Philippine Herald* said he might buy the "color pieces" she envisioned writing and gave her an accreditation letter. Naively, she entertained the possibility of trying to locate a group of Filipino doctors who had been captured by Pathet Lao guerrillas—doctors who were part of an Operation Brotherhood public health team. But she would have to find other work as well, despite the low cost of living. Making a living, however, seldom posed great hardships for women who landed in Southeast Asia. The availability of inexpensive apartments and cheap food, along with the PX (Post Exchange) privileges the U.S. military gave journalists it accredited, made Vietnam a bargain for Sanders and many other correspondents who worked there during the war.

Sanders hitched a ride from Manila to Bangkok on a military press plane accompanying the king and queen of Thailand on a review of South East Asian Treaty Organization forces. It was the first of many free rides she was to take during the next two years. She made her way to Udorn—again on military transport—where she found those U.S. Marines, the ones President Kennedy had just dispatched, "up to their asses in mud." A Marine helicopter ferried her to the Thai border, where she boarded a sampan to cross the Mekong River and landed in Laos. Later, she caught a ride to Vientiane in a taxi she shared with some Buddhist monks and old women selling fish.

Freelance work, as it turned out, was easy to find in Laos during those months of unrest in 1962. In short order, Sanders signed on as a stringer for the *New York Times* and *Time* magazine. The *Times* paid her a $50-a-month retainer. But since stringers' stories were, as a matter of practice, published without bylines and slugged "Special to the New York Times," there is no way to identify her articles in the newspaper's archive. Her economic stability came from *Time* magazine, then so rich and profligate that it usually paid her whether or not her material was used. She quickly learned the drill. Stringers for *Time* routinely filed suggestions for stories early each week. "You always had to make it sound as if war was about to break out so they would take your suggestion," she recalled, explaining how personal economics and political alarmism can sometimes converge. The more precarious the situation seemed, the more likely she would be assigned the story, which meant sufficient money to live on for another week. The three-way civil war Dickey Chapelle had encountered nearly a year earlier was still pitting the pro-Communist Pathet Lao forces, the U.S.-backed Royal Lao Army, and the country's neutralist government against one another. In 1962, Laos remained, at least in the Kennedy administration's view, the first in the line of dominoes that could, if it fell, put all of Asia under Communist control.

The United States was still trying to keep its involvement under wraps, but its presence in Laos was as unmistakable to Sanders as it had been to Chapelle. That "noisiest goddamned cease-fire" Chapelle witnessed in May 1961 was still breaking eardrums when Sanders claimed the beat in 1962. The skirmishing continued even after participants in the Geneva Conference agreed, in July 1962, on the neutrality of Laos and the creation of a coalition government. Rumors of coups circulated every day: A new government seemed to take power every week, Sanders recalled: "It was out of a Gilbert and Sullivan opera." The ongoing discord, along with the presence of an International Control Commission of Canadians, Indians, and Poles assigned to oversee the withdrawal of all foreign military personnel—including eight hundred American military advisors—provided Sanders with ample fodder. Laos always seemed to be on the brink of chaos, so it wasn't a huge stretch to suggest in her weekly files to *Time*'s editors that tensions between the country's warring factions might soon erupt into an armed confrontation.

Her reports so pleased *Time*'s editors in New York that she was mentioned in the weekly "Letter from the Publisher" in which noteworthy background information about the issue was featured. Using the familiar term of esteem and endearment in Southeast Asia, the "letter" characterized Sanders as "'Numbah One' in Laos as well as Viet Nam, Cambodia and Thailand," a stringer who "has taken part in countless dangerous missions in the past year."

Sanders was, in many ways, the antithesis of Deepe, the demure brunette who had lost little of the innocence so visible in her Belvidere High School yearbook photo. Sanders was blond and tall, and she well understood that her femininity could pay dividends. Where Deepe was reserved and private, Sanders was ebullient and approachable. Sanders, for example, cared little that her passion-filled but short-lived affair with the married *Time* magazine correspondent, Charles Mohr, was common knowledge in the insular Saigon press community. In the words of one historian, Sanders "was a one-woman Christmas show" in Southeast Asia. In Vientiane, she rented "a hovel next to a Buddhist temple" and bought a Honda motorcycle from a guard at the American embassy. The country offered Sanders a multitude of occasions on which she could envision her own death and witness that of others. She went on CIA Air America missions, flying up-country to drop rice supplies to refugees, often terrified by the dangers that the weather and the enemy created. In the monsoon season, visibility hardly reached beyond the nose of the plane. Laotians occasionally shot at the small aircraft in which she rode. Her greatest fear was that her pilot would be hit and she would have to land the plane alone. So, she recalled, "I asked one of the pilots to teach me how to use the radio." Unlike Deepe, Sanders had no intense commitment to journalism and no driving ambition to become a journalist. Journalism was simply a ticket—to adventure, thrills, free plane rides, and "a view of life at its most elemental and most meaningful."

Although Laos and Cambodia were her official beat, she made frequent trips to Saigon whenever events or staffing matters at *Time* demanded. She usually stayed at the Caravelle Hotel, and she quickly made an acquaintance with the men who later became famous for their coverage of the war— Browne, Halberstam, Sheehan, Arnett, and Faas. She found succor in the camaraderie that bound members of the group, much the way that Chapelle had been nurtured by the camaraderie she experienced with the U.S. Marines. Halberstam introduced her to everyone she needed to meet. He also helped arrange for her to interview Madame Nhu at the president's summer palace in Dalat. When Madame Nhu, the woman known in press circles as the "dragon lady," entered the elegant sitting room where Sanders waited, she was carrying a small handbag that matched her burgundy *ao dai*. Sanders remembered wondering whether the bag might contain a pearl-handled revolver; after all, Madame Nhu's often intemperate behavior "led one to contemplate such fanciful notions." The woman who served as Vietnam's first lady, by virtue of the president's being a bachelor, left Sanders with little doubt about her contempt for particular members of the press. She called Halberstam "that arrogant puppy," and she had little affection for his predecessor in the *New York Times* Saigon bureau, whom she mocked as "Omair Beegart, *quelle blague*" (Homer Bigart, what a joke), making a play on his name, Big-art.

In her encounters with the military, Sanders discovered, just as Deepe did, that young officers were sometimes loath to welcome her into their midst. In an encounter that she later depicted in her novel, *Miranda,* Sanders once accompanied Halberstam on an operation in My Tho, a Mekong Delta village where an operation directed by Army Lieutenant Colonel John Paul Vann was underway. Unnerved by Halberstam's suggestion that he let Sanders accompany his troops, Vann flew into a rage: "I've got the VC, the ARVN, and the Pentagon on my back—and now her!" he roared. "Shit! I'm telling you I don't want any goddamn women around here."

The South Vietnamese, in contrast, had fewer reservations about ambitious women than their American counterparts, in part because women in mid-twentieth-century Vietnamese society enjoyed considerable independence. In the early 1960s, Vietnamese women were joining the Women's Armed Forces Corps at the rate of ten volunteers for every one position, according to one of Deepe's early stories. Among the Viet Cong, Deepe also found women had taken up arms. Like other women drawn to journalism and the Vietnam War, neither Deepe nor Sanders affiliated herself with the growing feminist movement. Their reasons for cold-shouldering the cause seemed as different as their personalities. Sanders was intent on living life without the constraints that society had successfully placed on many women—including Deepe.

For all the barriers she was breaking with her success as a war correspondent in Vietnam, Deepe herself held a remarkably orthodox view of her role in a war zone. "Perhaps my biggest challenge as a woman correspondent is that most of the nearly 250,000 American troops stationed here expect me to be a living symbol of the wives and sweethearts they left behind. And they expect it even in the field," Deepe wrote early in 1966. Although she doubtless wanted the same freedoms and opportunities for which her feminist sisters would soon begin marching in America, Deepe clung to what she perceived as society's expectations for women: "I should be feminine, but not fragile; change from sport dress to flight suit as most women change from slacks to skirt; look fresh in fatigues during a downpour or scaling a slippery rice dike," she explained. For as much as she insisted on taking her place in a man's world of war correspondence, she also continued to accept male expectations. "Always, it's more important to wear lipstick than a pistol."

Sanders, in contrast, believed in the freedoms that the Betty Friedans and Gloria Steinems later demanded for women. But despite Sanders's admiration for America's leading feminists, she never joined the movement. "I guess I didn't think it had anything much to tell me," she said. "I admire them [Steinem and Friedan] because they are much less selfish than I am. They were out there fighting the battles for everyone. I just wanted what I wanted for me." Sanders also found the company of most women stultifying. Their conversations focused on little more than clothing and parties. Men, it seemed, were more inclined to talk about important matters. "They didn't ask about where you had your hair done."

So although Sanders became friends with the young male journalists who were known as the "Saigon commandos," Deepe's association with them was confined to professional interactions. Like Browne, her mentor in Vietnam, who went home to his apartment after work and savored the strains of Wagnerian opera, Deepe was something of a loner, apparently disinclined to mix business and pleasure. "I don't date. Men are a luxury I can't afford," she once told a *Time* magazine correspondent in 1965. "I'm a woman journalist, and I am competing with men." Nonetheless, Deepe, too, found romance in South Vietnam—with Lieutenant Colonel Charles Keever, a handsome U.S. Marine public information officer who, like Halberstam and Sheehan, was a Harvard graduate. Although associates occasionally saw her on what appeared to be a date in Saigon restaurants later in the 1960s, their courtship remained private. Keever had grown up in Kansas. His participation in Harvard's ROTC program earned him a commission as a second lieutenant. After fighting in the Korean War, he went to Harvard Law School and established a practice in Seattle. But, after seven years, he returned to active duty with the U.S. Marines and was sent to Vietnam, where he met Deepe. An associate recalls that they met in Da Nang sometime after the U.S. Marines were ordered to Vietnam by President Lyndon B. Johnson in 1965. Deepe's reports, which so often rankled American diplomats and military leaders, occasionally left Keever open to good-natured admonitions from his bosses, who wondered why he could not control his girlfriend. A hallmark of Deepe's romance with Keever, whom she later married, was discretion. She could no more have participated in the kind of public love affair that Pamela Sanders had with Charles Mohr than she could have walked into Belvidere High School dressed like a *Cosmo* girl.

Month by month, throughout 1962, as Deepe and Sanders turned out freelance stories, relations between the press corps and America's political and military leaders deteriorated. The U.S. State Department's infamous Cable 1006 had arrived at the American embassy in Saigon two weeks before Deepe landed in Vietnam. The cable counseled embassy officials to avoid taking correspondents "on missions whose nature [is] such that undesirable dispatches would be highly probable." It went on: "It is not—repeat not—in our interest to have stories indicating that Americans are leading and directing combat missions against the Viet Cong." Cable 1006 also suggested that military public affairs officers should emphasize to the Saigon press corps that "trifling or thoughtless criticism" of the South Vietnamese government made cooperation with President Diem problematic.

Cable 1006 became a sword in the hands of those already suited up for battle. Although the government billed it as a step to "liberalize" its press policies, the military brass took it as justification for banning reporters— especially those whose reports they found offensive—from helicopters, just when helicopters were becoming the primary mode of transport in a war in

which Americans were still ostensibly functioning only as advisors. Ultimately, the military placed the American airfield at Bien Hoa off limits to the
press, a move that further diminished the ability of reporters to observe the war.
The ban lasted until mid-1964.

It wasn't long before America fired up its propaganda machine to discredit
reports by journalists who remained skeptical about U.S. pronouncements.
Neither Deepe nor Sanders had much regard for most Americans assigned to
the embassy, which, with its endless litany of optimism and selective interpretation, "was the enemy," Sanders recalled. "It represented constant lies." Those
continuing lies helped lead the Saigon press corps to abandon the media's general inclination to support the government, a tradition reflected in the 1956
decision by the *New York Times* and other American newspapers to decline an
invitation from the Communist Chinese government to send correspondents
to China. Although this was the first time in seven years that the Chinese had
invited American journalists, the editors said no thank you. "We did not want
to embarrass our government," said Clifton Daniel, a *Times* editor. In the early
1960s, however, rather than show that kind of deference to their government,
members of the Saigon press corps began resisting military and diplomatic efforts to use them as propagandists.

Government efforts to rein in the press were conducted with secrecy and
deception. In January 1962, for example, just weeks after the United States
had suffered one of its earliest combat casualties in a jungle ambush outside
Saigon, Tom Wicker, a *New York Times* reporter, used the setting of a presidential press conference to pose a question he and his editors had "honed to a
fine point." "Mr. President," Wicker asked, "are American troops now in
combat in Vietnam?" Wicker said that Kennedy looked him "as if he thought
I might be crazy" and quickly dismissed the question with a monosyllable.
"No." He moved on to the next question.

In Vietnam, however, government efforts to keep evidence of its growing involvement out of the news were increasingly thwarted by reporters
such as Bigart, whose stories repeatedly cast doubt on the official line. In
mid-February 1962, for example, at a time when the Kennedy administration
was hiding its growing commitment, Bigart's story noted that the appointment of Army General Paul D. Harkins to head the new U.S. command "is
said to be a result of the growing extent of the United States' involvement in
support of military operations against the Communists." Although the Geneva
cease-fire agreement, which the United States did not sign, set the limit on
foreign military advisors at 685, Bigart's story noted that nearly 5,000 U.S.

troops were in Vietnam at the time. Five days later, another Bigart story explained that American officials had implied that their lack of candor was necessary to avoid hurting the feelings of Vietnam's leaders, who were touchy about suggestions that Americans rather than the Vietnamese were directing the fight against Communist insurgents.

The fundamental cause of the friction between correspondents and the U.S. mission, according to John Mecklin, a journalist to whom the State Department turned to resolve the "press mess," resulted from a pattern of lies told by diplomats and military leaders in Vietnam: "There had been so many little deceptions that they no longer believed anything we said on any subject." Mecklin, *Time* magazine's San Francisco bureau chief, had been persuaded to take a leave of absence to become the U.S. mission's chief of public affairs. In an early report to the State Department, Mecklin explained that "misunderstandings on all sides" had created the rancor. "While the Diem regime pridefully resented any form of hostile criticism," young reporters—"average age 27"—failed to note that the mark of a great nation was "tolerance and understanding of such tortured people as the Vietnamese," who often resorted to "petty, pathetic maneuvers to save face."

The Diem regime held the American press in even greater contempt than did American officials. The president repeatedly expelled American journalists whose reports displeased him. In this early period of the war, dispatches cabled out of the country were translated by South Vietnamese interpreters and sent to the presidential palace by the Saigon cable office. In August 1962, Diem's particular hatred for *Newsweek* provided a major break for Deepe, then still working as a freelancer. Earlier in the year, Diem targeted Bigart of the *New York Times* and Francois Sully of *Newsweek* for expulsion. Bigart was told he had "spread false information which is considered to be tendentious and against the government and people of Vietnam." Bigart later discovered that his offending language was contained in an article his newspaper had never used. Sully, a debonair French expatriate who was *Newsweek*'s longtime stringer in Saigon, hit the presidential family like a rash for which there was no balm. Sully, had been in Indochina since World War II and in the early 1960s reported information that repeatedly humiliated the Diem clan. In an effort to discredit him, government officials circulated rumors that he was a French spy, a Communist, an opium smuggler, and a participant in orgies.

Diem had to be convinced that although tossing a Frenchman out of Vietnam might merely cause a ripple, expelling a *New York Times* reporter, especially one of Bigart's stature, could have serious repercussions. The average

American might begin to wonder about his government's support for a regime predisposed to tampering with freedom of the press. U.S. Ambassador Frederick Nolting Jr. had to convince Diem that although members of the U.S. mission were equally exasperated by the newsmen, the dangers posed by an imbroglio with the American press were too risky. Several days after the government issued the initial expulsion order, Vietnamese authorities reversed it, saying they had acted on misinformation resulting from an error in the translation of one of Bigart's stories. Sully and Bigart were spared.

But when Sully and *Newsweek* again crossed the regime's often arbitrary line in a story that appeared in the magazine's August 20 issue, the Frenchman was doomed. Diem did not take kindly to Sully's observation that the war was "a losing proposition." And his sister-in-law, Madame Nhu, was inflamed by a photo caption that, in her view, demeaned her paramilitary women's group. She expressed "profound indignation" at *Newsweek*'s disrespect for Vietnamese womanhood. This time Ambassador Nolting's arguments with President Diem lacked the punch they had carried when Bigart was involved. The second expulsion order against Sully spurred the Vietnam Foreign Correspondents Association, of which Browne was president and Deepe secretary, to organize a protest. Despite considerable discord among its members, some of whom suspected that Sully might be a Communist or a French spy, the association rallied to his cause. Their letters of protest to President Diem and President Kennedy were ignored, however. Sully left the country on September 9 and soon settled in at Harvard University, where he became a *Newsweek*-sponsored Nieman Fellow. Deepe took his place. She had started doing freelance work for *Newsweek* well before Sully's ouster because the Frenchman "didn't write English all that well, so Beverly was hired to do some English-language reporting," recalled Robert McCabe, a *Newsweek* stringer based in Hong Kong.

After Sully's expulsion, Deepe found steady work with the magazine for more than a year. Stepping into the large footprints Sully left in Vietnam could not have been easy. His colleagues were exceptionally fond of the older, worldly Frenchman, whose exuberance and elan were magnetic. For his cohorts, he found girlfriends and opium, AP photographer Faas remembers. That his departure gave Deepe something of a respectable berth in the Saigon press corps rankled them a bit. Certainly, she had done some good work for AP at the outset, but for some members of the Saigon press corps it was unthinkable that the young woman Faas considered a "boring, farm-bred Nebraska girl" could step into Sully's shoes. Halberstam's take on Deepe was dismissive. He called her "a lost traveler" who left few traces on the journalistic terrain of the era. "She didn't know what was in her notebooks," he said in 1998. Although Halberstam's assessment might have had credence during the year he spent in South Vietnam, Deepe's later accomplishments proved otherwise. In the seven years she spent in Vietnam, Deepe worked for three of America's preeminent news organizations, one of which nominated her for a Pulitzer Prize.

The reports Deepe sent to *Newsweek* were hardly as bellicose as Sully's, but they maintained a critical edge. Although she observed the tenets of objectivity she had learned at Columbia, the skeptical undertone of many *Newsweek* reports, especially those that appeared later in 1963, suggests she had growing doubts. Although the routines of America's weekly news magazines often make the contributions of individual staffers difficult to trace, *Newsweek* occasionally published verbatim excerpts from Deepe's reports. She was sometimes listed as a contributing writer on a cover story, as was the case with *Newsweek*'s 1963 portrait of the crisis in South Vietnam. Generally, *Newsweek*, like *Time*, compiled a synopsis of news events that incorporated information from a correspondent's "file," related news stories, and background material assembled by its research staff in New York. Because *Time* seldom incorporated a correspondent's name in its reports, it is unknown whether Sanders's files were ever directly quoted.

One of the first reports that bore Deepe's name after Sully's departure involved the use of helicopters as a tool of war, the same subject featured in Chapelle's *National Geographic* cover story in November 1962. Deepe's article, "The New Metal Birds," published in October 1962, focused on three American airmen who died when their helicopter was shot down. *Newsweek*'s lead-in to Deepe's material questioned the role of American "advisors" in Vietnam. How was it that three pilots performing duties as advisors could be blasted out of the sky in the space of just seventy-two hours, *Newsweek* asked. The story incorporated Deepe's report on her visit to A Chau, a military base located 380 miles northwest of Saigon, near the Laotian border. Writing about the log cabin where the airmen lived, she interviewed three Americans who described the difficulties of outwitting their enemy. Helicopters were shot down with such frequency, one officer told Deepe, that pilots had taken to calling the area "Shotgun Alley."

By the closing months of 1962, life in Vietnam, particularly in Saigon, had become so risky that the U.S. Department of State had rated South Vietnam a maximum hardship post, a designation that entitled American diplomatic personnel stationed there an allowance of 25 percent above base salary.

Grenades, often aimed at Americans, were tossed into the city's restaurants, bars, and sidewalk cafes, and at passing American cars. Month by month, more than two years before the U.S. Marines came ashore at Da Nang, the war was intensifying; a U.S. withdrawal became unthinkable. The dangers Deepe and Sanders had faced in Southeast Asia in 1962 intensified in 1963, the year Secretary of State Dean Rusk called America's involvement in South Vietnam "a dirty, untidy, disagreeable war."

The situation in Saigon grew more tumultuous in the opening days of 1963 with the battle at Ap Bac, which further inflamed tensions between the press and American officials. From their own view of the battle on the ground, and from interviews with junior commanders in the field, Lieutenant Colonel Vann among them, American journalists learned—and later reported—that the battle amounted to "a miserable damn performance" by the South Vietnamese Army commanders and their units. Yet back in Saigon, American military authorities characterized the encounter as a South Vietnamese victory. Reporters who had witnessed the battle were enraged. Boiling over was a combination of resentment over President Diem's continuing harassment, lingering anger over the Sully expulsion, fury at Madame Nhu's charges that the entire American press was Communist, and bitterness about the way the American military mission handled the press.

Ap Bac marked the beginning of a year in which, according to the press historian William Prochnau, a small group of mostly young correspondents "dominated the words and the images sent home from the war." The rebellion among reporters against U.S. government efforts to manage news and to portray events in Vietnam as an American success story brought them a certain fame and celebrity. Deepe, less vocal than the likes of Halberstam, shared their sentiments and wrote stories that irritated the embassy staff and military leaders. By virtue of the Diem regime's continuing dislike of *Newsweek,* she was persona non grata at the presidential palace. The magazine's reports on the "press mess" listed Deepe's name among those permanent U.S. correspondents in Saigon whose dispatches were criticized as biased. What some saw as bias, however, others perceived as truth. Deepe's name appeared—along with those of Sully and Halberstam—in a letter to the editor of *Newsweek* from Vann, whose candor about battlefield operations had made him a rarity among officers and a favorite among reporters. Expressing a sentiment that contradicted the view of his superiors, Vann said of Deepe, Halberstam, and Sully, "I sincerely believe that the American press corps in Saigon has rendered a greater service to this country and to the fourteen million deserving Vietnamese citizens than any official American group a hundred times their number."

Developments in South Vietnam in early to mid-1963 kept Deepe's files pouring into *Newsweek*'s New York headquarters. Her name appeared in the magazine week after week: "*Newsweek*'s Beverly Deepe reported from . . ." "In Saigon, reports *Newsweek*'s Beverly Deepe . . ." "*Newsweek*'s Beverly Deepe cabled that . . ." In April 1963, Deepe reported from Laos, where once again the cease-fire established under the nine-month-old Geneva agreement was being broken. The neutralist army led by General Kong Le had come under attack by Communist Pathet Lao forces with help from North Vietnamese cadres. By mid-April, Kong Le's 2,500-man force was in retreat near the Plain of Jars. Deepe's report described the scene of defeat and withdrawal underway at a makeshift airstrip near Muong Phanh, northwest of Vientiane: "Around the airstrip, neutralist wives and children prepare to flee from tragedy to uncertainty," Deepe wrote. "A few miles down the road, a shorts-clad farmer herding his water buffalo looks up at the caravan of Soviet built jeeps and trucks carrying the neutralist army into the hills. In Kong Le's HQ only a few soldiers remain, stuffing papers into canvas bags. Behind a knotted curtain, Kong Le's small, dark room is empty, except for two pet hamsters."

Sanders, too, made a trip to the Plain of Jars. A Laotian pilot invited her along for the ride and they flew at night, through a huge thunderstorm. She spent five days at Kong Le's headquarters and, using information from her report on the trip, *Time* magazine described him as a man who "neither drinks, smokes nor gambles and is fanatic about health, honesty and cleanliness. He shares common Laotian superstitions, such as wearing a 'magic' ring and wrist amulet." When she spoke of that encounter several decades later, Sanders recalled, "Kong Le was pretty depressed in those days; it was the monsoon season and he was in retreat." But her visit seemed to cheer Kong Le and he invited her to stay. By way of enticement, he proposed marriage and offered her "some troops of my own to command." The marriage proposal had no appeal but the offer of troops was rather tempting, Sanders recollected. However, "the smell of those dried fish they ate every morning for breakfast" so sickened her that Sanders decided to forego Kong Le's offer.

By May, back in South Vietnam, the Diem regime had provoked a crisis among the nation's Buddhists, who were prevented from flying their flag in Hue during celebrations of Buddha's birthday on May 8. Nine demonstrators died when South Vietnamese soldiers opened fire on Buddhists participating in the celebration. President Diem justified the move by saying that Communists had infiltrated the temples. The discord grew in the following weeks and spread throughout the country. Although few of their number spoke English, the Buddhist opposition had a well-developed understanding of how to use the American media. Over several months, they made a practice of notifying American journalists of their plans for demonstrations; often messages on the banners they carried were in English. AP photographer Faas even recalled that one monk who routinely visited Browne in the AP office availed himself of Browne's knowledge of chemistry. The conversation Faas remembered involved a discussion of the speed with which certain gas mixtures ignited, but he never dreamed the use to which the holy man would put that information.

On the night of June 10, a dozen or more foreign correspondents in Saigon received telephone calls similar to ones they had received in the past. An important event would take place the following morning, they were advised. Alone among them, Browne went to the appointed place and was the only media witness to the first act of martyrdom. Standing at the intersection of Phan Dinh Phung and Le Van Duyet in the company of about a thousand monks and nuns, Browne watched an elderly monk assume the lotus position and, after allowing two young monks to douse him with gasoline, strike a match. As flames engulfed his body, two monks raised a cloth banner with the message (in English) "Priest burns for Buddhist demands." Browne recalled shooting "roll after roll" of film, photographs that made the front page of newspapers across the country. One of Browne's images prompted President Kennedy to ask, "What the hell is going on over there?" Throughout the year, Buddhists continued to use suicide as a political statement. As the weeks passed, each self-immolation further destabilized the Diem government. In face of this continuing chaos, in the summer of 1963, the *New York Herald Tribune* sent its star columnist to explain to its readers the roots of the Buddhist crisis and the continuing self-immolations. That decision provided the occasion for Beverly Deepe's only encounter with the role model who had inspired her to be a journalist, Marguerite Higgins.

Perhaps no other reporter in America had a familiarity with Vietnam comparable to that of Maggie Higgins. Her acquaintance with the country dated back to her infancy. She was born in Hong Kong, the daughter of an Irish American father who worked as a freight manager for the Pacific Mail Steamship Company, and a French-born mother whose own father—Count George de Godard—was a member of the French colonial forces that had fought the Vietnamese in the 1890s. In 1922, when Larry and Marguerite

Higgins's six-month-old baby was stricken with malaria, her parents followed the doctor's suggestion and took baby Marguerite to Dalat, Vietnam's mountain resort, where the cooler, clearer air would hasten her cure. Beginning in 1951, she went back to Vietnam ten times as a correspondent. Like the majority of Americans in her generation, Higgins was zealously anti-Communist, and she believed in the domino theory. As the granddaughter and wife of military men, she readily accepted military action as the price of preserving America's place in the world. Moreover, her understanding of the pacifist nature of the Buddhist religion and its precepts against suicide led her to question the underlying motives of monks whose grisly suicides were attracting world attention. She doubted the dark predictions of a looming American failure in Southeast Asia and was inclined to disbelieve reports of religious persecution by the Diem regime.

Her knowledge of the country and her stature as a journalist gave her an attitude of superiority over the Saigon press corps. She appeared to have arrived in Vietnam with the belief that she would correct all the false impressions those young upstart correspondents had created in America. As the high priestess of her profession, a journalist whose coverage of the Korean War had been honored with a Pulitzer Prize, she would give American readers the correct story.[1]

Befitting both her status and her ideology, it was natural that America's political and military leaders in Saigon would happily share their perspectives with her. Ambassador Nolting told Higgins that President Diem was deeply concerned with the lives of peasants and committed to improving them. Diem was a man who held deep moral convictions, Nolting insisted, not the rabid Roman Catholic that members of the American news media were portraying him to be. "The Viet Cong are losing because we are steadily decreasing their areas of maneuver and the terrain over which they can move at will," General Harkins, the top man in the Military Assistance Command Vietnam, told her. Harkins, her story noted, had been criticized by the resident American press corps for over-optimism, a charge that "left him unmoved." And after her five-hour interview with President Diem, who was soon to institute martial law throughout the country, Higgins wrote about his religious tolerance and made special note of his willingness to grant the Buddhist protesters their demands. The real motive driving their continued demonstra-

---

1. Higgins shared the Pulitzer Prize for international reporting with her archrival and fellow *Herald Tribune* correspondent, Homer Bigart, and three others.

tions, she concluded, had less to do with religious freedom than with a desire to bring about an overthrow of the Diem government.

In the countryside, far from all the chicanery and intrigue of competing interest groups in Saigon, Higgins found an old farmer in a Mekong Delta village who praised the Diem government's good intentions and told her that its aid programs never discriminated on the basis of religion. Catholics, Buddhists, and ancestor worshipers alike had all recently received pigs and bags of fertilizer in equal measure. Oh yes, they would like to be rid of the Viet Cong, who collected taxes and bags of rice from farmers, the old man said: "But we must be polite to the Viet Cong. Very polite. For they have weapons. . . . If we do not do what the Viet Cong say, they would kill us. So we have to be polite and obedient."

In a story about the suicide of a young monk in Pan Theit, Higgins described how a grisly, near tug-of-war erupted over the burned corpse as monks had tried to wrest the body from the young man's parents. Acting on orders from their highly politicized brethren in Saigon, Higgins charged, the Buddhists wanted to stage a funeral choreographed to further provoke anti-Diem demonstrations. By way of underscoring the dubious rationale for his self-immolation, she described how monks "at this pagoda could not offer any examples of discrimination in this rural province that could have triggered the tragedy."

Most women with designs on joining journalism's big leagues in the early 1960s always invoked the name of Maggie Higgins. "Being the Maggie Higgins of the Vietnam War was what women journalists talked about," recalled one distaff member of the Saigon press corps. "Who else was there. She had done it and so she was always held up as a model." Beverly Deepe, however, found herself disappointed with the woman whose career had once so inspired her. Higgins's take on the war so disturbed Deepe that, on the only occasion she saw Higgins in Saigon, she found that the vibrant young woman whose images she once saw in *Life* had vanished. Higgins, who was then forty-two, lacked the glow Deepe had discerned in Carl Mydans's photos. Deepe thought that she now looked mean. As much as she had been drawn to journalism by Higgins's example, and for all the esteem in which she had once held her, on the one occasion Deepe saw her, she walked away without introducing herself. She had no wish to shake hands with Higgins. Deepe's admiration for her sank in the summer of 1963 after she read a story posted on the bulletin board of the United States Information Service offices. That article, which advocated a deeper American commitment, was more propaganda than journalism, or at least the kind of journalism Deepe was practicing in Vietnam. Deepe's portrayal of those same events differed sharply from the Higgins story. Yet Higgins's stature led editors to question those young "commandos" about why their conclusions often seemed to contradict the message Higgins brought home from Vietnam. She took pains to suggest that news reports that contradicted her judgments were written by young, untested journalists whose patriotism was suspect. Higgins especially rankled Halberstam, who many years later said of her: "She was an embarrassment to herself. She was virtually working for MACV."

Following her return from Vietnam in August, the *Herald Tribune* ran a six-part series that promised Higgins would sort out the confusion surrounding events in Southeast Asia. They called it "Viet Nam—Fact and Fiction." In the first installment, Higgins presented a cross section of Vietnamese minorities whose collective praise for President Diem was summed up by a Buddhist monk contradicting claims of religious persecution made by his brethren in Saigon: "All this talk of discrimination has nothing to do with reality as we know it here in our village. The Catholics don't get more than we do and we don't get more than the Catholics do." Her series, which repeated information from the dispatches she had written in Saigon, ran just days after members of President Diem's private army undertook a brutal crackdown on the regime's Buddhist opponents. That crackdown began with raids on scores of pagodas in Saigon and Hue and ended with the imprisonment of several hundred Buddhist holy men. Her final installment was published one day after President Kennedy expressed impatience with the deteriorating mess in Saigon during an interview in Hyannis Port with Walter Cronkite. The president's words directly contradicted all the optimism and pro-Diem sentiments with which Higgins had laced her stories. "We are prepared to assist them, but I don't think the war can be won unless the people [of Vietnam] support the effort and, in my opinion, in the last two months, the government has gotten out of touch with the people." Then, in what has since been widely interpreted as a signal to Diem's opponents that the United States would take no steps to thwart a coup, Kennedy added: "With changes in policy and perhaps with personnel, I think it can. . . . It is their war to win."

Higgins's series largely ignored the fast-paced events that began unfolding after her departure. In August, for example, *Newsweek* ran Deepe's reports about the deepening religious crisis in Hue, noting that the continuing predicament was benefiting the Communists in the war effort. Her article also speculated about the possibility of a coup. A week later, she reported on raids against the Buddhists by heavily armed government troops who targeted 2,000 pagodas, including Saigon's Xa Loi Pagoda. Monks and nuns were dragged away by secret police and members of a Vietnamese special forces unit. At least thirty monks and nuns were believed to have died. Deepe's report on the attacks noted that the troops in Operation Pagoda had three characteristics: "They were Catholic, they were from Hue, and they were ruthless." The following month, *Newsweek*'s September 9 issue listed Deepe as a member of the "nine-man force" deployed to write a cover story on the Nhu family and its disastrous role in ruling the country.

The biggest story of 1963 was the overthrow of the Diem regime, carried out on November 1 with what has been widely considered to be the not-so-veiled blessing of the Kennedy administration. Deepe's account of the events filled nearly two columns in *Newsweek*. From the moment members of the 7th Vietnamese Army Division left their hideouts in the south of the city and set off for the heart of Saigon, Deepe appears to have witnessed the day's events. She reported that guards at the Gia Long palace strung barbed wire around the president's home and that loyal troops acted to halt the insurgents. By evening, rocket fire reverberated throughout the city and T-28 fighter bombers flew low over the palace, where 20 mm shells fired from rooftop gun emplacements warded them off. Dressed in clerical attire, President Diem and his brother left the palace and took sanctuary in a Catholic church in Cholon, Saigon's nearby twin city. After their surrender to an army unit, the brothers were assassinated: Diem was shot, his brother beaten and stabbed. On the day after the coup, Deepe entered the palace through a hole blown in its six-inch-thick wall. In the family quarters, she glimpsed Madame Nhu's pink bathtub and her wardrobe of embroidered *ao dais*. In President Diem's musty and dank room, which Deepe described as "unbelievably disorganized and littered with men's magazines," she saw a reflection of his style of government. A double-breasted white sharkskin jacket was flung on a rocking chair, and a French-language book, *Ils Arrivent* (They're Coming), lay on the desk.

When she finally returned home, Deepe found that her own apartment, just half a block from the presidential palace, had been "looted by fleeing Diemist troops and riddled with machine gun fire." One of the bullets, she noted, lodged in a book titled *Problems of Freedom: South Vietnam Since Independence*. That volume of scholarly essays, edited by Wesley R. Fishel, the Michigan State University professor who had functioned in various advisory roles in South Vietnam, is noteworthy for its clear-eyed but generally optimistic assessment that Vietnam would emerge as a democratic society.

Noting that President Diem had survived the near unanimous calls for his ouster in late 1954 and early 1955, Senator Mike Mansfield's introduction to the book observed, "What had seemed to be a nightmare of chaos one year earlier was then shaping into a solid, hopeful situation." Quoting a report he had written for the Senate Foreign Relations Committee, Mansfield added: "It has been gained largely through the dedication and courage of Ngo Dinh Diem." Now, a bullet hole obscured the book's message of hope; Diem lay in the morgue with a bullet in his head; and Deepe explained to *Newsweek* readers that the South Vietnamese "seemed delirious with excitement, and joy; laughing, crying, shouting slogans and waving banners."

As for Sanders, several months before the Diem regime was overthrown, she found herself haunted by the savagery and cruelty she had witnessed, and she began to contemplate leaving. Unlike many of the American journalists who became her friends in Southeast Asia, Sanders had an international perspective on events in the region. Her childhood in the Philippines and her acquaintance with how the former Spanish colony was annexed by America during the Spanish-American War in 1898 gave her a different view of America as a colonial power. In her opinion, the American victory in the Manila Bay battle in May 1898, when the U.S. Navy destroyed the Spanish fleet and acquired control over the Philippine Islands, had marked the moment when America became not only a major world power but also an imperialist power. The longer Sanders remained in Southeast Asia, the more convinced she became that America was wrong.

Those intellectual concepts, however, were at odds with her more immediate visceral experiences. "The guys on the missions were your pals," she said. "To talk about objectivity in that situation is ridiculous. You can't be objective. You weren't out there traveling with the Viet Cong. On a day-to-day basis, you still wanted to win." At the same time, she watched the destruction of a country and its people. "You were seeing Vietnamese being blown to hell. Houses going up in flames from napalm, or you saw a guy running across a rice paddy and you knew he was a farmer but he was gunned down. Well, he was running. Any male over the age of fifteen had to be Viet Cong." Slowly, she came to realize that "we would never win."

The early thrills of those Air America rice drops in Laos and, later, the bombing runs in Vietnam's Iron Triangle, a Communist base area northwest of Saigon, gave way to a rising sense of vulnerability as she traveled in two-seater fighter planes flown by South Vietnamese pilots. "It occurred to me that I might actually be killed," she recalled. One dive-bombing run was particularly terrifying, especially after an American pilot told her later that she was lucky to be alive. Moreover, her friend Halberstam kept telling her to get out. "Do I really want to die in Southeast Asia?" Sanders wondered. After she lost a couple of friends in the fighting, the question was no longer abstract. As Halberstam prepared to leave Vietnam in December 1963 at the end of his assignment for the *Times,* he kept saying the country had grown too risky. Her odds were dwindling, he counseled. Sanders was inclined to believe him.

Sanders finally acquiesced. Early in 1964, *Time* magazine in New York City hired her as a freelance reporter, but Southeast Asia and the war remained her preoccupation. She had endless arguments about the war with her associates at the magazine, including *Time*'s editor-in-chief, Henry Grunwald, a believer in both the domino theory and the peril of Communist China. "I felt that I had deserted one of my own family," Sanders said, recalling the emotional upheavals that afflicted her after her return from South Vietnam. "I could hardly bear to read about it."

Back in Vietnam after the overthrow of Diem, a military triumvirate led by Major General Duong Van Minh took over the leadership of the country. The new leaders allowed Francois Sully to return to South Vietnam and resume his work for *Newsweek.* How Beverly Deepe felt about the Frenchman's return is unclear. Her reports no longer appeared in *Newsweek,* however, and she soon became a special correspondent for the *New York Herald Tribune.* By then, Deepe had made Saigon her home. Unlike the many other correspondents whose lives in South Vietnam seemed so transient and temporary, Deepe's presence there had a sense of permanence. Instead of a room at the Continental Palace Hotel or the Caravelle, the hotels of choice for so many in the Saigon press corps, Deepe settled into a downtown apartment; later, she moved into a small villa where she employed a Vietnamese servant. The apartment at 32 Cong Ly was located between the presidential palace and the American embassy. She filled the place with tasteful furnishings and good books, including titles that underscored her interest in Vietnamese culture, politics, and history. The bats that Gloria Emerson had so feared several years before still populated the city and occasionally winged their way through her building. "Beverly lived in Saigon as opposed to being on assignment there," recalled a *Washington Post* correspondent who made her acquaintance in the mid-1960s. "Unlike the rest of us, Vietnam was her home. She was really dug in," said another. Elizabeth Pond, who arrived in Vietnam several years after Deepe, recalled that she appeared to be rooted in Saigon.

Deepe was also alone in the way she interacted with other female correspondents. Unlike some of the women who came later, Deepe apparently never deliberately distanced herself from her female colleagues; indeed, she is remembered with fondness by female peers in the Saigon press corps. They found in her a willingness to guide their early steps in a strange land. In contrast, Jurate Kazickas recalled how, in the atmosphere of competition, female correspondents seldom formed close friendships. "The women were never really a group," said Kazickas, whose two-year stay in Vietnam began in February 1967. She was accredited on the strength of referral letters from the North American Newspaper Alliance, *Maryknoll* magazine, and *Darbininkas* (Worker), a Lithuanian-language weekly newspaper. Gender, or so it seemed to Kazickas, was her ticket; it made her unusual and it gave her access. What she called "a Queen Bee syndrome" developed. "There was fierce competition between women. The last thing I wanted to see was another woman on the battlefield," Kazickas recalled. Denby Fawcett, who covered the war for the *Honolulu Advertiser,* was unable, years later, to pinpoint why she made no effort to befriend other female journalists in Vietnam and rued it as a missed opportunity for friendships among peers in an often lonely environment. "The first and last time," female reporters bonded as a group, Fawcett recalled, was in response to General Westmoreland's brief effort to ban them from over-nighting with the troops during military operations. That directive grew out of an encounter Westmoreland had with Fawcett, whose parents had been his neighbors in Hawaii. It was during his early morning visit in the Central Highlands with troops who had been badly mauled in an encounter with the North Vietnamese that Westmoreland first became aware that female reporters were spending nights in the field, just as their male colleagues did. The women took their fight against the no-overnight order all the way up the chain of command to Secretary of Defense Robert S. McNamara. Westmoreland's second in command received the women's letter of protest and let the general's order die without being implemented.

In creating her life in Saigon, Deepe also established a far-reaching circle of Vietnamese friends who helped her develop an understanding of the country's politics, economy, culture, and history. The most loyal among them was Pham Xuan An, whose affiliation with Americans in South Vietnam dated back to 1954 when he met and befriended Air Force Colonel Edward Lansdale, the man in charge of reshaping Vietnam to America's liking. An knew several of Lansdale's associates, including at least one of his elite CIA commando team, the Rover Boys. An had studied journalism at Orange County

Community College, and he had worked briefly at a Sacramento newspaper. He had also studied the United Nations' press operations in New York. Despite his circle of associations with men in the Saigon press corps, including Nick Turner of Reuters, Robert Shaplen of the *New Yorker,* later Morley Safer of CBS, and a succession of men *Time* sent to Saigon, An maintained a special admiration for the women who covered the war, especially Deepe. She apparently had a similar admiration for An. He had been not only astonished but also deeply touched when, soon after she began working for the *Tribune,* he had seen paperwork in her typewriter relating to the company's life insurance policy for employees. Deepe had filled in the names of her sister and An as beneficiaries. Not that Deepe ever told him she had done so; that would have been out of character for the woman who disliked drawing attention to herself.

An's admiration later extended to Elizabeth Pond, Deepe's colleague at the *Christian Science Monitor,* where she found a job after the *Herald Tribune* folded. Pond, who arrived in Saigon in 1967, had completed her master's degree in Soviet studies at Harvard and she now had a vague plan either to join the State Department or to become a correspondent in Moscow. Along the way, she fell in love with Eastern Europe, especially with Czechoslovakia. She believed in the concepts of containment, advanced by George Kennan in 1947, which became the foundation of the U.S. cold war policy with the Soviet Union. As Vietnam began to overshadow other world issues in 1967, Pond decided to leave her job with the *Monitor* in Europe and go and assess for herself the situation there. An editor, however, prevailed on her to spend six months in South Vietnam writing for the *Monitor.* She went a second time in 1969 with a research fellowship from the Alicia Patterson Foundation. She worked with An on both occasions. "She never stopped working," he recalled. Pond's interest in understanding the Vietnamese people, particularly the peasant society, made a special impression on An. "Frankie [FitzGerald] was exactly the same way," he added, speaking of Frances FitzGerald. And in both women he saw the same daring he had so often seen in Deepe: "Those ladies were so tough and courageous." It seemed to An that so many American and Vietnamese officials "ran after all the well-known correspondents—the men" who worked for the big-name media organizations. "But I would tell them, 'You are stupid. The tough people here are the lady correspondents.' They were very disciplined."

After the war, An was revealed to have been a Viet Cong agent. As with other American journalists with whom he was associated, Pond had no inkling of his double life. Nor, apparently, did Beverly Deepe. Her friendship with An began while she worked for *Newsweek* and he worked for Reuters, an office Deepe visited frequently because the magazine used its Telex machines to wire her dispatches to New York. An told his American biographer how he had guided Deepe in her early work as a correspondent and that he was proud of the results. He taught her the art of "cooking" stories, as he did for Reuters. "I showed her how we use cables and other information, throw them all in, stir things up for an hour, and then out comes the story line of the day." In May 1964, after Deepe had joined the *Tribune,* she became "my boss," as An put it. As he had once been at Reuters, An became Deepe's interpreter, sage, driver, and at times her guardian. On occasion he wrote stories for the *Herald Tribune,* as he did in July 1965, when the paper published his bylined story about the chances of a neutralist or Communist government takeover in South Vietnam. The *New York Times* Saigon bureau chief, Terence Smith, who wanted to hire An after he left Reuters, good-naturedly teased him, saying, "You must be in love with her." Why else would he pass up the offer of a lucrative *New York Times* job to work for Beverly Deepe? "She was a lady and she was alone," An explained, recalling his decision to decline Smith's offer. Deepe was admired by her Vietnamese friends because, An said, "she always dressed and acted like a lady; she never wore miniskirts," and her demeanor was always low-key.

By the time Deepe signed on with the *Herald Tribune,* she, like Sanders, had witnessed haunting scenes of war that would prowl her psyche for decades. "Of all the men I've met in Vietnam, it is the ones I knew only briefly that I remember best," she recalled. The young T-28 pilot who took her on a bombing raid in 1963 claimed a permanent place in her consciousness. Three missions later, he made a low strafing pass, she said, trying to cut off the heads of the Viet Cong with the plane's propellers. Unable to pull up after dipping so low, he came to his final resting place in a rice paddy dike. Nor has her encounter with a young medic named Levy ever left her. As he tenderly bandaged a blister on her foot just before a night patrol, Levy spoke as if her feet belonged to him. "You never take care of my footsies that way," he told her. Levy went home "under a 50-star flag," killed by friendly fire. In 1966, she wrote these words: "I live in a brown half-house made of teak, in a world made of tears, shattered dreams and everywhere the dead and the almost dead, where the American men are lonely and the Vietnamese are sad. My major personal difficulty is to laugh—if only occasionally—for all of Vietnam cries."

Yet even in the mid-1960s, Deepe seemed to have a sense of immunity to the terrible dangers of combat. When a battalion commander asked in 1965 whether she was certain she wanted to accompany a mission to relieve an armored column that had been encircled by Viet Cong for nearly thirty hours, her reply suggests she might have felt invulnerable, or at least was able to ignore her vulnerability. "Oh yes, we in the press are among the blessed," she said, drawing a halo above her head with her index finger. Days later, she doubtless pondered her own vulnerability when she learned that Dickey Chapelle had been killed by a land mine. Although the war had become what she called "a hellish dancing madness," Deepe endured.

By then she had been writing for the *Herald Tribune* for more than a year. First as a "special correspondent" and later as a member of the staff, Deepe scored a succession of big stories between early 1964 and April 1966, when she was the *Tribune*'s anchor in Saigon. Coverage of the war out of Washington was handled by the newspaper's A-team, but judging by the *Herald Tribune* microfilm of those years, Deepe appears to have written more stories with a Saigon dateline than any other *Trib* staffer. Although some of its star reporters and columnists, including Jimmy Breslin, made brief visits to Vietnam and wrote lengthy stories about the war, the *Herald Tribune* did not leave its mark on the Vietnam conflict as it had a decade earlier in the Korean War when it shared that Pulitzer. When Breslin arrived in Vietnam expecting the full resources of the *Trib*'s Saigon office to be at his disposal, Deepe infuriated him with her unwillingness to be used as a resource. She ignored him and went about her own work—little of which appears to have made the paper on days when Breslin's stories ran, usually on page one.

More impressive than any one story Deepe wrote for the *Tribune* between 1964 and 1966 is the near-limitless range of stories she produced, including a seven-part analysis of South Vietnam's instability a year after the fall of President Diem. That series, which ran from October 1964, illustrated how the country's non-Communist political factions seemed to hate one another as much as they hated the Communists. Rival cliques of military officers overthrew one another in quick succession. In the final installment, she described how, one year to the day after the coup, South Vietnam was starting over. The country's civilian High National Council had just named Tran Van Huong premier following the resignation of Lieutenant General Khanh. Recalling that just one month before his assassination, President Diem superciliously proclaimed—in an echo of Madame de Pompadour's eighteenth-century prophecy *"apres moi, le deluge"*—Deepe declared, "the deluge has descended."

In America's apparent inability or unwillingness to reverse three key failings in its approach to the war, the country was squandering its chances of winning, Deepe argued. Vietnam would be lost, she said, unless the United States began fighting a guerrilla-style war rather than sticking with the conventional, Korea-style approach it was taking. Moreover, the United States needed not only to formalize its alliance with South Vietnam but also to define specific responsibilities for each country. Third, the United States had to attach clear demands for reforming the South Vietnamese military and economy.

Perhaps the most celebrated story Deepe wrote as the *Tribune*'s correspondent revealed the rift between U.S. Ambassador Taylor and South Vietnam's Lieutenant General Khanh, a one-time Diem ally who had participated in the president's overthrow. In January 1964, barely three months after Diem's assassination, Khanh helped to topple the military junta that had taken power. That began a year of political turbulence in which Khanh led an ever-more shaky government in Saigon. The new constitution he imposed, one designed to make him a virtual dictator, was met with massive street protests that forced him to step aside. He became part of a triumvirate, in which he was named prime minister, that was to rule until a permanent government was created. That arrangement allowed him, temporarily at least, to re-establish his hold on power. Ambassador Taylor, frustrated by the ongoing factional disputes, grew increasingly impatient, particularly with Khanh, the government's intriguer-in-chief. Taylor was especially rankled by Khanh's insistence during an interview with Deepe that a regiment of Chinese troops had moved into North Vietnam and that the North Vietnamese army had moved three of its battalions into South Vietnam. Calls for retaliation among members of Khanh's government alarmed Taylor, who feared that the inflammatory rhetoric might be interpreted as a step to widen the war. The storm passed after American officials succeeded in having Khanh clarify his comments. But the calm that followed was short-lived. In December 1964, a pair of young generals dissolved the High National Council, placed several of its members under arrest, and replaced it with an Armed Forces Council. As it had in the past, the political unrest threatened to discourage the U.S. Congress from increasing its aid to Vietnam.

During a meeting with Khanh and the other leaders of the latest machinations, Taylor blew up. America's leaders were fed up with their coups, he seethed. Khanh, in turn, angered by Taylor's tongue-lashing, summoned Deepe for an exclusive interview on December 22. Khanh warned that if Taylor "does not act more intelligently, the United States will lose Southeast Asia and we will lose our freedom." He further criticized Taylor "for having engaged in 'activities beyond imagination' during American efforts to obtain the restoration of the civilian High National Council." Khanh, speaking of America and its leaders, added, "You have to be more realistic . . . you must be more practical and not have a dream of having Viet Nam be an image of the United States because the way of life and the people are entirely different."

The next day, Taylor held an off-the-record briefing at which he described to a select group of American journalists his recent talks with Khanh. Deepe was not among the eight reporters Taylor had invited and thus was not party to the guidelines requiring that none of his remarks were to be attributed to him or to any other American official. Taking full advantage of the liberty her absence from the background session provided, Deepe pumped one or more of the reporters who had attended for the substance of Taylor's comments, all of which subsequently appeared on page one of the *Tribune*'s Christmas Day edition in 1964. Taylor told the reporters that South Vietnam was facing "the most serious political situation since [he] arrived here five months ago." Taylor further suggested that the generals seemed to be devoting more energy to fighting him and members of Vietnam's civilian government than they were devoting to the fight against Communist guerrillas. Taylor, speaking of the generals, said that although some were absolutely first class, others bordered "on being nuts." Taylor later challenged the accuracy of Deepe's quote, and a press release from the American embassy dismissed it because it was "apparently based on inaccurate leaks from a background session to which the *Tribune*'s correspondent was not invited." Barry Zorthian, who became the "information czar" of the war effort in 1964, remembered how the leak of his comment and other Deepe stories had annoyed Taylor to the point the he tried to ban her from press briefings for a time. "I finally managed to talk the boss out of that," Zorthian recalled years later.

Time magazine took notice of Deepe's scoop in its January 8, 1965, edition, calling her interview with Khanh "a singular achievement for a girl who has yet to be accepted as a regular in the Saigon corps of regular correspondents." *Time* characterized Deepe, who had been in Vietnam for nearly three years, as "Saigon's prettiest Western correspondent." With characteristic modesty, Deepe credited her break to "luck and timing," but added that she had put in a request for an interview early in December. "I was sure that something like this was going to happen," she remarked. Deepe, the story noted, was accustomed to being the only reporter not invited to embassy briefings. "They don't like me because I won't say what they want me to say," she said of America's diplomatic staff. "They accuse me of giving the Vietnamese line, when in fact what I do is listen to them and then go out and find out for myself."

Deepe also established that she was as adept at covering American soldiers at war as she was at covering Vietnam's political battles. In June 1965, just three months after the Marines landed in Da Nang, the Viet Cong had mounted a series of attacks that led General William C. Westmoreland to conclude that the enemy "had the resources to attack at will in all four of South Vietnam's corps tactical zones." Deepe accompanied the Army's 173rd Airborne Brigade on a mission that marked America's first "official" search-and-destroy operation in South Vietnam. In what the *Herald Tribune* called "a new phase of the dirty little war," the operation involved from 120 to 150 helicopters and 2,800 American, Australian, and South Vietnamese soldiers. The paratroopers quickly realized that the Viet Cong knew in advance about the operation.

Several months later, Deepe accompanied U.S. Marines on a mission to retrieve some of the fifty-five Americans who had been killed fighting in "hell's valley" near Chu Lai. It was the largest American death toll for any operation to that date. Upwards of 5,000 Marines in the India and Hotel companies had trapped members of the Viet Cong 1st Regiment, which lost more than six hundred men in the battle. Trudging through bramble bushes that were as tall as they were, the American survivors returned to search for their dead, many of whom had been shot in the back by the enemy after marching past well-camouflaged tunnels and foxholes. In Michael Herr's description of the encounter, "the Marines were dying so incredibly fast, so far beyond the Command's allowance, that one of them got zipped into a body bag and tossed to the top of a pile of KIA while he was still alive."

Early in 1966, returning to a subject that had previously captured her attention, Deepe wrote about the "Communist military stranglehold" continuing to tighten around the heart of Saigon. She explained that American intelligence officials had established that the equivalent of a Viet Cong battalion—roughly six hundred men—was operating inside the city limits "as suicide squads, murder teams and sabotage units." In addition, six battalions made up of Viet Cong "hard-core regulars" were operating in locations just outside the city limits, including Tan Son Nhut Air Base, where pilots often made night landings without lights rather than risk becoming a target.

In yet another of her military stories, Deepe described the action aboard the aircraft carrier USS *Kitty Hawk* in February, when the United States resumed the bombing of North Vietnam after a pause that had begun on Christmas. In a story that received front-page play, Deepe explained how the first of those attacks was launched. At mid-month, she wrote about how red tape and infighting had stalled a pacification project dear to the heart of Pres-

ident Johnson. He had announced the creation of a $5-million rural electrifi-
cation project designed to bring low-cost electricity to 250,000 villagers in
three provinces. In mid-April, Deepe wrote what appears to have been her
last story for the *Trib*. In it, she described a new wave of political intimidation
carried out by members of Buddhist-backed, antigovernment action groups
in Da Nang who had taken twenty-two South Vietnamese civilians prisoner.
Worsening the situation, the Viet Cong had reportedly murdered eight pro-
government civilians. "The whole American community in Da Nang is in a
state of distress," Deepe quoted an American official as saying.

Deepe was researching a story in the Demilitarized Zone near the border
of North Vietnam when she learned, on April 23, that the *Herald Tribune*'s
presses had stopped. The *Tribune*'s editor-in-chief explained in a front-page
editorial that his efforts to ensure the newspaper's survival had "not been
completely successful." Once again, she was out of a steady outlet for her
work. Much in the way she had during the earliest months she spent in
Saigon, she appears to have cobbled together a succession of "strings"; this
time however, she had a vast understanding of the landscape in which she
worked. She was accredited—along with Pham Xuan An—to work for NBC
News in August 1966, a job that lasted just one month, according to military
accreditation files. Later that year, the North American Newspaper Alliance
notified the Joint U.S. Public Affairs Office in an accreditation request that
"she has provided and will continue to provide in 1967 a considerable volume
of material for N.A.N.A." An recalled that he made an offer to help ease the
financial difficulty she might face during those uncertain months, but she assured him she would be fine. She said an uncle had made a standing offer to
help her out in a financial pinch.

Beginning in the summer of 1967, when Deepe became a special correspondent for the *Monitor*, her byline was regularly featured on the front page.
Her stories reflected a thorough knowledge of Vietnam's political, military,
economic, and social issues. From her analysis of the country's September 1967
elections and its newly adopted constitution, and later her study of the siege
of Khe Sanh, through her dissection of the failing economy in early and mid-
1968, Deepe's stories revealed her understanding of the complex equation of
the war: the weaponry, the military tactics and strategy, and the history—as
well as the force of changing public opinion in America and its effect on
North Vietnam.

Deepe's page-one story about South Vietnam's presidential election explained how uncertainty surrounding "America's war-peace decision," namely,

whether President Johnson planned to pursue victory in the war or negotiate a peaceful end to it with the Communists, had created a mood of chaos in which "rumors multiply in geometric proportions." While American leaders claimed they backed neither the incumbent military ticket—General Nguyen Van Thieu and his running mate, Premier Nguyen Cao Ky—nor any of the ten civilian candidates challenging it, the Vietnamese were skeptical of their ally's motives.[2] "The net impact of all the rumors is to discredit virtually all the Vietnamese presidential candidates, chisel divisions among them, and make the American officialdom here appear as bumbling hillbillies in Ivy League suits," Deepe wrote in her analysis of the U.S. role in the election. Although it had originally been scheduled for the fall of 1966, the election was being held in 1965, Deepe explained, at the insistence of President Johnson. America, after all, had 470,000 troops in Vietnam, and to legalize its presence there it desperately needed a legitimate government in place.

In a three-part series published at year's end, Deepe recalled the events of 1967 and discussed the prospects for peace in Vietnam in the new year. Discord between the newly elected president, General Thieu, and his vice president, former Premier Ky, had all but immobilized the government since its inauguration on October 31. "It's not that Ky and Thieu are fighting with each other, anymore—they just ignore each other," one American diplomat told Deepe.

Deepe was in Da Nang when the Tet Offensive was launched on January 31, 1968, and, according to An, she hastily made her way back to Saigon. The *Christian Science Monitor*'s early coverage of the offensive was written in Washington. By February 2, however, Deepe's stories about the enemy's effort to stage a general uprising throughout the country began occupying space on the front page. In the first of her many *Monitor* stories about what she called the Communists' "blitz war," Deepe's view from Saigon suggested that the attacks had "opened up the possibility of the United States losing its first major war in history." In spite of its military power, America had become an underdog, and the chances of reversing the damage, according to Vietnamese insiders, was "highly debatable."

Street fighting still raged all over Saigon a week after the attack began. More than 100,000 refugees clogged the city. U.S. Army helicopters attacked the Viet Cong with machine guns, just as they had done in the countryside. Tanks and armored carriers clogged the narrow streets. The result was a cityscape of rubble and ashes. In a *Monitor* story published ten days after the

2. Air Vice Marshal Ky had taken over as prime minister of a military regime on June 11, 1965.

offensive began, Deepe wrote that "Communist mini-mobile warfare" was underway in the capital. Just as the Americans used tactics perfected in the countryside, so, too did the Communists. Defying the Saigon government's early predictions that the enemy would be driven out of the city in forty-eight hours, Communist squads in Cholon established a mobile front line. Indeed, Viet Cong forces had barricaded alleys and side streets around the city, leaving people "virtually at the mercy of the Communists—reminiscent of warfare in the rural areas for years." Assassination squads were also said to be roaming the streets to pick off officials and terrorize the citizenry.

Deepe also covered the even larger battle raging in Hue, Vietnam's ancient imperial capital, where the fighting lasted for four weeks. Deepe reported on efforts to retake the Citadel from its North Vietnamese occupiers. Built, as Deepe explained, to duplicate China's walled Forbidden City, the complex was an enormous warren of buildings situated along alleys and streets. She spent a day with a U.S. Marine battalion that had been fighting for the previous eleven days, block by block, house by house, to retake the cultural symbol of Vietnam. On that day, the battalion was positioned within two blocks of the Citadel's east and south walls. Her page one report in the *Monitor* described how Chinese mortars and rockets fired from inside the former royal compound landed within fifty to seventy-five meters of the Marine positions. At mid-morning, one of the rockets hit a tank, killing two Americans and wounding twelve. By afternoon, and until darkness fell, the Americans were on the attack, bombarding the North Vietnamese with heavy weapons. In the early morning, Deepe watched as South Vietnamese forces captured the palace moat and then the flagpole near the main gate where the North Vietnamese flag had flown for twenty-four days. At last, members of South Vietnamese army raised their own standard.

In a subsequent story about the South Vietnamese forces making their final drive on the former imperial palace, Deepe wrote that their charge through the main gate had met little resistance from the North Vietnamese, who apparently had abandoned the grounds through a small hole in the western wall. Later reports by senior Vietnamese officials that 140 Communists were killed on the palace grounds, her story noted, were dismissed by on-the-scene observers "as more fairy tale than fact."

Through the first half of 1968, Deepe made Khe Sanh one of her key interests. The U.S. Marine outpost in northeastern South Vietnam was, depending on which general you talked to, either "a crucial anchor of our defenses" or "a piece of terrain that wasn't worth a damn." Once a small U.S.

Special Forces redoubt in the Annamite mountain range, the hilltop garrison was taken over by the Marines in 1966 to frustrate North Vietnamese infiltration along the Ho Chi Minh Trail and to provide a base for operations across the Laotian border—just eight miles to the west. The Marines defended Khe Sanh in May 1967 in a series of savage battles for control of several surrounding hills. In mid-December 1967, in response to a build-up of North Vietnamese forces just across the Laotian border, the Marines began sending reinforcements to the base. What was to become a seventy-seven-day siege began on January 20, ten days before the Tet Offensive, when 15,000 to 20,000 North Vietnamese troops surrounded the base and began a continuing barrage of rocket and mortar fire. They destroyed several helicopters and a base mess hall, and, in a direct hit on the ammunition dump, destroyed 16,000 shells, setting off a series of explosions and fires that burned for forty-eight hours.

In the minds of the president, policymakers, military strategists, and the press, the attacks conjured visions of the French debacle at Dien Bien Phu. In worst-case-scenario discussions, military men talked about contingency plans for the use of nuclear weapons at Khe Sanh—adding further to the comparisons with Dien Bien Phu, where Americans had also contemplated using nuclear weapons to support the French. LBJ, who had a sand-table model of the Khe Sanh plateau in the White House Situation Room, was preoccupied with the prospect that General Vo Nguyen Giap, the mastermind of the French defeat in May 1954, was plotting to humiliate the United States and its president at Khe Sanh, just as he had humiliated the French. That analogy with "Dinbinphoo," as Johnson often pronounced it, attached a psychological significance to Khe Sanh that, in hindsight, perhaps far outweighed its strategic importance. Similarly, it received a disproportionate level of publicity. And why not, when the likes of General Westmoreland had boasted that "the amount of fire power put on that piece of real estate exceeded anything that has ever been seen before in history." Notwithstanding the doomsday scenarios envisioned by American military leaders and the huge force assembled by the North Vietnamese, the siege of Khe Sanh ended not with "the decisive set piece battle" Westmoreland had so hoped for but with quiet withdrawals on both sides. By early to mid-March, the North Vietnamese had pulled out more than half their forces, leaving just 6,000 to 8,000 troops surrounding the American base. The Marines destroyed the base and, in mid-June, staged a secret exodus of the forces.

Throughout, Deepe put her imprint on the story of Westmoreland's piece of prized real estate, making repeated visits to Khe Sanh aboard the C-130 and C-123 transport planes that fortified the base throughout the eleven-week siege, often landing under fire. Her stories probed Westmoreland's thinking in committing American men and resources to the base and questioned whether the North Vietnamese purpose in mounting the siege was a diversionary tactic or an effort to re-stage Dien Bien Phu. In one story, she characterized Khe Sanh as a "sliver of cheese in Westmoreland's mousetrap." In another, she explained that the 96,000 tons of bombs dropped during the siege amounted to "roughly the equivalent in tonnage to five atomic bombs of Hiroshima vintage." In other stories, she analyzed Westmoreland's thinking about the Korea-style battle he expected and questioned why the general, having reached that conclusion, had not better equipped the four-square-mile base to protect it from the North Vietnamese human-wave attacks he anticipated. And she asked questions that could be answered only in history: Why, as the chances of losing Khe Sanh grew less and less likely, did American political and military leaders repeatedly declare that it would be held at all costs, and in so doing attach undeserved importance to it?

Deepe's stories also illuminated the self-destructive deadend to which General Westmoreland's search-and-destroy strategy was leading. With the American dead numbering more than five hundred a week in early 1968, and a divisive presidential primary season underway, Khe Sanh would turn into a public relations debacle for the government. Deepe wrote that the Communist activity in Khe Sanh was a part of North Vietnam's effort to influence American public opinion and its expression in primary elections. The specter of Dien Bien Phu was never far from the minds of the military or the media during this time.

By mid-June, after Westmoreland was replaced by Creighton Abrams as America's commanding general in South Vietnam, the last Marines had been pulled out of Khe Sanh. Military crews were dispatched to bulldoze and blow up the base and destroy roadways and bridges that provided access to it. "Americans did not know about the pullout because news reporters were forbidden to write about it by the U.S. Command," Robert Pisor later wrote in *The End of the Line*. The decision to abandon the base was first revealed by John Carroll of the *Baltimore Sun*, after he saw the bombed-out bunkers and blown-up airfield. Carroll was reprimanded for "endangering the lives of American troops," and his press identification card was suspended. As for Deepe, her final analysis of Khe Sanh was that "the human cost exceeded the value of the prize." The *Christian Science Monitor* nominated her Khe Sanh stories for a Pulitzer Prize for international reporting.[3]

---

3. William Touhy of the *Los Angeles Times* won the prize in this category for his Vietnam correspondence that year.

In January 1969, after reporting on the war for seven years, Deepe finally left South Vietnam and moved to Washington after her Valentine's Day wedding to Lieutenant Colonel Charles Keever in a candlelight service in the Congregational United Church of Christ in Belvidere, Nebraska. The winter's worst snowstorm, driven by high winds, had started the day before and continued through Friday, leaving the wedding party and guests to slog though fourteen to sixteen inches of snow to get to the church for the 7:00 P.M. service. Deepe's was a traditional heartland wedding. With gardenias and white roses in her hair, a frothy confection of a gown, and an aisle-wide train behind her, Deepe walked to the altar on her father's arm. An assortment of young cousins lit the candles, carried the rings, and left the aisle strewn with red and pink rose petals. After the ceremony, the bride's aunts served cake, coffee, and punch in the "church parlors," according to a lengthy account of the event published in the *Hebron Journal Register*.

At the time Deepe returned home and married, Pamela Sanders, who remained haunted by Vietnam long after she left in 1964, had turned to fiction. By the late 1960s, with a small book advance, she began working on *Miranda*, a thinly veiled roman à clef in which she drew on her Vietnam experiences in 1962 and 1963. The narrative is heavily populated by her press corps colleagues, including David Halberstam, Peter Arnett, Horst Faas, and Neil Sheehan. Sanders herself appears as Miranda, the title character in a tale about Miranda Pickerel's life, first in the Philippines, later in New York, and finally in South Vietnam and Laos. Sanders's erstwhile lover, Mohr, appears as the Iowa-bred Harry Willard. Halberstam is Steve Zimmerman, and Faas takes the stage as an uncouth German named Hans Bieler who speaks with a phony Irish accent. Shaplen of the *New Yorker* becomes Bob Grayzel, Turner of Reuters is Nick Jenkins, and Sheehan is Sean Adams. "We're all in there," Halberstam once lamented. The book's jacket calls *Miranda* a "wonderfully deft novel about a liberated woman-before-her-time."

Sanders' own doubts about America's Southeast Asia policy are shared by Miranda, who agonizes about what is happening to the Vietnamese people on both sides of the conflict. Miranda bemoans the agony a superpower is inflicting on innocent people. Just as Sanders shared those sentiments with Halberstam while the two were in Vietnam, Miranda expresses those concerns to Steve Zimmerman. But Zimmerman tells her, "Don't feel sorry for Charley, Miranda. He's winning."

4

Challenging the
Conventional Wisdom

We were foreign invaders.
—DANIEL ELLSBERG

ABOUT SIX MONTHS after she returned from her life-transforming journey
to Vietnam, Frances FitzGerald traveled from her home in New York
City to Washington, D.C., in the spring of 1967 for a weekend visit with her
father. She carried with her the manuscript of an article soon to be published
in the *Atlantic* in which she explained, point by intricate point, how America's
policies in Southeast Asia were framed around a set of dangerously flawed assumptions, and how the war that had sundered Vietnamese society promised
no hope of a U.S. victory. There was no light at the end of the tunnel. Any
promise of victory was a chimera. America would never "attrit the enemy" as
the president, policymakers, and military leaders had vouchsafed to the
American people for five years. Her conclusions so sharply contradicted
the conventional wisdom that she feared her father might take strong exception
to her reasoning. He, after all, had a vested interest in the very policies that
she was denouncing as misguided.

Her father, Desmond FitzGerald, was the Central Intelligence Agency's director of operations—the organization's number three man. His knowledge of Asia went back to World War II. Moreover, during his sixteen-year career in the CIA, he had been a central figure in the gathering and analysis of intelligence that political leaders used to formulate America's Southeast Asia policy in the 1950s and 1960s. Frankie, as she was known among family and friends, wondered how he might respond to her view that America's leaders would never find answers in Vietnam because of their inability to postulate the appropriate questions. Furthermore, she described South Vietnam's government as a weightless shell. Neither President Nguyen Cao Ky nor the collection of feckless opportunists who surrounded him had the wherewithal to develop an acceptable alternative to the Viet Cong. "There was no political there, there," she reasoned. Ergo, American policies, developed with intelligence assembled under her father's oversight, were downright wrong-headed and destined to fail. Any hope of establishing a non-Communist government in the former French colony was "as improbable as an air-conditioned motel in the middle of a trackless jungle," her essay declared. Although Desmond FitzGerald had read and applauded other articles she had written about Vietnam during the ten months she spent there in 1966, those pieces had never so explicitly condemned American foreign policy. Now, in "The Struggle and the War," she had presented a scholarly study of the conflict. Desmond FitzGerald, a man of ideas, would surely find in his twenty-six-year-old daughter's article the kind of intellectual heft that he admired. Still, she wondered. Ultimately, her writing helped to upend so many of the government's assumptions and helped to define a new perspective of the American experience in Vietnam. For decades, her book, *Fire in the Lake*, which grew out of that *Atlantic* article, has been required reading for those seeking insight and an understanding of the Vietnam War.

Her trip to Vietnam in February 1966 was originally planned as a month-long interlude during which she would write a couple of articles and visit a few long-time friends posted to the American embassy in Saigon. Because she found reports from Vietnam in American newspapers so filled with ambiguity, she decided that seeing the situation for herself was the only way to understand a conflict that was fast becoming a threat to international stability. Four weeks, however, stretched into ten months. Vietnam—its people and America's war—became her epiphany. She found there what her father had so often told her was essential to one's work and one's life—a subject for which she could develop both "a passion and a commitment." The Asian nation held her in its grip for nine years. "It seemed impossible to concentrate on any other subject" until the war was finally over, she recalled many years later.

FitzGerald's father had found his own passion in Asia. He was a Harvard-educated, Wall Street lawyer who, during World War II, had been a liaison officer assigned to a Chinese battalion stationed in the China-Burma-India theater under General Joseph Stilwell. He and his wife, having married in 1939, divorced after World War II ended, when Frankie was six years old. In 1951, Desmond FitzGerald, perhaps searching for the same sense of mission that had energized him during the war, quit his lucrative law partnership and joined the Office of Policy Coordination, a clandestine agency that soon merged with the CIA. This new career perfectly suited the man who was once described as having "the imagination and dash of a Renaissance soldier of fortune." In his first CIA assignment, FitzGerald became an executive officer in the Far East Division. His work involved handling the Korean War and monitoring efforts by Communist insurgents across Southeast Asia, from the Philippines to Thailand. Although family members knew he worked for the CIA, neither his employer nor the nature of his work was ever acknowledged to outsiders. Her father simply "worked for the government," Frankie recalled. And back in the 1950s, that's all one needed to say. No one asked for details. Although Desmond occasionally told his second wife, Barbara (Frankie's stepmother), a few particulars about his often furtive travels, he never talked shop with her or any other family member.

Now, on her way to visit her father, Frankie anticipated another of the conversations about politics and world affairs that they had been having for years. After she graduated magna cum laude from Radcliffe in 1962, with a degree in Middle East studies, their discussions were especially edifying and amiable. In the spring of 1967, however, anticipating that they would find fault lines in their divergent views of the war, she wondered how their exchange would unfold. If America had indeed invented a different Vietnam, as her *Atlantic* article claimed, its inventors had suffered a startling failure of understanding. Her father and his peers had been blind to a reality that was so palpable to her: The village was the core of life in Vietnamese society. Family and ancient tradition bound the people of Vietnam. Without that understanding, American policy—the one that Desmond FitzGerald's work had helped to shape—was destined to fail, built as it was around the overarching notion that America's political structure could be grafted onto an ancient Asian culture. "I was worried about what he'd think," she recalled thirty years later. She knew he was not an optimist on Vietnam, "but he had been fairly close to it. He had known President Ngo Dinh Diem and his brother, Nhu, from the period when he was in Asia for the CIA."

Even so, Frankie heard only cryptic hints of her father's views on Vietnam. "When I talked with him about the war, it was clear that he was asking questions. You didn't get this gung-ho thing from him," she recalled. "He was on the team, but the CIA was always more skeptical about Vietnam than anyone else." Then again, he had occasionally demonstrated little patience for questions about the rectitude of American intervention in Vietnam. During a dinner party in November 1965 at the home of Joseph Alsop, the influential columnist who was a FitzGerald family friend, Desmond had listened to Alsop express delight with America's nation-building efforts in South Vietnam and praise the daring young men—whom he called "the Young Lords of the Delta"—who were carrying out that noble mission. However, Frankie and several of her contemporaries who were also Alsop's guests that night voiced their distaste for the war. In what soon became a high-decibel, gin-lubricated conversation, the young guests disagreed with Alsop's hawkish assumptions and told their host that the war was a "disaster." When one of the younger guests raised the issue of morality, Desmond FitzGerald irritably declared, "You're all so wet. You don't know what you are talking about." Two months later, Frankie left for Vietnam.

As the weekend visit with her father unfolded, in 1967, Frankie had second thoughts about presenting him with her manuscript. She was still uncertain about this essay, one of her early efforts at foreign policy analysis, and it had yet to be finalized. Her editors were still working on it. Perhaps she would feel better armed for the discussion after the piece was published, she rationalized. So she left Washington, unable to foresee as she returned to New York that another opportunity would never come. Weeks later, Desmond FitzGerald died of a heart attack on the tennis court of his summer home in Virginia.

"The Struggle and the War" became the foundation on which his daughter built her award-winning study of Vietnam. Whether he agreed with its premise or not, Desmond would surely have savored the widespread praise and many awards *Fire in the Lake* received. Frankie FitzGerald's interpretation of Vietnam became her enduring achievement. Yet, more than three decades after the war, she is still uncertain about whether her father would have accepted her analysis, especially her conclusion that a North Vietnamese victory would be the war's most desirable outcome. "I'm glad the test never came," she said.

Among the dozens of women who covered the Vietnam War, no name has remained more entwined with America's Vietnam experience than that of

Frances FitzGerald. She presented Americans with an alternate view of the war and—as her admirer, the famous war correspondent Martha Gellhorn, called *Fire in the Lake*—"a dazzling work." In the very way that Vietnam came to define David Halberstam, even though it consumed only a few years of his working life, the names FitzGerald and Vietnam are as tightly bound as a pair of crossed fingers.

Although Frances FitzGerald is significant for the reputation she established with her Vietnam reportage, at the time of her arrival she was a well-respected but little-known freelance writer. In contrast, two other women who arrived in Vietnam in 1966—Gellhorn and Ethel Payne—both enjoyed a considerable following, albeit among vastly different audiences. Gellhorn ranked as one of America's celebrity journalists. Her fame as a war correspondent reached back to the 1930s, when she covered the Spanish Civil War for *Collier's*, the same magazine that published her later reporting on World War II in Europe. Her five-year marriage to Ernest Hemingway further suffused her in an aura of glamour. Like FitzGerald, Gellhorn went to Vietnam to see the war for herself. She felt compelled to go because she "could not learn from anyone else what was happening to the voiceless Vietnamese people," even though she hardly wished, as she wrote in 1967, "to learn about new techniques of warfare, nor ever again see young men killing each other on the orders of old men." Gellhorn's antiwar sentiments were so widely known in journalism circles that she had difficulty finding a newspaper or magazine to underwrite her trip. When England's *Manchester Guardian* finally agreed to publish her stories from Vietnam, it was with the proviso that she travel there on her own dime. FitzGerald was moderately skeptical about the war when she arrived in Vietnam, but Gellhorn was appalled by its savagery well before her arrival. Television images of the fighting had convinced her that the war was immoral and racist. The two women were searching for answers to the same questions. Following different paths, both FitzGerald and Gellhorn concluded that America would never win the hearts and minds of the Vietnamese people. They also agreed that the war would bring dishonor to America in the process. Gellhorn's observations were passionate and filled with moral outrage; FitzGerald's work was cool-headed and cerebral.

Ethel Payne was a virtual unknown in white America in the 1960s, but among African Americans she was every bit as famous as Gellhorn and as widely respected as FitzGerald was soon to become. As a staff writer on the *Chicago Defender*, Payne had been covering national and international issues critical to life in black America for fifteen years. In part because her newspaper was a leading voice in the black media, she was esteemed by thousands of readers and was well known among black leaders in America and abroad. Her career in journalism had started when black Americans were still called "colored," before *Brown v. Board of Education* mandated the integration of public schools, before Rosa Parks refused to give up her seat on that bus in Montgomery, Alabama, and well before mainstream (white) American newspapers acknowledged that the "Negroes" in their midst deserved attention. Payne was one of the first black women to integrate the White House press corps. She covered every milestone in the struggle for civil rights from the Montgomery Bus Boycott in 1956 to the integration of the University of Alabama and Little Rock's Central High School. She joined demonstrations in Birmingham in 1963, participated in the March on Washington in the same year, and marched from Selma to Montgomery in 1965 with 15,000 others to demand voting rights for blacks. Payne was part of a network of news organizations that remained largely invisible to white America but that thrived in the first half of the twentieth century by affirming in black Americans a sense of identity and self-worth. And Payne was one of the few women reporters who never had to ask to cover the war in Vietnam but went instead at the behest of her publisher. In late 1966, when *Defender* publisher John Sengstacke singled out Payne to investigate the complaints of racism and discrimination against black troops in Vietnam, it was, as Payne observed years later, "a very daring thing to ask a woman to go to war." It was also a time when increasing numbers of African Americans involved in the fight for civil rights in America were turning against the war. A poster in the Student Nonviolent Coordinating Committee's office in Atlanta summed up the growing sentiment among young black men: "No Vietnamese ever called me nigger." When Payne accepted Sengstacke's proposal, she became both the first black woman and the first black reporter to cover the war.[1]

Perhaps no other trio of women who covered the Vietnam War demonstrate quite as vividly the polarity of backgrounds and diversity of interests that brought women to Vietnam. The luxury and privilege that Gellhorn and FitzGerald enjoyed as they grew up contrasted sharply with the second-class

---

1. Tom Johnson was assigned by the *New York Times* Saigon bureau from December 1967 until March 1968. Wallace Terry covered the war for *Time* magazine from 1967 until 1969. Philippa Schuyler, a concert pianist and sometime freelancer, wrote several articles about the war for the *Manchester Union-Leader*. Schuyler died in Vietnam in May of 1967, when she volunteered to help evacuate South Vietnamese orphans from Hue. She was killed when the Army helicopter ferrying the group to Da Nang crashed.

citizenship that characterized Payne's childhood. Desmond FitzGerald worked at the highest level of government; Ethel Payne's father was a Pullman car porter who endured the kind of servitude that can come with being denied a proper education. Martha Gellhorn's mother, Edna, marched in St. Louis wearing the yellow ribbon that was the symbol of support for women's suffrage. Long after her campaign was won in 1920, blacks remained disenfranchised, especially in the South where both men and women of color were denied voting rights. Ethel Payne's interests were tightly focused on the role of black soldiers fighting the war and on celebrating their contributions to that effort. FitzGerald, by contrast, was searching for larger, cosmic truths. For her part, Gellhorn brought her zealous opposition to war and an overriding concern with its impact on Vietnam's children.

All three women went to Vietnam in the face of America's rising commitment to the war. The death toll had more than tripled between 1965, when 1,863 American soldiers died, and 1966, when the total reached 6,143. In response to rising draft quotas, rowdy war protests across America were creating domestic tensions. American troop strength had reached 215,000 in the early weeks of 1966. In February, when FitzGerald left for Vietnam, the Senate Foreign Relations Committee began televised hearings to scrutinize the president's conduct of the war and examine the legality of using the 1964 Gulf of Tonkin Resolution to justify further escalation. In July, when Gellhorn made her month-long tour, America's B-52 bombers were hammering targets in Hanoi and Haiphong. The luckless few American pilots whose planes came within range of North Vietnam's then rather primitive antiaircraft emplacements were captured and paraded before angry mobs in the streets of Hanoi. By December, when Payne began her three-month stay, 389,000 American troops were "in-country" and the *New York Times* reporter Harrison Salisbury was reporting from Hanoi that American bombs had fallen on civilian targets.

In the early weeks of 1966, just before FitzGerald departed for Vietnam, an old family friend who worked at the American embassy in Saigon wrote to caution her: "I wish I could say you would not be consumed in this game as I am, but I fear I would be lying if I did," Frank Wisner Jr. wrote. "This is not your world—the guns, tanks and brutality all seem so pointless save in the very obvious point of it all, and the obvious is alive here." The bales of barbed wire lying about in the streets of Saigon were reminders that people were dying. Yet the city remained captivating; Americans worked and partied with equal zest. At times, the absurdity of it all intruded. But not often.

The war's strange juxtapositions hit FitzGerald just hours after she arrived in Saigon. The birthday party the NBC newsman Dean Brelis threw for his photographer girlfriend, Jill Krementz, that evening was "so glamorous," in FitzGerald's memory. One hundred guests, mostly American journalists and embassy staffers, drank champagne on the rooftop of the Caravelle Hotel, the downtown watering hole where Americans would "go and watch the war." In another time and place, the exploding mortar fire just across the Saigon River might have been alarming. But on this warm evening beneath a starry sky, the distant flares seemed to add a festive air to the celebration— more reminiscent of fireworks than a portent of death. When the party ebbed, Ward Just, the *Washington Post* correspondent in Saigon whose acquaintance FitzGerald made at the party, suggested they take a swim at the Cercle Sportif. They rode bicycles to the former country club where generations of French overlords had relaxed and dined. The gates, of course, were locked at that hour, so FitzGerald and Just scaled the compound wall and jumped into the same pool where, in daylight, U.S. Ambassador Henry Cabot Lodge took his afternoon swim. They assumed they were alone. Not so, they discovered when they returned to their clothing and found that Just's watch had been stolen. "I thought this was all pretty amazing," FitzGerald remembered. "It's not what I expected in Saigon."

When Frances FitzGerald was born in October 1940, the ancestry of both her parents placed her in the American aristocracy. In the 1990s, James Sterba, whom she married in 1990, once made a hunt for the quintessential "high WASP" his summer sport in Northeast Harbor, Maine, where her family had vacationed for generations. Sterba, a Midwesterner who was born in Detroit and had spent part of his childhood on a farm, had no interest in what he labeled "run-of-the-mill WASPS," those who might have been classified as "Wall Street riff-raff" by earlier generations of the town's summer inhabitants. No, Sterba, who had enthusiastically embraced the FitzGerald tradition of summering in Northeast Harbor, hoped to unearth either "proper Bostonians" or "snooty Philadelphians." Applying all the skills he might otherwise have brought to his work as a reporter for the *Wall Street Journal*, Sterba did his research in colonial history texts at the local library. He found a few clues in *Old Money: The Mythology of America's Upper Class*, which advised the reader to look for men who inhabited "somewhat seedy cottages and clubs" and who, above all, were "stuffy, pompous or stupid." Still at a loss to single out a perfect specimen, he finally asked a female acquaintance whose family had deep summer roots in Northeast Harbor where he should look for the elusive "high WASP." The answer astonished him. "Oh, that's easy," she said. "You're living with her."

FitzGerald grew up with an unobstructed view of the Establishment, one that gave her the perfect perspective from which later to judge who among its members had feet of clay. Her maternal ancestors are the Parkmans and the Peabodys, Puritan bloodlines that flowed back to a governor of the Massachusetts Bay Colony. The Peabodys tended to live as exemplars of parsimony and morality, but the wealthier Parkmans were quirky and self-indulgent. The staid likes of Endicott Peabody, Frankie's great-grandfather, who established Groton School in 1884 and served as its rector for fifty-six years, stood in stark contrast to such flamboyant characters as her great-grandmother, Frances Parker Parkman, whose "unusually close relationship" with a handsome American Indian who lived nearby is said to have scandalized Maine's Mount Desert Island in the nineteenth century. In contrast, Frankie's grandmother, Mary Elizabeth Parkman Peabody, was a "combination of salt, steel and Emersonian individualism." She taught her granddaughter self-discipline and notions of service to one's country. In a display of her own grit, at age seventy-two, Grandmother Peabody was arrested with members of the Southern Christian Leadership Conference, who were trying to integrate a St. Augustine motel in 1961. Their sit-in took place in the motel bar and it marked the first time Mrs. Peabody had ever been in a bar or a motel. It also marked the first time her grandmother had seen the inside of a jail—where she spent two days following her arrest.

Those bloodlines as manifested in Frankie's mother, Marietta Tree, produced a decided preference for flamboyance over moral rectitude. She scandalized her family when she divorced Desmond FitzGerald in 1947. No other Peabody marriage had ever ended in divorce. "You have let down your family, your society and your God," her mother told her. While Desmond was off in Asia fighting World War II for four years, Marietta became a stylish career woman in a job as a *Life* magazine researcher. She joined the New York society set and entered a liaison with the Hollywood director John Huston, who expected her to marry him. However, Marietta fell in love with and married Ronald Tree, the British-born heir to the Marshall Field fortune and a member of the British Parliament. Tree took his bride and new stepdaughter to live in England. There, they resided at Ditchley Park, an eighteenth-century manor house where Frankie occupied one of twenty-nine bedrooms. Several years later, her mother and stepfather returned to New York to a townhouse on Manhattan's Upper East Side, where they seemed to live in the old-money splendor of an Edith Wharton novel. Both in her mother's home and in the upscale Georgetown home where her father lived, Frankie's formal education was supplemented by dinner table conversations with leading artists, writers, journalists, political figures, and diplomats. At age eleven, she campaigned for her mother's friend, Adlai Stevenson, and at sixteen, on a trip to Africa, she visited with Albert Schweitzer. "Just being around people who were so articulate made a tremendous impression on me."

Among the thousands of young Americans who protested the war, her acts of rebellion were quietly intellectual, more effective, and more difficult to discredit than the acts of defiance other antiwar activists chose. Unlike other young Americans of the upper middle class who joined the Weather Underground and expressed their outrage with homemade bombs, FitzGerald could hardly be dismissed as the radical fringe. Nor did she embrace the counterculture and draw attention to herself with symbolic pranks like the one Abbie Hoffman engineered in the 1960s when he brought the New York Stock Exchange to a brief halt. With his keen understanding of capitalist instincts, Hoffman led a band of demonstrators to the balcony above the floor of the exchange where they dropped dollar bills and watched with delight as traders below lunged for them. Although Vietnam certainly did become something of an obsession for FitzGerald, it never led to the emotional extremes to which it took Norman R. Morrison, a pacifist Quaker from Baltimore, who sat in a small raised garden and lit a match after dousing himself with kerosene within clear view of office 3E880, the Pentagon suite occupied by Defense Secretary Robert S. McNamara. Although Desmond FitzGerald's onetime colleagues in government could dismiss those protests as acts of lawlessness, buffoonery, or desperation, Frankie FitzGerald's defiance was more formidable. She attacked the established order with her intellect. The bombs she fashioned were illuminating—an approach that reflected her ancestry.

To read in succession the articles FitzGerald wrote during the nine years when the war was her overriding preoccupation is to follow the arc of her intellectual growth and her evolving despair. Her earliest articles, published in the *Village Voice,* were perceptive and largely impressionistic, more filled with her stiletto wit than with the insights and scholarship that characterized her later work. After her visit to Laos in 1966, FitzGerald explained that the country's principal natural resource is gossip: "What Laos has to teach the world (a lesson worthy of a full-scale aid program) is that one statistic usually does quite as well as any other, and facts are not less spiritually nourishing for being cooked." Another article explained the political realities in Vietnam: "To come to Vietnam is to walk through the Looking Glass of print into a land beyond the vanishing point. Solid objects break loose from their lines of perspective, sensations collide. . . . In a state of persistent abnormality one makes periodic checks on oneself like an airline pilot before take-off." Noting the difficulties American officials confronted in explaining the Buddhist uprisings in the country's northern cities, FitzGerald wrote that American spokesmen had never given much effort to inventing new, official versions of the truth about Vietnam. "Since reliable facts are far and few, it takes but a sleight of hand to turn President Ngo Dinh Diem into a popular hero and dead Vietnamese into dead Viet Cong," she wrote. Those American spokesmen, she added, were out of practice thanks to a docile press corps and eight months of relative calm.

Articles published in *Vogue* in early 1967 reflect her increasingly somber assessment of events in Vietnam. Her understanding of and respect for Vietnamese culture is obvious, as is her emerging sense of hopelessness about the war. The Vietnamese, she understood, had little interest in being like Americans, an incomprehensible attitude to many in the United States at the time. In the article her father never read, "The Struggle and the War," FitzGerald accused the government of deceit: Although America might innocently have bumbled into the muck of Vietnam with the best intentions, along the way successive administrations had turned to lies and deception—not as a way of winning the war but as a way of saving face. In 1968, in a review of Bernard B. Fall's *Last Reflections on a War*, published a year after his death in Vietnam, FitzGerald mocked America's military leaders; they were, she said, waging a "war where events succeed each other without consequence like a series of ghastly traffic accidents." Two years later, with equal disdain, she mocked President Richard M. Nixon's "Vietnamization" policy. With its call for an anti-Communist government, its eagerness to enlarge the Vietnamese army, and its planned renewal of the counterinsurgency program, Nixon's approach precisely duplicated the failed strategies that America had put into practice after the French rout at Dien Bien Phu. And what had failed before would fail yet again, FitzGerald predicted. Later articles accused American leaders of deliberately pursuing evil ends. By 1975, with the spectacle of America's exit from Saigon playing out, FitzGerald wrote that "not one of the five Presidents who supported intervention had any confidence that the war could be won." Yet the conflict continued. In the end, perhaps even more than Nixon, she despised Nixon's national security advisor, Henry A. Kissinger, who later became secretary of state, with whom she had been acquainted at Harvard during her undergraduate years at Radcliffe. During the final months of the war, she recalled Kissinger's tortured claims about American credibility, the need to save face, and that old bugaboo the domino theory, all of which continued to justify the war. "To take it seriously," FitzGerald declared with obvious scorn, "is to believe that Kissinger looks at Indochina with the detachment of a schizophrenic." As the war progressed, all those articulate people whose conversations had once enriched her education became objects of her contempt. As she confronted the travesty that Vietnam had become and concluded that Americans pursuing it were immoral and perhaps evil, for a time she could not bear being in the company of the people whom her parents invited to dinner. She decided she would no longer speak to Henry Kissinger.

FitzGerald's rejection of her parents' friends was still years away in early 1966, when she planned her trip to Vietnam, a country that was "the center of our concerns," according to President Lyndon B. Johnson's State of the Union address that year. For FitzGerald, "Vietnam seemed like the biggest story of the moment. It seemed very important to me at the time that Americans learn something about the Vietnamese." Her journey came four years after she graduated from Radcliffe College. She had spent two years in Paris working for the Congress of Cultural Freedom, whose mission was to advance American ideas of liberty and deflate whatever appeal Western Europe's intellectuals, artists, and writers might find in Communism. She never knew until years later that the congress, founded in 1950, was a front organization for the CIA. After her return to the United States, she began writing profiles of personalities such as David Merrick, Philip Johnson, and Herman Kahn for the *New York Herald Tribune*'s trendy Sunday magazine. That association with the *Tribune* gave her access to the newspaper's Saigon bureau, where she became acquainted with Seymour Friedin, the foreign editor who ran the bureau, Beverly Deepe, Krementz, and Pham Xuan An.

The Joint U.S. Public Affairs Office gave FitzGerald press accreditation on the basis of letters from the *Village Voice* and *Vogue* magazine. In Vietnam, her fluency in French, her parents' associations in diplomatic circles, and her skills as a writer gave FitzGerald easy access to the Vietnamese as well as the Americans. Ward Just recalls Frankie's early days in Saigon: "I remember her as shy. I don't think she knew quite what she was after in Vietnam," he said. That uncertainty was short lived. She quickly became interested in the Viet Cong. "That wasn't a subject that interested most of us because it was so difficult to get at because they weren't inviting us over to dinner," Just recalled.

Soon after she arrived in Saigon, Desmond FitzGerald wrote to his daughter, encouraging her to pull strings where necessary to find herself a place to live, and he wished her success on the story she had written about Vietnam's president, Ky. "I fear that he will soon have to join that spectral crew of ex-chiefs of Vietnam," he noted. Despite the support and enthusiasm expressed in those letters from her father, her mother told Frankie many years later that Desmond FitzGerald was furious when he learned she planned to extend her stay in Vietnam indefinitely. Then again, as she learned over the years, "any communication between my mother and my father was suspect." Yet she knew he feared for her safety.

Both Desmond FitzGerald and the CIA station chief in Saigon imagined that she might be kidnapped by the Viet Cong if her family connection with the CIA were known. Frankie doubted that anyone in Saigon ever knew of that connection—including her canny friend Pham Xuan An, who after the war was identified as a North Vietnamese agent. An said he knew she was the daughter of an important CIA official, but added, "I doubt that members of the Provisional Revolutionary Government or anyone among the North Vietnamese forces would ever knew [*sic*] Frances' family connection to any U.S. intelligence organizations. I am sure that many of them knew that Frances is a cousin of the late John F. Kennedy." Apparently, An had confused the Peabody and Kennedy families. Even though he did know of FitzGerald's family connection with the CIA, FitzGerald insisted long after the war ended that An would never have reported such information to his contacts. He had a great fondness for American journalists, she explained. "He never talked about the reporters. The only information he provided was about the ARVN (Army of the Republic of Vietnam)." FitzGerald and An developed a friendship soon after she arrived. "He loved Doberman pinschers," FitzGerald recalled, "and he thought I had eyes like a Doberman. I don't really know why he thought that. I have green eyes."

By March 1966, a month after her arrival, the Buddhist crisis started to create havoc in the northern cities of Hue and Da Nang. Once again, the Johnson administration's efforts to convince Americans that its South Vietnamese ally was on its way to political and military stability looked spurious. After several weeks of inaction, President Ky dispatched government troops to quell the demonstrators who were once again protesting the government's crackdown on civil liberties. The Buddhists went underground. Nobody knew what the Buddhists cause was all about, FitzGerald remembered: "The crisis totally surprised everyone in the embassy." She joined Just on a trip to

Hue late in March. At about that time the regional government simply fell apart. "It was amazing. It was as if the war had disappeared. The city was operating as though it was another time," she wrote. By April, the country had become, in the words of James Reston, "a tangle of competing individuals, regions, religions, and sects."

That's when the reality of Vietnam began to hit FitzGerald. "This was not just a military matter," she said. "There was so much more to it. I realized how little I knew and at the same time how fascinating it was." A month, she realized, would never give her sufficient time to understand Vietnam. Even though she had settled in to a routine, the war began to challenge all her assumptions during these early months in Vietnam. From random notes typed in April, it is clear that FitzGerald had embarked on a journey that would take her from skepticism to rage. She ruminated about the complexities of the war: "You must not forget. You simply must not forget," she wrote, "that the greatest sin is to speak of politics in the abstract. That the containment (of communism) argument has much to be said of it. That those who have concentrated on Europe have a difficult time becoming relevant here. That nothing is simple as it might be made out to be. . . . That war is hell. That some peace is worse hell."

The next day, she observed that

> South Viet Nam is like one of those surprise boxes you keep opening and never reach the inside—the war within the war within the war within the war. U.S. containing China (and Russia). North Viet Nam against South VN, VC vs. RVN, Central VN against South VN, Struggle committees v. Ky. Thieu and American intervention. . . . Everyone has their own little war. It ought to make everyone happy. There is only one person not making war against anyone. The Vietnamese peasant. And he is not counted—in statistics—but counted en masse for each side.

Clearly, FitzGerald had begun to move away from a belief in the essential goodness of her country and its leaders. An anger about the vast deceptions that successive administrations appeared to have undertaken began to simmer.

Some of the hostility that characterized relations of the media with the military and diplomatic corps in South Vietnam had eased considerably by the time of FitzGerald's arrival. Part of that success belonged to Barry Zorthian, who became a kind of media czar overseeing all American press operations in 1964. Indeed, under his leadership, a sense of mutual respect slowly developed as a result of his efforts to decrease the secrecy and increase communication. He held background sessions with a cross section of media representatives every Thursday, and he often socialized with members of the press corps. Zorthian understood that public support for the war depended on having the war be open to the press. Even decades later, he spoke with pride about the unprecedented access afforded the press during the war and insisted that under his watch, at least, there was no conscious effort to mislead. "This notion of an immaculate press and mendacious government simply does not stand up to scrutiny," Zorthian said years later. "The government certainly made mistakes, but I reject the conventional wisdom that all the government did in Vietnam was lie."

Early in her stay in Saigon, FitzGerald took on the government and its curious use of numbers. Her colleagues in the media often focused on the numbers military briefers so religiously presented, but the body counts and casualty rates perplexed FitzGerald. It was always numbers and more numbers; the military said the numbers showed progress, the numbers demonstrated the enemy's weakness, the numbers promised victory. Week after week, using visual aids, a cast of spokesmen from the Joint U.S. Public Affairs Office held forth. Outsized map boards with little blue bombs denoted bombing missions over North Vietnam or B-52 raids in the South. Red and blue arrows pinpointed military operations—blue for the good guys and red for the Communists. The story line in each of these daily accounts always spotlighted the numbers as indicators of imminent success. Body counts—KIAs, WIAs, and MIAs of American, South Vietnamese, and North Vietnamese soldiers—were all-important. Invariably, what the military called the "kill ratio"—the number of American dead in relation to the number of enemy dead—cast the Americans as victors. Ward Just recalled with considerable amusement how FitzGerald's powers of observation changed the way military personnel presented the numbers. She began examining the numbers—years' worth of numbers. She divined from those records that the weekly totals never, ever ended in either five or zero. When she asked why, officials had no satisfactory answer. However, those two elusive numbers began showing up in the totals thereafter, Just recalled. FitzGerald soon dismissed the briefings as a waste of time.

These conclusions, however obvious they seemed decades after the war, were—like her belief in the need to honor Vietnam's people and their traditions—hardly the accepted wisdom in the mid-1960s. No less an eminence than the political journalist Stewart Alsop, the brother of family friend

Joseph Alsop, found truth and hope in the military statistics that FitzGerald dismissed as laughable. He analyzed the KIA numbers for 1964 and concluded in a *Saturday Evening Post* article that the figures accurately indicated that the war could be won if America succeeded in halting aggression from North Vietnam. Lamentable though it was that 141 Americans had been killed in action during that twelve-month period, Alsop said, the fatalities hardly represented "any very terrible strain on a nation of some 190 million." The South Vietnamese dead—7,000—amounted to less than a 2 percent casualty rate, a number he described as "a tolerable percentage." In the 17,000 Viet Cong KIA number—which, as Alsop noted, American officers "swear" is accurate—he saw evidence that without the continuing support of the North Vietnamese the Communist forces in South Vietnam could easily be defeated. "That is why President Johnson really had no choice but to order air strikes against the North, to force the North Vietnamese to pay a price for their oblique aggression. If the price is high enough they may halt the aggression," Alsop conjectured. For FitzGerald, in contrast, embedded in those same numbers that Alsop claimed were cause for optimism were "all the themes of comedy and tragedy in Vietnam."

Just as she brushed aside the numbers that so preoccupied her news media colleagues, FitzGerald recognized that battlefield encounters were equally worthless in understanding the war. On an operation she accompanied in 1966, she spent nine hours observing two U.S. Marine battalions as they marched inland from separate points on the coast of Vietnam. The day, as so many military operations do, mixed boredom, apprehension, and discomfort with tensions and moments of high drama. She described how members of the battalion encountered an apparently harmless old man who flashed his voting card as if it constituted a shield. Later, the group took half a dozen rounds of sniper fire coming from the direction of a shrine; in response, a lieutenant called for an artillery attack to destroy the "suspected Viet Cong structure." From 7:00 A.M., the Marines marched, their shirts dampening with sweat along the way. Finally, at 4:00 P.M., the two battalions met according to schedule at a rendezvous point called Flying Eagle. The commander who led the operation expressed satisfaction with its success. For FitzGerald, however, the day ended with a whimper rather than anything approaching a bang. Nothing had happened. But amidst the chaos that characterized all Vietnam, the day had unfolded in an orderly progression. And for the commander, that added up to success. Yet the order this young officer created, FitzGerald observed, was in no way connected to the nation whose landscape was being reduced to "points, lines, and spaces." In an article about the mission published in *Vogue* magazine, FitzGerald concluded that the Americans had created a linguistic illusion in Vietnam, "a terribly tidy place which in some degree resembles the American military system itself." Yet Vietnam continued to resist these efforts to superimpose a Western order on its society.

Although Frankie could intellectualize the meaninglessness of battles she witnessed, her body reacted independently to the gory side of war. That was the only plausible explanation she ever attached to the illness that began afflicting her in April 1966. After witnessing several battlefield operations, she experienced dizzy spells, high fevers, exhaustion, and uninterrupted menstrual bleeding. Perhaps it was the sight of blood that prompted the symptoms, she thought. Her condition worsened despite several weeks of medical treatment. Even after surgery, there was little immediate improvement. She resisted leaving Vietnam; indeed, it was psychologically difficult for her to pull herself away. "But I also became so sick that I became passive. I couldn't figure out how to get on the plane because I was so exhausted." Finally, her mother, who was touring Southeast Asia with a group from the Ford Foundation, received a telegram from the American embassy in Saigon informing her of her daughter's condition. FitzGerald, apparently afflicted with a postoperative infection, collapsed soon after her mother's arrival in Saigon. Marietta Tree was appalled by her daughter's appearance, and even more so by the city in which she was living. "I don't see how she has survived this long," she wrote in her log of the trip. "The city . . . is one big traffic jam, garbage piled high, no water and the necessities of life require bribery to get them." Without ado, she booked flights to Singapore, where her daughter spent ten days recovering in a first-class hotel. From there, mother and daughter went to Bangkok; FitzGerald stayed there until she felt strong enough to return to Saigon several weeks later.

FitzGerald continued exploring questions about the country's religious divisions, its historic traditions, its sociology. Frank Wisner, the friend in the American embassy who had warned her before she arrived in Vietnam that the country was "not [her] world," introduced her to Daniel Ellsberg. She quickly perceived him to be one of the more astute thinkers about America's role in Vietnam. Early in 1966, Ellsberg was an aide to Colonel Edward Lansdale, who by then had been sent back to Vietnam by the Pentagon. Lansdale and his dozen-member team were assigned to reform the Saigon government and establish an effective pacification program, problems for which

America had been seeking solutions since the mid-1950s. In 1966, Ellsberg, who had joined the Rand Corporation after earning his PhD at Harvard, was still a disciple of the American cause. And what Ellsberg believed, according to Neil Sheehan, "he believed completely and sought to propagate with missionary fervor."

In one of her early encounters with Ellsberg, FitzGerald recalls that she had traveled to My Tho, a Mekong Delta town two hours south of Saigon, with Jill Krementz, who was photographing for the *Herald Tribune*. They had helicoptered in to the thriving commercial and agricultural center where the French had established a garrison in 1860s. Through much of the 1960s, members of the Army of the Republic of Vietnam's 7th Infantry Division occupied the facility. The U.S. Army's 7th Division Advisory Detachment was assigned to help train members of the ARVN division. As Krementz and FitzGerald prepared to return to Saigon after a day of interaction between the two armies, they encountered Ellsberg, who invited them to ride with him back to the capital. For Krementz, who had arrived in Vietnam months before FitzGerald, the two-hour ride was ordinary. But for FitzGerald, it was a reminder that she was in a perilous place. "I remember sitting in the car and watching the grenades rolling around the floor. There was a rifle of some kind, too," she said. Krementz seemed unconcerned. "But I was very new. I kept wondering whether we were on a really dangerous road," FitzGerald recalled. Ellsberg, one of the few Americans who made a practice of driving—rather than using helicopters—to reach the countryside, explained years later that he kept a supply of grenades in the car in case of an ambush. Not that he had ever been ambushed.

Back in Saigon, the city's growing refugee problem appalled Ellsberg and FitzGerald. Together, they toured the fetid slums, where ankle-deep raw sewage coursed through the streets during the monsoon season. That a people so rooted in their land, so bound to the graves of their ancestors, would abandon their hamlets for this unrelenting squalor horrified them. Driving thousands of peasants to a place Ellsberg called "fields of shit" were the bombs America was dropping all over the countryside. Ellsberg and FitzGerald both recognized that no one with the power to improve the mess seemed to care. There was a symmetry to their shared anguish over the war. He, the Harvard-educated scholar who had put his intellect to work in the service of his government, and she, the daughter of a well-placed public servant whose work had framed the flawed policies that had given the Vietnam debacle whose work at least some of its contours, both wrestled with their doubts. They had grown up believing that Americans "cared." Day-by-day, they confronted mounting evidence that undermined their notions of what America stood for and—as a consequence—began to debase their identity as Americans.

In their conversations about the war, FitzGerald soon concluded that Ellsberg seemed to be the only person in the American embassy who read books. Both intuited that the war was not working, but the why of it was baffling. With his cold war ethos still firmly in place, Ellsberg believed—rather like Graham Greene's fictional Alden Pyle—that Communism was a legitimate menace. He thought his brilliant policy analyses would provide America's leaders with the information necessary to prevail in that struggle. FitzGerald, too, was essentially a liberal who embraced the conservative suppositions that defined the international order during the cold war, chief among them the supposition that America had to beat Communism by imposing its own order on the world. Indeed, to question that fundamental assumption during what the historian Godfrey Hodgson called "the age of consensus" was to "proclaim oneself irresponsible or ignorant." That supposition settled like a fog around the Vietnam debate.

For a time, pacification of Vietnam's countryside was a key point of disagreement between FitzGerald and Ellsberg. He held out hope for success; she saw only failure. In one form or another, pacification or counterinsurgency efforts in Vietnam stretched back to 1959. In all their incarnations, they amounted to little more than programs of rounding up peasants and placing them in moated, barbed-wire stockades where the people could be issued identity cards and be kept separated from the Viet Cong, who were so heavily dependent on them. Emptied hamlets became free-fire zones, places Americans bombed with abandon. The justification was simple: Anyone on the inside of the compounds embraced the Saigon government. Thus, anyone on the outside had to be the enemy.

In 1959, President Diem began experimenting with so-called "agrovilles" designed to bring the "light of civilization" to newly secured villages in Vietnam's countryside. By 1962, the American-inspired and American-financed Strategic Hamlet Program replaced the agrovilles. Again, the goal was to sever the connections between the Viet Cong and the South Vietnamese villagers. Schools and medical care were part of the counterinsurgency effort, as was protection by the army of South Vietnam, at least until the villagers were deemed sufficiently trained in the techniques of self-defense to resist enemy encroachment. Many peasants, however, resisted. Abandoning the graves of their ancestors was particularly loathsome to a people for whom ancestor worship was a centuries-old tradition. Some peasants were moved at gunpoint.

Strategic hamlets excited Americans. How better to go about winning hearts and minds? The idea was to offer the South Vietnamese peasant an alternative, one that would checkmate the revolution the National Liberation Front was trying to sell. But the Strategic Hamlet Program never won over the peasantry. By the time Diem was assassinated in November 1963, the program was "in a shambles, with many of the key hamlets in the critical Mekong Delta region having been torn down either by guerrillas or by their own occupants." Later in the war, Strategic Hamlets became New Life Hamlets. They, too, were only minimally successful. By the time Ky became president in 1965, the mission was repackaged under the name "Revolutionary Development." Even this pacification effort, led by Lansdale, who was convinced that an American victory depended on pacification rather than bombing the North, suffered no better a fate.

These efforts that so engaged Ellsberg all looked suspicious to FitzGerald: Didn't this staggering investment of American resources and the well-meaning efforts of generations of Daniel Ellsbergs amount to little more than a carousel? She began to find justification for her doubts when Ellsberg introduced her to John Paul Vann, the retired U.S. Army colonel who had been a favorite of so many American journalists during the Diem regime. Vann had found civilian life in America stifling after his retirement from the army. He returned to Vietnam in March 1965 as a province pacification officer with the Agency for International Development. FitzGerald was impressed with his knowledge of the Delta, but found that he continued to think about Vietnam in military terms at a time when she was beginning to recognize that the political dimensions of the conflict made the military side all but inconsequential. "Vann must have known that our policies were wrong, but he was something of a war lover," in FitzGerald's memory. Vann suggested she visit the village of Duc Lap, twenty-two miles north of Saigon, where he was assigned. On her first visit, she found that Vann was determined to root out corruption among the provincial leaders and to drive out the Viet Cong. At the time, Vann thought the war could be won militarily but, he insisted, it had to be done by the Vietnamese.

Duc Lap was a collection of twenty-five hamlets; their strategic location at the intersection of two supply routes—one used by ARVN troops and the other by the enemy—made the area contested territory. One of the first strategic hamlets had been built there in January 1962. The village was part of the Hau Nghia Province, created in December 1963 in an effort by the Saigon government to wrest control of the region from the Viet Cong. That is also when Duc Lap became part of the New Life Hamlet Program. By the time FitzGerald made her first visit—under the protection of a military escort—90 percent of the population were believed to be Viet Cong sympathizers.

In this upper Mekong Delta village, FitzGerald found a microcosm of the war and all its misconceptions. Although the village had been bypassed by the Japanese invasion during World War II, French forces re-established an outpost in 1947 after defeating a force of guerrillas who lived in nearby swamps. In the 1960s, however, as she learned, the routines of peasant life changed dramatically when villagers found themselves torn between the competing demands of the Viet Cong and the Diem regime as each side recruited young men for its armies. American aid compounded an already complex situation and undermined rather than aided villagers, FitzGerald explained in an article she wrote for the *New York Times Magazine* in 1966. Although ARVN units were based in the nearby provincial capital, the village was considered so insecure that soldiers who patrolled safer areas by day withdrew at night to the security of battalion headquarters in Bao Trai. Leaving the villagers to the Viet Cong at night meant that the village was insecure. Hence, the village received scant support from the provincial government whose leaders reasoned that any aid given Duc Lap ultimately helped the enemy. In effect, "the villagers of Duc Lap are paying twice for the Government's inability to defend them," FitzGerald explained. The very program designed to give the peasants a sanctuary had simultaneously "made the countryside a place of terror." As a result, all but the youngest, oldest, most infirm, and poorest peasants had abandoned their villages for the refugee encampments in Saigon. The real strategic hamlets in Vietnam, FitzGerald concluded, were in those disease-ridden, sewage-filled, densely populated urban slums.

FitzGerald's thinking about the war led her to the realization that America had "created a government out of nothing" in Vietnam. But during their occasional conversations, Ellsberg initially resisted her interpretation, she recalled. For a time, he continued to believe in America's obligation to fight the Communist threat. "With each step he went back and back, and finally he came out the other side," FitzGerald said. By the time her *Atlantic* article was published in 1967, Ellsberg, too, was beginning to acknowledge that the war was unwinnable. During the same year, he participated in compiling a top-secret analysis of the war commissioned by Secretary of Defense Robert McNamara. That undertaking completed his disillusionment. What America was doing in Vietnam, he ultimately realized, amounted to nothing more than empire building. Notwithstanding all the rationalizations served up by policymakers to justify their pursuit of victory in Vietnam and all the optimism about achieving that goal, America had become an imperial power in Southeast Asia. America's motives were no purer than those of the French had been, Ellsberg realized. For all the arguments he had heard over the years—"We're not racist," "We're not colonizers," "We'll win because we have helicopters," "Our weapons are automatic," "The French are garlicky ass holes," "We are the United States of America"—there was no way to ignore the fundamental truth that America was an occupying power in Vietnam and that the war could never be won. Further, Ellsberg ultimately realized that five American presidents knew the war was a futile, unwinnable exercise—indeed, they had known it all along. But each in his turn continued the fight, apparently willing to accept tens of thousands of military and civilian casualties rather than face the truth. That recognition shattered Ellsberg's abiding faith in his government and led him to leak the study that became known as the *Pentagon Papers* to the *New York Times* correspondent Neil Sheehan.

Martha Gellhorn's faith in her government had vanished decades before she landed in Saigon in the summer of 1966. It was the same month that President Charles DeGaulle of France visited Cambodia and called for the withdrawal of American troops from Vietnam. Like FitzGerald, Gellhorn, then fifty-eight, was interested in Vietnam's civilian tragedy. Her difficulty in finding a publication to underwrite her trip to Vietnam grew out of the comments she made during a visit to New York early in 1966 when she claimed that those who protested the Vietnam War would, years hence, be considered "good Americans, in the way those who had protested against Hitler decades earlier had come to be recognized as 'good Germans.'" In her novel *The Lowest Trees Have Tops*, which features a group of European exiles and expatriates living in the United States during the early 1950s, the growing clamor of Vietnam-era dissent was obvious in her descriptions of America's intolerance for foreigners. The kind of public hostility she expressed about America and Americans, especially in relation to Vietnam, made editors skittish about using her material, even though she had considerable experience as a war correspondent.

Despite the many parallels in their upbringing and their views of the war, FitzGerald didn't warm to Gellhorn instantly. "I think I was fairly put off by her at first," FitzGerald said. "She was barely there a day when she was the expert on all the suffering of the Vietnamese." Like FitzGerald, Gellhorn was born into a prominent family and a world of social activists who embraced the traditions of community service, Progressive politics, and social justice. Dr. George Gellhorn and his wife, Edna, were nonconformists who encouraged their four children to be outspoken. In St. Louis society, George and Edna were unique in their own ways. He spoke five languages and revered the works of Thomas Jefferson. She had gone to college—a rarity among women in that era. That she had gone East to college, to Bryn Mawr, further distinguished her. Unlike the Peabodys, the Gellhorns practiced no conventional religion and considered themselves atheists. Martha's grandparents, who were descended from Jewish immigrants, founded the St. Louis chapter of the Ethical Culture Society. Martha attended its Sunday school for several years. (The Ethical Society, founded in New York in 1876, observed "the supreme importance of the ethical factor in all relations of life.") Martha once claimed that hers was the only important family in St. Louis that did not join a country club. Her father simply refused after he discovered that the members devoted their days to playing golf. Anyway, he disliked exclusive clubs and dismissed them as undemocratic.

Like Mary Peabody, Edna Gellhorn took to the streets of St. Louis to lead the city's campaign for women's suffrage. She organized a demonstration of 7,000 women in March 1916 when Democratic Party leaders held their national convention in St. Louis to re-nominate President Woodrow Wilson. Women wearing yellow sashes and carrying yellow parasols lined the route along the street leading to the convention hall. A woman dressed as the Statue of Liberty stood at the top of the steps leading to the hall. Below her were seven women dressed in white, representing the states that had enacted women's suffrage; then came women dressed in gray, representing the states that leaned toward approval of the measure. On the bottom steps women dressed in mourning clothes represented the states that refused women the vote. Missouri was represented among the women wearing black. Martha stood somewhere among the yellow parasols that lined Locust Street. She was eight years old.

Later in life, however, Martha Gellhorn found little kinship among the women of her generation who were pushing to expand those equal opportunities for which her mother and grandmother had fought. Both Gellhorn and FitzGerald seemed disconcerted by the feminist movement of the 1960s. Frankie was generally indifferent to the cause, but Gellhorn was occasionally hostile to feminists. She "deplored the way that enterprising women were discussed rather as if they were performing dogs," according to Carl Rollyson, her biographer. Neither FitzGerald nor Gellhorn seemed to see a clash between being a woman and pursuing individual interests. Nor did Ethel Payne, for that matter, in part because black women were so widely accepted as equal to black men in the norms of their culture.

For Gellhorn, Vietnam was "the Spanish Civil War all over again," but this time, she felt she was, "for the first time in her life, on the wrong side." During the weeks she spent in South Vietnam, Gellhorn visited hospitals and refugee camps, spoke with amputees, victims of napalm and white phosphorus burns, people blinded by mortars and mines, orphans, and the homeless—all a side of the war that so many American journalists had ignored in the years since their president had sent U.S. Marines to fight in Asia. By then, she had witnessed wars in eight other countries. Later she concluded that the horrors she found in Vietnam had no parallel in the those earlier conflicts.

Early in her career, she brought to her work as a war correspondent the notion that a journalist's job was to bring news to the people, "to be eyes for their conscience." Her initiation was in Spain in 1936. During World War II, she saw war as "a malignant disease, an idiocy," but also as a part of the human condition and of human history. By 1959, when she wrote an introduction to the book she titled *The Face of War*, she had recognized that "the guiding light of journalism was no stronger than a glow-worm." Her profession, she concluded, was merely the act of keeping the record straight. Like FitzGerald, she thought journalists in Vietnam were hardly doing a very good job of it.

While FitzGerald was eyeing Gellhorn with skepticism, Just, whose coverage of the war for the *Washington Post* focused heavily on the battlefield, the bombing, and the military briefings, was entranced by his encounter with the legendary war correspondent. She seemed so unlike other famous writers, hardly taken with her own fame in the way he found that John Steinbeck and Mary McCarthy had been when he met them during their visits to Vietnam. Just has vivid recollections of having lunch with Gellhorn in Saigon, a get-together that followed the one trip she made to a battlefield. She spoke so eloquently about the soldiers she had met, contrasting their morale to that of the ones she had known during World War II, Just recalled: "She loved soldiers and seemed so happy to be among them again. She said the best of them had a kind of gaiety about them. I knew exactly what she meant—a jaunty, amused quality." She spoke, too, of the life she and Ernest Hemingway had shared in Spain during the Spanish Civil War, a subject that Just, who was something of a Hemingway scholar, found thrilling. In retrospect, Just said he was pleased that he and Gellhorn were chasing vastly different stories in Vietnam. "If Martha Gellhorn had chosen to go out and cover the battlefield, the rest of us would never have reached the hem of her dress," he said.

Back in London, Gellhorn began writing about Vietnam. Drawing on the five notebooks she had filled with her observations, she explained that what she had found in Vietnam was "a beautiful people, especially the children." The *Guardian* published six of Gellhorn's stories, the least scathing of which were later republished in the *St. Louis Post-Dispatch*. Drawing on an indoctrination lecture given American soldiers arriving in Vietnam, Gellhorn's first *Guardian* article explained the U.S. conviction that Vietnam represented "a new kind of war," one in which winning the hearts and minds of South Vietnam's peasants was as important as killing the enemy. The fundamental problem, she said, was that the Americans seemed to be killing and injuring countless civilians with their bombs and napalm, perhaps as many as three to four times more victims than the Viet Cong killed, she speculated. During a visit to one of the country's free civilian hospitals built by the French, Gellhorn described the unspeakable conditions and the horrific injuries civilians had suffered at the hands of the Americans. The crowding, the filth and squalor, conditions that doubtless existed in each of the country's forty-three provincial hospitals, she wrote, were akin to those in the era of the Crimean War. In a portrayal of three young victims, Gellhorn described a panorama of suffering and misery. "The most beautiful child in this ward was a little boy who looked about five years old, with plaster on both his legs to the hips. He and two little girls sat on the tile floor. . . . They simply sat, motionless and silent; the girls were also in plaster, a leg, and arm. The boy's eyes were enormous, dark, and hopelessly sad; no child should have such eyes," she wrote.

Even more searing was her portrayal of a Saigon orphanage. The compound run by thirty-six French Catholic nuns was one of the capital city's ten orphanages. In that "sorrowful corner of hell" hunger ruled and wizened babies were "too weak to move or cry." Children afflicted with leprosy, polio, tuberculosis, blindness, and an assortment of physical and mental war wounds populated the orphanage, she explained. Throwing the numbers game played by the American military back in their faces, Gellhorn wondered why, in light of the enormous weight they placed daily on KIAs, WIAs, and MIAs, was there so little interest in the country's 80,000 children who had been orphaned by the war, a number she claimed was rising at the rate of 2,000 a month.

In October of 1966, Gellhorn persuaded the editors of the *Ladies Home Journal* to publish her story about the multitudes of children who were being killed in the war every month. In January 1967, *Journal* readers learned about the mutilated babies Gellhorn had seen in Vietnam. "Suffer the Little Children" drew painful images of the war casualties that "nobody dare[d] talk about." Bombs, machine guns, mortar shells, and mines had left their victims silent, Gellhorn explained. "But their eyes talk for them. I take the anguish, grief, bewilderment in their eyes, rightly, as accusation." Like FitzGerald, Gellhorn came away from Vietnam realizing that Americans knew nothing about the Vietnamese, nor did they recognize how that ignorance so endangered their cause.

Years later, Gellhorn acknowledged that she had pulled punches in her stories. Had she described what the war was really doing to the South Vietnamese, she could have been dismissed as a Communist propagandist; to avoid being so labeled, she admitted, she had sugar-coated reality. "I wanted to be read, to be heard, and knew I had to write carefully. There are smarmy sentences in those reports that I wrote with gritted teeth," she said in the 1986 edition of *The Face of War*. For all its horrors, however, Gellhorn wanted desperately to return to what she called the show-off war into which America had waded with "buoyant arrogance." That wish, however, went unfulfilled. Her stories apparently so disturbed South Vietnamese leaders that she was never again able to secure a visa to reenter the country.

Just was fascinated by Gellhorn's stories. He found in them evidence of how his own stories fell short. Gellhorn, he said, "brought the news from the unexamined corners of Vietnam and it seemed to me that was highly valuable work." Like so many of his colleagues, he had largely ignored those corners, but later he appreciated Gellhorn's vision. His, however, was apparently a minority view, at least back in the 1960s. The AP photographer Horst Faas, for example, characterized Gellhorn's work as an irritating rehash of a subject that typically attracted female journalists: "For Christ sake, here we go again. We've seen this before, we know all this. Why do women always have to look for orphanages?" Faas fumed at the time. Later, he is said to have conceded that Gellhorn had, indeed, revealed an important and untold part of the war story.

FitzGerald stayed in Vietnam for two months after Gellhorn's leave taking in mid-September. She continued her visits to the village of Duc Lap, where little was happening. Defense Secretary McNamara visited in October 1966 and returned to the United States with a pessimistic report about the future of the war. By mid-November, with the number of U.S. troops reaching 385,000, FitzGerald went home.

Returning to America after ten months in Southeast Asia was a psychic jolt. Her anger over the war and a growing disdain for its architects began to consume her. Alongside that growing obsession, the matters that concerned her friends seemed banal. "The essence of the difficulty in returning was that most people, everyone except those who had been to Vietnam, simply weren't thinking about the war to that degree I was," she recalled. Gloria Emerson later encountered that same nonchalance in 1972 when she returned from her two-year assignment in the *New York Times* Saigon bureau. By chance, FitzGerald arrived in New York just in time for one of the decade's most fabled parties—Truman Capote's Black and White Ball, held in honor of Katharine Graham, the *Washington Post*'s publisher, at New York's Plaza Hotel, a place light years removed from Duc Lap. FitzGerald, her mother, her stepfather, and her half-sister, Penelope Tree, whose career as a model blossomed after the party, were among Capote's 540 guests dancing to the music of Peter Duchin's orchestra. Secretary McNamara was there. So was McGeorge Bundy, head of President Johnson's National Security staff. Unlike another famous partygoer who opposed the war, FitzGerald didn't speak with either man. A tipsy Norman Mailer argued vehemently with Bundy and invited him to go outside. "I could have killed him that night, I was so angry," Mailer said. As the critic Diana Trilling later noted, Capote's lavish party on which he spent $16,000 (the 2007 equivalent of nearly $100,000 in inflation-adjusted dollars) was "a very complicated moment in this country's social history." Frankie FitzGerald had an especially acute awareness of those complications.

In the December issue of the *Atlantic*, already on New York newsstands as Capote's guests at the Plaza were consuming 450 bottles of Tattinger's, FitzGerald had described how millions of Vietnamese refugees—people displaced by America's war—were crowding into ghettos on the fringes of every major city where "cholera, smallpox, and bubonic plague, as well as leprosy and typhoid [had] become endemic." All those numbers in which the likes of Stewart Alsop found significance never included tallies of these civilians.

FitzGerald, however, did consider those numbers, and she put a human face on them. The refugee-filled Vietnamese slums she described in "The Tragedy of Saigon" were filled with peasants from the agricultural villages that were once the soul of Vietnam. Now, these homeless millions had "nowhere to turn for justice, for material help or for a promise of security." In the tin and thatched-roofed shacks of Bui Phat, the Saigon refugee quarter built on mud banks that washed over with garbage and sewage during the monsoon season, FitzGerald saw a dangerous breeding ground. The displaced peasants knew only the ways of their villages, but the generation of children they were raising in this urban squalor, FitzGerald's article speculated, might soon become strangers to their own parents. But the Americans who lived around the refugee enclaves, or at least those "Americans who had spent time in their own city slums," she conjectured, were likely to find something familiar in the urchins of Bui Phat. The disconnect between the scene in Manhattan's Plaza Hotel on her first night home and her memories of places such as Bui Phat overwhelmed her on that night. "I wish I had been in a better mood for that kind of party. I really couldn't cope with it all," she said years later.

At about the time FitzGerald began to sort out the dissonance between life in Saigon and life in New York City, John Sengstacke, publisher of the *Chicago Defender* and founder of the Negro Newspaper Publishers Association, was telling Ethel Payne that "it would be a unique thing to have a woman cover the war." He wanted her to find answers to questions about the treatment of black soldiers in Vietnam, questions that were then widely ignored in the mainstream press. "Yes, I'll do it," she told Sengstacke. Payne considered herself a spiritual descendant of Frederick Douglass, who in 1847 founded the abolitionist newspaper the *North Star.* His admonition to "agitate, agitate, agitate" still resonated with her a century later, just as it did with many other staffers on America's dozen or more black daily and weekly newspapers. Their collective circulation, 1.2 million in the mid-1960s, was hardly a measure of their impact on America's black population. In the de-facto apartheid system that was a hallmark of black life in America, at least until the passage of civil rights legislation in 1964, reporters like Ethel Payne became unapologetic defenders of the interests of the country's poorest paid, least educated, and most disenfranchised people. She and her peers spoke to African Americans about themselves, their causes, their accomplishments, and their aspirations for equality. Among their readers, all the Ethel Paynes in the black press enjoyed the status of heroes.

One of that era's cultural quirks is that black women, segregated though they were from white society, enjoyed opportunities in their own society that were denied to white women in the framework of their cultural norms. For all the white women in America's mainstream media who begged, cajoled, or carped at their bosses for the Vietnam assignment, to say nothing of those who recognized the futility of such entreaties and went on their own, Ethel Payne never had to ask. Certainly the greater competition for plum assignments on a *New York Times*–sized publication severely diminished the odds of, say, a Gloria Emerson getting assigned to the newspaper's Saigon bureau. But unlike Emerson, Payne had the freedom to reject an assignment on the society pages, even though it was an important component of the news equation, just as it was in the white press.

What little scholarship exists on the black press in America suggests that a variety of forces combined to define gender-neutral policies. The *Chicago Defender*, like its counterparts in the mainstream (white) American media, was run by an all-male hierarchy. But those male editors never harbored the prejudices held by the layers of white male editors who doubted women's abilities to handle major news stories. Moreover, the same striving for justice and equality that gave birth to the black press itself also attracted reporters whose commitment to those aspirations transcended individual egos. Black men expended their energy fighting the oppression of white men. Jim Crow was the adversary, the only adversary, the one that journalists, men and women, joined forces to fight.

Ethel Payne grew up with none of the privileges and little of the promise that attached itself to upper-middle-class white girls in America. She was born and raised in a predominantly black neighborhood on the southwest side of Chicago, one she characterized as having been populated by "good burghers," hard-working, church-going, solid citizens who quietly suffered the many indignities of life in a segregated America. She was the granddaughter of slaves who had migrated North in search of work after the Civil War. Her father, William Payne, had a job with the railroad, one of the few secure positions for blacks and one that had considerable prestige among his peers. He was an imposing figure, one who took the same pride so many of his contemporaries did in his ability to support his family, meager though his wages were, while Ethel Payne's mother, Bessie Austin Payne, a Latin Scholar, stayed home with their six children. After William Payne's death, she became a cleaning woman to support her family.

Ethel Payne recalled spending her childhood in "a solid bastion of God and patriotism." The Paynes were a politically astute and racially conscious family, well aware of their status as second-class citizens but inclined to work for change within the system. Her mother believed in the power of prayer to right social wrongs. Ethel Payne's personal fight for equality was sometimes as basic as besting rock-throwing and epithet-spewing bullies through whose all-white neighborhood she had to walk through on her treks to high school.

The first hint that writing might shape her future came from her English teacher at Lindbolm High School who told her that her handwriting resembled that of her star pupil at another school, a man whose name would enter America's literary canon in the coming decade—Ernest Hemingway. Her early aspiration to be a lawyer grew out of a wish to defend the poor, but her lackluster high school grades and the lack of money following her father's untimely death combined to dash that hope. She applied to the University of Chicago Law School but was not accepted.

Boredom and a taste for adventure energized her decision to abandon a dull clerking job at the Chicago Public Library and join the U.S. Army Special Services, work that took her to occupied Japan in 1948. Payne's job involved organizing recreational activities for African American soldiers. That job became the springboard to her career in journalism. Payne began keeping a diary during the weeks she spent crossing the Pacific Ocean on her way to Japan, and she continued recording the events she witnessed in her new job. Japan's society, largely closed to the outside world long before the war, fascinated Payne, so much so that in her free time she sought out Mamoru Shigemitsu, the Japanese foreign minister who signed the surrender document aboard the USS *Missouri* in September 1945, and his aide in the foreign ministry, Toshikazu Kase.

Although President Harry S. Truman's 1948 Executive Order 9981 declared that "there shall be equality of treatment and opportunity for all persons in the armed services without regard to race, color, religion, or national origin," segregation in the services persisted systemically until Dwight D. Eisenhower became president in 1953. The black soldiers Payne encountered on the segregated base were "rough and tumble kids, very young . . . and it was a jolly good time we used to have." All the GIs had Japanese girlfriends, companions they called "moussimaes," with whom many of them lived off base. "Good living was the order of the day" during the early years of the Japanese occupation, according to Lieutenant Colonel Charles M. Bussey. The closest an American soldier came to conflict "was negotiating a price for a single night's pleasure."

That life of relative ease quickly changed when North Korean troops staged an attack across the 38th Parallel and struck South Korea on June 25, 1950. Payne documented the discontent among American servicemen and provided evidence that, in spite of President Truman's directive to military leaders to integrate the armed services, in Japan, it wasn't happening. As the fighting in Korea grew during the summer, legions of American reporters passed through Tokyo on their way to the battle lines. Payne met many of them at the city's overseas press club and shared her observations about Asia.

That's how she met Alex Wilson, a correspondent for the *Chicago Defender*. Drawing on the entries in her diary, Payne enlightened Wilson. "You know," Wilson told her, "the folks back home don't know what's going on." He convinced her that the information in her diaries would draw a huge readership in America, so she let Wilson take her diaries back to the United States. It was true: Americans had little knowledge of their country's occupation of Japan and knew even less about the liaisons between GIs and young Japanese women. Most important of all, "they didn't know much about how [MacArthur's] command was set up to keep it rigidly segregated." That meant President Truman's two-year-old executive order was being ignored.

Payne's diary notes, revised by the *Defender*'s editors into a news writing format, were a sensation. Copies of the newspaper "were just jumping off the stands," Payne recalled years later. One story published under her byline described how Japanese women exploited black soldiers, whom they called "Chocolate Joe." These same soldiers, another of Payne's stories explained, had fathered hundreds of babies, mixed-race children widely considered outcasts in Japan's social order, which placed high value on racial purity. As was a pattern in black newspapers of the day, the stories highlighted Ethel Payne's own role in the drama. Besides her byline, the headlines featured her name, too, as in "Ethel Payne, 'Says Japanese Girls Playing GIs for Suckers.'" To the delight of *The Defender*'s editors, circulation soared.

Military leaders, however, were anything but delighted. "It was just so explosive," she recalled. Indeed it was. Black soldiers in Korea were being courtmartialed—some of them with little in the way of due process—for misbehavior and disobedience with alarming frequency. Their sentences ranged from ten years at hard labor to death. The problem, the NAACP attorney Thurgood Marshall concluded after a six-week investigation in Korea, was military foot-dragging on Truman's desegregation order and a propensity of white commanders (many from the South) to find fault with black troops. "Next thing I knew, all hell broke loose at Supreme Allied," Payne recalled years later. Members of the high command threatened to fire her for demoralizing the troops—all of which Payne perceived as the military's way of covering up their failure to comply with the president's integration directive. She was chastised, humiliated, and isolated for her transgressions.

Payne was made a secretary at command headquarters, a position in which she could be kept under close scrutiny. That's when the *Defender*'s editor-in-chief offered her a job. "Come on home," Louis Martin urged her in a telephone call to Japan. "We've got a job for you." Martin, who had made a fortune buying and selling insurance companies, was a hard-headed, fun-loving character who was the *Defender*'s editor for twelve years. He was Payne's contemporary as well as her mentor. In later years, Martin was the civil rights liaison for the Kennedy and Johnson administrations, and he served as a special assistant to the president during the Carter administration. During the 1950s and 1960s, Payne became one of the most prominent black female reporters of her generation, even though she remained little known beyond readers of the *Defender* and her peers in the black press. With the radio and television commentaries she did between 1972 and 1978 for the CBS program "Spectrum," she became the first African American woman hired for such work by a national network, a position that made her a voice of America's black minority in the mainstream media. The three months she spent covering issues related to African American servicemen fighting the war in Vietnam, and the stories she wrote about her experiences, were but a small part of the four-decade-long, globe-trotting career in which she established an international reputation among both journalists and diplomats. Although Payne's "Vietnam Diary" was little more than an evanescent ripple—a simple, straightforward narrative similar to Beverly Deepe's earliest travelogues—its purpose had less to do with the sweep of history than it did with giving a long-overlooked minority proper credit for its endeavors. Eleven years after her death in 1991, in honor of her success as a journalist, Payne was one of four American women whose contributions to journalism were celebrated by the U.S. Postal Service in its 2002 Women in Journalism commemorative series. Payne's image, and those of three other American women, was printed on 61 million postage stamps. The other women journalists whose faces appeared on individual stamps in the series were Ida Tarbell, Nellie Bly, and Marguerite Higgins.

Both Payne and the *Chicago Defender* were part a network of black newspapers that in their earliest, pre-radio, pre-television years served as the only form of public communication—besides word of mouth—in the country's African American population. In Detroit, Baltimore, New York City, Norfolk, Pittsburgh, and Richmond, black-owned newspapers celebrated black achievement, railed against injustice, and fought for civil rights. The *Defender*, established by Robert Abbot, was one of many black newspapers that were considered subversive, especially south of the Mason-Dixon Line where, particularly during World War II, local officials made a special effort to halt their distribution. Abbot, a Georgia native, built his own base of readers in Chicago by encouraging the migration of Southern blacks to Northern cities. Using a variation of the formula that had served William Randolph Hearst so well, Abbot featured news of crime and discrimination on the *Defender's* front pages, giving it mass appeal among urban readers in Chicago. Thanks to Abbot's ingenuity in using a "vast network of black Pullman car porters"— people just like Ethel Payne's father—the newspaper circulated not only in Chicago but also throughout the South.

By the time Ethel Payne joined the *Defender's* staff in 1951, the black press in America was, in the words of the Swedish sociologist Gunnar Myrdal, "at the center of a developing Negro protest in the United States." The black press, as he explained in *An American Dilemma,* covered the country and the world from the perspective of race but also maintained the character of a small-town newspaper. Moreover, as Myrdal noted, "the black press also functioned to define the Negro community as an institutionalized society to the individual Negro who is excluded so much from white society and gives him a feeling of security and belongingness." So it was natural for reporters such as Ethel Payne to become heroes to their readers. Payne had both access to the nation's policymakers and the courage to ask questions for which blacks sought answers, questions that white reporters usually never thought to ask. With its commitment to advocacy journalism, an approach that Payne embraced with enthusiasm, the black press functioned as a moral force for African Americans throughout the civil rights movement and beyond.

Martin, the *Defender* editor who hired Payne and sent her to Washington in 1953, likened her to a racehorse. "You know, sometimes maybe you had to curb me a little bit. But he knew . . . that I liked to go after the unusual." Going after "the unusual" made her something of a legend in 1954, when she enraged President Eisenhower during one of his weekly press conferences with what she considered a simple, defensible question: She wanted to know when he planned to issue an executive order to end discrimination in interstate travel. The president's rage was palpable. With all the command of a four-star general lashing out at a lowly subordinate, to the astonishment of the White House press corps, he shouted at Payne. "What makes you think that I'm going to cater to any special interest," he demanded. "I'm the president of all the people." Ironically, members of the white male press corps cheered her on, but men in the black press chastised her as "over-assertive" and accused her of "show-boating." When Ike's outburst made national news, everyone was asking, "Who is that colored woman?" By 1966, "that colored woman" had scored uncounted numbers of firsts for women and people of color in American journalism with her continuing coverage of the White House, Congress, every notable milepost in the civil rights movement and numerous international trips.

Payne embraced the Vietnam assignment with the same "racehorse" enthusiasm that energized all her work. By then, she was known in the Washington press corps as "the First Lady of the Black Press." Vietnam marked the first war in American history in which black soldiers were fully integrated with their white counterparts. The affronts suffered by the 500,000 black servicemen and women who fought World War II in Europe and the Pacific were only marginally less onerous than those their World War I brethren had endured. In that earlier war, for example, unlike their white shipmates, black stevedores on U.S. naval vessels were not assigned to lifeboats but were expected to survive on floating debris.

Those World War I–era segregation customs were officially banned by the War Department in 1943, but the edict did not change the belittling practices of denying black soldiers access to transportation and entertainment on American military bases. Nor did the ban have any impact on those larger indignities, like denying blacks service awards for their acts of heroism. For African Americans, the fascist evils they were fighting in Germany, Italy, and France during World War II had a frightening parallel in their lives as soldiers and citizens. But although segregation still prevailed, the acceptance of black volunteers into the U.S. Marines, the elevation of black servicemen to the ranks of naval officers and fighter pilots, the inclusion of black women in the WACS and WAVES all counted as victories in the face of continuing disrespect.

After the war, whatever solace blacks might have taken from President Truman's Executive Order 9981, was quickly undone by General Eisenhower's protest and his support for the Army's insistence that "separate but equal was necessary to national defense." So the conflict in Korea began as a segregated war: Black servicemen were bedeviled by the familiar accusations of mental inferiority, insubordination, and cowardice. By the time a cease-fire was declared in the police action in 1953, however, the three-year-old experiment of integrated training on U.S. military bases had proven that fears of racial conflict between whites and blacks were misplaced. As president, Eisenhower changed his mind about segregation in the military; and less than a year after he took office, 95 percent of the Army's black troops had been integrated into white units. In 1954, the military's last segregated units were dissolved.

Thereafter, whites and blacks trained and fought side-by-side for the first time in Vietnam. From the time that American ground troops first landed in Vietnam, however, blacks suffered a disproportionate number of casualties compared with white troops. "In 1965 and 1966, nearly 25 percent of U.S. troops killed in action were black, more than twice the percentage of blacks in the population as a whole." Although the Defense Department hastily moved to correct that imbalance, those early figures created "an enduring impression that African Americans took unduly high losses throughout the conflict." That disparity combined with questions about why black men should fight for the liberty of Asian people on behalf of a country that denied them fundamental liberty at home were all part of the dynamic that propelled Ethel Payne during the three months she spent in Vietnam.

She landed in Saigon on Christmas Day in 1966 and was accompanied by military escorts to a USO show underway for wounded soldiers. Bob Hope and a band of entertainers were doing their annual gig at a base near Saigon. Her first glimpses of Americans in Vietnam were of injured young men, some of them paralyzed, others burned, some missing limbs. "So what was meant to be a pleasant occasion, a holiday, had this eerie dual quality that things in Vietnam always seemed to have," she recalled in an oral history years later. "Everything beautiful or pleasant was always tinged with something horrible. Everything was unmistakably touched by the war."

Payne's "Vietnam Diary" gave *Defender* readers none of the jolting insights that her diary entries about the lives of black soldiers in Korea had in the early 1950s. In 1966, her stories had a folksy, invitational take-a-seat-and-I'll-tell-you-a-story tone meant to bring the war home to her readers. She put them in touch with individual soldiers in the way Ernie Pyle's World War II stories had. Her coverage of Vietnam began with a historical primer setting "forth the terms of the problem which still remains hazy to millions of Americans." A reader's note also explained that Payne's mission in Vietnam was to search out the pitfalls and the probable final results from her "front-row seat in the coming months." She described the Vietnamese as "an abused people," and her focus on the country's 3,000-year history was heavy on details of World War II and its immediate aftermath. She also echoed the official American perspective. Her story spoke, for example, of North Vietnam's "aggressive program of wholesale violations of the Geneva agreements" and characterized the enemy as "insurgents whose tactics are similar to the terroristic methods of gang mobs."

Other articles revealed her commitment to celebrating the contributions of African American soldiers to the war effort. Even when race was not explicitly stated in Payne's stories, readers could reliably conclude that her subjects were black. One story explained the "big business" of distributing soldiers' paychecks and otherwise financing the war, duties carried out by members of the 10th Finance Section Disbursing Facility, an undertaking in which black soldiers from Detroit and Chicago were assigned major responsibilities. In a story about the army's main supply depot at Cam Ranh Bay, Payne described how servicemen from Chicago were "providing a big boost to the U.S. Army Support Command, a vital lifeline to the war effort in Vietnam." Beyond half a dozen descriptive paragraphs, Payne cited the names and duties of fifteen Chicago-area soldiers.

A story about her visit to the USS *Enterprise*, on a six-month deployment in the Gulf of Tonkin, celebrated the role of African Americans aboard "the mightiest ship afloat." That young black men from Blooming Grove, New York; Portsmouth, in Virginia; Memphis, and Charleston, were helping to operate the world's first nuclear-powered aircraft carrier gave readers a look at the war that few other American news outlets provided. Payne likened the ship to a skyscraper towering twenty-five stories and stretching five city blocks, drifting on the ocean. She said its bombing missions were designed "to interdict lines of communication which include highways and railroads."

On occasion, Payne reverted to the antiseptic language more common to military operation than journalistic writing. The *Enterprise* was actually a floating runway from which thousands upon thousands of bombing strikes on targets in South Vietnam had been launched. Indeed, the ship held a military record set early in December 1965 for having launched 125 sorties and dropped 176 tons of bombs and rockets in the vicinity of Bien Hoa Airport in one day. Payne's story, however, made no reference to bombs, bombing missions, air strikes, or the damage they were inflicting. John Sengstacke had sent Ethel Payne to Vietnam with a different assignment. Information that could raise questions about America's role in the war were best left for America's white newspapers to explore. The Reverend Dr. Martin Luther King Jr. had questioned the morality of the war since 1965 but had yet to declare his outright opposition to it. In April 1967, nearly a month after Ethel Payne's Vietnam assignment concluded, in a speech at Riverside Church in New York City, Dr. King declared that he opposed the war not just because of the disparity in black and white draft statistics and the fact that the war was bankrupting poverty programs. The war, he said, endangered America's soul, "lest it become totally poisoned."

The military appears to have lavished the same measure of attention on Payne that it had earlier lavished on the likes of Marguerite Higgins. Payne's itinerary was tightly programmed and designed to give her the "most positive and least dangerous" glimpses of the war. A few black officers she befriended, however, helped her make the occasional departure from her official program. In these unscripted encounters, she found they endured many of the same trials that black soldiers had endured in service of their country in prior wars. Although the Army had been integrated, the slights remained unchanged. They were labeled with the same stereotypes that soldiers Payne had known of in Korea. They complained to Payne about trumped-up charges of insubordination and misconduct brought by white officers who disdained "uppity" blacks. They spoke of being used as "cannon fodder."

Payne raised questions about these racial issues in an interview with General William Westmoreland, who, as she recalled years later, "was very sensitive to criticism of the military's handling of racial problems in Vietnam." After three months, she began to wonder whether the war "was really worth all the death." When she looked back on her work in Vietnam more than two decades later, Payne recalled that the experience "had a profound effect on me as a journalist." She wished, in retrospect, that she had taken a broader look at the scene. Although the story of the black soldier was significant, she realized later, "it was just one tragedy among many, many in Vietnam. I wish I had examined more of them."

By late March, as Ethel Payne was returning from Vietnam, the war Frankie FitzGerald had left months before continued to grip her. The more she studied Vietnamese political and cultural life, the more questions about America's role there seemed to plague her: Why were America's pacification efforts failing? Why did America's leaders allow so many soldiers to continue dying when there seemed to be so little purpose in the war? What did the domino theory really mean anyway? FitzGerald turned to books by French authors who had studied Vietnam during that country's century-long occupation of Indochina. The Americans, of course, believed that so little could be learned from the French experience in Vietnam that books by the most important French authors on the subject had yet to be translated into English. Beyond the translations of a few books by Bernard Fall and Jean Lacoutre, little had been written in English about Vietnamese history and culture.

The first result of her thinking was the long, scholarly examination of the war she wrote for the *Atlantic,* the article she had planned to discuss with her father before his death on that hot July weekend in 1967. That news reached her in Ireland. The CIA's London station called her at Glinn Castle, the FitzGeralds' ancestral family estate, where she was vacationing with her friend, Ward Just. It was, she wrote, "a small voice over the phone." She was inconsolable. She felt as if her stomach had been torn out. She felt deserted. One obituary writer characterized her father as "one of the most powerful, and least publicized, of high Government officials in Washington." After his death, President Johnson awarded Desmond FitzGerald the National Security Medal for his "exceptional competence and stimulating leadership for sixteen years as a member of the CIA." In subsequent years, Frankie FitzGerald had dreams about her father. She saw him in his trench coat. He was always leaving.

Even before "The Struggle and the War" was published in the August 1967 edition of the *Atlantic,* her editors proposed that she write a book about her perspective on the war. In pursuit of that idea, she began meeting with Paul Mus, a French historian and scholar who soon became an intellectual father figure to her. His book, *Vietnam: Sociologie d'une guerre,* published in 1952, is still considered a seminal analysis of the French war in Indochina. She had first seen the book while she was in Vietnam, and she read it after her return. John McAlister, a scholar at Princeton University's Woodrow Wilson Center who was translating Mus's book, introduced FitzGerald to Mus, who was teaching Asian studies at Yale.

In speaking about how he guided her research, FitzGerald recalled that "as a friend, we would just talk about Vietnam, and he would tell me things that would make things he wrote more accessible." She added, "He was such an incredible scholar of ancient languages that this would very much be caught up with his argument about his views on Vietnam today." Mus, who had been raised in Hanoi, served as a political advisor to French General Phillip Leclerc after World War II. He advocated granting independence to Vietnam, advice that his superiors ignored.

With Mus's guidance, FitzGerald mastered an understanding of *I Ching,* the ancient Chinese Book of Changes, a Confucian classic that defines a world order with symbolism and poetic language. In it she found "all the clues to the basic design of the Sino-Vietnamese world." At Mus's urging she also read, in French, Leopold Cadiere's three-volume *Croyances et pratiques religieuses des vientamiens;* Phillippe Devillers's *Histoire du Viet-Nam de 1940 a 1952;* and Le Thanh Khoi's *Le Viet-nam, histoire et civilisation.* Her thirst for information about Vietnam seemed, for a time, insatiable. As Mary Peabody once observed, her granddaughter went after scholarly research "in the way most women go after husbands."

Transforming all that knowledge into a clear and original statement, however, became an often painful five-year ordeal. With the kind of rigid self-discipline her great-grandfather had helped instill in generations of Groton students, FitzGerald labored daily at her old Remington. Living in a Manhattan apartment, she arose early and went at what she called her "typing." At times her ideas seemed too disjointed, perhaps because they remained so at odds with the conventional thinking. She was, after all, challenging the very language that military men and policymakers had used to frame their explanations of the war. Who was she, a twenty-seven-year-old skeptic, to question the wisdom of her father's generation and to declare them—and him—all wrong? Self-doubt sometimes beset her.

Reactions from readers of her early work on the book were especially discouraging. An editor at Atlantic Monthly Press who read the first chapter made no effort to hide his disappointment. FitzGerald recalled that he told her it was "terrible, it [didn't] make any sense." She thought he was about to cancel her contract. McAlister, at the Woodrow Wilson Center, was similarly dissatisfied with her early drafts. He wrote FitzGerald a lengthy memo in 1969 explaining his disappointment that she had not more closely followed her style in the *Atlantic* article. He suggested that she draw the same sharp differences between the Americans and Vietnamese that she had so clearly defined in that article. McAlister told her the manuscript lacked "coherence and any organizational structure."

Well-meaning friends were the source of still more discomfort. When will the book be finished, her New York pals incessantly asked. "The war will be over," they warned her, implying that thereafter anything she had to say would be irrelevant. In an act of self-preservation, she fled New York and found an apartment in Cambridge, where she had spent her college years. She returned to Harvard University's incomparable Widener Library where, during her years as an undergraduate at Radcliffe, she had become acquainted with the books that occupied miles and miles of shelf space. Yet, as she toiled in Widener's dusty nooks, nothing in the emerging policies of the Nixon administration indicated to FitzGerald that her friends' predictions about an imminent conclusion to the war would come to pass. Six months after he took office, President Richard Nixon began withdrawing American troops as part of his plan to "Vietnamize" the war. Against the backdrop of troop reductions, however, the 3rd Marine Division mounted an operation in Laos in February and the secret bombing of Cambodia began in March. By then, General Creighton W. Abrams had taken over command of the war from

General Westmoreland, but the fundamental strategy America had followed since the mid-1950s remained in place. By continuing their support for the anti-Communist government of President Nguyen Van Thieu, Nixon and National Security Advisor Henry Kissinger were "creating the conditions for an extended and bloody political conflict after an American withdrawal," FitzGerald concluded in early 1970 in the *New York Review of Books*.

Her anger over the war rose during the early years of the Nixon administration with the realization that what could have been excused as wrong-headed but well-intentioned bungling during the Johnson administration now seemed to border on immoral, even criminal, behavior. Was saving the illusion of American preeminence really worth so many American and Vietnamese lives?

In the early 1970s, as she began to grasp the evolution of the CIA-sponsored Phoenix program, that anger escalated. Phoenix, or "Phung Hoang," in Vietnamese, developed in 1967 as an extension of America's failure-haunted pacification effort. Its director, Robert Komer, was a former CIA official. The program's so-called "Hamlet Evaluation Surveys," which indicated that by the fall of 1967, 75 percent of the population was pacified, underscored the self-delusion afflicting so many American officials. The overarching goal of the Phoenix program was to eliminate the Viet Cong infrastructure, in part by centralizing South Vietnam's rival intelligence operations in one organization. American army advisors trained South Vietnamese police, government, and civilian officials to infiltrate the villages and identify Viet Cong operatives. The results were mixed. By 1969, Komer set a quota of 3,000 Viet Cong to be "neutralized" each month. Between 1968 and 1971, 20,000 enemy agents were reported to have been assassinated.

But Phoenix had "early on became an extortionist's paradise." Liberties the Phoenix program allowed resulted in the indiscriminate killing of tens of thousands of Vietnamese whose guilt or innocence of complicity with the enemy was never firmly established. Komer's quotas, along with the practice of rewarding informants and paying off "friendlies" who produced evidence of having killed a Viet Cong, corrupted the program. Torture techniques were monstrous. In testimony before Congress, one military intelligence officer described how a six-inch dowel inserted in a suspect's ear canal was tapped through his brain until he died. The Phoenix program's success, FitzGerald wrote, was in how it "eliminated the cumbersome category of 'civilian'; it gave the GVN, and initially the American troops, as well, license and justification for the arrest, torture, or killing of anyone in the country, whether or not the person was carrying a gun."

As she struggled to put her thoughts about the war on paper during those years, FitzGerald occasionally thought about her father. She once said that "it would have been bad" had he still been around after the book was published. Yet, in the year after his death, thanks to Stewart Alsop, the old family friend who saw victory in the numbers, she learned of Desmond's early skepticism about the war. In his book, *The Center: People and Power in Political Washington*, Alsop repeated an anecdote once related to him by Desmond FitzGerald, then head of the CIA's Far East Division. FitzGerald had told Alsop about a brief, private conversation he had with Secretary of Defense McNamara at the Pentagon in 1962, when McNamara lamented that he was having difficulty making sense of the war. FitzGerald, drawing on his experience in the Far East that began with the Chinese during World War II, cautioned the secretary that the numbers on which he relied so heavily as indicators of victory might be misleading, that the statistics from Vietnam were obscuring the underlying story of a people's revolution. "Facts and figures are useful, but you can't judge a war by them," FitzGerald warned. "You have to have an instinct, a feel. My instinct is that we're in for a much rougher time than your facts and figures indicate." FitzGerald counseled that "spirit," an unquantifiable element in the Vietnam equation, might prove more important than numbers. The secretary was incredulous and stared at him "as though FitzGerald had taken leave of his senses." He was never again asked to brief Robert McNamara. But although the Alsop anecdote finally provided a foundation for what she had perceived as her father's skepticism about the war, her uncertainty about how her father might have responded to her conclusions persisted as she wrote *Fire in the Lake*.

Even as she wrestled with her book, FitzGerald continued to write about Vietnam. Her own trip to Hanoi was still seven years away when Susan Sontag and Mary McCarthy went to North Vietnam in 1968 and 1969. For both women, the sojourn in Hanoi became a journey of introspection, and both published books about the experience. FitzGerald's essay in the *New York Review of Books* welcomed the new perspectives the two women defined—McCarthy in *Hanoi* and Sontag in *Trip to Hanoi*. The Vietnamese—both enemy and ally—had been lost in America's "preoccupation with the significance of its own action," FitzGerald wrote, likening that national sense of self-absorption to a patient in psychoanalysis. Both women, she explained, had wrestled with how to reach beyond the linguistic bombast and portraits of Joseph Stalin that they had heard and seen in Hanoi. Each woman, FitzGerald said, had to "re-create their culture for herself by an act of imagination." That was the very same task that FitzGerald confronted during the five years she spent writing *Fire in the Lake*. As that work neared completion in mid-1971, FitzGerald began planning her second trip to Vietnam.

She returned there with a plan to write a long piece for the *New Yorker*. The good times of 1966 in Saigon were long over by then. After the Tet Offensive, fear replaced the mood of gaiety in American circles. Anxiety replaced the sense of confidence. In the words of one observer, "Saigon was never the same after Tet." FitzGerald felt self-conscious as she walked around Saigon after her return. "The ugliness was stunning. . . . The streets were full of wounded Vietnamese soldiers without an arm or a leg, begging. After a while, you looked odd to yourself because you had all four of your limbs." The countryside and coastal regions of Vietnam that had been so beautiful in 1966 were strewn with equipment and barbed wire left behind by the Americans. The site of the country's Cham temples, architectural treasures built between the seventh and twelfth centuries by a people who inhabited coastal regions of southern Vietnam, had been mercilessly bombed by the Americans, who had no sense of their cultural significance. It all left FitzGerald heartbroken.

Yet at another level, especially in the countryside, "Vietnam was returning to itself," she recalled. With so little of the fighting that had characterized her travels in 1966, in 1971, "it was fairly easy to move around. In the countryside life was so much better. The farmers were planting rice again in the Delta, television antennas were visible. There was prosperity." She traveled all over Vietnam, sometimes by bus, other times by car. FitzGerald visited healers in the Delta, Hoa Hao doctors, and Buddhist monks. American troop strength had fallen steadily after Richard Nixon instituted his "Vietnamization" policy. By late 1971, only 140,000 American soldiers remained in Vietnam, down from a high of 540,000 in mid-to-late 1968. A few American troops were still stationed in Cam Ranh Bay, once the Army's Biggest supply base in Vietnam. In a conversation with a Catholic priest who lived near the base, FitzGerald was unable to convince him that the Americans would soon be pulling out. It was utterly inconceivable to him that anyone would build what Ethel Payne described in one of her stories as "a colossus," and then abandon it, FitzGerald recalled. The priest's disbelief was yet another demonstration of the disconnect between the American and Vietnamese lifestyles in their most basic expectations. Everywhere she looked during that six-month stay in Vietnam, the changes she encountered seemed "like water running out of the bath."

Even in Duc Lap, the village so scarred by the war in 1966, the place that had become the yardstick by which FitzGerald judged the progress of the war, life seemed to have improved immeasurably. The place that had once suffered so from its unfortunate location at the intersection of two major supply routes used by the opposing armies had come back to life, particularly in the outer hamlets. It was no longer the dangerous place she had described to American readers in September 1966. On one occasion, FitzGerald and her interpreter, Tran Ba Loc, crossed one of the Delta's many invisible lines and realized that they were in a Viet Cong enclave. Very little distinguished the opposing forces in those days; the peasants looked, dressed, and acted much like each other. But, FitzGerald remembered, "they spoke in a way that I did realize they belonged to the other side." It was the first time she knew for certain that she was in the presence of "the enemy."

Loc, FitzGerald discovered, was an especially effective interpreter on those forays outside of Saigon in 1971. That he spoke French rather than English, she realized, changed the dynamic of their interviews. An odd, colonial issue sometimes complicated the way English-speaking interpreters did their work because Vietnamese who had learned English had usually done so out of a wish to get ahead in the new system. The misgivings many of them felt about those motivations sometimes tainted their translations of the thoughts Vietnamese subjects expressed. With Loc, an older man who had learned French as a child, nothing was held back. He unselfconsciously translated everything and enlarged FitzGerald's understanding of how the peasants viewed this interlude of calm and the future they anticipated. After her return to the United States early in 1972, she labored on her *New Yorker* article for weeks. Unfortunately, soon after it was completed but before it was published, the North Vietnamese crossed the Demilitarized Zone on March 30 and launched their Easter Offensive, a major operation that had been long awaited in the South. Everything she had written about the new face of Vietnam and its future was made moot by the renewed fighting. The article was never published.

Fire in the Lake was published in August 1972. The result of all the years of research and writing was a triumph. Although she has written three other books (on subjects far removed from Vietnam) and countless articles since, *Fire in the Lake* will doubtless remain the work for which FitzGerald will be best remembered.

No less a luminary than Stanley Hoffmann, FitzGerald's former professor at Harvard, wrote on page one of the *New York Times Book Review* that she had written "a compassionate and penetrating account of the collision of two societies that remain untranslatable to one another." That review gave her special pleasure because Hoffmann's judgment of her work had not always been so laudatory. During her undergraduate years at Radcliffe, she took his French intellectual history course and recalled getting a C, either on a term paper or perhaps even for the course itself. Some of America's most respected voices echoed Hoffmann's praise for *Fire*. Writing in the *Washington Monthly*, the author Taylor Branch called FitzGerald "a poetess." He praised her for sticking to the Vietnam perspective of the war rather than heeding the views of the experts in Washington, who were far removed from the consequences of their decisions. "There was a powerful but camouflaged impact on the other end of all those LBJ orders and McNamara memos, and *Fire in the Lake* is a vitally important ground-level view of the awesome effect that even bumbling governments can have on the lives and reality far away from those who make the decisions." Reviews in *Newsweek* and in *Time,* so long a defender of the war, were equally generous. *Newsweek*'s reviewer praised the book: "FitzGerald fills in an enormous gap by explaining the Vietnamese from their own point of view and by describing the war from the perspective of Vietnamese culture. She asserts that American ignorance of cultural differences eventually led to moral and political catastrophe." *Time* applauded her for the "sense of historic perspective that she brings to a roiling subject."

Even the CIA recognized the value of her work. A few months after *Fire in The Lake* was published, an unnamed CIA officer suggested that she be invited to speak at the agency's Senior Seminar. A CIA memo written on December 6, 1972, stated: "Despite Subject's well-known anti-U.S. attitude regarding the Vietnam War, it is not believed that her appearance at the Senior Seminar would cause embarrassment to the Agency. It is, therefore recommended that she be Security Approved for this activity." FitzGerald was flattered to be invited and accepted the invitation. Years later, she recalled that the seminar participants had asked "tough" questions. After its publication, excerpts of FitzGerald's book were published in Hanoi newspapers. When FitzGerald was invited to visit Hanoi in 1974 with several members of America's anti-war movement, the itinerary included a seminar on *Fire in the Lake* in which she participated. Clearly, the North Vietnamese applauded her work.

At the time of its publication, a few critics weighed in with less than positive appraisals. The *New Republic* faulted *Fire in the Lake* for relying too much on generalities. Predictably perhaps, the conservative *National Review* called it the newest of many "cleverly written and emphatically pessimistic accounts" of Vietnam. The book, it concluded, had occasionally indulged in "blatantly rhetorical overkill." Nonetheless, the reviewer conceded that "there has been to this point no book on recent Vietnam with the power and conviction of *Fire in the Lake.*" Robert Komer, the Phoenix program director, took particular exception to FitzGerald's depictions of the pacification program in Vietnam. In a letter to Hoffmann at Harvard, Komer said that FitzGerald's analysis was flawed.

In a more private appraisal, Martha Gellhorn applauded the book in a letter to FitzGerald: "I cannot express my admiration and also my gratitude," Gellhorn wrote. "It is a dazzling work. If you were run over by a bus tomorrow, you would have paid your full entrance fee to life, having made something entirely your own, entirely valuable and unique and permanent." The intensity of both women's opposition to the war and their anger with the political leaders who continued to pursue victory despite clear evidence that success was impossible, led them to campaign for U.S. Senator George McGovern, the Democrat who challenged Richard Nixon's bid for reelection in 1972.

Despite all the praise, and even after her book made the best-seller lists in 1972, FitzGerald remained dubious about the value and acceptance of its conclusions. In fact, she could barely believe her good fortune when a representative of the Pulitzer Prize committee called her in April 1973 to tell her that *Fire in the Lake* had won the 1972 prize for nonfiction. Indeed, the import of the news initially eluded her. She gave her thanks, hung up the phone, and went back to her "typing." FitzGerald's Pulitzer medallion strung on a red ribbon was, for a time, draped around the bust of a Buddha in her New York apartment. In addition to the Pulitzer, *Fire in the Lake* won the 1972 Bancroft Prize for History, a National Book Award, the Sidney Hillman Award, and a George Polk Award. But the prizes meant little at a time when her despair over the war festered. "I was glad," she recalled. "But you have to understand that I continued to be obsessed about the war, so that everything that happened to this book of mine was hardly as important as what was happening in Vietnam."

FitzGerald held the press partially responsible for the tragedy the war had become. Her general view was that in its coverage of the war, the press had functioned as a handmaiden of government interests by parroting the huge deceptions served up by a succession of American leaders. What she derisively called the media's "obsequious posture" had distorted news of the war by "presenting the views of the Administration officials on the front page, those of congressional critics on the back pages and those of people leading large demonstrations nowhere at all." Television, she added, by "bending over double in the direction of the Administration," had failed to live up to its promise to change the nature of foreign reporting and the relationship of Americans to war. "The medium proved incapable of describing the situation or presenting the issues in comprehensible form." The images shown in American living rooms might as well have been stills, she insisted. "Soldiers hanging on the helicopter struts, refugees running down a road." The same scenes were shot a hundred times during the war, and now, as ever, it was not at all clear what was happening." Further, television reports mindlessly repeated a precise, uncritical echo of the administration interests. Perhaps television executives decided the war was simply too hot a political issue on which to take a position for fear of offending some of their viewers, she conjectured. But, "in refusing to take a point of view, they robbed meaning from the lives of everyone who had ever fought in the war or protested against it."

As the Watergate scandal unfolded in the early 1970s, she sometimes wished that its dramatic formula could be grafted on to the Vietnam War—then maybe the press would step up to the challenges. She applauded Bob Woodward and Carl Bernstein, the journalists who had so methodically uncovered the story in the *Washington Post*. FitzGerald saw in that scandal all the qualities of drama—"time, place, character and justice done." What had started with a seemingly innocuous burglary at Democratic national headquarters at the Watergate Hotel in June 1972, finally resulted, after two years of manipulation, stalling, and dissembling, in the first-ever resignation of an American president who was facing certain impeachment.

In unpublished notes in her archive, FitzGerald recorded her lament that, unlike Watergate, Vietnam had "none of the same dramatic unities. And no denouement." The war instead "became something we live with—college seniors were not born when the involvement began. And deception as normal. . . . From the Tonkin Gulf Resolution to the cover-up of the investigation of the Mylai massacre to the covert bombing by Gen. Lavalle of NVN in winter 1972."

In both the war and the Watergate scandal, espionage tactics were employed to take away the rights of people. Both situations stood as examples of the "use of presidential power against the constitution and the laws of the land for the sole purpose of maintaining personal power, personal prestige."

Although no one had died in the Watergate shenanigans, she noted, "Indochinese are still dying under our bombs, not only in Cambodia but in Vietnam. And they will continue to do so unless Congress can cut off the appropriations."

To those who mouthed the familiar refrain about the possibilities of a bloodbath in the face of an American withdrawal, FitzGerald had an exquisitely simple answer. She once questioned a Vietnamese associate about what he thought would happen if the United States withdrew. He told her: "Don't ask us that. It's none of your business. We just want you to leave." Adding her own view to her notes of that conversation, FitzGerald wrote: "And I agree."

5

Foreign Journalists Report the War

What a bloody awful waste.
—KATE WEBB

KATE WEBB WAS losing her nerve. As she sat at the bar of Hong Kong's August Moon Hotel, each gulp of beer brought her closer to aborting her journey. Suddenly, her plan to go to Saigon and become a war correspondent seemed overwhelming, even foolhardy. Returning home to Sydney was looking more like the sensible move, even though doing so might mean she would never be able to understand the war that was affecting the lives of so many Australians. Hours earlier, she had learned that Bernard B. Fall, the Vietnam scholar and journalist whose war reportage she so admired, the man whose writing embodied all that she aspired to become in Vietnam, had been killed by a land mine during an operation with the U.S. Marines in Vietnam. Fall, a Frenchman, died along South Vietnam's Highway 1, a road he had famously named the Street Without Joy in his book about the French war in Indochina. Her plan was to follow in his footsteps. Now the hope that she someday might meet Fall, perhaps somewhere along that street without joy, and learn from him still more about Southeast Asia, evaporated. Now that

Fall was dead, she began to wonder whether her plan to cover the war bordered on madness.

Moments later, three young U.S. Air Force pilots at the bar jerked Kate Webb's thoughts into reverse. "Where are you going?" they asked. In that instant, her plan was back on track. "To Saigon," she told them confidently. With no job prospects, $200 in her pocket, and an old Remington portable typewriter her father had given her, Webb flew to Saigon the next day. She was twenty-three. Officially, Webb was on vacation from her job with the *Daily Mirror,* a newspaper in Sydney, Australia. She had not had the nerve to resign before she set off for Hong Kong because an explanation would have been required. If she had had to admit she was setting off to become a war correspondent in South Vietnam, she feared, "I'd be laughed out of court."

Between early March 1967 until the war ended in March 1975, Webb spent several years in Southeast Asia covering the conflict for United Press International. Indeed, she is said to have been the first woman to become a resident correspondent for an American wire service. Her description of the American embassy in the hours after the Tet Offensive began in early 1968 is widely quoted in histories of the war. The compound "was like a butcher shop in Eden, beautiful but ghastly," she wrote. "The green lawns and white ornamental fountains were strewn with bodies." In 1971, she had the distinction of reading her own obituaries that had run in newspapers around the world two weeks after she disappeared in Cambodia. In those reports of her death, Webb was praised as "one of the keenest war reporters in Indochina, and one of the most attractive, even in combat fatigues." By the time the war was over, no less a light than Gloria Emerson praised her as the reporter who wrote the best military stories in Cambodia.

As one of several foreign journalists who reported the war in American newspapers and magazines, Webb's work gave American readers an international perspective of the war, in an approach that lacked some of the cold war fervor then so entwined in America's thinking about the world. Oriana Fallaci, the idiosyncratic Italian writer whose interviews with world leaders often made front-page news, and Catherine Leroy, a budding French photojournalist, both viewed the war through a European lens. Webb—by virtue of her British parents, her birth in New Zealand, and her upbringing in Australia—had the advantage of a unique Euro-Asian outlook. She understood the deep longings in Asian countries to rid themselves of their colonial overlords. Leroy, who grew up in Paris, had a clear memory of the fall of

Dien Bien Phu, and she understood how deeply that defeat had wounded France's spirit.

Unlike Fallaci, Webb and Leroy arrived in South Vietnam as unknown and near-destitute would-be freelancers, much in the way Emerson had arrived in 1956. Webb's often anonymous daily dispatches for UPI ran in newspapers around the world. Leroy's freelance photographs appeared on the Associated Press wires and in America's most distinguished picture magazines. In the daring she brought to her work, Webb was to Vietnam what Maggie Higgins had been to Korea. In the enduring quality of the images of combat she captured, Leroy was Southeast Asia's Margaret Bourke-White. Both Webb and Leroy were raised by bright, well-educated mothers who placed few boundaries on their daughters' aspirations. New Zealand, where Webb was born, and Australia, where she spent much of her early life, were especially progressive societies in the context of women's rights. What little the two women read or heard about feminism in Saigon left them with a sense that it had no relevance to their lives. Neither woman encountered the difficulties that so many men in the military had anticipated the presence of women would create. Webb quickly learned that "taking a pee" in the field without attracting undue attention was simply a matter of donning a lightweight poncho and discreetly squatting. So much for all those military officials who had fretted for so many decades about facilities for women. Days and nights spent out in the field with soldiers had a way of obliterating gender. "Basically, you're just trying to survive," Leroy explained. "You're just as miserable as the men—and you smell bad anyway." Only after Webb visited the United States did she begin to understand why so many American women had embraced feminism. Both women covered the everyday grind of the war in ways that won the admiration of their colleagues in the Saigon press corps. They were a pair of spitfires whose war coverage is certain to endure because of the clarity and insight of their words and pictures.[1]

In her neatly ironed cotton sun dresses and sandals, Kate Webb always looked like a cross between a waif and a school girl on the streets of Saigon. Her feet were almost as dirty as the sidewalks. A shy, unprepossessing exterior served to mask her intelligence and deep understanding of Asians' world views. It also masked her will. Although the expletive-filled vocabulary of her later years was still undeveloped, and she wasn't yet known to punch adver-

---

1. Catherine Leroy, who lived in Los Angeles, died of cancer in 2006. Kate Webb died of cancer in Australia in 2007.

saries in the face, as she would later in her four-decade career as a journalist, her work in Vietnam and, later, Cambodia, established Webb as a formidable presence. Southeast Asia's landscape and climate, its culture and politics, its geography and people—with their yearning for independence—had long been familiar to Webb when she set off for Saigon. Besides her heavy type-writer, Webb took along her fascination with the crumbling colonial empires of post–World War II Asia—another subject she had hoped to discuss with Bernard Fall. She had a nuanced view of the war and an understanding that the leaders of Southeast Asia's changing societies often exploited Communism as a way to serve the nationalist aspirations that so many countries in the re-gion entertained after World War II. Webb had first encountered the rem-nants of colonialism in 1957 during a stop in Singapore on a family journey to Europe. She sensed stirrings of discord between the country's wealthy white masters and the hordes of impoverished coolies who served them. On a visit to Malaya in 1959, she got an even closer look at the region's often ago-nizing struggles. At her father's urging, as a college student, she had explored Muslim sentiments in the mosques. She understood that Southeast Asia's eleven nations each had a distinct identity. In the late 1950s and early 1960s, she studied the emerging independence movements in Malaya, Singapore, and Indonesia. Partly because the Americans and British saw those move-ments as a danger to the delicate balance between the superpowers, they questioned whether the former colonies were capable of self-rule. But Webb understood that from the perspective of those seeking independence, ques-tions about an individual nation's capabilities were no one's business but their own. She recognized those widening movements not as simple clashes that pitted Communism against democracy but rather as complicated and often highly individual struggles by indigenous peoples trying to rid themselves of the colonial overlords who had milked their abundant natural resources and of the feudal sovereigns who had served those overlords. "In the immediate postwar period, there was this huge hope in all of their countries," Webb ex-plained. They had the sense that 'we are free, colonialism is over.'"

Among the colonial powers of Western Europe, however, fighting World War II never meant that they would lose their colonies, Webb explained. And because America was showing no inclination to leave the Philippines, the ques-tion the European powers asked was simple: "You intend to stay in the Philip-pines, so why can't the rest of us go back?" The French returned to Indochina, the British to Malaya, the Dutch to Indonesia, all supported in large part by the United States. Communism was the convenient rationale each country used to reclaim its former colony. But even though fears of Communist expansion were hardly groundless, Webb knew that indigenous leaders such as Ho Chi Minh were, above all else, pragmatists. They were not artless innocents but cagey and forward-thinking strategists who perceived Communism not necessarily as a desirable form of government but rather as a step in the journey to independence. Anti-colonialism and Communism "got all mixed up in Western eyes," Webb explained. "Communism's appeal to native populations was its advocacy of anti-colonial and anti-feudal policies. It's easy to see now, but it was very complicated back then." Webb also understood that the Vietnamese were hardly the guileless children of the American imagination, likely to be duped by the Moscow-Beijing axis. In no way were they a people too backward to assume self-rule, contrary to the description of them in a U.S. State Department report on the region.

Webb's grasp of Southeast Asian history and understanding of the shifting geopolitical relationships in the postwar years gave her a perspective of the war that most of her American colleagues lacked. An Australian citizen living in South Vietnam explained those shifts to the *New York Times* reporter R. W. Apple in the mid-1960s: "Before 1945, we tended to think of ourselves as European, however absurd that may seem. Since the end of the war, we've had no doubt that we are Asians."

Webb's family ties to England further nourished her understanding of international politics. Her parents were descended from two prominent British families. Their own wide-ranging interests taught Kate to look around the world with a studious eye. Webb's father, Leicester Webb, was just a year old when his own father left England to become a land surveyor in Wellington, on New Zealand's North Island. Leicester Webb was assigned to duty with the Army Education Center during World War II and later became a highly respected political scientist. In the immediate aftermath of the war, he was always off to Geneva or Taiwan or Korea to attend conferences where he was either a representative of or an observer for New Zealand's government. He worked with New Zealand's Department of Stabilisation on issues involving emergency marketing, the government office that administered rationing policies during and after the war.

Her mother, Caroline Mabel West-Watson, emigrated to Christchurch from England when she was eighteen, when her father was named the Anglican bishop for New Zealand. He assumed the additional title of archbishop and held both offices after 1940. She returned to England, where she attended the London School of Economics, and later, in the 1930s, she traveled to Canton to study Asian history. One of the most enduring lessons Kate learned from her mother was how to study history. Kate was twelve when her mother watched her at her homework one evening, poring over a history book about the Philippine Islands. She was "sitting there reading one of those big print history books for kids," when her mother said: "Don't ever read just one version of history." No single history text can provide a thorough understanding of the past, she counseled. With that, her mother went to the family's book collection and brought down the Cambridge Modern History editions of Filipino history, one that incorporated the American perspective, and translations of the German, Japanese, and Spanish viewpoints in three other volumes. From those books Webb learned something important about the United States: "America argued that it had to occupy the Philippines, otherwise the Germans would. It was the same argument they later made about South Vietnam."

Dinner table conversation in the Webb household invariably centered on international affairs. Rachel Miller, Webb's older sister, remembers how her school friends later told her that as youngsters, "they always loved to come to our house for dinner. They said, 'Your parents talked about such interesting things.' Their own parents' conversations seemed to be quite dull in contrast." In Miller's recollection, Webb and their father seemed to have a special affinity for discussions about international politics. "I remember them going for long evening walks together talking about politics, the meaning of life, and everything else," Miller remembered. "They also used to go fishing together."

Their father joined the political science faculty at the Australian National University in Canberra in 1951. When Kate was thirteen, he took a year-long sabbatical to travel through Europe with his wife and three children. During that journey in the mid-1950s, so many of the countries they had talked about, places well beyond Asia and the Pacific, came to life. England was an awakening for the Webb siblings. Their parents had always spoken of England as home. "It was quite an amazing thing for us to see where our family had come from," Miller recalled. That trip "certainly opened up different worlds for us." In Italy, their father analyzed the country's growing Communist movement and the prospect that the Vatican might ultimately be surrounded by a sea of red. From Rome, where the family had lived in inexpensive pensiones, the family traveled to France and Germany, where Kate Webb spent several months in school. At every stop on their year-long odyssey, the ruin and rubble of World War II were still very much in evidence.

Webb started college when she was sixteen; she attended Australian National University, and later transferred to Melbourne National University, where she earned a degree in symbolic logic, a discipline in philosophy grounded in the question of why "A plus B doesn't necessarily add up to C," Webb explained. "I guess I was trying to learn how to think." She was occasionally dissatisfied with her studies; she longed for more discussion, a larger exchange of ideas. When she shared those sentiments with her father, he told her: "It's all there, just go out and find it." She was eighteen when her parents were killed in a car crash. Later, she was unable to identify the year in which they had died—1960 or 1961. "I blotted it out," she said.

Happenstance and Saint George led Webb to her career in journalism. By the time she graduated from college in 1964, her decision to become an artist led her to seek an apprenticeship with a painter in Sydney. But when she reached the city, she discovered that the artist under whose tutelage she was to work had left town. She apprenticed herself to a stained glass artist instead and worked as a waitress in a hamburger joint to support her minimal needs. But an accident in the artist's workshop suddenly created a need for much more money than she earned in tips. A large stained glass panel depicting Saint George, a warrior reputed to have slain a dragon and later died a martyr's death and became the patron saint of England, slipped from her grasp as she removed it from a kiln. In those shards of blue and red and yellow glass lay her future as a journalist.

Webb's boss demanded reimbursement for the loss, about $1,000. That is when she applied for a secretarial position with the *Sydney Daily Mirror* but stumbled instead into a writing job after she flunked a typing test. "So they shipped me off to the newsroom to be a reporter," Webb remembered. She joined an apprentice program with five other aspiring journalists. For several months, she learned shorthand, studied newspaper style, and joined the newspaper's staffers as they covered beats in City Hall, the courts, education, crime, sports, and fashion. She worked at the usual drudgery reserved for a newsroom's newest and lowliest recruits. Besides running a reporter's typed stories to an editor on the desk, her duties included writing abbreviated descriptions of movies listed in the newspaper's television program guide. At the time, the *Mirror* had one female editorial writer and a few women on the copy desk. Most others wrote for the women's page. Following standard practice, she joined the newsroom staff after her apprenticeship in the entry-level classification of a "D-grade" reporter. "So I went to work for Rupert Murdoch before he was Rupert Murdoch," as Webb liked to tell it.

Straight news began evolving as her forte. Her first beat was education and the church, with occasional assignments in fashion, but Webb kept gravitating to the police beat. Ride-alongs with the cops on their rounds were a "big thing" for her in those early years. Out in the field with the cops, she used the police radio to dictate her stories to a rewrite man back in the office. She covered bush fires outside the city and recalled how on one assignment her high heels melted into the ground; she flew by light plane to the outback where a drought was in progress; she buddied up with the newspaper's photographers, who seemed to be in on all the biggest action stories. "I'd take shit jobs just to be around them," she recalled.

Webb also read and analyzed stories written by Peter Gladwyn, the *Mirror* senior writer whose dispatches she admired. "I loved reading his work," she recalled. "It was like layer cake. If you didn't know much about the subject, you could just lick off the cream and understand it. But if you were an expert on the issue, you could read the story and have the whole cake." He became her role model, the reporter whose work so often made her wish, "Oh, if I could only write like that." To her great joy, her first bylined article ran as a sidebar to an article Gladwyn wrote about the India-Pakistan War. Her story described the reaction to the war among Indian and Pakistani students studying in Australia.

As a cold war ally of the United States, Australia had sent 4,500 troops to Vietnam: the 1st Battalion of the Royal Australian Infantry as well as supporting units. Some Australians maintained a sense of splendid isolation, secure in their distance from so many of the world's trouble spots, according to Webb. During the years when American school children held dress rehearsals for a nuclear attack by huddling beneath their desks, the Aussies looked at the world with a view that resembled an "On the Beach" scenario. They would survive as the earth's last living inhabitants. Others, however, echoed American fears that Communists could overrun their western beachheads. Those Australians appeared to think of Communism as an enemy better confronted in Vietnam than in their front yards. So, although the military and Prime Minister Henry Holt might declare that Australia "will be all the way with LBJ," popular sentiment at home reflected no unanimity on the war.

Webb's first encounter with the Vietnam story came in October 1966 during President Lyndon B. Johnson's three-day state visit to Australia. LBJ and Lady Bird Johnson received an enthusiastic welcome from the country's leaders, and record-breaking crowds welcomed them in Melbourne, Sydney, and Brisbane. At the same time, the many Australians who opposed their country's participation in the war also took to the streets. Others jeered the president and tussled with members of the Secret Service detail. The most intense demonstrations were staged in Sydney by protesters who broke through police lines and lay down in front of the motorcade. In the city's Hyde Park area, demonstrators hurled paint balls at the presidential limousine, shouted derisive slogans, and carried banners denouncing the president: "Tomorrow's Hitler Today's Johnson."

"There was an enormous police crackdown," recalled Webb, one of several reporters assigned to the story. "We managed to get photographers stationed at a few key areas." She, meanwhile, was trying to stay close to the American president, an effort that earned her a kick in the shins from Rufus Youngblood, one of Johnson's Secret Service agents, who was on foot alongside the bubbletop limousine as the paint balls landed on his head. By then, war and the idea of covering it as a journalist had started to intrigue Webb. In her office, she overheard editors tell never-ending war stories about their adventures in World War II. Most of the men had served either in the Australian army, navy, or air force. War began sounding like the ultimate ride-along.

Not long after the LBJ visit, Webb started asking her editors why they hadn't assigned a reporter to Vietnam. "We had troops there, but nobody seemed interested in covering them." The idea that she could do the job kept growing. Only later, in South Vietnam, did she discover that the Australian army had a rigid "no women" rule for reporters.[2] Getting nowhere with her own editors, she began asking around the three wire service offices in Sydney. She'd like to go to Vietnam, she told them; what were the possibilities? "They just laughed," she recalled, "not in an unkind way, but they told me that a big war like Vietnam takes experts."

Rather than shake her growing fascination with the war and the possibility of covering it, all the negative responses made the idea more irresistible. That left her with the only option open to most women: She would find her way to South Vietnam on her own. Unwittingly, Maury Wilmott, a UPI photographer on a short visit to his home in Sydney, provided the last bit of encouragement. Webb overheard him describing to her male colleagues all the stringer jobs that were to be had for people who simply showed up in Saigon. "I thought he must be full of shit," Webb remembered. She went anyway.

---

2. Commanders of the troops from New Zealand had the same rule, and Korean military enforced a "no reporter" rule.

Webb made her move in February 1967. At the August Moon Hotel in Hong Kong, she wrote a resignation letter, pounding out the terse sentences on her father's old typewriter. Recalling her decision many decades later, Webb said, "I was nuts." In retrospect, Rachel Miller was hardly surprised that her sister would go off to Vietnam. "I don't think she has ever been conventional," she said. Miller has no memory of knowing about her sister's intention. Although Webb might have dropped some obscure hint, Miller recalled, "she never made it plain what she was doing. If she had, I'd certainly recall being worried."

Webb's only recollection of her arrival in Saigon was that the streets of the city looked so busy. On the ride into town from the airport, she was astonished by the convoys of American-made military trucks and Jeeps that filled the air with fumes, the locust swarms of motor scooters that darted through the streets, and all the honking taxi cabs and other cars that clogged the streets. Her first move was to find Wilmott, who had by then returned to South Vietnam. He seemed taken aback by her arrival, perhaps because he barely knew her.

Before she left Sydney, Webb had set her sights on writing for UPI. She had worked for a time on her newspaper's wire desk, and it always struck her that the UPI copy was crisper and more comprehensive than that of the Associated Press and Reuters. So in Saigon she sought out Bryce Miller, UPI's Saigon bureau chief. His response to her request for stringer assignments was hardly encouraging. In Webb's recollection, Miller was especially reluctant to gamble on her because he was dissatisfied with the results of stringer assignments he had given the wife of a UPI photographer in Saigon. Beyond that, Miller had still another problem: Although she was twenty-three, Webb looked more like a sixteen-year-old kid. "What do I want with a girl?" he asked. Of course, plenty of "girls" were covering the Vietnam War by then: Frankie FitzGerald, Catherine Leroy, Jurate Kazickas, and Beverly Deepe, to name a few. Still, the permanent full-time positions in the AP and UPI Saigon bureaus were all held by men in 1967.

Joining a wire service was a huge ambition for a fledgling journalist in the 1960s, especially for a woman. During the Vietnam era, competition between America's two major wire services was merciless. Years after the war, John Macbeth of the *Far Eastern Economic Review*, in a tribute on the occasion of Webb's retirement from Agence France-Presse, wrote that the services were king in the 1960s. "In those days in Asia, at the height of the Indochina War, the real war was between UPI and AP. Winning was an all-consuming passion.

It was competition at its best." Peter Arnett, for example, noted in his memoir that Associated Press beat United Press International by a full five minutes in breaking the story of the surrender of the South Vietnamese government in April 1975, "proving again that while wars may start and end and leaders rise and fall, the only important determinant in the news business is to be first with the story."

Despite his doubts about Webb, by early April, Miller sent a letter to the Military Assistance Command Vietnam Office of Information explaining that Webb was being considered for employment and requesting temporary accreditation "so that we may view her work." Miller's letter, along with one from Ann Bryan, editor of the *Overseas Weekly,* were the start Webb needed. Bryan, Webb recalls, "saved my life. She made me a reporter."

Bryan was a gutsy young American who had been writing in Germany for the *Overseas Weekly,* a small-circulation underground newspaper established in the late 1950s as an alternative to the more establishment-oriented voice of *Stars and Stripes,* published by the U.S. Army. Bryan began working for the privately owned weekly in Frankfurt in 1959. In late 1965, she was assigned to open a bureau in Saigon where, in later years, she became something of a "mother figure" to young women like Webb who were chasing their dreams of covering the war. Initially, the U.S. military had tried to block the *Weekly*'s distribution to soldiers in Vietnam by banning it in the PX (Post Exchange) system. Only after the paper won a lawsuit against Secretary of Defense Robert S. McNamara for violating the First Amendment and the due process clause of the Constitution was it sold on PX newsstands in Vietnam. Its nickname among GIs, *Oversexed Weekly,* was a barometer of the ease with which it took on issues likely to be ignored by its more staid counterpart. As America committed hundreds of thousands of soldiers to the fight in Vietnam, the paper's hard-edged reporting earned it a wide following among grunts who welcomed its candor on issues critical to them: drug abuse, assorted courts-martial, and, in a practice unique to the latter stages of Vietnam War, the fragging—or assassination—of an officer in one's own fighting unit. Those killings were often accomplished with a fragmentation grenade, hence the origin of the term. Years later, the newspaper was praised for the way it "best conveyed the real, as opposed to the official, picture of the war as it affected American GIs."

When Kate Webb arrived at the *Weekly* office, as so many freelancers did, Bryan explained the paper's mission. It was determined "to ferret out the truth of events by interviewing the grunts and enlisted men who were actually there on the spot." And she reminded Webb that "the job description of the information officers said that journalists should get access only to people, places, and information that would support the official version of events."

During Webb's early months in Vietnam, Miller at UPI assigned her small stories. Most were inconsequential home-towners, stories about average-Joe American soldiers in Vietnam that were aimed at local readers of regional newspapers across America. She also wrote for English-language Vietnamese newspapers, which paid her pennies per column inch.

Webb's big break came from a tip Bryan handed her about the alleged defection of an American GI who opposed the war on moral grounds. Webb recalls making her way to Cam Ranh Bay, where the young soldier had been stationed. He was a Korean War orphan who had been adopted by an American major. Like his father, he had chosen life in the military. When Webb arrived, the military brass "were all off at some big piss-up." That gave her unfettered access to the GIs who had known the young defector. They showed her his locker and told her how he had jumped on a Japan-bound cargo ship and taken refuge there in the Cuban embassy. The soldier, they said, had become increasingly upset by the U.S. treatment of Vietnamese civilians and had slowly stopped talking to his compatriots. Back in Saigon, Bryce Miller liked Webb's story, and the "brownie points" she scored brought her closer to her dream.

In the same way Bryan had a year before, Webb found a cold-water room above a shoe repair shop located on a small side street not far from the UPI office. The most important feature of these digs was the willingness of the shoe shop owners who lived downstairs to lend her their iron. Although colleagues in later years claimed never to have seen Webb wearing a dress—one insisted that that prospect was less likely than the "pope conducting Mass in a leather jock strap"—in South Vietnam, her wardrobe was a concern. "I wore cotton dresses and I always wanted my dresses ironed," she said. Though living in Saigon in those years was cheap, Webb endured lean times during the first months of her Vietnam adventure. Even though one could eat at outdoor food stalls for little more than pennies, she said, "I was quite often hungry during those early days. I had what I called my chicken and no rice days."

One big break with UPI came in November 1967 when Jacqueline Kennedy visited Angkor Wat, Cambodia. Webb was assigned to work the story with Ray Herndon, based in UPI's Singapore bureau. At the time, Cambodian visa regulations banned entry to Americans living in Vietnam. With her British passport and fluency in French, Webb was hired as a freelancer to cover the story in Phnom Penh. Jackie, then still Mrs. Kennedy, had accepted Prince Norodom Sihanouk's invitation for a "private visit" to Cambodia. The theatrical prince, however, staged an extravaganza that captured the world's attention. During the welcoming ceremony at his palace, Sihanouk, with a microphone in hand, announced, "And now Mrs. Kennedy will feed the sacred elephants!" As though by magic, the crowds parted and huge painted elephants appeared in a cloud of dust, their trunks curled upward in a gesture of which Rudyard Kipling would have approved. Mrs. Kennedy managed to maintain a slightly strained but still dazzling smile. The microphones, however, picked up her despairing groan, "Oh, no."

As Beverly Deepe had earlier in the decade, Webb was determined to develop friends and acquaintances among the Vietnamese people. She came to know bar girls and priests, students and soldiers, street kids and military policemen. The Vietnamese journalists she befriended were especially helpful. "There were lots of issues they could not write about," she explained. So they fed her tips on stories that were off limits to them. Too often, however, those stories were of little interest to her American employers. "It was difficult to put stories about Vietnamese politics into language that UPI and the Americans thought was significant."

Stories in the American press occasionally had dire consequences for Vietnamese nationals. A peace candidate opposing President Nguyen Van Thieu, for example, was sentenced to hard labor after telling a UPI reporter that a coalition government with the North was a desirable possibility. The verdict inflamed Webb. "He was convicted on our story," she said later. She was so angry that she kicked a step outside her office and broke a toe. In the weeks that she hobbled around Saigon, occasionally exchanging a crutch wave with one of the many amputees who were part of Saigon's street scene, she met a man who became one of her best Vietnamese sources—one of Thieu's bodyguards whom she occasionally joined on evening forays to opium dens. He taught her about Vietnam's neutralist Hoa Hao sect, to which he belonged. And he occasionally provided her with terrific inside information, which she appropriately attributed to "sources close to President Thieu."

The first military operation Webb joined was with a platoon in the 25th Division. On a mission at a rubber plantation near Cu Chi, not far from Saigon, she didn't see much action, but she did learn about how to equip herself for field operations. "The first sergeant taught me how to assemble a light pack." Instead of the bulky, blow-up mattress that she was toting, he suggested a hammock made of sturdy but lightweight parachute silk. He taught her how to use mosquito repellent to get leeches off her skin. He showed her how to use an entrenching tool to dig a foxhole and one's own latrine hole. When she first witnessed combat, a small fire fight during a patrol, Webb said, "I was so scared that I wet my pants. I hoped the GIs would think that it was sweat and that no one would notice. Then I saw that some of the GIs had wet pants, too, and it didn't matter any more."

The war, at least as it played out for Webb, never had the narcotic quality that it had had for Dickey Chapelle. Battle seemed more likely to sicken rather than exhilarate Webb. She participated in military missions to bear witness rather than to glorify war and the men who fought it. She consciously sought to build a wall between the horrors of what she saw in battle and her very different life in Saigon. "Whenever I came back to Saigon, I'd always try to go home and shower before I went to the office to file my story," Webb explained. "It came to represent a separation from what I had seen."

As time allowed, she developed an acquaintance with dozens of journalists in the Saigon press corps. She never hung around with the big names in town, she said, referring to the likes of *New York Times* correspondents and the stars of network news. "I was much too shy and I would have felt like an idiot trying to be part of that." Besides, having no expense account, she couldn't afford to drink at their favorite watering holes. She did, however, know many of the women in the Saigon press corps. Besides Ann Bryan, she knew Beverly Deepe, and Catherine Leroy, the French photojournalist, who had arrived in Saigon on the familiar one-way ticket. Leroy's pockets were as empty as Webb's when she passed through Tan Son Nhut Airport with about $200. Instead of the battered portable typewriter that Webb had dragged along, Leroy came equipped with a Leica camera. Unlike Webb, however, she had no experience in journalism and barely spoke English. Still, her vision of the war would leave its imprint on the pages of America's two great photojournalism magazines, *Life* and *Look*.

As with Webb, Leroy's diminutive stature (five feet tall, eighty-five pounds) and her youth (age twenty-one), tended to obscure her tenacity and courage. She often braided her blond hair and looked, a Vietnam-era *Newsweek* reporter once wrote, as if her "battle fatigues could have come from a stylish Paris store specializing in children's uniforms." Webb arrived about a year after Leroy, and by then, "the French girl photographer" had stamped her imprint on the history of the war. She had established a reputation as the photographer who spent more time at the front than any other woman in the Saigon press corps. As experienced a hand as the AP photographer Horst

Faas considered her "one of the best four or five freelancers" covering the war. He had first hired her in 1966 when she walked into the AP bureau looking for work. Faas gave her the standard commitment of $15 for a usable picture. "Some weeks I sold more than $200 worth of pictures," Leroy said.

Although her dream of becoming a photojournalist in Vietnam took hold before her teens, most of Leroy's experience with a camera prior to Vietnam consisted of "portraits of friends and my cat." The work of Robert Capa and Henri Cartier-Bresson inspired her. Because expensive photography books were beyond her budget, Leroy spent hours in Paris book shops studying their work. After her graduation, she toiled away at a hostess job in Paris for eight months to save for her Leica and her airfare from Vientiane, where she waited for a visa for nearly a month, before she flew to Saigon. She told her parents that she was going to Vietnam to do a story on Vietnamese women, "keeping the subject matter as vague as possible." In reality, she had no idea what she would do there. She arrived with no particular feelings about the war. "It was very abstract," she recalled. A Frenchman she met on the flight from Vientiane to Saigon introduced her to Charles Bonnay, a photographer for *Life* who "offered me his hospitality for a month, the time for me to get my feet on the ground." Early in his career, Bonnay had parachuted into Dien Bien Phu to take photographs for the French army.

In Southeast Asia, memories of her "difficult childhood" faded. Her middle-class parents had sent her to Catholic boarding schools from elementary school through part of high school. She hated the uniforms, the dormitories, attending Mass at 6:30 A.M., and the constant demand to "submit to authority." She ran away on numerous occasions; sometimes her destination was the Club Saint Germain on the Left Bank where she listened to jazz. "All I wanted to do [was] sing the blues," an abiding passion, she said, since she had turned eleven. In part because she had grown up in a family of musicians, Leroy started playing the piano at the age of four. She recalls being a gifted student, even though she was lax about practicing. She was raised listening to classical music, but lost all interest in it once she discovered jazz. The program *Pour ceux qui aiment le Jazz* (For Those Who Like Jazz) on French radio entranced her. Abandoning the classical pieces that interested her piano teacher, Leroy spent her practice sessions playing tunes like Billie Holiday's "It's My Man." Her mother was aghast. "Do you want to end up in a brothel?" she demanded one day when she discovered her daughter playing a jazz tune and lip-syncing. Leroy recalled, "I closed the piano and I have never since touched it."

Leroy was just nine years old when French military forces were defeated at Dien Bien Phu. Years later, she still recalled the picture stories of the siege that ran for months in *Paris Match,* the weekly French photojournalism magazine. Although her parents never expressed their political opinions and politics was never a topic for dinner table conversation, the fifty-six-day siege evoked intense emotions among the French, especially in her father. She found his reaction curious because, until the 1950s, average people in France seemed to have had little interest in Indochina. "The French army was there. They were professional soldiers, unlike Algeria, where conscripts were called to serve," which created public controversy, she explained.

In November 1953, the French began occupying Dien Bien Phu, a town in a valley near the Laotian border. Listening to French radio news reports of the ensuing siege by Ho Chi Minh's nationalist Viet Minh became a nightly ritual in the Leroy household. The French military hoped to thwart the enemy's access to supply lines that stretched into Laos. French forces occupied the eleven-mile valley with 13,000 troops and further fortified their position with artillery bases in the surrounding hills—bases that the commanding officer, Colonel Christian de La Croix de Castries, purportedly named for his mistresses. That the Viet Minh could move enough men and artillery to mount a successful attack in the mountains above the village was simply unimaginable to the French. But, to their everlasting astonishment, General Vo Nguyen Giap successfully placed an army of 50,000 in those hills. An estimated 200,000 Vietnamese peasants, using bicycles and shoulder poles, moved tons of ammunition and food supplies into position for the Viet Minh. One contemporary military historian called Dien Bien Phu "one of the most spectacular logistical feats in the history of warfare." In preliminary assaults that began in January, the Viet Minh used "human wave" tactics; but, because the casualty rate was so high, they later adopted a more cautious approach. The battle that the French army had so anxiously awaited and had expected would be a quick rout finally began in March 1954. To French amazement, the Viet Minh overran two of the three artillery bases—Beatrice and Gabrielle—in two days. Soon after, the enemy also knocked out the airfield on which the French relied for the delivery of supplies, leaving them to depend on parachute drops for the paratroopers, ammunition, and food they soon desperately needed at their last remaining stronghold, Isabelle. Fearing they might be shot down, pilots of the French C-47 transport aircraft were reluctant to fly re-supply missions. Between mid-March and May 7, when the last stronghold was overrun, the battle became a living hell for the thousands of isolated French soldiers.

"I remember my father crying when Dien Bien Phu fell," Leroy recalled. "He was listening to the radio and hearing about the fall of Isabelle." By then, May 8, 1954, "the siege had lasted one hundred and seventy days, with the last fifty-seven days and nights of hell." After the last radio report, "the room was silent," she recalled. "My father thought that the French soldiers had been abandoned." French military leaders felt they, too, had been abandoned— by the United States, to which they had turned in desperation and begged for air support as the prospect of a Viet Minh victory grew more likely. From the French perspective, the battle for Dien Bien Phu was part of a larger war that the United States had encouraged France—its ally—to fight. That victory over the French marked the end of the First Indochina War and the first time that nationalist forces in a colonial nation had bested their Western European occupiers.

Twelve years later, Catherine Leroy began covering the Second Indochina War, a war in which the adversaries had changed from the French Foreign Legion fighting the Viet Minh to the Americans fighting the Viet Cong and the North Vietnamese army. The war, however, remained essentially the same. Leroy first took photos for a small Paris agency, but soon grew tired of waiting to be paid for her work. "So I pushed the door of the Associated Press," she recalled. When she asked Horst Faas what he needed her to photograph, he showed her a stack of pictures. "I knew immediately what I had to do," she recalled. She discovered in herself a gift for composition. "It's not something I learned. It was just there." Her first AP assignment was the 1966 Buddhist uprising in Da Nang, the same Buddhist demonstrations that drew Frances FitzGerald. Faas soon began buying her photographs.

Leroy's recollections of her first experience in combat were fuzzy more than forty years later. She had no memory of precisely where or when the battle took place, but the sounds and images of it remained with her. She had accompanied a group of American soldiers on a helicopter mission and was immediately pinned down after the landing: "I couldn't see anything. The sound of machine gun fire and explosions was indescribable." Officers were yelling orders, wounded soldiers were screaming in pain, friendly fire was passing above her head and exploding just a few hundred yards away. "I learned quickly to recognize the sounds of war. In fact, I learned to sleep rocked by the sound of artillery shells. It was reassuring."

Her first battle pictures earned her $1,000 from the Associated Press and *Paris Match*. That success, however, had apparently come at the price of alienating a number of people in the U.S. military, a few of whom suggested that her press accreditation to cover the war should be withdrawn. She was, it appears, as unwilling to submit to the authority of the U.S. Army as she had been to submit to the nuns who ran the boarding schools she attended in her childhood. In his Vietnam memoir, Peter Arnett made an observation, substantiated by several memoranda in her accreditation files, that the polite vocabulary she had brought with her from France was soon augmented with a selection of choice epithets; further, she didn't hesitate to hurl them liberally at anyone who tried to block her path to the battlefield. "Peter Arnett is a good friend," Leroy remarked in 2002, "but he is also a male chauvinist," suggesting that the same behavior in male reporters would be acceptable. Besides, what did they expect? She had learned most of her English from the U.S. Marines, she said. As she had for years, Leroy denied that her behavior was improper and insisted that she patterned her actions after the behavior of male correspondents she had witnessed. "My English was very limited," she recalled. "I heard cussing all the time. Yes, I cussed, but no more than anybody else. What is considered perfectly admissible for a man, becomes suddenly unacceptable for a woman. English had become for me the language of violence, and I was repeating what I was listening to all day long."

Her behavior was the subject of a series of letters and memos written between the end of October and mid-December 1966. In memos exchanged by members of the military, she was alternately referred to as "The Unwashed One" and "The Ugly Caucasian." Indeed, her conduct had upset not only the U.S. military public affairs officials but also a few of her own colleagues in the news media who feared that she might get them all barred. One report claimed that on a mission with the U.S. Marines, Leroy had tried to "force her way aboard a helicopter which had already allotted five spaces to correspondents" who had made advance arrangements. When the commander insisted that he could not carry yet another member of the press, "she proceeded to revile him with foul language." The report further noted that this was one of several occasions on which Leroy had berated field and aircraft commanders who did not "acquiesce to her demands." Similar complaints were made about her behavior during a visit aboard the hospital ship USS *Repose,* also in October 1966. A member of the 3rd Marine Amphibious Force denounced her manner as "arrogant and obnoxious" and declared: "Miss LeRoy [*sic*] is not welcome aboard the ship again." Several memoranda in her file indicate that MACV declined to renew her accreditation when it lapsed at the end of October, but decided about a month later to reinstate it on a month-by-month basis. She was banned from I Corps for six months.

Despite those encounters with military officials, Leroy's pace appears to have quickened rather than diminished. In a move that recalled the combat traditions of the photojournalist Dickey Chapelle, who had been killed several months before Leroy's arrival, she earned her paratrooper's wings after she jumped with the 173rd Airborne Brigade in February 1967 on a search-and-destroy mission named Operation Junction City. Parachuting had been her hobby in France, where she had jumped eighty-four times. Operation Junction City was her eighty-fifth jump and, she said, it ranked as her "best souvenir" of Vietnam. On the following morning, Brigadier General John R. Dean came up to her in the jungle and pinned to her fatigues the paratroopers wings with a gold star in honor of that first combat jump.

Leroy had never heard of Dickey Chapelle and knew nothing about her death before she got to South Vietnam. The Marines whom she accompanied on missions, however, soon told her about Chapelle: "They greatly admired her and loved her." Unlike Chapelle's photographs, which tended to glorify war, the images Leroy made often illustrated the terrible physical and emotional wounds war left on those who fought it. Ideology, however, had nothing to do with her work. Although she certainly developed a distaste for the war, it never extended to those who were fighting it, men with whom she had a strong bond. "Friendship, camaraderie, generosity—all of this is what you have in time of war. The GIs were like my brothers. We were the same age and I loved them."

Sometimes Leroy would feel guilty about leaving the troops behind and going back to Saigon where the food was hot and the sheets were clean. Although she avoided a show of emotion out in the field, when she got back to her tiny third-floor flat in Cholon, "sometimes with human brain on my fatigues, the horror of it would hit me and I would sleep for twenty, thirty hours straight." She spent so little time in Saigon between her trips to the field that what little she saw of her neighbors led her to believe that she was surrounded by students who had fled the country's war zones. She learned otherwise one day when she heard a fracas outside her door and discovered three MPs. "Sorry ma'am," one apologized as she opened the door. "We're checking all the whorehouses." There she was in a brothel, just as her mother had predicted. But she wasn't playing jazz.

By 1967, her images of the war were in demand by the photo editors of America's best-read picture magazines. In May 1967, *Life* ran a six-page spread of photographs Leroy took of a battle in which the U.S. Marines suffered their heaviest losses in two years. Leroy was with the second wave of

Marines who stormed Hill 881, one of three hills that became the objects of a bloody twelve-day assault near the Khe Sanh Valley in northwestern South Vietnam. The fight for Hills 861, 881 North, and 881 South, named for their height above sea level, marked some of the most brutal fighting of the war. "I was with Gold Company, 2nd Battalion 3rd Marines when we took off from Hill 861 going to 881. We were hit on the way, but not badly, and reached the hill in a few hours," Leroy recalled. The battle, waged from hilltops surrounding a valley, was eerily similar to the fight for Dien Bien Phu. But the air power the French had lacked thirteen years before was in abundant supply in 1967. The Marines fought for control of Hill 881 in what Robert Pisor of the *Detroit News* later described as "toe-to-toe slugging matches between the shock troops of two nations." As the fighting continued, Leroy took some of her finest photographs of the war, all of them made in some of the most dangerous conditions she ever experienced. It was one of those occasions when she was scared, so scared that "I never thought I was going to get out of this alive." In the inevitable rush that came with survival, those moments of recognition in which she realized she was alive and unhurt, Leroy once explained, "you are alive like you've never felt alive before. It's not something pleasurable in a sensual sense. It's pleasurable in the sense of sheer animal survival. . . . It's very low and very primal." Her photo of the battle, which appeared in *Life*, showed a sequence of images in which a navy medical corpsman reaches a dead Marine and cradles the man in his arm as he searches for a sign of life. Then, with his arm draped gently over the man's body, the young medic casts an anguished gaze into the distance, as if searching for but failing to find a measure of understanding. That image, titled *Corpsman in Anguish*, was part of a body of work that "brought a sensitivity to the war and to the brutality," ruminated Ken Light, director of the University of California at Berkeley's Center for Photography, and the curator of a 2006 university exhibit of Leroy's photos. "I hate to say it, but it's a woman's eye. It was very different than what the men were doing at the time."

Those photographs won Leroy won the 1967 George Polk Award for news photography. "By the time the two and a half weeks of fighting for the hills had ended, the bodies of one hundred and fifty-five Marines had been carried to the graves registration point at Khe Sanh airstrip and four hundred and twenty-five had been wounded, the worst Marine losses for any single battle of the war thus far," according to Neil Sheehan's account of that battle for the hills.

Just as Dickey Chapelle had before her, Leroy developed an affection for the Leathernecks whose courage she chronicled on Hill 881. After that battle, she said she began to think of them in the same way the French thought of their Foreign Legionnaires: "des grandes queules au coeur d'or," or "the big mouths with hearts of gold."

Just two weeks later at a Special Forces camp in Con Thien near the Demilitarized Zone, she was hit by an enemy mortar barrage on her way toward the front lines with Marines. "In my head it was a big sound . . . like a gong. I knew I was hit but was still on my feet. I felt nothing but noticed my right pigtail was all blood. My three cameras were also bloody. . . . They had been high and probably saved my life. I was in bad shape." When the medics arrived, "they started to cut off my fatigues and take off my bra. I was never so embarrassed in my life and kept saying no, no, no." Finally someone declared, "'This is not a time for modesty' and then it was all right." She was evacuated to the navy hospital ship USS *Sanctuary*, where she underwent surgery to remove shrapnel. She spent several weeks recovering aboard the ship, then returned to Saigon looking rather like a "broken bird," one colleague recalled. Without hesitation, she headed right back to the fighting. "Although I am afraid," she told an interviewer that year, "I have to be there when the killing starts. I want people who see my pictures to hate war as I do."

Webb, too, had learned to hate war by late in 1967. Her stories for UPI had impressed Bryce Miller so much that, in October, he made her part of the Saigon bureau's permanent staff. During the next year, Webb's stories continued to receive Miller's stamp of approval—the one that read "above and beyond." His other stamp, the one he used on stories that didn't measure up, was expressed in one word: "horseshit." Webb remembered with a note of pride, "I got lots of above and beyonds." Her work seldom dealt with politics but led her instead to the battlefield, or to Vietnamese citizens, to the lives of American soldiers. There was never a routine in her days. "Things always seemed to come in rushes." she recalled. "You'd be somewhere and there was an attack and you were the closest to it, you covered it. It was all a case of whatever body was available."

By the closing months of 1967, American troop strength was approaching 500,000 and American optimism was reaching its zenith. General William C. Westmoreland told the National Press Club during his November visit to Washington that Vietnam had entered a new phase "when the end begins to come into view." At a Pentagon briefing the following day, Westmoreland said a battle underway at Dak To in Vietnam's Central Highlands marked "the beginning of a great defeat for the enemy." LBJ and his military commanders hoped that the battle, which marked some of the fiercest fighting of the war, would stand as an affirmation of their upbeat outlook. But the press, particularly United Press International and Associated Press, dispatched stories suggesting that American troops had been trapped by enemy fire. More than 300 American soldiers died during the three-week battle and more than 1,000 were wounded. The Military Assistance Command Vietnam put enemy losses at sixteen hundred. What no one knew until months later was that the fighting at Dak To and a similar enemy campaign in Khe Sanh were part of North Vietnam's grand strategy to divert U.S. forces and leave the cities of South Vietnam vulnerable to the full-scale offensive planned for the opening weeks of 1968. For Webb and Leroy, that turning point in the war also marked a time of extraordinary professional achievement.

Working in different parts of the country when the Tet Offensive began in the early morning hours of January 31, Webb and Leroy earned an enduring place not only in the history of journalism but also the history of the war. Webb covered the attack in Saigon as UPI's first and main presence at the American embassy. Leroy was in Da Nang when the offensive began and quickly took off for Hue, believing that the city was in enemy hands and expecting that the biggest battle of the war would be fought there. In a great stroke of professional and personal luck, Leroy was detained briefly by North Vietnamese soldiers who had captured a U.S. tank in their assault on the city. First she charmed them into allowing her to photograph them, then she walked away with a smile and warm *au revoir.*

While most of Saigon slept on that first morning of Tet, the three-day lunar new year celebration, Webb arose and was on the street at 3:00 A.M. to fly to Pleiku, where she had been assigned to investigate rumors of a major Viet Cong attack on the largest military base in South Vietnam's Central Highlands. Along with widespread speculation about an attack on Saigon in the days before Tet, rumors of an attack in Hue, South Vietnam's imperial city, also swirled like the bush fires Webb had once covered in the Australian outback. The rumors were ignored, even though a captured Viet Cong document translated and released twenty-five days before the offensive began indicated that the enemy planned "very strong military attacks" on Saigon and other South Vietnamese cities on some undisclosed date. The document's predictions of a "general uprising" by the population in towns and cities throughout South Vietnam helped to undermine its credibility, as did the extraordinary and unbelievable scope of the plan. Moreover, in a tradition established several years before, the Communist and Saigon governments had declared a Tet cease-fire.

But the celebrations that marked the beginning of Tet Nham Than, the Year of the Monkey, were, in fact, a prelude to what became the "battle of all battles" in the Second Indochina War. Leaders of the North Vietnamese and Viet Cong forces dispatched an estimated 67,000 soldiers to attack one hundred cities and towns, thirty-nine of the country's forty-four provincial capitals, seventy-one district capitals, and the headquarters of all four military regions. Ten thousand of them were sent to Saigon to create havoc. Of that number, fewer than twenty were ordered to attack the American embassy. Although those twenty enemy soldiers were all repulsed and died in the attack, their defeat became the enemy's psychological victory, one that led many Americans to the conclusion that, despite President Johnson's protestations to the contrary, there was no light at the end of the tunnel. That the enemy could stage an attack in South Vietnam's capital city and hold the American embassy grounds for six hours left many Americans thunderstruck. And Kate Webb was one of its first witnesses. Her description of the scene is enshrined in the history of that battle to retake the embassy grounds.

Webb thought Saigon's streets seemed unusually empty and quiet at 3:00 A.M. that morning as she searched for a cab to take her to Tan Son Nhut Airport. From there, she would hitch a ride on a military transport plane to reach her assignment in Pleiku. "It was funny," she recalled, "I couldn't find a cab." Then an army Jeep rushed past her. Just as the driver told her he was heading for the embassy, she heard shots coming from that direction. "First I had to undo my pot [helmet] from my pack." Her first thought was to get back to the UPI office to tell them about the embassy attack. Unlike their brethren at Associated Press, many UPI staffers lived "above the store" on the floors above their office in a building at 19 Ngo Duc Ke street.

The attacks on Saigon began not long after the late-night Tet revelries wound down. Before dawn, red tracer bullets were visible in the sky near the presidential palace. The echoes of hand grenades and rocket fire could be heard at a dozen locations around the capital city. Because firecrackers, believed to ward off the evil spirits, are so much a part of a Tet celebration, few realized that a deadly battle had begun.

The most audacious attack of the offensive began unfolding shortly before Webb started looking for a cab. The U.S. Marine guards stationed at the embassy gate had sounded the alarm at 2:47 A.M.; the walled compound was under enemy attack. The four South Vietnamese policemen on duty outside the embassy either fled the scene or hid until the danger subsided. The two U.S. Marines posted at the gate were probably already dead by the time Webb heard the sounds of gunfire from the direction of the embassy. Just moments after Specialist Fourth Class Charles L. Daniel and Private First Class William E. Sebast radioed for reinforcements, a bazooka rocket blew a three-foot-hole in the protective wall that surrounded the embassy. Daniel and Sebast fired at the enemy soldiers as they scrambled through the hole and are believed to have killed two of the fewer than twenty men who pulled off the daring embassy raid. But the Marines soon fell, too: Daniel died of bullet wounds in his head, Sebast of chest wounds. At the American ambassador's residence about five blocks from the embassy, Ellsworth Bunker later recalled, "a fucking great black MP sergeant burst into my bedroom . . . and said, 'Mr. Ambassador, we're going to get you the fuck out of here' and hustled me away to safety in my pajamas in an armored car." Bunker took refuge in the home of the embassy's chief of security. Ironically, just two months before the American ambassador was so unceremoniously hustled out of his residence, General Westmoreland had told the National Press Club that the enemy was incapable of conducting large-unit operations near South Vietnam's cities.

Webb meanwhile was making her way to the embassy grounds located nearly two kilometers away from her office, often crawling on all fours to avoid exchanges of gunfire on the streets. A helicopter carrying American paratroopers tried to land on the embassy rooftop but was driven away by automatic weapons fire from the guerrillas. Reporters were also unable to reach the embassy grounds in the early hours of the fighting. They waited, clustered on a street corner about one hundred meters from the compound, until American military police in rammed open the embassy's front gate in what amounted to an assault on their own compound. At about the same time, just after 8:30 A.M. Saigon time, a platoon from the 101st Airborne Division landed on the rooftop. As Webb and other reporters entered the embassy grounds, a lone Marine fired from inside the buildings. "He was alone downstairs, fending off what he thought were the Viet Cong," Webb said. "All the other embassy personnel had retreated to the second floor." On the lawns, two Marines lay dead on the pavement near the embassy's side gate. Webb saw the bodies of dead Viet Cong, who wore red armbands on their gray-and-brown uniforms. The green lawns of the embassy grounds looked so lush, the landscaping so pristine, yet the scene was littered with corpses. It all seemed so incongruous. The body of an enemy soldier hung over the side of what appeared to be a marble fountain; his blood dripped down its white surface. That sight conjured images of slaughter and led her to write the widely quoted words that described the scene. To Webb, it all looked "like a butcher shop in Eden, beautiful but ghastly."

The battered and bullet-scarred Great Seal of the United States had been knocked from its place near the embassy's main entrance, the symbolism of which was hardly lost on news photographers at the scene. Besides the bazooka blast that tore a hole in the wall around the embassy, which had given the raiding party access to the compound, a Soviet-designed B-40 tank had heavily damaged the embassy building. About six and a half hours after the Marine guards had put out their first call for help, the embassy was declared secure at 9:15 A.M. Parts of the chancery building's first floor were smoldering. The North Vietnamese later reported that in their "fierce lightning attack" they had stormed through the embassy and killed more than two hundred Americans, "most of them holding key posts in the American ruling machinery." The death toll at the embassy was, in fact, seven.

General Westmoreland arrived at the embassy minutes after it was secured. In his comments to reporters, he dismissed the significance of the attack and subsequent stand-off. Here, in the midst of the "beautiful but ghastly" scene described by Kate Webb, while the bodies of the enemy dead were being removed, Westmoreland was essentially telling journalists that "we won." The reporters who listened were astonished. How could this be counted as a victory? A ragtag band of fewer than twenty Viet Cong soldiers armed with Soviet weapons had entered the grounds of the American embassy, killed two Marines, and nearly made it into the chancery building. Did he really believe his own words? He probably did. An article published in the *New York Times* six weeks later revealed that in a year-end report about the progress of the war, Westmoreland had unrealistically predicted "gains for 1968 far in excess of anything the United States had achieved in South Vietnam in 1967." The article contrasted the report's optimism with the realities of Tet and concluded that America had, in fact, "suffered a massive intelligence failure." Yet, on that first morning of the Tet Offensive, Ambassador Bunker echoed Westmoreland's sentiments when he visited the grounds several hours later. The Viet Cong attack had failed, Bunker declared, "because they were never able to enter the chancery building."

Webb had already left the embassy grounds by the time Westmoreland spoke. Believing that she had to report on the recapture of the embassy, she returned to the UPI office. Getting there posed yet another challenge: "The biggest dilemma was the two-kilometer distance between the embassy and the office," she recalled. "I had to let them know what was happening, but it was so difficult in all the gunfire and the confusion in the streets." Pockets of fighting persisted all over the city for more than a week. Bodies were strewn

Gloria Emerson went to Vietnam in 1956 hoping to be a journalist. Much of her work there was with Operation Brotherhood, a group of Filipino doctors and nurses who ministered to Vietnamese peasants. COURTESY OF PETER GATES

Gloria Emerson and her beau, John M. Gates Jr., who worked for the CIA in South Vietnam, traveled through the Middle East and Europe on their way home in 1956. One of their stops was in Tivoli. COURTESY OF JOYCE HOFFMANN

Dickey Chapelle wore combat gear and kid gloves with equal ease and felt most at home in the field with the men she liked to call "my Marines," many of whom were young enough to be her sons. COURTESY OF THE ASSOCIATED PRESS

Photojournalist Dickey Chapelle, who made five trips to Vietnam between 1961 and 1965, was killed during a combat operation. To this day, she remains the only American woman working as a journalist to die on assignment. COURTESY OF THE WISCONSIN HISTORICAL SOCIETY

Flora Lewis, seen here in 1985 when she received the Fourth Estate Award from the National Press Club, went to Vietnam during her years as a *Newsday* columnist in the late 1960s and covered the Paris Peace Talks for the *New York Times* in the 1970s. Applauding Mrs. Lewis are long-time UPI correspondent Helen Thomas and foreign affairs expert Zbigniew Brzezinski. COURTESY OF LINDSEY GRUSON

Beverly Deepe planned to spend a month in South Vietnam when she arrived in February 1962. She stayed for seven years, working first as a freelancer for the Associated Press and later for three major American news organizations —*Newsweek*, the *Herald Tribune*, and the *Christian Science Monitor*. COURTESY OF THE ASSOCIATED PRESS

Frances FitzGerald arrived in South Vietnam in February 1966 and found a culture and a people who became her lifelong fascination. Her work helped to upend all the conventional wisdom about the war. COURTESY OF THE HOWARD GOTTLIEB ARCHIVAL LIBRARY, BOSTON UNIVERSITY

Like so many of the women who reported from Vietnam, Frances FitzGerald found that although the military brass shuddered at their presence, especially on military operations, the average American GIs welcomed them. COURTESY OF THE HOWARD GOTTLIEB ARCHIVAL LIBRARY, BOSTON UNIVERSITY

Kate Webb landed in Vietnam in 1967 with a battered typewriter, two hundred dollars, and no job prospects. Born in New Zealand and raised in Australia, she brought an international perspective to her coverage of the war, one that many American colleagues lacked. She always looked like a cross between a waif and a school girl on the streets of Saigon, but she built a reputation as "one of the keenest war reporters in Indochina." COURTESY OF RACHEL MILLER

Jill Krementz accompanied NBC newsman Dean Brelis to Vietnam in 1965. Her key interest was the impact of the war on civilians, especially the children. COURTESY OF JILL KREMENTZ

Pham Xuan An, the Vietnamese employee of several American news organizations who was later revealed to have been a North Vietnamese spy, and Seymour Friedin, the *Herald Tribune's* foreign editor, with Jill Krementz, *left*, Frances FitzGerald, *center*, and Beverly Deepe. COURTESY OF JILL KREMENTZ

Ethel Payne, a reporter with the *Chicago Defender*, spent three months in Vietnam in 1967. She was the only woman whose publisher asked her to take the assignment and the only black newswoman to cover the war. COURTESY OF SMITHSONIAN'S ANACOSTIA COMMUNITY MUSEUM ARCHIVES, ETHEL PAYNE PAPERS

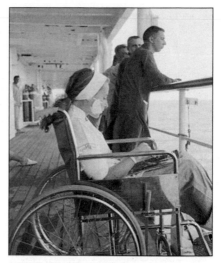

Freelance French photojournalist Cathy Leroy took some of the Vietnam War's most gripping photographs. "I want people who see my pictures to hate war as I do," she once said. COURTESY OF THE ASSOCIATED PRESS

Cathy Leroy was wounded in an enemy mortar barrage near Con Thien in 1967. She spent several weeks recovering from her injuries aboard a Navy hospital ship and returned to Saigon looking like "a broken bird." COURTESY OF THE ASSOCIATED PRESS

Christian Science Monitor reporter Elizabeth Pond and Richard Dudman of the *St. Louis Post-Dispatch* were captured in Cambodia in May 1970 and held for forty days. They are seen here soon after their release. COURTESY OF THE ASSOCIATED PRESS

When NBC newswoman Liz Trotta was sent to Vietnam in August 1968, she became the first woman assigned to cover combat by a network news operation in what was television's first war. COURTESY OF LIZ TROTTA

ABC Radio hired Laura Palmer in South Vietnam in 1972, a time when women in the American media were agitating for equal pay and expanded career opportunities. Despite her minimal qualifications for the job, Palmer said she was hired because "having a woman on the air from Saigon was a quick way to look good." COURTESY OF LAURA PALMER

Liz Trotta, who thought combat was the "only story" in Vietnam, said "war makes you grow up" and "turns you into a much, much better reporter." Her work in Vietnam won her an Emmy and an Overseas Press Club award. COURTESY OF LIZ TROTTA

Laura Palmer, *left*, and Tad Bartimus, "two good middle-class Midwestern girls," became Saigon soul-mates during the year they spent together covering the war—Palmer as a radio broadcaster and Bartimus as an AP correspondent. COURTESY OF LAURA PALMER

Tad Bartimus, *left*, and Laura Palmer, shown here with CBS newsman Ed Bradley at Tan Son Nhut airbase where, following the withdrawal of American troops, representatives of the Provisional Revolutionary Government held press conferences every Saturday. COURTESY OF LAURA PALMER

Gloria Emerson with freelance photographer Denis Cameron, who admired the "cyclopean eye" she brought to her work as a journalist in Vietnam. COURTESY OF MARC CAMERON

As a *New York Times* correspondent in Saigon, Gloria Emerson depended on her trusted friend and interpreter, Nguyen Ngoc Luong, seen here with her in a South Vietnamese cemetery. "The reporting depended so much on him," she once said. "He was more important than I was." COURTESY OF MARC CAMERON

along streets, some of them bloody, bloated, and rotting. Rockets and mortar fire had pocked buildings.

Retelling specific details of the Tet Offensive seemed difficult for Webb, for whom other memories of the war remained vivid all of her life. She said she blotted out precise memories of those days and grew edgy when pressed for details. During those days of chaos "some people cracked," Webb recalled. "But I guess I don't want to say any more about that." She kept herself busy "doing the things women do to keep going. I organized the kids to burn the rubbish that was piling up in the streets. I guess it's part of a woman's thing—keep busy and you don't get nervous. I can't remember how many days passed. The details of it are all a blur." She finally did make it to Pleiku, which was one of the first cities to come under attack in the Tet Offensive. Later in the month, she wrote stories about the bombing of North Vietnam and on the evacuation of dependents of the diplomatic corps.

Catherine Leroy, in Da Nang when the offensive began, encountered the *Newsweek* journalist Edward Behr at the press camp located on a riverbank in the center of town. Standing near the corpses of North Vietnamese soldiers whose suicide attack on the camp had failed, Leroy invited Behr to join her adventure. "Come with me to Hue," she said. "I am leaving now and we could have fun." She planned to catch a helicopter to a support base and travel on to Hue in an army convoy. "Hue," she declared with enthusiasm, "is in the hands of the North Vietnamese. It's the biggest battle of the whole war." She ranked among Behr's favorite colleagues, and her invitation certainly tempted him. But, as *Newsweek*'s acting bureau chief, he had to get back to Saigon. Leroy set off for Hue alone, but she soon teamed up with Francois Mazur, a fellow French reporter with Agence France-Presse—a colleague who had earlier expressed concerns about Leroy's behavior to American officials.

Together they made their way to a Marine base, Phu Bai, and hitched a ride with a Marine convoy to a spot about four miles south of Hue. They left the convoy and, fearing they might be entering hostile territory, changed into civilian clothing. On a tandem bicycle they rented from a Vietnamese man, Leroy and Mazur headed toward the fighting. When gunfire erupted as they reached a market place, the twosome shouted a phrase they would use frequently, *Phap bao chi bale!* ("French press from Paris"). No one in the clusters of people in the marketplace looked at them. Leroy and Mazur watched South Vietnamese fighter-bombers pass overhead and drop bombs on the Citadel about one mile north of where they stood. It was clear that they had landed in a Communist-controlled section of the city. When they took refuge in a nearby cathedral, a French-speaking priest invited them to spend the night. Although Mazur kept reciting the mantra *Phap bao chi bale!*, the Vietnamese among them were sullen and appeared resentful of their presence. All night, as they tried to sleep in a room the priest had offered them, Leroy and Mazur heard priests reciting loud prayers in Vietnamese, supplications that were drowned out by bursts of gunfire. By morning, nearly 4,000 Vietnamese women, children, and old men had taken refuge inside the cathedral and on its grounds. The "whites" among them, many of them feared, would enrage the North Vietnamese, the French-speaking priest told them. They had to leave. With a white flag, a letter from the priest explaining their identity in Vietnamese, and signs reading "*Phap bao chi bale!*" pinned to their chests, Mazur and Leroy left the cathedral accompanied by a young boy who promised to lead them to an American military compound.

Just a short distance from the cathedral, three men armed with AK-47s and dressed in khaki uniforms, attire that identified them as North Vietnamese soldiers, stopped Leroy and Mazur. The threesome took their cameras and tied their hands behind their backs. Their letter from the priest made little or no impression. Left in a garden outside a grand villa, they watched an American spotter plane cross overhead and a South Vietnamese bomber circle. Their immediate prospects looked bleak. If the North Vietnamese didn't imprison or kill them, a firefight might break out if the Americans or South Vietnamese happened to drive up. Leroy recalls shaking with fear. As the two were hustled inside the villa into what looked like servants' quarters, she encountered a Frenchman. His wife, a Vietnamese woman, "saved our lives." She asked the captors to summon an officer; in short order, the two were unbound and their cameras returned. When Leroy casually asked to take some pictures, the officer obligingly escorted them around the grounds. The soldiers seemed delighted to have their photographs taken. Finally, Mazur casually remarked, "Well, we have to get back to Paris with our story, so we'll be running along now." As they made their way through territory held by the North Vietnamese, through the no-man's land that separated the two sides, Leroy kept telling Mazur, "I'll kiss the first two Americans I meet."

Just over a week later, *Life* filled eight pages with Leroy's photographs of the battle for Hue, the most merciless encounter of the Tet Offensive. An editor's note in the front of the magazine introduced her as "A Tiny Girl with Paratroopers' Wings," and gave readers a thumbnail biography of the woman who by then had spent fifteen months covering the war.

Look magazine soon contracted Leroy to provide photographs for a story about how "the helicopter offers American soldiers dramatic new mobility." The text that accompanied Leroy's photos, written by Harvey Meyerson, detailed a fearsome battle in which four Americans died, twelve were injured, and three helicopters were destroyed in a "hot" landing zone where they came under heavy enemy machine-gun fire. The story was reminiscent of Dickey Chapelle's inclination to ennoble Americans in combat in her 1962 *National Geographic* cover story about how helicopters, with their mobility and speed, had become an essential tool in fighting a guerrilla war. Leroy's photos demonstrated the same atmosphere of pitched battle and individual bravery that Chapelle had captured years earlier. But Leroy's photos also caught the face of fear in both in the American fighting men and in the enemy soldiers they were holding prisoner. The final photo in the spread portrays an anguished peasant woman standing in a rice paddy with her hands clasped in supplication as the helicopter carrying her husband lifts off the ground.

Two weeks later, in *Look*'s May 16, 1968, issue, Leroy's photographs once again stood as a testament to the brutality of the war. This time, she wrote the brief text that accompanied her photographs. The young men depicted in the photos, Leroy wrote, "are boys of 20, with the idealism of their age, but they are fighting a war without glory. They all look the same, from the 1st Cav to the Marines, and they are united without discrimination by life and death." She wrote, too, of the disunity among Vietnamese soldiers. "I believe that about 20 percent of them are Vietcong—once underestimated as fighters, now overestimated—20 perent are strongly anti-Communist, and 60 percent are being crucified in a land of steel and fire, with their only political feeling a hope to survive." Her photo essay was followed by an editorial in which the editors of *Look* explained that Leroy's photos stood as a reminder "that people and nations make mistakes . . . and that in the process of rectifying a mistake, a person or a nation can grow in wisdom and strength. The Vietnam war has been a mistake, destroying something precious in the word 'America.'" The editorial concluded: "We at *Look* believe that the most important national business before us in this year of political debate is to wind up our involvement in the Vietnam war as quickly and honorably as possible." It was an echo of Walter Cronkite's earlier declaration that the war had reached a bloody stalemate and, as a matter of honor, America's leaders had to find a graceful way to exit the mess.

Not long after the Tet Offensive, Leroy wound up her personal involvement in Vietnam. Like many women who covered the war, removing herself from the physical space of Vietnam did not remove her from the experience. War continued to be the centerpiece of her professional life. Like Chapelle's, her travels were a road map to world unrest in the mid-to-late twentieth century: a civil war in Lebanon, a hijacking in Mogadishu, the revolution in Iran, never-ending unrest in Northern Ireland, Libya, and Afghanistan, and "a few wars in Africa," she recalled several years before her death in 2006. "To be a photojournalist is to be possessed somewhat. There is no looking back. You are there or you have missed it. You are constantly over-exposed and in harm's way."

As Kate Webb's work in Vietnam continued, it became clear that harm's way could extend beyond the battlefield. In 1969, Webb spent every spare moment pursuing a story about Vietnam's black market, an effort that never made it into print. She had heard about scandals at the PX, stories about how huge amounts of merchandise simply vanished, only to turn up in Saigon's street markets. She had also heard rumors about a black market operation involving shipments of artillery shells to the Philippines. She suspected that Americans had to be involved. How could they not know that so many shells were disappearing from their bases? They were worth so much money. "Lots of people had to be in on it," Webb recalled. Perhaps people in the South Vietnamese government and the military, surely port authority officials familiar with the assorted cargo entering and leaving the country. "People I talked to initially later warned me off the story," she recalled. At that time, after working late one night at the UPI office, Webb reached home and discovered a bullet hole in her apartment door and a .45-caliber slug lodged in the wall above her bed. Webb always believed that the bullet was fired as a warning to her to stop nosing around in the black market story. "There were so many stories that were never fully explained," Webb said. "We'll never know the whys. You could follow these stories for a lifetime. There are people, I call them the old dogs of war, who pursue such questions. But the decision I made was that I needed to move on." Some of the war's mysteries would remain forever unexplained.

Unanswered questions also surround the so-called "Green Beret Affair," in which eight members of America's Special Forces were charged with murdering a Vietnamese civilian who may or may not have been a double agent. Webb learned of the story several months after she started spending more and more time with the Green Berets, finding she was "comfortable around them."

Like other colleagues in the Saigon press corps, she soon fell in love with an American officer stationed outside Saigon. Through her lover, whom she declined to name, she learned in July 1969 that the military was soon to bring charges against members of the 5th Special Forces Group for the murder of a

South Vietnamese national, Thai Khac Chuyen, a suspected double agent, whose body they subsequently dumped at sea. Ironically, the case against Colonel Robert Rheault and seven of his men came at a time when U.S. officials were pressuring the North Vietnamese government to demonstrate moderation in the treatment of American prisoners of war. After interrogating the agent for more than ten days, three of the men were said to have drugged him, taken him to the bay off the shore of Nha Trang, fired two bullets into his head, and dropped him overboard after chaining two tire rims to the corpse. In an apparent violation of the Uniform Code of Military Justice, the eight men accused of the atrocity were placed in solitary confinement and held incommunicado at Long Binh's American military prison.

"I've always been hesitant to talk about it," Webb said decades later. "A number of people in the stockade with Rheault died later in accidents." Claims that the CIA had ordered the killing of Thai Khac Chuyen complicated the case. Although the agency denied involvement, it refused to provide the military prosecutors with the appropriate evidence. Efforts by the military to keep information about the June 30 arrests confidential unraveled after questions from a *New York Times* reporter forced military public affairs staffers to release limited details about the case. The case continued to occupy the media as the trial date approached; meanwhile, the accused men were freed from their tiny, tin-roofed cells. On the floor of the House of Representatives, Peter Rodino declared that "one of the weirdest—and probably the cruelest—trials in military history of the nation" was about to begin. Less than a week later, on September 29, in part because of the CIA's continued refusal to participate and questions about the possibility of a fair trial, Army Secretary Stanley R. Resor dismissed charges. But, Resor warned, "this Army will not and cannot condone unlawful acts of the kind alleged." Two months later, the story of how a company of American soldiers had killed nearly 350 South Vietnamese civilians at My Lai was told for the first time by Seymour Hersh through Dispatch News Service.

By then, Webb was about to leave South Vietnam. She followed her Green Beret lover back to the United States, anticipating that they would soon marry. The romance, however, fell apart, and Webb returned to work for UPI, filling the agency's only open slot at the time, a job in Pittsburgh. She worked on the story of the murder of Joseph Yablonski, president of the United Mine Workers, and his wife and daughter at their home in January 1970.

The other major story she covered in Pittsburgh put her, in essence, back in the middle of the Vietnam War, albeit on American soil. President Richard

M. Nixon's decision early in 1970 to widen the war into Cambodia fueled the protest movement at home. The once-secret bombing of Communist sanctuaries along Cambodia's border with South Vietnam became official U.S. policy and was carried out in the open. The invasion, Nixon told the country in a televised speech, would destroy the sanctuaries being used to stage attacks on South Vietnam. The U.S. military was also looking for North Vietnam's Central Office for South Vietnam, an installation presumed to be a vast underground bunker that served as headquarters for the North Vietnamese command—something like a mini-Pentagon in the jungles of Indochina. As it turned out, that central office existed only in the imaginations of American military personnel, who, in an observation made later by Frances FitzGerald, both enlarged and diminished the enemy with such hypotheses. Nixon's decision to move the war into Cambodia ignited protests on college campuses across America, including one at Kent State University in Ohio. Webb was on the UPI team that covered the story of how edgy National Guardsmen called out to maintain order on the campus had opened fire and killed four students in a crowd of demonstrators.

Outrage over the Kent State debacle was just beginning to ebb when UPI reassigned Webb to Southeast Asia. Frank Frosch, UPI Phnom Penh bureau chief, had called for reinforcements to cover the widening war and asked specifically for Webb. The unraveling of Cambodia had begun in March 1970 following a coup staged while its leader, Prince Sihanouk, was out of the country. He was overthrown by his prime minister, Lon Nol, who was unable to maintain the prince's fragile success in keeping his country out of the Vietnam war. Cambodia's neutrality, of course, had been a farce all along. Not only did the Ho Chi Minh Trail run for many miles along the country's five-hundred-mile eastern border with South Vietnam but North Vietnam had long used its bases in Cambodia as a staging area for its attacks in the South. U.S. Special Forces teams began staging secret missions into Cambodia as early as May 1967. President Nixon authorized the first secret B-52 strikes inside Cambodia less than a month after his inauguration.

Cambodia became an especially dangerous assignment for journalists after April 30, 1970, when President Nixon presented the once-secret attacks as a new initiative against North Vietnamese bases inside Cambodia. Unlike their colleagues in South Vietnam, where journalists accompanied U.S. troops on military operations, in Cambodia, the press was on its own. Reporters went off singly or in small groups to pursue the murky Khmer Rouge forces, then allied with the North Vietnamese, who were vying for control of the country with government forces controlled by Lon Nol's army. The reporters called themselves the Mercedes Marauders after the rented four-door diesel sedans many used for transportation. In these rented cars, or on motor scooters, they roamed the countryside in search of stories in a war that had no borders. There was no safety net.

Because a sense of war weariness among Americans had led many editors to turn their attention away from Vietnam, reporters on the scene, especially those in the rabidly competitive business of television news, are said to have taken ever greater risks in their search for deadly combat situations. In an echo of the accusation made against Dickey Chapelle after her capture in Hungary in 1956, the CBS reporter John Laurence in his book, *The Cat From Hue,* claimed that "trying to get captured and released was an option most journalists in Phnom Penh had considered," apparently believing it would make a great story and enhance their careers.

"I don't believe that," Webb declared years later. "Journalists were simply trying to cover the other side. No one was trying to get captured." Sean Flynn and Dana Stone were among the first Americans to disappear in Cambodia. The two freelancers were last seen riding rented motorcycles along Highway 1 near the South Vietnamese border, according to Laurence. These "Easy Riders," as Flynn and Stone were called, "appeared to be trying to become the first American journalists to be taken and released by the other side," according to Laurence. Four months after Webb returned to Southeast Asia, her boss, Frank Frosch, and the UPI photographer Kyoichi Sawada were killed in an ambush near Takeao along Highway 2 on October 28. That's when Webb, as she recalled years later, stepped into a dead man's shoes. Even more than in Vietnam, in Cambodia—to use a phrase that once headlined an article by Gloria Emerson—each day was a separate ordeal. The days that marked Webb's biggest Southeast Asian ordeal began about six months after Frosch and Sawada died.

By the spring of 1971, capture in Cambodia had become an almost certain death sentence for journalists. Of the more than two dozen who had fallen into the hands of the North Vietnamese or Khmer Rouge troops, only three were released. Twenty-five were dead or missing and presumed dead. No one then understood what distinguished the three journalists who were released from all the others. But the safe return in June 1970 of Elizabeth Pond of the *Christian Science Monitor,* Richard Dudman of the *St. Louis Post Dispatch,* and Michael Morrow of Dispatch News Service, after five weeks of captivity, had allowed others to hope, though most of them did so in vain.

In April 1971, Webb, now Phnom Penh bureau chief, and UPI's driver-interpreter Chimm Sarath, were captured and held for twenty-three days. They had traveled down Highway 4 on a hot afternoon—that fry-an-egg-on-the-pavement kind of heat. Sweat ran into her eyes, down her arms, and onto her camera. Like many journalists, she was driven by a desire for front-page play; inside pages really didn't count. Why bother, she decided after reckoning that her chances looked pretty slim that day. Pakistan was boiling over again in yet another skirmish over Kashmir. "To heck with this," she thought. Pakistan was sure to take page one. But before she could act on the thought, "the world exploded." Small arms fire, mortars, and automatic weapons sent her diving for cover in a nearby ditch. The area around milepost 95.5 on Cambodia's Highway 4 had become a shooting gallery with the Cambodian army firing from one direction and the North Vietnamese and Viet Cong from the other. Webb lit a cigarette and thought, "This is it." Caught in the crossfire with Webb and Sarath were four others: Tea Kim Heang, the photographer known among his American colleagues as "Moonface," whose week-old bullet wounds received in an earlier skirmish opened again and seeped blood through his bandages; Eang Charoon, a twenty-seven-year-old newspaper photographer; Toshiichi Suzuki, a correspondent with a Japanese news film agency; and Suzuki's interpreter. Together, the six journalists alternately hid in the jungle or wandered in search of the way back to Phnom Penh. Nearly twenty-four hours after the firing started, the six found themselves face-to-face with two young North Vietnamese soldiers who were pointing AK-47 rifles at their heads. *"Bao chi, bao chi,"* they pleaded, identifying themselves as members of the press. The two young soldiers bound Webb's arms behind her back with vines, tape, and ropes, and, once they had done the same with her companions, ordered them at gunpoint into a bunker. After collecting the cash and valuables from their captives, the two soldiers brought canteens of water.

No less than it had been for Beth Pond and her colleagues the year before, the early hours of captivity for Webb and her five companions were the most frightening, the time when they came closest to being killed. Although Webb's captivity was measurably shorter than Pond's, twenty-three days versus forty, in many ways it was more brutal largely because of the primitive, often deplorable, conditions of their imprisonment.

Pond's most harrowing hours came on the first day, when she was separated from Dudman and Morrow and taken to an empty school house. That is when an armed young man angrily tore her rings from her fingers and seemed intent on raping her. "Whatever happens," she told herself as fear began to overwhelm her, "I am not going to hate anyone. I am not going to let myself believe that men are evil." Pond and her would-be attacker did not speak a mutual language, but she quietly told him, "You are my brother. You have everything you need as the son of God." In that instant, his rage seemed to ebb. "He repeated the word God," and ever so gently returned her rings. Pond was elated. "He had not been hypnotized by this atmosphere of war and enmity." Pond and her companions were placed in the custody of two members of the National Liberation Front, two Cambodians, and a North Vietnamese political officer.

Although Webb never faced the threat of rape, her captivity was grueling in other ways. She and her five colleagues spent nine days walking, mostly through the jungle, much of the time in bare feet. On that first day, with each of them bound individually, then chained together in groups of three, they marched for hours, herded like sheep by their six guards. American observation planes flew over them at treetop level but never spotted the journalists. In an echo of the order directed at Pond, Dudman, and Morrow the year before, they were told, "If you run from the planes, we will shoot." Webb lost her shoes on the first day. Nonetheless, the group continued walking over the stubbled trails until dusk. That night, to her amusement, Webb watched not only the enemy "grunts" hurriedly moving in and out of the forest but also the supply trucks, their lights shaded, doing the same—none of which was spotted by those piloting the American planes. One night she saw an elephant dragging what appeared to be an artillery piece through the jungle growth. Just how do elephants hide from observation planes? she wondered. And still the captives kept walking, across creek beds, deep into the mountains, always heading uphill. After forty hours, the six had their first meal—bowls of rice and pork-fat soup. Webb threw up.

They walked again the next night, and the next; four nights straight, it turned out. The rest stops were brief, just long enough to smoke a cigarette. The encounters with angry villagers and the proximity of the bombs dropped by American planes terrified Webb. They would all die, she thought, shot perhaps by their captors or blown to smithereens in a bombing raid. Even when the bombs crashed just fifty to one hundred yards away, she saw with amazement that the young soldiers were not only indifferent to the danger but amused by the fear so evident in the way Webb and the others reacted.

Her feet, those ever-dirty size eights, soon became as big a problem as her fear. Having lost her shoes, the "shower shoes" she was given by her captors became her most valuable possession. Still, the sandals cut her feet so badly that at times she simply went barefoot. After several days one of her toes was turning black and oozed pus. She wanted to cut a piece off with a razor blade, but the guard said no. They would soon reach a place where she could see a doctor. Her feet looked like a mass of bloodied pulp. But she wasn't alone. All the guerrillas had "gaping ulcers and scars from their toes to their knees."

A year earlier, Pond and her colleagues had been moved from village to village during the early weeks of their captivity, invariably transported in cars and trucks. Most of their moves seemed to come without warning; they were told to pull together their belongings, often late at night, and taken to another village where they stayed with yet other villagers. Later, the captives learned that more than one of those moves had come just hours before an enemy attack. By dawn after one of the middle-of-the-night moves, the hut in which they had stayed was hit. The final week of their captivity was spent in one place.

For Webb, the walking in those early days seemed endless, and the tough regimen weakened her. She lost twenty pounds and suffered from an assortment of fevers and headaches. The doctors treated her with rudimentary medications and cautioned her: "Don't get sick. If you get really sick there is nothing we can do." After those long days on the march, the group arrived in a place named the Press Village, a small compound of thatched-roof huts scattered beneath trees. It was there that the six spent the remainder of their captivity.

From a distance, the site looked like another clump of trees. After Webb had taken her first bath in a week, an experience that brought her to tears, she and Suzuki were moved to an open-sided hut furnished with a metal bed and a new mat cover. She rejoiced at the aroma of fresh straw and leaves. The camp had two pet dogs, Bunker, apparently named for the American ambassador, and Ky, no doubt a mockery of the vice president of South Vietnam. A tailor arrived to measure them for clothes, and, before long, Webb was dressed in the familiar black pajamas of the Vietnamese peasant.

For Webb and Pond, their respective interrogations evoked a strange mix of emotions. Those proceedings were among the most unpleasant periods of their captivity because they were grounded in the question of whether the journalists were spies. Their lives depended on proving they were not. But amazingly, while they were trying to detach themselves from the consequences of failing to prove to their captors that they were neutral journalists, they also appreciated the rich potential these scenes had as stories.

Pond's interrogation sessions were never the hours-long ordeals that they often were for Webb. A few hostile sessions at the outset left Pond wondering whether she and her colleagues might be framed on some trumped-up charges of espionage. Later, however, Pond began to perceive the process as a holding pattern, a way of maintaining a certain threat level while their captors awaited word from Hanoi about what to do with them. When the sessions were conducted in Vietnamese, her colleague Michael Morrow served as translator. When they were conducted in French, Pond translated. Pond's thirty- to-sixty-minute interrogations were conducted by people who arrived almost daily on motorbikes, but Webb's questioners, who exhausted her with day-long interrogations in French, appeared to live in the same jungle camp where she and her colleagues were being held.

Both women were required to fill out lengthy questionnaires. Pond had been asked to provide information about her newspaper, a description of the articles she had written, and the names of "especially progressive" journalists who could vouch for her. Webb's captors wanted to know much more— information about her family, her salary, her biography, and her feelings about the war. From memory, Webb tried to rewrite the last stories she had written for UPI on the military situation in Cambodia.

In one day-long grilling, Webb was asked, "Why would you risk your life if you are not with the CIA? Why are you working for the American imperialists?" Sometimes she answered with questions of her own. The answers she heard, along with the scenes she witnessed around her, began to give Webb an understanding of how and why these men fought. It was their spirit, the same spirit Frankie FitzGerald's father had hoped to impress upon Secretary of Defense McNamara in the conversation that marked their last discussion of Vietnam policy.

Over time, however, Webb, like Pond before her, found that her role as a journalist was accepted by her interrogators, a transformation that gave rise to increasingly frequent—and welcome—conversations about ideology. Webb's effort during one of those sessions to explain the concept of objectivity, the centerpiece of American journalism, underscored all the conclusions that Frankie FitzGerald reached about how the differing mindsets of the Americans and Vietnamese made a common understanding all but impossible.

"You must be very brave to go down the highway for no other reason than to get the truth. This is hard to believe."

"I went down the highway because it is the only way to find out what was really happening. How else can I find out?"

"You can listen to what the government says."

"The government gives its version, you give yours, so we must find out what is really happening."

"But this United Press, it is American?"

"Yes, American."

"So you work for the American government."

"No, I don't work for the American government. It's called United Press International. It is broadcast all over the world . . . and we write about what is happening, not our opinions . . . that's why I was down Highway 4, because I had to find out about what was happening, not what someone on one side said was happening."

The idea that American journalists could maintain autonomy vis-à-vis the government was a dubious concept to her interrogators. "You cannot be a neutral observer in this war. Everyone is on one side or another," her questioner insisted. Webb, however, maintained it was true.

Those occasional good-natured exchanges, however, never obscured their respective roles. Her fear that she might be killed steadily diminished, but the reality that these interrogators were in charge of her fate never left her consciousness. Their captors had repeatedly told Webb and her colleagues that, as a routine, they turned over all their prisoners to the Cambodians. The Khmer Rouge considered journalists to be "imperialist spies." And, one guard explained more than once, they would kill all of them, "especially Mademoiselle," he added, sometimes drawing an index finger across his neck for emphasis. On another occasion, an elderly interrogator whom Webb had nicknamed Dad, asked her, "Do you realize you are a prisoner of war, that one shot through the head could finish you just like that?" Webb grinned and replied, "I'm in your hands. That's up to you now; there's nothing I can do about it. Besides, I don't consider myself a prisoner of war, I'm not a soldier." In a counter parry, the old man asked, "Then consider yourself an invited guest."

One day, an interrogator she called "the Finger" challenged her: If she was objective, as she professed, then surely, having already spent so much time with their enemies, Webb must want to remain with the North Vietnamese. She was being baited with her own words. Her answer had better be sincere. She was simultaneously fearful of and fascinated by her situation. Captivity was depleting her physically, yet the journalist in her resisted letting go of a great story. "I'd like to stay with you for a few weeks, and then return home," she told him.

In casual conversations with her guards, Webb realized that the individual North Vietnamese soldier in Cambodia was not so unlike the average American GI in South Vietnam. Each one was far from home, in a strange country; neither understood the language; one gleaned a touch of home from Radio Hanoi, the other from Armed Forces Radio. Like American soldiers, the North Vietnamese spoke, often longingly, of home and family. Echoes of the poignancy in Erich Maria Remarque's *All Quiet on the Western Front* ring softly through Webb's later depictions of the shared fear, boredom, homesickness, and longing for family she discerned in so many North Vietnamese soldiers. She welcomed these glimpses of soldiers on the other side. She had written so many stories about America's GIs and the South Vietnamese soldiers. "Can you go home for visits?" Webb asked the guard she called Mr. Liberation, the one who at every turn laced his sentences with "American imperialist aggressors and their lackeys." "Make that walk?" he asked incredulously, referring to the 1,000-mile round-trip trek. "We are allowed, of course. I would like to see them, of course . . . but that walk, I would never walk all that way and back again."

A year earlier, Pond, too, had savored the experience of her close association with the forces that were fighting the Americans. "We lived, to some extent, on the 'other side' of this bitter war with an immediacy that we had never imagined possible," she wrote after her release. She learned about the personal lives of her captors and discerned in each of them a psychology that was "less that of a natural warrior than of the single-minded revolutionary, with a vast capacity to sacrifice for the cause." Most of the five guards who remained with them for forty days, Pond discovered, had not seen their wives or children for periods ranging up to ten or eleven years. Some of them were battle veterans who had suffered wounds several times. She admired the discipline she saw in their ranks, the singlemindedness of their commitment. They had the spirit it would take to win this war.

Captivity began to take on distinctive routines for both women. The curious reversal of day and night hit them, in the darkness they found comfort rather than peril. For Pond, that was the time she was allowed some freedom outdoors, a time to savor the full moon shimmering over a rice paddy or the sounds of bull frogs in the ponds after a heavy rain. In the collective boredom that came of their having to stay indoors during daylight hours, Pond, Dudman, and Morrow carved a miniature chess set from green tree branches, and their hosts provided a makeshift board drawn on the floor with chalk. The captives even taught their guards how to play, and in doing so helped them all occupy many hours. Both women also spent time writing.

For Webb, those interludes of relative ease were too often overshadowed by her worries about the UPI staff in Phnom Penh. She understood the horrifying emotions associated with losing a colleague—the scramble to pull every official string imaginable, the business of notifying their families, the desperate search for some back channel, perhaps through a diplomatic contact—to secure a colleague's release. And then there was her family. In Canberra, Webb's sister, Rachel Miller, who had first learned of the situation from a staffer in UPI's Sydney bureau, continued to hope. Australia's foreign affairs office undertook behind-the-scenes efforts. Radio Australia did the same. It was all "a dreadful time of wondering," recalled Miller.

All hope that Webb and her colleagues might be found alive evaporated when, weeks after their capture, several bodies were discovered near the site of their disappearance. A female Caucasian corpse with a bullet in her chest was identified as Kate Webb. News organizations across America and Australia reported her death.

But in Canberra, even after the body found fifty-five miles south of Phnom Penh was identified as Webb's and even as Rachel Miller sat in church during the memorial service, she continued to believe that her sister was still alive. "I always thought that I would know inside that she was dead. I never felt that," Miller remembered. Preposterous though it was, the sisters connected their worries and hopes for each other to an unlikely piece of clothing. During a visit to New York several years before, Rachel had sent Kate a pair of Pucci underpants, not quite bikini-sized swirls of fuchsia, turquoise, and purple nylon. "I remember how I kept hoping that she was wearing that underwear when she was captured," Rachel said. And, in fact, Kate was. When the captives were finally allowed to bathe after their first march, the guard assigned to watch Webb registered astonishment at the sight of her psychedelic undies. Later, on those long and wearisome days of her captivity, Kate would, as Rachel said "direct thought messages to me via the Pucci underwear."

As the tension of their earliest days as captives began to ease and a level of amicability developed in their interrogations, Pond, and later Webb, dared to imagine that they would survive after all. And if they did, when and under what circumstances might they be released? For Pond, Dudman, and Morrow, the end came abruptly. On June 9, the thirty-fourth day of their captivity, they had been taken for a pre-dawn walk in the woods to a tiny thatched hut, where they were to spend the day. It was the day they eluded an American helicopter search mission that was combing the jungle in search of enemy targets, the day they had been warned, "No matter what happens, don't run."

In a postscript to that warning, their guard later explained, "I want you to live. I want to see you safely back with your families. . . . Sooner or later you will be released." Seven days later they were free. For Webb and her colleagues, early tantalizing hints that they would be released never materialized. The disappointment tested her patience and her spirits.

Both in 1970 and again in 1971, before their release, the groups of captives were feted like celebrities during elaborate ceremonies that featured special food, speeches, toasts, picture-taking, and pleas for understanding. For Pond, it was a gala farewell dinner and the menu was braised dog, steamed rice, and boiled greens with an assortment of seasonings on the side. "Just about every front official we had met in our 5½ weeks showed up," Pond wrote. The captives offered as gifts some of their personal possessions, but those tokens were politely refused, all except the chess set that a few of their guards had learned to use. In comments made before he presented the gift, Richard Dudman, who noted that the chess pieces were made of green wood and would likely disintegrate soon, spoke of his hope that "by the time they have fallen to pieces your struggle for freedom and independence will have reached its successful conclusion." In turn, Ba, a South Vietnamese who was a commander in the Provisional Revolutionary Government (PRG), told Pond, Dudman, and Morrow, "We consider you not prisoners of war but as travelers who have lost their way . . . now, as you are preparing to go back to your country or back to your work, in our eyes you have crossed over and we now consider you as our friends." Before taking their leave, the journalists asked about the fate of their colleagues, twenty of whom remained in captivity. The question went unanswered.

In 1971, with equal extravagance, given the penury in which these guerrilla forces lived, Webb and her group were served tea, candy, and bananas. The ceremony made her think of the Mad Hatter's tea party, and she felt like Alice. That ceremony of farewell also featured speeches, words of friendship, hopes for peace, all spiced with dashes of propaganda. Each of the six was given a full package of cigarettes. With her forty- to fifty-a-day habit, Webb vowed to ration them; she wouldn't light the last one until her first moment of freedom. As the departure ceremony drew to its close, they asked about the other seventeen journalists then missing in Cambodia. With a look of what Webb described as embarrassment, the captives were told that "the liberation forces could not be held responsible for journalists who followed the Lon Nol troops." The first installment of the four-part series Webb later wrote about her imprisonment began with the last words spoken to her before her release:

"Tell the truth about us. Tell the truth," an officer had implored. "You may have to be very brave, but tell the truth."

For Pond and her colleagues, the road back to safety in 1970 was less dangerous and punishing than the one Webb's group traveled in 1971. Once again, Pond's group traveled by taxi, bus, and motor bike. Webb and her group made the journey back on foot.

Even as Webb and the others walked away from their imprisonment at 5:40 P.M. on Thursday, April 29, their captivity was hardly over. Among the six men who led them to freedom were several of the soldiers who had guarded them during their captivity. Continuing fevers made Webb's head swim, and she kept falling as they walked through the darkness. She was drenched in sweat; a blister on the back of her foot broke; a scorpion stung her.

Why, she kept wondering, would any army "risk the lives of six of its men to get prisoners to safety?" They were in territory controlled by the Khmer Rouge and near the end of their march; the guards were as nervous as their captives were fearful. They heard the sounds of fighting just three hundred yards away. Webb's pessimism mounted. "We've been too lucky; something's bound to happen . . . we're going to get bombed or shot or fall into a government ambush," she kept thinking. Their hope was to meet up with friendly Cambodian army troops before members of the homicidal Khmer Rouge troops found them.

When they reached Trappeang Kralaing on Highway 4, not far from where they had been captured, the group separated. A round of handshakes marked their first moment of freedom. But being free did not equate to being safe. As dawn broke, they stripped off their Viet Cong clothing and donned the clothes they were wearing when they were captured. With a swatch of white parachute silk tied to the end of a stick, they set off on the highway with Webb in the lead. A column of troops appeared at the crest of a hill ahead of them. Were they government troops or the Khmer? The journalists' two Cambodian colleagues knew instantly they were facing friendlies. Nearing the uniformed column, they shouted, "Press, we're press." Webb, it turned out, knew an officer in the group from an earlier encounter. As her eyes filled with tears, he said, "Miss Webb? You're supposed to be dead. It is Miss Webb? It is, isn't it?" With shaking hands, she pulled out her last cigarette and a young Cambodian soldier gave her a light.

Little more than a week after the body identified as Webb's had been cremated, the telephone rang in UPI's Phnom Penh bureau. With barely contained joy, Webb told Khauuv Bun Keang, the resident interpreter, that she was "alive and well." Taking the call for a sick joke, he hung up. He was still grieving for his dead bureau chief on that May morning. But with a second telephone call, he accepted the news of Webb's survival. Word spread through the city; a cheer went up in the nearby Reuters bureau. So when Webb and her fellow captors arrived by military helicopter, a crowd of journalists were at the airport to greet them. As her joyful colleagues began asking questions, a UPI colleague muttered a word of caution. "This is our story." Yes, it was. And back-from-the-dead tales are a sure way to make page one.

The circumstances of their releases puzzled both women for decades. Was it because they were women? Maybe. Of all the journalists who were captured in Vietnam and Cambodia, two women and three men returned— and two of those men were with Beth Pond. Webb thought her nationality might have been her armor. She was Australian, and none of the others were American, either. However, a list of those who died before her capture provides little support for the theory that non-Americans had a better chance at survival. Like Suzuki, some of those already killed were Japanese. On that same list of the missing were the names of French, Austrian, Dutch, German, Swiss, and Indian employees of international media organizations. However, it was, as Webb suggested, good luck that she was captured by North Vietnamese troops rather than by their Khmer Rouge allies.

Richard Dudman thought the "deluge of appeals" from his wife, his employer, contacts in the American embassy in Saigon, and sources in the State Department that inundated the North Vietnamese and the National Liberation Front in Hanoi and Paris, as well as the appeals made to Cambodia's Prince Sihanouk in Peking, had the greatest impact. Were that the case, surely the many appeals made by an equal number of family members, colleagues, and contacts on behalf of the CBS and NBC television news crews, eight men in all, who vanished on May 31, 1970, while Dudman, Pond, and Morrow were still in captivity, would have been successful, as well. They were not.

Pond asked the question, "Why us?" in an article for the *Monitor* shortly after her release. Were they a precedent or an exception, she wondered then and years later. "And if precedent, what kind of precedent?" In 2002, Pham Xuan An, Pond's Vietnamese translator and admirer, offered an answer, one that neither she nor Dudman nor any other American associated with the vast efforts to secure the release of captives had ever heard. In a lengthy interview in Saigon in February of that year, An revealed that he had intervened with his North Vietnamese and Viet Cong contacts to secure her release. It was apparently the first time, but not the last, that An risked exposure and certain death on behalf of an American colleague. An had great respect for Pond, whose intellectual interests in the Vietnamese people and their politics reached well beyond that of most reporters. Her serious and gentle nature, her courage and industry, and the determination and honesty she brought to her work had impressed An. He was, after all, a man who esteemed women and cherished womanhood. An had first met Pond in 1967, when she spent six months in Vietnam. Pond returned in 1969 to further understand and explain the structure of Vietnamese politics and explore the nuances of the country's village society. An was delighted with this new opportunity to serve as her translator as she pursued stories around Saigon. Her capture distressed him. To those who wondered about An's divided loyalties after his work as a spy was revealed in the 1980s there was no enigma or contradiction in his willingness to help Pond. Friendship never trumped ideology in his mind. He loved his country and wanted to see it free of foreign rule. He admired America and loved many of his American friends. These were the two fundamental truths of An's life. Neither one negated the other in An's mind. Much in the way he would do several months later on behalf of *Time* reporter Robert Sam Anson, An sent word to those "on the other side:" Pond had to be released unharmed. Because of An's stature as a colonel in the revolutionary army, that command came with considerable authority. Yet using that authority to secure the release of captured Americans put his life, his family, and his cause in grave danger. Fear was a perpetual state in his life throughout the war, An confessed years later to Morley Safer, the CBS newsman. "Constantly," he said. "I was terrified." The logistics of his intercessions had the cloak-and-dagger qualities of a John LeCarré mission. As An later explained to his American biographer shortly before his death in 2005, his routine in communicating with his contacts involved the writing of messages in invisible ink on paper that was then used as a wrapping—perhaps for egg rolls—and passed to Mrs. Ba, the nondescript older woman who worked as his courier for all his years in Saigon. An's answer to Pond's "why us?" question was so simple: "If any harm had come to her, I could not live quietly," he said in 2002.

Kate Webb, on the other hand, was left to wonder. The whys of her release remain among those unanswered questions about the war, questions that she pondered for the rest of her life. Just days after her release, Webb holed up in a Hong Kong hotel room and wrote her four-part series relating the details of her capture and imprisonment; the stories ran in newspapers in around the world, about 2,000 in all. Many American newspapers put her on page one and topped the stories with melodramatic headlines. In New York, the *Long Island Press* headlined her first report "The Unsinkable Kate Webb: Gal in War Jam." In the *Cleveland Press,* the headline read, "Kate Tells of Viet Capture: Bullets, Blood, Thirst, Fear," and the *St. Louis Post-Dispatch* made a boldface declaration: "Kate Webb: Back From the Dead."

In Japan, Webb received more attention than Toshiichi Suzuki. She, however, paid tribute to him with one of her familiar grace notes. Without Suzuki's company and his ability to speak Vietnamese, she said in the opening of her series, those three weeks on the other side would have been like a silent movie. "There will remain a bond between us, more real than the ropes that at times bound us together," she wrote. "I am forever in his debt." Until her death, she and Suzuki contacted each other every May 1 to commemorate their long-ago day of good fortune. In many ways, however, Webb was put off by all the attention. Among the scores of letters she received, some addressed to "Kate Webb, Phnom Penh," there were marriage proposals, advice on the appropriate *f*-stop for shooting photos in the jungle, and even a jocular note from an old friend who enclosed the liquor bill he had racked up mourning her death.

The story Webb wrote about her capture and release reflected what was the greatest strength of her Vietnam reportage, her neutrality. Webb never embraced one side or the other in the conflict. The labels "hawk" and "dove," which had long since entered the American lexicon, never had meaning in the context of Webb's view of the war. Objectivity transcended ideology. Her sense of the conflict had more to do with a personal philosophy than politics. "I still don't lean to one side or the other in this war," she told Tony Clifton. "My reaction is a woman's reaction: how very sad it all is, what a bloody awful waste."

On a trip to New York City soon after her series appeared, Webb was offered a $76,000 advance for her story by editors at Doubleday Books. In 1971, that was a minor fortune for a wire service reporter, especially one who worked for United Press International, universally known for its tight-fisted and miserly ways with employees. She was wined and dined at the Four Seasons while editors explained the deal to her. The story, they said, lacked just one crucial element—a love angle. That, they said, would really sell the book. They proposed that she incorporate a tale about how she had fallen in love with one of her Communist captors. Maybe they believed Dad would do; her series had indicated she was often in tune with him. Her response was classic Kate Webb. How could she fabricate a story? she asked. Certainly she had come to respect and even like her captors, but any suggestion that she had fallen in love would be a fiction. First and always, she was a journalist.

Her work had to be factual. The Doubleday crowd appeared to consider that an irrelevant detail. They implored her editors at UPI to help her see the light. She was astonished when several fellow journalists suggested that she just take the money and tell the story the way Doubleday wanted. What, a few of them wondered, was the big deal? For Kate Webb, however, the idea was unthinkable. Never, not for a millisecond, was there a shred of hope that she would acquiesce. The Doubleday deal collapsed.

Webb settled instead for a $14,000 advance from Quadrangle Books, a contract that made no demands on her to embroider the truth. For Webb, that was well worth $62,000. So it was an irony that the book's subtitle misstated a fact. She had certainly been *On the Other Side*, but the part about *23 Days with the Viet Cong* was incorrect. It should have read "with the North Vietnamese."

It was also during that New York trip that Webb discovered that the excruciating headaches and fevers she had begun experiencing in the jungle were associated with malaria. After collapsing in her New York hotel and being taken by two wire service friends to a nearby hospital, she was diagnosed with two strains of malaria—vivax and cerebral. In a coma, with her temperature hovering around 108, doctors wondered whether she might be brain-dead. She was placed in a tub of iced alcohol to lower her fever. "That's when I was a living martini," she said.

Webb's intention was always to return to her duties as UPI bureau chief in Cambodia, even though her bosses had reservations because they had heard about "intelligence reports indicating the North Vietnamese had it in for [her]." But she put those bosses in a bind when she announced during an appearance on the David Frost Show that "I really have to go back." With the understanding of the enemy she had gained from her captivity, Webb believed she could report the war more objectively. What she did not anticipate, however, was the emotional and physical toll that the subsequent disappearance of other journalists would take. Not long after her return to UPI's Phnom Penh, Chimm Sarath, the UPI interpreter and driver with whom Webb had been captured earlier in the year, disappeared for a second time. Wire service tradition made a bureau chief responsible for the welfare of his or her staff. Finding "Jimmy," as he was known in the bureau, became something of an obsession. Securing his release became her single mission. She owed it to his wife and five children to find him. She made contact with every government source she had ever cultivated. She pleaded with anyone who would listen to help secure his release. She tried contacting Lon Nol and Prince Sihanouk. She dispatched monks to make contact with troops in the countryside, believing that, unlike Cambodian civilians, they could travel freely. But on two occasions, monks searching for Jimmy were killed. Finally, she confronted the reality that her preoccupation was hurting the UPI bureau staff. "I said, 'It's time for me to leave.'" Her bosses at UPI gave her a leave of six months, during which she spent part of the time in the Himalayas. "There is something about the mountains that puts you back to middle size," she recalled.

But the war did not end for Webb. The fall of Saigon still awaited her.

6

The War on Television

At least she's not a lollipop.
—William R. McAndrew, NBC News

THE ASSOCIATED PRESS photographer Horst Faas had Liz Trotta focused dead center in his telephoto lens. The NBC newswoman was crossing an open field where American troops were fighting a North Vietnamese battalion entrenched on a hillside near Tay Ninh. Trotta, Vo Huynh, the network's Vietnamese cameraman, and a sound man moved in tandem toward the shelter of a school building where Faas was protected from enemy fire. Trotta wanted desperately to run, but Huynh had ordered her to walk. Although obedience was seldom her inclination, neither on this day nor on others did she question Huyhn's commands. An eternity later, when the threesome finally closed the distance, Faas's greeting seemed laced with disappointment. "You know the NVA had you in clear sight walking across that field," he told Trotta. "Dammit, I thought I had the best picture of the war. . . . Of you getting hit." Faas seemed serious. "Very funny, Horst," she told him dryly.

Trotta had arrived in Vietnam in August 1968, just six weeks before this encounter. As the first female correspondent assigned to cover the war by a television news network, she probably reported on more military operations than any other woman who worked on-camera in Vietnam. Her first glimpse of combat had come a week before this trip to Tay Ninh in a place with the unlikely name of Trang Bang. That first taste of combat taught her that covering what in America had come to be called "television's first war" was enormously complicated. The choreography of television, with its need for three people to work in unison, created difficulties and dangers that print journalists never faced. Unlike her earlier taste of combat, at Trang Bang, the encounter at Tay Ninh required American air strikes. Amidst enemy machine-gun fire, the U.S. Air Force was dropping napalm and 750-pound bombs. Despite the air cover, South Vietnam's regional forces were overpowered. Facing a decision about how close they should get to the battle, Trotta was beginning to falter. Huynh was cold and curt: "Either you get it or you don't." Trotta wasn't sure, either then or now, whether he was referring to getting killed or getting film. His meaning didn't matter. Because he was one of those rare people whose judgment she trusted, Trotta swallowed her rising fear.

By nature, she rejected authority and trusted only her own instincts. That, after all, is how she got to Vietnam in the first place. As the Tet Offensive had unfolded months earlier, Trotta fumed that the story belonged to others. Her bosses had first recoiled at the idea of assigning a woman to the war. Her badgering and begging continued unabated. NBC's bosses, however, stood firm. With an equal absence of subtlety, she dropped years-old clippings of Marguerite Higgins's Korean War articles on their desks. Six months after Tet, those bosses finally relented—in part because of her persistence but largely because they were running out of warm male bodies who wanted the assignment. The two other newswomen who had preceded her to Southeast Asia, unlike Trotta, focused on the human interest side of the war. Trotta, in contrast, hungered to witness combat. For her, that was the only story worth telling in Vietnam. In less than three months, Trotta, with her camera and sound men in tow, had witnessed terrifying helicopter assaults under enemy rocket and mortar fire, seen the dying and the dead, and learned to hold her fear in check.

Beyond Higgins and Dickey Chapelle, both of whom had died about three years before Trotta won the assignment, few women embraced combat with Trotta's zeal. Her success marked a triumph for women in television news. Almost instinctively, her bosses had resisted exposing women to danger, but that is precisely what Trotta found so alluring. From the time she had learned to walk atop picket fences in her childhood, Trotta enjoyed courting danger—on the battlefield and sometimes off. Vietnam became her shining moment. She won three Emmys and two Overseas Press Club awards during her television career, one of each for her Vietnam-war reporting.

In her embrace of truths that were neither conventional nor popular, Trotta had a kinship with Saint Jude, the patron saint of hopeless causes, who seemed to lurk backstage as an unacknowledged yet commanding presence in her life. The eleventh of Christ's twelve apostles, according to the New Testament, Jude preached that the faithful were required to persevere even in the face of harsh and desperate circumstances, even when their beliefs were called into question—as they sometimes were. One of the hallmarks of Trotta's character—both before Vietnam and after—is her determination to fight for her own truth, unpopular though it often was.

Television came late to Vietnam, and women in television came even later. Although print news organizations had begun sending full-time staffers to Vietnam in the early 1960s, the attention television paid to the conflict focused on spot news and was a hit-or-miss proposition until 1965. Before his assassination in 1963, President Ngo Dinh Diem, who apparently understood the power of the medium early on, kept television reporting teams under strict surveillance in Saigon and limited their opportunities to cover stories in the countryside. The weight and bulk of camera and sound equipment also restricted television's range in those early days.

Until 1965, the networks dispatched teams from their Hong Kong or Tokyo bureaus as events demanded. Peter Kalischer was frequently sent to Saigon by CBS, and Lou Cioffi represented ABC, which, during the war years, was an also-ran news operation. John Sharkey, an NBC stringer in 1962 and 1963, recalls doing considerably more radio reporting than television broadcasts from Saigon. He covered assorted breaking news stories, the Buddhist demonstrations, and the occasional foray with a U.S. military operation. "You'd spend all day trudging around in combat boots and fatigues, but it generally turned out to be a dry run because the Viet Cong seemed to already know what was coming," Sharkey said. But if he—or any other network correspondent—did get film footage of breaking news, the challenge was to get it back to New York in a hurry. "You would throw it in a sack. Each network had their own color; NBC's was red, and you had to get it out on one of two Pan American flights out of Saigon." Sending it to Tokyo was another option, one used only in a pinch, Sharkey explained. Above all, even though the material might be from thirty-six to forty-eight hours old, one wanted "a story to be pretty ripe by the time it reached New York City."

Another regular NBC visitor in Saigon was Jim Robinson, a teacher in China before Mao Tse-Tung came to power and, later, the Hong Kong bureau chief. He was expelled by the Diem regime in 1963 when word got back to Madame Nhu that after a lengthy interview with her, Robinson told a colleague the session had been "a waste of time." NBC's Garrick Utley was the first permanent television correspondent assigned to the war in July 1964 when his six-week tryout in Saigon turned into a year. From March 1966, when ABC News sent Marlene Sanders to Vietnam for a month, and April 1975, when Sanders's ABC colleague Hilary Brown was evacuated from Saigon, the networks assigned only a handful of women to their Saigon bureaus.[1] Generally, women's tours in the bureau were shorter than those of their male colleagues. Trotta, the only woman NBC News sent to Vietnam, began her six-month tour in 1968 and returned twice in subsequent years.

Trotta's view that combat was "the only story" put her at odds with other women who covered the war, most notably among her broadcast colleagues, the women who preceded her to Vietnam. Sanders thought covering combat "tells you absolutely nothing." She concentrated instead on stories about Americans working at a Vietnamese orphanage, civilian casualties, the injured and sick Montagnards. However, because network executives preferred the "bang-bang," Sanders's stories were largely consigned to the little-watched weekend news shows—to her great disgust: "I thought their judgment was very poor, simple-minded, and I was really very angry when I got back to find how little of it had been used."

Anne Morrissy Merick was similarly disappointed in ABC's preoccupation with combat. The "stories behind the story," which she produced in Vietnam for the network's news programs between January and September 1967, were seldom showcased on ABC's evening news report. Merick began her journalism career in Paris as sports editor of the *International Herald Tribune,* continued as a freelancer in the Middle East, and then proceeded to ABC, where she was a correspondent on *American Newsstand,* a daily news program for teenagers. Later, as a producer for ABC's Special Events Unit, she had covered the civil rights movement, nearly a dozen space missions, and elections, yet she never imagined she would be sent overseas. She was overjoyed when her boss asked her to join the staff in Saigon. In her work as

---

1. Several local stations, including ones in Texas, Louisiana, and California, sent women mostly to do feature pieces about local soldiers who were fighting the war.

a correspondent, field producer, and on-camera reporter, she soon realized that the network's night-after-night combat stories showing the correspondent hunkered down and whispering hoarsely into the camera, "We're at hill number so and so, and there's incoming," never provided viewers with the necessary context, Merick explained. "The war was just chopped into little pieces of bang-bang every night for dinner entertainment." Trotta, in contrast, thought Vietnam was all about the battlefield. With her near-exclusive interest in covering combat, and the aggressive behavior she sometimes displayed in pursuit of those stories, Trotta brought to television reporting the same approach the Frenchwoman Catherine Leroy brought to still photography. In wanting to cover Vietnam in the way Higgins had covered Korea, Trotta dovetailed perfectly with the men who produced the *Huntley-Brinkley Report*, the network's highly popular evening news broadcast. They loved the bang-bang.

At Tay Ninh, danger and romance were overshadowed by the prospect of imminent death. Just before Trotta and her team set out across the field for the schoolhouse, Huynh, who saw terrific visuals in the mortar fire around them, had encouraged her to record an on-camera report. Too afraid to stand as Huynh had suggested, she crouched close to the ground and spoke to the camera. Her voice was a near whisper—breathless and hurried—as she described the fighting around her. Her face was mud-covered, the lipstick she had applied was smudged around her chin. Sweat poured off her. But the luck of a quick ride back to Saigon and the delivery of her material to a Tokyo-bound flight put NBC ahead of CBS and ABC in reporting the Tay Ninh story. Beating their rivals always counted as a coup in broadcast journalism, just as it did for Kate Webb and her wire service colleagues. Alone and exhausted, Trotta returned to her "lumpy bed" in Saigon's Continental Palace Hotel. The restless sleep that followed was marked by a nightmare, her first war nightmare. "No plot, no cast of characters," she recalled in her memoir. "Just an endless expanse of blanched bodies stretching into infinity under a low gray sky."

The primal nature of the war she experienced in Vietnam gave Trotta a fuller understanding of herself. "War makes you grow up. In war, I think you really learn how to be alone," she recalled more than a quarter century after she reported from the battlefields. Somehow, amidst all the terror, "you still function. And that's how war makes you a better person. And it also turns you into a better reporter, a much, much better reporter." Amidst the chaos and ceaseless noise in every battle situation, Trotta always felt a sinking loneliness; a sense that "'this is really it and I'm going to fall apart. The next thing I'm going to see is all black.'" In those moments of overwhelming fear she felt the spirit of her dead father near her. And she prayed to him.

Gaetano (Thomas) Trotta had died in 1966, two years before she left for Vietnam. But her mother was still back in Connecticut, saying novenas for her every day. He was the son of a penniless Italian shepherd who had emigrated from Amalfi to America during his childhood. Gaetano started out as a six-year-old shoe-shine boy who supported his crippled father, mother, and three siblings. By the time he married Lillian Theresa Mazzacane, who also had emigrated from Italy during her childhood, Thomas Trotta had become a classic New World success story. He was a prosperous New Haven pharmacist who had little patience for frivolities and scorned taxpayer financed-assistance programs. By 1937, when Elizabeth was born, Thomas Trotta was making enough money to provide his family with a comfortable, middle-class life. The enormous self-discipline Liz Trotta brought to her career in journalism grew out of her parents' example of hard work and her Catholic upbringing. She speaks of her parents with reverence, praising her father for the rigid rules he imposed on her as she grew up and her mother for the ladylike example she always set. "I suppose it's terribly unfashionable," she said, mocking—as she so often does—society's twenty-first-century conventions. "I loved my parents and don't have any dysfunctional story to tell."

Ballet was Trotta's first career choice, one she made as a child. The lessons she began taking as a nine-year-old at Madame Annette's School of Dance, she said, taught her the kind of persistence and determination that are journalism's essential survival skills. Betty, as she was known in her family, often spent four or five hours a day practicing her pliés and pirouettes at a barre in a basement room. In daydreams that played out during these sessions, Trotta saw herself dancing on the world's great stages, perhaps in London's Sadler's Wells Theatre or at the Metropolitan Opera House as the prima ballerina in Tchaikovsky's *Swan Lake*. Even in these reveries, however, the cold war put Moscow's Bolshoi Theater, the ballet world mecca, off limits. In one capital or the other, she would star in the dance adaptation of *Carmen*, Georges Bizet's famous opera about a gypsy outcast who longed for acceptance. Trotta had seen Reneé (ZiZi) Jeanmaire, a famous French ballerina, dance as Carmen at New Haven's Schubert Theater. But a hometown stage, even one where all Broadway-bound shows did try-outs, was far too small for Trotta's ambitions. She needed grander surroundings. And in these fantasies she was "always a solo," she recalled with a burst of laughter. "I wasn't going to share the spotlight with anyone." *The Red Shoes*, a film "which probably introduced more people to ballet than any other event," enchanted Trotta. Somehow the reality that Victoria Page, the prima ballerina played by Moira Shearer, was ultimately devoured by the urge to dance didn't deter Trotta and the legions of other American girls who dreamed of becoming dancers. Although Trotta had the will, the discipline, and the stamina needed to be a ballet dancer, as a teenager she recognized that her reach exceeded her grasp. When she was thirteen, she spent a day practicing in New York at the School of American Ballet. Afterward, Trotta performed a bit of self-analysis and, in the take-no-prisoners style that became so familiar to colleagues at NBC, she faced reality: "I didn't have the talent. I was good for New Haven, but I'd never make it in the big time." Besides, her "Mediterranean body" would never grow the long legs dancers required. With that realization, her visions of *pointe* shoes and tutus vanished.

And just as well perhaps. Her father had no intention of letting her become a dancer. That was show business, a disreputable career. Dancing was out of the question; she could be a doctor or a criminal lawyer. "This is not a democracy," he declared. "If you want to be a dancer and go into show business, that's fine, but you're not in this house anymore." And in the Trotta household, his edicts were non-negotiable. That's when she turned to journalism, even though it was a distant second to her original aspiration. Trotta first confronted journalism's gender barriers as a teenager at the *New Haven Register*, where she tried to get summer job in journalism's lowliest ranks. "You hire copy boys, don't you?" she flippantly asked the man in charge of summer hiring. Yes, he acknowledged, "but they're not girls." She reluctantly spent the summer working in the *Register*'s advertising department. By then, she was also developing a rebellious spirit and a taste for the conservative politics she had learned at her father's knee. As an immigrant who had been given nothing beyond the opportunity to work hard, Thomas Trotta scorned President Franklin D. Roosevelt and the New Deal with the same zeal his daughter later deployed in scorning the antiwar movement in the Vietnam era. "He just did not understand handouts, he really didn't," Trotta said of her father. "No one had ever given him anything." Nor did he think anyone should. America stood for opportunity; that was all the nation was obliged to offer its citizens and its immigrants, he insisted.

That conservative outlook gelled further in her late teens after she read William F. Buckley's *God and Man at Yale*. By then an aspiring writer herself, she delighted in his use of language and his wit. Even on paper, that arched patrician eyebrow so familiar to those who later witnessed his television appearances seemed visible. Trotta found a kindred spirit in his Catholicism and conservatism. Perhaps she heard echoes of her father's views in Buckley's criticism of his alma mater, particularly when he excoriated Yale University's economics curriculum for its use of textbooks that advocated notions of collectivism, socialism, and government control of the economy. "How is it that a Department of Economics that once upheld individual self-reliance and limited government—but for few exceptions—now dedicated to collectivism in various degrees?" Buckley asked.

That her own future might be quite different from her mother's life as a housewife and caregiver first struck her in Troup Junior High School. Ida Himmelfarb, in Trotta's description, was the school's "most feared English teacher." She worked to inspire in her female students aspirations on the far side of traditional female pursuits. Himmelfarb wanted teenaged girls to reach beyond those trammeled ambitions that had beset the girls in Gloria Emerson's graduating class at New York's Washington Irving High School—girls whose sights were set on jobs as telephone operators and receptionists. Although Himmelfarb understood that women in the early 1950s "dared not invade the upper reaches of any profession," she strove to kindle in her students the idea that women could not and should not constrain their ambitions. "What you are to be, you are now becoming," Himmelfarb told her seventh-grade students. "I was stopped cold," Trotta recalls. "Suddenly I realized that this is serious, it's like writing in wet cement. It's all going to dry one day." Junior high school also gave Trotta her first opportunity to practice journalism. Armed with her yellow *Troup Trumpet* press pass, she elbowed her way through the backstage door at the Schubert Theater whenever big shows passed through town. "I was so star-struck in those days," she recalled. "I would wander around and interview everybody."

High school, however, was another story. Certain that a wild streak he discerned in his daughter boded trouble if left unchecked, Thomas Trotta decreed that she would attend St. Mary's Academy, a Catholic high school run by Dominican nuns. Her strongest recollection of those four years is Sister Camillus, her English teacher, who, Trotta noted, "really taught me how to perform on TV." She required students to memorize and recite a long short story, something twenty pages or more. "It taught me so much about poise and confidence and the power of memory." The College of New Rochelle, another Catholic school that Thomas Trotta chose for his still rebellious daughter, gave her a glimpse of the conventional future she realized she did not want. The institution's fundamental lesson seemed to be that marriage—to a Catholic, of course—was the most desirable destiny to which a woman could aspire. "It seemed a terrible waste of time, putting in four years of brainwork and then holding out for the bridal registry at Tiffany's," Trotta concluded. "It was a giant failure of imagination, a buying-in to a system and an attitude that held up as models women such as Jean Kerr and Clare Booth Luce: "very talented, but more important, Catholic, married, and rich."

In Trotta's memory, the academic curriculum at the College of New Rochelle was stultifying. One of the restraints placed on students by the college library, for example, demanded written parental permission to sign out books by James Joyce and Voltaire. To the horror of the Ursuline nuns who ran the college, Trotta adorned her dorm room with a life-sized poster of a lustful-looking Elvis Presley whose pouty lips, unbuttoned shirt, and parted legs left them aghast. She told them "the King" was her fiancé. By the end of her sophomore year, the nuns had had enough. Her acts of insubordination, to her delight, led school officials to ask her not to return. She finished her undergraduate studies at Boston University, where she was no less unruly. She and a like-minded classmate, Rick Gelinas, published the *Razor's Edge,* an underground newspaper that challenged, among other things, "the 1950s sweetheart of Sigma Chi campus ethic." Trotta recalled it as "a mixture of trendy philosophical thought, very earnest fiction, Beat Generation essays, satires of the rah-rah student leaders, university officials, and philosophy professors." The *Razor's Edge* and its message of protest, however, quickly became a victim of censorship. At a time when the First Amendment rights of students had yet to be tested in the U.S. Supreme Court, Trotta and Gelinas deferred to university officials who threatened to expel them if a second edition appeared. By the time the rest of the country caught up with her discontent in the antiwar movement nearly a decade later, Trotta appears to have lost all patience for the kind of crusade that had fired her in the late 1950s.

She perceives no parallel between the way she rebelled in one decade and how another generation of students rebelled a decade later. Her own youthful protests were entirely different, she insists. She was not trying to upend the foundations of societal values and norms, Trotta explained. "Yes, I was certainly about challenging authority because I had a healthy skepticism about authority. But not all authority and I certainly wasn't tearing down all authority. I didn't challenge my church because I believed in my church." In Trotta's mind, protesters in the 1960s used the Vietnam War as a ruse:

The antiwar movement was about not attending school. It was about taking drugs and running wild and not taking any responsibility. Those people at the barricades who were portrayed as so heroic really didn't have any consequences to pay. In the '60s, the sense of tearing down came with the attitude that it was fun. It also came out of an ignorance of what was going on in Southeast Asia. That ignorance was gigantic.

With her degree from Boston University in hand, Trotta sought the imprimatur of Columbia University, whose graduate program in journalism still remained the model for the academic programs it had spawned after its creation in 1903. "It was very tough to get into Columbia in those days," she recalled. Indeed, her first application was rejected. Get some writing experience, the we-regret-to-inform-you letter advised. In her ensuing job hunt, Trotta learned that little had changed since she had asked to be hired as a copy boy at the *New Haven Register*. Employers were reluctant to hire women because they "leave and have babies." Her long search ended when Hillman Publications, a company whose specialty was confessional magazines, made her an editorial assistant. She wrote seductive cover blurbs for *Real Romance* and *Real Story*, catchy lines designed to stimulate an impulse purchase at supermarket checkout lines. She also wrote suggestive captions for the illustrations that accompanied stories of love, lust, and loss, work that admissions officials at Columbia apparently found impressive. A year later, she was among the dozen or so women at Columbia generally admitted to its seventy-five-member classes.

Columbia's graduate program "was run like a trade course, probably the best trade course in the country," recalled Trotta's classmate, Christopher Wren, who spent much of his career at the *New York Times*. Richard Duncan, another classmate and Trotta friend, who later became the chief of correspondents at *Time* magazine, said that hard news and news writing were central to the curriculum. John Hohenberg, Columbia's legendary teacher, "was a wire service guy who focused on 'writing first lead, second lead, go with what you've got on deadline approach to journalism,'" Duncan said. Jack Shepherd, another of Trotta's classmates, said the program was so focused on the rudiments that the professors "almost told you where to keep your pen and put your notebook." Professor Hohenberg, recalled Shepherd, "would tell you, 'Don't forget to wear a hat, don't forget to take an extra pen, and don't forget to read [what's on] the top of the desk.'"

Comparing the public regard for journalism—and journalists—in the late 1950s and early 1960s with the "access" culture that beset the profession in the 1980s and 1990s, Wren recalled how "journalists were admitted to the tradesmen's entrance. In my day you expected to be fed in the kitchen. We reveled in being outsiders, in being paid to satisfy our curiosity." Columbia's program, in Shepherd's recollection, "was a mixture between the Hemingway kind of journalism and the more academic level." Much was made of how the Columbia student armed with a master's degree was certain to become a unique figure in America's newsrooms, most of which in those days were filled with men whose formal education had ended with a high school diploma. "Somehow we were made to feel that we were going to be extraordinary," Shepherd said. Trotta, too, recalls feeling that "we were special."

Wren and Shepherd said Trotta thrived in Columbia's "newsroom" environment where three other women who became Vietnam-era journalists—Higgins, Flora Lewis, and Beverly Deepe—launched their careers. Assignments were distributed daily, and students were expected to deliver stories by a late afternoon deadline. The reputation Trotta quickly established as competitive and audacious led Wren to nickname her "Scoopie." She would charge through a wall for a story, both he and Shepherd remembered. "She loved deadline journalism. There was no question that of all the women in our class, she was going to be a journalist," Shepherd said. Wren remembers her "slightly hard-nosed, sassy attitude." He rather admired it.

The 1960 presidential election campaign provided Columbia's young journalists with an abundance of story opportunities, as did the many international events that took place in New York City. With her official-looking but phony press pass establishing her as a member of the Columbia Press Association, Trotta tried—unsuccessfully—to slip through the police cordon around the United Nations on the October day in 1960 when Soviet Premier Nikita Khrushchev banged his shoe on the table in response to a Philippine delegate who accused the Soviet Union of imperialism in Eastern Europe. She sought out interviews with the likes of Nelson Rockefeller and John F. Kennedy, then the Democratic presidential candidate. She covered trials, press conferences, and police stories.

Her friends have no recollection of her conservatism during their graduate school days together. To them, Trotta seemed to have few interests beyond her career. "Politics wasn't important in the context of what we were doing at Columbia," Wren remembered. In Shepherd's recollection she was "quietly proud of her Roman Catholic heritage." Based on his vague realization of her background as the daughter of immigrants, Shepherd assumed she was a liberal and presumed she was a JFK supporter. But Trotta considered Kennedy "a fake prince." Wren and Shepherd have difficulty imagining that Trotta cast her vote for Nixon in 1960, the first presidential election in which she participated. Shepherd also has difficulty fathoming that she could be anything but a moderate Republican whose political views were "somewhere in the center of the spectrum." Trotta maintains she was anything but. While she was studying at Columbia, she joined what she called the "wild-eyed conservatives" in the Young Americans for Freedom during the first week of the organization's existence. Politics, however, remained a minor preoccupation in the context of her studies. Becoming a journalist was all that mattered to Trotta.

George Barrett did more than any other Columbia faculty member to help her achieve that goal. The *Times*man, whom Trotta described as a William Faulkner look-alike and a man to whom romantic tales attached themselves, became her guru at Columbia. Since Barrett was the professional who stripped journalism of all its glamour, Trotta understood that the life he had led covering Paris after World War II, his posting at the front lines in the Korean War, and his assignment to report on the early stirrings of America's civil rights movement often made for grinding work and an empty personal life. "Being a reporter means leaving airports with no one to say 'Goodbye,' and arriving at airports with no one to say 'Hello,'" Barrett told Trotta. Her commitment to the profession remained unshaken.

Journalism in the early 1960s was still all about print, about words rather than pictures. Radio was the only important source of broadcast news. Despite its twelve-year history, television news was still in its infancy when Trotta joined Columbia's Class of 1961. There were few hints that the medium would, in less than a decade, begin to eclipse newspapers as the nation's most important source of news. Indeed, the nation's premier journalism program offered only one course on the subject: "a throwaway," as Trotta described it. Network successes in live coverage of the 1948 Republican and Democratic national conventions led CBS and NBC to launch nightly news broadcasts that year. Those fifteen-minute programs, *Douglas Edwards and the News* on CBS and later *Camel Caravan of News with John Cameron Swayze* on NBC, never gained the esteem in which the nation's major newspapers were held. Advertiser sponsorship—Oldsmobile at CBS and Camel cigarettes at NBC—made for occasional difficulties. The manufacturers of Camel cigarettes, for example, invoked a ban on broadcasting images of anyone smoking a cigar. Consequently, Winston Churchill, England's World

War II–era prime minister who remained in the news long after the war, was never seen on Swayze's broadcast—because he always had a cigar in hand. When Reuven Frank became the program's writer in 1951, he won a special dispensation for Churchill. Other cigar smokers, Groucho Marx, for example, remained outcasts.

The *Camel News Caravan* and John Cameron Swayze, whose trademark was a fresh flower in his lapel and a new tie every day, was replaced by the *Huntley-Brinkley Report* replaced in 1956. With the novelty of Chet Huntley reporting from New York and his partner, David Brinkley, reporting from Washington, the program remained a fifteen-minute "headline news service." So did *Douglas Edwards and the News,* even after Edwards was replaced by Walter Cronkite as the CBS news anchor in 1962. The fifteen-minute news broadcasts expanded to thirty minutes within a week of each other in September 1963, a move that injected a new set of parameters into the nation's media equation. Walter Cronkite's Labor Day broadcast featured an interview with President Kennedy to mark the debut of its expanded format. Days later, the new thirty-minute *Huntley-Brinkley Report* also featured an interview with the president. Media historians delineate that week as the time when television news shed its identity as a derivative of radio. News in the thirty-minute format gained increasing legitimacy with viewers who numbered in the millions every night. The number of American households with television had first surpassed the number of those households that received a daily newspaper in 1957. Newspaper readership had continued to grow, but television ownership grew even faster. The supremacy of print was in doubt. That reality had yet to penetrate the Columbia curriculum when Trotta was a student there on 1961. The single television news course Columbia offered was "a hoot" in Trotta's memory. Her only recollection of it was writing and recording a narrative for pieces of film: "It was sort of a joke, a toy course because back then you wanted to write and you didn't find real writers in television," she said. So it meant little when her professor, Dallas Townsend of CBS News, told her: "You have a wonderful voice; you would be a natural on television." News on television was a tainted commodity; it seemed more like show business than journalism, Trotta thought. She told Townsend she wanted to be a "newspaper woman, not a performer."

She was drawn to more complex subjects than the kinds of stories that lent themselves to a television format. Her graduate thesis project, for example, the capstone assignment in Columbia's program, was an investigative report on an urban renewal project proposed for her own Greenwich Village neighborhood. "Title I On Trial," Trotta's twenty-page article, examined the New York City Planning Commission's proposal to raze a fourteen-square-block "blighted" area. Militant protests, parochialism, charges of fraud, and threats to take the case all the way to the U.S. Supreme Court were of part of the saga. The controversy ultimately became one of the most important real estate fracases in New York, one that taught city residents they could fight City Hall and win. Her thesis advisor, Penn Kimball, gave her little guidance and was unimpressed with her finished product, Trotta recalled. Not only was he George Barrett's polar opposite, he seemed to her to be a pretentious liberal, the kind she would soon come to despise. "The trouble with you is that you're Catholic and Catholics can't write," he told her. He said her mind had been stifled by "all that parochial training." The experience, Trotta said years later, taught her "a valuable lesson about American political thought." The lesson she took from the encounter was that liberals had a dangerous capacity for intolerance and even tyranny. She later judged the antiwar crowd by that yardstick.

Despite the Columbia pedigree that the school's professors insisted would make its students "anointed ones," graduates in the early 1960s discovered that their degrees did not guarantee them a special place in America's newsrooms. Journalism jobs were hard to find in 1961. The New York City newspaper market was shrinking in the early 1960s, and the number of American cities with competing daily newspapers had dropped from a high of 181 in 1940 to 61 in 1961, a downward spiral that continued in subsequent decades. "Most of us did not get a job with a major newspaper right out of Columbia," Richard Duncan remembered. Trotta, however, was one of the few who did. She landed in Chicago, in a job that some classmates envied.

She found a place at the *Chicago Tribune,* the newspaper Colonel Robert McCormick had built in the windswept city of gangsters and bootleg liquor. By any standard, the job put her in the big leagues, even though she wrote for one of its suburban weekly supplements. In that familiar proving ground for all new recruits, Trotta was assigned to cover town meetings, the local school board, and, that most dreaded assignment of all, zoning hearings. Stories about the installation of some new type of sewer plant in a proposed development, the merger of three North Side neighborhoods into a "super community," or a quarrel about closing a city street were hardly the pinnacle of her aspirations as a writer. "I thought it was beneath me," she recalled. "I was annoyed. I belonged in the main newsroom."

Trotta wanted a future that reached well beyond a weekly suburban section—even though that section was tucked inside the *Chicago Tribune.*

And she was one of the increasing number of women who dared to ask for what they wanted. Of the two women in the *Trib* newsroom, both World War II–era holdovers, one wrote feature stories and the other wrote about pets—hardly the size stage Trotta needed to accommodate her ambitions. When she heard about the newspaper's plans to open a New York office, Trotta went straight to the executive editor to plead her cause. Clayton Kirkpatrick was dismissive. "It's not a job for a woman," he told her.

In frustration, Trotta quit after less than two years. She took a job with the Associated Press in its Miami bureau. During a short-lived career as a wire service reporter, she wrote about robberies and murders. Her real break came in 1963 when she joined *Newsday,* the Long Island newspaper Alicia Patterson had founded in 1940 and built in the face of objections and doubts registered by her father, Joseph Medill Patterson, a co-owner with his cousin—McCormick of the *Chicago Tribune* and the *New York Daily News.* Alicia Patterson made *Newsday* an award-winner—and, like Horace Greeley and his successors at the *International Herald Tribune,* she rejected prevailing notions about women and their competence as reporters.

Trotta arrived at *Newsday* the same year that Marguerite Higgins became a staff correspondent. Higgins took the job after her twenty-two year association with the *New York Herald Tribune* ended. Editors there were said to have been embarrassed by the role she played in the battle royal with the South Vietnam's resident correspondents in the summer of 1963, and by the ideological spin on her stories about the war. She left the newspaper, according to her biographer, after her editorial page column was dropped "for lack of space." According to David Halberstam, one *Tribune* editor who was angry about the slant of her Vietnam dispatches vowed: "That woman will never piss outside the United States again." At *Newsday,* Higgins wrote three columns a week, and once again she was spending considerable time in Southeast Asia. On rare occasions, an article by Trotta would run alongside one by Higgins. But Trotta was only dimly aware of the conflict in Vietnam. It was President Kennedy and his empowerment of the Green Berets that first brought Vietnam to her attention, Trotta recalled.

Trotta's first assignment at *Newsday* was the entertainment beat. Perhaps because she had seen too many stars backstage at the Schubert in New Haven, the often vapid comments of Broadway and Hollywood types quickly bored her. She interviewed Liza Minnelli, the seventeen-year-old daughter of Judy Garland whose blatherings about all the advice "Momma" had given her included "always be feminine" and "don't let people use you." She interviewed the original, alluring James Bond—Sean Connery. Her story noted the Scottish actor's "bedroom eyes," the presence of "three models assigned to escort him" on his Manhattan rounds, and his vacuous observation, "Yes, I do identify with Bond. I, too, enjoy drinking, women, eating."

She asked the entertainment editor to give her a meatier assignment. "Go get yourself a job in a dime-a-dance hall in Times Square," snapped Lou Schwartz. Never one to pass up a challenge, Trotta rented herself a sequined gown, supplemented her minimal natural endowments with wads of Kleenex, and waltzed around a seedy Seventh Avenue dance hall with anyone who plunked down their dollars. At last, she had found a story that no male reporter could have researched or written—a three-part series that resulted in action by New York's city council. Former Columbia classmates Wren and Shepherd were in awe of Trotta when they read her stories. The early 1960s were still a buttoned-down era. "This was a sexually conservative time when people were still chaperoned in dorms. And here was a woman going into the fringe of a red-light district—going places that I wouldn't have gone at the time," Shepherd said. "We thought it was a great risk. It was a defining moment."

Trotta's series exposed the world of Manhattan's dance halls, places where women hired themselves out, most often to lechers who wanted more than a brief foxtrot around the slippery dance floor. And the women who made their living in dance halls wanted more, too. For both sides, it was a con game. Most of the men hoped for an after-work encounter, and the women hoped for money—without the after-work encounter. Women doing all that dancing and conning earned between $50 and $150 a week. Trotta, in her slinky, strapless dress, danced her way to a $70 paycheck in the seven days she worked at the Parisian Danceland. As it turned out, the dime-a-dance price tag was itself a con. Trotta's story explained how all those men she danced with, "old and young, fat and lean, rich and poor from Boise to Brooklyn" paid $1.35 to get in the door, a fee that bought ten tickets and entitled the holder to two dances. Every two additional dances cost $1.25. Better money was made by talking customers into "sitting at the tables," an option that cost fifty tickets ($6.25) per half hour. Earning the big bucks involved "propping," or propositioning, a customer. That was agreeing to meet a customer after hours for an encounter that would involve sex. The con was that he had to pay up front, usually $25 to $50, and she never showed. Apparently the number of hoodwinked customers who returned to demand a refund was minimal.

Not long after her stories were published, New York City revoked the licenses of dancing establishments for practicing "lewd, obscene and immoral dancing and acts offensive to public decency." The *New York Times* noted in a story about the closing of a Seventh Avenue dance hall that "Miss Elizabeth Trotta, who by way of researching a story about dance halls, got a job as a dancer," had been called as a witness at a city License Commission hearing.

Several months later, in a foretaste of the marathon work days she would endure in Vietnam, Trotta spent all but a few hours at her desk during the November 1963 weekend when President Kennedy was assassinated. In an extra edition published on the day the president died, Trotta shared a byline with two other reporters on a story about the impact of the assassination on Long Islanders. "Businesses closed, traffic stopped, and people wept openly," the story explained. The region's political leaders weighed in with expressions of grief, sympathy for the family, and support for President Johnson. Later that weekend, Trotta wrote about the eight "stately geldings" that drew the caisson carrying President Kennedy's casket to Arlington National Cemetery. The horses and the soldiers astride four of them were part of the U.S. Army's ceremonial unit and were otherwise involved in an average of three military funerals every day, Trotta's story explained. Their head trainer likened the horses to people, saying they were "just like human beings. If they stay in one place too long, they get jittery and restless."

While Trotta and her peers in newsrooms across the country scrambled to put out extra editions to keep readers abreast of developments, television was delivering a more visceral and immediate brand of news. If any event marked the moment television news achieved legitimacy, it was the hours and days that followed the news flashes of the assassination in Dallas. From the moment that Walter Cronkite removed his black rimmed glasses and swallowed his emotions on Friday afternoon after he relayed the news of the president's death until darkness fell on the newly ignited eternal flame late Monday, television usurped the moment. How could Trotta's story of a horse trainer talking about his eight jittery geldings compete, for example, with television's image of the symbolic riderless horse, Black Jack, majestic, taut, and unruly as he followed the caisson along Pennsylvania Avenue. Trotta's words on the pages of *Newsday* amounted to little more than a horse story, but the images of Black Jack reached the dimension of allegory. The succession of spectral images left Americans spellbound: the bronze casket being removed from Air Force One in the darkness, a new president asking for God's help, Lee Harvey Oswald taking a bullet in the abdomen, a little boy's endearing salute to his father's flag-draped coffin, a vibrant, young first lady in widow's weeds. All were delivered in an instant, long before the morning and afternoon newspapers arrived on America's doorsteps. Neither in words nor in photographs—all printed in black-and-white—could any daily newspaper compete with the power of those televised images. Even on the pages of the wildly popular *Life* magazine, with its oversized color photographs, the action remained frozen and inert. For four days, television transfixed the nation.

Barely two years later, television and its growing ability to bring visual reports from distant battlefields into viewers' homes began to distinguish Vietnam from every previous American war. Vietnam was to become, as Michael Arlen so memorably put it, America's "living room war." The insistent nature of those distant images seen on daily news broadcasts had a net effect that could be measured only in hindsight. Their closest approximation was the newsreel footage, often shot by military cameramen, of battles in World War II and Korea that were shown in America's movie theaters. Rather than build support for war, as so many of those earlier film clips had, war on the small screen, inside the homes of millions of viewers, became too close and too constant. Television in the end changed the equation of war and had a profound impact on public support. In combination with the entertainment side of television programming—where truth and justice inevitably prevailed usually in thirty, or, at most, sixty, minutes—the war made for increasingly uncomfortable viewing. It lacked the kind of resolution viewers had been conditioned to expect from the small screen. The distasteful tactics common to every war were suddenly visible in one's living room. In moving images, one saw a young Marine, equipped with a familiar Zippo lighter, set fire to a thatched-roof hut as anguished peasants looked on. The scenes, which lacked any sense of proportion, imprinted themselves on the national psyche. Hulking, healthy-looking soldiers in olive drabs towered over tiny people dressed in black pajamas. And they all looked so terrified of the soldiers who were supposed to be saving them from the ravages of Communism. Something was out of kilter. Night after night, America's pursuit of victory was unfulfilled. Indeed, as improbable as it seemed, the enemy so often invisible to viewers on television, an enemy who fought the war with bamboo spikes and AK-47s from the Soviet Union, appeared capable of besting all the Sherman tanks and B-52 bombers let loose by the most powerful army in the world. Night after night, the questions festered.

This was the milieu into which Liz Trotta walked when she made her giant leap from print to broadcast news in April 1965. The growth of television during and immediately after World War II, combined with the absence of men to fill the new jobs it created, was a bonanza for women. Women occupied positions at every level of network and local station operations in the mid-to-late 1940s. By the mid-1950s, however, those jobs as producers, directors, writers, engineers, and announcers were evaporating despite the growth of television. The few women who survived were slowly consigned to represent their gender's interests. "There was at least one woman on the staff of every television studio, large or small, to handle the woman's angle." By the early 1960s, however, that pattern began to change . . . ever so slowly.

Television's stature as a news medium had risen since Trotta's grad school days at Columbia, and to her it was no longer out of the question. The half-hour news broadcasts on NBC and CBS had crossed a frontier of professionalism in 1963 as a result of their shift from a fifteen-minute format. "Real writers" were doing television news. Trotta had watched the televised reports of the Kennedy assassination and its aftermath; their reach and intensity impressed her. The medium itself made Black Jack a big story, bigger than her own horse story could ever be, confined as its distribution was to the newspaper's Long Island readers. "The sun had come out and television news was big," she recalled. By late in 1964, the tedium of working nights, her growing dislike of *Newsday*'s city editor, and her need for some new challenge put all the pieces in place. Why couldn't she stare into a camera lens, grip a microphone, and deliver news to the multitudes? Hadn't Dallas Townsend told her she had a great voice? And the money—well, the money was big. Her annual income might leap by as much as $15,000. But best of all, television offered her a national stage, maybe even an international one—and she would do stand-up solo performances, rather like the those she had envisioned in her daydreams of ballet stardom. So when an acquaintance working at NBC's local news operation in New York told her his bosses were looking for a female reporter, Trotta was ready. Early in 1965, Robert Kintner, president of NBC News, had put out word to his management team: "Find me a girl reporter." By then, the CBS local news operation in New York had placed a woman in front of the camera, and Kintner apparently thought it was time to catch up with the competition. Fifty women auditioned, and Trotta was offered the job. "Back then you didn't have to look like a mermaid," said Trotta years later, wryly disparaging some of her female successors. "If you were not Quasimodo you had a shot at a job in [television] journalism."

Among those who had already established a foothold in television when Trotta was hired at NBC were Pauline Frederick, who joined ABC News in 1948 as a radio reporter and later covered the United Nations with savvy and intelligence. Frederick joined the NBC news operation in 1953. Nancy Dickerson had become a major player on the White House beat for NBC in the 1960s. Marlene Sanders had a daytime news program on ABC and was the first woman to anchor an evening news program. At the time, most of these women were routinely urged to color their hair, remove their glasses, and change their wardrobes. Although just a few of them had made the network ranks of on-air talent, women had more than proven their abilities as television reporters. Nonetheless, news directors were predisposed to exclude women from broadcast jobs. Men sounded more authoritative, according to public opinion surveys. In the 1970s, that view was echoed by Reuven Frank, NBC News president, when he told a *Newsweek* interviewer, "Audiences are less prepared to accept news from a woman's voice than from a man's." Women couldn't handle the assignments and, besides, women let their personal problems affect their jobs, according to editors who responded to one of the surveys.

On her first assignment, Trotta proved her mettle. She was sent off to the Waldorf-Astoria to cover a speech by Congressman John V. Lindsay and get him to answer a few questions. She approached Lindsay as he entered the Waldorf to ask whether he had a moment to answer a few questions. The congressman never broke stride and uttered a curt "no" as he passed her and the camera crew. When she called the news desk to apprise her assignment editor of the brush-off, his instructions were to go on the offensive after the speech: "Chase the bastard to hell if you have to. Just keep asking questions." That required "going portable." It meant that Trotta, with microphone in hand, would lead a chase, with her camera and sound men following in hot pursuit—a three-member unit bound together by cables. Lindsay, apparently determined to avoid the cameras that day, hadn't reckoned with Trotta's tenacity. As she gave chase, her prey headed for a staircase, but appeared to become confused about which way was out. After a go up and down the Waldorf's red-carpeted stairs, and uttering an angry "no comment" to every one of Trotta's questions as he went, he demanded in a moment of rage to know her name. He then declared, "Your station will hear about this." Trotta appealed for his understanding, telling Lindsay it was her first day out in the field and she was just trying to do her job. Unmoved, he sputtered about her unseemly behavior, unaware perhaps that the cameras were running. It was Trotta's first ambush interview and it led the Sixth Hour News in New York that night. William R. McAndrew, president of the news division, as Trotta later told the story, "bolted from his office to exclaim to his attendant cronies, 'Well, at least she's not a lollipop.'"

Trotta soon discovered that inside the newsroom and in pursuit of stories the news was very much a man's business. The insults and sexist put-downs she endured as the rare woman in the man's world of television news stretched across years. Both from her own colleagues in the news business and from the subjects she covered, behavior that would in a later decade become grounds for a legal action was commonplace. When she covered Lindsay's 1966 campaign for mayor of New York, both the candidate and her colleagues in the media were ever ready to have a laugh at her expense. During a campaign appearance at which Trotta was the only woman in the press entourage, the candidate covered the NBC microphone with his hand and declared, "Women should only be allowed in the bedroom and the kitchen." Her male colleagues roared with laughter at Lindsay's stag-party wisecrack. In Trotta's telling, even men one presumed might have some sympathy for and understanding of the women's movement would invariably revert to boys-will-be-boys behavior when they were in a group setting.

In April 1968, in another of her assignments, Trotta encountered the same behavior when she was assigned to Senator Eugene McCarthy's romantic but ill-starred bid for the Democratic presidential nomination. On her first day aboard the campaign plane, an aide attempted to introduce Trotta to the Minnesota senator; however, rather than shake her outstretched hand, McCarthy turned to her competitor from CBS News and announced, "Well, well, NBC's gotten so desperate, they've sent a girl." Her own producer joined in the laughter, Trotta noted in her memoir. Camera crews, Trotta also discovered, could be just as implacable. Unlike her subjects and her bosses who harbored doubts about a woman's ability to do the work, most of the men responsible for producing the pictures and sound were blue-collar types who didn't much like working with women. The perception that "she's got balls" seemed to allay their resentments, but that process took years. It was only after she returned from Vietnam that she began to win their acceptance and respect.

Even in her early years as a lowly staffer for WNBC, the network's New York affiliate, Trotta put her bosses straight about her ambitions. Their first taste of Trotta's intransigence left them stunned. It came in the summer of 1965 when a network producer organizing NBC's coverage of the marriage of Lynda Bird Johnson, the president's daughter, to U.S. Marine Captain Charles Robb asked Trotta to ferret out a story about Johnson's wedding dress. It was "shaping up as a hell of a story," he told her. The producer, of course, thought he was doing Trotta, a mere New York affiliate staffer, a huge favor. "But I don't do weddings," Trotta told him. "I don't work on women's stories." The next day, a network vice president tried to put her back in her place. As "just a local reporter," she should be grateful, he told her. Trotta was having none of it. "Don't you understand," she said, "I want to cover a war—not a wedding." Word slowly began to get around: "Trotta is trouble."

She was no less defiant in 1970 when NBC was preparing to mark the fiftieth anniversary of the enactment of women's suffrage. Trotta discovered her name in the pages of the New York *Daily News* in a story drawn from a network press release outlining NBC's plan to revamp the *Today* show to celebrate the occasion. All the men who had on-camera jobs would be replaced by women on August 27, 1970, the story explained. Pauline Frederick, Nancy Dickerson, Aline Saarinen, and Trotta were to join Barbara Walters, then a *Today* show regular, as cohosts and anchors. Trotta exploded. The blatant tokenism that framed the idea enraged her. Worse still, the men who had conceived of the idea were astonished by her reaction. The *Today* show's executive producer, Stuart Schulberg, was flabbergasted. In response to her tirade, he said, "I had no idea anyone would feel this way." Trotta recalled that Saarinen shared her contempt for what Trotta labeled the network's "Aunt Jemima plan." Saarinen suggested that "they might just as well ask all the blacks on the staff to do the news" on Lincoln's birthday. Trotta, who stood by her principles, refused to participate in the network's celebration.

Neither early in her career nor later, Trotta said, did she find women who could serve as her role models. When pressed to name a woman who might have influenced her career, Trotta cannot come up with a single name. Not even Marguerite Higgins, whose style and whose stories she so admired. Who was her role model? "ME," she declared without hesitation. "It's pretentious but it's true," she conceded. Her heroes, she confessed, "were guys." After surveying the feminist movement in the mid-1960s, Trotta quickly surmised that she would manage on her own. Being a woman was irrelevant, she insisted years later. She was a journalist, and journalism was profession that transcended gender. Certainly the growing force of women's lib put pressure on her network bosses. Still, she was disdainful of what she called the movement's "noisy posturing and its excessively liberal demands." The National Organization for Women, in her view, "seemed more bent on arguing who's on top sexually than on the less glamorous issues of pay equality," an issue in which Trotta had a keen interest.

One of the most noteworthy early coups she scored in her television career came in the opening days of 1966 when she was assigned to cover the bargaining talks aimed at settling a transit workers strike that had left New

York City on the brink of disaster. For reasons she still cannot fully explain, a federal mediator involved in the talks agreed to an interview with Trotta. Nathan Feinsinger was attempting to frighten both sides into serious negotiation. Trotta's unlikely reasoning was that he "took pity" on her as the talks dragged on because he had so often seen her elbowed aside by her male colleagues. NBC broke into its regular programming to broadcast Trotta's live interview with Feinsinger. By the time the strike was settled on January 13, her work in covering it left network executives considering whether it was time to place "a girl" on their reporting staff. Only on rare occasions did local reporters scale the wall that separated the galley slaves doing local news from the network's team of elites. Although Trotta did finally breach that divide, she spent two more years in local news before joining television journalism's "royal company."

As a local reporter, her growing ambition to cover the war was so ridiculous on its face that even Saint Jude could have offered little help. However, once she informally joined the network in March 1968, she saw a slim chance. Her temporary assignment was covering Senator McGovern's presidential bid. Nonetheless, she began reading the classic backgrounders on Vietnam, *Street Without Joy* and *Hell in a Very Small Place* by Bernard B. Fall, *The Vietnamese and Their Revolution,* coauthored by the French scholar Paul Mus. Trotta's envy for the NBC reporters Garrick Utley and Dean Brelis, who were covering Vietnam, grew. Neither the scenes from the battlefields, where American casualties began reaching into the thousands, nor images of mayhem in the streets of Saigon dampened her longing. She had some vague knowledge that Dickey Chapelle had died covering combat in 1965 but had no idea that two Associated Press photographers had died the month before Chapelle. And Robert Capa's death at Dien Bien Phu in 1954 had happened so long before that it hardly seemed real.[2] Even the pictures of her NBC colleague Howard Tuckner lying wounded on a Saigon street in the days following the Tet Offensive left Trotta undaunted.

Vietnam was the story she had to cover. There was no way around it. "I was twenty-seven at the time and not to want to go to Vietnam didn't make any sense to me. It was the biggest story going in the second half of the twentieth century," she recalled. Getting there as an NBC news correspondent, however, turned out to be an Everest-like challenge. "Don't ask to be sent,"

---

2. According to the Center of Military History, thirty-one journalists were killed and twenty-three more are listed as missing in Vietnam, Laos, and Cambodia.

counseled George Barrett, her former Columbia professor who became a life-long friend. "Just tell everyone you want to go. Not the brass—because it will eventually get back to them and that's the point of the exercise."

Just as Barrett predicted, word soon reached her bosses. Bill Corrigan, NBC's vice president in charge of Asia coverage, asked her whether the rumor about her wish to cover the war was true. But the plan faltered when Ron Stein-man, NBC's Saigon bureau chief, told Corrigan he would "be on the first plane back" if Trotta or any other woman showed up in the Saigon bureau. He didn't want to deal with the problems of having a woman covering war. "I don't apologize for it. It was a different era, a different time," Steinman said decades later.

Steinman was adamant. A woman would not cover the war on his watch, even if she had scored some notable news coups back in the United States. He was also opposed to allowing correspondents' wives to live in Saigon. "It was a dreadful mistake to have wives accompany their husbands. You aren't going to a nine-to-five job. To have the pressure of a spouse sitting in a hotel room twiddling her thumbs while you are out covering a war is too difficult," Steinman said. Trotta recalled that she was "broken hearted. But I was mad, too. And I went on a campaign." By her own description, that campaign was waged like the war itself, "first a guerrilla action and then an all-out offensive with major battles." She made herself "a general pain in the ass" on the subject—nagging, bitching, and complaining through much of 1968. "It made them go through the ceiling," she recalled.

Inadvertently perhaps, Reuven Frank, the NBC news president, aided her cause. Early on he had instituted a policy that no reporter would be forced to take the Vietnam assignment. In contrast, at CBS all the big-name reporters were expected to take their turn at what Frank considered "a lousy assignment in a lousy place." Years later, he concluded that the "volunteers only" policy was probably one of his worst mistakes. By 1968, the volunteers were growing thin. In June, the news bosses finally relented. Trotta's chance to become a war correspondent emerged when Steinman left Saigon for Hong Kong to become director of Far East news. His replacement, Frank Donghi, had none of Steinman's aversion to a woman's covering battle. Although as president of NBC News, Frank would surely have given the final okay to assign Trotta to the Saigon bureau, years later he said he had no memory of the decision and is certain that her gender would not have been an issue for him. "I assume Bill Corrigan came in and said Trotta wanted to go and I said, 'Why not?'" It was the same nonchalance that editors at the *New York Times* claimed character-ized their decision to send Gloria Emerson to Vietnam in 1970s. That, of course, was the same year that Frank observed in a *Newsweek* interview that television audiences found a man's voice was more acceptable than a woman's in delivering the news. But Frank Donghi liked Trotta. Indeed, during the months Donghi had lobbied to become Saigon bureau chief, he had quietly assured Trotta that he would push to have her assigned there.

By then, of course, Beverly Deepe had been on the scene for years, Kate Webb was working for UPI, and Catherine Leroy had long since demonstrated that women could bring no less courage and talent to covering war than men. Frances FitzGerald had written analyses of the Vietnamese culture. When network news directors first warmed to the idea of assigning a woman to Saigon, like their peers in the print media, that acceptance stopped short of combat coverage. Trotta was probably the first woman in network news to show her skittish bosses that it could be done—again, and again, and again.

A network producer was conscripted to brief Trotta about Vietnam and the business of covering a war. His lessons ranged from the necessary to the arcane: How to keep her mind focused when the bullets fly to the Tu Do Street address of Mr. Minh, the Saigon tailor who had cornered the American correspondents' market with his excellent bush jackets. Preparing to leave also involved the predictable assortment of inoculations. And, perhaps because one NBC correspondent was brought back to the United States in a straitjacket, the network required that every Vietnam-bound correspondent undergo a psychiatric examination. Company policy, Trotta was told. She had a fit. The psychiatrist seemed to share the same doubts that preoccupied her bosses about why a woman would want to cover a war. "The guy was so patronizing," Trotta recalled. "He asked questions about my parents; he wanted to know what kind of dreams I had." Perhaps a frustrated libido was driving her, he suggested. The session was "something out of a Woody Allen movie, and he hated me because I thought it was so funny," Trotta added.

Up in Westville, Connecticut, unmoved by her daughter's assurances that "it really wasn't going to be dangerous," Trotta's sixty-six-year-old mother had her rosary beads out. Liz Trotta's father had died in her arms of a heart attack on Christmas Eve in 1966. Had he still been alive, her leave-taking would have been more difficult. His realm of understanding would not have accepted that his daughter was going to war. He likely would have fought the idea, just as he had fought her ambition to be a dancer years earlier. By 1968, however, Trotta thinks she would have defied her father's wishes despite her admiration and affection for him. He had never wanted her to be a reporter. "He knew it would break my heart . . . and it did. It breaks everyone's heart."

Her bosses, Trotta later learned, had grave doubts about her ability to handle the assignment. In her memoir, Trotta recalled that Les Crystal, the second in command of NBC's *Huntley-Brinkley Report,* had made a prediction: "I don't think she's going to make it out there. The story's too big and too tough." Crystal, who later became president of NBC News, made the comment to Bill Corrigan, who passed it on to Trotta many months later. Years later, Crystal had no recollection of making that comment. In fact, he added, "it flies in the face of logic for me to have said something like that." One well-meaning colleague best summed up the newsroom's low expectations with a parting observation: "If you do half as well as the worst guy out there, you will succeed," he said. In contrast, at the *New York Times,* Wren, the Columbia classmate who called her "Scoopie," reached the opposite conclusion: "I remember thinking, 'She's going to pull it off,'" he said later.

On August 4, 1968, she finally cut loose. At Kennedy International Airport, Barrett, the dapper professor who had once warned her about the life of solitary departures and arrivals, came to the airport for a farewell. "This is an exception," he told her. "We've got to get you launched as a foreign correspondent, so just this one time." She flew to Hong Kong on Japan Airlines; two days later, she traveled to Saigon. Although Trotta saw the same beauty in Vietnam that so many of her colleagues described, the squalor and filth repulsed her. In the place where the landscape had delighted Gloria Emerson, where the refinement of the Vietnamese people had charmed Martha Gellhorn, Trotta, as she wrote in her memoir, saw instead fist-sized cockroaches that scaled her shower curtain, the unmistakable stench of the Third World, and a place where people and garbage live side by side. She wrote of the ants in her baguette and registered disgust at the sight of geckos copulating on the wall near her table in a Saigon restaurant.

By the time Trotta was assigned to Saigon, American officialdom had already recognized the power of television over the printed word in shaping public sentiment. As a result, the men—and few women—who stood in front of the cameras enjoyed growing prominence. "Television was gaining in importance and prestige after 1965. Print was still powerful, but the balance began to shift, particularly if you were with a major news organization," recalled Utley. By the end of 1967, the three networks were spending around $5 million between them to cover the war. The need to justify their huge budgets meant that reports from Vietnam appeared frequently on the nightly news. And that made a posting to Saigon all the more alluring for young reporters on the make. During the Tet Offensive, the NBC staff in Saigon had grown to nearly seventy. By August, it had shrunk to its more standard size of about twenty-five. NBC's Saigon staff included cameramen, sound men, editors, producers, and an assortment of Vietnamese office staffers, drivers, and interpreters.

One continuing headache for a bureau chief, Ron Steinman explained, was the fear of emotional breakdowns among staffers. In the NBC bureau there were at least two men who were overwhelmed by the assignment. A woman, he feared, might be especially vulnerable to the fate that Lem Tucker and Howard Tuckner had endured. Still another concern, he added, was the possibility that correspondents would become hooked on war. "There were people who actually got high on battle and that often skewed their views and their reporting in terms of what the war was all about." The exhilaration of television reporting, especially combat reporting, was a unique danger. "It's very heady to know that you are on television when the bullets are going over your head and you can show everybody what you are doing and how you are doing it," Steinman said. Trotta acknowledged years later that the war did become a narcotic for her. Being the first woman on network television when "the bullets are going over your head" kept her adrenaline pumping. Not that she ever indicated as much in her letters home.

"First of all—stop worrying," Trotta wrote to her mother from Saigon on August 10. She was ensconced in Room 54 of the Continental Palace and her balcony overlooked the opera house on Lam Son Square. Reports her mother might hear about attacks on the city were nothing to be alarmed about, Trotta explained. Regardless of what the Communists tried, "they'll never get into the city as they did in the early part of this year." Eleven days later, the Continental Palace was hit in a rocket attack on central Saigon. The Russian-manufactured 122 mm rockets shattered her glass balcony doors and the earth seemed to shudder beneath her. Out in the hall, on her way to a safer place, the scene might have been scripted for a comic opera. A German journalist listened to the aircraft overhead and reassured her, "Zee Americans are in za air." As the rockets continued to explode on the streets, she spied Barbara Gluck, a freelance photographer, in a baby-doll nightgown, looking for *New York Times* correspondent Joe Treaster, whom she was soon to marry. "Where's Treaster," she shouted again and again. Despite the pandemonium, one NBC staffer claimed to have slept through the attack. Trotta never wrote to her mother about that "grotesque, funny and terrifying" night.

By the closing months of 1968, American troop strength had reached 540,000, nearly 36,000 American lives had been lost in the fighting, and, thanks in part to television, public support for the war was fragmenting. But Trotta was convinced, just as Chapelle had been earlier in the decade, that all Americans, journalists included, had a responsibility to support American foreign policy. As widespread as that conviction had been during World War II and Korea, by the time Trotta found her desk in the Eden Building, that attitude made her something of an oddity in the Saigon press corps. The Deepes and Halberstams had all believed early on that the war was a necessary endeavor, that Communism was a menace that had to be vanquished. But by 1968, many journalists had reexamined those assumptions and concluded that their patriotism did not require them to give voice to what they believed were government lies. Trotta, however, shared the beliefs espoused earlier by Maggie Higgins, the woman she honored as "one of the bravest correspondents of all."

Television's ceaseless lust for action made combat the perfect story. The battlefield was uncomplicated and dramatic in ways that stories about rice yields, the vagaries of Vietnamese politics, and the cultural practices of ethnic tribesmen could never match, especially when American GIs were confronting the evils of Communism. The grainy old black-and-white picture screens of the late 1950s were, by the 1960s, being replaced by color sets, making the images of Southeast Asia even more vivid. For as much criticism as television has taken for showing war at its most grim, news editors in New York had a squeamish side. Television news hardly carried all the battlefield blood and gore its cameramen shot. Historians who have studied media portrayals of the war insist that the networks imposed a self-censorship that eliminated some of the worst carnage.

During the Tet Offensive, for example, a South Vietnamese cameraman employed by NBC was on the Saigon street where Brigadier General Nguyen Ngoc Loan executed a Viet Cong suspect. Eddie Adams, the AP photographer who shot the still photograph of the moment, won a Pulitzer Prize. The NBC tape of the same scene shot by the NBC cameraman, Vo Suu, reached New York two days after the Adams photo had run on the front page of newspapers around the world. Robert Northshield, the executive producer of the *Huntley-Brinkley Report*, was appalled by the footage. Reuven Frank and John Chancellor were equally horrified. In the final frames, blood was spurting from the dead man's head. "It was too much for me," Northshield said years later. Chancellor, who had been viewing the tape with him, could hardly speak. He said, "I thought that was awfully rough." Northshield decided to cut the tape when the victim hit the ground. "We went to black,"

Northshield said. The spurting blood was too much for supper-hour viewing. Still, a craving for the bang-bang continued.

Trotta's first chance to cover combat in Vietnam for NBC viewers came when Donghi, the bureau chief, told her on August 30, "You'll be going out with Vo Huynh tomorrow." She was off for Trang Bang. Following an office tradition that Steinman had established, the cameraman whom Trotta described as the "brain and guts of the Saigon staff" always accompanied newcomers on their first assignments in the field. Huynh, a Northerner who emigrated to the South in 1955 after the Viet Minh killed his grandfather, had started working for NBC in the early 1960s. He soon became "one of the best combat photographers who ever lived," Steinman recalled. The NBC newsman Jack Reynolds called Huynh "the Godfather." Utley considered him such a crucial part of NBC's Saigon operation that he moved Huynh into one of the two apartments that NBC rented above its office in the Eden Building. "He was so indispensable, I wanted him right nearby," Utley recalled. Huynh would tell the first-timers when to duck and where to stand. To Trotta's great satisfaction, Huynh was the cameraman who most often accompanied her on battlefield forays throughout her six months in Vietnam.

Before that first combat assignment, after studying the oversized map that hung on the bureau's wall, Huynh assured Trotta that they were likely to find a good firefight. The routine for these trips into the field was a 4:00 A.M. wakeup call, a cab ride to Tan Son Nhut Airport, a seemingly interminable wait for the mission to begin, and then a helicopter ride to the site of the action. The ride to Trang Bang took an hour; when they arrived, Trotta, Huynh, and Hugh Van Ness, the Dutch-born sound man, joined a unit from the U.S. Army's 101st Airborne Division.

During a firefight with the Viet Cong the night before, eight Americans in the unit had been killed and twenty-six wounded. Among the Alpha Company survivors, Trotta first saw the aftermath of battle; young soldiers standing among their fallen brothers, stunned by the finality of death, overwhelmed by the enormity of their grief. The company commander explained that the day's mission was to search out the enemy. As the march began, Trotta saw the enemy dead, chalk white, blood-stained, some with half-opened eyes. The corpses lay along the trail as she marched through the jungle. She had fallen in step behind the company's radioman, but Huynh pulled her away. "Don't walk with the radioman," he cautioned her. "The VC always try to kill him first to knock out communication."

The danger, she recalled in her memoir, seemed to transform Huynh into a cunning jungle creature, one who recognized just how terrified she was. Surviving the first shot, he told her, was the key. "The first shot is the one that they aim at you and you don't see them." With that one out of the way, he assured her, she'd be okay. Then she would know where the gunfire was coming from. As they approached a clearing, Trotta was about to witness her first firefight. U.S. soldiers were firing M-16s and machine guns at figures fleeing toward the tree line. Huynh stood up to take pictures. Trotta was hunkered down in a foxhole next to a young colonel from Connecticut. "Sure isn't like this in Westport," he quipped. She silently recited a few Hail Marys. In those moments when she grasped that her survival hung in the balance, Trotta first experienced the kind of battlefield ecstasy that becomes addictive.

In the "stand-upper" she wrote to conclude the report, she delivered the timeless commentary that television news required of those whose reports might not be aired for at least two days. The Viet Cong soldiers who had been assaulted, she said, were "trying to make their way back to Saigon for another Tet attack." She interviewed the company commander, a crisp, handsome West Pointer who managed a smile despite his apparent weariness. Several of his men talked about the nature of "Charlie's" surprise attacks and their fears. By mid-afternoon, a monsoon deluge had sent them all into a huddle. By nightfall, Trotta and her crew were back in the Saigon bureau where she recorded her script, which would be shipped with the film to New York the following morning. Twenty years later, when she was writing her memoir, Trotta first saw the two-minute-twenty-five-second report from Trang Bang that marked her baptism as a combat correspondent. In the case of Trang Bang, she concluded, "I wrote it straight and dully competent." Six days later, the men of Alpha Company were overrun near Trang Bang in a surprise attack by hundreds of Viet Cong and North Vietnamese soldiers. Twenty-seven soldiers were wounded and thirty-one were killed, among them the smiling company commander, whose body was identifiable only by his fingerprints. That's when Trotta first recognized the senselessness and sheer randomness of war. Six days earlier, all the ingredients had been the same, but then everyone had shared those moments of rapture that accompany survival.

Battlefield assignments soon became the routine for Trotta, although the work itself always engendered fear. Beating the competition drove her and sometimes displaced that fear. When she went off to Tay Ninh, for example, Donghi, with an expression that bespoke his concern, had warned her:

"You are walking right into a firefight." Tay Ninh was surrounded, Donghi told her. That meant that ABC and CBS would be there, too. Added to the list of worries familiar to reporters of both genders—will I get it right, will the camera jam, will the helicopter arrive, will my bosses like it—Trotta had an added anxiety. "If I fail, they'll say it's because I'm a woman." Tay Ninh, according to her memoir, was the test. She traveled by troop transport helicopter to the city, sixty miles northwest of Saigon near the Cambodian border. The chopper made a "hot landing," Trotta's first; its occupants came under fire as the craft landed and the soldiers exited. She was stepping into what quickly became a "Miltonian hell." Over the next ten hours, as she stared into the prospect of dying, fear nearly paralyzed her.

Yet for all its horror, Tay Ninh was also a professional triumph, judging by the network's "play reports"—a yardstick by which television journalists measured their success. The daily reports, Telexed to Saigon every morning, answered two all-important questions: On which of the network's news broadcasts had the story played, and for how long? Morning newscasts were decidedly inferior to the evening programs, even though a story was likely to be given considerably more airtime in the morning. At NBC, where America's most popular news program, the *Huntley-Brinkley Report,* was the crown jewel, airtime on *H-B* stood as the peak of success. In the daily routine at NBC's Saigon bureau, every morning correspondents reached for the play reports before work began. "We would casually scramble over and look at the list," Trotta explained. "We didn't want to look too anxious, but everybody wanted to see if they made 'H-B.'" On the morning after her return from Tay Ninh, Trotta discovered that her story had led the previous day's program and that a full twenty-five seconds of her "crouching stand-upper" was incorporated in the report. The next day, a congratulatory message from Chet Huntley said that reaction to her story had been great. "Proud of you," he concluded. She had succeeded. Her day at Tay Ninh had demonstrated that a woman could hold herself together and deliver a television news report that was every bit as good as any report a male colleague could produce. Still, the experience enveloped her in shadows. The nightmare that followed her safe return was the first of many.

A few weeks later she again found herself in what Nghia, another of the bureau's Vietnamese cameramen, called a "numbah ten situation" at Thuong Duc, near the Laotian border. A U.S. Special Forces camp was under siege. Mortars and rockets greeted the arrival of the NBC team; the attack was so intense that it seemed to Trotta she would never reach the bunkers, which were about a hundred yards away. She did. From that vantage point, she watched the supply helicopter that had just brought her to this inferno take enemy fire and crash. No one aboard survived. By evening, a Special Forces sergeant gathered the visitors at his camp and instructed them on "how to get the hell out of there when the bad guys overran the perimeter." The danger made her throat close and her insides shake. The awful loneliness she felt in these moments returned. And with it came her father's presence. He was her only hope for pulling through. Her mind fixed on a scene from her childhood. She was ice skating at Edgewood Avenue Park in New Haven. He stood at the bank of the pond, fearful that the ice was too thin, prepared to rescue her if his unspoken worries proved true. As she endured that overpowering sense of loneliness in Thuong Duc, she felt his presence. She knew he was out there somewhere, ready to rescue her, just as he had been that day when he sensed the ice might give way. The following morning she was rescued.

Trotta covered battles in the Central Highlands and the Demilitarized Zone, accompanying the U.S. Marines on missions to retake territory that had once been conquered only to be later reoccupied by the enemy. From those battles, she began to understand what she saw as larger truths about the fundamental differences between men and women. Whenever the shooting started, her basic instinct was to retreat. She was certain that "no course in basic training would have changed that." Men, however, were driven by primeval instinct to "take territory and defend it against an outside threat." The erotic rush that accompanied males into battle seemed to marry war with sex. "Let me tell you, when a real good firefight gets going," one young lieutenant told her, "it's like screwing six women at the same time."

Between late August when she first entered this world of men at war and mid-October when she flew off to Hong Kong for her first ten-day R&R Trotta had tasted war's discomforts, large and small. Foot blisters, leeches, red ants, thirst, motion sickness, and the fear of wetting her pants were among the physical menaces she had encountered. She had learned to dive into a bunker when the incoming started, she had learned how to watch for tripwires on land mines, and she learned that Hollywood's John Wayne–style soldier existed only on celluloid. She had also learned tricks unique to her gender, particularly in handling matters for which there were "no facilities." In mastering a technique she called "thinking dry," Trotta claims to have minimized the need for toilet trips into the bush. Every now and then she wondered what she was doing in Vietnam. "And the answer was always the same: You're covering a story. And remember, you volunteered."

In November, after she had returned from Hong Kong, NBC's news executives issued new instructions to the network's Saigon bureau. Staffers should diminish the attention paid to combat and focus instead on stories associated with negotiations underway in Paris. ABC news executives had issued similar instructions to their Saigon bureau eight months earlier when they asked reporters to begin doing stories on non-combat subjects such as the black market, opposition to President Nguyen Van Thieu, the effectiveness of the country's bureaucracy, and medical care for civilians. During the next two months, according to one media historian, NBC producers ran combat footage on the evening news only three times. NBC's new focus on "cosmic analysis," as Trotta called it, made little sense to her. Vietnam was all about combat. The search for some larger context was futile, she believed. "Nobody I knew had a clue as to what the Big Picture was. The little pieces, the disjointed firefights, were the context of the war. It was all about a tiny, determined nation ready to struggle to the death against a dazed giant growing weary of battle."

Trotta found that the bang-bang intruded even as the search for that "Big Picture" was underway. On patrol with the 9th Infantry Division in the Mekong Delta's Kien Hoa Province, Trotta joined Operation Tiger Claw as its men pursued a Viet Cong battalion thought to be in the area. On a day-long trek though the jungle, where the danger of booby traps was ever present, she trudged through chest-deep water and mud, wondering how many leeches were sucking on the skin beneath her clothes. Yanichi Yasuda, her cameraman that day, shook his head as he followed her. "Crazy American woman," he muttered. Five hours into the hot, soggy hike, a sniper took aim at the column of soldiers and a long blast of return fire followed.

That was the day when Trotta learned how easy it was to shoot at Vietnamese civilians and how difficult it was not to. Late in the day, after American infantrymen began firing mortars and machine guns at three people running for a tree line, a South Vietnamese soldier screamed, "Why you shoot? How do you know who they were?" It happened all the time, the soldier later told Trotta. The American battalion commander conceded that the three might not have been VC. But "you can't always ask questions first," he told her. "When to shoot or not to shoot is the grayest area in the war—and it will always be." Her report on the Mekong Delta battle led *H-B* that night. Another triumph. It ran for two minutes and forty-five seconds. The death of innocents tormented her, as did the abandoned Amerasian children she saw in villages. So many Vietnamese children had been scarred and maimed by war. "Combat wasn't as lethal as thinking about these children could be," Trotta said.

But neither those horrors nor Hong Kong's peaceful and idyllic surroundings quelled her urge to return. A friend told her that she was on the Vietnam needle. She wanted another fix. Adding to the war's allure were the congratulatory telephone calls she had received in Hong Kong from her bosses in New York. They massaged her ego and fired her ambition. She wanted more. And she got it. For all this she received $100 a month in combat pay, bringing her salary in 1968 to $25,521. "I knew I was getting paid less than my male colleagues, but I wanted the story so bad, wanted to be a correspondent so much, that I never complained about money."

For as much as she admired America's fighting men, endorsed America's struggle against Communism, and criticized participants in the antiwar movement, her acid tongue and occasionally demanding attitude, like that of Catherine Leroy, rankled even those whose work she wished to celebrate. A memorandum in her military accreditation file in the National Archives bears witness to her capacity for hostile behavior with public information officers when they gave her less than instant cooperation. Major Thomas P. Malloy complained in a memo that during her visit to the Ban Me Thuot press camp and subsequent trip to Bu Prang, Trotta was "discourteous, unethical, and most inconsiderate." Trotta had asked Malloy to arrange an interview for her with a member of the U.S. Special Forces. When he questioned her about the scope of the interview, Trotta told him, "It's none of your God Damn business." Later, she fingered through the papers on his desk, and when he cautioned her that such conduct was improper, "she became highly incensed at my action." When technical difficulties prevented her from putting a call through to Saigon, she resorted to "vulgar" speech and conduct that was "repugnant." Even the NBC camera crew "seemed to accept her conduct as, 'That's just the way she is,'" Malloy's report concluded.

Despite the early skepticism among her bosses at NBC about her ability to handle the assignment and the reservations enumerated in memos sent to New York, her work was so good that in December her bosses began pleading with Trotta to extend her stay for another six months. But Donghi, the bureau chief who had engineered her Vietnam assignment, had slowly fallen apart in Saigon and was relieved of the job midway through Trotta's six-month tour. He was replaced by Jack Reynolds, a one-time producer of public affairs programs of whom Trotta observed years later, "Our loathing was mutual." Besides, her gut kept telling her to leave. She had tempted the gods long enough. Why push her luck? Her final assignment was a three-part series to mark the first anniversary of the Tet Offensive. With an NBC colleague, Jake Burn, the producer who had once been the love of her life, Trotta traveled the length of South Vietnam looking for stories. She and Burn had exchanged letters during her six months in Vietnam. By the time he arrived from New York to work with her on this final assignment, however, it was clear that little was left of the relationship they had once enjoyed. Trotta concluded, just as Dickey Chapelle had years earlier, that romance and a commitment to a career in journalism were mutually exclusive. The professional demands of television news, at least as Trotta pursued them, were inimical to life as a couple. "Most of the time men see you at your worst: harried by deadlines, sweating in haste, hair wild in flight, make-up long erased, clothes disheveled, snapping orders, cussing in rage, and no time for the flirty demure stuff."

By the time the Tet anniversary special was in the can and she had turned the key in the lock of Room 54 for the last time, Trotta had lost twenty-three pounds and a fair share of her innocence. She thought she had had enough of war and vowed never to return. She arrived back in New York on a snowy February day in 1969 to a homecoming sweetened by the news of her Overseas Press Club Award for her reporting from Vietnam. Just as Gloria Emerson would discover several years later, against the backdrop of what she had witnessed in Vietnam, life in New York seemed so superficial, so frivolous. The war's presence remained ubiquitous, even though Trotta's dreams of those chalk-white bodies went away after her return. The transition from the Eden Building to 30 Rockefeller Plaza was vexing at best. She remained, as she had been before her departure for Saigon, a member of the local New York news staff. Although she was assured by those in a position to make it happen that she was "going network," her early assignments were confined to the city. From Room 520, the center of all NBC news operations, she was dispatched to cover stories that bored her. Even one of New York's most exciting and news-filled mayoral races—one that pitted her old nemesis, now-incumbent John Lindsay, against a pair of media darlings, Jimmy Breslin and Norman Mailer—seemed vapid.

Trotta joined occasional network talent tours designed by the corporate press department to heighten the NBC profile in the hinterland and offer affiliate owners a chance to schmooze with the news stars. In the on-air interviews that were routine on these trips, Trotta was repeatedly questioned about the female presence in what had for so long been a male occupation. These "obligatory feminist observations," as she called them, taxed her patience—

always in short supply in the best of circumstances. Barely six months after she returned, Trotta began realizing that she wanted more of the war. By midsummer, a chance, "holy shit" assignment allowed her to avoid confronting this growing restlessness. She happened into NBC's Washington, D.C., newsroom on a mid-July weekend after attending a colleague's wedding in the capital. She was the first warm body to fall under the assignment editor's gaze after he had received word of an accident on Cape Cod involving Senator Edward Kennedy of Massachusetts. Trotta was dispatched forthwith to some place called Chappaquiddick.

There, on the same weekend that America's first astronauts landed on the moon, Ted Kennedy had driven off a rickety plank bridge and plunged his car into the drink. A twenty-something staffer, one of the "boiler-room girls" who had worked on his brother's presidential campaign earlier that year, was drowned. The youngest brother of the man Trotta had once dismissed as a "fake prince" had left the scene of the accident and then failed to report it to police until the following morning—nine hours after the fact. Later that day, police fished the body of Mary Jo Kopechne and the black Oldsmobile Kennedy had been driving from the waters of Nantucket Sound. The unfolding playscript certainly quickened Trotta's pulse. Nothing in her approach to the story contradicted her reputation as a hard-hitting reporter. For Trotta, the media preoccupation with the impact of the accident on Kennedy's political fortunes overlooked an essential issue: A young woman had died. No Kennedy connection, no Kennedy PR effort, no Kennedy family myth, and none of Kennedy's dubious explanations could obscure that crucial fact for Trotta. By midweek, Kennedy's invisibility and silence had left the press in a near frenzy. As he stepped off the family jet in Hyannis after attending the Kopechne funeral in Pennsylvania, Kennedy once again refused to comment. But the ever-determined Trotta, who thought Kennedy's account of the accident and his delay in reporting it was "preposterous," was undeterred. Did Kennedy think the accident would derail his political ambitions, she asked. The senator, in Trotta's memory, turned scarlet and snarled at her, "I've just come from the funeral of a very lovely young lady, and this is not the appropriate time for such questions." Trotta's cameraman caught that intemperate moment on film. Apparently Kennedy and members of his coterie were so angered by what they considered her antagonistic questions that one of them asked an NBC vice president not only to remove Trotta from the Chappaquiddick story but also to fire her. NBC resisted; her bosses kept her on the network staff and on the story.

But through the long Kennedy melodrama that involved months of legal wrangling the war kept tugging at her. Her Kennedy stories got lots of attention, but she missed the chaos of Saigon, the life-and-death clarity of the battlefield. So when her bosses asked her to return to Saigon for a month to relieve staffers there, Trotta was ready. "Just one more time. I missed covering the story," she reasoned. An additional 9,000 or so American soldiers had died between the time she left in late January and her return on November 3. The danger energized Trotta. Her one-month assignment lasted nearly three.

One day in the countryside, the reality that America could not win struck her. As Trotta and Vo Huynh trudged through the muck and the mud of the Mekong Delta, her foot hit a rusted Coca-Cola can in the tall grass. This relic of some previous American patrol emerged for her as a symbol of America's impotence in fighting the war. "I picked it up and held it in my hand like a dead bird. It didn't matter anymore. The war was over."

Not really, and certainly not for Trotta. After her return to New York in January 1970, the war at home consumed her professional life for more than a year. She interviewed men in a Bronx veterans hospital after receiving a tip that some of them were being mistreated. She was dispatched to cover an antiwar demonstration on Wall Street and watched as hundreds of construction workers in hardhats, some carrying American flags, charged the demonstrators. Fists flew. Both the demonstrators and the police sometimes attacked journalists, especially television crews, apparently believing that by simply covering an event the media demonstrated they were in league with one side or the other.

Early in 1971, Trotta went to Fort Benning, Georgia, to cover the court-martial of Lieutenant William L. Calley Jr. for his role in the murder of as many as 350 unarmed civilians in the village of My Lai. After seventy-nine hours of deliberation, the six-member jury found Calley guilty. He was sentenced to life in prison. (A day later, President Nixon ordered his release, pending an appeal. Following that review, he served three and a half years under house arrest at Fort Benning.) Trotta, however, thought Calley deserved the life sentence: "Good soldiers don't do what he did," she said years later. "He was a punk."

Trotta's judgments about her colleagues in the media—especially those who turned against America's involvement in Southeast Asia—were as unforgiving as her judgment of Calley. Although her dedication to objectivity never faltered in her newscasts, her decidedly conservative political views often put her at odds with her colleagues and bosses. Those who sympathized with the North Vietnamese—including anyone who served up charitable portrayals of the enemy following visits to Hanoi—were "frigging traitors," she said years later. She praised the "dash and depth" of some network colleagues, including Dean Brelis and Welles Hangen of NBC and Charles Collingwood and Peter Kalischer of CBS, but Trotta thought a majority of the reporters who covered the war were unworthy of their profession.

She could heap scorn on the likes of Morley Safer who, she insisted, thought the war belonged exclusively to him. She thought Harrison Salisbury's stories from Hanoi during his 1966 visit were "by most measures unbalanced." It was, she added, "a spectacular example of how ideological considerations on both sides had infected coverage of the war." The "voguishly bohemian and religiously radical" Gloria Emerson was the "debutante at war," in Trotta's telling. Her reports for the *New York Times* were "a great read on the Perrier-with-lime circuit." She perceived Emerson's work as dogmatic and intolerant—the same kind of intolerance she had first encountered in Penn Kimball in her graduate school days at Columbia when he told her that "Catholics can't write." There was, she decided, a kind of tyranny of the Left that epitomized the same doctrinaire views that liberals claimed to find so repugnant in those right-wingers whose orthodoxies they mocked.

At the same time, however, Trotta also had little regard for some of the journalists who shared her views on Vietnam. The likes of Joe Alsop and Henry Luce were "all pensive elder statesmen of a press elite traditionally on the team." Further, they had all traded their integrity for access: "They were newsmen who co-opted authority from the powerful men they covered long before TV journalists of the sixties caught on to the game and dealt into it for themselves." Even as her stature grew, especially after the Vietnam assignments, so to did her demanding persona.

As the first woman network correspondent assigned to cover combat, Trotta had survived months of battlefield action and her reports won prestigious awards. On her home turf, however, in the often mortal combat of the newsroom, she was less adept. Despite her awards, she was demoted and ultimately forced out of NBC in the 1970s. Her single-mindedness carried with it echoes of *The Red Shoes*, the movie that had so enthralled her in the 1940s. Ironically, the standards she set for herself and others undermined the goal for which she had struggled for so long. In many ways, Trotta, like the ballerina, was devoured by her professional ambitions. She sacrificed her romances and her family life, and she tossed social niceties to the wind. Her intolerance for anything less than perfection left her bosses doubting that she could be a team player. Female colleagues applauded her successes but privately cringed at her occasionally demanding nature. "She was a terrific journalist," explained Gloria Clyne, a long-time employee of NBC's news operation. "All the women supported her professionally . . . but she was just too much trouble." Trotta, who invariably has a rejoinder, would argue that her bosses could not tolerate in a woman qualities that were entirely acceptable in a man. Her view, as she once explained to a *Los Angeles Times* interviewer, was that women in television news could be criticized with impunity, but "if she criticizes back, she's labeled a prima donna or a bitch. If a man loses his temper, he is described a someone fighting for a cause, doing the manly thing." To some degree, Trotta became a victim of that reality.

In her position as NBC's Singapore bureau chief in the early months of 1973, she was in place to participate in the coverage of Operation Homecoming, the four-stage release of American prisoners of war by the North Vietnamese. She had hoped to be the lead reporter on the story of the first released, when 143 prisoners were freed. For years, the prisoners had been her special interest. She could identify them on sight, she had studied their biographies, and she even knew what most of them liked to eat for breakfast. To her dismay, however, Jack Perkins was assigned to anchor NBC's live coverage. Nonetheless, she was part of the team that covered the homecoming at Clark Air Base in the Philippines.

Her turn came with the fourth and final prisoner release, which Trotta was assigned to cover in Hanoi. At the Lan Xan Hotel in Vientiane, Laos, the take-off point for reporters assigned to cover the release, Trotta discovered that no less a light than Walter Cronkite was covering the story for CBS. She admired him as "a journalist who had earned his reputation," but her sassy impulses kicked in. "It's about time your shop sent me some competition," she told one of America's most respected and influential news correspondents. A fleeting look of confusion crossed Cronkite's face, she recalled. He smiled and told her, "We'll see."

Days later, during the release ceremony at Hanoi's airport, she encountered a pilot, Don D'Amico, whom she had befriended in Da Nang. He had been her subject in a story about fighter pilots. Later he was shot down and severely injured near Da Nang, but now he was flying one of the two C-141s that were carrying war prisonerss to freedom, the last story of the Vietnam War Trotta would cover. Her joyful reunion with D'Amico took place inside the barriers the North Vietnamese had set up to contain the press. Once the last soldier had been escorted to the plane, the reporters surged forward.

When a North Vietnamese soldier pointed his AK-47 at Trotta and D'Amico and ordered them to move back behind the barrier, Trotta turned on him and thundered, "Get away from me you son of a bitch or I'll knock your head off." The North Vietnamese soldier with the AK-47 retreated.

That kind of gutsy and abrasive behavior had been leaving her bosses slack-jawed for several years. On the night when Governor Nelson Rockefeller of New York was reelected to his fourth term in 1970, Trotta had staked out her ground at the hotel where he was to give his victory speech. Moments before his arrival, a campaign groupie tried to shove her out of her forward position. When Trotta shoved back, the woman raked her long fingernails across Trotta's face. In a battle-hardened reaction, Trotta smashed her steel microphone into her assailant's face and knocked out two front teeth. It was, then, no wonder that when one of her bosses in New York learned she had been arrested in the Philippines while attempting to cover the imposition of martial law by President Ferdinand Marcos he muttered: "God, let's pray they keep her."

She created something of an international incident when, after being thwarted for weeks in her requests for an interview with Prime Minister Indira Gandhi, she posed as an American tourist to gain access to one of Gandhi's weekly sessions with Indian citizens. Alone with Mrs. Gandhi in the room where she granted audiences, Trotta explained her ruse and made her interview request face-to-face. The prime minister was noncommittal, but a week later Trotta learned that the Indian government had made a formal protest to officials at the U.S. State Department. Just a bit more finesse, her boss advised, might be appropriate on the foreign stage, especially with international leaders.

When her Singapore assignment ended in 1974, Trotta was posted in NBC's London bureau, an assignment that bespoke success. Of all the foreign bureaus in any news organization, London inevitably had a special cachet. Echoes of Murrow's World War II broadcasts for CBS, the allure of British royalty, the old world of gentlemen's clubs, country estates, and the lingering majesty of an empire on which the sun had never set all combined to inspire the sense that one had arrived professionally. For Trotta, it was a logical next step toward the dream that she could follow in Murrow's footsteps to become the voice that would make sense of world affairs and their impact on America for NBC viewers.

From London, Trotta covered the war in Northern Ireland. As she shifted in and out of Ulster, Belfast, and Londonderry, she confronted the incongruity of Catholics who were capable of murder. Not something she'd learned in her catechism classes in New Haven. She was part of the NBC team that covered the Yom Kippur War in Israel, a conflict she said played out like a Cecil B. DeMille production. Familiar faces from Vietnam all kept showing up in the Golan Heights or the Sinai Peninsula, among them Horst Faas, the AP photographer who had had Trotta in focus back in Tay Ninh, ready to open his shutter the moment a bullet cut her down. His ghoulish nature remained intact, Trotta discovered. "If your escort gets killed," he told her in Israel, "that's when you'll get good pictures."

The more benign of her assignments were subjects such as life aboard a North Sea oil rig and Japanese tourists in search of the Loch Ness monster. The story she considered her personal triumph was a series on the Sahara Desert, another war story, but this time it was man against nature rather than nation against nation. As the result of a drought that had persisted for years, the desert was overrunning countries in upper West Africa. From Mauritania to Timbuktu, she and the NBC crew taped images of starving children, hungry camels, and abandoned French Foreign Legion posts, all against the backdrop of the desert's arid beauty. "This was TV journalism as it was supposed to be," she wrote years later. The story won her a second Emmy and a second Overseas Press Club Award in 1975.

Saigon had fallen to the Communists by the time her London assignment concluded in June 1975. But rather than catapult her to the top echelon of NBC reporters, London was her last triumph at NBC. When she asked one of the New York bosses what she'd be doing when she returned to headquarters, he told her testily, "Nobody back here wants you." So Trotta left London with a sense of foreboding. Not only was her job in jeopardy, but she also felt uneasy about her plans to marry an American expatriate writer with whom she had had a romance in London. They made plans to marry after their return to America. Weeks later, after being purged from the network news team, Trotta gamely returned to the newsroom where her television career had started nearly eleven years earlier. Local news, she quickly realized, simply was not her business. Moreover, it was a humiliation, a manifestation of failure. She gave it nearly three years before imploring her indifferent former bosses to let her come back to the network, a campaign that ended in failure. Les Crystal, by this time the president of NBC News, told her that she would first have to audition for six months before being reconsidered for a network job. Audition? No way, she thought, not after thirteen years, not after her Emmys and Overseas Press Club awards. She left NBC. Her father had been right. Journalism did break her heart, just as he had predicted. By then her marriage plans had fallen apart; her expatriate lover decided he couldn't handle living back in the United States. But being spurned by NBC was by far the greater heartbreak—indeed, far worse than any of her failed romances. "I was devastated," she said more than a quarter of a century later. "I don't think I've ever gotten over it."

As she surveyed what little was left of her dream, Trotta concluded that there were two ways she could look at life: "through the tears of a Victorian novel's long-suffering heroine or with the survival skills of Job in drag." She opted for Job. Of course, she did survive—and in the end she thrived.

7

A Force
of Nature

Oh, John Pareham, what are you doing here?
He died.
—GLORIA EMERSON

RALPH BLUMENTHAL HAS an unsettled memory of Gloria Emerson's arrival in Saigon in February 1970. He and the *New York Times* Saigon bureau chief, Terence Smith, drove to Tan Son Nhut Airport to meet the first
woman his newspaper had assigned to cover a war. Unlike Blumenthal, who
had been assigned to Vietnam without having asked for the posting, Emerson had spent four years begging to join the regiment of mostly younger men
the *Times* began sending to Saigon in 1962. Smith, who befriended Emerson
in 1968 when he covered the peace talks in Paris, was overjoyed by the new
dimension her vision was about to add to his bureau's coverage. En route to
the airport, Blumenthal, who had never met Emerson but was familiar with
her reputation as "a rather forceful personality," decided to add a touch of
peril to her welcome. As she climbed into the Jeep for the ride into town, he
thrust a rifle at her, insinuating that she would soon have use for it. "You
handle the right side and I'll handle the left side," he snapped, repeating a fa-

miliar greeting that veteran correspondents had been using on new arrivals for several years. In fact, the six-mile trip from Tan Son Nhut to downtown Saigon was "as safe as the ride from LaGuardia into Manhattan," Blumenthal explained years later.

But after describing that long-ago scene with little apparent uncertainty, Blumenthal hesitated. Did Emerson's arrival play out that way? he wondered aloud. "I'm not entirely positive that it really happened," he said. "It may be that we just joked about it and we didn't really do it." Indeed, Terence Smith has no memory of Emerson with a rifle in hand during that ride to the *Times*'s downtown headquarters. Then again, Saigon in those days—as Gloria Emerson was soon to discover—had a way of muddling up reality.

Once she reached the heart of Saigon, the place of her distant memories, Emerson discovered it had become "a malignant city," one that "demanded constant suspicion." Too many of the mango, flame, and tamarind trees that lined the streets back in 1956 were gone—cut down to accommodate American military traffic. The glamorous, Ivy League–educated Rover Boys who had worked with Colonel Edward G. Lansdale in the noble fight against Communism had been replaced by GIs who prowled Saigon's streets in search of bars, brothels, and drugs. The city's nightclubs rang out with the strains of "Have You Ever Seen the Rain?" and "Proud Mary" sung by South Vietnamese singers who called themselves Elvis Phuong and Candy Xuan. By 1970, many American diplomats, civil servants, and military leaders had become members of the Cercle Sportif, the French-built country club that some Americans had avoided in the 1950s for fear that its insinuations of colonial rule would tarnish them in the eyes of the Vietnamese. The razor wire that encircled so many buildings was a new sight, too. By her own count, Emerson lived 730 days in the city's now noisy and vulgar atmosphere. Years after her return to the United States in 1972, she described Saigon as a place where "you could never quite sort out the horrors fast enough."

One of her earliest stories bearing a Saigon dateline recalled the city's bygone glories. She wrote about the few French people who had remained there so many years after Dien Bien Phu, people much like those she had known in 1956. Little of France's imprint stamped on Vietnam during a century of colonial rule was still visible. On Tu Do Street, the old Rue Catinat where Emerson had lived in a fifth-floor walk-up, the shops where she bought baguettes, French perfumes, and silk scarves now hawked Big Boy Hamburgers and pizza. The sentiments of a Frenchwoman who owned a flower shop on Tu Do Street might well have echoed Emerson's own reaction to the transformation of South Vietnam's capital city. "Saigon?" asked Mrs. Aimee Galaup in Emerson's story. "Ah, it was a paradise when I came here, a paradise. And now—well, look at it. It is not even clean." The tone of mild disbelief evident in her early stories later turned to melancholy, then to despair, and finally to hopelessness. Gloria Emerson, with her hyper temperament and jangled nerves, found a long-sought purpose during those 730 days. Vietnam became her life's transcendent moment against which every other experience would forever be measured.

On the day of her arrival, February 18, 1970, "she swept into the office in that high state of excitement that was Gloria's permanent state," Terence Smith recalled. "She was thrilled to be back." And well she should have been. The day marked the fulfillment of her professional aspirations. Emerson had finally overcome the reservations of those many *Times* editors who doubted the wisdom of assigning a woman—any woman—to a war zone. At last she had escaped what for her had become the mindless drudgery of stories about pleated skirts and patent espadrilles, about Emanuel Ungaro's "schizophrenic" hemlines and about "the fresher kind of prettiness" on display in the newest Givenchy collection. That the *Times* had assigned her to cover the spring-summer haute couture shows in Paris and Rome in the weeks before she left for Vietnam surely made her escape all the sweeter. *Times Talk,* the *New York Times'* in-house newsletter, made special note of Emerson's new assignment. "The *Times* has sent its first woman reporter to Vietnam," noted the column titled "Our Far-flung Correspondents." In explaining that she was "to join the three-man Saigon staff as a war correspondent," the article noted that she had been a freelance correspondent in Vietnam in the late 1950s. "She prefers rice paddies to skyscrapers and had been angling for some time to get back to the Far East."

Given the *Times'* historic institutional doubts about the capabilities of women, the decision marked an epic breakthrough in gender attitudes. Adolph Ochs, who purchased the near-bankrupt newspaper in 1896 and remained its publisher until 1935, was loath to hire women in the newsroom or anywhere else in his operation. The newspaper's conservative editorial voice opposed women's suffrage and applauded the defeat of New York State's suffrage amendment in 1915. After Ochs retired, however, his son-in-law and successor, Arthur Hays Sulzberger reversed that tradition when he appointed a woman to the *Times* editorial board. Anne O'Hare McCormick, a freelance writer whose news stories from Europe began appearing in the

Times in 1921, was widely considered to be one of the best journalists of her day. Yet Ochs's antipathy toward hiring women had precluded her from full-fledged membership on the *Times* staff despite her many illuminating articles, including interviews with Adolf Hitler and Benito Mussolini. Soon after Sulzberger appointed her to the editorial board in 1936, her signed column, "Foreign Affairs," began alternating with Arthur Krock's column.[1]

Emerson had started angling for the Saigon posting in 1966, thirty years after McCormick's breakthrough. If "how she got there" is half the story, as David Halberstam claimed in speaking about the women who covered Vietnam, then Emerson's tale is one of unflinching tenacity in the face of well-meaning but stubborn editors whose concern for her safety outweighed any consideration of her aptitude. Halberstam, who had joined the *New York Times* staff in 1961, was the newspaper's man in the Congo in early 1962, when he began voicing his interest in being assigned to Indochina. By late July, five months later, he was offered the assignment. Emerson, however, had to wait. For four years, her ever more urgent appeals to be released from the fashion beat invariably began: "Please, you have to get me out of here." Although she did win assignments in Central Africa and Ireland during those years, they did not lessen her desire to be assigned to Vietnam.

That urgency was perhaps heightened by the work of other women who were covering the war. Emerson was reading Beverly Deepe's dispatches and hoping that she "might do as well as this enterprising and smart reporter who covered politics and the fighting." Martha Gellhorn, whose war reportage Emerson had long admired, was writing with her familiar "poetic fury" about the smallest victims of the conflict, the children in Saigon's hospitals for children. Oriana Fallaci's sassy interviews with North Vietnam's General Vo Nguyen Giap and South Vietnam's President Nguyen Van Thieu were widely read in America and Europe. As the ubiquitous fashion shows were juxtaposed against the ever more dramatic news from Southeast Asia, the urgency of Emerson's supplications heightened.

When Emerson finally overcame the resistance and doubts of so many *New York Times* bosses, men whose acceptance of women in the newsroom had been glacial at best, her triumph was seismic. Furthermore, measured against both the stature of the reporters the *Times* sent to Vietnam and the tradition of quality that the newspaper brought to its coverage of every twentieth-century war, her assignment amounted to a badge of honor.

---

1. In 1937, McCormick became the first woman to win a Pulitzer Prize in journalism.

That the *Times* had chosen a pair of highly accomplished firebrands in Homer Bigart, who had covered wars for twenty years, and his successor, the more bombastic and headstrong Halberstam, as its first two resident correspondents set a high standard for the colleagues who followed them to Saigon. Among his peers, Bigart was considered "the best war correspondent of an embattled generation," a journalist willing to risk the wrath of generals when he discerned their blunders. Among the American diplomats and military officials he so often offended, he was considered the "big rat," a designation invented by transposing two letters in his last name. Halberstam carried on his predecessor's scrappy, self-assertive style with political and military leaders in Saigon. And his scorn for members of the *Times* foreign copy desk back in New York outpaced even Bigart's seldom disguised contempt for those staffers. The young Harvard graduate whom the *Times* had first assigned to cover civil rights in Mississippi seemed ever ready to answer small, BB gun-sized challenges with multiple rounds of semiautomatic weapons fire. Halberstam won a Pulitzer Prize for his coverage of the overthrow and assassination of President Ngo Dinh Diem in 1963. In later years, Neil Sheehan, Charles Mohr, Craig Whitney, Sydney Schanberg, Henry Kamm, and Fox Butterfield left their distinct imprints on the Indochina story as it was told on the pages of the *New York Times*. In February 1970, Emerson was at last offered a chance to do the same.

Before her Vietnam assignment, Emerson had spent six years in the *Times*' Paris and London bureaus, among the most coveted positions in the thirty-four foreign bureaus that the newspaper maintained in the 1960s. For the forty-five regular correspondents assigned to those bureaus, freedom, prestige, top salaries, and generous expense accounts came with the territory. "It was always presumed that those working abroad would be people of a certain exaggerated metabolism, nourished by crisis and more by chaos," Emerson once wrote of the many *Times*men and few *Times*women assigned to the foreign bureaus. "It was not unlike joining the army, to be sure; the rank was decent, but one never knew what the final cost would be." Over and above the distinction that a foreign assignment bestowed on a newsroom staffer, being tapped to cover a war elevated one's professional stock still further, in part because of the newspapers reputation in its war correspondence.

Since World War I, when the newspaper spent $750,000 a year to transmit its stories from Europe via cable, the *New York Times* had been a major force in American journalism. Carr Van Anda, the editorial genius who oversaw the *Times* newsroom from 1904 until 1932, papered his office walls with maps of Europe and transformed himself into a military strategist. Van Anda's skill in outwitting press censors further burnished the newspaper's reputation for getting the best stories first. He began the tradition of printing transcripts of official government reports and speeches. The *Times*' coverage, more expansive than that of any newspaper in England, according to a British press historian, won the newspaper its first Pulitzer Prize in 1918.

In the decade that preceded World War II, the *Times* assigned reporters to capitals across Europe and Asia. From the earliest demonstrations of megalomania by Hitler and Mussolini in the mid-1930s until the Japanese surrendered aboard the USS *Missouri* on September 4, 1945, the *Times* routinely outshone its rivals in America and around the world. In 1935, for example, Herbert L. Matthews was the only reporter to accompany an Italian troop ship with a brigade of Mussolini's Blackshirts bent on conquering Ethiopia. In a description of Ethiopia that Emerson might have written more than twenty years later from Saigon, Matthews described "a hellish country—in a nightmare land that swarmed with sticky flies and countless vermin, where the day's heat made men's tongues hang from dry lips, where there were only bad odors and no modern comforts." During the final days of World War II, the newspaper scored a historic coup when its science reporter, William Laurence, became the only journalist to witness the dropping of an atomic bomb. In the spring of 1945, Laurence had been recruited by the director of the Manhattan Project to write a secret history of America's development of the bomb. On August 9, 1945, "Atomic Bill," as he came to be called, had a seat aboard the instrument plane accompanying the B-29 bomber that carried the atomic bomb dropped on Nagasaki. The eleven-part series he wrote about the bomb and its use won Laurence a Pulitzer Prize for reporting in 1946.

The *Times*' spare-no-expense commitment to covering wars invariably paid huge dividends in circulation growth. For Adolph Ochs and Arthur O. Sulzberger, however, that commitment to quality was not all about profit. They were driven by patriotic impulses and a belief that their newspaper had a duty to serve the national interest, especially in times of peril. Sulzberger, according to a colleague, came out of World War II believing that "the *Times* had a responsibility to serve as a guardian of freedom." So it was entirely predictable that the longest war in American history also became the most expensive war in *New York Times* history. From March 1962, when Homer Bigart took up residence in the Continental Palace Hotel, until April 29,

1975, when Malcolm Browne and Fox Butterfield fled Saigon (in such a hurry that Butterfield forgot to pay his bill at that same hotel), the reporters who covered Southeast Asia comprise a gallery of the *Times'* own best and brightest. Collectively, those three dozen or more men and one woman were instrumental in defining American journalism in the late twentieth century.

Seldom had any other bureau of a newspaper caused such consternation for so many political and military leaders in a time of war. And Gloria Emerson quickly became part of that tradition. President John F. Kennedy helped cement Halberstam's status as a legend in Vietnam War reportage after he suggested to Sulzberger, the *Times* publisher, in October 1963 that Halberstam should be given a vacation from his duties in Saigon. Sulzberger famously ignored the president's advice. Several years later, President Lyndon B. Johnson is said to have lamented, prophetically perhaps, "I can't fight this war without the support of the *New York Times.*" Although the *Times* never sought that position of power vis-à-vis the White House, the inordinate importance the Sulzberger family placed on serving the national interest together with the newspaper's reputation made it a media powerhouse without equal during this period of American history.

Then, even much more so than now, to have the ear of a *New York Times* reporter was highly prized, especially among young diplomats and military men who entertained high aspirations. Peter Grose, one of Halberstam's successors in Saigon, recalls with passing amusement how a young American Foreign Service officer seemed unusually eager to meet him on the day he landed in Saigon on December 31, 1963. As Grose stepped out of the Caravelle Hotel hours after his arrival, he encountered Hedrick Smith, the *Times*man whom he was replacing. At his side was the Foreign Service officer, who eagerly invited Grose to visit the Mekong Delta provinces assigned to his oversight. Grose, of course, understood the strategy. A story in the *New York Times* about his work would grab the attention of the young diplomat's State Department superiors in Washington far faster than any communication sent through the sclerotic diplomatic channels he otherwise used. "That young Foreign Service officer was Richard Holbrooke," Grose recalled. In the early 1960s, service in Vietnam was a requisite resume builder for aspiring diplomats and military men seeking a fast track as well as for journalists eyeing the big leagues. For Emerson, the assignment would engage her in the decade's biggest story, in a country to which she had longed to return.

But in the meantime, her ceaseless pleas to be relieved of her fashion beat responsibilities apparently had earned her tickets to a couple of world hot spots—Central Africa in 1968 and Northern Ireland in 1969. In a prelude to her work in Vietnam, Emerson went to Africa with Denis Cameron, the freelance photographer she had first met "one dark night in Paris" during the student riots of 1968. Emerson was covering the street protests for the *New York Times* and Cameron had been hired to photograph the melee, also for the *Times*. Later, Cameron recalled, Emerson "picked me out from the mob and asked me if I wanted to go to Africa with her on assignment." Together, they covered the famine in Biafra. Back then, he wondered whether his background as a photojournalist who covered war would mesh with Emerson's experience as a fashion writer. "We didn't work in the same circles," Cameron remembered. He soon discovered that she was "splendid" at covering conflict. Just a few days into their Africa assignment, Cameron realized, "She had a cyclopean eye that zeroed in on an objective and then went at it like a terrier goes at a bone."

Her stories described the tribal hatreds that had led to civil war and the secession of Biafra from Nigeria a year earlier. Her story about Biafra's capital city, Enugu, a town abandoned by its 140,000 residents, was a foretaste of the vision she brought to her work in Vietnam. "In a country where, in spite of civil war, life goes on, Enugu is a grave," she wrote. "Only the wind and the insects of Africa touch the wrecked furniture, the slashed mattresses, the shredded books, the broken pictures inside the houses. The wild grass is tall where once there were only neat lawns." In Nigeria's capital, however, Emerson noted that the war counted as little more than an inconvenience.

From Nigeria, Emerson traveled to Kenya, Senegal, Liberia, Cameroon, and Mali, where she wrote about considerably lighter subjects. In a dispatch from Nairobi, she observed that Kenyan men all seemed to dress like John Wayne. And in a story from the town whose name has long been synonymous with the far reaches of the earth, Emerson described the shy young man in a long white robe who greeted passengers disembarking from the flight from Mali's capital: "I am from the tourist office," he said in halting English. "Welcome to Timbuktu." Her greeter, Mohammed Ali, worked for the Mali Tourist Office, an organization "that defeats its purpose with stunning consistency," Emerson quickly discovered. "Campement," the town's only hotel, had "pink sheets, electricity, frogs in the showers and no hot water."

In Northern Ireland the following year, Emerson wrote about a demonstration by Protestant extremists who were tear-gassed by British troops assigned to keep peace between Protestants and the country's Roman Catholic minority. The five hours of street fighting between the troops and demonstrators marked the first anniversary of the outbreak of violence in Londonderry. "Belfast remains a city of constant and unpredictable outbursts of rioting for reasons that cannot be coherently explained by participants," according to Emerson's story. Other stories Emerson wrote from Belfast put a human face on the story of the decades-old conflict in the way her stories from Vietnam would soon do. In one of those stories, she described the fears that had become a part of daily life for Frank and Kathleen McGrillen, a Catholic couple. At dusk each day, Frank announced his intention to close and bolt the shutters on the ground floor windows of their small home. "It's to protect you and the children," he told his wife. But Kathleen always protested, arguing that the move would simply advertise their fears to the Protestant mobs. With their seven children possibly at risk, she explained, "I don't sleep good. I doze a little, then I wake when I hear a noise and start smoking and walking about."

Emerson's crack at covering the war in Vietnam finally began to take shape late in 1969 when the idea came under discussion among her editors. Oddly, although Emerson's close associates on the *Times* remember her campaign to join the Saigon bureau as a prolonged battle, all three editors who made the assignment contend that their decision was quite unremarkable. Contrary to Craig Whitney's recollection that Emerson had "had to fight like hell to get the assignment in Saigon and the one that had preceded it in Africa," A. M. Rosenthal, the executive editor at the time she got Saigon, claimed that the newspaper "sent a number of women to foreign posts. I was involved in all foreign assignments, but I do not recall anything particularly special about the decision to send Gloria Emerson to Vietnam." In an echo of Whitney's recollection, Terence Smith's memory also contradicts his top editors: "I knew she had been agitating for it (the Saigon assignment) for some time. The record speaks for itself," he said. "The *New York Times* had not sent a woman to a war zone before that." However, Seymour Topping, foreign editor in the late 1960s, insisted that gender was never a consideration and that Emerson's own ambivalence prolonged the decision. "When Gloria expressed an interest in going to Vietnam, I told her repeatedly that this was entirely possible and when she finally made up her mind that she really wanted to go, to get back to me." Any delay in sending her, he added, was the result of an "inner struggle on her part about going to Vietnam."

By late 1969, when James Greenfield replaced Topping as foreign editor, the idea of sending Emerson to Vietnam emerged from his discussions with Rosenthal and Topping about widening the *Times*'s perspective in its coverage of the war. They wanted to go beyond the numbers, the official battlefield reports, the daily briefings, the American embassy's relentless optimism, and the Saigon government's pronouncements. For years they had reported those stories in depth. Now they wanted good writing about the war, Greenfield explained. He studied scores of Emerson's clips. Clearly, she was a writer. "We wanted to catch the atmosphere, catch the themes. We knew she could do that," he said. Then again, "a lot of people thought of her as testy and a lot of people were probably not anxious to send a woman to Vietnam," he added. In the end, Greenfield recalled, her extraordinary talent negated every argument against sending her. "It was not a great decision for us. For her, of course, it was a big thing because she had wanted the assignment for so long." In the first line of her Vietnam memoir, Emerson gave him full credit: "James Greenfield, the foreign editor of the *New York Times*, assigned me to Vietnam in 1970. I had long wanted to go back there to write about the Vietnamese, been refused by other editors, and at last was able to do it."

Smith remembers getting a telephone call from Greenfield in late 1969, a rather surprising move in itself because telephone calls to the bureau had to be routed through the American military communications system, a step usually taken only in extraordinary circumstances. "Hear me out," Greenfield told Smith, sounding as if he expected an instant rejection. Smith was overjoyed; adding Emerson's voice to the Saigon coverage was the best news he had heard in a long time. "What a wonderful, totally fresh eye she would bring," Smith recalled telling Greenfield. "I believe I surprised him. No one was more suited for the assignment than Emerson," he said many years later. She had occasionally regaled Smith with stories of her time in Vietnam a decade earlier. The romantic French colonial scene sounded exotic, yet her description was tinged with an underlying mood of corruption and decay, Smith recalled.

By the late 1960s, Emerson's full-throated liberal ideology had been a legend in the *New York Times* newsroom. Long gone were the days when she seldom questioned government officials and bestowed blanket approval on her country's self-appointed role as world protector. Her belief in capitalism had waned and her embrace of socialist causes had grown more impassioned. One colleague remembers a fiery newsroom exchange between Emerson and Allan Siegal about the merits of Communism. "She was wearing a mink coat at the time," the colleague recalled. "Siegal told her if she was going to be a Communist she shouldn't be wearing a mink coat." Emerson argued otherwise. "She insisted that she could and would be a Communist with a mink coat." Similar ideological passions about the war divided the *Times* newsroom staff and members of the Sulzberger family, no less than it had divided the country in the 1960s.

If Emerson's doubts about America's role in Vietnam had begun to grow in 1964, when Congress approved the Gulf of Tonkin Resolution, by the time she arrived in Saigon, her opinion reflected the same skepticism and doubt that Bigart and Halberstam had developed in the early 1960s. Along with the yellow seersucker bedspread and eleven books, which she never found time to read, a hatred of war and an abhorrence of the government that pursued it were all part of Emerson's baggage. Her experiences in Africa and Northern Ireland had prepared her for Vietnam, or so she thought. Unlike so many of the young men who covered the war, men who had show themselves as audacious and unafraid, Emerson arrived with a sense that she had nothing to prove. "I knew who I was—the bravest woman in the whole world. That was the lie I told myself," she recalled years later. More than 11,000 American soldiers had died during the year before her arrival, bringing the total American deaths close to 48,000. In the 730 days she spent covering the war, Emerson witnessed President Richard Nixon's dual effort to reduce American troop strength in Vietnam even as he periodically escalated the violence in an effort to bludgeon the North Vietnamese into submission. By the time the assignment she had sought for so long was winding down, she understood exactly why American GIs counted the days until the end of their tours. Emerson, too, found herself counting the days, "for I was stupid enough to think that leaving would be the cure." By her leavetaking in February of 1972, 8,440 more Americans had died.

The *Times* bureau at which Emerson arrived after the not-so-harrowing trip from Tan Son Nhut Airport was located on the second floor of a standard French colonial structure built in the 1920s. "The entryway was really grungy," recalled Bernard Weinraub, who covered the war for the *Times* during the Tet Offensive and beyond. "You had to walk up a twisting staircase. It was very Graham Greene." The bureau had three adjoining rooms which overlooked Tu Do Street just opposite the Continental Palace, where Bigart had opened the first *Times* "bureau." The office had wooden desks, Underwood typewriters set on rickety metal tables, and two telephones. Air conditioners stuck in the floor-to-ceiling windows made the French fans that still hung overhead obsolete. The floors were patterned ceramic tile. The space was close to luxurious by Vietnamese standards, but simply comfortable and functional in the context of American expectations. In this setting, reporters routinely worked seven days a week and, because of the twelve-hour time difference between Saigon and New York, were on call twenty-four hours a day. Room 53 of the Continental Palace was Emerson's first home on this, her second stay in Saigon. But she soon grew tired of its bad food and down-at-the-heels environment and moved to "a cheerful apartment" on the top floor of Saigon's tallest building opposite of the *Times* offices, where a maid tended to her daily needs. As events allowed, every eight or ten weeks, staffers would leave Saigon for a week of rest and relaxation. Emerson's destination of choice was usually Hong Kong.

Imagining the primitive technology journalists relied upon in the 1960s is close to impossible for reporters whose cell phones and Internet connections became essential professional tools in the 1990s. Bigart and his successors operated in the Pleistocene age of Telex machines and unreliable telephone connections. In the early years, stories typed in duplicate were hand delivered to Saigon's central post office, where they were encoded into sets of holes on ticker tape and transmitted to New York. Later, after Reuters, the British news service, established its own twenty-four-hour Telex operation, *Times* stories were transmitted from that office. "We had Reuters Telex operators. Often you'd get the operator out of bed, or maybe the Vietnamese Telex operator, who was always in his pajamas, was dozing off when we got there," recalled Alvin Shuster, a *Times*man who became bureau chief in 1970 following Smith's departure. Until the mid-1960s, *Times*men in the Saigon bureau waited from ten days to two weeks for the arrival of the international edition to learn whether their stories had landed on page one. Peter Grose still recalls with considerable pride the "great coup" he scored as the *Times'* man in Vietnam—successfully arranging the delivery of two copies of the *Times* to the Saigon bureau by a Pan American Airlines staff member. He had befriended a Saigon representative of Pan Am, whose Clipper service landed in Saigon daily, and offered him a deal: In exchange for a complimentary subscription, Grose had two copies of the paper delivered to the bureau daily by a Pan Am staffer. "It was such a joy to have this little messenger arrive every day with yesterday's newspaper," he said.

Colleagues remember the dazzle Emerson brought to the *Times'* drab offices. She was forty, older than the three other staffers assigned to the bureau. The combination of her pale complexion, the dark brown hair she wore in a pageboy, her deep blue eyes, and those still-perfectly manicured, carmine-red fingernails was as striking to the young *Times*men as they had been to Demi Gates in the mid-1950s, especially when her two index fingers were racing around a keyboard. Colleagues were charmed by her penchant for drama, her marvelous wit, and her gifts as a writer. By turns, the younger men she joined in the bureau found her beguiling, intense, amusing, and, occasionally, intimidating or downright irritating.

As bureau chief, Smith was lead man in the troika that Emerson joined in Saigon. He had run the office since December 1968. Before Emerson arrived, Smith recalled, the Saigon bureau was "a boys' club, a young boys' club." Indeed, much of the Saigon press corps was a boys' club. The *Washington Post* bureau, which also occupied space at 203 Tu Do Street, was known in Saigon press circles as "the Nazi bureau," so named in jest for its three German American staffers—Robert Kaiser, Don Oberdorfer, and David Hoffman. With the departure of Liz Trotta in January 1969, the NBC bureau in the nearby Eden Building had again become an all-male redoubt. The bosses at Associated Press, whose offices were also in the building, routinely bought stories and photographs from female freelancers who showed up in Saigon, but the first woman from the United States to join the AP team arrived in 1972, after Emerson's two-year assignment had ended.

Blumenthal was enchanted by Emerson's many eccentricities. He remembers their frequent lunches during those early months. She would tell him in her richly theatrical voice, "Ralph, Ralph, what shall we do? You are so young. What shall we do? Oh, Ralph," he recalled. "Then she would roll her eyes and smoke." That she had been in Vietnam back in what he called the romantic Graham Greene years intrigued Blumenthal in the same way it did Smith. No less intriguing were her occasional comments about American intelligence operations in the 1950s. So, too, were the fleeting references she made about her second husband, some Italian count "or something," as Blumenthal remembered. "She talked about him in a fond and almost mocking way. She was always satirical, never bitter," Blumenthal said. She had a name for him, "something like tippo or beppo or hippo." After Emerson resigned from the *Times* in the early 1960s, she married Charles A. Brofferio and lived in Brussels for a time. She divorced Brofferio the following year after discovering that he was "an ill-suited husband." She once told a friend with considerable horror that he had expected her to cook meals. "It's easy to understand that she might find marriage incompatible with her lifestyle," Blumenthal observed. "It's hard to imagine her as a homemaker. She was a force of nature." By 1964, she had rejoined the *Times* as a staffer in Paris.

James Sterba, the third member of the Saigon staff, appreciated Emerson's "incredible sense of humor," but because he also knew that her intensity could make for uneasy moments, he held her at arm's length. His wariness grew out of an encounter he had had with her in 1969. During a stopover in London on his way to begin his assignment in the Saigon bureau, he had glimpsed her cantankerous side. With evident envy that he, rather than she, was en route to cover the war, she asked him, in a tone that dripped with sarcasm, "How many books have you read by Graham Greene?" Her manner was at once humorous and contemptuous as she declared, "Oh, they are sending you," with an unspoken but clear implication that the bosses were "scraping the bottom of the barrel." She spoke of how she had already been in Vietnam and knew the country and had read all the books and that they should be sending her instead, Sterba recalled. She might as well have just said it outright: "Why are they sending you, another stupid white male who doesn't know anything?"

Sterba also recalled how, following her arrival in Saigon, Emerson's conversations with friends, colleagues, or news sources often began with abundant measures of charm, humor, and understanding. But sometimes her conviviality ebbed. She turned somber and her words became sharp. Yet she seemed oblivious to the wounds she inflicted on her often unsuspecting targets. "She had a way of making people squirm, which was great fun to behold when she was dealing with some hapless Army major but no fun if the squirmee was you," Sterba said.

Iver Peterson, who rejoined the Saigon bureau in the fall of 1970, remembers that Emerson was the first political reporter he had ever met. She introduced him to journalism with an attitude. Gloria was different, recalled Peterson, who had first arrived in Vietnam in the fall of 1967 as an employee of the United States Information Agency. In January 1969, the *Times* hired him as a stringer in Saigon. He was the only staffer who spoke fluent Vietnamese. Peterson, who had been diagnosed with Addison's disease, was hospitalized in the United States in early 1970 when Emerson arrived in Saigon. When he returned in October, she befriended him and quickly conjured a name for him, as she so frequently did with friends. She called him "a wounded Confederate officer," meaning he was a little weak and a little effete. "I love her, I hated her a lot of the time, but I love her deeply. She is a sparkly human being. She is always in the story and in the moment. She had flair. She was so exotic and womanly and she was beautiful."

On the day after she landed in Saigon, Emerson applied for press accreditation from the Joint United States Public Affairs Office (JUSPAO), or "Juicy Pow," as she liked to call it. As Smith had anticipated, Emerson's vision focused on story ideas that her colleagues had overlooked. Blumenthal remembers how astonished Emerson was when she spotted the war-related picture postcards in Saigon's souvenir shops. No one else in the bureau had considered their implications in quite the way Gloria instantly did. "I remember her picking through all of them and gasping, 'Oh Ralph, Ralph, did you see this one, did you see this one?' She got all excited." Her story about the postcards described them as part of "a curious war." The apparent favorites among American GIs were "Direct Hit," "Mine Detecting," and "Night Convoy Moving Cautiously." Blumenthal remembered that other reporters had either laughed off or ignored those postcards: "She took it all as quite striking, which, of course, it was. She perceived them as an indication of how the war had corrupted everyone's sensibility."

Just as Smith had anticipated, Emerson quickly demonstrated her mastery at finding stories, her keen skills as an interviewer, and her singular ability to craft an engaging narrative. And she was able to do it again and again and again. The postcard story reflected precisely the kind of vision Smith expected when Greenfield had proposed sending her to Vietnam.

The two bureau chiefs who succeeded him, first Shuster and later Whitney, shared Smith's enthusiasm for Emerson's journalistic sensibilities. Years later, Shuster spoke of how quickly those editors who had resisted sending her to Vietnam had to acknowledge "that she should have been there long before." Whitney thought she had no equal in her ability to pinpoint the underlying themes of the war. "None of us did this Vietnamese angle as well as Gloria. We were all so proud to be working with her."

But coupled with her capacity for those keen insights was a temperamental streak. She often grew depressed or argumentative with those who haphazardly edited the stories she had crafted with such great care. In replicating a role that Halberstam had played in the early 1960s, Emerson thought the foreign desk editors in New York, the men who judged her work and had the authority to change it, were "cretins who existed solely to flatten her copy. Gloria was always wounded by the editing process, and she talked about the barbarians back on the desk," recalled Smith. But the arguments she might have had with her editors in New York paled in comparison to the disagreements that she and other Saigon reporters had with their official sources.

The hostility that had characterized relations between the Saigon press corps and America's diplomatic and military leaders in the early 1960s—most particularly when Halberstam was the *Times'* one-man show in Saigon—had eased. The intense secrecy that marked the Kennedy and early Johnson years diminished after America sent troops into combat in 1965. Yet an atmosphere of confrontation reemerged in 1970 with the implementation of President Nixon's Vietnamization policy. One military historian theorized that the cumulative effect of fatigue and declining morale both among information officers and reporters in Vietnam once again created hostility between the two groups. Smith recalled that relations with diplomats and military men in 1970 were highly problematic—with the war being fought by a diminishing number of Americans, with lies still being told at MACV's (Military Assistance Command Vietnam) daily briefings, with Ambassador Ellsworth Bunker and others like him still so determined that the war would succeed that they quashed all contrary information. "And into this complex, intense situation comes Gloria Emerson with her eye for the people, the tone, and the smell and fabric of the place, and with a completely different approach to her coverage," Smith remembered. "She was a fairly flamboyant figure at this stage of her life." In a more terse, wire-service-style observation, Richard Pyle, chief of the AP's Saigon bureau, recalled that Emerson "hit Saigon like a goddamned storm."

The *Times* routinely covered Vietnam on two levels. As the self-proclaimed "newspaper of record," it monitored the evolving battlefield action and documented the day-by-day pronouncements of both South Vietnamese government officials and American diplomatic and military leaders. A mainstay in the routine in the bureau was the daily briefing by military spokesmen in a ritual that journalists had nicknamed the Five O'Clock Follies. A *Times* representative always attended the briefings, staged by MACV in downtown Saigon. "The newspaper of record, bless its heart, had to cover that briefing every day. It was probably the only newspaper that had it," recalled Iver Peterson, who was often assigned to that story. Among other *Times* staffers who covered such briefings were Drummond Ayres, Joseph Treaster, and Weinraub, all soldiers-turned-journalists, a background sometimes favored by the *Times* for its war correspondents. Ayers was a graduate of the tradition-bound Virginia Military Institute and had served with the U.S. Marines. Joe Treaster was "hired out of the field" where, in Peterson's memory, he had served with the First Cavalry or the First Infantry Division. Like Peterson, both journalists "were fairly committed to the war," in large measure because they were anti-Communists. At one level, the daily briefing was a desirable assignment because the story inevitably landed on page one, recalled Weinraub, a Korean War veteran who was assigned to Saigon in 1967. "But I realized quickly that it wasn't a good story to write," he said of the Follies. "You had to take at face value what people were saying. You had no idea of what was really happening from reading those stories. They were stories without any soul to them."

Colleagues soon deduced that Emerson's contempt for the military brass made her ill-suited for the daily briefing and, early on, she was excused. Blumenthal attended a press conference with Emerson not long after her arrival: "She asked some very aggressive and strident questions of the briefing officer and I remember him turning to an aide afterward and asking, 'Who is that woman?'" he recalled. Her colleague Fox Butterfield said that by the time he was assigned to Saigon in 1971 "there was an edict from the foreign editor that Gloria was never to do the war story because she had such strong views." He added: "She didn't want to and couldn't write a straight news story. She would write it as a diatribe." Then again, she had not been sent to Vietnam to do the straight news stories. "Gloria was the Maureen Dowd of her time. She was there to write the color story, the greater truth that couldn't be captured in standard news format," he explained.

Emerson excelled in pinpointing those greater truths. To be sure, other Saigon bureau staffers, like good reporters everywhere, routinely pursued the not-so-obvious but telling stories that provided larger insights into the war. Few, however, did so with Emerson's level of consistency and success. In his daily operation of the bureau, Smith, in consultation with his staff, usually made decisions on specific assignments. Occasionally Greenfield, the foreign editor, would cable story suggestions, but usually individual correspondents came up with their own story ideas. "And Gloria always had a list as long as her arm," Smith remembered. Like any good editor or bureau chief, Smith trusted his reporters. Besides, as Sydney Schanberg, another *Times* correspondent in Southeast Asia, observed, "Terence Smith would have quickly given up trying to rein in Gloria."

Schanberg encountered Emerson in all her flamboyance on one of her trips to Cambodia during the dangerous weeks after the overthrow of Prince Norodom Sihanouk in March 1970 and President Nixon's decision in April to bomb Communist sanctuaries there. The same carrot-and-stick approach that President Johnson had taken in response to Tet also became the standard for the Nixon administration. LBJ's efforts to entice the North Vietnamese to begin peace talks in 1968, for example, had accompanied a decision to increase American troop strength by about 40,000. Soon after Nixon took office, in a step to make good on his promise to end the war, he announced his plan to withdraw 60,000 U.S. troops by the end of 1969. He called it Vietnamization—a policy that shifted the burden of fighting the war to the South

Vietnamese. In a shorthand reading of its intent, Ambassador Bunker said the policy's net result would be changing "the color of corpses." North Vietnam apparently thought so, too. Radio Hanoi denounced the new policy, saying it was not a plan to end the war "but to replace the war of aggression fought by U.S. troops with a war of aggression fought by a puppet army of the United States." With the help of a sometimes acquiescent press, Nixon made war and successfully called it the pursuit of peace. Behind the scenes, Nixon had initiated Operation Menu, the secret bombing of Communist camps in Cambodia, just two months before the new Vietnamization policy was unveiled. Thanks to Sihanouk's tacit approval, the administration was able to keep the raids secret for a time. A system of dual reporting was developed by the Pentagon to "divert information on the air strikes from normal channels." North Vietnam remained silent about the attacks because to have done otherwise would have been an acknowledgment that it, too, was violating Cambodia's neutrality. In April 1970—two months after Henry Kissinger, the national security advisor, began secret talks with North Vietnamese representatives in Paris—Nixon announced the U.S. ground invasion of Cambodia, complete with round-the-clock B-52 raids. The decision to take the war into Cambodia marked the first time that America bombed an officially neutral country.

In May and June, Emerson was assigned to Phnom Penh to cover the fighting that overtook the country in the wake of the air strikes. Schanberg had been sent to Cambodia from his post in India and was already ensconced in the Hotel Royale when Emerson arrived. He was laboring on two daily spreads and a weekend article that was two days late when Emerson unexpectedly swept into his room to tell him "with forlorn but firm sweetness" that she would be staying with him because there were no other rooms. A half dozen youngsters trailed in behind her, bearing her suitcases. "Sydney, Sydney. What are we going to do?" she lamented. "There's death all around us. Oh, Sydney."

After assuring him that he needed to pay her no heed, "Gloria, with her entourage of smiling boys, rearranged all the furniture, nailed up maps, changed drapes, stowed my laundry in unknown drawers and arrayed her 50 pounds of cosmetics and bathroom paraphernalia in a display that would have blinded Walgreen's," Schanberg wrote months later in *Times Talk*. He described how Emerson plucked from her just-unpacked toiletries what he described as her prize possession, a plastic box in which small cylinders were arranged like toy soldiers. They were electric hair curlers, she explained. Once plugged in, they first glowed red, then black. They were, he declared in a tone of good-natured mockery, "a calming, psycho-sexual experience."

Schanberg knew this description of Emerson's arrival in Phnom Penh might offend her, yet he expected she would understand the parody. She did not. And her fury astonished him. "She said I trivialized her work and it hurt her because it made her appear to be a crazy woman—which she was, but she was also a great correspondent," Schanberg recalled. In her rage, Emerson declared that she would not speak to him for two years. A year and nine months later, she relented.

In keeping with the *Times* practice of allowing writers to select their own photographers for their stories, Emerson had asked Denis Cameron to join her on the Cambodia assignment. Cameron, who had been Emerson's photographer of choice for her 1968 trip to Africa, had arrived in Indochina late in 1969 and soon began selling his work to *Time, Newsweek,* and the *New York Times.* On their second day in Cambodia, he and Emerson began making plans to travel to Siem Reap, where, in June, Communist forces had seized the famous Angkor Wat temples built by the Khmer kings between the ninth and twelfth centuries. Claiming control of the ancient temples provided the Communists with an important psychological trophy, one that recalled the glories of Cambodia's greatest era. Since Emerson maintained that Schanberg was her "bureau chief," she began angling for his approval of the trip. It was really Cameron who wanted to go, Emerson explained. Schanberg, however, thought Cameron was a man who gloried in taking unnecessary risks. Schanberg began to wonder whether Emerson was too much like Cameron. Was she a "cowboy" too, a journalist who was far too eager to tempt fate? In Schanberg's mind, "Cameron didn't have both feet on the ground." Schanberg's fears for Emerson's safety were well-grounded. On the other hand, "it was common knowledge that Sydney Schanberg did not often put himself in danger, and Gloria would certainly have known that," Cameron claimed. He nonetheless acknowledged years later that he often took risks that many other journalists avoided. "It was almost as though I had an appetite for fear." And he thought Emerson did, too.

But, given the enormous dangers involved, covering the war in Cambodia required acts of courage and bravery; indeed, one needed something of an "appetite for fear," especially when group after group of colleagues never returned from forays into the field, as happened in those months after the United States began bombing Cambodia. Terence Smith remembers how a pall enveloped so many members of the Southeast Asia press corps as their colleagues disappeared, especially as the fruitless searches for Gerald Miller, George Syvertsen, and Welles Hangen were underway. Even the release of

Elizabeth Pond, Richard Dudman, and Michael Morrow offered only a measure of solace, given the number of journalists who did not return. "I remember Gloria sharing our general anxiety about them," Smith said. In his memory, she was not a reporter who took unnecessary chances. "'Unnecessary' suggests that it was frivolous," Smith explained. "If you acknowledge that her purpose was to get as close to the story as she possibly could, the chances she took weren't unnecessary. They were chances, of course, and she did not hesitate. Gloria was a smart and worldly person."

But Schanberg recalled that Emerson appeared oblivious to the dangers. As she continued to harangue him about going to Siem Reap, he finally told her, "Well, Gloria, the bureau chief says this is an unwise trip. There's too much risk for too little in the way of a story. Find another story." That conversation took place at 2:00 A.M. When Schanberg arose the next morning, he found a note from Emerson explaining that she and Cameron had taken off at 6:00 A.M. "So much for the bureau chief's advice," Schanberg said. The 150-mile trip from Phnom Penh to Siem Reap almost ended in disaster, Cameron said. He recalled rounding a sharp bend in their rented Peugot 402 and suddenly encountering a bus surrounded by Khmer Rouge soldiers. With their hands held high, Cambodian civilians were stepping off the bus at gunpoint. "I knew that if they stopped us, we were dead, so I just accelerated around the corner. They swung around with their weapons as I swept around the bend. Suddenly a monsoon rain opened up and we were safe."

In one story Emerson wrote about the trip, she described how members of the Cambodian army had put on display the corpses of two recently slain enemy soldiers. "The Cambodians clustered around a truck to stare at the two dead men sprawled in the back as if something could still be learned from their gray faces and cold bodies," she wrote. The body of a North Vietnamese soldier and a second Vietnamese described as a Viet Cong were doubtless the first enemy soldiers most Cambodians in the area had seen, the story speculated. With perhaps as many as 12,000 Communist troops in the region, the Cambodian army was outnumbered and underequipped, Emerson wrote. Requests for help from the South Vietnamese army had done little to ease the dangers. Most of the civilian population in Siem Reap had abandoned their homes and moved to a pagoda guarded by the Cambodian army.

In a subsequent story, Emerson explained that the Cambodians were helpless in the face of outside forces. They were, she said, "bewildered by the violence and the rapidity of the Communist attacks throughout the country and numbed by their belief that Cambodia is in a war she did not want."

President Nixon's goal was to rid the country's eastern regions of Communist refuges, but now the North Vietnamese army was everywhere in Cambodia. Large chunks of the country were either under Communist control or at risk of falling to the Communists. Even in Phnom Penh, an imminent attack seemed possible, or so many Cambodians feared. Cambodians dared not give voice to their anger with the United States, Emerson's story explained. However, one young official with the country's information ministry spoke of the grim future he feared might await his country—a future that Schanberg would cover with great distinction five years later with the publication of his story "The Killing Fields." America's leaders had recklessly risked all of Cambodia for their own purposes, the young information official told Emerson. "We were not even consulted about it, and the biggest gift we could make to the Americans was to let them come into our country. But now we are facing the consequences and they are not good."

Cameron thought he and Emerson were kindred spirits not only in their taste for danger and hatred of war but also in their perceptions of the average soldier, the GI conscripted out of the lower socioeconomic class, who was fighting and dying in Southeast Asia. "Here were young men who couldn't afford a new pair of pants to die in," Cameron lamented years later. "So I felt it was important for me to record their passing." What Cameron captured in his photographs, Emerson later presented in her book *Winners & Losers*—portraits of the young men, draftees mostly, who had become the war's fodder. Those "grunts," the word James Sterba made immortal in his coverage of American soldiers, were, in Emerson's thinking, disdained by their superiors who had no appreciation for their sacrifices, and later disrespected at home. It was they who paid for the ghastly policies adopted by successive American presidents and carried out by the generals, she believed. Cameron shared Emerson's antiwar sentiments but was less willing to see only evil in America's policy decisions. He told Emerson that the enemy was capable of as much, or more, evil as the American policymakers she so despised. "She would tell me, 'It doesn't matter.' Sure, the opposing side did things that were as bad or worse as the Americans did. But she would say, 'I don't care about what the thieves and murderers on the other side are doing, I care only about my side,'" Cameron recalled. She held South Vietnam's leaders in equal contempt. President Thieu seemed to care little for his own people, even those who did his bidding. "He did not even seem to like them very much if they were poor or frightened or sad," she once wrote.

The American bombing campaign in Cambodia was especially noteworthy for Emerson because it was there that, for the first time, an American soldier died in her presence. His name, she learned from the tag tied to his blood-stained fatigues, was John Pareham. He had a head wound, and it was obvious he was dying when Emerson saw him lying on a stretcher in a medical evacuation helicopter. Her impulses told her to hold his hand "as a black medic worked over him, trying so hard to give John Pareham a little string of life again," Emerson wrote. "He looked very long and very frail, with his eyes shut and his brown curly hair wet and clotted from his blood. Oh, John Pareham, what are you doing here? He died."[2]

Emerson's deep sympathy for these John Parhams, the American nobodies on the front lines, was one of two major themes evident in the scores of stories she wrote from Southeast Asia. Even stronger was her abiding concern for the Vietnamese whose interests America was purportedly defending. Dr. Gerald Hickey, an American anthropologist whose acquaintance Emerson had first made in 1956, sensed that her fascination with the Vietnamese peasant was part of her larger affinity for the downtrodden. He teased Emerson, telling her she was the illegitimate daughter of Nellie Bly, the nineteenth-century journalist whose stories in Joseph Pulitzer's *New York World* made her name a synonym for reportorial derring-do. Bly's best-remembered story was about a globe-circling journey in which she beat the hero of Jules Verne's *Around the World in Eighty Days* by shaving nearly eight days off Phileas Fogg's fictional record. The other side of Nellie Bly, the one that Hickey saw reflected in Emerson, was a sense of sympathy for society's underdogs. Bly, whose real name was Elizabeth Cochrane, faked insanity in order to be committed to a New York City insane asylum. Her celebrated exposé revealed the deplorable state in which patients lived and prompted a grand jury investigation that resulted in improved living conditions.[3]

Hickey could easily imagine Emerson tackling the same stories that captured Bly's interest—New York City's sweatshops and jails, and the state's corrupt legislature. The downtrodden whom Emerson sought out in the far reaches of South Vietnam were American grunts and Vietnamese peasants.

---

2. Emerson appears to be referring here to John Holt Parham III, a twenty-two-year-old sergeant from Atlanta, Georgia, who arrived in South Vietnam on April 9, 1970, and died in Cambodia on May 28, 1970, according to U.S. Army records. Those records indicate that his head wound was inflicted by small-arms fire. Parham's name is listed on Panel 10W, Row 15, on the Vietnam Veterans Memorial.

3. Nellie Bly's collected stories were published in *Ten Days in an Insane Asylum* in 1887.

Hickey recalled with fondness the only concession Emerson ever made to creature comforts on her many trips to the countryside. She sometimes spent the night in the dirty, grim, and rat-infested hooches at U.S. Special Forces camps. "It was terribly hot and dusty in some places, or it could be very cold in the mountains at night," Hickey explained. So she carried a clean sheet to avoid direct contact with the often filthy army blankets given her by her soldier hosts.

Emerson held Hickey in equal esteem. From their earliest acquaintance, when he was studying Vietnam's ethnic tribes in the mid-1950s, she considered Hickey different from his peers. Other Americans had come to Vietnam believing that they could bring salvation to the country simply by teaching its people Western values, but Hickey, who spoke French and Vietnamese, had come with a wish to learn from the Vietnamese. His 1964 book, *The Village in Vietnam,* introduced American readers to the lives of peasants, who accounted for 80 percent of the population. That study of the Vietnamese began in 1958 and focused on the Mekong Delta village of Khanh Hau in Long An Province, a place to which he returned for several years. It became his microcosm because it embodied the typical lifestyles, agricultural practices, religious customs, and administrative and legal systems of the Vietnamese peasant. By 1970, Hickey had been coming to Vietnam for sixteen years in one capacity or another. As they recalled their memories of an earlier decade in the country whose people they both held dear, Hickey told Emerson, "You and I are ghosts." She agreed.

In a story Emerson wrote about Hickey several weeks before he returned to the United States to testify before the Senate Foreign Relations Committee, she explained his concerns about the forced relocation of South Vietnam's ethnic tribesmen. The Montagnards, or mountain people, as they were collectively known, were generally disliked by the other Vietnamese for their primitive lifestyles and independence. Yet their needs, like those of South Vietnam's many political parties and movements, Hickey would tell Congress, had to be accommodated if a lasting settlement to the conflict was to be reached. Hickey also answered Emerson's question about the greatest failing of American advisors in Vietnam: "It is that we never care about the ordinary people. We never saw the necessity of understanding them. We are so ethnocentric."

Years later, Hickey recalled Emerson's elegance, sparkling intellect, and irreverence towards authority. With a burst of laughter, he related how on an afternoon stroll through downtown Saigon, he and Emerson encountered a small group of diplomatic wives who made loud comments about Emerson's antiwar sentiments. "Oh, there she is, the sob sister, all she does is write negative stories abut the war," one American woman declared to another. In Hickey's memory, Emerson was unabashed. "She told them, 'Go fuck off.'" On a sadder note, Hickey also recalled visiting Emerson on the day in the summer of 1970 when she received the news that her father, William B. Emerson, had died. "Gloria's father was a problem for her," Hickey recalled. "She was very bitter about him. I bought her some flowers and took them to the *New York Times* office. She couldn't talk. She was swept away with the thought that her father's life had been wasted." In her own recollection of her father's death, Emerson portrayed it as insignificant—less important than a middle-of-the-night call from an editor in New York with questions about one of her stories. The telephone call came to the Continental Palace, very late at night, from Mr. Lee, a Reuters employee who spoke little English. He had to read the cable three times, and when she finally understood the message, "I went back to sleep in relief. There was no problem with a story, no inserts, no new facts needed. It was only another death, and not an unfair one, not a Vietnamese ending," she wrote nearly two years later.

Few friends glimpsed the personal side of Emerson's life that Hickey saw. She so artfully lured people into divulging their most closely held secrets, but seldom disclosed details about her own background. Even on casual social encounters with friends, she mined far more information from a dinner partner than she ever volunteered about herself. "You'd give her all the intimate details of your life and then you might say, 'Well, were you married' and she'd say, 'Oh yes, for one week because I had a bad cold.' She would serve up a single sentence, then fend off the inquisitor," Halberstam said, explaining her technique. Only a few friends and associates appear to know that she was married twice. Those familiar with the details of her brief first marriage in 1954 to Andrew A. Znamiecki often know very little about her second marriage, to Charles Brofferio. Friends and colleagues always remained wary about breaching her armor of privacy. She might taunt an associate with some flip remark about how one of her husbands had committed suicide, relating the event with measured indifference. Or she might tell the tale of how one unidentified suitor made her so angry that she dropped a flower pot off a balcony, hoping to hit him on the head, but missed. But the people to whom these revelations were confided would never dare ask for details.

Nancy Moran, who was married to Iver Peterson and worked as a freelance photographer in Saigon, also remembered how Emerson teased people with remarks about her personal life but repulsed any pursuit of details.

Moran knew that Emerson was acquainted with Jacqueline Kennedy Onassis, remembers that Demi Gates was her great love, and that she never quite stopped wanting to be a part of that world. "Then you'd hear the story about the husband who committed suicide by sticking his head in the oven. She told the story as if it was about someone else. We all used to listen but never really inquired too much into them," Moran remembered.

Emerson's long-time friend Don Luce, a humanitarian aid worker who went to South Vietnam with the International Voluntary Services, claims that no one would dare question Emerson about her age. "You ask Gloria serious questions," he said. "To her, age is a trivial subject." She was, in fact, so secretive that friends were left to guess—or sneak a peek at her passport—as Moran once did in the Saigon bureau.

Still, this carefully camouflaged woman revealed tantalizing snippets about herself in her books and magazine articles. She is a crier, she confessed in one *Esquire* essay, an inconsolable and disruptive weeper who was once asked by an usher in a Manhattan theater either to pull herself together or to retreat to the ladies' room during the scene in *For Whom the Bell Tolls* when Gary Cooper tells Ingrid Bergman to leave him behind. The oak-paneled environs of New York's Harvard Club and the elegant Carlyle Hotel were also among her favored weeping locales, she disclosed. In her book *Some American Men,* she revealed that she nearly died of meningitis in Thailand. In a 1963 *Reader's Digest* article, she recounted her effort to quit smoking in a London antismoking clinic. Confessing that she belonged to the "desperate breed of cigarette smokers who want to quit but can't," Emerson wrote that her smokers' cough and fear of lung cancer had driven her to the seven-week program. She succeeded in kicking her fifty-cigarette-a-day habit for a while in the early 1960s. But the seductive-looking jacket photo on the cover of *Winners & Losers,* in which she holds a smoldering cigarette between her index and middle fingers—with those flawlessly lacquered nails—suggests that she lost her resolve.

Emerson was also well acquainted with John F. Kennedy. They dated in the early 1950s, according to Demi Gates. Later, Emerson befriended Jacqueline Kennedy after her marriage to the Massachusetts senator in 1952. Emerson repeatedly resisted the entreaties of *Times* editors who wanted her to write about the Kennedys during the 1960 presidential campaign. Years later, however, in a *McCall's* article pegged to Mrs. Onassis's forty-fifth birthday, Emerson described a 1972 dinner party at New York's El Morocco where she was among the sixty-two guests invited to celebrate the fourth anniversary of her friend's marriage to Aristotle Onassis. Sometime after Mrs. Onassis died in 1994, Emerson appears to have spoken at length to Seymour Hersh about John Kennedy's sexual magnetism, his penchant for philandering, and his astonishing indifference to the women with whom he had intimate relationships.

Her colleague and admirer, Craig Whitney, knew little about Emerson's past or her life outside the office. He thought that perhaps she found parts of her personal life too painful to share. "But I think most of her reticence comes from a belief that she herself isn't important—it's her work, the subjects of her work, that she wants us to concentrate on," Whitney explained. Occasionally, he said, Emerson mentioned that she had not graduated from college, mostly as a way of establishing "her distance from the 'best and brightest' Harvard, etc. crowd that got the U.S. into the Vietnam War."

Emerson put her uncommon skills at interviewing to their best use on the soldiers who fought the war, according to Halberstam. "She was marvelous about getting men to talk to her, and she had a great capacity to identify with the young kids there," he explained. "She was very skillful. I can just imagine that she became a girlfriend, sister, and mother all wrapped up in one with the young kids she would interview."

One of her most celebrated successes grew out of interviews with those "young kids," who told her all about how they had been ordered to fabricate a citation detailing acts of heroism and valor so that a brigadier general could be awarded a Silver Star. Emerson learned about the trumped-up citation from the six young soldiers who had first written to Representative Mendel Rivers, chairman of the House Armed Services Committee, expecting him to be upset. Rivers was not. Emerson was. Her story detailed how Private James Olstad, aged twenty-two, and five members of the army's Awards and Decorations Office in Bien Hoa received orders to "prepare a descriptive narrative of his supposed acts of valor" on behalf of Brigadier General Eugene P. Forrester, assistant division commander for the First Cavalry Division (Airmobile). Because no one had collected the required eyewitness accounts normally used in the preparation of such citations, the men said, they were ordered to concoct a story. With all the imagination and skill of Hollywood screen writers, they developed a tale about how, in Cambodia on June 9 (a date chosen because one soldier said it was his birthday), while flying with a copilot in his command helicopter near Fire Support Base Bronco, General Forrester "came under fire but remained in position to call in and adjust artillery fire on the enemy positions." The soldiers told Emerson how they also commended the general for delivering ammunition and evacuating casualties from that unit. The end product of their fictional handiwork read: "Brigadier General Forrester's conspicuous gallantry and decisive leadership were the deciding factors in turning a desperate situation into a defeat of a determined enemy force. His inspired performance of duty is in keeping with the highest traditions of military service and reflects great credit upon himself, the First Cavalry Division (Airmobile) and the United States Army."

As she dug into the story, the First Cav colonel who had issued the order for the citation asked Emerson and Alvin Shuster, the *Times* Saigon bureau chief, to join him for a chat. On what she later wrote "must have been the ugliest day of his life," the officer who had so badly bungled what should have been a routine award made a desperate—and almost pathetic—plea: "If you print this story, think of how it will affect the mothers of all our dead boys who won decorations," he said. Emerson was unmoved.

For her, it was a matter of another corrupt American general selfishly using GIs for purposes that had nothing to do with the war and everything to do with getting himself promoted. The story appeared on October 21, just a few days after the forty-four-year-old general received the commendation, one of the army's most coveted awards. General Forrester, unavailable for comment according to Emerson's story, returned the Silver Star.

A few months after her return from Vietnam, Emerson wrote that the fraudulent award had destroyed the last shred of admiration she had for the leadership of the U.S. military. Her memories of World War II movies had made her believe that "American officers were splendid, sensitive and unselfish." In Vietnam, her view changed. She learned that the Army "was not the bravest and best among us." That insight became one of the bases on which she rejected the feminist movement. "I have never known a woman who was as helpless as a draftee, as humiliated and hassled as he is, or one who had so few choices. The real victims of men are other men."

Some colleagues criticized Emerson for routinely dismissing career military men as "stunted and simpleminded souls," "liars and lunatics," men who had mindlessly sent tens of thousands of young Americans—mostly draftees—to their deaths, and almost killed a country in the process. On the other hand, although only a few examples exist, Emerson could write about the military brass with considerable admiration when she encountered one who contradicted the pompous prototype into which she thought most top military men fit. In a brief profile of Army Brigadier General John G. Hill Jr., whom she praised as anything but an "aloof, imperious figure, intent on his image," Emerson's respect was palpable. She found symbolism in a remark about the general made by one of his junior officers who described him as "a no starch man." At nightfall, she noted approvingly, General Hill, a West Point graduate, did not retreat to the comfort and safety of some distant command post but rather stayed in the field with his men. Hot coffee, cooked on a small burner in his one-room trailer, was the general's only indulgence. For the most part, however, Emerson's stories were more likely to rankle than please military and political leaders in Washington and Saigon. In their estimation—and sometimes that of her own colleagues—her stories were rife with antiwar sentiments and sympathy for the enemy. That judgment reached right into the Oval Office, where President Richard M. Nixon can be heard on the infamous White House tapes calling her "bitch." Not long after John Kerry helped found the Vietnam Veterans Against the War that year, a group of pro-war and pro-Vietnamization veterans organized to neutralize the VVAW. The White House set up a humanitarian mission for the pro-administration group, described by one of its participants as "a right-wing Habitat for Humanity club." A ten-member anti-Kerry team was sent off to Vietnam to build housing for South Vietnamese veterans in a village on the outskirts of Saigon. President Nixon received the group in the White House after their return. One of its members described Gloria Emerson's visit to the village and told Nixon that he sensed she wanted him to acknowledge the guilt he harbored about his actions in Vietnam. Nixon is said to have sneered. "Yeah, of course, she's a total bitch. She's been writing that stuff for years in the *Times*—totally inaccurate, totally distorted."

Among her colleagues, Malcolm Browne, who spent years in Vietnam, first as an AP correspondent and later as a *New York Times* staffer, thought Emerson's stories lacked the requisite skepticism, a sentiment he shared with other colleagues. "One of the things that had always irked me about her was her continuing and unyielding defense of those who she thought of as victims of the war. She was ardently defending people who were real rats and charlatans." Similarly, Fox Butterfield recalled Emerson's rigid views on so many subjects. "It was hard to talk to Gloria," he explained. "She had no patience for people who disagreed with her. She had high standards, but they were arbitrary." Her relentless concern for the Vietnamese people provoked one conservative political observer in America to denigrate her as her generation's Tokyo Rose, the World War II–era Japanese radio announcer whose English-speaking broadcasts were designed to lower morale among American troops.

Emerson, for example, described a South Vietnamese army captain who wished aloud for an injury that would render him unfit to serve. He wondered what life would be like without an eye, an arm, or a leg. In another story, she described a weeping Vietnamese mother arranging gifts at the grave of her dead son, a twenty-one-year-old corporal who was killed in Cambodia: "Son, son, why are you dead so soon?" she lamented. "Come back, take my gifts, do you hear me, Thu?" In Pleiku, Emerson found a former peasant working as a prostitute near the American military base. "Her face and her voice show nothing," Emerson wrote, "for she has the apathy of the peasants who do not believe that life really offers that much choice." In Saigon's poorest districts, she found groups of Vietnamese who had embraced a movement called Doi Moi (new life) and deliberately shunned American aid in favor of building self-reliance. Emerson's report seemed to quietly applaud their independence: "Despite the immense United States presence here, there are Vietnamese who do not need to be motivated by Americans, and who do not want to be advised, assisted or coddled by them."

Writing in the *National Review,* Gerry Kirk called these kinds of stories "soggy Saigon specials" and charged her with having an "undeviating devotion to the principle that bad news (for our side) is good news." Other press critics, however, praised these kinds of stories for casting a spotlight on the Vietnamese whose lives were forever disrupted by a war that few of them understood. What Kirk had dismissed as "soggy stories" were praised by, among others, Robert Shaplen, who reported on the war for the *New Yorker.* In a 1970 article in the *Columbia Journalism Review,* Shaplen deplored the media's almost exclusive focus on American issues in Vietnam while they had for so long ignored the human and social impact of the war on the country. Gloria Emerson's more reflective stories, Shaplen wrote, were one of the rare exceptions to this pattern. He applauded Emerson, and with her, *Times* colleague Bernard Weinraub, Ward Just of the *Washington Post,* and William Tuohy of the *Los Angeles Times,* for "some of the most subtle and poignant reporting" about the war.

Emerson's concern for the human and social impact of the war was never more obvious than in the celebrated stories she wrote in July 1970 about the imprisonment of enemies of South Vietnam's President Thieu in the so-called "tiger cages." Don Luce, by then a correspondent in Vietnam for the Ecumenical Press Service, had a lifelong friendship with Emerson after she made public on the pages of the *New York Times* the inhumane conditions he had helped to uncover in a one-time French penal colony on Con Son Island.

Luce told Emerson about the prison where President Thieu's enemies were held in undersized, isolated stone compartments. He visited the island, located just off the country's southeast coast, accompanied by two U.S. congressmen, Augustus F. Hawkins of Iowa and William R. Anderson of Tennessee, and an aide. Soon after their arrival, Thomas Harkin, the congressional aide who was elected a congressman and later a senator from Iowa, interrupted the polite conversation in which the prison warden and his American visitors were engaged. Harkin asked the warden about six prisoners in the island's Camp Four section, where Luce believed the prisoners were being held. The warden said special permission would be needed from the Ministry of the Interior in Saigon. He sent a telegram, and the planned—sanitized—tour of the prison began while they awaited a response. The visitors remained insistent. The warden protested, but Luce, who had a description of its location, spotted a small door between two walls. Behind it they discovered "airless, hot, filthy stone compartments" measuring five by nine feet each holding three or four prisoners. Their legs were bolted to the floor and their wrists were handcuffed to a rod. Among the prisoners, the group found four students and the editor of a newspaper shut down by the Thieu regime.

"These were the tiger cages which are not supposed to exist anymore," Luce told Emerson. Prisoners complained that they were being beaten, were urinated on by the guards, were denied water, proper food, and medical treatment. Congressman Hawkins said after the tour, "It is an atrocious way to treat human beings, no matter what their offense might be." Tom Harkin took pictures.

Luce had first come to Vietnam in 1958 as an agricultural extension worker and became director of International Voluntary Services in Vietnam in 1961. After six years, he resigned, loudly protesting the war in a letter to President Johnson in which he said the conflict had become "an overwhelming atrocity." His doubts about the war, along with his ability to speak the language, had helped him establish friendships with students, Buddhists, and other elements in Vietnamese society, giving him broad understanding of the country. Luce was driven by a desire to have Americans recognize that the Vietnamese were "a people who loved their land, their trees, their poetry, their music, their language."

Emerson first met Luce shortly after the congressional delegation left Vietnam. She visited him at his apartment on Rue Pasteur, located six floors above a dance hall and brothel. Because his radical activities in Vietnam sometimes put him under police surveillance, the location was a perfect cover, Luce recalled years later. "People would come over and not raise any suspicion because the police wouldn't know if a person was coming to see me or visit the dance hall." Like Gerald Hickey, the anthropologist, Luce quickly grew to respect Emerson's tenacity and her deep sympathy for the war's victims.

Emerson's stories about the tiger cages reverberated in capitals around the world. In Washington, news of the inhumane facility, financed with American tax dollars, caused considerable embarrassment. One Democratic member of the House of Representatives called on President Nixon to set up a commission to examine all of South Vietnam's political prisons. The White House remained mute. A U.S. State Department spokesman announced that the American embassy in Saigon was asked to make inquiries about the prison and report back. The Saigon government was said to be investigating the charges. A day later, the *Times* reported that the United States was trying to persuade President Thieu's government to do away with the tiger cages. In Geneva, the Red Cross said the United States was "at least morally responsible for the treatment of any American-captured North Vietnamese or Viet Cong if they were transferred to the tiger cages." At the peace talks in Paris, two Communist delegations pointed to conditions at Con Son Island as evidence that the United States and its "puppet" government in Saigon were pursuing a barbarous war against the Vietnamese people. Luce recalled how Emerson stayed with the tiger-cage story long after the initial splash, and he applauded her interest in meeting former prisoners. "One of her great strengths was follow-up," Luce remembered. "She wanted to see what happened afterwards, how the U.S. and Saigon governments treated the issue." With his help, she found a one-time tailor whose long imprisonment in the tiger cages had paralyzed his legs. Ba said he was rounded up by South Vietnamese police in 1965 after a clash between the Viet Cong and members of the South Vietnamese army. Although he insisted he was sewing in his house and had no connections with the enemy, Ba was brought to trial in Saigon as a Viet Cong agent and sentenced to five years. His withered calves were no larger than Emerson's wrist, and the deep rings around his ankles would be a lifelong reminder of the time he was shackled in a three-foot by six-foot cell in the company of three, or occasionally four, other prisoners.

Ba, who, of course, could not walk after his release, spoke to Emerson of his impending trip home, which would require a bus ride of many hours. When she asked how he would maneuver the distance from the bus stop to his home, he responded, "I will crawl." Emerson wanted to help. Yet she understood that to give Ba anything more than a few cigarettes would wound his pride. Luce recalled the encounter decades later, describing it as a demonstration of her extraordinary compassion and her keen understanding of human nature. Emerson gave Luce money to give to a group of students who would them pass it on to Ba. "Certainly many of the journalists there were compassionate people," Luce recalled. "But I never saw anyone with that combined depth of compassion and depth of understanding about people's pride." Emerson went to Ba's village in the months after he left Saigon, but discovered through relatives that he had never returned.[4]

Emerson's largesse with Ba was part of a pattern repeated dozens of times with needy Vietnamese people for whom she became something of a ministering angel. Her colleagues in the Saigon bureau all have memories of her extraordinary generosity. After one of her periodic R&R trips to Hong Kong, Emerson returned with two wheelchairs for disabled patients she had met in a Saigon hospital.

"Part of her heart was always wrapped up in children," Nancy Moran remembered. *Times* colleague, James Sterba, recalled the frequent collections she took for the needy people she encountered on her assignments. She often sent telegrams or pictures to the mothers and girlfriends of young American soldiers she met in the field. Many colleagues laugh at how Emerson frequently dragged a gaggle of street children into the *New York Times* office and, to her colleagues' dismay, had them shower in the outsized bathroom that doubled as the bureau's photo lab. Ralph Blumenthal said, "Her heart went out to people, and once she seized on to you, you were a goner. She was always getting people out of places."

Perhaps that reputation prompted a Cambodian soldier to approach her during an outdoor press conference in Phnom Penh. Blumenthal recalled the scene: As a Cambodian military official, the unfortunately named Major Am Rong, stood in front of a map, pointer in hand, and droned on about the day's victories, his desperate subordinate, Captain Song, sidled up to Emerson. "Are you Gloria Emerson of the *New York Times?*" he asked.

"Yes I am."

"You've got to get me out of here."

Emerson credited her many successes with the Southeast Asian subjects of her articles to her assistant, Nguyen Ngoc Luong, who often served as her driver and interpreter. "The reporting depended so much on him," Emerson

---

4. The South Vietnamese government ordered Don Luce to leave Vietnam in April 1971.

said. "He was more important than I was." Their friendship was considered rather odd in its intensity by some of her colleagues. One *Times* reporter in the Saigon bureau viewed her association with Mr. Luong as big-heartedness and a concern for underdogs; another wondered whether she was infatuated, or perhaps even in love with him. Then again, this same colleague added, maybe the friendship "was totally on a spiritual level." Foreign correspondents in unfamiliar environments invariably availed themselves of intelligent, well-connected, and savvy English-speaking helpers, essential for reporters who needed to find their way through the country's political, linguistic, military, religious, and social thicket. The best of them were men such as Luong, Dith Pran, who worked with Sydney Schanberg in Cambodia, and Pham Xuan An in Vietnam, all of them experienced journalists. Sometimes putting their own lives in jeopardy in service of their American colleagues, they simultaneously functioned as translators, photographers, drivers, protectors, and Mr. Fix-its. Their photographs received credit lines and on occasion, their bylines appeared on stories.

Luong first sought work at the *Times* bureau in late 1968, sometime after his employer, the *Saigon Daily News,* was closed by President Thieu for three months because its editors offended him by giving greater play to remarks made by Clark M. Clifford, the American secretary of state, than to Thieu's responses. Luong was finally hired by the *Times* in 1970. By all accounts, Emerson bonded instantly with him, perhaps because he reminded her of Mr. Luoc, the young man to whom she had given her watch in 1956. Luong had grown up in Hanoi, where he studied English during World War II. He told Emerson about his glee as a child when he witnessed the Japanese humiliating the French.

Craig Whitney, who became Saigon bureau chief in 1971, remembers that Luong was unique among his peers in the way he did his own reporting before going out with the *Times* reporters. "He would spend hours hanging around with people the correspondents wanted to interview to find out as much as he could about what they really thought and did, and then tell the correspondent what he found," recalled Whitney. This made the questioning much more intelligent and the answers much more interesting and profound. "He had a musical ear for both English and Vietnamese, and he was a great photographer." Whitney once said that Luong's gift for interpreting the "English stylistic equivalent of the Vietnamese answer" went well beyond the abstract summaries that were the standard for many of the Vietnamese interpreters who worked with American reporters. And the friendship that several *Times* reporters developed with Luong went well beyond the standard, too, Whitney recalled.

One of the most painful days they spent together was in September 1970, when Luong accompanied Emerson and Ronald Ridenhour to My Lai. Ridenhour had repeatedly heard about the 1968 massacre of several hundred civilians at My Lai during his year-long tour of duty in Vietnam in 1968; later, in his role as a journalist, he worked to bring the atrocity to light following his discharge in 1969. He returned to Vietnam in fall of 1970, several months after Seymour Hersh first broke the story. For Luong, translating the anguished memories of survivors of the slaughter was one of his most distressing days as a *Times* employee.

Denis Cameron accompanied Luong and Emerson on several assignments and remembers their relationship of mutual admiration and respect. Luong seemed to have had as complex a personality as Emerson, Cameron recalled. They shared a sense of sorrow for the victims of the war. Luong had a wiry build and wore outsized glasses that seemed too large for his elongated face. He had a special fondness for black soldiers in the American Army. So many of them were large men, and their size astonished him—so much so that he seemed unable to believe that blacks in America often lived in underprivileged environments. He also marveled at the abundance he saw on American military bases. Could he really eat one apple in the Army mess hall and stick a second one in his pocket for later, he wondered. Apples were so expensive in Vietnam that they normally were given only to invalids. Colleagues guessed that Emerson made certain the bureau paid Luong well. She often contrived to find work for him for which she paid him personally.

Emerson sometimes worried about what personal consequences Luong might endure after the war because he had worked for an American news operation: "Yet I never worried so much that I let him go." Luong kept the Saigon bureau open for weeks after the last two *Times* reporters—Malcolm Browne and Fox Butterfield—left the city in April 1975. At his own choosing, Luong stayed behind. Having seen his country at war for so many years, he wanted to witness the long-awaited peace. "It was so like Luong to stay behind," Whitney remembered decades later. Once the victors shut down the bureau, however, Luong did not fare well: "He had too many of the wrong connections," Whitney later wrote of his former colleague and dear friend. He never had a real job again but survived selling trinkets and playing his bamboo flute for street audiences. "He had no idea how much personal hardship he and his children would suffer because of his association with foreigners and his previous service with the Army of the Republic of Vietnam," Whitney recalled in 2005. "Communist societies all visit the ideological sins of the fathers on their sons and daughters, and his were not allowed to study, so they ended up working with him at home making handicraft objects to sell to foreign tourists, once tourists started coming back."

In her book, Emerson explained that she had no address for him other than the Saigon office of the *New York Times*. "The expert reporter thought that would always be enough," she wrote with a touch of self-mockery. "I didn't think there would be a time when I didn't know him." In a letter to Emerson after the fall of Saigon, Luong explained that he had continued to take photographs after the American exodus; but even though there was no immediate way to transmit them to New York, he had declined an offer from the Associated Press to buy them. Since he was still with the *New York Times*, the photos rightfully belonged to the *Times*, he explained. "And I thought of those pix in a very sentimental way," Luong wrote, "a message to the paper, to friends like you, iver, craig, joe and barbara treaster . . . those I have worked with, liked and loved, and I don't think that I would see again." Emerson also lavished her generous spirit on colleagues in the Saigon bureau. She took Butterfield in hand right after his arrival, advising him on how to buy a field kit, military uniform, and combat boots on the black market. When she urged him to go out immediately on a military mission, he headed for Da Nang and spent a week with a remnant of Lieutenant William Calley's unit. When he returned, Emerson read a draft of his story. "Gloria told me I wrote a terrible lead; she introduced the note of irony into the scene. . . . She was able to show me some fairly simple tricks of the trade," Butterfield said.

Nancy Moran has similar memories. "Gloria took me under her wing and helped me," recalled Moran, twenty-six at the time. Moran thinks Emerson was especially sympathetic because the *Times*' marriage and gender policies had short-circuited her own promising career in journalism when she married Iver Peterson, her *Times* colleague. Because *Times* rules then precluded married couples from serving in the same bureau, Moran quit reporting and took up photography when she accompanied Peterson back to his Saigon assignment in October 1970. With Emerson's help, she soon found that she could make $150 a day taking photographs as a freelancer for the *Times*. Back in New York, she had earned $250 a week. At times it seemed to Moran that she and Emerson were the only women in Saigon. "I had such a good time because of her friendship, but I didn't realize it at the time."

Decades after the war, Moran recalled Emerson's quirky personality, from the fashion statements she made in her choice of clothing to the occasional dust-ups with colleagues in the bureau. "She always dressed up and she always looked so neat and clean," Moran marveled decades later. The fatigues she wore on forays into the field were tailored in Hong Kong. In Saigon, her shirtwaist dresses were invariably complemented with matching bandanas. Emerson's angry exchanges with Alvin Shuster, the bureau chief, were sometimes especially shrill, as they were when she demanded—after she had been tear-gassed while covering a demonstration—that he provide staffers with gas masks. Shuster, who seldom succumbed to Emerson's fury, refused. And then there were those sweet, memorable moments when a colleague off on an assignment away from Saigon would receive a message with affectionate regards from Emerson. "You'd be somewhere and some Vietnamese man would show up and say, 'Long Lady send message.'"

But by the close of 1970, a year in which 4,221 Americans were killed in battle and 30,643 were wounded, echoes of despair and hopelessness became increasingly evident in Emerson's stories. At year's end, she wrote about a despairing Vietnamese man who looked back on a decade of war and its transformation of his family. Le Van Phuoc was one of the 17 million Vietnamese peasants who had been forced to leave their villages. With Luong at her side translating Phuoc's words, Emerson learned how an American air strike, undertaken in retaliation after a military unit came under Viet Cong attack, had destroyed his home. With it, Phuoc lost his past. Emerson cast him as an emblematic character because the war had disrupted his family and its ties to the land—the two deepest themes in the lives of the Vietnamese. Yet for all the hardships and deprivations the war had inflicted on him, Le Van Phuoc told Emerson that he knew very little about the war.

In the week of Emerson's first anniversary in Saigon, she learned that she had received the George Polk Memorial Award for foreign reporting: "for her series of articles, spanning almost a year, about the effects of the war on the South Vietnamese as individuals." At about that same time, Emerson wrote another of her more celebrated stories—this one about the easy accessibility of heroin and its growing use among American troops. To prove her point, Emerson herself bought $3 vials of heroin available "in a dozen conspicuous places within a few minutes" along the fifteen-mile Bien Hoa highway outside Saigon. Shuster shuddered at Emerson's blase attitude about legalities. He once told her she would give him a heart attack before he was forty. Her story was an early example of the increased attention the press began paying by mid-1971 to the widespread drug abuse among American soldiers. At the time, army estimates of heroin users among enlisted men were 10 to 15 percent—25,000 to 37,000 men. Indeed, during some years of the war's Vietnamization period, more soldiers were being evacuated from Vietnam for drug problems than for wounds.

Serious heroin use took hold in the spring of 1970, and it fast became a plague among enlisted men. "You can salute an officer with your right hand and take a hit with your left hand," one young GI told her. Some soldiers traded cigarettes for heroin; others paid anywhere from $3 to $6 a vial. Compared to the price at home, heroin was a cheap high. Maids who worked on military bases sold it to GIs. Vietnamese children sold heroin and marijuana at makeshift roadside stands set up outside the American base at Long Binh, the largest U.S. military installation in Vietnam. Along highways away from the base, adolescent girls commonly sold heroin to soldiers passing in convoys. "It's harder for boys to approach military convoys because they might be though of as Viet Cong," an older woman told Emerson. The families of all those children were making small fortunes.

By far the biggest story during the opening weeks of 1971 was the South Vietnamese invasion of southern Laos, an operation undertaken to disrupt the flow of enemy supplies along the Ho Chi Minh Trail, near Tchepone, twenty-five miles from the border of South Vietnam. The operation, called Lam Son 719, or Dewey Canyon II by the Americans, was well underway by the first anniversary of Emerson's arrival in Vietnam. Although no American ground troops crossed the border into Laos, U.S. forces did provide air cover and transportation. The congressional edict barring Americans from crossing Indochinese borders made Lam Son 719 the South Vietnamese army's opportunity to demonstrate its ability to carry out major military operations at a time when American troop strength had plunged—from 543,500 in April 1969 to just under 280,000 less than two years later. It would, President Nixon and Secretary of State Henry A. Kissinger hoped, demonstrate the viability of their Vietnamization strategy and set the North Vietnamese back two years.

The *Times* coverage of the operation was reminiscent of the saturation approach perfected by Carr Van Anda during World War I. Editors dispatched their heavy-hitters to cover every detail of the ten-week operation. Stories speculating on the likelihood of an offensive began to surface in the *Times* late in January, even though the political and military officials in Saigon and Washington embargoed all information about operations near the

Laotian border. Public information officers in Saigon even embargoed the embargo—forbidding journalists to report on the blackout itself. However, heavy troop movements made the plan obvious, and word of the plan reached the North Vietnamese. To the chagrin of the Saigon press corps, information about the plan was more easily accessed in Washington than in Southeast Asia. On January 31, Craig Whitney reported that saturation bombing raids in southern Laos by American B-52s were underway. But because of the embargo, Whitney's story could give no indication that "one of the most intensive aerial campaigns of the Indochina war" signaled a new offensive. Yet Terence Smith, a former Saigon bureau chief, now writing from Washington, echoed Whitney's report of round-the-clock B-52 raids across the Laotian border. In a hint to readers that some action was imminent, Smith added that North Vietnam Radio had denounced the long-rumored invasion as a "bold intensification of the war."

Tillman Durdin, the paper's long-time Asia correspondent, was sent to Vientiane, Laos, where he reported that President Souvanna Phouma had questioned officials at the American embassy about the rumors of an offensive inside his country's borders. He reportedly was told that "nothing was known at the moment of any South Vietnamese incursion." This at the same time Ralph Blumenthal wrote about reports by American pilots that 5,000 Soviet-made trucks had been destroyed by B-52 bombers at bases along the Ho Chi Minh Trail. The embargo, finally lifted on February 4, had created six days of "confusion [and] cloak and dagger secrecy" even though knowledge of plans for the invasion and the invasion itself was widespread, both in North and South Vietnam. Another story by Blumenthal noted that an American soldier on a brief visit to Saigon had, despite all the secrecy, heard about the plan from "the mama-san who cleans my hooch," he explained.

On many days, the *Times* front page carried two stories about the campaign. The one from Indochina, which opened with datelines such as "Khe Sanh," or "Banhouekatang," or "Vientiane," or "Phnom Penh," or "Quang Tri," was written by one of the stars on the foreign staff. The other, invariably datelined "Washington, D.C.," described the political implications of those far-away events on the presidency and Congress. On the inside pages, news analyses and background stories put the battle in context. Maps detailed the invasion routes. Brief stories datelined "Moscow" or "Hong Kong" or "Warsaw" or "Paris" reported reactions to the offensive in world capitals. The People's Republic of China weighed in with a denunciation of the United States for "savage crimes of aggression against Laos." In the Soviet Union, officials charged that the neutrality of Laos had been violated. The government of Poland, in its role as a member of the International Control Commission, protested the American military intervention. Polish diplomats said the U.S. intervention was pushing Laos "into the tragedy of civil war." Even the seemingly insignificant name of the operation, Dewey Canyon II, rated a four-column-inch explanation because it was the name given a 1969 undertaking by U.S. Marines who "seized several hilltops just inside the Laotian border," the story explained. The name of that mission appeared to have been inspired by the region's wet weather, but the "dewy" part was misspelled.

Khe Sanh, the American stronghold that had been abandoned after a ninety-plus-day siege during and after the Tet Offensive in 1968, had come to life again as the staging area for American bombing operations inside Laos. As Lam Son 719 got underway, Emerson recalled Khe Sanh's history and the many American casualties suffered there: Between January 23 and April 26, 1968, 300 U.S. Marines had died and 2,200 had been wounded. Emerson's story also recalled that beneath the red clay soil, underground tunnels laced the terrain. In subsequent stories about the base, Emerson described how, in the span of just two hours, helicopters flown by American crews delivered thirty dead and two hundred wounded Vietnamese soldiers from the fighting inside Laos to an improvised field hospital where they were treated by Vietnamese doctors. She called it "a small despairing scene repeated every day in the face of mounting Communist resistance." One of South Vietnam's elite Rangers who was wounded by the North Vietnamese during Lam Son 719 told Emerson that the enemy was "frightening." Many of his fellow Rangers hoped to be ordered to withdraw "because all of us are surrounded and cannot figure out a way to fight back against the North Vietnamese. They don't fear air strikes or artillery. I am convinced that we cannot fight them in Laos."

The sixty Vietnamese pilots participating in Lam Son 719 had flown about 1,000 missions compared to the twelve hundred American pilots who made 20,000 flights in the same operation. Critics blamed the poor performance of South Vietnamese pilots on a variety of problems, including a language barrier, poor maintenance, and the reduction by more than half in the flight time required to qualify pilots. In a story Emerson wrote about the American-trained South Vietnamese pilots, the Americans were highly critical of their performance in the Laos mission. Four photojournalists, including two of America's top photographers, were killed when their helicopter, piloted by a Vietnamese crew, crashed after getting lost over Laos. Larry Burrows, a *Life* photographer, and Henri Huet, the Associated Press photographer who had photographed Dickey Chapelle as she lay dying, both died.

Several weeks later, Emerson returned to Khe Sanh and wrote about the dwindling morale of the South Vietnamese military units fighting in Laos. Even soldiers in the Republic of Vietnam's finest military units had been forced to run "like ants"—sometimes over the bodies of their own dead and wounded—in the face of unbeatable enemy advances. "They were so daring," even in the face of B-52 bombing raids, one South Vietnamese soldier said of the enemy. "Their firepower was so enormous, and their shelling was so accurate, that what could we do except run for our lives?" Most demoralizing, however, was the large number of their own wounded troops left behind in the rout. "They lay there, crying, knowing the B-52 bombs would fall on them," one soldier told Emerson. "They asked buddies to shoot them but none of us could bring himself to do that." He added that "the wounded cried out for grenades" so they could commit suicide.

Back again in Khe Sanh in late March, seven weeks after the Lam Son 719 operation began, Emerson again wrote about the dead and wounded. This time they were Americans. At an emergency field hospital called B Med, three weary American doctors and twelve medics were treating soldiers defending the base from increasingly intense enemy attacks. Helicopter pilots were facing some of the worst counterattacks of the war. In one of the most poignant quotations in all the hundreds of stories she wrote during her two-year assignment, Emerson recounted the words of an American doctor, Captain Robert Roth, a San Francisco pediatrician, who was haunted by the memory of a twenty-year-old American soldier who had lost both legs and an arm in a landing zone near the Laotian border. "First this kid said, 'Pray with me,'" the doctor recalled. "Then he asked me, 'Will my parents treat me the same?'"

The South Vietnamese forces that invaded Laos were 17,000 of country's best-trained soldiers. They fared well during the opening days of the offensive, with a "kill ratio" reported to be two-to-one: Two enemy dead for every South Vietnamese dead. Later, however, as resistance from North Vietnamese forces grew and the operation stalled, South Vietnam's political and military leaders lost their resolve. Unbeknownst to the Americans, President Thieu ordered his generals to remain at a standstill when casualties reached 3,000. That order was issued on February 12, just four days after the offensive began. In another secret directive issued March 8, the president ordered his forces to retreat. "By this time," wrote Gabriel Kolko years later, "only massive U.S. air support prevented a complete disaster for the badly coordinated and frightened elite ARVN units." Nearly 9,000 South Vietnamese soldiers were killed or wounded during the offensive. On the American side, sixty-five helicopter crewmen died, 818 soldiers were wounded, and 42 were missing in action. More than 500 helicopters were damaged and 106 destroyed between January 30 and March 24, 1971. Clearly, Lam Son 719, named for the Vietnamese victory over China, never lived up to the expectations America had for it. Undaunted by a defeat so obvious to others, President Nixon's jubilant declaration in a televised speech—"I can report that Vietnamization has succeeded"—hardly reflected reality. And in another of his routine attacks on the news media, he criticized their preoccupation with "a few horrible scenes."

By the conclusion of Lam Son 719, the length of the war, its daily horrors, and the deaths and disappearances of so many colleagues combined to create measures of burn-out and fatigue in many reporters. Increasingly, the war demoralized participants and observers alike. "The longer you were covering the war, the more you realized how totally screwed up it was, especially in the military," recalled Emerson's colleague James Sterba. By way of underscoring the point, Sterba described how recruiting sergeants arrived at battle sites on medical evacuation helicopters. Their message was simple and straightforward: Re-up for two years and we'll get you off the battlefield. "Here were these grunts who were totally frazzled and they'd be asked to sign up for more time in the military as a way to get out of the field," Sterba said thirty years later, still sounding amazed at the absurdity of it all.

Alvin Shuster's recollections of what he called "the crazy atmosphere" of the Saigon bureau are an echo of Sterba's memories. Shuster, who replaced Terence Smith as bureau chief in the summer of 1970, was one of several *Times* men who had to be coaxed into the assignment. Indeed, he was a bit ambivalent when A. M. Rosenthal, by now the executive editor, proposed the move. Quite settled into his life in London, with season tickets to the Royal Opera House at Covent Garden and a membership in one of London's famous clubs, he consulted his old friend James Reston in the *Times's* Washington bureau. "It's the story of your newspaper generation," Reston told him. "You cannot turn it down." The refinement of London made the madness of Saigon all the more astonishing. His earliest encounter with that madness came when he opened the bottom drawer of the bureau chief's desk. He couldn't believe what he was seeing—a pistol. Why would a *New York Times* bureau chief ever need a gun, he wondered. He never asked about its origins.

Terence Smith had found the gun, left for him by his predecessor, Charles Mohr. "Yes, I left it for Al, just as Charlie Mohr had left it for me nearly two years earlier," Smith explained. "We worked late in the bureau in those days because of the twelve-hour time difference. There were a lot of odd characters about, and on various occasions people came into the office looking for money." On a couple of occasions, staffers showed people out of the office. The gun, he concluded, provided a little psychological comfort. For Shuster, who saw "correspondents working twenty-four hours a day, seven days a week covering an elusive war in dangerous, mysterious places and some of them dying as they did so," the pistol offered little or no comfort.

On occasion, however, the grim atmosphere gave way to merriment at the assortment of parties held to celebrate the arrivals and departures of correspondents, many of them documented by bulk purchases of liquor from the PX (Post Exchange) in Saigon. Typical of those requests, found in correspondent accreditation files, was one filed by Craig Whitney and Peter Jay of the *Washington Post* early in October 1971 for liquor to accommodate an estimated one hundred guests. They requested five bottles of gin, four each of Scotch, vodka, and bourbon, and three bottles of vermouth.

On a more regular basis, newsmen and women gathered at the outdoor restaurant in the Continental Palace, a place known as the Continental Shelf, for interludes of relaxation after deadlines. Richard Pyle, AP bureau chief during part of Emerson's time in Vietnam, recalled that she fancied his Bloody Marys, so much so that she routinely instructed the bartender to assemble the ingredients for her drink of choice and deliver them to Pyle's table, where he was expected to work his magic. "It was a bit much," Pyle recalled years later. Then again, he added, "Gloria herself was a bit much."

Holidays were similarly cause for celebration. New Year's Day parties, at least the ones held at 47 Phan Thanh Gia, a villa leased by the American embassy and occupied by a succession of Foreign Service officers, have assumed near-mythic status among reporters who covered the war in the late 1960s and early 1970s. Smith remembers how those alcohol-sodden, year-end celebrations began in mid-afternoon and continued until the following morning. Drugs were standard fare, too. The invitation bade guests to join in celebrating the arrival of 1971: "The Flower People of Saigon invite you to see 'The Light at the End of the Tunnel, Act Four.'" In Emerson's description, "there was nothing else quite like that villa" where the Cambodian silver animals always looked polished and the manservant wore a white coat. With its flowers, pillows, good towels and wine, the place, she added, "had a fluffed up feeling."

Emerson herself recounted the memorable Thanksgiving party held by the *Newsweek* correspondent Kevin Buckley, one of her cherished friends, and Frankie FitzGerald. The friendship Emerson cemented with Buckley in Vietnam lasted until she died in 2004, a time when she had broken contact with many other friends and acquaintances. In her memoir, Emerson described Buckley as "a young, witty, wildly good-looking raconteur and correspondent for *Newsweek*." They shared a passion for the novels of Graham Greene; both were fans of the British novelist and playwright W. Somerset Maugham. Evelyn Waugh's novels captivated them, too. In fact, it was in his 1930 novel, *Vile Bodies,* that Buckley found a nickname for Emerson. She became Agatha Runcible, the scatter-brained debutante whose character is among those satirized in Waugh's story about the vacuous lives of café society. Emerson, in turn, tagged Buckley as Basil Seal, the dissolute 1920s bounder and intellectual poseur who is a recurring presence in several of Waugh's social comedies. In *Black Mischief,* a spoof on the British Empire's naive colonial aspirations, Seal unwittingly dines on the flesh of his fiancée, Prudence, at a cannibal feast in a fictional African country. In *Put Out More Flags,* Basil is cast as a former leader writer for the fictional *Daily Beast* who finds meaning in his life after being overtaken with burst of patriotism on the eve of World War II.

Beyond their shared literary tastes, Emerson and Buckley, who spent four years as a correspondent in Saigon from 1968 to 1972, had a mutual skepticism about the war and disdain for what they saw as the timidity of their publications to reveal America's deliberate lies about the course of the war. In 1971, Buckley and a colleague spent two months investigating a story about how the reports of 11,000 enemy killed in action during the American campaign called Operation Speedy Express in late 1968 probably included about 5,000 noncombatants. Buckley told his editors in New York that this was not another My Lai featuring GIs killing innocent children. "But this was killing on a much larger scale. This was policy. This was the stuff the war had been made of." What he considered a major, prize-winning investigation was greeted with apathy by the foreign editor after Buckley submitted the story in January 1972. A shorter and "savagely" edited version of the story finally ran six months later. "Looking back, what I remember most vividly was that the editor seemed to view the story not only with indifference but with utter boredom," Buckley recalled.

As her two-year assignment dwindled to its last weeks and days, Emerson's stories confronted the parade of follies, lies, evasions, and missteps made by leaders in Saigon and Washington. One story revealed the corruption in every level of the Vietnam government, right down to the office clerks who demanded bribes from new war widows seeking application forms for widows' benefits. She wrote, too, about the disquiet among GIs who objected when members of the Nixon administration claimed that American forces remaining in Vietnam were "no longer fighting the war." According to those claims, members of the American military had instead adopted a "defensive" posture. But how could that be, wondered one GI quoted Emerson's story. Didn't those folks in the government know he was still carrying an M-16 rifle through the jungle in search of the enemy? In yet another piece, Emerson wondered about the fate of hundreds of refugees being relocated because the fighting around Quang Tri (in the country's northernmost province) had made life too dangerous to remain. Would the government keep its many promises to these peasants, some of whom had already been moved once, after they reached the resettlement area 450 miles to the south?

During the first week in 1972, a story published in the *Times* echoed the same hopelessness embodied in Emerson's first story of 1971. This time she wrote about a young woman imprisoned for her efforts to prevent President Nguyen Van Thieu from running for reelection in another one-man race in the October 1971 election. The woman confessed to organizing street protests, but she hardly played a major role in the violence that later erupted. Speaking in front of American television cameras during the street demonstrations, she denounced the Americans in Vietnam as "blood-thirsty." Now, in the cell she shared with twelve other women in Saigon's Thu Duc prison, Gai, a graduate of the University of Saigon, had slowly been forced to accept her worst fear that the crusade she had joined to bring about change had failed. Now, at last, her need to suffer for her country was being satisfied. Emerson quoted Gai's sister, who explained that on a recent visit Gai had told her, "It does not make any difference now whether I am in prison or out of it."

One of the last stories Emerson wrote under a Saigon dateline ran on the pages that she had worked so hard to escape—Food Fashions Family Furnishings. Her story featured the youngest and most innocent victims of the war, the thousands of mixed-race infants and children whose dark skin would forever make them outcasts in Vietnamese society. In an orphanage she visited, Emerson found dozens of children born of liaisons between black American soldiers and Vietnamese women. "Any child who grows up without a family which is the focus of Vietnamese life, and is also black, confronts obstacles that a Westerner cannot easily imagine," she wrote. Emerson also described the Southern Christian Leadership Conference's plans to create the Martin Luther King Home for Children to house a few of Vietnam's many mixed-race orphans. Her story concluded with an anecdote about a mixed-race infant whose adoption was delayed because of the bureaucracy involved in Vietnamese adoption procedures. As that process dragged on, the little girl, according to Emerson's story, died from malnutrition and otherwise inadequate care.

In an odd counterpoint, the orphan article appeared just above a story that spoke volumes about the world to which Emerson was about to return, a world that was indifferent to and perhaps even ignorant of the suffering she had witnessed in Vietnam. In an echo of the subject that had once been her beat, the story noted the "romantic" mood of new summer fashions and explained that they would soon replace the industry's "dalliance with various weird looks." The writer described creations with batwing-sleeved jackets, off-the-shoulder dresses, and the girlish pinafores that fashionable women would likely be buying. Backgrounds of "raging color" were set off against black and white in some of the new summer collections. The preferred color in the new season's designs was "dead white."

Just before Emerson had left Paris for Saigon in the early weeks of 1970, Harrison Salisbury, her colleague at the *New York Times*, asked her, "What will a year in Vietnam do to you?" Perhaps it would make her a better person, she told him, drawing on the notion that "suffering makes us more human." Seven hundred and thirty days later, just before she left Saigon, Denis Cameron gave Emerson a farewell gift, a Zippo lighter from the U.S. aircraft carrier *Constellation*, just like the ones carried by pilots who bombed North Vietnam and the pilots who searched for comrades who were shot down on those missions. It was engraved with the phrase used on those search missions. As they swept over the jungles trying to pinpoint downed planes, pilots radioed, "Give me voice or give me beeper." Again and again, they would radio those same seven words, hoping for a response from the downed airmen. "There may be no other sentence in our language that cuts me as much," Emerson said. For the meaning of that sentence, "Tell me if you are really alive," reminded her that, after Vietnam, she was never "really alive" again.

Back in New York, Emerson found cab drivers who told her to "have a nice day" and colleagues who seemed most interested in what she had worn to officer's dances. Indeed, even Iphigene Sulzberger, the redoubtable mother of the *New York Times* publisher Arthur Sulzberger, who had invited Emerson to dinner, asked her what she thought of the military balls in Saigon. In later years, Emerson, who could be every bit as imperious as her hostess, liked to regale friends with the rejoinder she served up that evening: "In Saigon, Mrs. Sulzberger, the American military have no balls."

What little laughter returned to Emerson's life, however, came much later. Friends who conjectured that she might leave the war behind and resume a normal life soon realized they were wrong. As her friend Luong observed in a letter she received months after she left Vietnam: "You are the only one who cannot overcome your Vietnam experience. There is an acute lack of forgetfulness in you about Vietnam." The war never faded from her consciousness, as her friends had hoped it would. It preoccupied her for much of the rest of her life, often invoking the fury that gripped her in Vietnam. After leaving the *New York Times* staff, she traveled the country for several years in search of Vietnam veterans and incorporated dozens of their stories in her memoir *Winners & Losers,* published in 1977. A long-time friend soon concluded that Gloria Emerson had become one of the war's many casualties.

8

A Place in History

There are some events that overwhelm destiny.
—A Saigon fortune-teller, April 1975

THE LETTER FROM Saigon left Laura Palmer thunderstruck. In an instant, her friend's message of despair and foreboding eliminated all the doubts she had harbored about returning to South Vietnam. She was, of course, familiar with the deteriorating situation in Southeast Asia in those early days of the Paris spring. Indeed, in her freelance broadcasting job with NBC Radio she had been reporting on the ever-bleaker outlook. Once Hue fell to the Communist assault in late March 1975, and then Da Nang four days later, on Easter Sunday, the entire northern half of the country had come under enemy control. Palmer, in fact, had reported on reaction among the French to the collapse of Da Nang, where events unraveled so quickly that America's consul general "damned near didn't get out."

Nearly 1 million refugees were fleeing south. Scenes on American television showed evacuation boats packed with refugees from Hue. To the south, desperate mobs clawed or kicked or stomped their way aboard buses, boats, and evacuation flights out of Da Nang. In the city where the U.S. Marines had first gone ashore ten years earlier, South Vietnamese soldiers were seen trampling women and children in their rush to board U.S. chartered planes.

For weeks, Palmer had wrestled with the idea of returning. Saigon, after all, had come to feel like home during the two years she had spent there. With the country's collapse growing more and more likely, she yearned to bear witness to its agony. But uncertainty about whether she could find work had left the question of returning unresolved. Still, nothing had quite prepared her for the sense of panic in Bich Dao's words on that tissue-thin blue aerogram; they overtook all her misgivings: "If this is the last letter you ever get from me, know that I have loved you as a sister. . . . The bottom of our world has fallen out and we are floating, floating, but I don't know where," her friend had written. The words dissolved Palmer's apprehensions. She would somehow find work, just as Gloria Emerson had in 1956, Beverly Deepe had in 1962, and just as she herself had in 1972, when her chances of success were even more improbable than those of the two women who had preceded her to Vietnam. She would return to help her friend, before it was too late.

Palmer had left Saigon with few qualms in August 1974, after having parlayed her liberal arts degree from Oberlin College into a job as a radio news broadcaster with one, then another, of America's major networks. But after two years, the incessant horrors had begun to darken her world. The daily cruelties drained away all the exhilaration she had once found in covering the war. Her choices then were stark and simple. Flee this benighted place or risk spending the rest of her life as a war junkie. So she retreated to Paris, and to another job as a freelance radio reporter for NBC News.

She had come as a "tourist," one who by happenstance became a journalist. Her boyfriend, a pediatrician, suggested that she accompany him on his six-month tour with Children's Medical Relief International in Saigon. She had graduated from college twelve weeks earlier, and no commitments constrained her. After landing in Saigon, she winnowed her job prospects to two choices, the American government or the American media. The first was a decidedly unlikely option, given her long and passionate opposition to the war. But considering that she had even less experience than Beverly Deepe had had a decade earlier, the second option was implausibe. A summer stint as "the first girl copy boy at NBC News in Washington, D.C.," hardly qualified one to cover a war. As she prepared to leave Paris for Vietnam in 1975, however, she had credentials and contacts. Although friendship was driving her to Vietnam, the professional journalist she had become recognized the possibilities and had the skill to tell the story of what was about to unfold. Palmer asked Paul Scanlon, her editor at *Rolling Stone,* the magazine that had given her the thrill of seeing her first byline in May 1974, whether Frankie FitzGerald and Hunter Thompson were already on their way to Saigon. He assured her they were not and asked to see anything she wrote in the coming weeks. So much for her worries about finding work. Palmer hastily quit her job with NBC Radio and bought a round-trip ticket to Saigon for $600. It was the last time she qualified for a youth-fare ticket. She was twenty-five.

Palmer's first inkling of the doomsday scenario unfolding in South Vietnam hit her before she reached Saigon. As she changed planes in Bangkok, the bold-faced headlines assailed her with news that 150 Vietnamese orphans en route to the United States had died when their transport plane crashed in a rice paddy moments after take-off from Tan Son Nhut. Fifty adults also died. Ninety-three orphans survived. The airlift characterized the hysteria of America's last rush to shape Vietnam's destiny. One embittered Vietnamese official commented to the *New York Times* after the crash, "It's good that the American people are taking the children. They are good souvenirs, like the ceramic elephants you like so much. It's too bad that some of them broke today, but don't worry, we have many more." For all their preoccupation with bringing hundreds of adoptable children to America, officials in Washington and Saigon simultaneously ignored the need to evacuate the many Vietnamese nationals who had worked for the American government and expected to face reprisals—perhaps even death—after the Communist takeover that was beginning to appear inevitable. A *New York Times* editorial criticized the "exaggerated importance assigned . . . to the orphans' airlift" while it ignored the growing humanitarian crisis and the need to evacuate those at risk.

Gloria Emerson, whose ire over the war had festered from the moment she left Saigon, endorsed those editorial sentiments. Emerson, who was no longer on the *New York Times* staff, saw the baby lift as one more spectacle in America's fruitless search for a happy ending in a place it had so systematically destroyed. Why indeed, she sarcastically wondered in an essay in the *New Republic,* had America come so late to concern itself with these victims of the war? Babies, she concluded, made for a happier story than "the 26 million [bomb] craters we have given South Vietnam, nicer than the 10,000 amputees in that wretched country, more fun to read about than the 14 million acres of defoliated forest." Evidence that Vietnamese officials saw the airlift as "a good way to get sympathy for additional American aid to Saigon" soon surfaced. Graham Martin, the U.S. ambassador, had told South Vietnam's deputy prime minister that the mass movement of orphans would "help swing American public opinion to the advantage of the Republic of Vietnam."

The newspaper headlines and photos of the wreckage Palmer glimpsed when she changed planes in Bangkok were reminders of a reality that made her apprehensive. The death of so many children struck her as a slaughter. "Oh, my God," she thought. "This is war, this is real, and you are going back into it." The crumpled cargo liner in which the children had died was still smoldering near the runway when Palmer's flight landed in Saigon. She expected to find a mood of desperation or panic on the ground; but, as it had so often, Vietnam confounded her. Life and death had always co-existed here in ways that were disconcerting, at least to her Western sensibilities. Just as it had when she arrived there in 1972, Vietnam in 1975 still had the quality of a jump cut, a sequence of discordant images that made no sense. The kind of sequential logic so necessary in a succession of video images, as Palmer learned in her later work as a television producer, was seldom part of life in Vietnam. Improbably to her, the airport was in a state in relative calm. Downtown Saigon, she mused, would surely be different. There she would find evidence of fear. But again, the reality defied her expectations: "I got into downtown Saigon and everything looked the same, no visible panic, in fact, nothing beyond the ordinary chaotic atmosphere," she recalled, the same atmosphere she had encountered when she first arrived in mid-1972, several months after Emerson's two-year assignment ended.

By the time of Emerson's departure early in 1972 and Palmer's arrival some months later, the novelty of women covering war was starting to fade. Saigon assignments for women had become increasingly commonplace. Yet, for all their successes, few women covered the fall of Saigon, a final act that was as sullied as the war that preceded it. Most of them watched the events from a distance as Americans were driven out of a country so many of them, as young journalists, had come to love. A few gave voice to their sadness and anger on op-ed pages and in magazine articles. Kate Webb, who had been assigned to UPI's Los Angeles bureau after leaving Phomh Penh in 1972, was aboard an American aircraft carrier during the helter-skelter evacuation. Ann Bryan Mariano, who was living in Hong Kong, went to Saigon to help a Vietnamese friend, a long-time ABC staffer, get out of Saigon with his family. With her mission accomplished, she fled the city shortly before the end. Laura Palmer and Hilary Brown of ABC News departed in the helicopter evacuation of the city on April 29 as Saigon fell. Palmer left from Tan Son Nhut Airport; Brown left from the American embassy in downtown Saigon.

Although the Associated Press, a notable holdout in assigning women to Vietnam, had no women covering the fall of Saigon, nearly three years before, the agency had finally removed the barrier that had disqualified virtually all women from foreign assignments. AP's first female staffer assigned to the bureau arrived in Vietnam in October 1972. One rule, however, remained constant at AP and United Press International (the latter had dismantled its gender barriers in 1970 with the appointment of Margaret Kilgore to its Saigon bureau). For all the successes Kate Webb, Jurate Kazickas, and other itinerant freelancers had scored in their combat coverage for the wire services, AP and UPI were adamant: Women sent from its offices in the United States were not to cover combat. Although that dictate remained firmly in place right up to the end, two wire service women, Tracy Wood and Tad Bartimus, successfully circumvented it.

That new willingness to widen opportunities for women at the AP and other news organizations, coincidentally or not, came at a time when women seeking equal treatment organized at several major media companies. The most notable of those groups was the *New York Times'* Women's Caucus, established in 1972 after women in an assortment of departments had concluded that, despite the paper's public image of integrity and fairness, *Times*women were consigned to a second-class status in both salaries and opportunities. During that same year, women at the Associated Press filed a complaint with the U.S. Equal Employment Opportunity Commission challenging the company's promotion practices. By 1978, when the suit women finally brought against the *New York Times* reached a last-minute out-of-court settlement, a collection of lawsuits and official complaints of sex discrimination had also been filed by female employees at NBC, the *Washington Post, Reader's Digest, Newsday,* and *Time.* The gender disparities highlighted in those legal actions brought a few hasty high-profile promotions—some of which placed women right out front, in the store window. In a rush to demonstrate a willingness to assign women to positions that had once been reserved exclusively for men, the *Times,* for example, installed Flora Lewis as the first female bureau chief in its Paris office, one of the newspaper's most coveted positions. Efforts by major media organizations to present an appearance of gender neutrality also began to characterize assignment decisions at America's major networks, which, according to Laura Palmer, was why ABC News took her on as a radio broadcaster in Saigon.

Between mid-1972 and America's exit from Saigon in April 1975, women found a climate of wider acceptance in media circles, both in Southeast Asia and in Paris, where intense diplomatic efforts were underway to end the war. Media interest in the peace talks intensified as interest in the Saigon story ebbed, especially after President Richard Nixon's "Vietnamization" policy resulted in sharp reductions in American troop levels there. By shifting the burden of ground combat to the South Vietnamese, and lowering American casualties in the process, the administration succeeded in diminishing American interest in the war. As a result, news organizations began shrinking the size of their Saigon operations and shifting their focus to Paris, where talks had been held in fits and starts since 1968. Although there had been little to show for the nearly 150 meetings, the story in Paris, unlike the one in Saigon, offered hope for a long-awaited conclusion, especially as the pace of those talks quickened in the months before the 1972 presidential election.

The rising expectations that media attention on the talks created during the summer of 1972 dovetailed with the arrival of Lewis, the new chief of the *Times*' Paris bureau, whose specialty was diplomacy, yet another mostly-male realm in journalism. In the estimation of her peers, she was, by most measures, one of the great voices in American journalism. When the *New York Times* belatedly opened its doors to her in 1972, she had a reputation in international diplomatic circles that had been built on a distinguished twenty-five-year career; during those years, she had reported from across Europe and the Middle East, and throughout the Soviet Union and Southeast Asia. When A. M. Rosenthal, then a rising star at the *Times*, was named to succeed Lewis's husband, Sydney Gruson, in the newspaper's Warsaw bureau in the mid-1950s, he feared that he might not measure up. "It wasn't Sydney's act I was afraid to follow; it was Flora's," he explained years later. In Rosenthal's estimation, Lewis was "the best damned diplomatic correspondent on earth." In spite of that encomium from a man known for his disinclination to lavish praise, especially on a woman, the *Times* had remained off limits to Lewis for much of her career. If the *Times* was indeed "the kingdom," as Gloria Emerson once claimed, the executive editor Turner Catledge's longstanding rule barring *Times* wives from jobs on the newspaper ensured that Lewis would never cross its moat. Not long after she married Gruson in 1945, Catledge had let her know where she stood. "Over my dead body" would she be hired at the *Times*, he told her. "As far as I'm concerned, you married the wrong man."

By then, Lewis was inured to such rejections based on gender. Her early aspirations to become a diplomat withered when she received a form letter from the U.S. Department of State in response to her inquiries about the Foreign Service. It said, in essence, that "women need not apply." In fact, the rules imposed a penalty on women's test scores that sorely diminished their chances. Recalling that penalty years later, Lewis said, "I vaguely remember twenty per cent; maybe it was ten per cent . . . because you are a woman." After that, Lewis concluded, "journalism sounded like a lot more fun." She graduated summa cum laude from the University of California at Los Angeles when she was nineteen, and she enrolled in Columbia University's graduate program in 1941, believing it was a certain ticket to a job. Her career began at the Associated Press in the early 1940s. That she was assigned to the London bureau just days after World War II ended, made her an exception to the AP rule that denied women any position on its foreign staff. She landed in London on the day before V-J Day in August 1945, where her suitor, Gruson, was working for the *New York Times*. They married in a civil ceremony during their lunch hour.

Throughout her twenty-seven-year marriage to Gruson, the *Times'* managers were grudging in their willingness to accommodate her desire to pursue her own career. His contract with the *Times*, for example, precluded her from working for any *Times* competitor, a proviso that initially put the *New York Herald Tribune*, and later the *Washington Post*, off limits.

As Gruson received a succession of career-enhancing assignments, he, Lewis, and their three children moved seventeen times in twenty years. She was usually left to piece together a new set of "strings" in yet another foreign capital. In her ever-dauntless style, Lewis wrote stories by candlelight from battle-ruined Warsaw; from Berlin during the tense days of the airlift in 1947; from Israel just after the siege of Jerusalem. Her work was published by the *Chicago Tribune*, *Newsday*, the *Los Angeles Times*, *Time* magazine, the *Washington Post*, and at least half a dozen foreign newspapers and journals. In 1958, she was named the *Post's* first foreign correspondent. Much of her work in the early decades of her career was done, in the words of her friend Craig Whitney, "when foreign policy was made by men who thought women had no place in the world of diplomacy." The major journalism awards she won, the first of which was the 1956 Overseas Press Club award for best interpretation of foreign affairs, belied that perception.

In 1966, Gruson negotiated a contract that required the *Times* to offer Lewis a job if it refused to let her work for a competitor. Sure that her job with the *Washington Post* would force Catledge to acquiesce, she came away from a meeting with him realizing that women were still supposed to settle for whatever scraps the men tossed their way. Catledge had been painfully blunt. He wasn't going to offer her the kind of job he would give her "if we really wanted you," he said. To her great satisfaction, Lewis already had an offer in her pocket. She became a syndicated columnist for *Newsday*, a role in which she often wrote about the war in her thrice-weekly column, "Today Abroad," in commentaries that originated in Washington or an assortment of other world capitals, including Saigon.

In what became an annual ritual, Lewis made her first trip to South Vietnam as a *Newsday* columnist early in 1968, arriving there a few days after the Tet Offensive exploded. She landed on a military flight after dark and spent the night because "you could travel to Saigon from the airport only in a convoy and not at night," she recalled. By the time she reached Saigon, the American embassy had been liberated from enemy soldiers, but fighting was still underway on the streets of nearby Cholon. In conversations with members of the American diplomatic corps, she began to discern a baffling lack of clarity about the war. More astonishing still, Lewis recalled long after the war ended, that lack of clarity persisted for decades. Of her annual one- to two-month trips during the late 1960s and early 1970s, Lewis recalled, "I found that at the junior level, diplomats and military people in Saigon and Washington had a clear idea of what was going on." But in her conversations with the likes of Ambassador Ellsworth Bunker and New York Senator Robert F. Kennedy during the war, and with two secretaries of defense, Robert S. McNamara and Clark M. Clifford, in the years after it ended, Lewis sensed they lacked a clear-eyed grasp of the realities she perceived.

Senator Kennedy amazed Lewis when she asked him sometime in the mid-1960s why he thought America could win the war when the French, who knew Vietnam so much better than Americans did, had fared so badly. His response, as she related it nearly three decades later, seemed to stupefy her every bit as much as it had when he first uttered it: "Helicopters," Kennedy told her. Helicopters would win the war. "We have them. The French did not." She rolled her eyes in wonder as she repeated his response. Long after the war ended, Lewis was similarly amazed by McNamara's blindness to what she considered the most significant impact of the Vietnam War on American life: the distrust of government it had engendered. Lewis recalled a conversation she had with him in 1995 soon after the publication of *In Retrospect,* his mea culpa for the role he had played in escalating the war. At a time when McNamara's critics were dismissing the book as too little too late, Lewis commended him for revisiting the most unpleasant chapter of his life. But the book's one shortcoming, she told him, was his failure to address the major lesson of Vietnam, "that the government lied to the people." Indeed, those lies had turned the press and the public against the war, she added. "And as a result, people are much more skeptical about government." McNamara's answer was as simple and as wrongheaded as the one Kennedy had uttered years earlier. "He said the government didn't lie. He simply didn't understand the destruction of public confidence."

In one of her first columns from Saigon, Lewis noted that in the chaotic aftermath of the Tet Offensive, as President Nguyen Van Thieu's government moved to impose increased military powers throughout the country, the constitutional democracy that was America's creation in South Vietnam had been eroding. She questioned the continuing effort to impose democratic ideals on an ancient and complex Asian society, one where "always precise and quite clear rules, and an intricate structure of regulations provided order." The American vision of democracy, she concluded "cannot be the alternative way of doing the job necessary at this stage."

In another of those early commentaries from Saigon, Lewis took issue with General William C. Westmoreland's theory that the Tet Offensive demonstrated the degree to which Hanoi was losing its spirit for the war and had been driven by its mounting casualties and failed expectations to "go for broke" in a desperate lunge for victory. Lewis was buying none of what she called "Westmoreland's immutable optimism." Although the enemy had failed in its effort to ignite a popular uprising, it had successfully attacked cities all over South Vietnam while simultaneously maintaining its ability to attack again, she argued. "It takes willful refusal to look at the situation (and) not to conclude that Hanoi was going for what it considered a good chance of speeding victory rather than for a last-ditch gamble."

Ambassador Bunker also surprised Lewis in the same way Kennedy had. She questioned Bunker about siege of Khe Sanh, the American base in the northern reaches of South Vietnam, which was being widely compared at the time to the French battle for Dien Bien Phu. With so many Americans dying at a base that was accessible only by air, Lewis asked Bunker in February 1968 to explain the importance of Khe Sanh. "Bunker looked at me in his avuncular way. He took out a piece of blank paper and looked as if he had to explain something fundamental to someone who had not an inkling of what was going on," Lewis recalled. He drew two Xs on the page, several inches apart, and explained as if speaking to an imbecile that one represented Khe Sanh and the other Hue. "We need to defend Khe Sanh so that the Viet Cong do not overrun Hue," Bunker told her. Yet, on that very day, Lewis informed Bunker, American military men were trying to rid Hue of the enemy forces that had been occupying the city since the start of the Tet Offensive weeks before. "I had the impression that he thought, 'What a stupid woman. She doesn't understand anything about the military.'"

Although she had no interest in covering combat, because, as she said years later, "I was tired of reading about bullets that whoosh and Marines screaming in anguish," she did have a keen sense of military strategy. Indeed, had Bunker read her commentary on Khe Sanh, he might have realized how thoroughly he had underestimated Lewis's knowledge of history, war, and strategic thinking. What Lewis saw in Khe Sanh was the dangerous possibility that the Americans were allowing themselves to be drawn into a "do-or-die" confrontation at a marginal outpost that they had vowed to defend at all costs. In an earlier decade, she noted, the French had endowed a similarly remote and inconsequential base at Dien Bien Phu with the very same "apocalyptic quality." "The French Army was not defeated at Dien Bien Phu," Lewis wrote. "There was nothing militarily decisive about the battle. It was rather the unexpected loss of a post that had been ordered to defend itself at all costs that broke France's will to fight." The United States, she observed, was creating the very same risks in attaching such overwhelming importance to Khe Sanh.

Lewis also quickly grasped the fundamental flaw in the policy decision that limited troops to one-year tours and how it blurred the continuing seesaw nature of the war. Often meaningless territorial objectives—such as Hamburger Hill—were taken at great cost, subsequently relinquished, only to be taken again with a new batch of recruits at some later time. "America's capacity to sustain the war was the rotation system. . . . [T]hey [the soldiers] didn't know they were fighting a battle for a town that had been taken and lost before, maybe a few times."

Just as Frances FitzGerald had in 1966, Flora Lewis found the best place to measure the war's progress was in the countryside. FitzGerald had made Duc Lop the touchstone by which she judged the country's fortunes. Lewis found a similar point of reference in Cai Be, a village in the Plain of Jars close to an area controlled by the Viet Cong. Cai Be was in dire economic straits when she first visited in 1968, its people clearly undernourished. She first reached Cai Be by helicopter because the Viet Cong presence made traveling by car too dangerous. In later years, however, thanks to improved security, she was able to drive. Signs of prosperity were also visible in those later years. In

1971, on her last trip, Lewis saw from her car window what appeared to be snow-covered ground in the village. The white fluff she had glimpsed was, in fact, ducklings, scores and scores of them, eating the rice left behind after the harvest. "That was a tremendous sign of economic improvement," she recalled, "The fact that they had the resources to raise ducklings was a sign of remarkable progress."

In 1972, when Lewis divorced Sydney Gruson, Rosenthal, the managing editor, finally invited her to cross the moat. The bonus attached to hiring someone he so admired was that naming Lewis as the newspaper's first female bureau chief in Paris gave Rosenthal an opportunity to undermine the newly organized Women's Caucus and its charges of gender discrimination. Rosenthal, who Gloria Emerson believed was instrumental in thwarting her early efforts to be assigned to cover the war, was by turns dismissive, obstinate, and downright hostile toward the women who led the movement for equal opportunity at the *Times*. Because the inequities the women unearthed seemed so blatant, and the individual efforts of so many women had been for so long cold-shouldered by the newsroom bosses, the new group took its grievances directly to the publisher. The request for that meeting with Arthur O. Sulzberger, the man whose family had owned the *Times* for three generations, upended decades of tradition; indeed, the women essentially stiff-armed every department head in the organization. The newspaper had operated for more than half a century on a system that was less a corporate structure than it was a collection of fiefdoms presided over by middle managers who reported to department heads, and department heads who reported to vice presidents, who alone spoke to the liege lord. The break in corporate protocol was especially offensive to Rosenthal, who declined to attend the epoch-making July 19 session in which women spelled out their grievances to their publisher.[1]

Lewis's appointment as Paris bureau chief came just a few weeks before the Women's Caucus met with Sulzberger. She, of course, saw right through Rosenthal's strategy. "The women had come out in the open, the management was about to meet with them, and now the *Times* could say with great glee, 'Ha, ha—we have a woman bureau chief.'" The decision to place Lewis on the "publisher's payroll" added further plausibility to her hypothesis. That

---

1. Gloria Emerson, whose return from Vietnam preceded the formation of the Women's Caucus, was cool about joining when first approached by Betsy Wade, a key organizer. "Oh, dear," Emerson lamented, "they've let me ride my water buffalo, why should I get involved in this?" When Wade explained that she had probably earned less than her male counterparts, Emerson responded, "Oh, all right, all right, goddamit. I'll sign it."

distinction, reserved for the newspaper's long-established or rising stars, came with higher-than-average salaries and bonuses, the occasional bestowal of company stock, and enhanced health and pension benefits. Among the ninety-five employees in that elite circle, three were women.

Lewis took over her duties in Paris in July, just as peace talks between the United States and North Vietnam were reaching a critical juncture. The talks, begun in secret years before, had gone nowhere until President Nixon's revelation in January 1972 that Henry A. Kissinger and Le Duc Tho were working together to find an agreement. The on-again, off-again negotiations had been halted by the United States in May as a signal of its dissatisfaction with the lack of progress. Renewed negotiations, which began in mid-July, were so intense, and they occupied so much of Lewis's time during her early weeks in the bureau, that she often said, "I'm covering Saigon, France, and I'd like to get to Paris some day." Her previous trips to Southeast Asia had provided a rich background against which she could judge the progress of the talks.

When the principals met in Paris at the Hotel Majestic in mid-July for the 150th time, Lewis wrote that intransigence defined the mood, just as it had on so many earlier occasions. The two sides faced each other like a pair of mimes so frozen that the merest tremor on either side was construed as a noteworthy portent. North Vietnam and the National Liberation Front persisted in their demand for the ouster of President Thieu in South Vietnam as a condition to an agreement. The Americans insinuated that they might not oppose Communist participation in a government in the South, but they would make no overture to enable a takeover. "Despite the urging of any interested powers," Lewis explained, "there was still no hint that next week's session, or the ones after it, would bring a difference."

In a later story about the talks, Lewis's profile of the National Liberation Front's chief delegate, Nguyen Thi Bich, injected the peace process with a human dynamic. Pragmatic, level-headed, clear-spoken, Bich "looked much fresher than her forty-five years and the hard life of a guerrilla would seem to have warranted," according to Lewis. The National Liberation Front's goal, Lewis explained, was to defeat Vietnamization, a policy sustained by continued bombing of both the North and the South, and huge American subsidies for "the Saigon army."

Late in October, the announcement that an agreement had finally been reached was greeted with a mixture of joy and relief until Kissinger's famous declaration, "Peace is at hand," turned out to be premature. The peace agreement he and Le Duc Tho had negotiated evaporated in the face of President

Thieu's rejection of its provisions. He likened the agreement to suicide. Among the terms that outraged Thieu were provisions that North Vietnamese troops were to remain in the South and the Provisional Revolutionary Government, the administrative arm of the Viet Cong, would have a voice in the future leadership of the South.

As Lewis maneuvered her way through the permutations of the peace talks underway in Saigon, France, during the summer and fall of 1972, Laura Palmer negotiated her way around Saigon, South Vietnam, a city that had first revealed itself to her as "a bad girl with a Buddhist soul." Before she had time to ruminate about its malevolence and understand what she later recognized as all its "trapdoors," she had fallen through one. For all its wretchedness and vulgarity, Palmer was no less charmed than Emerson had been by the elegant place she had found there in 1956. Just as Emerson and FitzGerald had in earlier decades, Palmer fell in love with the ethereal state of mind she discerned in Saigon. "I missed the sign that said 'Stay away or be prepared to stay forever,'" she wrote years later.

In an echo of the conclusion Flora Lewis had drawn about the agenda behind her appointment as the *Times'* Paris bureau chief, Palmer, too, was certain that credit for her first job in journalism belonged to the Women's Caucus at the *New York Times*. She had landed in Saigon armed only with a liberal arts degree from Oberlin College. She had majored in government, not journalism. She had never written a word for her college student newspaper. She knew zero about the military. She had met her college language requirement with Spanish rather than French. In short, she was among the least qualified people who had ever knocked on the door of any news organization in Saigon. But with debtors awaiting repayment of her college loans, Palmer's only choice was to persist. Nothing, save perhaps her gender, qualified her for the radio stringer job that ABC News in Saigon needed to fill. And ABC's bureau chief in Saigon told her so. ABC bosses in New York, however, overrode the objections of their Saigon staff and ordered that Palmer be hired because "having a woman on the air from Saigon was a quick way to look good," as she explained it years later. "The courage behind my work in Vietnam belongs only to a heroic band of women at *The New York Times* who filed a landmark sexual discrimination suit against the paper at great professional sacrifice to themselves."

Throughout her college years, Palmer hated the war and participated in every major demonstration against it. She embraced the antiwar movement in the belief that her voice and others that spoke the same message might be heard. Finding a sense of catharsis in public expression, she marched in the rain, the snow, and the sun. In Washington, she was tear-gassed in front of the U.S. Department of Justice. Knowing that the police had used the same c2 gas that was used against the enemy in Vietnam "created a feeling of solidarity and oneness with the Vietnamese." She and her fellow activists patted themselves on the back when the media declared they had helped to "dump Johnson." All that euphoria over the purported impact of their efforts was shattered, however, on a sunny May afternoon in Ohio when National Guardsmen opened fire on antiwar demonstrators at Kent State University. The four young men and women who died on the campus lawn were shot by their contemporaries, really, young men called to the campus to keep order in a time of disorder. Palmer stopped going to demonstrations after Kent State because, she said, "I stopped thinking I mattered. I stopped believing anything could change."

Palmer's opposition, however, never translated into a desire to see firsthand just how war was fought, nor did she share the desire of some antiwar activists to meet with North Vietnam's leaders in Hanoi. She had never been drawn to journalism and to war in the same way Beverly Deepe or Tad Bartimus, the AP reporter whom she befriended in 1973, had been. She never pictured herself as a journalist, even after she graduated from college. Indeed, other than some tentative thoughts about law school, she hadn't really mapped out a future for herself when her boyfriend called and asked her to go to Saigon with him.

Journalism, however, certainly made sense in the framework of her interests and her spirit. She was drawn to the idea of "being in the mix of big adventures" in the same way that fictional icon of her childhood, Nancy Drew, was in the many mysteries she so skillfully solved. As a child in Evanston, Illinois, Palmer began to perceive history as a succession of momentous events, geographic discoveries, scientific breakthroughs, international crises, wars, and sweeping acts of nature. But with that recognition came twinges of regret. All the epoch-making events, those hinges on which history had turned, the revolutions that had changed mankind, the wars that had reordered the world, the discoveries and inventions that had altered life, all of them had already taken place. Her own life, she fretted, was likely to be lived out in ordinary times. She would have no chance to be in the mix of big adventures. That fear, however, vaporized with the inauguration of John F. Kennedy, an occasion when her parents, Frank and Helen Palmer, allowed her to skip a few hours of school to watch the event on television. When the president was assassinated a thousand days later, Palmer knew for certain that history had waited for her coming of age.

During her earliest months in Saigon, Palmer felt like the rookie in a world of pros. She abandoned the easygoing take on the world that she had often impressed upon her sister, the one that held "things always happen when they should and work themselves out." The intensity of her work for ABC Radio and her boss's occasional impatience with her inexperience made her apprenticeship excruciating. Quitting, however, was not an option. She needed shelter, food, and $34.10 for the monthly installment on her college loan. The uncertainties of life in Saigon added a touch of anxiety to the mix. When the pace of negotiations quickened before the 1972 presidential election, Palmer wrote her family that the "secret" peace talks created an abundance of confusion. "No one knows if there will be a cease-fire or an attack on Saigon."

In her earliest reports, Palmer tracked the daily military briefings, those attenuated snapshots of the day-to-day events served up by a U.S. Army spokesman, the ones so many journalists derided. The carefully staged Five O'Clock Follies made for rather formulaic and easily mastered forty-second spot news reports. But Palmer quickly recognized, as had countless journalists before her, that although those briefings provided fleeting glimpses of the action, they offered little in the way of understanding. Still, they gave her the opportunity to master radio reporting. Her first real reporting assignment, one that required her to find people to interview, took her to Saigon's USO in search of GIs who were spending Thanksgiving away from home. The entirely predictable answers she received to her entirely predictable questions once again made for an easily manageable, by-the-book radio news report.

Palmer had far less experience than the three wire-service women whose assignments in Saigon overlapped her two-year stay in Vietnam from 1972 until 1974. In the two news organizations where who was first mattered greatly, United Press International won the race. UPI sent two stateside reporters to Vietnam well before AP got around to assigning its first woman to cover the war. Margaret Kilgore's assignment began in 1970. She spent two years covering the political and diplomatic rather than the military side of the war. She was replaced in 1972 by Tracy Wood, who arrived with a determination to change the rules. UPI's foreign editor, William Landry, and its Saigon bureau chief, Arthur Higbee, were kindred spirits on the issue of women covering war. Higbee's instructions were unequivocal. Politics, diplomatic functions, and stories about refugees, nurses, and hospitals were okay. War stories were not. Wood was to stay away from combat. "You are too feminine," he said, and clearly he wanted her to stay that way.

Wood, however, had no intention of allowing her gender to circumscribe her Vietnam assignment. If she did her boss's bidding and limited her work to the assignments he defined, she would never be a "full reporter." During a tour of Hue, where Wood had been sent to get a sense of the country's geography, Barney Seibert, an overweight, middle-aged, chain-smoking colleague who was a master of all things military, quietly taught her the rudiments of covering—and surviving—combat. In the months that followed, although Wood's reports often originated from remote fire bases and hilltop outposts around Hue or Da Nang or Quang Tri, she and Higbee never had a direct, one-on-one conversation about her coverage of combat and her sometimes close encounters with death.

Associated Press, the last holdout in bringing women into its Saigon bureau, finally set aside the many restrictions it had placed on women and assigned Edith Lederer to the bureau in October 1972. Just as Kilgore had when she was assigned to UPI's Saigon bureau in 1970, Lederer abided by the rules and stayed away from the battlefield. Those rare occasions when she did face danger were a matter of happenstance. On the other hand, Tad Bartimus, who replaced Lederer in May 1973, was as determined as Wood to thwart her bosses' efforts to limit her work to safe assignments inside Saigon.

It was Richard Pyle, the AP bureau chief in Saigon from 1970 until 1973, who succeeded in having the first female staffer assigned to Vietnam. He played a crucial role in reversing a long-standing policy that banned the assignment of women to foreign bureaus. Bringing a woman to Saigon was one of the goals Pyle had when he was named bureau chief. He had met Kate Webb of UPI on his second day in Saigon in 1968 and was instantly impressed. She was dressed in fatigues, seated at the table in the Continental Palace Hotel where Pyle and a colleague were having a drink. As Webb stared at him across the table, Pyle was uncomfortably aware of his status, in the argot of the press corps oldtimers, as an FNG, a "fucking new guy." After a few minutes passed, she leaned over and, with her lips barely moving, told him, "I hear you're hot shit," Pyle remembered. "With that remark she established both a friendship and put me in my place all at once." Forever after, Pyle held Webb in high esteem and considered her work "absolutely top notch."

Webb was a ubiquitous reminder to him that AP was deficient in not having a woman on its Saigon staff. Only Kelly Tunney Smith, who had been attached to the bureau for four months in 1967, when she did a special series with Peter Arnett, had been there. Pyle thought a woman's voice would bring a new dimension to the AP's Vietnam reportage—the same thought that led

Terence Smith to welcome Emerson to the *Times* bureau in 1970. "We didn't need a woman combat reporter. We needed a different eye and ear and voice on the effects of the war on the civilian population," Pyle recalled many years later. He wanted AP to produce more stories about the Vietnamese people and believed that a woman would outperform a man in that arena. "My feeling was that people tend to trust a woman and are more inclined to talk to somebody who didn't have the appearance of a tough guy. Men cannot get the same trust from people that women do. That is just a fact," Pyle said.

When he sent the request to Wes Gallagher, AP's president, Pyle asked specifically for Edie Lederer, described once by her friend and colleague Bartimus as "a tiny woman with big hair, baby wrists and perfectly lacquered red nails." Lederer had wowed Pyle during the summer of 1971 when she made a stop in Saigon on her round-the-world vacation trip with her friend Nancy Goebner. Although she had traveled widely in Europe and the Middle East, because Lederer had seen little of Asia, her itinerary was determined by the destinations that could be reached via the Pan American Airlines Clipper service on that continent. In Vietnam, as she did at all their other destinations, Lederer touched base with colleagues in the AP bureau. Thanks to Pyle, who accompanied Lederer and her friend on a helicopter tour of the Mekong Delta, she caught a distant glimpse of combat and left the country feeling rather like a "war tourist." Lederer's vacation jaunt struck Pyle as adventuresome, and her curiosity about the country impressed him. Still, Saigon ranked second on Lederer's list of most exciting places. Kabul, Afghanistan, where two women were stoned by a group of men who apparently took issue with their attire, took top billing.

Gallagher's decision to assign a woman to Saigon was a stunning reversal for an organization where women had yet to join the ranks of foreign correspondents, let alone war correspondents. Years before, in a fiat that paralleled "Catledge's rule," Ben Bassett, the foreign editor, had banned women from AP's foreign desk. Since a turn on the foreign desk was a precondition for a foreign assignment, Bassett's policy effectively made women ineligible for jobs outside the United States. Gallagher's intervention, however, outflanked Bassett. Nonetheless, Gallagher drew boundaries around Lederer's assignment. He unequivocally put to rest any secret longings she might have harbored about covering combat. "Neither he [Pyle] nor I want you popping in and out of the fronts just to prove you can do everything that one of our veteran war correspondents can do. You are being sent there to do a job on special coverage, not to go into any combat coverage," he wrote to Lederer before she departed for Saigon. And, in a conclusion that might have raised eyebrows among AP legends like Peter Arnett and Horst Faas, Gallagher added, "You are too valuable."

A year had passed by the time Gallagher approved Pyle's request. America was in the midst of its unprecedented diplomatic push to end the war. President Nixon wanted "peace with honor," a key component of which was securing the release of American prisoners of war held by the North Vietnamese and their allies in the South. The International Control Commission was established to oversee the cease-fire and to serve as a buffer between the South Vietnamese government and the newly recognized Provisional Revolutionary Government. All this, in Pyle's mind, played into Lederer's greatest strengths. "Edie established sources in the diplomatic community. She was extremely effective," Pyle recalled. "She was aggressive, but not obnoxiously so. She got information that others couldn't or wouldn't get. I recognized early on how smart she made me look."

In Saigon, Lederer joined what Pyle described as "the greatest war bureau ever." The collective depth and breadth of experience embodied in AP's thirty or so staffers was unparalleled anywhere in the world. The principles of the operation had been established by Malcolm Browne in 1962, back when it was still a one-man operation. In the decade that followed, the bureau had grown into an "international stew" with a changing cast that at any given moment might include British, French, German, Japanese, Dutch, New Zealand, South African, and Vietnamese staffers working alongside the Americans. In Pyle's thinking, the sense of collegiality among AP staffers made it unlike other news operations in Saigon. At the television network offices in particular, "long knives and internecine rivalries" were the standard among sharp-elbowed wannabes who would all but kill for those precious minute-and-a-fraction time slots on the Huntley-Brinkley or Cronkite broadcasts. By comparison, AP staffers were often anonymous. The nature of their responsibilities demanded teamwork. "Everybody gave ground to other people. We all pitched in when a crisis occurred," Pyle recalled. Getting the story, getting it right, and getting it first transcended individual egos. Lederer, Pyle recalled, "caught the sense of it right away." She soon became an eager participant in those often fierce, Vietnam-era wire service wars in which "scooping the competition was the equivalent of a battlefield victory."

When Horst Faas, AP's German-born Pulitzer Prize-winning photographer, first laid eyes on Edie Lederer he thought, "My God, what has Gallagher sent us now." She struck him as a bit bizarre, with her high heels, heavy make-up, short skirt, and a hairdo that he thought "looked like a tower." She also brought a set of talents tailor-made for a wire service a operation. Faas quickly realized that his newest colleague was a highly professional "workhorse," someone who "was great in getting out the story and getting it out quickly."

Lederer spent her first day in Saigon writing a "peace related" story about a Vietnamese woman who had lost three sons in the war. In the days that followed, she visited the carrier USS *America,* where she talked to pilots whose bombing runs had become increasingly dangerous in the face of ever-more aggressive antiaircraft weapons fire by the North Vietnamese. She also wrote about a reconstructive surgery center for Vietnamese children maimed or disfigured by bombs, napalm, and gunfire. The scene overwhelmed her emotions. It was harder to take than all the murders and dead bodies she had seen in her previous six years of stateside crime reporting. Beyond the rocket and mortar attacks she heard in her downtown Saigon apartment and the American bombs she saw dropping in the distance on forays outside the city, Lederer's encounters with combat were minimal. What she quickly realized was that the bureau was still in what she called the "muddy-boots mode" that covering combat had for so long required, and was less than fully prepared for the cease-fire. As Pyle had anticipated, Lederer was quick to establish a network of contacts in the diplomatic community.

Lederer arrived less than a week before Kissinger's premature "peace is at hand" declaration and stayed through one of the liveliest news periods of the war. Kissinger's ill-timed comment brought hordes of journalists back to Saigon. "Old Vietnam hands" in the press corps returned anticipating that the coming peace would surely be both the story of the decade and the final chapter of the story that had, in varying ways, defined their careers. After the breakdown of the Paris talks in October and President Nixon's landslide re-election in November, major events of the war unfolded in rapid succession: the Christmas bombing of Hanoi and Haiphong in December 1972, the signing of a peace agreement in January, the release of American prisoners of war, and the withdrawal of the last American ground troops on March 29. At various times, Laura Palmer, Edie Lederer, and Tracy Wood took part in covering those stories.

The media descent on Saigon in October to cover "the peace" left Laura Palmer bemused. She wanted to believe—as all of them seemed to—that peace would come. But believing required an intellectual leap, one she could not make. "I wanted to be swept into their abyss of optimism, but I could not," she wrote at the time. She watched as the ranks of the "old Vietnam hands" swelled in anticipation of a big story. "You know, for us," some of them told her, "there will never be another story like this again." The camaraderie and spirit on display as they greeted one another reminded Palmer of the esprit among veterans of the antiwar movement. She had watched the energy of her fellow demonstrators run high—an enthusiasm that was ephemeral. Peace, it turned out, was not at hand. Richard Nixon had other ideas. No other moment in the war caused outrage equal to that of the Christmas bombing of Hanoi and Haiphong in December 1972. Undertaken by the president in what one historian called "one of his Patton moods," the bombing was scripted as an effort to bring the North Vietnamese back to the bargaining table after talks deadlocked in early December. Rather than renegotiate the few remaining points that, once concluded, would have cemented the agreement, Kissinger instead tried to reopen major issues in the pact and threatened "savage bombing" if Hanoi refused. In short, "the Nixon Administration had it both ways, the illusion of peace, the reality of ongoing war," according to one historian. For twelve days just before and immediately after Christmas Day, Nixon unleashed the most relentless air attacks of the war. Hundreds of U.S. Air Force, Navy, and Marine fighter-bombers were joined, for the first time, by B-52 bombers, two hundred in all, each armed with two dozen 500-pound bombs and forty 750-pound bombs. Day after day, in round-the-clock raids, 36,000 tons of bombs were dropped, more than the total tonnage dropped between 1969 and 1971. The North Vietnamese in turn had probably never put their Soviet-made surface-to-air missiles to better use. American losses were high, twenty-six aircraft, fifteen of them B-52s—valued at $8 million each. The loss of U.S. airmen, ninety-three, was unprecedented in such a short time. The thirty-one pilots who were captured raised by 10 percent the number of American prisoners of war held by the enemy. That aerial bludgeoning, according to historians, had two objectives: Nixon hoped to blast the North Vietnamese back to the bargaining table and simultaneously demonstrate to President Thieu his commitment to intervene if the North violated any future peace agreement.

In the days just before Christmas, Palmer was dispatched to Laos with an ABC television crew to cover the arrival of passengers on the once-a-week flight from Hanoi—including Joan Baez, the singer and pacifist who had traveled there before the bombing began. Palmer and throngs of other reporters hoped to learn about the impact of the military operation named Linebacker II. Baez and other antiwar activists who accompanied her to

Hanoi reported that heavy damage had been done to civilian targets, including a hospital that was, according to the Columbia University law professor Telford Taylor, "blown to smithereens." After leaving Hanoi, Baez spoke of the "hideousness of it all." The Pentagon, however, maintained that only military installations were being targeted. In an odd counterpoint to mayhem underway in Hanoi, in Vientiane, Palmer was savoring her first taste of the expense-account lifestyle that came with the territory in television news. "I've felt like Eloise at the Plaza," she wrote to a friend on stationery from the Lane-Xang Hotel. Aside from doing "some radio," Palmer wrote, "for the first time I've lived a completely self-indulgent luxurious week—like a rich lady—and it's been fun." But the indolence also made her restless and anxious to return to work, she told her friend. "This kind of life is not fulfilling." In America and around the world, on editorial pages and elsewhere the bombing operation was denounced as barbarous. An interfaith group of forty-one American religious leaders signed a pastoral letter that declared: "The bombing must be stopped. The war must be ended." A German newspaper called the attacks "a crime against humanity." Premier Olof Palme of Sweden compared the bombing campaign to the Nazi massacres of World War II.

The speedy resumption of the peace talks in January gave rise in some quarters to the reasoning that the bombing had accomplished its purpose, especially after an agreement was sealed within days of that resumption. The accord called for a cease-fire in South Vietnam, and the release of all American prisoners of war by North Vietnam within sixty days. In return, America agreed, to President Thieu's consternation, that North Vietnam was permitted to leave its forces in place in regions under its control in the South at the time of the cease-fire. At the time, an estimated 150,000 North Vietnamese soldiers were in the South. The agreement further stipulated that the role of American combat forces would end, but that American military assistance in the South would remain almost unrestricted. Against this backdrop, on January 20 President Nixon declared: "We have finally achieved peace with honor."

Flora Lewis's *New York Times* story about the signing of the cease-fire agreement in Paris on January 27, 1973, described the "cold, gloomy atmosphere" of the setting in which U.S. Secretary of State William P. Rogers wrote his name sixty-two times on copies of an agreement that was as rich in ambiguities as the conflict itself had been. Although what had been "the longest, most divisive foreign war in America's history" was purportedly over, the struggle between the two Vietnamese sides would, in all likelihood, continue. Optimists among participants to the peace agreement hoped the continuing issues would be resolved in the political arena rather than on the battlefield. Lewis's story noted that the document was "signed here today in eerie silence, without a word or gesture to express the world's relief that the years of war were officially ending." But like so many of her colleagues, she understood that the peace envisioned in the agreement was an illusion. In the end, firepower rather than civil discourse would settle the conflict.

The next day, an hour before the cease-fire was set to begin at 8:00 A.M., Tan Son Nhut Airport was hit by rocket attacks. Later that day, Lederer covered the arrival of the flight from Bangkok carrying the Viet Cong representatives who now, according to the terms of the peace agreement, were allowed to have an official presence on South Vietnamese soil. After two planes carrying the North Vietnamese and Viet Cong representatives landed, Lederer watched a diplomatic contretemps play out as members of both delegations, reluctant to cede authority to the South Vietnamese, stayed aboard their respective airplanes rather than submit to the indignity of showing their passports to South Vietnamese customs officials. When the "plane-ins" finally ended, the North Vietnamese and Viet Cong delegations were escorted to the utterly Spartan living quarters chosen for them by the South Vietnamese.

On the day the peace agreement was to take effect, Frances FitzGerald weighed in with her prediction that it would bring no honor and very little peace to Vietnam. In a *Washington Post* commentary, she wrote that the implied commonalities in the agreement's reference to two "parties" simply did not exist. On one hand, the Provisional Revolutionary Government (PRG) was "a political party with a relatively small military force . . . but with strong roots in the countryside of the South"; on the other hand, President Thieu's regime had "no responsibility to its own people and no coherent interest except in maintaining the flow of American aid." In fact, its survival would depend on "maintaining a state of hostility," FitzGerald wrote. The agreement's ambiguous and potentially deceptive language gave no indication whether America sought simply to end its role in the war or genuinely wanted peace. The latter would require an American willingness to lead the Thieu regime on a path to its own dissolution. And that was a highly unlikely scenario, she insisted. Just as President Ngo Dinh Diem had thumbed his nose at the provision in the Geneva Accords that called for nationwide elections in 1956, President Thieu resisted any move toward the kind of power sharing incorporated in the language Kissinger and Le Duc Tho had negotiated. The war in Indochina, once again, almost seemed to double back on itself. The 1973 cease-fire brought to mind the one Dickey Chapelle had witnessed in

Laos in 1962, the one she had described eleven years earlier as "the noisiest goddamn cease-fire I've ever covered." FitzGerald concluded that the agreement signed in Paris left unanswered the central question: Who controlled South Vietnam?

Few Americans pondered that question, especially between mid-February and late March of 1973 when the North Vietnamese released the 591 American prisoners of war. After so many years of mounting impatience and cynicism over the war, at last Americans found reason to rejoice, if only for a few weeks, about something that looked like an American triumph. By then, Nixon seemed to be making the case that the safe return of America's POWs was reason enough to continue fighting the war. By early 1973, it was "perhaps the only war aim that had not lost credibility with the public." The government's carefully stage-managed succession of prisoner releases were made-for-television melodramas. One hundred and seventy newsmen and women were accredited to cover the arrival of the first 143 American prisoners, some of whom had been held for more than eight years. In a succession of four releases between February 12 and March 29, prisoners boarded U.S. Air Force C-141 Starlifter hospital aircraft in Hanoi and were taken to Clark Air Base in the Philippines. Through perseverance, luck, and ingenuity, Tracy Wood pulled off two trips to Hanoi to cover the first and last of the four prisoner releases for UPI.

The key to landing that coup, Wood recalled much later, was time she had spent on the telephone in long and occasionally vacuous conversations with the bored and isolated representatives of the PRG, who were holed up in a barracks near Saigon's airport and allowed out only for official meetings. Those hours seldom yielded anything newsworthy. But Wood persisted in cultivating these potentially valuable sources, even when it meant indulging in an hour-long discussion of the appropriate uses of Mrs., Miss, and Ms. The payoff was sweet. Among the hundreds of requests from Western journalists who wanted to cover the first prisoner release in Hanoi, the North Vietnamese issued only three visas—one of them to Wood. The others went to two foreign newsmen working for American media organizations, Horst Faas of AP and Chris Callery, a British cameraman for NBC.

The first prisoner release was the most dramatic. Because the POWs were released in the order in which they had been captured, those who had been imprisoned the longest were the first to be repatriated. In Hanoi, a day before the first prisoner release, Wood, Faas, and Callery were given a tour of the prison where the POWs were held. It was last day these men would spend in the baggy gray-and-red striped prison uniforms. Following the orders from their guards, none of the Americans spoke with the three journalists. A few even avoided eye contact. The next morning, the prisoners were bused in groups of twenty-two at Hanoi's Gia Lam Airport, where the damage wrought by the Christmas bombing was evident. American and North Vietnamese officials presided over a brief ceremony. One by one, a North Vietnamese military officer presented each of the prisoners by name to an American military official; each man was then escorted by an American serviceman to one of the three airplanes that arrived and departed in succession. As Wood watched the procession of prisoners make their way from the camouflage-painted buses past the table where each name was announced, and finally on to the waiting hospital planes, it struck her that these prisoners all looked the same. They lacked any trace of individuality. The long years during which the need to remain obscure was critical to survival, Wood concluded, had left all these men with the same posture, the same way of walking, and the same expressionless faces. The ceremony began at 12:30 P.M. By 1:45 P.M. the last prisoner was airborne.

When Wood asked her contacts in North Vietnam for permission to return to Hanoi, their response came as a surprise. Wood, they said, could return to Hanoi to witness the release of the last sixty-seven American prisoners and she could bring along other journalists. The only stipulation, however, was that the trip must be limited to one day. Since the only commercial airline flying to and from Hanoi made the trip once a week, the provision necessitated chartering an airplane. UPI briefly considered the idea, but when the bosses learned the price tag was $7,000, Wood asked permission to invite colleagues from other news organizations to share the cost. Wood's coup was nearly derailed by CBS and its pursuit of an exclusive for Walter Cronkite, star of the network's evening news program and by then an American icon. UPI discovered that no planes were available for charter within a reasonable range of Vientiane or Hanoi. CBS, with its enormous bankroll, had reserved them all. Walter Cronkite's bosses wanted—and could afford—to leave the network's rivals, NBC and ABC, on the tarmac in Laos. But the North Vietnamese refused Cronkite's request for a visa. So CBS had the planes and UPI had the visas. UPI did not want AP along for the ride any more than CBS wanted ABC and NBC aboard. While the U.S. and North Vietnamese governments haggled over the terms of the final release— including visas for CBS—Wood found herself in the middle of negotiations with Cronkite, his producer, and two North Vietnamese officials. Calling what amounted to a twenty-four-hour truce in the news wire and television wars, UPI executives agreed to make space for two reporters and a photographer from AP; CBS accepted the inclusion of reporters from NBC and ABC. On the flight to Hanoi, many of the journalists awaiting their big story on enemy soil were tense and moody. Then, minutes before landing, the plane turned sharply and went into a steep descent. The pilot, the journalists later learned, was trying to evade ground fire from farmers who were following their practice of shooting at American aircraft. News of the truce had not reached them.

The journalists' hosts in Hanoi once again took the reporters on a city tour, showing the "massive damage" done to civilian targets by the bombs dropped from planes piloted by the likes of the American airmen who were about to be released. During a briefing at the prison where the last American POWs were being held, the North Vietnamese harangued their audience at length about the care and comforts American prisoners had enjoyed during their captivity. Later, in a room inside the prison compound, two dozen reporters, photographers, and television crew members crowded around an equal number of POWs. The men seemed confused and apprehensive; most were afraid to speak. A few took the cigarettes offered by the journalists. One prisoner staring through the barred window suddenly recognized a face. The POW's expression and his words conveyed disbelief: "Is that really Walter Cronkite?" The crowd of wonder-struck prisoners stared at the television news guru, whom some had not seen for years. Cronkite, ever gracious, pretended not to notice and went about asking his questions, just like any other journalist. Wood thought, "In the strange world of prisoner releases, this moment was one of the most extraordinary."

After the final prisoner release, Frances FitzGerald returned to Vietnam to see firsthand what shape the so-called peace was taking. She set off with David Greenway, a *Washington Post* reporter, and an interpreter, to find those cadres of the "enemy" whose presence in the South had been legitimized by the accords. A clause in the agreement allowed both the North Vietnamese and representatives of the Provisional Revolutionary Government to establish offices in the South. Thanks to their South Vietnamese hosts, the barbed-wire-enclosed barracks near Tan Son Nhut airport gave the Communists their first official presence in the South. An additional provision that allowed for the PRG to remain in place in regions under its control made the "enemy" easily accessible to reporters for the first time. Although a few reporters had made contact with the resistance fighters before the cease-fire, for most the Communists were a shadowy presence whose operations were carried out beyond the tree line. Fearing that a sympathetic portrait might legitimize the enemy, members of South Vietnam's military and civilian leaders took a dim view of these encounters and tried to thwart such trips by American journalists. Sympathizers were easy to find, but FitzGerald and Greenway had hoped to make contact with troops from North Vietnam and the National Liberation Front. In Chuong Thien in the Mekong Delta, where nighttime echoes of artillery fire indicated that the war was still going on, they stumbled into a large PRG military base. For five hours through the afternoon and much of the evening, they talked with a commander of the region's reserve troops and later to his superior. The Thieu regime routinely violated the terms of the cease-fire, the two men charged. They wondered aloud whether Thieu and the United States would "tear up the [peace] agreement" and wage war again. South Vietnam's president, declared a man who called himself Nam, "is a corpse because all the people hate him and his only power comes from American aid." Around midnight, word came that some "high officials of the PRG" wanted to see the two visitors. They moved by sampan to a remote jungle shelter and, once back on land, were led to a building where six uniformed men sat in wooden armchairs (the chairs reminded FitzGerald of the ones so common where she had summered). She and Greenway marveled that everything—the soldiers' uniforms, weapons, ammunition, two-way radios, and even the Coleman lamp that illuminated the thatched-roof enclosure— were American-made. The six soldiers spoke about the victory they had won over the American imperialists. The Paris peace agreement, they insisted, was an admission of defeat by the Americans. They would soon meet President Thieu's continuing violations of the cease-fire head on, they declared. "Today you see us in the forest, but tomorrow you will see us in the cities," said one.

Although the last American soldiers had withdrawn, it was obvious that neither side thought the war was over. And not every American soldier, as Laura Palmer discovered weeks before the final pullout, was all that eager to go home. On Tan My Island, near Da Nang, she spoke with a group of helicopter pilots, all of whom were delighted to "talk to anything with round eyes." When she asked their thoughts about the peace agreement, their responses contradicted all her assumptions about the basic goodness of Americans in uniform. They wanted to stay in Vietnam, they told her. They wanted to settle scores. Besides, they were having a good time "killing dinks." She added: "For these chopper pilots, some of whom were on their second or third tours in Vietnam, the war had reduced the enemy to gooks, dinks, slant-eyes, and gooners."

Still, after the last troops had left and her pediatrician boyfriend had returned home, Palmer remained enchanted with Vietnam. By then, her mastery of radio was such that in one letter she could tell her mother that the day's radio logs in her office showed her "all over the dials, as we say in the trade . . . feels great." In letters home to family and friends, she shared her joys, her moments of discovery, and the growing independence that life in the Saigon press corps was affording her. She gloried in the occasional dinner-party encounters with the likes of Frankie FitzGerald, whom she met soon after *Fire in the Lake* was published. "What a fantastic lady," Palmer wrote to her friend Elly about the occasion. "That is what I really love about my little life here in Saigon . . . intellectual stimulation . . . being around people who are so much more intellectual in the sense of being more experienced and older. . . . I am learning so much."

After ABC eliminated her job in September 1973, she soon found work with NBC Radio. Palmer, with her new-found confidence as a radio news broadcaster, began to think she had more to say about the war and the politics of Southeast Asia than could be crammed into forty-second radio spot news reports. She worked on a television report about Vietnam's mixed-race orphans and began stretching herself as a writer with submissions to *Harper's*, the *Atlantic*, and, later, *Rolling Stone*. She began stringing for *Time* magazine and started writing about some of the war's more complicated and curious issues, including the orphan crisis, President Thieu's national police, and Pentecostalism in South Vietnam. In the *Time* magazine office, she first met Pham Xuan An, and soon became, along with Deepe and Pond and FitzGerald and Webb, one of the young women whose friendship he held dear. Their paths crossed frequently as *Time* assigned Palmer more and more work.

She also met a French journalist who worked for Agence France-Presse, mostly out of Phnom Penh, a city she soon began visiting twice a month and where, like scores of journalists before them, they became habitues of Chantal's, the opium den of choice among Westerners. In the aftermath of the peace agreement, the intensity of life around Saigon diminished appreciably. "It was a war we didn't see," Palmer recalled. "It was a war we didn't care about as much, at least for the editors in New York." With the POWs safely repatriated, Americans, of course, wanted to forget the war. The unseen war in Vietnam and the increasingly visible war in Cambodia continued to be major stories even as news organizations made staff cuts in their Saigon bureaus. The political fortunes of the American-backed government in Saigon deteriorated. The hope that Asian nations would engage in "self-help" and shape their own destinies never took hold. Instead, President Thieu's addiction to American aid grew and demanded ever greater fixes. More M-16 rifles. More M-79 grenade launchers. More tanks and trucks. More howitzers and helicopters. Besides the weaponry of war, Thieu became dependent on what he perceived as America's willingness to resume bombing targets in the North, the South, and in Cambodia, if conditions demanded. Still, the reality did not change. South Vietnam kept losing ground. The Army of the Republic of South Vietnam could not score a significant victory.

In Paris, talks aimed at framing a political solution to the issues that had kept the countries at war in spite of the accords signed in January 1973 began with little promise and continued with little progress. Both sides took steps that ignored both the letter and the spirit of the agreement, as Flora Lewis reported. The pace of meetings between the four parties to the agreement quickened to the point where Lewis might have felt she was once again in Saigon, France. Even the cast of characters was occasionally the same: Henry Kissinger aided by Ambassador William H. Sullivan on one side and Le Duc Tho accompanied by Nguyen Cao Thach on the other.

Each side charged the other with failing to meet the pledges spelled out in the peace agreement. America continued to supply its South Vietnamese ally with war materiel, and the Soviet Union did the same for its client state, North Vietnam. A representative of the Provisional Revolutionary Government contended that the United States was stalling on its commitment to remove the many mines it had planted in Haiphong Harbor. The Americans and South Vietnamese countered that North Vietnam was bringing in men and equipment to strengthen its forces in the South. Although the Americans had pledged to withdraw their troops, upwards of 9,000 "civilian" advisors remained, many of whom had quickly received military discharges and were placed on civilian payrolls. The Communist delegates complained of bad faith in the treatment of the North Vietnamese and PRG representatives whose presence in the South was sanctioned by the peace agreement. They were virtually imprisoned in the barracks at Tan Son Nhut, isolated even from journalists who sought to interview them. America also brushed aside its promise to dismantle its military bases. Those bases were instead turned over to the Saigon government before the start of the cease-fire, which exempted them from its terms. The equipment and supplies left behind were labeled "nonmilitary," still another step to fortify President Thieu's army for the fight to come. American reconnaissance flights over North Vietnam continued, as did American bombing raids in Cambodia. As Lewis explained in one of her analyses, the accord signed in January "was a compromise of words but not of intentions." It all added up to a war masquerading as peace. The ruse was carried out mostly for the benefit of Americans who had had enough of Vietnam. "It is obvious that the fighting is continuing," Lewis wrote from Paris ninety days after the agreement was signed. Once again, Vietnam had become a looking glass in which a war that was not a war persisted and the peace to which the parties had agreed never materialized.

Tad Bartimus arrived in Saigon just as this strange reality began to emerge in 1973. For years, dissonant perceptions of the war had torn at the fabric of her family just as they had torn at the fabric of the nation. Her father, a U.S. Air Force fighter pilot in North Africa during World War II, flew missions to Vietnam in the 1960s. Only after he died did Bartimus learn that the cargo on many of his return trips was flag-draped coffins—probably hundreds of them in all. Her mother, a woman of liberal inclinations, hated the war for personal reasons: a draft-aged son who was a likely conscript. Her maternal instincts occasionally bred hawkish tendencies, such as the thought that maybe President Lyndon B. Johnson should just drop an atomic bomb so that the fight would end quickly—before her son graduated from college and was forced to join the fight. That son, Tad's brother, was decidedly supportive of U.S. policy, a position that too often sparked shouting matches with his sister. Most Americans were fed up with the war by 1973, but Bartimus still hungered to see it, or at least what was left of it.

She had made a vow to become a war correspondent in Vietnam when she was sixteen. News junkie that she was, she started spying Kate Webb's UPI byline on page one for her hometown newspaper. Photo spreads of the war she saw in the pages of *Life* were often the work of Catherine Leroy. "I was totally aware of Kate and her work," Bartimus recalled. "I was obsessed with her work and with Cathy Leroy's work. They were the only role models." During her college years, she refined that dream still further. She wanted to write about the war with the purity she had discerned in Elizabeth Pond's *Christian Science Monitor* articles, in which the prose was always so precise and clean. "I hoped that I could bring the same kind of integrity to my work," Bartimus said.

Bartimus imagined herself in Southeast Asia writing about soldiers from America's heartland, Midwesterners fighting the war, "folks who looked like me, grew up like me, thought like me." An encounter with Larry Burrows in 1967, during her sophomore year in college, cemented her ambitions. She told Burrows of her aspirations during his visit to the University of Missouri in 1967 to accept the school's Photographer of the Year award. Fearful that the war would end before she had a chance to cover it, she told Burrows that she planned to quit school. Burrows responded with "a scathing look" and a three-word rebuke: "You will not!" he thundered. She needed to finish her education first, he said, because the last thing anyone needed in Vietnam was another stringer getting killed for twenty-five dollars a day. As he departed, he encouraged Bartimus "to drop me a line once in a while" and promised that when she was sent to Vietnam, "I'll make sure we all try to keep you alive." By the time she reached Vietnam six years later, Burrows was dead, killed in February 1971—along with three other photographers—in the crash of a South Vietnamese army helicopter in Laos.

By then Bartimus had been an AP staffer for nearly two years, and had spent much of that time badgering Wes Gallagher, the AP president, to send her to Vietnam. AP hadn't sent a woman to Vietnam "because there was no safety anywhere," Gallagher wrote in response to one of her occasional blandishments. During still another joust about her desire to become a war correspondent, Gallagher demanded, "If you got killed what would I tell your mother?" To which Bartimus responded, "What did you tell Henri Huet's?"—a reference to the AP photographer who perished in the same helicopter crash that killed Burrows.

In the end, Bartimus was assigned to replace Edie Lederer; she became the second woman AP sent to its Saigon bureau. Her arrival in April 1973, followed by one month the arrival of Graham Martin as ambassador. It also coincided with the beginning of the "decent interval," the period of relative quiet—with a few notable exceptions—that followed the cease-fire of January 1973 and the start of the North Vietnamese offensive that ended with the fall of Saigon. A long, slow-motion goodbye played out in those months. With the departure of American troops, the Five O'Clock Follies were no more. The war was no longer being fought by young men from America's heartland. The corpses of young Asian men were filling the body bags instead.

After Graham Martin replaced Ellsworth Bunker as U.S. ambassador to South Vietnam in April 1973, relations between American news organizations and the embassy staff again sank to the nadir they had occupied in 1962–1963. Critics and admirers alike were certain Bunker had been sent to Vietnam because of a belief that "he was the next best thing to a B-52," according to Frank Snepp, a CIA officer who worked with Martin until the end. The public information policy Martin established was unsparing in the restrictions it imposed on contacts that embassy staffers were permitted to have with the Saigon press corps. Moreover, journalists were virtually denied access to the Defense Attaché's Office, headquarters of the military mission that stayed in Vietnam after the truce. That office's 159 embassy guards and fifty other members of the military were the only uniformed Americans who remained in Vietnam. Coupled with that circumscribed access, Martin's uncritical support of the Thieu government and his relentless optimism about its ability to hold diminished his credibility with the Saigon press corps. He was certain that irresponsible reporting had damaged America's efforts in Vietnam, and he even lectured visitors about that belief.

The team that Ambassador Martin assembled to take over the key positions in the embassy included Marshall Brement, a member of the Foreign Service who became the embassy's public affairs officer. Brement's new bride, Pamela Sanders, had first come to Vietnam as a freelance journalist in 1962, but left in sorrow the following year. A decade later, she accompanied her husband back to Saigon and his new assignment. She had worked at *Time* after leaving Saigon in late 1963, not long after the assassination of President Diem. By 1968, Sanders began working full time on a novel. That work became a self-portrait, one that placed a spotlight on the life she had led in Southeast Asia in 1963. She carried those memories gently; they were like fragile dried flowers sheathed and pressed between the pages of a favorite poetry book. Her new husband was well aware of the bitterness she felt about what America, in the name of democracy, was doing in Southeast Asia. "Marshall and I spent our first year of marriage arguing about Vietnam, re-fighting the war every night at dinner," said Sanders. She sympathized with the members of the Saigon press corps, and he took the side of the government.

"It was very strange," she said, to be back in Vietnam in the persona of an embassy wife. The role reversal it represented from her earlier identity, when she had little more than contempt for everyone in the American diplomatic corps, was always a bit jarring. Back then, everyone who worked in the embassy had represented "the enemy." All they did, in her mind at least, was "lie about the war." Now, her husband was serving the man whose contempt for the press exceeded that of all his predecessors, even that of the one who had occupied the ambassador's office in 1962, when Sanders was part of the Southeast Asia press corps. Frederick Nolting, the genteel Virginian whose scorn for journalists ranked with Martin's, had once grown so annoyed with David Halberstam's questions during an interview that he took Halberstam by the arm, lifted him out of his chair, and escorted him out the door. Martin, in the mold of his predecessor, is said to have longed for the old days, when journalists were "men who believed that their work should of course further their government's policies when those policies were sound—as they damned well were whenever he was in charge." Although Sanders found likeable qualities in Martin and believed he had been saddled by Nixon and Kissinger with a set of no-win options, she thought the way he handled the American press was nothing short of peculiar. "He was unquestionably paranoid about the press," Sanders recalled. "He was adamant about concealing everything, about keeping the press as ignorant as possible. I truly believe that Graham Martin thought every journalist was a Communist—or at least a Communist sympathizer."

Neither Bartimus nor Palmer had much contact with the embassy and its staffers, in part because their assignments seldom required their interaction with the diplomatic community. Then again, as Pham Xuan An had observed years before when he worked with Deepe and Pond, South Vietnamese and American officials alike invariably sought out male reporters representing the major print and broadcast operations. Palmer, in particular, apparently offended many embassy staffers who perhaps attached inordinate significance to a chance exchange she had had with two young Viet Cong soldiers not long after Martin's team began running the embassy. In one of ABC's standing Saturday assignments, Palmer was covering the weekly press conference staged by the Provisional Revolutionary Government at its headquarters at Camp Davis near Tan Son Nhut Airport. Those sessions usually replicated all the tedium and self-serving dimensions once reserved for the now defunct Five O'Clock Follies. So it was little wonder that both Palmer and her colleagues welcomed the diversion offered up when, during a break in the news conference, she was invited to meet with two National Liberation Front soldiers—young women outfitted in uniforms and pith helmets. With smiles all around, one woman placed her helmet on Palmer's head and asked her to extend their greetings to American women, especially those who had supported their revolutionary endeavors. The scene as captured by photographers in attendance soon reached a worldwide audience thanks to UPI, whose photo caption read, "East meets west in Saigon as a Viet Cong woman soldier admired the bra-less look of ABC correspondent." Whether it was the helmet on Palmer's head, her warm smile, or her arm on the shoulder of the woman whose helmet she was wearing, American embassy officials were not amused. Frank Snepp called it Palmer's "stunt with the helmet"; he claimed that it "famously destroyed her relationship with the U.S. establishment in Saigon," whose members interpreted her behavior as a gesture of support for the PRG. No one in the embassy was about to embrace another Jane Fonda.

Bartimus, who arrived shortly before Palmer's moment in the media spotlight, had been promised "complete freedom" to cover stories throughout Vietnam, Cambodia, and Laos with no restrictions because of her gender. In reality, Wes Gallagher was no more predisposed to allow her to cover combat than he had been with Edie Lederer. In fact, he had ordered the Saigon bureau chief to limit her to safe assignments within the confines of the capital. Just as Wood had done in 1972 with UPI, Bartimus quickly set about ignoring that edict, and George Esper, who was bureau chief by then, made no effort to stop her. On a trip to Cambodia shortly after her arrival, when Bartimus and Edie Lederer were sent to mind the store so that AP's Phnom Penh bureau chief could take a day off, rockets aimed at nearby oil tanks missed the mark and began falling around the bureau. When it was all over, the two women wrote the story; a third, Christine Spengler, a freelance photographer from Holland, went off to take pictures. Their work landed on the front page of the *New York Times*. So much for Wes Gallagher and his "no combat" edicts.

Bartimus often felt that Saigon was a vastly more dangerous place than the distant outposts to which she traveled in pursuit of stories. Esper had cautioned her, just as he did with every new arrival, that she would be under scrutiny by the government at every moment. Indeed, the AP office itself probably had government spies and North Vietnamese spies among its staffers. Behavior that offended the government might result in deportation; in the worst-case scenario, the bureau itself might be shut down. For Bartimus, it was quite terrifying. She was equally daunted by the sexist attitudes she perceived in some of her male colleagues. Dead women who had covered the war—Dickey Chapelle for example—were exalted, but the live ones who were still among them were subjects of merciless gossip and criticism, or so it seemed to Bartimus. They mocked Oriana Fallaci and Cathy Leroy, and seemed to hate Liz Trotta, she recalled. "If you went into the field and you were pushy, then you were 'that bitch' and very aggressive. If you took advantage of help from soldiers, then you didn't carry your own weight and you were a burden. If you stayed in Saigon, you were sleeping with the military to get your stories. You really couldn't win."

All those currents inside Saigon made assignments in the countryside all the more inviting, even when they were dangerous. In the most dangerous of those trips, Bartimus traveled along Highway 13, just outside Vientiane, a strip of roadway that at the time was a bombed-out track laced with mines. Once, she boarded a leaky boat for a trip up the Mekong River in search of the CIA-trained Hmong people who were fighting the Communist Pathet

Lao in a remote corner of Laos. Most of her stories, however, were devoid of rocket fire and bomb-pocked roads. She wrote about a leper colony run by Canadian nuns. In Hue, where she had been sent to write about the restoration of the old imperial city, she found a pianist playing a grand piano in the rubble and the aging Queen Mother of Vietnam absorbed in reading her Bible.

Of the many stories Bartimus wrote in Vietnam, the last of her big stories stayed with her; and ever after, its scene of carnage stalked her memory. The time was mid-March 1974; the place was Cai Lay in the Mekong Delta; the story was the death and injury of scores of children. The "how" of it all was never clear. Had the Communists fired the single 82mm artillery shell into the schoolyard, as the Saigon government charged? Or had the explosion been staged to look as if they had done so in a bid to get more American aid, as the Communists claimed? Bartimus never knew for certain. What she did know was that the sight of twenty-three dead children whose bodies had been "shredded" and eighty-six others who had been injured by shrapnel sickened and infuriated her. Days later, after listening to the familiar invective at the weekly, three-hour PRG press conference, she pulled aside a Viet Cong colonel and demanded to know whether the Viet Cong fired that shell: "I'd heard all the goddamn propaganda I wanted to listen to, now I wanted a straight answer from him, a military officer who professed to live by a code of honor," she recalled. Did his troops kill those kids, she asked. The blood was pounding in her temples as she awaited an answer. "No, Ms. Bartimus," he re sponded, addressing her in English for the first time. He gave her his word. It was not the Viet Cong.

The competition between the wire services was such that neither Edie Lederer nor Tad Bartimus struck up a friendship with UPI's Tracy Wood during the time the three spent in Vietnam. Wood finally became acquainted with her arch competitors more than thirty years after the war ended when they collaborated on the book *War Torn,* a collection of stories by nine female journalists who covered various phases of the war. Speaking of their professional rivalry years later, Bartimus said, "Tracy and I competed head-to-head. We did not know each other. You did not acknowledge the presence of anyone else. We did everything we could to thwart each other." Indeed, she confessed during a radio interview in which Wood also participated, that she "stole" Wood's jeep one evening in pursuit of a story when she could find no other means of transportation.

That competitive fervor, however, did not extend to colleagues who reported on the radio. When Bartimus arrived, Laura Palmer ranked as something of a regular in the Saigon press corps. The two women quickly warmed to each other and became Saigon soul-mates, then life-long friends. Bartimus perceived them as "two good middle-class, Midwestern girls who also happened to be independent, strong-willed, feminine, vulnerable, tough, and oddities in an alien place." They found support and solace in each other; they celebrated each other's triumphs and consoled each other in moments of disquiet.

In May 1974, Palmer's efforts to interest a major magazine in her work finally paid off. That month, she savored the thrill of seeing her first byline on the pages of *Rolling Stone*. It appeared among the magazine's commentary pieces and was presented as "A Small Journal." Palmer described the surrealism of life in Saigon and the leaps of rationalization required to maintain a measure of sanity. Even the irony seemed to be drained out of Saigon, for irony demands a measure of logic. That was nowhere to be found in the city Palmer described. Both Saigon and the country beyond it were an unconnected series of contortions, each one having less appeal than the previous one. Survival required detachment. Rationalizations helped, too, but not much. In Saigon, life was reduced to the lowest common denominator. "Living in black and white, without the chiaroscuro." The half-page, pen-and-ink graphic that ran with her story was a variation on the theme of Picasso's *Guernica*—with a dash of Asia. Assorted figures stand against a backdrop of scattered teardrops—a woman in a string bikini, two figures wearing conical hats, a head with a fat, outstretched tongue, a man with the Stars and Stripes tattooed on his chest, snakes, and distorted faces. The graphic perfectly matched the sense of Palmer's story.

Her frequent trips to Cambodia gave her the insights she crafted into another piece for *Rolling Stone*, "Life, and War, Go On in Cambodia." If Saigon was surrealistic, Phnom Penh was positively schizophrenic in Palmer's telling. President Nixon's declaration in November 1971 that "Cambodia is the Nixon Doctrine in its purest form" now rang with connotations of betrayal. The war, like the moon rock in the city's National Museum, was a perverse gift from the United States. In a glass case alongside the chunk of rock lay the Khmer flag that flew to the moon aboard Apollo 17. The letter from President Nixon that accompanied the rock said, "It is given as a symbol of the unity of human endeavor and carries with it the hope of the American people for a world at peace." The war in Cambodia had become a spectator sport, Palmer's story explained. In a readily available chauffeur-driven Mercedes Benz, one could reach the fighting in as little as twenty minutes. Earlier in the year, Khmer Rouge rebels, using a strategy similar to America's bombing of Hanoi, staged a massive attack on Phnom Penh. The aim, Palmer explained, was "terror." It was successful to the degree that it drove the baby buyers out of town.

After two years, Saigon was sapping Palmer's spirit. Her friend Tad Bartimus left in May, debilitated by the collection of symptoms that had alternately been diagnosed as parasites, a tropical disease, a virus, or an illness of unknown origin. In April, her ailments—swollen legs and lymph nodes, fevers, exhaustion, diarrhea, and skin irritation—started to grow more severe. It had become impossible to hide her failing health from her AP colleagues. Reports of her depleted physical condition had so alarmed Wes Gallagher that he called from New York to order that she return home "before you die like Maggie Higgins." Bartimus left, believing that after a diagnosis and brief recovery in the States, she would be back in Saigon in short order.

Palmer occasionally felt depleted, too, but her condition was more emotional than physical. The first hint had come after the interviews she did with those U.S. airmen who were less than keen about the peace agreement and the prospect of going home. That afternoon, Palmer had begun to understand that, in war, death can either come in an instant or crawl slowly over the soul to shroud a life in darkness. One spring afternoon in 1974, her thoughts about leaving began to take shape as she realized that for all its charm and beauty, the environment in which she lived also had a capacity for malevolence and cruelty. An otherwise ordinary walk home underlined that reality with such power that it set in motion her journey back to a world where war was a distant rather than immediate fact of life. Just before she reached her building at 6 Thi Sach, Palmer spied a Vietnamese woman squatting at the curb with a club in one hand and a puppy in the other. After a few swift and well-placed blows, the animal fell limp. "It felt like it was time to leave," Palmer said years later.

In one of her last broadcasts from Saigon, Palmer reported on President Nixon's resignation and its potential impact on South Vietnam's future. President Thieu was losing one of his staunchest allies, Palmer's report explained: "Government officials sense that the era of massive and total American commitment to South Vietnam is declining." In subsequent reports, Palmer noted that the resignation was hardly a surprise in Saigon, where developments in the Watergate scandal and the growing likelihood of impeachment had been widely reported in the local media. Radio Hanoi took the opportunity to condemn Nixon's aggressive and warlike policies, a reflection of the

Communist belief that Nixon was forced out of office because of his failed Asian policies.

For the North Vietnamese, Nixon's banishment removed their continuing fears that he might easily be provoked into reentering the war. In the aftermath of the Paris Peace Accords, Nixon had maintained his "madman" pose in all the government's behind-the-scene contacts as a way of keeping violations of the peace provisions to a minimum. No one wanted Nixon to send in the bombers again. With President Gerald Ford in the Oval Office and President Nixon safely neutralized in San Clemente, the North Vietnamese "began to think that the road to Saigon might be open."

Palmer went to France to join her beau, Philippe Debeusscher, following his assignment in Cambodia. She found work as a freelance radio correspondent with NBC News. For a time, at least, the seasons in Paris engaged her and she was able to put the war aside. March 1975 turned into a busy and profitable month for Palmer. The illness and death of Aristotle Onassis in a Paris hospital at mid-month made news around the world. Rumors that Onassis had been estranged from his wife, Jacqueline, combined with her absence from his bedside, heightened interest in the story. Its widespread use on radio stations around the world meant a fattened paycheck for Palmer. Thus, she had a stash of several hundred dollars when Bich Dao's letter arrived. That "Onassis money," as she called it, paid for her plane ticket back to Saigon.

By the early days of April, when both Laura Palmer and Hilary Brown of ABC News reached South Vietnam, Saigon, in the words of one embassy staffer, was becoming "a Brechtian scene." Lines outside the American embassy, peopled for the most part by thousands of anxious South Vietnamese in search of visas, began stretching for blocks on every street approaching the compound. Day after day, the numbers of people and their sense of desperation climbed. Ambassador Martin's hope in the prospect that holding on to the southern reaches of South Vietnam—from Nha Trang through the rice-rich Mekong Delta—an idea he cited in a television interview with NBC's Garrick Utley, had waned by mid-month. Now Martin and members of the embassy staff talked about the likelihood that the end would come in June or July, even though a CIA analysis indicated that the situation could collapse in three or four weeks. Publicly, Martin kept insisting that with additional U.S. aid, the situation could be stabilized. Even more incredibly, Martin's deputy, Wolfgang Lehmann, told an embassy gathering that "militarily, the North Vietnamese [did] not have the capability to launch an offensive against Saigon." The South Vietnamese, however, knew what the Americans refused to acknowledge. The end was near. Renegade American embassy staffers, unbeknownst to Martin, were secretly evacuating hundreds of Vietnamese who feared that their associations with Americans would place them in grave danger when the Communists took control of the country. The director of the Defense Attaché's Office, whose operation was located at Tan Son Nhut, was getting its people out beyond the oversight of Martin and the embassy.

Palmer returned to Saigon in April 1975 not as the inexperienced, freshly minted liberal arts grad whose major concern was repaying her college loan; this time, she came with a sense of having earned herself a place at journalism's table. She had mastered the profession's demands, was respected by her peers, and was well aware of the potential story that awaited her telling once she had succeeded in helping her friend. She moved into a room at the Continental Palace and in short order resumed her stringing duties for *Time*. The detailed notes she kept of her experiences, reactions, and conversations during those days were useful later when she wrote two articles for *Rolling Stone*. But Bich Dao was her first concern. Palmer was intent on helping her find a way out while there was still time. And that was in short supply. The North Vietnamese and their allies occupied the northern half of South Vietnam and virtually controlled the rest. South Vietnamese and American intelligence officials conceded to at least one reporter in the early days of April that Saigon was likely to fall in just twelve hours if the North Vietnamese decided to attack. Indeed, the defense of South Vietnam was so weak that the North would need only 20,000 troops to capture the capital. The most momentous three weeks in Palmer's life were about to play out.

At Dao's behest, they visited a fortune-teller so that she could ask about her brother, a soldier in the Army of the Republic of Vietnam whose whereabouts were unknown. The fortune-teller assured Dao that her brother was safe and was making his way back to Saigon. When their conversation turned to the future of Vietnam, the fortune-teller grew somber. Her words gave voice to the dread with which so many Saigonaise anticipated a Communist takeover. If that happened, the fortune-teller vowed, she and her husband would poison their five children and themselves. Palmer wanted to know whether that was because her clairvoyant powers gave her knowledge of events to come. The fortune-teller shrugged and said, "There are some events that overwhelm destiny." Palmer had never heard a more apt explanation of the Vietnam War.

The next time Palmer and her friend met some days later, Bich Dao arrived unannounced in the *Time* offices. Palmer was scrambling to finish the daily report that each person in the bureau filed on whichever event he or she had covered that day. Dao arrived at night, late. The bureau was on deadline. Palmer was scrambling to finish her file and was wound tight. So was Dao, she quickly intuited. Standing in front of Palmer's desk, Dao explained that her family had it on good authority that the negotiated settlement on which so many hopes relied was no longer a possibility. The Communists planned to sweep into Saigon. Her words were halting and choked. Would Palmer stay in touch with her family in her absence, Dao wanted to know. That's when the realization hit Palmer. Her friend was contemplating suicide. And, as a medical student, how easy that would be for her. "Dao, listen to me," Palmer implored. "Promise me it won't be tonight. Promise me you will meet me here tomorrow. . . . Okay?" Fearing that her friend remained resolute, Palmer turned to threats. "If you don't," she said, "I will never see your family, I will never see them, never, ever help them. Promise me you will come tomorrow." Dao promised. But when Palmer reached her office the next day, a note from her friend explained that "something comes up suddenly I left." As it turned out, Dao's sister in Washington, D.C., was married to an American who was able to pull the appropriate strings and get the family out on an unofficial evacuation flight—one that Graham Martin was not supposed to know about.

One of Hilary Brown's first reports from Saigon for ABC News early in April brought to life the anxieties that Dao and other South Vietnamese had about the prospect of a Communist bloodbath. Her story profiled a young translator who feared that his work for the Americans marked him for imprisonment or death when the North Vietnamese overran Saigon—an outcome that now seemed certain. Like so many other Vietnamese, he was trying to find a way out for himself and his young family. Brown was impressed that he had the courage to allow her to use his name. Another of her reports from Saigon, aired April 9, was a narration of video footage taken by East German television showing refugees who had fled Hue for Da Nang during the assault on the city several weeks earlier. The images of smiling people and soldiers holding babies were meant to demonstrate that life in the so-called liberated areas of South Vietnam had returned to normal. The refugees, Brown explained, were returning to their homes. Shops and factories also appeared to be open, signs from the old regime were being painted over, and leaflets explaining the revolution were being distributed to people in the street, according to Brown. She noted that many people remembered how, during the Tet Offensive in 1968, the Communists had also taken over the city. The Americans, however, ultimately drove out the Communists. "This time," she concluded, "they appear to be here to stay."

Full-blown panic was taking hold of the Saigon's 2.5 million residents by the time Brown's next report aired on April 24. In it, she revealed that American officials had, for the first time, acknowledged that a large-scale airlift evacuation of Vietnamese was underway. Video images showed hundreds, if not thousands, of people camped out at Tan Son Nhut Airport, all of them obviously hoping that the Americans would help them get aboard one of the military flights out. To underscore the desperation many of them felt, Brown told the story of a Vietnamese woman who asked an American acquaintance, a fifty-year-old man, to adopt her daughter as a way of assuring that the youngster would escape harm. With the number of exits from the country diminishing swiftly and the number of rumors predicting mayhem by the Communists spiking ever higher, those without the appropriate connections or cash to get a seat aboard one of the flights out were said to be buying large quantities of sleeping pills, thus giving themselves the wherewithal to commit suicide should their worst fears be realized. Two days later, on April 25, President Thieu left the country and the durable General Duong Van Minh, who had led the country following the overthrow of President Diem in 1963, was sworn in as chief of state. His tenure was to last five days.

During that same week, Hunter Thompson showed up in Saigon, to Palmer's initial dismay. Competitive impulses were part of the package that came with the journalism skills she had so carefully honed. His arrival sent an electric charge through the male-dominated press corps whose members, in Palmer's telling, ranked Thompson as "their alter ego, the person many fantasized they would be if they didn't have wives, children, and mortgages." Palmer's fears that Thompson might usurp the story were misplaced, however. Rather than undermine her prospects for bylines in *Rolling Stone,* Thompson invited her to join his team. A partnership with Thompson, however, proved a dubious and short-lived honor. For as much as members of the (male) press corps might have envied his irreverence, hanging around with him was just too dangerous. Ron Yates, a *Chicago Tribune* reporter who met Thompson on the day he arrived in Saigon, recalled that the Gonzo man had joined him on a foray outside Saigon. Yates, however, feared for Thompson's safety, a fear shared by a few other colleagues whom Thompson accompanied on jaunts outside Saigon. "All of us were terrified that we might be the one who took Hunter Thompson out and got him killed." They were thankful that Thompson seemed content to stay in Saigon, where the familiar mix of alcohol, drugs, and women occupied his time.

As it turned out, Palmer was made of sterner stuff than Thompson who, after what amounted to a brief walk-on role, hastily retreated to the safety of Hong Kong. "Frankly, he was scared to death in Saigon," recalled *Time* bureau chief Roy Rowan. "Here he was, this big macho man who left town. . . . He covered the end of the war from Hong Kong."

For much of April, most of the women who had reported on the war in earlier years watched from a distance, many of them in sorrow, some in anger, most in disbelief, and a few with regrets that they, too, were not there. So many of them had found their first professional success, had experienced the most exhilarating time of their lives in Saigon and had left a little of themselves there. Both in America and abroad, the likes of Frances FitzGerald, Elizabeth Pond, Pamela Sanders, Liz Trotta, Tad Bartimus, and Beverly Deepe observed, commented on, or played a bit part in the drama. It is likely they would have agreed with Gloria Emerson's reflection that those last days "nearly stopped the heart."

Frances FitzGerald, whose vision was always fixed on history, saw precise links with the past in the events overtaking Vietnam. The collapse of American authority was a reminder of the collapse of French authority in the aftermath of Dien Bien Phu a quarter century before, as she explained in an essay in the *New Republic*. The increasing obstinacy and isolation of President Thieu in 1975 replicated the posture of President Diem in the months preceding his assassination in 1963. Ambassador Martin seemed to be clinging to Thieu in precisely the way Ambassador Nolting had clung to President Diem. What was falling in South Vietnam in the spring of 1975, she wrote, was not so much individual cities such as Da Nang or Hue but rather "the world of illusions" that a succession of five American presidents had created.

FitzGerald was far from the reach of news reports on the day the last Americans left Saigon. She was vacationing on a Caribbean island that week, the same week, coincidentally, that the *New Yorker* was running her article about the trip she had taken to Hanoi in the fall of 1974. "I longed to be in Saigon, but knew I couldn't get there quickly enough—even if the *New Yorker* had agreed to send me," she said more than thirty years later. Without television, and with access only to the occasional newspaper, a full understanding of the situation eluded her. FitzGerald cannot recollect her precise reaction to the events. It was neither joy nor despair, she said, "but something more complicated." Whatever relief the war's end brought her was dwarfed by apprehension. Her dread, of course, was justified, given the fate that befell so many South Vietnamese, especially those considered tainted by their associations with Americans. "If only the U.S. had agreed to a coalition government in the South while it still had some influence there we might have mitigated this terrible denouement."

Elizabeth Pond was deeply absorbed in her work as the *Christian Science Monitor* correspondent in Moscow during that last week in April. Vietnam was far away, and not only in the geographic sense. Pond's experiences in Central Europe had a much more lasting impact on her life. Czechoslovakia's short-lived flirtation with democracy in 1968 came to have the same powerful hold on her intellectual interests that Vietnam had on many of the other women who reported on it. That flirtation—a period known as the Prague Spring—during which the country attempted a process of reform that threatened to break the Soviet Union's hold on its satellite states in Eastern Europe, ultimately brought about the same reaction that Hungary had endured in 1956 when its people attempted to loosen the Soviet hold on their nation. For Pond, the absence of easy access to news reports from Vietnam further removed the story from her reality.

Pamela Sanders, whose husband had been transferred to Moscow after his Saigon assignment, was monitoring the developments in Vietnam on the United States Information Service wireless radio and in copies of the *New York Times* received at the American embassy. As the Communist offensive washed over the country, Sanders felt a yearning to return. Unlike Palmer, however, she could not act. The wife of a high-profile member of America's diplomatic community could hardly go flitting off to a country where Americans and their allies were in the midst of an evacuation. By the last days of April, Sanders and Marshall Brement were in Warsaw. The luncheon companion scheduled to meet them at the Writer's Club arrived late, delayed, he explained, by the latest news from Saigon. The country had fallen, he told them. "I burst into tears," Sanders recalled. She mourned for all the helpless people who had been caught in a geopolitical drama in which they had no influence. "Vietnam and Cambodia and Laos were victimized and manipulated in a way that was truly, truly terrible," she said. "The ghastliness of the war was matched only by awful horror at the end."

Liz Trotta, who was just returning to New York from her assignment in London with CBS, felt disconnected from the scenes she watched on her television screen. "I guess I had washed Vietnam out of my system," she recalled. "Or so I thought." Although the war had not remained a big part of her life in the way it had for others, a sense of guilt started to creep into her consciousness as the message those television images presented grew increasingly dire. "I started to feel guilty about not being there. Every story has an end and this was the end."

Tad Bartimus, who was then Anchorage, Alaska, bureau chief for the AP, became heavily involved in the effort to bring Vietnamese orphans to America. She helped members of the Anchorage Junior Chamber of Commerce organize and raise funds for one of the airlifts from Saigon. Her efforts violated all the AP rules about its employee participation in news events. The major concern underlying all her efforts was Trung, an eleven-year-old orphan boy whose guardian angel she had become in Saigon. When her deteriorating health forced her to leave the country in May 1974, Bartimus never said goodbye to Trung even though she had promised him that she would never leave without doing so. She had told herself she'd be back in short order, so really there was no need. It was, she acknowledged, an act of cowardice; and with that memory still alive as Vietnam fell, Bartimus was determined to help him escape. She wanted to see him to safety, even if that meant adopting him herself. Trung, whose lot in life had endowed him with street smarts that far exceeded his years, turned to Bartimus's colleagues in the AP bureau, George Esper, chief among them. With his intercession, Trung was placed aboard one of the orphan flights and made it to Los Angeles, where, through a series of missteps, he arrived alone. He had Bartimus's telephone number in his pocket. He also had the number of a Hollywood director who had once filmed a documentary about the war's orphans in Saigon. And David Seltzer's number was a local call. Seltzer adopted Trung.

Beverly Deepe, who was then living in Washington, D.C., found herself with five house guests soon after the fall of Saigon. With the help of *Time* magazine, Pham Xuan An had sent his wife, Thu Nhan, and four children out of the country, a move he made in part to allay suspicion about his double life. An's family had left Saigon on April 23, but he stayed behind, telling anyone who asked that he could not leave his aging mother. His family spent a week in Guam, then continued on to California for processing when it became clear that An would not be following. *Time* underwrote their relocation and agreed to sponsor the family. Initially, they stayed in a Los Angeles motel with other members of the magazine's Vietnamese staff, then requested that *Time* allow them to go to Virginia, where Deepe and her husband, Charles Keever, who lived in Arlington, took them in. The children, then twelve, eleven, ten, and eight, soon enrolled in Patrick Henry Elementary School. Thu Nhan and the children stayed with Deepe for three months.

Even with An's family gone and the downward spiral quickening, Palmer never contemplated the possibility that the Saigon government might collapse and leave her and all the other Americans to flee the city. That An had allowed *Time* magazine to evacuate his family seemed like a prudent move in Palmer's judgment. They could always come back when the situation had stabilized, as surely it would, or so she thought. She had assured her mother in a letter written just before she left Paris that as long as the American embassy continued to function, her safety in Saigon was assured. Moreover, Palmer was certain that an accord would be reached at the eleventh hour. Ambassador Graham Martin, after all, kept holding out the possibility of a negotiated settlement, an accommodation that would result in a three-way power-sharing agreement and provide for a continued U.S. diplomatic presence. People around the embassy were talking about a cease-fire and the creation of a coalition government. Besides, hadn't Saigon been defying doomsday predictions for decades? Twenty-one years before, in 1954, Peggy Durdin had written that Saigon, with its corrupt and dissolute ways, was a "tragic city, hovering on the edge of disaster." She conjectured that the Communists were surely "eyeing [the city] with self-confident anticipation." In 1975, they were eyeing the city once again, and this time their self-confidence was well placed. Nowhere was that more obvious than during the press conference held on April 27 for a group of correspondents and television crews at Camp Davis, the PRG and North Vietnamese compound at Tan Son Nhut. Noting the departure of President Thieu the day before, a move that elevated Vice President Tran Van Huong to the presidency, Hilary Brown asked about the prospects for a negotiated settlement and whether President Huong would be acceptable as a member of a coalition government. Pham Van Ba told Brown that "Messieurs Huong et Thieu sont bonnet bleu et bonnet blanc [Tweedledum and Tweedledee]." Other journalists pressed Ba for assurances about the outlook for their personal safety if they stayed behind once the Communists took over. "Anyone who earns an honest living will be welcome," he said. Although the end was fast approaching, Palmer, like so many others in the city, continued to think there was time.

Hilary Brown's April 28 broadcast on ABC News underscored the reality that the unraveling was irreversible. Hoping to reach the Bien Hoa airbase, she and her crew traveled north on Highway 1, which had been under enemy attack for several days. Their encounter with what she called "a tidal wave of refugees," tens of thousands of people heading south stretched over a dozen miles, brought their car to a standstill. "They moved mostly on foot, strangely silent, at a jog-trot pace—men, women, children old people, wheeling their few possessions on handcarts, raising clouds of dust as they headed toward the supposed safety of the city," Brown recalled a decade later. As Brown and her crew retreated toward the city, they were beset by a strike force of North Vietnamese and Viet Cong soldiers who had set up a machine-gun nest in the middle of the arching New Port Bridge that spanned the Saigon River. She did her stand-upper in a crouch and grimaced each time a shell exploded nearby as she explained that the battle for Saigon had begun. With fifteen divisions closing in on the city, "this is the closest the Communist offensive has come to Saigon since the Tet Offensive," she explained. The sound of gunfire all around her, she added, "is proof, if any proof is needed, that the Communist forces are finally closing in on the capital." Communist commandos with grenades and AK-47 rifles were dug in beneath the bridge and on its strut-work; above it a South Vietnamese helicopter sprayed the enemy emplacements with machine gun and rocket fire as it swooped and wheeled to avoid the gunfire from below. A small corps of newsmen and women, Brown explained, "were foolish enough to get themselves caught in the crossfire." Malcolm Browne, who had first met Hilary Brown in 1971 when both were assigned to cover the war between Pakistan and India, was part of the group at the bridge. Her cool-headed performance impressed him, recalled Browne, who was by then a reporter for the *New York Times*. "She was under direct fire," he said. "She was on the bridge as the fire came in and she continued on with her stand-upper which I found quite impressive."

Improbably, that night in the Caravelle bar, conversations among press corps suggested that a cease-fire and the creation of a coalition government were still viable prospects. When Thieu's successor, Vice President Tran Van Huong, resigned and the redoubtable General Duong Van Minh became president on April 28, hopes for a settlement kindled—at least in the minds of these Americans. Brown, having seen the fighting so close to the city, was skeptical. The end came the following morning. There would be no coalition government and no continued American presence. This time, the North Vietnamese army and its allies in the South would not be repulsed as they had been during the Tet Offensive, the only other occasion when the war had really come to Saigon in a significant way. This time, the enemy came to stay.

Laura Palmer awakened to the sounds of explosions on the morning of April 29. It was 4:00 A.M. Although they seemed closer and louder than they had on previous nights, she reckoned, in her semiconscious state, that the attack was still five miles away from her room at the Continental Palace. The makeshift barricade she had erected on the room's second twin bed had seemed like a good idea the night before. But with the rocket fire still so distant, the two vinyl-covered armchairs perched atop the mattress now seemed devoid of purpose. No shrapnel and shards of flying glass would endanger her—for the time being. Even then, in the early morning darkness, Palmer was still unaware that by evening she would be gone from the country that had seduced her and from the place that "had always blown like an unexpected wind in my life, pushing me into deeper waters."

Out at Tan Son Nhut, at the same early hour when Palmer had stirred, the rocket fire began just as a C-130 transport plane had almost finished loading its cargo of more than 150 evacuees. Somehow, inside this thunderstorm of rockets and mortars, U.S. Air Force Captain Arthur Mallano managed to take off. A fuel truck exploded; rockets blew the wing off a C-130 ready to load the next evacuees, and the control tower was destroyed. The attack that left the runways of Tan Son Nhut damaged and strewn with debris also destroyed the fixed-wing evacuation plan to run sixty C-130 sorties out of the airport that day—planes that were to carry thousands people out of the country. At the embassy in downtown Saigon, however, Ambassador Martin doubted that the runways were unusable, and he balked at implementing the alternative plan, a total helicopter evacuation. He refused to give the order until he had traveled out to Tan Son Nhut to see the damage for himself. Only then did he signal the okay to carry out Option Four.

At the Continental, the knock on Palmer's door came at 6:00 A.M. "We're all getting out of here," her NBC colleague Dennis Troute said. "Pack your things. The airport is burning." Time had run out. Now she was entering a world without gravity. Packing was a strange ordeal. As she prepared to run for her life, she was forced to confront all that was expendable. "Parts of a part of you that suddenly clashes and glares," as she described it later. Out in the hall, a few reporters told her that a few hours remained. That left time for breakfast and good-byes. She walked across the square to the Caravelle Hotel and went to its famous rooftop to watch the war for one last time. From here she could see death in the distance over croissants and coffee. The journalists talked about Graham Martin's early-morning trip to the airport and wondered whether they had been "left in the hands of a madman."

Facing the friends she would leave behind was excruciating. There was danger in even a single tear, for it might let loose the floodgates of her emotions. The first was the maimed, mute young beggar whose shoes slapped the pavement as he shuffled on his way, and hence commonly known among Westerners as Slappy. He was a dear, a sweet soul who perhaps had no way of grasping the depths of fear in the hearts of those around him. He had often walked alongside Palmer in Saigon, shooing away any beggars who might confront her. Palmer held herself in check when she saw him, for an even more difficult encounter awaited her. Saying good-bye to Pham Xuan An was the saddest moment of her final hours in Saigon. She cherished An's friendship. He had always believed in her and in her potential. Not that he had ever put that thought into words. There was no need to do so; she knew it in her bones. An's wisdom, his serenity and incandescent spirit had engaged her. She admired his Confucian aplomb and understood his wish to remain behind and witness the outcome: "Perhaps he knew he would never be happy again if he left." An's authenticity was, for Palmer, his most endearing quality. Later, when she discovered his double life and considered how paradoxical it was that a spy could have such authenticity, she decided: "That was the magic of An."

Because she had no inkling on that day of An's work for the North Vietnamese, she feared for his safety. She wondered what would happen to him when the North Vietnamese arrived. Surely his long associations with Americans would create difficulties. He would certainly be questioned, maybe even imprisoned, or worse. The fact that his wife and children were in America complicated his situation still further, or so Palmer thought. So great was her fear for his future that she gave An a pseudonym in her story about those last hours in Saigon. Palmer said that she "never felt betrayed" when she later learned of his work as a spy. "It made him more interesting to me. It was consistent with his intellect and with his heart . . . his overriding goal was to have Vietnam returned to the Vietnamese." Years later, An told her how he had wanted to console her that day, to assure her that he had nothing to fear, that the anticipated bloodbath was unlikely. He also wanted to tell her that she would be safe in Saigon, that she could stay behind because he could guarantee her safety. But her youth and its promise stopped him. "I wanted you to go on in life and have a family." So he held back. The rest of the day played out in seconds of fear and hours of sadness. By late morning, both Palmer and Brown had assembled designated pick-up points where they boarded evacuation buses for what would quickly become the most hair-raising rides of their lives. Mobs of Vietnamese crowded around each bus, but only Westerners were allowed to board—a nervous but well-armed, young Marine who stood at the door made sure of that. In all the chaos, the young translator whom

Brown had profiled days before found her and implored her to take him and his family aboard. Brown thought it was "madness." She had already seen the U.S. Marines kicking hysterical Vietnamese away from the embassy wall. "I wasn't sure I could get him away," Brown recalled. "I thought he'd be better off in Saigon than on some aircraft carrier in the South China Sea. I told him I couldn't do it. I shall never forget the look of supplication in his eyes and in the eyes of his wife and children."

Brown's ride began with what seemed to be an aimless tour of the city. Inexplicably, the first stop was the port, "where two decrepit barges were tied up." Having already seen the fate of dozens of refugees who died as they tried to leave Da Nang on overcrowded river boats two weeks earlier, the Westerners aboard the bus were adamant. They were not leaving.

The bus meandered through the streets, all congested with desperate Vietnamese. Some clawed at the mesh-covered window, others managed to reach in and tried to grab watches and jewelry. The panicky driver put the bus in reverse and backed over something, or maybe someone. "It's a child," someone yelled, "he's run over a child." Finally, they reached the American embassy, where the scene was even more frenzied than it had been in the streets. The compound was surrounded by thousands of Vietnamese. Only the Marines who guarded the gates and the barbed wire atop the high walls kept them out. Brown and the others had to fight their way though the crowd to the gate, where just two Marines "were hauling up the round eyes." Westerners got in, everyone else was kicked away. With a boost from her cameraman, Brown scaled its height. A Marine on the other side grabbed her arm and hauled her over.

The first thing Brown saw when she landed inside the embassy compound was a staffer throwing American currency into an improvised incinerator. Brown was incredulous and asked the woman what she was doing. "Whadya want us to do," she barked, "leave it to the goddam Commies?" Brown spent several hours inside the compound, watching what she later called "a terrible, terrible scene. I remember thinking America's final hour in Vietnam is not its finest." By late afternoon, Brown had boarded one of the huge transport helicopters that flew 630 sorties and evacuated more that 7,000 people from Vietnam that day.

Palmer, meanwhile, boarded a huge black bus, its grimy windows meshed with heavy chicken wire and took a seat near Robert Shaplen. Malcolm Browne was on board, too. It was not clear why he was wearing a World War II–era German helmet. "Okay ladies and gentlemen. I just want you to know that I've never driven one of these things," the driver announced as he threaded through downtown Saigon. "Last night they gave me an M-16; this morning they gave me a bus." This driver, too, seemed to be lost. At least that is what Robert Wiener of NBC Radio thought. He recalled how, as the bus inched its way through the crowds, desperate Vietnamese civilians offered up their children to its passengers. If these Saigonaise could not reach safety themselves, they apparently hoped that some soft hearted American might impulsively reach out and take a child to a more secure life somewhere beyond this dark and uncertain place. The danger that the Vietnamese might turn on the fleeing Americans was a distinct possibility. Many Americans were surprised they did not do so. Beyond Wiener's uneasiness about attacks by civilians being left behind in downtown Saigon, he worried too about whether the armed South Vietnamese soldiers guarding the gates at Tan Son Nhut would allow the bus to pass. They did get through, but still another surprise awaited them.

Moments before they passed through the gate, two rockets had crashed near the Defense Attaché's Office "so everybody ran like crazy to get into the building," Wiener remembered. Inside, Palmer and Shaplen and Browne and Wiener joined several thousand people awaiting evacuation. They were lined up along the walls in an endless succession of corridors. About nine hundred Marines—a battalion and a half—carried out the operation with an efficiency that impressed Palmer. The first order was a call for the evacuees to divest themselves of weapons, ammunition, explosives, and knives. As she watched a box fill up and considered the hundreds and hundreds of others around her who wanted out, she realized, recalling the panic in Da Nang a few weeks before, that "there is a little Da Nang inside us all." She came face to face with her own baser instincts: She knew that "if panic broke out the fittest and strongest would survive." And she intended to be among the survivors. Yes, if she had to, she, too, would push and shove, kick and stomp. Palmer, the woman who had opposed the war because she abhorred violence, confronted the uncomfortable truth about the power of fear and its capacity to twist the soul.

As the line moved slowly through the windowless, fluorescent-lit corridors, the din overhead sounded as if it were raining helicopters outside. The evacuees were clumped into groups of fifty, "tagged" for shipment, and herded into holding areas. At the final corner, a hulking Marine moved along the line. No luggage. Just people. Drop the bags. Leave them here. Finally, it was time for Palmer and her colleagues to make their dash to the chopper. A Marine was shouting, "You fifteen people on that chopper. Run. Now. Go. Run." They dashed across the tarmac toward a Sea Stallion. The tailgate was already up, but someone grabbed her and pulled her aboard. She found a seat next to Bob Shaplen. She clutched his hand and a hush surrounded them as the chopper left the ground. Together, they spanned three decades of the American experience in Vietnam. If Shaplen, who began writing about Vietnam in 1946—before Palmer was born—was the beginning, then Palmer—among the youngest journalists in Saigon—was the end. Together, the oldest and the youngest. The helicopter climbed to 1,500 feet, above the many landmarks so familiar to both of them, and headed toward the refuge of the South China Sea. Palmer and Shaplen glanced at each other with tear-filled eyes, but just for an instant. The moment was too powerful to sustain that gaze. For Palmer, there was something hallowed and prayerful about this metal compartment with fifty-some human beings who had become "a mosaic of faces, confusion, and fears." They were all being lifted heavenward, to safety. Palmer felt that she was in a cathedral. Other than the screaming Vietnamese babies whose mothers tried in vain to comfort them, silence prevailed. Palmer understood that she was bearing witness to something monumental and sacred. "It was sacred because it was beyond words; you stand in the mystery, you stand with humility, and you stand with awe." Laura Palmer knew she was living a moment in history.

Epilogue

Los Angeles Times book critic Richard Eder once asked, "Will the Vietnam conflict be the first war recorded better by women than by men?" That question, posed in his 1986 review of *Shallow Graves, Two Women and Vietnam,* was grounded in the notion that the story of war and the story of men at war are distinctly different. Women, he suggested, were at least as good as men in telling the story of the latter. Although Eder saluted the brilliance of *Dispatches* by Michael Herr and *Going After Cacciato* by Tim O'Brien, both Vietnam War classics, he theorized that telling the story of war required making "wider connections." *Shallow Graves,* by Wendy Wilder Larsen and Tran Thi Nga, Eder said, along with *Fire in the Lake* by Frances FitzGerald, *Winners and Losers* by Gloria Emerson, and Bobbie Ann Mason's 1972 novel, *In Country,* all captured those wider connections "in words and images that we have not seen and that make it understandable in a way we have not known."

Eder's respect for the achievements of these writers is a summons to consider the richness women brought to America's perceptions of the war in all its dimensions. The idea that the Vietnam War might have been "recorded better by women than by men" is unlikely to withstand scrutiny. However, women, by exploiting the singular circumstances presented by the conflict in Southeast Asia, established themselves as equals to their male peers. In doing so, they staked out a lasting place for their gender on the landscape of war. Evidence of that success, though tentative at first, began emerging in subsequent conflicts in Israel, Central America, India, Pakistan, Afghanistan, the Balkans, and Lebanon. Today, five years into the Iraq War, women journalists have been so integrated into its coverage that they appear to be accepted with little more than a shrug. Although something of a male ethos still hangs over war correspondence, women no longer have to "fight like hell" for the assignment.

In many ways it is difficult to remember the media landscape when, even just a decade ago, this subject seemed to have a measure of considerably more urgency than it does in today's climate of greater gender neutrality. That so many women have been assigned to the Iraq War, and that so little note appears to be taken of their presence, suggests that gender is overshadowed by other considerations in making combat assignments. Much of the credit for that shift belongs to the dozens of women whose curiosity and courage led them to take on the challenge of reporting on the Vietnam War. Together, they succeeded in changing the nature of journalism. The futures they pursued after the war were as diverse as the assignments they chased during the war.

With the exception of Dickey Chapelle, who was a casualty of the war, among the fifteen women whose stories are told in varying detail on the preceding pages, six have died since the fall of Saigon. Three died of cancer; Flora Lewis at age eighty-nine in 2002; Catherine Leroy at sixty in 2005; and Kate Webb at sixty-three in 2007. Two others committed suicide: Martha Gellhorn in 1998 and Gloria Emerson in 2004. Ethel Payne died in her sleep of an apparent heart attack at seventy-nine in 1991. In the aftermath of Vietnam, they all continued to write and photograph, some as daily journalists, others as magazine contributors. A few women turned to teaching, either as a full-time endeavor or as a sideline to writing. Ten women wrote books on an array of subjects, a total of twenty-eight between them. In addition to studies of both Vietnam and later conflicts, subjects of those volumes range from explorations of international policy questions, American defense, education, health and social issues, religion, and media, to novels, novellas, and two collections of war photography.

Vietnam remained a powerful force that shaped their lives in an assortment of ways. Two women, Catherine Leroy and Jurate Kazickas, left Vietnam with shrapnel embedded in their flesh, fragments that became, over the years, ever-present reminders of the war. Equally permanent was the psychic shrapnel that others carried in their heads and hearts. Although none of them appears to share Gloria Emerson's long-held conviction that she would never recover from the experience, for most the war helped to define the futures that awaited these women after April 1975. Some continued to make war their professional specialty. For others, Vietnam was their first and last war. Catherine Leroy, for example, spent nearly a decade covering subsequent wars in Africa, Asia, and the Middle East. And so did Liz Trotta—the Yom Kippur War, the India-Pakistan War, the "troubles" in Northern Ireland, and what little there was to cover of the invasion of Grenada. Flora Lewis and Elizabeth Pond, in contrast, built reputations as foreign policy analysts whose insights into the nuances of global issues won them respect in international diplomatic circles. Frances FitzGerald initially turned her attention to an analysis of the teaching of history in American public schools. At least one, Tad Bartimus, has battled an assortment of health problems, doubtless related to the year she spent in Vietnam. Laura Palmer, after working for many years as an author and a producer for *Nightline*, took the first step toward a career in ministry in 2006, when she began pursuing a master's degree in theology at Union Theological Seminary.

Most of the women have returned to Vietnam for occasional visits, trips that began in the 1980s and 1990s when visa restrictions on American visitors eased considerably. Three women, Gloria Emerson, Martha Gellhorn, and Elizabeth Pond, never made that journey. One or two return with some regularity, usually to mark the anniversary of the fall of Saigon. For others, the memories are still too tender to permit the revelries that invariably accompany those anniversary observances. They have returned alone.

Until the 2002 publication of *War Torn*, a collection of autobiographical essays by nine women correspondents who covered the war, only two female correspondents had recounted their Vietnam experiences, one in a memoir, the other in a novel. Liz Trotta made her role as the first woman assigned to cover battlefield operations for a television network the centerpiece of her 1991 memoir, *Fighting for Air*. Pamela Sanders did likewise in her autobiographical novel, *Miranda*, published in 1978. Emerson incorporated recollections of her own Vietnam experiences in *Winners & Losers*, but veterans of the war were her principal focus.

Emerson's fury over the war framed the rest of her life. Her demand for retribution from those she considered responsible for the debacle remained forever undiminished. A decade after the fall of Saigon, she vented her rage on the pages of *Newsweek:* "Take all of them, all of them who gave us the war—all of them who, like [Robert S.] McNamara, began to doubt that the war could be won and still kept it going," she demanded. "Chain them to the memorial for several days, if need be, and have them read each name aloud. Wouldn't that be something? Justice at last." She had left the *New York Times* by then, driven away, in part, by her unwillingness to accommodate journalism's demand for neutrality. Detachment was anathema to Emerson. Ever emotional and sometimes irascible, she spent the next three decades crying out against injustice and defending the downtrodden.

In her early post-Vietnam years, her work fused teaching, first at Harvard and later at Princeton, with writing. She authored four books between 1978 and 2002, each of which touched on war in an assortment of ways. Her first, *Winners & Losers,* which won a National Book Award, explored the afterburn of Vietnam on the lives of those who fought there. It remains one of the classics of Vietnam-era journalism. Like Frankie FitzGerald's *Fire in the Lake,* it is regularly listed among the "must-read" books about the war. Reviewers of her second book, *Some Men,* tempered the enthusiasm that greeted her earlier work. Some said they were unable to divine what Emerson was trying to say about the changing definition of masculinity during a time when the women's movement had brought about new expectations and social norms. In *Gaza: A Year in the Intifada,* Emerson portrayed Palestinians not as violent radicals but rather as a sympathetic people whose yearnings and dreams of a homeland were no less valid that those of the Israelis. Her conclusions, based on having spent the year 1989 living in the Gaza Strip, were criticized as a one-sided, anti-Israeli account of the occupation. From the time of its publication in 1991 right up until her death, Emerson challenged critics of the book, arguing that it was her effort to provide an understanding of the region's many complexities. Her novel, *Loving Graham Greene,* is a morality play driven by the same ethos that shaped *The Quiet American,* that literary classic written by her idol, Graham Greene. Emerson's Molly Benson, a well-intentioned idealist whose efforts to heal suffering and right injustice complicate rather than clarify the cause she hopes to serve, might have been a distant fictional cousin to Graham Greene's Alden Pyle.

Beverly Deepe straddled the worlds of teaching and news writing after she returned from Vietnam. Both before and after she worked for Capitol Hill News Service, a Ralph Nader–inspired news distribution service designed to provide small media outlets with skilled coverage of Washington, D.C., Deepe pursued an academic career. Drawing largely on her Vietnam experience, Deepe began teaching at Northwestern University's Medill Graduate School of Journalism and continued at the University of Maryland in its Far East Division in Okinawa. She joined the University of Hawaii faculty in 1980, where she is still a professor. She co-authored a study, published in 1997, that examined the way mainstream media covered the nation's minorities of African, Asian, Hispanic, and Native American descent between 1934 and 1996. In 2002, she was prominently featured in the

Newseum's exhibit about war correspondence. More recently, her 2004 book, *News Zero: New York Times and the Bomb,* took on the *New York Times* in the same way she had taken on Ambassador Maxwell Taylor decades before in Vietnam. The self-proclaimed "newspaper of record," she charged, allowed itself to become a lapdog for the thermonuclear industry by ignoring questions about the dangers of radiation exposure. In its coverage, first of the bomb's use on Hiroshima and Nagasaki and later on the scores of nuclear weapons tests carried out on islands in the South Pacific, the *Times,* she charged, acquiesced in the government's near-obsessive secrecy. Instead of investigating the clear evidence of radiation sickness, it instead served up rhapsodies to the promise of nuclear power that suggested these weapons of mass destruction offered a potential boon for mankind. Deepe's book was published just a few months after the newspaper belatedly acknowledged its complicity in misleading the American public about the existence of a later generation of WMDs in Iraq.

In the years after the fall of Saigon, Frances FitzGerald became what David Halberstam once characterized as "a cultural anthropologist working as a journalist." She continued to write on an array of international issues and personalities: the Iran Contra scandal, Fidel Castro, and Nancy Drew in the 1980s; the evangelical movement, and George H. W. Bush's presidency in the 1990s; and evangelical Christians, Wesley Clark, and the George W. Bush presidency in the early years of the new millennium. Her stories appeared in nearly a dozen magazines that ranged from *Redbook* to *Foreign Policy; Architectural Digest* to the *New York Review of Books;* and *Vogue* to *Rolling Stone, Esquire,* the *Nation, Harper's,* and the *New Yorker.* A study of textbooks used in the teaching of American history in public schools engaged her in the late 1970s. She explored how marketing forces and political pressures combined with demands for multiethnic representations left America's history texts rife with generalities, short on the necessary ingredients for critical thinking, and relentlessly dull. *America Revised,* published in 1979, argued that the inadequacies of textbooks and the teaching of history in public schools nurtured one of the country's most critical shortcomings, an unsatisfactory understanding of the past. Her 1986 book, *Way Out There in the Blue,* was an investigation of the origins of President Ronald Reagan's Strategic Defense Initiative (SDI). In tying SDI to the larger social and cultural history of the late twentieth century, FitzGerald explained how the idea of isolating America from outside perils had a unique appeal in the Reagan notions of America's place in the world. That the "Star Wars" shield was a pie-in-the-sky concept mattered little. It perfectly fit all the cinematic qualities that characterized Reagan's personality, according to FitzGerald.

Yet, even in the face of these successes, Vietnam continues to define FitzGerald's identity. In recent years, she has written the text for the *Vietnam: Spirits of the Earth*, a photo essay on contemporary Vietnam published in 2001. In 2007, she wrote an introduction to the English translation of *Last Night I Dreamed of Peace*, a diary written between 1968 and 1970 by the North Vietnamese doctor Dang Thuy Tram, who worked in a battlefield hospital in South Vietnam. The book became a bestseller in Vietnam after its publication in 2005.

Martha Gellhorn's commitment to covering war and her passionate opposition to it continued long after her 1966 trip to Vietnam in the same way it did with Gloria Emerson. She covered the Six-Day War in the Middle East in 1967 and the civil wars in Central America in the mid-1980s. She traveled to Panama in 1989, at age eighty-one, to cover the U.S. invasion and the capture of General Manuel Noriega. Three years later, however, when war broke out in Bosnia, she acknowledged that age had finally become a hindrance. "You need to be nimble," she conceded. In the 1987 re-issue of her book *The New Face of War*, Gellhorn appended the chapter: "Last Words on Vietnam, 1987." In it she declared that America's failed crusade against Communism in Southeast Asia "did irreparable damage to America in history." In the weeks before her death in 1998, ill with cancer and nearly blind, Gellhorn wrote that Vietnam was the only war she had reported "from the wrong side."

Ethel Payne continued to cover international events for the *Chicago Defender*, including the Nigerian Civil War in 1969. In the 1970s, she accompanied two American secretaries of state, William P. Rogers and Henry Kissinger, on tours of Africa. She added broadcast commentary to her repertoire in the early 1970s when she became the first African American woman to discuss public affairs, first on the CBS radio network and later on television. In both those outlets, she continued addressing issues of interest to America's black community. Her commitment to racial justice never flagged, and she often participated in the events she covered as a journalist. She never saw her crusading as a conflict with her professional duties. She would, in fact, have argued that fighting prejudice, whether it was against blacks, Jews, gays, or women, was her professional responsibility. Her assignments continued to take her abroad and put her in the company of world leaders up until the 1980s. To the end, she remained unapologetic about her commitment to racial equality and civil liberties.

By the time the war was over, Kate Webb, the shy, soft-spoken waif who had shown up in Vietnam in 1967, had become a intrepid war correspondent. When she landed back in Hong Kong after covering the evacuation of Saigon aboard the USS *Blue Ridge,* Webb possessed the classic style of the war correspondent. She was tough, hard-drinking, at times foul-mouthed, and ever unwilling to suffer fools. Her talent for what Peter Arnett called "the vivid phrase" never faltered, and her impatience with inaccuracies could be intimidating. She remained with UPI for a time, but took her leave after one of her legendary spats with her boss. She moved to Jakarta in 1977 and joined Agence Presse-France in 1985. For the next sixteen years, war, unrest, and disorder were her specialty, whether it was in Indonesia, India, Pakistan, Afghanistan, South Korea, Sri Lanka, or East Timor.

At the end of 2001, with little idea of what she would do next, Webb retired after concluding that she was "too old to keep up with frontline reporting and that was the only kind I liked." In retirement, she taught for a time in Ohio, traveled, and indulged in writing something longer than the daily wire service dispatches that were her specialty. In "High Pockets," the chapter she contributed to *War Torn,* she revisited her Vietnam experience from the distance of a quarter of a century. Beyond writing, teaching, and traveling, Webb, in the spirit of *Candide,* "tended her garden," both in the physical space of her backyard, where she cultivated vegetables, and in a spiritual space, where she nurtured her many friendships. Her funeral service in Sydney, Australia, in May 2007, ended with Edith Piaf's recording of "Non! Je ne regrette rien."

War defined Leroy's career for more than a decade after she left Vietnam in 1969. Her coverage of the war in Lebanon in 1975 and 1976 won her the Robert Capa Award for exceptional courage and enterprise, marking the first time the prize was given to a woman.

Operating on the same fearless style that characterized her work in Vietnam, from the mid-1970s to the early 1980s, Leroy covered the conflict in Northern Ireland, the fighting in Libya, the ongoing discord in Iran and Iraq, the Russian misadventure in Afghanistan, among other hot spots. After photographing the Israeli siege of West Beirut and massacre of Palestinians in the Sabra and Shatila camps in 1982, Leroy swore off war and moved to Los Angeles.

Although she removed herself from the battlefield, war photography continued to engage her. Leroy and her colleague Tony Clifton, then with *Newsweek,* collaborated on the book *God Cried,* a volume of photos and essays about the civil war in Lebanon. In 2005, she edited a volume titled *Under Fire: Great Photographers and Writers in Vietnam*, which showcased the work of war photographers, including her own.

Leroy lived long enough she see her work celebrated at the University of California at Berkeley thirty years after the war ended. Ken Light, curator of an exhibit of her combat photographs, spoke of Leroy's sensitive portrayals of the brutality of war: "I hate to say it, but it's a woman's eye. It was very different than what the men were doing at the time." Speaking about Leroy's contribution to the genre, Susan Moeller of the University of Maryland explained that she turned away from the World War II–style focus on war's triumphant moments, which had produced images such as the flag raising at Iwo Jima. Leroy trained her lens instead on the "random moments" of combat, according to Moeller. The difference between those approaches is the difference between an image of a child at the end of a piano recital and one of the same child throwing a tantrum at the dinner table. In Moeller's view, "With Catherine Leroy, we got the tantrums at the dinner table." In 2005, she tried, without success, to stage an exhibit of war photographs at the Vietnam Veterans Memorial in Washington. At the time of her death in 2006, she was working on a book about the environment titled *The Earth Is Sick*.

After a two-year assignment in Moscow with the *Christian Science Monitor*, Elizabeth Pond moved to Bonn in 1976, where she spent another twelve years as the newspaper's European correspondent. With her deep understanding of how history, politics, and economic realities shaped Europe's evolution in the twentieth century, she became a respected geopolitical thinker in foreign policy circles, both in America and on the Continent. The John D. and Catherine T. MacArthur Foundation named her a Fellow in Central Europe in the early 1990s, and an assortment of think tanks have funded many of the scholarly studies she has undertaken in recent decades. She has written eight books (and co-authored a ninth) in the past twenty-five years, on Russia, the reunification of Germany and its consequences, and the emergence of Europe as a world power. Her most recent book, *Endgame in the Balkans*, was published in 2006 by the Brookings Institution Press. Daniel Hamilton of Johns Hopkins University called it "a masterful survey of Europe's most turbulent region." Another reviewer said that "this is vintage Pond at her best—always insightful, consistently fair-minded and judicious." She belongs to the Council on Foreign Relations and the German Council on Foreign Relations. Her intense preoccupation with Europe usually crowds out most memories of her years in Vietnam. She has never returned to Vietnam. "I got swept in other directions—Japan, the Soviet Union, Europe," she explained. When Jill Carroll, a freelance journalist working for the Christian Science Monitor was kidnapped in Baghdad in 2006, Pond said, she was brought back, as she is whenever a journalist is taken hostage somewhere in the world, to her own weeks as a captive in Southeast Asia. "And I hope and pray that they too will come out of their experience undamaged and enriched."

Seventeen years after Liz Trotta began her first assignment in Vietnam in 1968, she returned to cover the tenth anniversary of the fall of Saigon for CBS News. In her second job in television network news, which began in 1979, Trotta remained committed to the idea that there was something worthy, perhaps even noble, about the neutral pursuit of truth and heaped scorn on the widening intersection of news and entertainment. During the so-called "Rather (as in Dan) years," at CBS, when who reported a story became increasingly more important than the story, Trotta grew less and less willing or able to contain what she called her "native prickliness."

When she arrived at CBS, Cronkite, whom she had had the temerity to sass during the final release of American prisoners in North Vietnam, warmly welcomed her to the news operation. But by the early to middle 1980s, with Cronkite in retirement, Trotta soon became the "brunette wading into middle age" at a time when news bosses seemed to be searching out blondes with pin-up potential. Her Vietnam assignment in 1985 was one of the last big stories she reported. Six months later, she lost her job at CBS in one of its massive downsizing efforts. She soon joined the *Washington Times* as its New York bureau chief and paired that newspaper job with television commentary for Fox News. Although she officially retired in 2006, she continued to do commentary on Fox News, and she delighted in calling herself "the oldest person in television news."

Flora Lewis must have felt she had returned to Saigon, France, in the weeks before the city of the same name in Southeast Asia fell. Although with less intensity than in 1972, when the Paris Peace Talks occupied her for about six months, she once again found herself reporting on the pronouncements made by representatives of the country's two governments. Early in the month, a representative of the Provisional Revolutionary Government in Paris called for the immediate withdrawal from South Vietnam of 25,000 U.S. military personnel "disguised as civilians." She also reported on the deteriorating situation in Phnom Penh, where hundreds of foreigners from twenty countries had taken refuge in the French embassy after the Khmer Rouge take-over of the government early in April. Five Americans were among the 610 people awaiting evacuation from the compound. Later, after the dramatic endings had played out in Saigon and Phnom Penh, Lewis wrote another of her thoughtful analyses of the events.

When she was named an op-ed columnist for the *Times* five years later, that decade-long endeavor began with an exploration of an ongoing debate over French defense policies. She noted that France was broadening its spectrum of arms and upping its supply of warheads while simultaneously calling for disarmament—to the chagrin of the United States. America's protestations notwithstanding, Lewis reasoned that the parallel pursuit of a strong defense and disarmament made perfect sense in the light of Moscow's invasion of Afghanistan and its arms build-up in Africa, Asia, and Latin America. The next year, the French government awarded Lewis its Chevalier of the Legion of Honor. It was one of dozens of such honors she received during her long career. For ten years, she brought an intelligence, once described as nimble and ferocious, to her twice-weekly examinations of foreign affairs. When she wrote her last regular column for the *Times* in December 1990, Lewis looked back with a touch of awe at all she had witnessed and the insights she had drawn from those experiences. The old idea that history was all about those dazzling few kings or popes, she wrote, had given way to the more modern idea that history was as likely to turn on economics, geography, or climate. For years, she said, she had watched the "individuals who reach the heights of command and the swelling crowds who set the direction." History, she said, was no longer faceless: "What a wonderful time to have been able to watch up close." She continued to write until just a few months before her death. Until the end, she remained, as one obituary writer observed, "a beauty who could out-talk, out-charm and, if necessary, out-drink anyone who came within her magic circle."

The first two women to cover the war for the Associated Press remained with the wire service in careers that spanned decades: Edie Lederer for more than four and Tad Bartimus for two and a half. Lederer believes that Vietnam shaped the rest of her life as a journalist. In a matter of months after she left Saigon she covered the Yom Kippur War in 1973. In 1980, AP dispatched her to Kabul to cover the Soviet invasion of Afghanistan; and in 1991, she covered the Persian Gulf War. She also covered the unrest in Northern Ireland, conflicts in Bosnia and Somalia, and the genocide in Rwanda. Still other assignments took her to North Korea, Romania, the Soviet Union, and North Africa. In 1998, she was named AP's United Nations correspondent.

Tad Bartimus, who in the spring of 1975 in Anchorage, Alaska, where she was AP's bureau chief, had so anxiously awaited the arrival of her friend Laura Palmer to hear all about those last days in Saigon, remained with AP until 1992. In addition to becoming the service's first female bureau chief, Bartimus was assigned to cover the violent upheavals in Northern Ireland and guerrilla forces living in the jungles of Latin America during the 1980s. The debilitating symptoms that she had first experienced in Vietnam returned. Finally, in 1992, the same doctor who had pronounced her to be in excellent health before she left for Vietnam in 1973 determined that her repeated bouts of pneumonia and frequent inability to walk were caused by an acute onset of autoimmune disease. Her AP career ended a year later when the doctor found she was incapacitated. Nonetheless, she built a rich life around those disabilities. Back in Anchorage, she taught journalism at the University of Alaska for three years. She shared the 1998 Overseas Press Club Award and the George Polk Award with David Halberstam, Horst Faas, and Tim Page for *Requiem,* one of the most exquisite photo collections of the Vietnam War. In it, Bartimus profiled many of the book's photographers, all of whom died in Indochina. "Among Friends," the column she launched in early 1990s, is a weekly take on life's routines, both grim and joyful. Dave Barry, her friend and fellow columnist, said that in the more than five hundred columns she had written by early 2008 "she mines wisdom, humor and smack-your-forehead truths."

On the first anniversary of the fall of Saigon, Laura Palmer saw for the first time what had happened beyond her own narrow view of the events in which she had been a player. She had heard and read about the scene at the American embassy. But the video images replayed on the anniversary astounded her: "I really saw how frightening it was," she said. In the years that followed, Palmer established herself as a freelance producer who worked almost exclusively for ABC's *Nightline* program with Ted Koppel. There she found the interest and the space to take television news to its richest potential. When Koppel left the program in 2005, Palmer felt that "television had abandoned me, so I abandoned television." She has written three books in the past twenty years, the first of which is her most enduring contribution to the collective understanding America's experience in Vietnam.

More than any of her long-forgotten radio news broadcasts and her impressionistic essays published in *Rolling Stone* during her years in Saigon, *Shrapnel in the Heart* diagnosed America's unending Vietnam affliction. In it, she explained how "each bullet that took a life in Vietnam stopped several other lives dead in their tracks." The grasp she developed in the 1970s of the war and of the Americans who fought it were the foundation of the epiphany she experienced during her first visit to the Vietnam memorial on New Year's Day in 1986. In the many messages and mementos left at the base of that huge, granite wedge, Palmer discerned the deep, unhealed wounds among the survivors of those whose names are etched in black granite. The notes and poems and teddy bears and flowers were, for Palmer, all manifestations of endless mourning. The book that grew out of that recognition gave voice to the mothers, fathers, siblings, friends, and fellow soldiers who lost loved ones but whose anguish had been muted by public diffidence about the war, one born of a collective wish to forget. Twenty years after her book was published, Palmer was still awed by the enormity of what she had discovered: "There was so much pain and no one knew it."

For Gloria Emerson, the challenge facing every writer who aspires to cover war is finding a way to make war imaginable, "for in the detail is the horror." Telling the story of war, she once insisted in an interview with National Public Radio, should not be left only to men. Too many of them, she explained, were "boys at heart who got dazzled by guns and uniforms." Although it was she, among all these women, who most despised being distinguished by gender, it was Emerson who acknowledged in that same NPR interview that it was "important for women to cover wars."

Notes

Introduction

1   *"fight like hell to get the assignment."* Craig Whitney, e-mail correspondence with the author, 4 November 1998.

2   *"that I never even asked."* Nancy Dickerson, *Among Those Present* (New York: Random House, 1976), p. 31.

2   *Obscure news operations.* Donna Jones Born, "The Reporting of American Women Correspondents from the Vietnam War" (PhD diss., Michigan State University, 1987), pp. 191–198.

2   *"Can you imagine."* Jurate Kazickas, ed., "These Hills Called Khe Sanh," *War Torn* (New York: Random House, 2002), p. 95.

3   *Scholars have identified approximately 70 women.* Jones Born, p. 5; Virginia Edyth Elwood-Akers, "Women Correspondents in the Vietnam War" (master's thesis, California State University, Northridge, 1981), p. 1; Christine Martin, "The Women Correspondents in Vietnam: Historical Analysis and Oral Histories" (master's thesis, University of Maryland, 1988), p. 56.

3   *Margaret Fuller as a foreign correspondent.* Marion Marzolf, *Up from the Footnote* (New York: Hastings House, 1977), p. 14.

3   *Dakota Sioux uprisings.* Douglas C. Jones, "Teresa Dean: Lady Correspondent Among the Sioux Indians," *Journalism Quarterly* (Winter 1972): p. 656.

3   *"That's the worst of being a woman."* Maurine H. Beasley and Sheila J. Gibbons, *Taking Their Place* (Washington, DC: American University Press, 1993), p. 139.

3   *The first woman accredited.* Jones Born, p. 84.

4   *"Massive inequality between the sexes."* Ibid., p. 85.

4   *"the woman's angle."* Patricia Bradley, *Women and the Press: A Struggle for Equality* (Evanston, IL: Northwestern University Press, 2005), p. 226.

4   *"at a rate 75 percent higher than men."* William Chafe, *The Unfinished Journey* (New York: Oxford University Press, 1986), p. 84.

5   *"big stories of the day."* Kay Mills, *A Place in the News* (New York: Dodd, Mead & Company, 1988), p. 200.

5   *"I was the best writer they had."* Rodger Streitmatter, "No Taste for Fluff: Ethel L. Payne, African-American Journalist," *Journalism Quarterly* 68, no. 3 (Fall 1991): p. 529.

5   *"women got work."* Anne Morrisey Merick, quoted in Martin, p. 156.

5   *She reminded him of his daughter.* Tracy Wood, "Spies, Lovers, and Prisoners of War," in *War Torn*, p. 224.

5   *Westmoreland tried to ban overnight stays by women.* Denby Fawcett, "Walking Point," in *War Torn*, p. 13; Shirley Biagi, Interview 2 with Tad Bartimus, April 26, 1994, Washington, DC, for the Women in Journalism Oral History Project of the Washington Press Club Foundation, in the Oral History Collection of the National Press Club Archives, Washington, DC, p. 58.

6   *Earn the confidence of European government officials.* Marzolf, p. 85.

6   *No aptitude for executive roles.* Maurine H. Beasley and Sheila J. Gibbons, *Taking Their Place* (Washington, DC: American University Press, 1993), p. 33.

6   *"no U.S. textbooks had been written."* Quoted in Larry Berman, *Perfect Spy* (New York: Smithsonian Books, 2007), p. 163.

7   *"if you had your mind made up."* Elizabeth Pond, author interview, 12 July 1997.

7   *"The correspondent assigned to."* Margaret Kilgore, "The Female War Correspondent in Vietnam," *The Quill* (May 1972): p. 9.

8   *"the first war recorded better by women than by men?"* Richard Eder, "Shallow Graves," *Los Angeles Times Book Review*, 20 April 1986, Sec. V, p. 3.

8   *"more generous curves of the Western world."* Richard Tregaskis, *Vietnam Diary* (New York: Holt Rinehart & Winston, 1963), p. 98.

8   *"bored, distracted, frightened, unhappy."* Michael Herr, *Dispatches* (New York: Alfred A. Knopf, 1978), p. 224.

8   *"lovely female journalists."* Edith Lederer, "My First War," in *War Torn*, p. 175.

9   *"Who was there besides Frankie and Gloria?"* Stanley Karnow, author interview, 6 April 2000.

9   *"at the risk of being humiliated and patronized."* Peter Arnett, *Live From the Battlefield* (New York: Simon & Schuster, 1994), p. 220.

9   *"donut dollies and do-gooders."* Horst Faas, author interview, 9 January 2002.

9   *Legend of the Trung Sisters.* George Herring, *America's Longest War*, 4th ed. (Boston: McGraw-Hill Higher Education, 2002), p. 4.

9   *Ensure the safe return of Elizabeth Pond.* Pham Xuan An, author interview, 22 February 2002.

10   *Terror, comradeship, and eroticism.* J. Glenn Gray, *The Warriors* (New York: Harper & Row, 1970), p. 25.

10   *"rebellion of white, middle-class girls."* Wini Breines, *Young, White, and Miserable* (Boston: Beacon Press, 1992), p. 10.

11   *"the taste of their tuna casseroles."* Betty Friedan, *The Feminine Mystique* (New York: W.W. Norton and Company, 1963), p. 243.

11   *Containment of women and minorities.* Breines, p. 11.

12   *"fiercely fashionable advocates of women's lib."* Gloria Emerson, "Hey, Lady. What Are You Doing Here?" *McCall's*, August 1971, p. 61.

14   *"you will turn to a different time."* Gloria Emerson, letter to the author, 17 February 1997.

14   *"There isn't any way for you to understand those years in Vietnam."* Gloria Emerson, letter to the author, 4 November 2000.

15   *"I don't know what possessed me."* Pamela Sanders, author interview, 26 June 1997.

15   *"I knew I had met my destiny."* Barbara Gluck, author interview, 6 September 2007.

Chapter 1

16   *All the manners of a Vassar girl* and *"the chemistry must have been fairly instantaneous."* John M. Gates Jr., author interview, 14 October 1999.

17   *His bravado caught and held her.* Gloria Emerson, *Winners & Losers* (New York: Random House, 1977), p. 292.

17   *WASP-ish Groton-Yale type.* Marylin Bender, author interview, 18 July 2000.

17   *"hello-how-are-you letters."* Gates Jr. interview, 14 October 1999.

17   *Demobilization information.* Ibid., 20 June 2000.

18   *A passion-filled but fleeting romance.* Ibid., 14 October 1999.

18   *Arrive unannounced on his doorstep.* Ibid., 20 June 2002.

18   *"Hanoi is completely safe now."* Charlotte Ebener, *No Facilities for Women* (New York: Alfred A. Knopf, 1955), p. 91.

18   *"wanting to be a journalist and not knowing how you do it."* Gloria Emerson, *Vietnam: A History in Documents*, Gareth Porter, ed. (New York: New American Library, 1979), p. xxii.

18   *"most significant choice" she had ever made.* Barbaralee Diamonstein, *Open Secrets* (New York: Viking Press, 1970), p. 114.

18   *The New York Journal-American.* Nan Robertson, author interview, 20 September 1999.

19   *"a great place to leave."* Bender interview, 18 July 2000.

19   *"don't go off the deep end about world affairs."* Carolyn Warmbold, "Women of the Mosquito Press" (PhD diss., University of Texas, Austin, 1990), p. 37.

19   *"could not have known how exciting it would be."* Bender interview, 18 July 2000.

19   *"the prospect appalls me."* Gloria Emerson, letter to the author, 17 February 1997.

20   *"I think she seemed healthier."* David Halberstam, author interview, 7 January 1998.

20   *"Just my awful luck."* Gates Jr. interview, 16 May 2001.

21   *"a rabid [Francisco] Franco supporter."* Ibid., 14 October 1999.

21   *Anti-Communist Spanish-language comic books.* Peter Gates, author interview, 18 July 2000.

21   *"He was very close-mouthed."* Ibid.

21   *"An original and romantic man."* Emerson, *Winners & Losers*, p. 294.

21 *Her trip to Vietnam was inspired by her widely traveled grandmother.* Ibid., p. 291.

21 *Bessie Benson's travels.* "Mrs. C. F. Emerson to Cruise the World," *Titusville Herald,* 27 January 1923, p. 3.

21 *"exceptional cultural attainments."* "One of Best Known Women of City Dies," *Titusville Herald,* 23 July 1932, p. 3.

22 *Description of Emerson's ancestry.* Edmund K. Swigart, *An Emerson-Benson Saga* (Baltimore: Gateway Press, 1994), p. 623.

22 *"defined the cultured person for mid-nineteenth-century Americans."* Joan Shelley Rubin, *The Making of Middlebrow Culture* (Chapel Hill: University of North Carolina Press, 1992), p. 8.

22 *Established the Benson family fortune.* Ida M. Tarbell, *The History of Standard Oil Company,* vol. 2 (Gloucester, MA: P. Smith, 1963), p. 23.

22 *"It was a great jumble."* Typed manuscript of an undated conversation between Gloria Emerson and Charlotte Salisbury. Unnumbered folder labeled "Charlotte Salisbury," Gloria Emerson Archive, Mugar Library, Boston University.

22 *"a rich man who inherited lots of Tide Water shares."* Ibid.

23 *"Tide Water shares would not sink as long as he did."* Gloria Emerson, "Who Will Save Us from Fear?" *Esquire,* December 1973, p. 225.

23 *"stage-door Johnny."* Gates Jr. interview, 20 June 2000.

23 *It was "quite a relief."* Transcript of Emerson and Salisbury conversation.

23 *"was oppressed—by herself."* Diamonstein, p. 112.

23 *Jackie Onassis parallel and "bent twig."* Bender interview, 10 July 2000.

23 *Information on Washington Irving High School.* Robert Durkin, principal, author interview, 18 July 2000.

23 *"smiling crescent moon."* Gloria Emerson, "Rebellion," *Washington Irving Sketchbook* (Spring 1944): p. 22.

24 *"you know I am living with."* Gloria Emerson, "I Am Introduced to Noel Coward," *Washington Irving Sketchbook* (undated): p. 39.

24 *Characterizations of Gloria Emerson in high school.* Author interviews with Maybelle Lum, Frances Burnett, and Josephine Rey, undated.

25 *"faith in our country and its history."* Mary E. Meade, "Our Leading Lady," *Daisy,* 1946, p. 14.

26 *Vassar College and Beloit College.* Registrar's offices at both colleges state that their records indicate Emerson never attended either school.

26 *An opening at* Promenade. Craig Whitney, "Gloria Emerson, Chronicler of War's Damage, Dies at 75," *New York Times,* 5 August 2004.

26 *"splashy, almost unsightly" appearance.* Richard Kluger, *The Paper* (New York: Alfred A. Knopf, 1986), p. 433.

26 *"the dismal arts."* Warmbold, p. 30.

26 *"pretense, mystique, and flash."* Nan Robertson, author interview, 10 October 2001.

27 *Information on the operation of New York Journal-American fashion pages.* Bender interview, 19 October 2001.

27 *"You would never take your mother there."* David Anderson, author interview, undated.

27 *"A time of starting over."* Bender interview, 10 July 2000.

27 *"She was the breadwinner."* Gates Jr. interview, 14 October 1999.

28 *"Should Meg Marry Peter?"* New York *Journal-American,* 10 October 1955, p. 18.

28 *New York* Journal-American *Pulitzer Prize.* William Randolph Hearst Jr. and Jack Casserly, *The Hearsts: Father and Son* (Niwot, CO: Roberts Rinehart, 1991), p. 68.

28 *"kicked the hell out of."* Ibid.

28 *Gallup poll. Public Opinion, 1935–1971,* vol. 2 (New York: Random House, 1972), p. 1982.

29 *Haw River.* Edwin Yoder Jr., *Joseph Alsop's Cold War* (Chapel Hill: University of North Carolina Press, 1995), p. 118.

29 *would have told her, "Don't come."* Gates Jr. interview, 14 October 1999.

29 *Targeting only the French.* Anne Westerfield, author interview, 12 April 2006.

30 *"malignant and frightening" time.* Emerson, *Winners & Losers,* p. 292.

30 *"tidy up the world."* Ibid., p. 291.

30   *"we cannot ignore its needs."* John F. Kennedy, "America's Stake in Vietnam," *Vital Speeches of the Day,* 1 August 1956, p. 617.

31   *Having created the nation of South Vietnam.* Neil Sheehan, *A Bright Shining Lie* (New York: Random House, 1988*),* p. 138.

31   *Description of Edward G. Lansdale.* Frances FitzGerald, *Fire in the Lake* (Boston: Atlantic Monthly Press Book, 1972*);* Sheehan, *A Bright Shining Lie;* Cecil Currey, *Edward Lansdale: The Unquiet American* (Boston: Houghton Mifflin, 1988).

32   *Gates's first encounter with Lansdale.* Gates Jr. interview, 16 May 2001.

32   *Packed Bohannan and Gates off to his staff house at 24 Rue Tabard.* Edward G. Lansdale, *In The Midst of Wars* (New York: Harper & Row, 1972), p. 290.

32   *Glo-Glo and Ed.* Letter from Gloria Emerson to Edward Lansdale, 13 August 1966; Lansdale letter to Emerson, 4 September 1966, Edward G. Lansdale Papers, The Hoover Institution on War, Revolution and Peace, Box 51, Folder 1404.

32   *"building a tidy financial empire."* "The Gregorys of Saigon," *Newsweek,* 23 September 1962.

33   *Dai Viet Party.* William Duiker, *Ho Chi Minh: A Life* (New York: Hyperion, 2000), pp. xiv, 275, 338.

33   *The Westerfields' lifestyle.* Gloria Emerson, "Mlle Readers in Saigon," *Mademoiselle,* March 1957, p. 128.

33   *"We were saving the world."* Westerfield interview.

34   *The language . . . too difficult to be mastered.* Paul Mus, quoted in Gerald Hickey, *The Village in Vietnam* (New Haven, CT: Yale University Press, 1964), p. xi.

34   *Arellano as "charming con artist."* Gates Jr. interview, 19 October 1999.

35   *"Arellano caught fire as he listened."* Lansdale, p. 214.

35   *"the noisiest building in the city."* Emerson, *Winners & Losers,* p. 292.

36   *Emerson as "a thoroughbred."* Emma Valeriano, author interview, 10 September 2000.

36   *"She was a queen bee."* Gates Jr. interview, 14 October 1999.

36   *"Everything she touched just lit up."* Arthur Arundel, author interview, 19 October 2001.

36   *Operation Brotherhood mission.* Gloria Emerson, "Doctors, Thank You!" *Rotarian,* November 1956, p. 28; "Doctors—Thank You!" *Reader's Digest,* November 1956, p. 12.

37   *"gifted and inexhaustible man."* Emerson, *Winners & Losers,* p. 293.

37   *"was life in Technicolor."* Ogden Williams, in *Strange Ground,* Henry Maurer, ed., (New York: Avon Books, 1989), p. 83.

38   *Saigon architecture.* Helen West, ed., *Insight Guides: Vietnam* (Hong Kong: APA Publications, 1991), pp. 257–259.

38   *"totally in love with John."* Elyette Conein, author interview, 9 September 2000.

39   *Land reform in North Vietnam.* Stanley Karnow, *Vietnam: A History* (New York: Viking Press, 1983), pp. 230–231; Marilyn Young, *The Vietnam Wars 1945–1990* (New York: Harper Collins, 1991), pp. 55–57.

39   *Maintained a veneer of calm and normalcy.* Peggy Durdin, "Saigon: New Focus of Tension in Asia," *New York Times Magazine,* 14 January 1951, p. 7.

39   *"a smell of doom about it."* Peggy Durdin, "Saigon in the Shadow of Doom," *New York Times Magazine,* 21 November 1954, p. 7.

40   *"Catledge's Rule."* Nan Robertson, *Girls in the Balcony* (New York: Random House, 1992), p. 152.

40   *The Binh Xuyen uprising.* A. M. Rosenthal, "Crisis Deepening in South Vietnam," *New York Times,* 21 April 1955, p. 1; A. M. Rosenthal, "Vietnamese Army Winning Saigon Fight with Rebels, Premier Rebuffs Bao Dai," *New York Times,* 30 April 1955, p. 1.

40   *Referendum that President Diem arranged.* Henry Lieberman, "Diem Wins Poll in South Vietnam," *New York Times,* 24 October 1955, p. 1.

40   *"no free election."* "A Visit to Vietnam," *New York Times,* 4 July 1956, p. 20.

40   *Address the South Vietnamese National Constituent Assembly.* Robert Alden, "Nixon Hails Diem On Visit To Saigon," *New York Times,* 7 July 1956, p. 4.

40   *"biased news."* "Saigon Bans Press Bias," *New York Times,* 23 February 1956, p. 4.

41   *Vote on the Constitution.* Bernard Kalb, "Vietnamese Law To Be Set Forth," *New York Times,* 25 October 1956, p. 19.

41 *"have given the world an object lesson."* "Vietnam Constitution," *New York Times*, 26 October 1956, p. 27.

41 *Vietnamizing French names.* "New Names for Vietnamese," *New York Times*, 31 August 1956, p. 4.

41 *"they will not be happy here."* Emerson, *Winners & Losers*, p. 273.

42 *View of Vietnamese in U.S. diplomatic circles.* Christian G. Appy, ed., *Cold War Constructions* (Amherst: University of Massachusetts Press, 2000), p. 27.

42 *Incapable of self-governance.* Mark Phillip Bradley, *Imagining Vietnam & America* (Chapel Hill: University of North Carolina Press, 2000), p. 47.

43 *"covers everything but hides nothing."* Insight Guide: Vietnam (Hong Kong, APA Publications, 1991), p. 133.

43 *Emerson's interview with President Diem.* Emerson, *Winners & Losers*, p. 292.

44 *Description of demilitarized zone.* Ibid., p. 291.

45 *Description of Mr. Luoc.* Ibid., p. 292.

46 *"lying at night under mosquito netting."* Porter, p. xxiii.

46 *"brilliant but cynical."* Emerson, *Winners & Losers*, p. 298.

46 *A giddy high-schooler on a first date.* Laura Palmer, author interview, 11 September 2007.

46 *"How could you not love him?"* Gloria Emerson, interview with *FEED* magazine in 2002. http://web.archive.org/web/20001206033900/http://www.feedmag.com.

46 *"just one layer removed from biography."* Phyllis Levin, author interview, 17 October, 2001.

46 *"a pointless person."* Gloria Emerson, book promotion appearance at The Corner Book Store, New York City, 24 October 2000.

47 *"your correspondent is completely wrong."* John Clark Pratt, ed., *The Quiet American: Text and Criticism* (New York: Penguin Books, 1996), p. 349.

47 *"We had long conversations."* Gates Jr. interview, 14 October 1999.

48 *Peter Gates's view of John Gates's work in the CIA.* Peter Gates, author interview.

48 *"designed for weeping."* Ibid.

49 *Pot-throwing anecdote.* Gates Jr. and Peter Gates interviews.

49 *Emerson's left-leaning politics.* Peter Gates interview.

50 *Emerson's opinion of Eleanor Roosevelt.* Gates Jr. interview, 16 May 2001.

50 *"Plato said poverty makes men emotional."* Diamonstein, p. 115.

51 *Information on Emerson/Gates itinerary.* Drawn from a photo album Emerson compiled for Gates in 1957.

51 *He would line his pockets with the losses of lesser men.* Emerson, *Winners & Losers*, p. 294.

51 *"coping with life here and abroad."* Gloria Emerson, "Mlle Readers in Saigon," *Mademoiselle*, March 1957, p. 128.

51 *"might end up on the cover of Time magazine."* Gloria Emerson, "The Lives of a New York Career Girl," *Holiday*, May 1958, p. 80.

51 *Description of Mrs. Howkins and Times women's staff.* Robertson, p. 79.

51 *"The women's department was a different planet."* Sydney Schanberg, author interview, 7 April 2000.

52 *"Gloria's Flighty Personality."* Mary Marshall Clark, Interview 4 with Betsy Wade, 13 November 1992, New York. Women in Journalism Oral History Project, p. 99.

52 *"the kingdom."* Gloria Emerson, *Some Men* (New York: Simon & Schuster, 1985), p. 89.

52 *"Every one of us wanted a wider world."* Robertson interview, 20 September 2001.

53 *Parachute jump.* Gloria Emerson, "Collegians Jumping for Joy in New Sport of Parachuting," *New York Times*, 10 May 1959, p. 57; Gloria Emerson, "I Was the World's Most Scared Skydiver," *Reader's Digest*, March 1963, p. 88; Gloria Emerson, "Take the Plunge . . . " *Esquire*, May 1976, p. 93.

53 *"One of the great figures of 20th-century war correspondence."* Craig Whitney, e-mail to the author, 31 October 1998.

54 *"little brown brothers,"* Robertson interview, 20 September 2001.

Chapter 2

57 *"as good as any man on earth."* Richard Starnes, "A Lady Among the Warriors," November 10, 1965, Dickey Chapelle Papers, Box 1, Folder 1, State Historical Society of Wisconsin. (The Chapelle Papers are hereafter noted as DCP.)

57   *"own private appointment in Samarra."*"Chat with Miss Chapelle," *The Keukonian*, 17 October 1958, DCP, Box 1, Folder 1.

57   *"If you don't, someone else will."* Ibid.

58   *"floppy, go-to-hell kind of hat."* Dean Brelis, author interview, 25 September 2001.

58   *A gift from a fellow photographer.* Roberta Ostroff, *Fire in the Wind: The life of Dickey Chapelle* (New York: Ballantine Books, 1992), p. 16.

58   *"It's Dean, can you hear me?"* Jill Krementz, letter to Nancy Palmer, 6 November 1965, DCP, Box 1, Folder 4.

58   *"a sort of valentine."* Brelis interview.

59   *"casualties occurred at 0822."* Combat After-Action Report (Operation Black Ferret), 1st Battalion, 7th Marines.

59   *And called it her "Hilltop Hilton."* Ernest B. Ferguson, "How Dickey Chapelle Spent Her Last Hours," *Milwaukee Sentinel*, 6 November 1965.

59   *An "old war dog."* Malcolm Browne, *Muddy Boots and Red Socks* (New York: Random House, 1993), p. 192.

60   *"It would please my aunt."* Ernest Zaugg, "War Seemed Like a Dream," *Milwaukee Journal Sentinel*, 12 December 1965, DCP, Box 1, Folder 3.

60   *Her mother back in Milwaukee.* Dickey Chapelle, letter to Edna Meyer, DCP, Box 3.

60   *"She was a Marine."* Bev Deepe, "An Extra Round of Drinks," *Overseas Press Club Bulletin*, 20 November 1965, p. 1, DCP, Box 1, Folder 3.

60   *"to try to stop the bleeding."* Zoe Smith, "Dickey Chapelle, Pioneer in Combat," *Visual Communication Quarterly* 1, no. 2 (April 1994): p. 4.

60   *Someone told her Aunt Louise back in Milwaukee.* Ostroff, p. 24.

61   *"we are killing more of them."* Jean Dietrich, "Complexities of Vietnam Denied by Observer," *Courier-Journal*, 6 February 1965, DCP, Box 1, Folder 1.

62   *"take no favors from you or anybody."* William Giles, "Dickey Chapelle and an Editor's Observations," *The National Observer*, DCP, Box 1, Folder 1.

62   *"she was in the right place."* Wilbur Garrett, author interview, 20 September 2006.

63   *The melodramatic "I-was-there" style.* Hobart Lewis, letter to Dickey Chapelle, 5 June 1963, DCP, Box 7, Folder 3.

63   *"Aren't these sovereign people?"* "TV Under Parr," *New Republic*, March 6 1962, p. 6.

63   *Draft laws in 1848.* Dickey Chapelle, *What's a Woman Doing Here?* (New York: William Morrow and Company, 1962), p. 19.

63   *Midwestern breeze.* Ostroff, p. 27.

64   *Lessons in sewing doll clothes.* Chapelle, p. 17.

64   *"a little scary to younger kids."* Mary Holgate Dohmen, author interview, 2 June 2003.

64   *"putting her hair up in curlers."* Florence V. Lindsay, author interview, 17 June 2003.

65   *"yearbook entry quite like hers."* Margaret Harrigan, author interview, 19 June 2003.

65   *Never to look down.* Julia Edwards, *Women of the World* (Boston: Houghton Mifflin Publishing, 1988), p. 23.

66   *"Dad, can't we go to the airport?"* G. L. Meyer, "Why We Want to Fly, by One of Us, Age Fourteen," *U.S. Air Services*, September 1933.

66   *"we'll get us some Victor Charlies."* Dickey Chapelle, "Searching Vietnam for Victor Charlie," *National Observer*, 8 November, 1965, p. 2.

66   *"won't come out and fight us here."* Ibid.

67   *"preferred black lingerie."* Lindsay interview.

68   *"would do anything for money."* Federal Bureau of Investigation, File Number 100-HQ-216903, Confidential Memorandum, 3 December 1948.

68   *"charm the tits off a brass monkey."* Ostroff, p. 72.

68   *"between God's and Humphrey Bogart's."* Ibid., p. 73.

69   *"Any of those islands will do."* Ibid., p. 88.

69   *Red Cross blood donor photo.* Edwards, p. 209.

70   *"bodies of the dead who were buried at sea."* Dickey Chapelle, "The Quality of Mercy," *Reader's Digest*, October 1957, p. 33.

70   *"You look like another damn Marine."* Elizabeth Deadman, "Dickey Chapelle: Photo-Journalist," *Feminist Connection,* July–August 1982, p. 13. DCP, Box 1, Folder 6.

70   *"the unmentionable war filling out papers!"* Dickey Chapelle, "The Answer Is No, Admiral," unpublished manuscript, DCP, Box 11, Folder 4.

70   *MARCH 5 UNDER FIRE.* Chapelle, p. 95.

71   *"about as badly as an epidemic."* Ibid., p. 114.

71   *"Okinawa, Miss Dickey Chapelle."* Nancy Sorel, *The Women Who Wrote the War* (New York: Arcade Publishing, 1999), p. 378.

71   *"largely because of her sex."* Ostroff, p. 124.

72   *"unprettied pictures of the wounded."* Chapelle, p. 129.

72   *"to spread perpetual peace."* Ostroff, p. 142.

73   *"the remark rings like a bell."* Chapelle, p. 142.

74   *"substantial amount of money with her."* Ostroff, p. 192.

74   *Refugees to freedom in Austria.* James Michener, *The Bridge at Andau* (New York: Random House, 1957), p. 198.

74   *"was not her finest hour."* Edwards, p. 209.

74   *"freedom-fighter doctor."* Chapelle, p. 158.

75   *"occasionally up to the bridge."* Michener, p. 226.

75   *"got what she deserved."* Ostroff, p. 206.

75   *So that she could write about it.* Edwards, pp. 209–210.

76   *Chapelle put on her pearl earrings with shaking hands.* Chapelle, p. 216.

76   *"would not be found stripped of honor."* Ibid., p. 82.

76   *Chapelle's release from Fo Street prison.* Memorandum from J. Edgar Hoover to E. Tomlin Bailey, U.S. Department of State, 2 February 1957, Federal Bureau of Investigation, File Number 100-HQ-429675.

76   *"damn Hungarian cornfield in the first place."* Dickey Chapelle, letter to Robert Meyer, March 1967, DCP, Box 4.

76   *"could have been a spider's web draped over the globe."* Deadman, DCP, Box 1, Folder 6.

76   *"as sex seemed to be to other teenagers."* Chapelle, p. 19.

77   *The great press failures of the second half of the twentieth century.* Philip Knightley, *The First Casualty* (New York: Harcourt Brace Jovanovich, 1975), p. 368.

77   *Who then lived in Algeria.* "Algeria and the UN," *New York Times,* 4 February 1957.

77   *"then they'll say we did it."* Dickey Chapelle, "I Know Why the Algerians Fight," *Pageant,* April 1958.

78   *"she would faint without them."* Ibid.

78   *"can kill but cannot frighten him."* Arthur Lubow, *The Reporter Who Would Be King* (New York: Charles Scribners Sons, 1992), p. 141.

79   *"the courage to face death unafraid."* Dickey Chapelle, "I Roam The Edge of Freedom," *Coronet,* February 1961.

79   *"wherever a gun was fired."* Edwards, p. 21.

79   *"There is hope of democracy in the air."* Dickey Chapelle, "Remember the 26th of July," *Reader's Digest,* April 1959.

79   *"some challenge every waking moment."* Dickey Chapelle, "Cuba: One Year After," *Reader's Digest,* January 1960.

80   *Hard at masking its presence.* Dickey Chapelle, letter to Hobart Lewis, DCP, 29 June 1961, Box 6, Folder 1.

81   *Involve longer-term consequences in Vietnam.* George C. Herring, *America's Longest War* (New York: McGraw-Hill, 1996), p. 93.

81   *Ratchet up America's commitment to Vietnam.* Gabriel Kolko, *Anatomy of a War* (New York: New Press, 1985), p. 113.

81   *Supported by North Vietnam and the Soviet Union.* James R. Arnold, *First Domino* (New York: William Morrow, 1991), p. 376.

81   *"the noisiest goddamn cease-fire."* Dickey Chapelle, letter to Selma Blick, 29 June 1961, DCP, Box 5, Folder 7.

82   *"what my own eyes have taught me."* Dickey Chapelle, letter to Aunt Lutie, 26 June 1961, DCP, Box 5, Folder 7.

82   *"leadership of the free world."* Dickey Chapelle, letter to Hobart Lewis, 29 June 1961, DCP, Box 6, Folder 1.

82   *What was training and what was fighting.* Draft of unpublished manuscript, "The Men Who Didn't Give Up on Laos," DCP, Box 11, Folder 10.

83   *"a story-teller of integrity."* Chapelle letter to Lawrence Hughes, 28 September 1961, DCP, Box 6, Folder 1.

84   *"goes over better with American readers."* Bernard Yoh, letter to Chapelle, 9 March 1963, DCP, Box 7, Folder 1.

84   *"Who can serve a greater cause?"* Dickey Chapelle, "The Fighting Priest of South Vietnam," *Reader's Digest,* July 1963, p. 200.

84   *"decide to start winning NOW."* Dickey Chapelle, letter to Lt. Gen. Wallace M. Greene Jr., 3 December 1961, DCP, Box 5, Folder 7.

85   *Nearly 6,000 from December 1961.* Herring, p. 104.

85   *"Sure did like it!"* Edward G. Lansdale, letter to Dickey Chapelle, 26 December 1961, Lansdale Archive, Hoover Institution.

85   *"the ground war in World War II."* Edward G. Lansdale, letter to General Curtis LeMay, 1 April 1964, DCP, Box 7, Folder 4.

86   *"protect [the information] from unauthorized disclosure."* Kathryn I. Dyer, CIA Information and Privacy Coordinator, letter to the author dated 26 July 2000.

86   *"I call it doing my duty as a citizen."* Carl Bernstein, "The CIA and the Media," *Rolling Stone,* 22 October 1977.

87   *"many women are much equaler than others."* Charles Poore, "Books of the Times," *New York Times,* 1 February 1962, p. 26.

87   *That her work indeed had merit.* Dickey Chapelle, letter to Nancy Palmer, March 1963, DCP, Box 6, Folder 4.

87   *"we may get the stupid problem solved."* Dickey Chapelle, letter to Nancy Palmer, 25 February 1962, DCP, Box 6, Folder 2.

88   *"had so much to do with my getting the award."* Dickey Chapelle, letter to Selma Blick, 1 April 1962, DCP, Box 6, Folder 4.

88   *"do it again the next day."* Archie Clapp, author interview, 2 November 2003.

88   *In his esteem as Chapelle.* Ibid.

89   *"Communists would surely dominate all Viet Nam."* Dickey Chapelle, "The Helicopter War," *National Geographic,* November 1962, p. 723.

89   *"the most important thing she left behind."* Horst Faas, author interview, 15–16 October 2007.

89   *The editors refused.* Zoe Smith, "Dickey Chapelle, Pioneer in Combat," *Visual Communication Quarterly* (Spring 1994): p. 4.

90   *Shocked the photo editor of Life.* Ibid.

91   *"candle of freedom flickering."* Letter from Hobart Lewis to Dickey Chapelle, 19 April 1963, DCP, Box 7, Folder 3.

91   *"the American freelance writer."* Leighton McLaughlin, "Cuban Raiders' Hialeah Bomb Factory Raided," *Miami News,* 22 September 1963.

91   *Moored along the Miami River.* Dom Bonafede, "Boat Seizure Rapped," *Miami News,* 23 October 1963.

92   *"my cameras . . . were in the bow."* "Twas Major Blast for Mrs. Chapelle," *Milwaukee Sentinel,* 7 January 1964.

92   *"thus the silence."* Quoted in Frederick R. Ellis, "Dickey Chapelle: A Reporter and Her Work" (master's thesis, University of Wisconsin, 1972).

93   *"the least objective observers around."* Dickey Chapelle, undated manuscript, DCP, Box 7, Folder 1.

93   *America's involvement in Vietnam.* Ibid.

93   *"rather than of democratic government."* Hanson W. Baldwin, "Managed News," *Atlantic Monthly,* April 1963, p. 53.

93   *Anything less endangered democracy.* Dickey Chapelle, "Open Letter to President Kennedy," undated, DCP, Box 7, Folder 2.

94   *"at least one American's idea—mine."* Dickey Chapelle, "Water War in Vietnam," *National Geographic,* February 1966.

95   *"everything we're trying to do."* Bette McNear, "War Correspondent: Tougher Army Needed," *Wilmington (DE) Morning News,* 5 April 1965.

95   *"throw me in prison tomorrow."* DCP, Box 1, Folder 1.

95   *"men serving in VietNam."* Esther Brightman, "War's Seen Better Now Than Later," *Plain Dealer,* 8 April 1965, DCP, Box 1, Folder 1.

96   *"brother and sister in every sense of the word."* "Brother Remembers Dickey As an Exciting Personality," *Milwaukee Sentinel,* 4 November 1965.

96   *"It was all such fun."* Marion Meyer, author interview, 8 August 2000.

96   *"Aren't they tough enough for you?"* Ostroff, p. 379.

97   *"for them to come back."* Dickey Chapelle, "It's Mostly the Pros Who Say Farewell," *National Observer,* 11 October 1965, p. 10.

97   Sought any of the privileges of her sex. "A Reporter's Death," *Newsweek,* 15 November 1965, DCP, Box 1, Folder 3.

97   *"about the fight for freedom."* Associated Press report, DCP, Box 1, Folder 3.

97   *"she had decided on the former."* "Brother Remembers Dickey as an Exciting Personality," *Milwaukee Sentinel,* 4 November 1965.

97   *"doing things the hard way."* S.L.A. Marshall, "Death, Too, Slighted Dickey Chapelle," *Los Angeles Times,* 21 November 1965, sec. H, p. 6.

98   *"as a monument to a cause."* "Rites Will Be Friday for Dickey Chapelle," *Milwaukee Journal,* 9 November 1965. Dickey Chapelle Collection, Shorewood Historical Society.

98   *"center of any upcoming action."* Chapelle, p. 95.

98   *"and we will miss her."* "Rites will be Friday for Dickey Chapelle," *Milwaukee Journal,* 9 November 1965, Dickey Chapelle Collection, Shorewood Historical Society.

98   *"as she saw it for all Americans."* Dohman interview, 12 June 2003.

Chapter 3

100   *"what a place for her to be in."* Malcolm Browne, author interview, 16 December 1997.

100   *"a story that just grew and grew."* Karen Griess, "Vietnam 'a Story That Grew' for Journalist from Hebron," *Lincoln Journal Star,* 14 August 1998, p. 1B.

102   *"Beverly knew from day one."* Ibid.

102   *"rewards of taking well-calculated risks."* Beverly Deepe, "Adventures of the Young Journalist," *Alumni News,* University of Nebraska (Winter 1999): p. 15.

102   Beverly *"always tended to business."* Grace Lake, author interview, 17 October 2001.

103   *"the ladies would fix meals."* James Hudson, author interview, 18 November 2001.

103   Nettlesome disciplinary problems. Lake interview.

104   *"visitors at the M. J. Widler home."* "Carleton," *Hebron Journal Register,* 24 January 1951.

104   *"You didn't do sleepovers."* Elizabeth Beechner, author interview, 4 November 2001.

104   Demanded academic excellence. Jackie Williamson, author interview, 5 November 2001.

105   *"in forty-eight years of teaching."* Lake interview.

105   *"Higgins still manages to look attractive."* Carl Mydans, "Girl War Correspondent," *Life,* 2 October 1950, p. 51.

106   *"there is no way to change her mind."* Neale Copple, author interview, 14 November 2001.

107   *"operated on a level that was close to perfection."* James Boylan, "Declarations of Independence," *Columbia Journalism Review* (November–December 1986): p. 30.

107   *"I'd probably fritter the money away."* Griess.

108   *"a war we can't afford to lose."* Daniel Hallin, *The "Uncensored" War* (New York: Oxford University Press, 1986), p. 37.

108   *"led to U.S. disengagement from Vietnam."* Ibid., p. 49.

109   *"morning sunlight accented a solitary junk."* Beverly Deepe, "Porthole View of Red China," *Sunday World-Herald Magazine,* 3 September 1961, p. 18.

110   *"wiping out the country's leadership."* Homer Bigart, "Saigon Discounts Pilots' Raid on Presidential Palace," *New York Times,* 28 February 1962, p. 1.

110   *"divine protection."* Stanley Karnow, *Vietnam: A History* (New York: Viking Press, 1983), p. 264.

110 *"writing too much about American casualties."* Homer Bigart, "M'Namara Terms Saigon Aid Ample," *New York Times,* 12 May, 1962, p. 1.

110 *"on the roads outside the city."* Browne interview, 22 December 1997.

111 *"We don't want women with legs down here."* Beverly Deepe, "The Woman Correspondent," *Dateline,* January 1966, p. 95.

111 *Too many uncomfortable questions.* "Women War Correspondents: Vietnam Version," *Matrix* 58 (Winter 1972–1973): p. 5.

111 *Drove without an escort along Route 19.* Browne interview.

111 *"uninterested in helping them out with the authorities."* Arnett, p. 230.

112 *"curves in the right places."* Richard Tregaskis, *Vietnam Diary* (New York: Holt Rinehart and Winston, 1963), pp. 97–103.

113 *Prevent any further Communist aggression in Laos.* http://www.presidency.ucsb.edu/ws /index.php?pid=8657.

113 *"'Wow! I can do that.'"* Pamela Sanders, author interview, 26–27 June 1997.

113 *"My father was dubious."* Ibid.

114 *"up to their asses in mud."* Pamela Sanders, *Miranda* (Boston: Little, Brown and Company, 1978), p. 157.

114 *Work routines of Time stringers.* Sanders interview.

115 *"'Numbah One' in Laos."* "A Letter from the Publisher, *Time,* 5 July 1963, p. 11.

115 *"was a one-woman Christmas show."* William Prochnau, *Once Upon a Distant War* (New York: Vintage Books, 1995), p. 207.

116 *"I asked one of the pilots to teach me."* Sanders interview.

116 *"led one to contemplate such fanciful notions."* John Mecklin, *Mission in Torment* (New York: Doubleday, 1965), p. 55.

116 *"I don't want any goddamn women around here."* Sanders, p. 223.

116 *Women in mid-twentieth century Vietnamese society.* Beverly Deepe, "Vietnam WACs: Too Many Volunteer," *Herald Tribune,* 23 November 1965, p. 2; "Viet Women, Life of Conflict," *Herald Tribune,* 21 December 1965, p. 8.

117 *"Always, it's more important to wear lipstick than a pistol."* Deepe, "The Woman Correspondent," p. 95.

117 *"They didn't ask about where you had your hair done."* Sanders interview.

118 *"I don't date. Men are a luxury I can't afford."* "Foreign Correspondents: Self-Reliance in Saigon," *Time,* 8 January 1965, p. 38.

118 *Why he could not control her.* Pham Xuan An, author interview, 22 February 2002.

118 *"trifling or thoughtless criticism."* Mecklin, p. 3.

119 *"It represented constant lies."* Sanders interview.

119 *"We did not want to embarrass our government."* Gay Talese, *The Kingdom and the Power* (New York: World, 1969), p. 5.

119 *"are American troops now in combat in Vietnam?"* Tom Wicker, *On Press* (New York: Viking, 1978), p. 92.

119 *Bigart's story noted.* Homer Bigart, "U.S. Expanding Role in Vietnam," *New York Times,* 10 February 1962, p. 5.

119 *"There had been so many little deceptions."* Mecklin, p. 122.

119 *"petty, pathetic maneuvers to save face."* William M. Hammond, *Public Affairs: The Military and the Media* (Washington, DC: Center for Military History, United States Army 1962–1968, 1988), pp. 37–38.

120 *Expulsion of Bigart and Sully.* Prochnau, p. 50.

120 *An article his newspaper never used.* Homer Bigart, "Bigart Tangles with Red Tape in Vietnam Jungle," *Times Talk,* April 1962, in *Forward Positions,* edited by Betsy Wade (University of Arkansas Press, 1992), p. 198.

121 *"didn't write English all that well."* Robert McCabe, author interview, 31 May 2002.

121 *"boring, farm-bred Nebraska girl."* Horst Faas, author interview, 2 January 2002.

122 *"She didn't know what was in her notebooks."* David Halberstam, author interview, 7 January 1998.

122 *"Shotgun Alley."* "The New Metal Birds," *Newsweek,* 29 October 1962, p. 37.

122   *A maximum hardship post.* Mecklin, p. 32.

123   *"dirty, untidy, disagreeable war."* Emmet John Hughes, "A Lesson from Vietnam," *Newsweek,* 9 September 1963, p. 17.

123   *The press coverage of Ap Bac.* Hammond, p. 35.

123   *Correspondents in Saigon whose dispatches were criticized as biased. Newsweek,* 7 October, p. 98.

123   *"American press corps in Saigon."* "War of Words," *Newsweek,* 21 October 1963, p. 7.

124   *"Kong Le's small, dark room is empty."* "On the Laotian Brink," *Newsweek,* 29 April 1963, p. 33.

124   *"neither drinks, smokes nor gambles."* "Evil Spirits on the Plain," *Time,* 5 July 1963, p. 32.

124   *"some troops of my own to command."* Pamela Sanders, e-mail message to the author, 27 February 2008.

125   *Higgins's childhood and work in South Vietnam.* Antoinette May, *Witness to War* (New York: Beaufort Books, 1983), p. 233.

126   *Harkins criticized for over optimism.* Marguerite Higgins, "Diem and the Buddhists," *New York Herald Tribune,* 14 August 1963; "Diem's Version of Buddhist Dispute," *New York Herald Tribune,* 9 August 1963.

127   *"So we have to be polite and obedient."* Marguerite Higgins, "Farmer on the People's Fate," *New York Herald Tribune,* 4 August 1963, p. 1.

127   *Story of monk's suicide.* Marguerite Higgins, "The Two Living Pyres that Sear Diem," *New York Herald Tribune,* 6 August 1963.

127   *She had no wish to shake her hand.* Prochnau, p. 333.

128   *"She was virtually working for MACV."* Halberstam interview, 7 January 1998.

128   *"talk of discrimination has nothing to do with reality."* Marguerite Higgins, "Viet Nam—Fact and Fiction," *New York Herald Tribune,* 26 August 1963.

128   *Speculated about the possibility of a coup.* "Vietnam's Future: 'All Bets Are Off,'" *Newsweek,* 26 August 1963, p. 35.

129   *"they were from Hue, and they were ruthless."* "War in the Pagodas: Who is the Enemy?" *Newsweek,* 2 September 1963, p. 35.

129   *Nhu family and its disastrous role in ruling the country.* "Vietnam: Getting to Know the Nhus," *Newsweek,* 9 September 1963, p. 33.

129   *President Diem's musty and dank room.* "The Fall of the House of Ngo," *Newsweek,* 11 November 1963, p. 27.

129   *Deepe's apartment looted.* Deepe, "The Woman Correspondent."

130   *"shaping into a solid, hopeful situation."* Mike Mansfield, foreward to Wesley Fishel, ed., *Problems of Freedom: South Vietnam Since Independence* (New York: Free Press of Glencoe, 1961), p. ix.

130   *"shouting slogans and waving banners."* "The Fall of the House of Ngo," p. 27.

130   *"We would never win."* Sanders interview.

131   *"hardly bear to read about it."* Ibid.

131   *"Beverly lived in Saigon as opposed to."* John Sharkey, author interview, 12 December 2001.

131   *"She was really dug in."* Ward Just, author interview, 20 October 1999.

132   *"There was fierce competition between women."* Jurate Kazickas, author interview, 30 May 1997.

133   *Pond's Vietnam trips.* Elizabeth Pond, author interview, 12 July 1997.

133   *"she never stopped working."* An interview, 22 February 2002.

133   *"They were very disciplined."* Ibid.

134   *"You must be in love with her."* Ibid.

134   *His final resting place in a rice paddy dike.* Deepe, "Adventures of the Young Journalist," p. 15.

134   *"for all of Vietnam cries."* Deepe, "The Woman Correspondent," p. 95.

135   *"a hellish dancing madness."* Ibid., 97.

135   *Deepe infuriated Breslin.* Barry Zorthian, author interview, 22 October 2007.

135   *"the deluge has descended."* Beverly Deepe, "Vietnam a Year After Diem—His Dire Prophecy Coming True," *New York Herald Tribune,* 1 November 1964, p. 14.

136   *Khanh–Taylor contretemps.* "Viet Strongman Defies on Civilian Rule," *New York Herald Tribune,* 23 December 1964, p. 1.

137   *Some bordered on "being nuts."* Beverly Deepe, "Taylor Rips Mask off Khanh," *New York Herald Tribune,* 25 December 1964, p. 1.

137   *Deepe stories had annoyed Taylor.* Zorthian interview, 22 October 1999.

137   *"a singular achievement for a girl."* "Foreign Correspondents, Self Reliance in Saigon," *Time,* 8 January 1965, p. 38.

138   *"dirty little war."* Beverly Deepe, "Viet Jungle Sweep: The Surprise That Wasn't," *Herald Tribune,* 8 July 1965, p. 1.

138   *Largest American death toll for any operation.* Hammond, p. 199.

138   *"Marines were dying so incredibly fast."* Michael Herr, "Dispatches," in *Reporting Vietnam, 1969–1975* (New York: Library of America, 1998), p. 737.

138   *"Communist military stranglehold."* Beverly Deepe, "The Red Noose Around Saigon," *Herald Tribune,* 30 January 1966, p. 15.

138   *Aircraft carrier USS Kitty Hawk.* Beverly Deepe, "On the Carrier As Raids Resume," *Herald Tribune,* 2 February 1966, p. 1.

139   *Rural electrification project.* Beverly Deepe, "Red Tape Snarls Viet Farm Aid," *Herald Tribune,* 15 February 1966, p. 2.

139   *Anti-government action groups.* Beverly Deepe, "Ky Loyalists Under Attack in DaNang," *Herald Tribune,* 17 April 1966, p. 1.

139   *"America's war-peace decision."* Beverly Deepe, "U.S. Role in Vietnam pivots on election." *Christian Science Monitor,* 31 July 1967, p. 1.

140   *"they just ignore each other."* Beverly Deepe, "Saigon Effectiveness Seen Crucial to War," *Christian Science Monitor,* 2 January 1968, p. 3.

140   *Communists' "blitz war."* Beverly Deepe, "Blitz Erodes U.S. Position in Vietnam," *Christian Science Monitor,* 3 February 1968, p. 1.

140   *Cityscape of rubble and ashes.* Arnett, p. 252.

141   *"Communist mini-mobile warfare."* Beverly Deepe, "Viet Cong in Saigon Hits and Hides," *Christian Science Monitor,* 9 February 1968, p. 1.

141   *"as more fairy tale than fact."* Beverly Deepe, "Assault Ends with a Whimper," *Christian Science Monitor,* 29 February 1968, p. 2.

141   *"a crucial anchor of our defenses."* Peter Braestrup, *Big Story* (New Haven, CT: Yale University Press, 1983), p. 260.

142   *Destruction of Hue by North Vietnamese forces.* Peter Brush, "The Battle for Khe Sanh," in *The Tet Offensive,* Marc Jason Gilbert and William Head, eds. (Westport, CT: Praeger, 1996), p. 195.

142   *Nuclear weapons to support the French.* Peter Brush, Ibid., p. 201.

142   *"Dinbinphoo."* Berman, Larry, "The Tet Offensive." Gilbert and Head, p. 18.

142   *"exceeded anything that has ever been seen before."* Robert Pisor, *The End of the Line* (New York: W.W. Norton, 1982), p. 261.

143   *"five atomic bombs of Hiroshima vintage."* Beverly Deepe, "How B-52's protected Khe Sanh," *Herald Tribune,* 28 June 1968, p. 1.

143   *"news reporters were forbidden to write about it."* Pisor, p. 256.

143   *"the human cost exceeded the value."* Beverly Deepe "Khe Sanh, Legacy of Westmoreland," *Christian Science Monitor,* 27 March 1968.

144   *Deepe's wedding ceremony.* "Deepe-Keever," *Hebron Journal,* Deepe Family Collection, Thayer County Historical Society, Hebron, Nebraska.

144   *"Don't feel sorry for Charley."* Sanders, p. 256.

Chapter 4

146   *"motel in the middle of a trackless jungle."* Frances FitzGerald, "The Struggle and the War," *Atlantic Monthly,* August 1967, p. 72.

146   *"a passion and a commitment."* Frances FitzGerald, author interview, 12 November 2004.

147   *"a Renaissance soldier of fortune."* Evan Thomas, *The Very Best Men* (New York: Simon & Schuster, 1995), p. 44.

147   *From the Philippines to Thailand.* Ibid., p. 50.

148   *"always more skeptical about Vietnam than anyone else."* FitzGerald interview, 12 June 1997.

148   *"know what you are talking about."* Thomas, p. 322.

148 *"I'm glad the test never came."* Claudia Dreifus, "Frances FitzGerald," *Long Islander,* 17 February 1980, p. 23.

149 *"a dazzling work."* Martha Gellhorn, letter to Frances FitzGerald, 1 January 1973, Frances FitzGerald Archive, Mugar Library, Boston University (hereafter referred to as FFA), Box 25, Folder 6.

149 *"on the orders of old men."* Martha Gellhorn, *The Face of War* (London: Hart-Davis, 1959), p. 224.

149 *Travel there on her own dime.* Caroline Moorehead, *Gellhorn* (New York: Henry Holt, 2003), p. 348.

150 *"daring thing to ask a woman to go to war."* Ethel Payne quoted in Christine Martin, "Women Correspondents in Vietnam: Historical Analysis and Oral Histories" (master's thesis, University of Maryland, 1988), p. 131.

151 *To justify further escalation.* William Hammond, *Public Affairs: The Military and the Media, 1962–1968* (Washington, DC: Center of Military History, U.S. Army, 1988), p. 247.

151 *"and the obvious is alive here."* Frank Wisner Jr., letter to Frances FitzGerald, 21 December 1965, FFA, Box 23, Folder 12.

152 *"It's not what I expected in Saigon."* FitzGerald interview, 12 November 2002.

153 *"You're living with her."* Jim Sterba, *Frankie's Place* (New York: Grove Press, 2003), p. 158.

153 *Scandalized Maine's Mount Desert Island.* Caroline Seebohm, *No Regrets* (New York: Simon & Schuster, 2003), p. 24.

153 *"salt, steel and Emersonian individualism."* T. Charlton Henry, "The Grandes Dame Who Grace America," *Life,* February 1968.

153 *"let down your family, your society and your God."* Seebohm, p. 161.

153 *Mary Peabody's arrest in a motel bar.* Frances FitzGerald, e-mail message to the author, 17 February 2008.

152 *Expected her to marry him.* John Huston, *An Open Book* (New York: Alfred A. Knopf, 1980), p. 121.

154 *"made a tremendous impression on me."* Robert Friedman, "Frances FitzGerald Is Fascinated with Failure," *Esquire,* July 1980, p. 51.

154 *"not less spiritually nourishing for being cooked."* Frances FitzGerald, "Comparative Calm in the Hurricane's Eye," *Village Voice,* 24 March 1966, p. 3.

155 *"like an airline pilot before take-off."* Frances FitzGerald, "Background of Crisis, The Trivia in Truth," *Village Voice,* 28 April 1966, p. 7.

155 *Eight months of relative calm.* Frances FitzGerald, "The Hopeful Americans & The Weightless Mr. Ky," *Village Voice,* 21 April 1966, p. 6.

155 *"of ghastly traffic accidents."* Frances FitzGerald, "Death of a Chronicler," *Commentary,* March 1968, p. 93.

155 *After the French rout at Dien Bien Phu.* Frances FitzGerald, "Vietnam: The Future," *New York Review of Books,* March 1970, p. 4–10.

156 *"with the detachment of a schizophrenic."* Frances FitzGerald, "The End is the Beginning," *New Republic,* 3 May 1975, p. 7.

156 *People whom her parents invited to dinner.* FitzGerald interview, 12 June 1997.

156 *"Americans learn something about the Vietnamese."* FitzGerald, author interview, 12 November 2002.

156 *"they weren't inviting us over to dinner."* Ward Just, author interview, 22 October 1999.

157 *Pull strings where necessary.* Desmond FitzGerald, letter to Frances FitzGerald, 6 April 1966, FFA, Box 23, Folder 1.

157 *"spectral crew of ex-chiefs of Vietnam."* Letter from Desmond FitzGerald to Frances FitzGerald, 10 September 1966, FFA, Box 23, Folder 1.

157 *"any communication between my mother and my father."* FitzGerald interview, 12 June 1997.

157 *"cousin of the late John F. Kennedy."* Pham Xuan An, e-mail correspondence with the author, 16 May 2005.

157 *"I have green eyes."* FitzGerald interview, 28 November 2004.

157 *"The crisis totally surprised everyone."* Ibid., 12 November 2002.

158 *"tangle of competing individuals, regions, religions."* James Reston, "Vietnam: War Within War," *New York Times,* 4 April 1966.

158   *"That war is hell."* Frances FitzGerald, notes in archive, FFA, Box 15.

159   *"an immaculate press and a mendacious government."* Zorthian interview, 22 October 1999.

159   *Ended in either five or zero.* Just interview.

160   *"they may halt the aggression."* Stewart Alsop, "The Meaning of the Dead," *Saturday Evening Post,* 24 April 1965, p. 16.

160   *"themes of comedy and tragedy."* Frances FitzGerald, "Vietnam—The People," *Vogue,* May 1967, p. 262.

161   *"the American military system itself."* Frances FitzGerald, "The Long Fear," *Vogue,* January 1967, p. 110.

161   *"because I was so exhausted."* FitzGerald interview, 30 November 2004.

161   *"necessities of life require bribery."* Seebohm, p. 291.

162   *"sought to propagate with missionary fervor."* Neil Sheehan, *A Bright Shining Lie,* p. 13.

162   *"whether we were on really dangerous road."* FitzGerald interview, 12 November 2002.

163   *"proclaim oneself irresponsible or ignorant."* Godfrey Hodgson, *America in Our Time* (New York: Vintage Books, 1976), p. 72.

164   *"but he was something of a war lover."* FitzGerald interview, 12 November 2002.

165   *90 percent believed to be Viet Cong sympathizers.* Frances FitzGerald, "The Village of Duc Lap," *New York Times,* 4 September 1966, p. 14.

165   *"finally he came out the other side."* FitzGerald interview, 12 November 2002.

166   *"We're not racist," "We're not colonizers."* Daniel Ellsberg, author interview, 19 October 2007.

166   *"recognized as 'good Germans.'"* Carl Rollyson, *Nothing Ever Happens to the Brave* (New York: St. Martin's Press, 1990), p. 291.

166   *"Fairly put off by her at first."* FitzGerald interview, 12 November 2004.

167   *Dismissed them as undemocratic.* Rollyson, p. 10.

167   *Suffrage demonstration.* Moorehead, p. 18.

168   *"the first time in her life, on the wrong side."* Ibid., p. 351.

168   *"to be eyes for their conscience."* Gellhorn, *The Face of War,* p. 1.

168   *"jaunty, amused quality."* Just interview.

169   *"reached the hem of her dress."* Ibid.

169   *"no child should have such eyes."* Gellhorn, *The Face of War,* p. 230.

170   *"in their eyes, rightly, as accusation."* Martha Gellhorn, "Suffer the Children," *Ladies Home Journal,* January 1967, p. 57.

170   *"I wanted to be read."* Gellhorn, *The Face of War,* p. 262.

170   *"Here we go again."* Moorehead, p. 355.

171   *"have killed him that night, I was so angry."* http://www.usatoday.com/life/books/excerpts/2004–09–29-truman-capote_x.htm.

171   *"very complicated moment in this country's history."* Diana Trilling, http://blogs.salon.com/0003974/2004/10/18.html.

171   *"nowhere to turn for justice."* Frances FitzGerald, "Tragedy of Saigon," *Atlantic Monthly,* November 1966, p. 59.

172   *"I really couldn't cope with it all."* FitzGerald interview, 12 November 2002.

172   *"Yes, I'll do it."* Kathleen Currie, interview 5 with Ethel Payne, September 24, 1987, Washington DC, for the Women in Journalism Oral History Project of the Washington Press Club Foundation, in the Oral History Collection of the National Press Club Archives, Washington, DC, p. 92.

173   *The oppression of white men.* Rodger Streitmatter, p. 528.

173   *Payne's recollections of her childhood.* Kathleen Currie, interview 1 with Ethel Payne, Ethel Payne, 25 August 1987, Women in Journalism Oral History Project of the Washington Press Club Foundation, pp. 1–8.

173   *"without regard to race, color, religion, or national origin."* Gail Buckley, *American Patriots* (New York: Random House, 2001), p. 339.

174   *"for a single night's pleasure."* Ibid., p. 350.

175   *"were just jumping off the stands."* Kathleen Currie, interview 2 with Ethel Payne, September 8, 1987, Women in Journalism Oral History Project of the Washington Press Club Foundation, p. 31.

175   *Sentences ranged from ten years at hard labor to death.* Richard Kluger, *Simple Justice* (New York: Alfred A. Knopf, 1976), p. 332.

175   *"It was just so explosive."* Currie, interview 2 with Ethel Payne, p. 32.

176   *"Come on home."* Currie, interview 2 with Ethel Payne, p. 33.

177   *"circulated not only in Chicago but also throughout the South."* David Halberstam, *The Fifties* (New York: Villard Books, 1993), p. 444.

177   *"at the center of a developing Negro protest."* Quoted in Gene Roberts and Hank Klibanoff, *The Race Beat* (New York: Alfred A. Knopf, 2006), p. 10.

177   *"feeling of security and belongingness."* Gunnar Myrdal, *An American Dilemma* (New York: Harper, 1944), p. 920.

177   *"had to curb me a little bit."* Currie, interview 2 with Ethel Payne, p. 34.

177   *Accused her of "show-boating."* Streitmatter, p. 532.

177   *"Who is that colored woman?"* Martin, p. 129.

178   *"was necessary to national defense."* Buckley, p. 338.

178   *Segregated units were dissolved.* Ibid., p. 367.

179   *"unduly high losses throughout the conflict."* Arnold Isaacs, *Vietnam Shadows* (Baltimore: Johns Hopkins University Press, 1997), p. 17.

179   *"unmistakably touched by the war."* Martin, p. 132.

179   *"terroristic methods of gang mobs."* Ethel Payne, "Vietnam: The History of An Abused People," *Chicago Defender,* 7–13 January 1967, p. 28.

180   *Assigned major responsibilities.* Ethel Payne, "It's Big Job, Paying Troops," *Daily Defender,* February 1967, p. 11.

180   *Duties of fifteen Chicago-area soldiers.* Ethel Payne, "Chicago GI's Doing Their Share in Vietnam Warfare," *Daily Defender,* 18 March 1967, p. 1.

180   *"which include highways and railroads."* Ethel Payne, "Mightiest Ship Afloat: We Visit the Enterprise," *Daily Defender,* 14 January 1967, p. 11.

180   *"lest it become totally poisoned."* Buckley, p. 408.

181   *Being used as "cannon fodder."* Martin, p. 135.

181   *"was very sensitive to criticism."* Ibid.

181   *"handling of racial problems in Vietnam."* Ibid.

181   *"had examined more of them."* Martin, p. 139.

182   *"high Government officials in Washington."* "Desmond FitzGerald Dies at 57, Chief of CIA Secret Operations," *Washington Post,* 24 July 1967, p. B2.

182   *"exceptional competence and stimulating leadership."* "Late CIA Aide Honored," *New York Times,* 16 September 1967, p. 24.

182   *"his views on Vietnam today."* FitzGerald interview, 12 November 2002.

182   *"in the way most women go after husbands."* Judy Bachrach, "Frankie FitzGerald—the Family Is Puzzled," *Washington Star,* 14 October 1979.

183   *"coherence and any organizational structure."* FFA, Box 3, Folder 4.

184   *"extended and bloody political conflict."* Frances FitzGerald, "Vietnam: The Future," *New York Review of Books,* 26 March 1970, p. 4.

184   *Identify Viet Cong operatives.* Karnow, p. 601.

184   *"early on became an extortionist's paradise."* Young, p. 213.

184   *Tapped through his brain until he died.* Ibid.

185   *"person was carrying a gun."* FitzGerald, *Fire in the Lake,* p. 413.

185   *"taken leave of his senses."* Stewart Alsop, *The Center* (New York: Harper & Row, 1968), p. 157.

186   *"by an act of imagination."* Frances FitzGerald, "A Nice Place to Visit," *New York Review of Books,* 13 March 1969, p. 28.

186   *"never the same after Tet."* Julie Kayan, quoted in Henry Maurer, ed., *Strange Ground* (New York: Avon Books, 1989), p. 481.

186   *"The ugliness was stunning."* FitzGerald interview, 12 November 2004.

186   *By bus, other times by car.* FitzGerald interview, 15 May 2007.

187   *"like water running out of the bath."* Ibid.

188   *"that remain untranslatable to one another."* Stanley Hoffmann, "Fire in the Lake," *New York*

Times Book Review, 27 August 1972, p. 1.

188   *"from those who make the decisions."* Taylor Branch, "Halberstam, FitzGerald and Ellsberg, Reporter, Poetess and Analyst," *Washington Monthly,* March 1973, p. 27.

188   *Newsweek* and *Time* reviews. Kevin P. Buckley, "Reporter at a Fire," *Newsweek,* 7 August 1972, p. 58; Martha Duffy, "The Big Attrit," *Time* 28 August 1972, p. 60.

188   *"Security Approved for this activity."* Frances FitzGerald's CIA file, FFA, Box 44.

188   *Asked "tough" questions.* FitzGerald interview, 12 November 2002.

189   *Critical appraisals of* Fire in the Lake. Tom Geoghegan, "For Tao and Countryside, *New Republic,* 16 September 1972, p. 28; David Brudnoy, "The New Anti-Vietnam Bible, *National Review,* 29 September 1972, p. 1968.

189   *FitzGerald's analysis was flawed.* Robert Komer letter to Stanley Hoffmann, 14 September 1972, FFA, Box 26, Folder 1.

189   *"entirely valuable and unique and permanent."* Martha Gellhorn letter to Frances FitzGerald, 1 January, 1973, FFA, Box 25, Folder 6.

189   *"as what was happening in Vietnam."* FitzGerald interview, 12 November 2002.

190   *"or protested against it."* Frances FitzGerald, "Vietnam and the Press," *More,* July 1975.

190   *"none of the same dramatic unities."* FFA, Notebook in Box 15.

190   *"Gen. Lavalle of NVN in winter."* Ibid.

191   *"And I agree."* Ibid.

Chapter 5

193   *Bordered on madness.* Kate Webb, author interview, 16–20 February 2002.

193   *"I'd be laughed out of court."* Kate Webb, "Highpockets," in *War Torn* (New York: Random House, 2002), p. 61.

193   *"like a butcher shop in Eden."* Philip Knightley, *The First Casualty* (New York: Harcourt Brace Jovanovich, 1975), p. 418.

193   *"even in combat fatigues."* "Transition," *Newsweek,* 3 May 1971, p. 12.

193   *Best military stories in Cambodia.* Donna Jones Born, "The Reporting of American Women Correspondents from the Vietnam War" (PhD diss., Michigan State University, 1987), p. 167.

194   *"and you smell bad anyway."* Peter Howe, *Shooting Under Fire* (New York: Artisan, 2002), p. 109.

194   *A cross between a waif and a school girl.* Douglas Robinson, "Missing U.P.I. Correspondent Is Reported Dead in Cambodia," *New York Times,* 21 April 1971, p. 18.

196   *"it was very complicated back then."* Webb interview.

196   *"we've had no doubt that we are Asians."* R. W. Apple, "Aussie Force Is Gallant—Learns American, Too," *New York Times,* 7 May 1966, p. 5.

197   *"the same argument they later made about South Vietnam."* Webb interview.

197   *"going for long evening walks together."* Rachel Miller, author interview, 21 March 2002.

197   *"certainly opened up different worlds."* Ibid.

198   *"trying to learn how to think."* Webb interview.

198   *"I blotted it out."* Vaudine England, "Being Where the Action Is," *Correspondent,* December–January 2002, p. 15.

198   *"So they shipped me off to the newsroom."* Webb interview.

199   *Peter Gladwyn stories.* Ibid.

199   *LBJ state visit to Australia.* "Johnson Renews His Offer to Halt Bombing in North," *New York Times,* 23 October 1966, p. 1.

200   *"Tomorrow's Hitler, Today's Johnson."* Tillman Durdin, "Throng in Sydney Greets Johnson But Some protest," *New York Times,* 22 October 1966, p. 1.

200   *"We had troops there."* Webb interview.

201   *"I was nuts."* Ibid.

201   *"certainly recall being worried."* Miller interview.

202   *"It was competition at its best."* John Macbeth, "Tributes," *Correspondent,* December 2001–January 2002, p. 16.

202   *"to be first with the story."* Peter Arnett, *Live from the Battlefield* (New York: Simon & Schuster,

1994), p. 302.

202 *"so that we may view her work."* Bryce Miller letter, National Archives accreditation files.

202 *"She made me a reporter."* Webb interview.

202 *Their dreams of covering the war.* "All the News Fit to Collect," *Manuscript Collection News,* no. 9 [Western Historical Manuscript Collection—Columbia, University of Missouri] (Winter 2004): p. 2.

202 *"as it affected American GIs.* Edward Behr, *Bearings* (New York: Viking Press, 1998), p. 241.

202 *"the official version of events."* Ann Bryan Mariano, "Vietnam Is Where I Found My Family," in *War Torn,* p. 42.

203 *"Mass in a leather jock strap."* Tony Clifton, "Tributes," *Correspondent,* December 2001–January 2002, p. 16.

204 *Despairing groan, "Oh, no."* Behr, p. 309.

204 *Street kids and military policemen.* Kate Webb, "Highpockets," in *War Torn,* p. 63.

205 *"so scared that I wet my pants."* Knightley, p. 418.

205 *"It came to represent separation."* Webb interview.

205 *"specializing in children's uniforms."* Behr, p. 270.

206 *"more than $200 worth of pictures."* Catherine Leroy, e-mail correspondence with the author, 28 March 2002.

206 *"Do you want to end up in a brothel?"* Ibid.

207 *"human wave" tactics.* William J. Duiker, *Ho Chi Minh* (New York: Hyperion, 2000), p. 454.

207 *Giap placed an army of 50,000.* George Herring, *America's Longest War,* 4th ed. (Boston: McGraw-Hill, 2002), p. 45.

208 *"I remember my father crying."* Leroy, e-mail correspondence.

208 *Encouraged France—its ally—to fight.* Bernard Fall, *Hell in a Very Small Place* (New York: Vintage Books, 1968), p. 461.

208 *"So I pushed the door of the Associated Press."* Leroy, e-mail correspondence.

208 *"It was just there."* Peter Howe, *Shooting Under Fire* (New York: Artisan, 2002), p. 98.

208 *"he is also a male chauvinist."* Leroy, e-mail correspondence.

209 *"what I was listening to all day long."* Ibid.

209 *Who did not "acquiesce to her demands."* National Archives, Catherine Leroy accreditation file.

209 *"not welcome aboard the ship again."* Letter from T. M. Fields to Col. Rodger Bankson, MACV, National Archives, accreditation files.

210 *In honor of her first combat jump.* George P. Hunt, "A Tiny Girl with Paratroopers' Wings," *Life,* 16 February, 1968, p. 3.

210 *"We were the same age and I loved them."* Howe, p. 100.

210 *"sleep for twenty, thirty hours straight."* Ibid.

211 *"the shock troops of two nations."* Pisor, p. 19.

211 *"very low and very primal."* Peter Howe, "The Death of a Fighter," *The Digital Journalist,* August 2006, http://www.digitaljournalist.org/issue0608/the-death-of-a-fighter.html.

211 *"it's a woman's eye."* Valerie Nelson, "Catherine Leroy, 60, War Photographer," *Los Angeles Times,* 11 July 2006, p. 10.

211 *"the worst Marine losses for any single battle."* Neil Sheehan, *A Bright Shining Lie* (New York: Random House, 1988), p. 649.

212 *"This is not a time for modesty.'"* Russ Havonrd, "Lensgirl Faces Peril to 'Make It,'" *Stars and Stripes,* 16 June 1967.

212 *"to hate war as I do."* *Observer,* 3 September 1967, p. 26.

212 *"Things always seemed to come in rushes."* Webb interview.

212 *"a great defeat for the enemy."* Hedrick Smith, "Westmoreland Says Ranks of Vietcong Thin Steadily," *New York Times,* 22 November 1965, p. 1.

212 *Put enemy losses at sixteen hundred.* William Hammond, *Public Affairs: The Military and the Media, 1962–1968* (Washington, DC: Center of Military History, U.S. Army, 1988), p. 332.

212 *On some undisclosed date.* Don Oberdorfer, *Tet!* (Garden City, NJ: Doubleday, 1971), p. 119.

214 *"First I had to undo my pot."* Webb interview.

214 *Near the presidential palace.* Arnett, p. 240.

215 *"in my pajamas in an armored car."* Behr, p. 265.

215   *Large-unit operations near South Vietnam's cities.* Hammond, p. 387.

215   *Weapons fire from the guerrillas.* Charles Mohr, "U.S. Aide in Embassy Villa Kills Guerrilla with Pistol," *New York Times*, 1 February 1968, p. 1.

215   *Landed on the rooftop.* Braestrup, p. 90.

216   *"we won."* Ibid., p. 120.

216   *"suffered a massive intelligence failure."* Hammond, p. 382.

216   *"never able to enter the Chancery building."* Oberdorfer, p. 35.

216   *"The details of it are all a blur."* Webb interview.

218   *Vietnamese woman "saved our lives."* Howe, p. 102.

218   *"so we'll be running along now."* Catherine Leroy, "A tense interlude with the enemy in Hue," *Life,* 16 February 1968, p. 22.

219   *As the helicopter carrying her husband.* Harvey Meyerson, "Choppers," *Look,* 30 April 1968, p. 92.

219   *"discrimination by life and death."* Catherine Leroy, "This is that war," *Look,* 16 May 1968, p. 10.

219   *"as quickly and honorably as possible."* "An Editorial," *Look,* 16 May 1968, p. 33.

220   *"over-exposed and in harm's way."* Leroy, e-mail correspondence.

220   *Stop nosing around in the black market story.* Webb interview.

221   *Chaining two tire rims to the corpse.* Homer Bigart, "Beret Affair: Step by Step," *New York Times,* 6 October 1969, p. 1.

221   *"cannot condone unlawful acts of the kind alleged."* Ibid.

222   *Diminished the enemy with such hypotheses.* Frances FitzGerald, *Fire in the Lake* (New York: Atlantic Monthly Press, 1972), p. 139.

222   *Less than a month after his inauguration.* William Shawcross, *Sideshow* (New York: Simon & Schuster, 1979), p. 24.

223   *"trying to get captured and released."* John Laurence, *The Cat from Hue* (New York: PublicAffairs, 2002), p. 665.

223   *"I don't believe that."* Webb interview.

223   *Dead or missing and presumed dead.* Kurt Volkert and T. Jeff Williams, *A Cambodian Odyssey* (Lincoln, Nebraska: Writer's Showcase, 2001), p. 9.

224   *"the world exploded."* Kate Webb, *On the Other Side: 23 Days With the Viet Cong* (New York: Quadrangle Books, 1971), p. 9.

225   *"atmosphere of war and enmity."* Elizabeth Pond, e-mail correspondence with the author, 23 June 1997.

225   *"If you run from the planes we will shoot."* Kate Webb. *On the Other Side of the War,* United Press International, 1971, p. 7.

226   *"scars from their toes to their knees."* Ibid., 40.

226   *Just hours before an enemy attack.* Elizabeth Pond, "We Are Part of the Revolution," *Christian Science Monitor,* 24 June 1970, p. 1.

227   *"especially progressive" journalists.* Elizabeth Pond, "Out from Cambodian Captivity," *Christian Science Monitor,* 22 June 1970.

227   *"working for the American imperialists?"* Webb, p. 104.

228   *"You cannot be a neutral observer in this war."* Ibid.

229   *"that we had never imagined possible."* Elizabeth Pond, "Why Us? Asks Journalist Freed from Cambodia Detention," *Christian Science Monitor,* 26 June 1970, p. 1.

229   *"a vast capacity to sacrifice for the cause."* Elizabeth Pond, "Journalists' Captors: 'We Are Part of the Revolution,'" *Christian Science Monitor,* 24 June 1970, p. 1.

230   *"direct thought messages to me."* Miller interview.

231   *"have reached its successful conclusion."* Richard Dudman, *40 Days with the Enemy* (New York: Liveright, 1971), p. 144.

231   *"consider you as our friends."* Ibid., p. 145.

232   *"be very brave, but tell the truth."* "Kate Webb's Story," *Newsweek,* 24 May 1971, p. 59.

232   *"shot or fall into a government ambush."* Webb, p. 149.

232   *A young Cambodian soldier gave her a light.* Ibid., p. 153.

233   *Had the greatest impact.* Richard Dudman, author interview, 28 September 2007.

233   *"And if precedent, what kind of precedent?"* Elizabeth Pond, "Freed journalist's question 'Why us?'" *Christian Science Monitor,* 26 June 1970.

234   *An risked exposure and certain death on behalf of an American colleague.* Pham Xuan An, author interview, 22 February 2002.

234   *For all his years in Saigon.* Larry Berman, *Perfect Spy* (New York: HarperCollins/Smithsonian Books, 2007), p. 39.

234   *"I was terrified."* Morley Safer, *Flashbacks* (New York: Random House, 1990), p. 179.

234   *"I could not live quietly."* An interview.

235   *"I am forever in his debt."* Webb interview.

235   *Had racked up mourning her death.* Craig Tomlinson, "Kate Webb prefers anonymity to fame," *Editor & Publisher,* 19 July 1971, p. 20.

235   *"what a bloody awful waste."* "Kate Webb's Story," *Newsweek,* 24 May 1971, p. 59.

236   *The idea was unthinkable.* Webb interview.

236   *"I was a living martini."* Ibid.

237   *"puts you back to middle size."* Ibid.

Chapter 6

238   *"Very funny, Horst."* Liz Trotta, *Fighting for Air* (Columbia: University of Missouri Press, 1994), p. 125.

239   *"Either you get it or you don't."* Liz Trotta, "Of Arms and the Woman," *New York Times,* 15 December 1968.

240   *Cover stories in the countryside.* Garrick Utley, *You Should Have Been Here Yesterday* (New York: Public Affairs, 2000), p. 38.

240   *"by the time it reached New York City."* John Sharkey, author interview, 14 June 2002.

241   *The session had been "a waste of time."* William Prochnau, *Once Upon a Distant War* (New York: Times Books, 1995), p. 179.

241   *Covering combat "tells you absolutely nothing."* Donna Jones Born, "The Reporting of American Women Foreign Correspondents from the Vietnam War" (PhD diss., Michigan State University, 1987), p. 140.

241   *"how little of it had been used."* Ibid., 141.

241   *Asked her to join the staff in Saigon.* Anne Morriooy Merick, "My Love Affair with Vietnam," in *War Torn* (New York: Random House, 2002), p. 92.

242   *"little pieces of bang-bang every night."* Christine Martin, "Women Correspondents in Vietnam: Historical Analysis and Oral Histories" (master's thesis, University of Maryland, 1988), p. 157.

242   *"Just an endless expanse of blanched bodies."* Trotta, p. 128.

243   *And she prayed to him.* Liz Trotta, author interview, 30 April 2002.

244   *"share the spotlight with anyone."* Ibid.

244   *"introduced more people to ballet."* Mary Clarke and David Vaughn, eds., *The Encyclopedia of Dance and Ballet* (London: Pitman, 1977), p. 308.

244   *His edicts were non-negotiable.* Trotta interview, 30 April 2002.

244   *"He just did not understand handouts."* Ibid.

245   *"How is it that a Department of Economics."* William F. Buckley, *God and Man at Yale* (Chicago: Regnery, 1951), p. 96.

245   *"It's all going to dry one day."* Trotta interview, 30 April 2002.

246   *"Catholic, married, and rich."* Trotta, p. 71.

246   *"the King" was her fiancé.* Ibid.

246   *"and philosophy professors."* Trotta interview, 30 April 2002.

247   *"That ignorance was gigantic."* Ibid.

247   *"you've got a deadline approach to journalism."* Richard Duncan, author interview, 31 May 2002.

247   *"don't forget to read [what's on] the top of the desk."* Jack Shepherd, author interview, 25 May 2002.

248   *Charge through a wall for a story.* Christopher Wren, author interview, 30 May 2002, and Shepherd interview.

249   *Joined . . . the Young Americans for Freedom.* Trotta, p. 19.

249   *George Barrett as Trotta's mentor.* Ibid., p. 17.

250   *Groucho Marx, for example, remained outcasts.* Reuven Frank, *Out of Thin Air* (New York: Simon & Schuster, 1991), p. 41.

250   *Shed its identity as a derivative of radio.* David Halberstam, *The Powers That Be* (New York: Alfred A. Knopf, 1979), p. 408.

250   *Television ownership grew even faster.* Gene Roberts and Hank Klibanoff, *The Race Beat* (New York: Alfred A. Knopf, 2006), p. 156.

250   *"you would be a natural on television."* Trotta, p. 17.

251   *Greenwich Village neighborhood.* Elizabeth Trotta, "Title I on Trial" (master's thesis, Columbia University, 1961).

251   *"all that parochial training."* Trotta, p. 18.

251   *Judged the antiwar crowd.* Trotta interview, 26 June 2002.

251   *Downward spiral that continued.* Edwin Emery, *The Press and America* (Englewood Cliffs, NJ: Prentice-Hall, 1972), p. 623.

251   *"I belonged in the main newsroom."* Liz Trotta, 26 June 2002.

252   *"It's not a job for a woman."* Trotta, p. 21.

252   *Dropped "for lack of space."* Antoinette May, *Witness to War* (New York: Beaufort Books, 1983), p. 231.

252   *"That woman will never piss outside the United States again."* David Halberstam, author interview, 7 January 1998.

252   *His empowerment of the Green Berets.* Trotta interview, 26 June 2002.

252   *"don't let people use you."* Elizabeth Trotta, "Talent Rubs Off on Judy's Teen Daughter," *Newsday*, Liz Trotta private papers.

253   *"Go get yourself a job."* Trotta, p. 24.

253   *"It was a defining moment."* Jack Shepherd, author interview, 25 May 2002.

253   *"entitled the holder to two dances."* Liz Trotta, "Many Dimes a Dance," *Newsday*, 25 July 1963, sec. C, p. 1.

254   *A city License Commission hearing.* Gay Talese, "Dime-a-Dance Girls Twirling Into Oblivion, Employers Fear," *New York Times*, 16 January 1964, p. B1.

254   *"people wept openly."* Kenneth Byerly, Elizabeth Trotta, and Richard Kwartler, "Long Island Stunned, Grieves with Nation," *Newsday*, 23 November 1963, p. 7.

254   *"they get jittery and restless."* Elizabeth Trotta, "Skilled Team of Geldings Draws Caissons," *Newsday*, 26 November 1963, p. 2.

256   *"to handle the woman's angle."* Marion Marzolf, *Up from the Footnote* (New York: Hastings House, 1977), p. 157.

256   *"Back then you didn't have to look like a mermaid."* Trotta interview, 23 March 2007.

257   *"from a woman's voice than from a man's."* Marzolf, p. 175.

257   *According to editors who responded.* Ibid., p. 149.

257   *"Chase the bastard to hell."* Trotta, p. 30.

257   *"'Well, at least she's not a lollipop.'"* Ibid., p. 31.

258   *"allowed in the bedroom and the kitchen."* Trotta, p. 34.

258   *"NBC's gotten so desperate, they've sent a girl."* Ibid., p. 66.

259   *"I don't work on women's stories."* Ibid., p. 58.

259   *"I had no idea anyone would feel this way."* Ibid.

259   *Her heroes, she confessed, "were guys."* Trotta interview, 26 June 2002.

259   *"less glamorous issues of pay equality."* Trotta, p. 206.

261   *"that's the point of the exercise."* Ibid., p. 57.

261   *"be on the first plane back if."* Ibid.

261   *"are out covering a war."* Ron Steinman, author interview, June 2002.

261   *"And I went on a campaign."* Julia Edwards, *Women of the World* (Boston: Houghton Mifflin Publishing, 1988), p. 232.

261   *Probably one of his worst mistakes.* Frank, p. 315.

261   *"and I said, 'Why not?'"* Reuven Frank, author interview, 20 June 2002.

262 *"because I thought it was so funny."* Trotta interview, 26 June 2002.

262 *"It breaks everyone's heart."* Trotta interview, 30 April 2002.

263 *"it flies in the face of logic."* Les Crystal, author interview, 17 July 2002.

263 *"'She's going to pull it off.'"* Wren interview, 30 May 2002.

263 *Refinement of the Vietnamese people had charmed.* Carl Rollyson, *Nothing Ever Happens to the Brave* (New York: St. Martin's Press, 1990), p. 292.

263 *"the balance began to shift."* Garrick Utley, author interview, 13 June 2002.

263 *Spending around $5 million between them.* Godfrey Hodgson, *America in Our Time* (New York: Vintage Books, 1976), p. 149.

264 *"people who actually got high on battle."* Steinman interview.

264 *"grotesque, funny and terrifying"* night. Trotta, p. 88.

265 *"one of the bravest correspondents of all."* Jones Born, p. 142.

265 *"We went to black,"* Peter Braestrup, *Big Story*, p. 100.

266 *"I wanted him right nearby."* Utley interview.

267 *"it straight and dully competent."* Trotta, p. 116.

268 *"they'll say it's because I'm a woman."* Trotta, p. 123.

268 *"casually scramble over and look."* Trotta interview, 30 April 2002.

269 *"bad guys overran the perimeter."* Trotta, p. 142.

269 *"like screwing six women at the same time."* Ibid., 133.

270 *Ran combat footage on the evening news.* William M. Hammond, *Public Affairs: The Military and the Media 1968–1973* (Washington, DC: Center of Military History, 1996), p. 103.

270 *"growing weary of battle."* Trotta, p. 157.

270 *"and it will always be."* Liz Trotta, "Hey, Fellows, Chet and David Have Sent a Woman," *TV Guide,* 19 April, 1969, p. 10.

270 *Two minutes and forty-five seconds.* Trotta, 161.

271 *"Combat wasn't as lethal as thinking about these children could be."* Trotta, p. 134.

271 *"I never complained about money."* Trotta, p. 132.

271 *"'That's just the way she is.'"* Maj. Thomas P. Malloy, memorandum, 10 December 1969, "NBC News Team Visit to Ban Me Thout," U.S. Army accreditation files.

271 *"Our loathing was mutual."* Trotta, p. 165.

272 *"no time for the flirty demure stuff."* Ibid., p. 166.

273 *The senator . . . turned scarlet and snarled.* Ibid., p. 181.

274 *"I missed covering the story."* Ibid., p. 185.

274 *"The war was over."* Ibid., 190.

274 *"He was a punk."* Trotta interview, 1 June 2004.

275 *"on the Perrier-with-lime circuit."* Trotta, p. 362.

275 *"dealt into it for themselves."* Ibid., p. 162.

276 *"She was just too much trouble."* Gloria Clyne, author interview, 30 May 2002.

276 *"doing the manly thing."* Trotta, p. 176.

276 *"We'll see."* Ibid., p. 237.

277 *"or I'll knock your head off."* Ibid., p. 239.

277 *"God, let's pray they keep her."* Ibid., p. 219.

278 *"TV journalism as it was supposed to be."* Ibid., p. 269.

279 *"I was devastated."* Trotta interview, 30 April 2002.

279 *"skills of Job in drag."* Trotta, p. 280.

Chapter 7

281 *"It may be that we just joked about it."* Ralph Blumenthal, author interview, 9 February 1999.

281 *Terence Smith has no memory of Emerson with a rifle.* Terence Smith, author interview, 4 January 2006.

281 *"a malignant city."* Gloria Emerson, *Winners & Losers* (New York: Random House, 1976), p. 361.

281 *"you could never quite sort out the horrors."* Gloria Emerson, "Hey Lady, What Are You Doing Here?" *McCall's,* August 1971, p. 61.

282 *"Ah, it was a paradise."* Gloria Emerson, "French Living in Saigon Cherish Old Memories," *New York Times,* 5 March 1970, p. 3.

282 *"She was thrilled to be back."* Smith interview, 23 July 1999.

282 *"schizophrenic" hemlines.* Gloria Emerson, "From Ungaro, Soft Angles and Curves," *New York Times,* 2 January 1970, p. 40.

282 *"the fresher kind of prettiness."* Gloria Emerson, "Givenchy, 1970: The Approach Is Positive, the Look Is Softer," *New York Times,* 31 January 1970, p. 22.

282 *"The* Times *has sent its first woman."* Times Talk, "Our far-flung correspondents." Jan/Feb. 1970, p. 3.

283 *Appointed a woman to the Times editorial board.* Susan Tifft and Alex Jones, *The Trust* (Boston: Little, Brown, 1999), p. 235.

283 *He was offered the assignment.* David Halberstam, *The Making of a Quagmire* (New York: Random House, 1964), p. 23.

283 *"you have to get me out of here."* Smith interview, 23 July 1999.

283 Her familiar "poetic fury." Gloria Emerson, "Remembering Women Correspondents in Vietnam," in *War Torn* (New York: Random House, 2002).

284 *Willing to risk the wrath of generals.* Betsy Wade, ed. *Forward Positions* (Fayetteville: University of Arkansas Press, 1992), p. xv.

284 *Scorn for members of the* Times *foreign desk.* William Prochnau, *Once Upon a Distant War* (New York: Times Books, 1995), p. 179.

284 *"It was not unlike joining the army."* Gloria Emerson, *Some American Men* (New York: Simon & Schuster, 1985), p. 85.

285 *Larger than that of any newspaper in England.* Philip Knightley, *The First Casualty* (New York: Harcourt Brace Jovanovich, 1975), p. 114.

285 *"only bad odors and no modern comforts."* Meyer Berger, *The Story of the New York Times* (New York: Simon & Schuster, 1951), p. 567.

285 *"serve as a guardian of freedom."* Tifft and Jones, p. 235.

286 *"I can't fight this war without the support of the* New York Times," Tifft and Jones, p. 442.

286 *"That young Foreign Service officer was Richard Holbrooke."* Peter Grose, author interview, 11 August 1999.

287 *"She had a cyclopean eye."* Denis Cameron, author interview, 16 July 2005.

287 *"Only the wind and the insects of Africa."* Gloria Emerson, "Enugu, Nigeria: Silence in War's Wake," *New York Times,* 13 October 1968, p. 1.

287 *"Welcome to Timbuktu."* Gloria Emerson, "In That Far, Faraway Timbuktu," *New York Times,* 2 November 1968, p. 17.

288 *"a city of constant and unpredictable outbursts."* Gloria Emerson, "Tear Gas Breaks Up Protestant March in Ulster," *New York Times,* 6 October 1969, p. 1.

288 *"I don't sleep good."* Gloria Emerson, "In Belfast, the Time of Troubles Becomes a Family's Way of Life," *New York Times,* 13 October 1969, p. 58.

288 *"had to fight like hell to get the assignment."* Craig Whitney, e-mail correspondence with the author, 31 October 1998.

288 *"I do not recall anything particularly special."* A. M. Rosenthal, letter to the author, 16 October 1999.

288 *"The record speaks for itself."* Terence Smith, author interview, 23 July 1999.

288 *"inner struggle on her part."* Seymour Topping, author interview, 16 October 1999.

289 *"probably not anxious to send a woman to Vietnam."* James Greenfield, author interview, 20 November 1998.

289 *"and at last was able to do it."* Emerson, *Winners & Losers,* p. ix.

289 *"I believe I surprised him."* Smith interview, 4 January 2006.

289 *"would be a Communist with a mink coat."* Nancy Moran, author interview, 10 April 1999.

290 *"That was the lie I told myself."* Gloria Emerson, *Patriots,* Christian Appy, ed. (New York: Viking, 2003), p. 371.

290 *"leaving would be the cure."* Emerson, *Winners & Losers,* p. 109.

290 *"It was very Graham Greene."* Bernard Weinraub, author interview, 9 August 1999.

291 *"you'd get the operator out of bed."* Alvin Shuster, author interview, undated.

291 *"arrive every day with yesterday's newspaper."* Grose interview.

292 *"the Nazi bureau."* Smith interview, 23 July 1999.

292 *"Ralph, what shall we do?"* Blumenthal interview.

292 *"She was a force of nature."* Ibid.

293 *"another stupid white male who doesn't know anything."* James Sterba, author interview, 25 July 2005.

293 *"but no fun if the squirmee was you."* James Sterba, e-mail correspondence with the author, 26 July 2005.

293 *"She was so exotic and womanly."* Iver Peterson, author interview, 14 July 1999.

294 *"Night Convoy Moving Cautiously."* Gloria Emerson, "Even the Postcards in Saigon Depict G.I.s in Battle," *New York Times,* 7 March 1970, p. 5.

294 *"she should have been there long before."* Shuster interview.

294 *"We were all so proud to be working with her."* Craig Whitney, e-mail correspondence with the author, 5 July 2005.

294 *"Gloria was always wounded by the editing process."* Smith interview, 23 July 1999.

295 *"She was a fairly flamboyant figure."* Ibid.

295 *A new level of hostility between the two groups.* William Hammond, *Public Affairs: The Military and the Media 1968–1973* (Washington, DC: U.S. Army Center for Military History, 1996), p. 359.

295 *"She was a fairly flamboyant figure."* Smith interview, 23 July 1999.

295 *"hit Saigon like a goddamned storm."* Richard Pyle, author interview, 24 July 2007.

295 *"The newspaper of record, bless its heart."* Iver Peterson, author interview, 20 November 1998.

296 *"They were stories without any soul."* Weinraub interview, 23 June 1999.

296 *"Who is that woman?"* Blumenthal interview.

296 *"Gloria was the Maureen Dowd of her time."* Fox Butterfield, author interview, 14 July 1999.

296 *"quickly given up trying to rein in Gloria."* Sydney Schanberg, author interview, 7 April 2000.

297 *Changing "the color of corpses"* and *"a war of aggression fought by a puppet army."* William H. Chafe, *The Unfinished Journey* (New York: Oxford University Press, 1986), p. 390.

297 *"divert information on the air strikes from normal channels."* Stanley Karnow, *Vietnam: A History* (New York: Viking Press, 1983), p. 592.

297 *"a calming, psycho-sexual experience."* Sydney Schanberg, "Glorious Gloria: war is enough to curl her hair." *Times Talk,* 2 November 1970.

298 *A year and nine months later, she relented.* Schanberg interview.

298 *"Cameron didn't have both feet on the ground."* Ibid.

299 *"almost as though I had an appetite for fear."* Cameron interview, 12 and 15 July 2005.

299 *"Gloria was a smart and worldly person."* Smith interview, 16 October 1999.

299 *"Find another story."* Schanberg interview.

299 *"if they stopped us, we were dead."* Cameron interview, 15 July 2005.

299 *And moved to a pagoda guarded by the Cambodian army.* Gloria Emerson, "Prestige Termed Reds' Aim in Angkor Wat Area," *New York Times,* 12 June 1970, p. 1.

300 *"facing the consequences and they are not good."* Gloria Emerson, "Cambodians Now Expecting Long Years of Strife," *New York Times,* 13 June 1970, p. 3.

300 *Was less willing to see only evil in America's policy.* Cameron interview, 15 July 2005.

300 *"He did not even seem to like them."* Gloria Emerson, "This Symbol of American Power in Vietnam," *New York Times,* 7 April 1975, p. 31.

301 *"John Pareham, what are you doing here? He died."* Gloria Emerson, "Hey Lady, What Are You Doing Here?" *McCall's,* August 1971, p. 61.

301 *The illegitimate daughter of Nellie Bly.* Gerald Hickey, author interview, 14 October 2005.

302 *"You and I are ghosts."* Emerson, *Winners & Losers,* p. 279.

302 *"We are so ethnocentric."* Gloria Emerson, "After Decade in Vietnam: An Anthropologist's View," *New York Times,* 25 April 1971, p. 3.

303 *"there she is, the sob sister."* Hickey interview, 14 October 2005.

303 *"Gloria's father was a problem for her."* Ibid.

303   *"not a Vietnamese ending."* Gloria Emerson, "We Are All 'Bui Doi,'" *Reporting Vietnam, Part II* (New York: The Library of America, 1998), p. 257.

303   *"then fend off the inquisitor."* David Halberstam, author interview, 7 January 1998.

304   *"but never really inquired too much."* Moran interview.

304   *"You ask Gloria serious questions."* Don Luce, author interview, 9 September 1998.

304   *An inconsolable and disruptive weeper.* Gloria Emerson, "A Few Words on Crying," *Esquire,* June 1974, p. 113.

304   *"desperate breed of cigarette smokers."* Gloria Emerson, "A New Way to Quit Smoking," *Reader's Digest,* October 1963, p. 100.

304   *Dinner party at New York's El Morocco.* Gloria Emerson, "Jacqueline Onassis at 45," *McCall's,* July 1974, p. 91.

305   *John Kennedy's sexual magnetism.* Seymour Hersh, *The Dark Side of Camelot* (Boston: Little, Brown, 1997), p. 24.

305   *"the 'best and brightest' Harvard, etc. crowd."* Craig Whitney, e-mail correspondence with the author, 5 July 2005.

305   *"she became a girlfriend, sister, and mother."* Halberstam interview.

306   *"Brigadier General Forrester's conspicuous gallantry."* Gloria Emerson, "Army to Conduct Inquiry on Medal," *New York Times,* 22 October 1970, p. 6.

306   *"think of how it will affect the mothers."* Emerson, *Winners & Losers,* p. 251.

306   *"The real victims of men are other men."* Gloria Emerson, "Arms and the Woman," *Harpers,* April 1972, p. 40.

307   *"a no starch man."* Gloria Emerson, "Unstarchy U.S. General in Vietnam," *New York Times,* 16 February 1971, p. 32.

307   *"totally inaccurate, totally distorted."* Douglas Brinkley, *Tour of Duty: John Kerry and the Vietnam War* (New York: William Morrow, 2004), p. 397.

307   *"people who were real rats and charlatans."* Malcolm Browne, author interview, 22 December 1997.

307   *"high standards, but they were arbitrary."* Butterfield interview.

308   *What life would be like without an eye.* Gloria Emerson, "A Saigon Captain Sees War Devouring His Life," *New York Times,* 21 July 1970, p. 14.

308   *"do you hear me, Thu?"* Gloria Emerson, "A South Vietnamese Widow Mourns Her Only Son, Killed in Cambodia," *New York Times,* 17 July 1970, p. 2.

308   *"that bad news (for our side) is good news."* Gerry Kirk, "As Seen by Gloomy Gloria," *National Review,* 20 April 1971, p. 426.

308   *"the most subtle and poignant reporting."* Robert Shaplen, "The Challenge Ahead," *Columbia Journalism Review* (Winter 1970–1971), p. 40.

309   *"an atrocious way to treat human beings."* Gloria Emerson, "Americans Find Brutality in South Vietnamese Jail," *New York Times,* 7 July 1970, p. 3.

309   *"a people who loved their land, their trees, their poetry."* Emerson, *Winners & Losers,* p. 350.

310   *"put him under police surveillance."* Luce interview, 18 September 1998.

310   *"at least morally responsible."* Thomas Hamilton, "Red Cross Aide Comments," *New York Times,* 10 July 1970, p. 10.

310   *"to see what happened afterwards."* Luce interview, 18 September 1998.

311   *"understanding of people's pride."* Ibid.

311   *"her heart was always wrapped up in children."* Moran interview.

311   *"Her heart went out to people."* Blumenthal interview.

311   *"You've got to get me out of here."* Schanberg interview.

312   *"more important than I was."* Emerson, *Winners & Losers,* p. 13.

312   *"was totally on a spiritual level."* Weinraub interview, 9 August 1999.

312   *"He had a musical ear."* Craig Whitney, "The Friend Who Stayed Behind," *Times Talk,* January/February, 1998.

313   *"I never worried so much."* Emerson, *Winners & Losers,* p. 309.

314   *"the ideological sins of the fathers."* Craig Whitney, author interview, 5 July 2005.

314   *"those I have worked with, liked and loved."* Emerson, *Winners & Losers,* p. 13.

314   *"fairly simple tricks of the trade."* Butterfield interview.

315 *"Long Lady send message.'"* Moran interview.

315 *He knew very little about the war.* Gloria Emerson, "In Vietnam, a Weary Look Back at a Harsh Decade," *New York Times*, 1 January 1971, p. 3.

316 *10 to 15 percent of enlisted men . . . were heroin users.* Alfred W. McCoy, *The Politics of Heroin in Southeast Asia* (New York: Harper & Row, 1972), p. 181.

316 *Children were making small fortunes.* Gloria Emerson, "G.I.s in Vietnam Get Heroin Easily," *New York Times*, 25 February 1971.

317 *A new offensive in the war.* Craig Whitney, "U.S. Saturation Air Raids Continuing in South Laos," *New York Times*, 30 January 1971, p. 1.

317 *"any South Vietnamese incursion."* Tillman Durdin, "Laotians Report No Word of an Incursion by Saigon," *New York Times*, 1 February 1971, p. 10.

317 *"destroyed by B-52 bombers."* Ralph Blumenthal, "Heavy Toll Reported," *New York Times*, 1 February 1971, p. 3.

317 *"The mama-san who cleans my hooch."* Ralph Blumenthal, "U.S. News Blackout in Saigon Tried to Keep Even Its Existence Secret," *New York Times*, 5 February 1971, p. 10.

318 *The "dewy" part was misspelled.* "Name of Drive by Allies Ties to Wet '60 Battle," *New York Times*, 6 February 1971, p. 4.

318 *Underground tunnels laced the terrain.* Gloria Emerson, "Khesanh Then and Now: Dust and Mud and Airstrip on a Windswept Plateau," *New York Times*, 5 February 1971, p. 11.

318 *"we cannot fight them in Laos."* Gloria Emerson, "Copters Return From Laos with the Dead," *New York Times*, 3 March 1971, p. 3.

318 *Poor performance of South Vietnamese pilots.* Gloria Emerson, "Saigon's Copter Pilots Are Criticized," *New York Times*, 5 March 1971, p. 1.

319 *"the wounded cried out for grenades."* Gloria Emerson, "Spirit of Saigon's Army Shaken in Laos," *New York Times*, 28 March 1971, p. 1.

319 *"Will my parents treat me the same?"* Gloria Emerson, "'Who could Conceive of This?' Asks Army Doctor at Khesanh," *New York Times*, 4 April 1971, p. 2.

320 *"massive U.S. air support prevented a complete disaster."* Gabriel Kolko, *Anatomy of a War* (New York: New Press, 1994), p. 74.

320 *"recruiting sergeants arrived at battle sites."* Sterba interview.

320 *"You cannot turn it down."* Shuster interview.

321 *Provided a little psychological comfort.* Terence Smith, e-mail correspondence with the author, 29 November 2005.

321 *Drugs were standard fare, too.* Ibid.

321 *"had a fluffed up feeling."* Emerson, *Winners & Losers*, p. 322.

322 *"a young, witty, wildly good-looking."* Ibid., p. 321.

322 *Evelyn Waugh's novels captured them.* Hickey interview, 14 September 2005.

322 *"with utter boredom."* Knightley, pp. 399–400.

323 *"no longer fighting the war."* Gloria Emerson, "'Grunts' Wonder When Their Fighting Became 'Defensive,'" *New York Times*, 22 January 1972, p. 9.

323 *Would the government keep its many promises.* Gloria Emerson, "Refugees in Quangtri Begin Shift to South," *New York Times*, 10 January 1972, p. 3.

323 *"It does not make any difference."* Gloria Emerson, "A Jailed Crusader Loses Hope in Vietnam," *New York Times*, 2 January 1972, p. 3.

324 *"died from malnutrition."* Gloria Emerson, "Part Black—and Orphans," *New York Times*, 7 February 1972, p. 26.

324 *Preferred color . . . was "dead white."* Bernadine Morris, "The Mood for Summer: Fashions That Are Romantic," *New York Times*, 7 February 1972, p. 26.

324 *"Give me voice or give me beeper."* Gloria Emerson, "Getting Back," *Esquire*, December 1972, p. 179.

325 *"the American military have no balls."* David Patrick, Columbia's Social Diary, http://www.newyorksocialdiary.com/socialdiary/2004/08_23_04/socialdiary08_23_04.php.

325 *"acute lack of forgetfulness."* Emerson, *Winners & Losers*, p. 9.

326 *One of the war's many casualties.* Phyllis Levin, author interview, 24 October 2001.

Chapter 8

327   *"If this is the last letter."* Laura Palmer, "Mystery Is the Precinct Where I Found Peace," in *War Torn* (New York: Random House, 2002), p. 265.

327   *Long and passionate opposition to the war.* Ibid., p. 253.

327   *Asked Paul Scanlon.* Ibid., p. 265.

328   *"They are good souvenirs."* Malcolm Brown, "A Deep Bitterness Toward U.S.," *New York Times,* 5 April 1975, p. 1.

328   *"14 million acres of defoliated forest."* Gloria Emerson, "Operation Babylift," *New Republic,* April 1975, p. 8.

329   *"help swing American public opinion."* Fox Butterfield, "Orphans of Vietnam: One Last Agonizing Issue," *New York Times,* 13 April 1975, p. 1.

329   *"This is war, this is real."* Laura Palmer, author interview, 20 August 2007.

329   *Fled the city shortly before the end.* Ann Bryan Mariano, "Vietnam Is Where I Found My Family," in *War Torn,* p. 48.

330   *A collection of lawsuits and official complaints.* Lindsay Van Gelder, "Women vs. The New York Times," *Ms.,* September 1978, p. 56.

331   *"best damned diplomatic correspondent."* Nan Robertson, *The Girls in the Balcony* (New York: Random House, 1992), p. 152.

331   *"you married the wrong man."* Ibid., p. 57.

332   *"journalism sounded like a lot more fun."* Kathleen Currie, Interview 1 with Flora Lewis, November 28, 1990, Washington, DC, for the Women in Journalism Oral History Project of the Washington Press Club Foundation, in the Oral History Collection of the National Press Club Archives, Washington, DC, p. 9.

332   *"women had no place in the world of diplomacy."* Craig Whitney, "Flora Lewis, 79, Dies; Keen Observer of World Affairs," *New York Times,* 3 June 2002, p. B7.

333   *"If we really wanted you."* Flora Lewis, author interview, 19 June 1997.

333   *"only in a convoy and not at night."* Kathleen Currie, Interview 3 with Flora Lewis, December 2, 1990, Washington DC, for the Women in Journalism Oral History Project of the Washington Press Club Foundation, in the Oral History Collection of the National Press Club Archives, Washington, DC, p. 67.

333   *Helicopters would win the war.* Lewis interview.

334   *"He simply didn't understand."* Ibid.

334   *"the alternative way of doing the job."* Flora Lewis, "Viet Democracy Wounded, Some Hope Fatally," *Newsday,* 12 February 1968, p. 26.

334   *"rather than for a last-ditch gamble."* Flora Lewis, "New Strategy Shows Hanoi's Optimism," *Newsday,* 14 February 1968, p. 4.

334   *"We need to defend Khe Sanh."* Lewis interview.

335   *"that broke France's will to fight."* Flora Lewis, "Red Delay at Khe Sanh Increases U.S. Anxiety," *Newsday,* 21 February 1968, p. 34.

335   *"America's capacity to sustain the war."* Lewis interview.

336   *"a tremendous sign of economic improvement."* Ibid.

336   *"they've let me ride my water buffalo."* Robertson, p. 146.

336   *"'Ha, ha—we have a woman bureau chief.'"* Ibid., p. 153.

337   *Three were women.* Ibid., p. 182.

337   *"would bring a difference."* Flora Lewis, "No Sign of Progress, but They're Glad to Be Back," *New York Times,* 16 July 1972, p. E3.

337   *"the Saigon army."* Flora Lewis, "Mrs. Binh Says Key Issue In Talks Is Saigon's Rule," *New York Times,* 12 August, 1972, p. 1.

338   *"'be prepared to stay forever.'"* Palmer, "Mystery," in *War Torn,* p. 254.

338   *"to a heroic band of women at* The New York Times.*"* Ibid., p. 255.

339   *"a feeling of solidarity and oneness."* Laura Palmer, unpublished manuscript, Laura Palmer's personal papers made available to the author, p. 2.

339   *"stopped believing anything could change."* Ibid., p. 3.

339   *"in the mix of big adventures."* Palmer interview, 11 September 2007.

339   *History had waited for her.* Ibid.
340   *"cease-fire or an attack on Saigon."* Laura Palmer, undated letter to Helen Palmer, Palmer's personal papers.
340   *"You are too feminine."* Tracy Wood, "Spies, Lovers and Prisoners of War," in *War Torn*, p. 234.
341   *"I hear you're hot shit."* Richard Pyle, author interview, 24 July 2007.
342   "We needed a different eye and ear." Pyle interview.
342   *"A tiny woman with big hair, baby wrists."* Tad Bartimus, "In Country," in *War Torn*, p. 205.
342   *Feeling rather like a "war tourist."* Lederer, "My First War," in *War Torn*, p. 168.
342   *Two women were stoned.* Edith Lederer, author interview, 19 October 2007.
343   *"You are too valuable."* Lederer, "My First War," in *War Torn*, p. 159.
343   *"how smart she made me look."* Pyle interview.
343   *"the greatest war bureau ever."* Horst Faas, author interview, 15 October 2007.
343   *"the equivalent of a battlefield victory."* Lederer, "My First War," in *War Torn*, p. 168.
343   *"what has Gallagher sent us now."* Ibid.
344   *"muddy-boots mode."* Ibid., p. 162.
344   *"wanted to be swept into their abyss of optimism."* Laura Palmer, unpublished manuscript, Palmer's personal papers, p. 2.
345   *"one of his Patton moods."* Stanley Karnow, *Vietnam: A History* (New York: Viking, 1983), p. 652.
345   *"the illusion of peace, the reality of ongoing war."* Marilyn Young, *The Vietnam Wars* (New York: HarperPerennial, 1991), p. 277.
345   *36,000 tons of bombs were dropped.* George Herring, *America's Longest War*, 4th ed. (New York: McGraw-Hill, 2000), p. 316.
345   *"raised by 10 percent the number of American prisoners of war."* Joseph Treaster, "Trial By Fire for the North," *New York Times*, 31 December 1972, p. 3.
346   *"blown to smithereens"* and *"hideousness of it all."* Seymour Hersh, "U.S. Aides Differ Sharply Over Value of the Raids," *New York Times*, 31 December 1972, p. 1.
346   *"like a rich lady."* Laura Palmer, letter to Elly, 28 December 1971, Palmer's personal papers.
346   *"The bombing must be stopped."* "Urge End to War," *New York Times*, 23 December 1972, p. 1.
346   *"a crime against humanity."* Dana Drenkowski, in Henry Maurer, ed., *Strange Ground: An Oral History of Americans in Vietnam* (New York: Avon Books, 1989), p. 549.
346   *Nazi massacres of World War II.* Robert H. Phelps, "U.S., Criticized on Raids, Rebuffs Sweden on Envoy," *New York Times*, 30 December 1972, p. 1.
346   *150,000 North Vietnamese soldiers were in the South.* Christian G. Appy, ed., *Patriots* (New York: Viking, 2003), p. 461.
347   *"signed here today in eerie silence."* Flora Lewis, "Vietnam Peace Pacts Signed; America's Longest War Halts," *New York Times*, 27 January 1973, p. 1.
347   *"maintaining a state of hostility."* Frances FitzGerald, "A Long Way From Peace," *Washington Post*, 28 January 1973, p. B1.
348   *"only war aim that had not lost credibility with the public."* Appy, p. 470.
348   *Description of the first prisoner release.* "Release of Prisoners in Hanoi is Simple and Swift," *New York Times*, 13 February 1973, p. 1.
349   *"and the same expressionless faces."* Tracy Wood, "Spies, Lovers, and Prisoners of War," in *War Torn*, p. 243.
349   *CBS/UPI negotiations for flight to Hanoi.* Ibid., p. 247.
350   *"Is that really Walter Cronkite."* Liz Trotta, *Fighting for Air* (Columbia: University of Missouri Press, 1994), p. 237.
350   *"This moment was one of the most extraordinary."* Ibid., p. 245.
351   *"his only power comes from American aid."* Frances FitzGerald, "Vietnam, Behind the Lines of the 'Cease-Fire' War," *Atlantic*, April 1974, p. 4–18.
351   *"Today you see us in the forest."* H.D.S. Greenway, "A Long Night Visit with the Vietcong," *Washington Post*, 15 March 1973, p. 1.
351   *"talk to anything with round eyes."* Palmer interview, September 11, 2007.
351   *Showed her "all over the dials."* Laura Palmer, letter to Helen Palmer, Laura Palmer's personal papers.

353   *South Vietnam kept losing ground.* Herring, p. 326.

353   *Ignored both the letter and spirit.* Flora Lewis, "A Return to Talking," *New York Times, News of the Week in Review,* 20 May 1975, p. 3.

353   *Even the cast of characters was occasionally the same.* Flora Lewis, "Kissinger and Tho End Talks in Paris," *New York Times,* 24 May 1973, p. 1.

354   *"the fighting is continuing."* Flora Lewis, "Vietnam Now: Pact but No Peace," *New York Times,* 27 April 1970, p. 1.

354   *"I was totally aware of Kate and her work."* Shirley Biagi, Interview 1 with Tad Bartimus, April 25, 1994, Washington DC, for the Women in Journalism Oral History Project of the Washington Press Club Foundation, in the Oral History Collection of the National Press Club Archives, Washington, DC, p. 45.

354   *"folks who looked like me."* Tad Bartimus, "In Country," in *War Torn,* p. 188.

355   *"You will not!"* Ibid., p. 192.

355   *"What did you tell Henri Huet's?"* Ibid., p. 195.

355   *"decent interval."* Ibid., p. 214.

355   *"next best thing to a B-52."* Frank Snepp, in Appy, p. 498.

356   *He even lectured visitors.* James Markham, "U.S. Envoy Runs Right Saigon Ship; Curbs News, Strongly backs Thieu," *New York Times,* 17 January 1974, p. 2.

356   *"It was very strange."* Pamela Sanders, author interview, 26–27 June 1997.

356   *He took Halberstam by the arm.* William Prochnau, *Once Upon a Distant War* (New York: Times Books, 1995), p. 172.

357   *"whenever he was in charge."* David Butler, *The Fall of Saigon* (New York: Simon & Schuster, 1985), p. 435.

357   *"or at least a Communist sympathizer."* Sanders interview.

357   *"stunt with the helmet."* Frank Snepp, author interview, 5 October 2007.

358   *Stories Bartimus pursued.* Bartimus, "In Country," in *War Torn,* p. 208.

358   *"You really couldn't win."* Shirley Biagi, Interview 2 with Tad Bartimus, April 26, 1994, Washington, DC, for the Women in Journalism Oral History Project of the Washington Press Club Foundation, in the Oral History Collection of the National Press Club Archives, Washington, DC, p. 58.

359   *Shelling of Cai Lay schoolyard.* Ibid., p. 217.

359   *"Tracy and I competed head-to-head."* Tad Bartimus, Leonard Lopate Show, WNYC Radio, New York, http://www.wnyc.org/shows/lopate/episodes/2002/12/24/segments/9353.

360   *"without the chiaroscuro."* Laura Palmer, "Saigon: March 1974," *Rolling Stone,* May 9, 1974, p. 10.

360   *"the Nixon Doctrine in its purest form."* Laura Palmer, "Life, and War, Go on in Cambodia," *Rolling Stone,* 26 September 1974, p. 28.

361   *"Before you die like Maggie Higgins."* Tad Bartimus, Oral History, Interview 2, p. 70.

361   *"felt like it was time to leave."* Palmer interview, 20 August 2007.

361   *Manuscripts of broadcasts from Saigon.* Laura Palmer's personal papers made available to the author.

362   *"Onassis money."* Palmer, "Mystery," in *War Torn,* p. 264.

362   *Through the rice-rich Mekong Delta.* David Butler, p. 216.

362   *"to launch an offensive against Saigon."* Arnold Isaacs, *Without Honor* (New York: Vintage Books, 1984), p. 398.

363   *North would need only 20,000 troops.* Ron Yates, "Reds could take capital in 12 hours—U.S. aide," *Chicago Tribune,* April 6, 1975, p. 1.

363   *Would poison their five children and themselves.* Palmer, "Mystery," in *War Torn,* p. 265.

364   *"Promise me it won't be tonight."* Ibid.

364   *Prospect of a Communist bloodbath.* Hilary Brown, ABC News videotape, Vanderbilt Television Archive, 4 April 1975.

364   *"This time they appear to be here to stay."* Hilary Brown, ABC News videotape, Vanderbilt Television Archive, 9 April 1975.

365   *Buying large quantities of sleeping pills.* Ibid., 24 April 1975.

365   *"the one who took Hunter Thompson out."* Ron Yates, author interview, 5 October 2007.

366   *"Frankly, he was scared to death."* Roy Rowan, author interview, 11 May 2007.

366   *"nearly stopped the heart,"* Gloria Emerson, book jacket comment for *The Fall of Saigon*, by David Butler.

366   *"the world of illusions."* Frances FitzGerald, "The End Is the Beginning," *New Republic*, 3 May 1975, p. 7.

366   *"I longed to be in Saigon."* Frances FitzGerald, e-mail to the author, 21 September 2007.

367   *Removed the story from her reality.* Beth Pond, e-mail to the author, 19 October 2007.

367   *"The ghastliness of the war."* Sanders interview.

368   *"I started to feel guilty."* Liz Trotta, author interview, 25 September 2007.

368   *Bartimus in Anchorage and Trung story.* "In Country," in *War Torn*, p. 219.

368   *Relocation of An's family to Washington.* Larry Berman, *Perfect Spy* (New York: Smithsonian Books/Collins, 2007), p. 231.

369   *Certain that an accord would be reached.* Palmer interview, 22 September 2007.

369   *"hovering on the edge of disaster."* Peggy Durdin, "Saigon in the Shadow of Doom," *New York Times Magazine*, 21 November 1954, p. 7.

369   *Tweedledum and Tweedledee.* Dirck Halstead, "White Christmas: The Fall of Saigon," *Digital Journalist*, http://digitaljournalist.org/issue0005/ch5.htm.

370   *"They moved mostly on foot."* Hilary Brown, "Vietnam 10 Years Later," *Globe and Mail*, 27 April 1985, p. 16.

370   *"I found quite impressive."* Malcolm Browne, author interview, 22 December 1997.

371   *"pushing me into deeper waters."* Palmer, "Mystery," in *War Torn*, p. 273.

371   *Martin doubted the runways were unusable.* Butler, p. 387.

371   *"Pack your things."* Laura Palmer, "Drowning in a Sea of Sadness," *Rolling Stone*, 22 June 1975.

371   *"left in the hands of a madman."* Ibid.

372   *"never felt betrayed."* Palmer interview, 11 September 2007.

372   *Had wanted to console her that day.* Palmer, "Mystery," in *War Torn*, p. 277.

373   *"I shall never forget."* Hilary Brown, "Seeking Forgiveness for a Saigon Family," *Toronto Star*, 29 July 1989, p. F 1, http://web.lexis-nexis.com.proxy.lib.odu.edu/universe/document?_m =cld79bcf818bc9f5.

373   *"It's a child."* Hilary Brown, "Vietnam 10 Years Later," p. 16, http://global.activs.com/ proxy.lib.odu.edu/ha/dfault.aspx.

373   *"Leave it to the goddam Commies?"* Ibid.

374   *"Last night they gave me an M-16."* Palmer, "Drowning in a Sea of Sadness," *Rolling Stone*, 22 June 1975.

374   *"Soldiers guarding the gates of Tan Son Nhut."* Robert Wiener, author interview, 7 October 2007.

374   *"everybody ran like crazy."* Ibid.

374   *She, too, would push and shove.* Palmer, "Drowning in a Sea of Sadness."

375   *"You fifteen people on that chopper. Run, Now, Go, Run."* Ibid.

375   *She clutched his hand.* Laura Palmer, "Mystery," in *War Torn*, p. 270.

375   *"and you stand with awe."* Palmer, author interview, 11 September 2007.

Epilogue

377   *"recorded better by women."* Richard Eder, "Shallow Graves," *Los Angeles Times*, 20 April 1986, Sec. V, p. 3

379   *"Chain them to the memorial."* "We're Still Prisoners of War," *Newsweek*, 15 April 1985, p. 34.

381   *"cultural anthropologist."* David Halberstam, author interview, 7 January 1997.

382   *"You need to be nimble."* Rick Lyman, "Martha Gellhorn, Daring Writer, Dies at 89." *New York Times*, 17 February 1998, p. 1.

382   *"did irreparable damage to America in history."* Martha Gellhorn, *The Face of War* (New York: Atlantic Monthly Press, 1988), p. 275.

383   *"too old to keep up with frontline reporting."* Kate Webb, author interview, 17–20 February 2002.

383   *"Non! Je ne regrette rien."* "No Regrets," *Correspondent*, May–June 2007, p. 7.

384   *"the tantrums at the dinner table."* Carol Pogash, "The Other Veterans: Reflecting on the

Shooting Through Decades of Battle," *New York Times,* 21 April, 2005.

384   *U.C. Berkeley exhibit information.* Steven Winn, "What Can Photos Teach Us About War? Have a Look." *San Francisco Chronicle,* 19 April 2005, p. E1.

384   *"This is vintage Pond at her best."* http://www.brookings.edu/press/Books/2006/endgamein thebalkans.aspx.

385   *"Japan, the Soviet Union, Europe."* Elizabeth Pond, e-mail correspondence with the author, 11 February 2008.

385   *The "brunette wading into middle age."* Liz Trotta, *Fighting for Air* (Columbia: University of Missouri Press, 1994), p. 322.

386   *610 people awaiting evacuation from the compound.* Flora Lewis, "Cambodia Orders Foreigners Out," *New York Times,* 30 April 1975, p. 1.

386   *Debate over French defense policies.* Flora Lewis, "Arms and Detente for France," *New York Times,* 6 June 1980, p. 27.

386   *Nimble and ferocious.* "1922–2002, Flora Lewis—an Appreciation," *International Herald Tribune,* 3 June 2002, www.iht.com/articles/2002/06/03/edflora_ed3_.php.

386   *"What a wonderful time."* Flora Lewis, "Foreign Affairs: People Make History," *New York Times,* 29 December 1990, p. 27.

386   *"out-drink anyone who came within her magic circle."* "1922–2002, Flora Lewis—an Appreciation."

387   *"so I abandoned television."* Laura Palmer, author interview, 20 August 2007.

388   *"each bullet that took a life."* Laura Palmer, *Shrapnel in the Heart* (New York: Random House, 1987), p. xiv.

388   *"There was so much pain and no one knew it."* Palmer interview, 11 September 2007.

388   *"boys at heart who got dazzled."* Scott Simon, National Public Radio, *Weekend Edition,* 7 August 2004, http://global.factiva.com/ha/default.aspx.

Selected Bibliography

Alsop, Stewart. *The Center: People and Power in Political Washington.* New York: Harper & Row, 1968.

Anson, Robert Sam. *War News: A Young Reporter in Indochina.* New York: Simon & Schuster, 1989.

Appy, Christian G. *Patriots, The Vietnam War Remembered from All Sides.* New York: Viking, 2003.

Appy, Chris, ed. *Cold War Constructions.* Amherst: University of Massachusetts Press, 2000.

Arnett, Peter. *Live From the Battlefield: From Vietnam to Baghdad, 35 Years in the World's War Zones.* New York: Simon & Schuster, 1994.

Arnold, James R. *First Domino, Eisenhower, The Military and America's Intervention in Vietnam.* New York: William Morrow and Company, 1991.

Beasley, Maurine H. and Sheila J. Gibbons. *Taking Their Place: A Documentary History of Women and Journalism.* Washington, D.C.: American University Press, 1993.

Behr, Edward. *Bearings: A Foreign Correspondent's Life Behind the Lines.* New York: The Viking Press, 1978.

Berger, Meyer. *The Story of the New York Times.* New York: Simon & Schuster, 1951.

Berman, Larry. *Perfect Spy: The Incredible Double Life of Pham Xuan An.* New York: Smithsonian Books, 2007.

Born, Donna Jones, "The Reporting of American Women Correspondents from the Vietnam War." PhD diss., Michigan State University, 1987.

Boylan, James. *Pulitzer's School: Columbia University's School of Journalism, 1903–2003.* New York: Columbia University Press, 2003.

Bradley, Mark Philip. *Imagining Vietnam & America: The Making of Post Colonial Vietnam, 1919–1950.* Chapel Hill: University of North Carolina Press, 2000.

Bradley, Patricia. *Women and the Press: A Struggle for Equality.* Evanston: Northwestern University Press, 2005.

Braestrup, Peter. *Big Story: How the American Press and Television Reported and Interpreted the Crisis of Tet 1968 in Vietnam and Washington.* New Haven: Yale University Press, 1983.

Breines, Wini. *Young, White and Miserable.* Boston: Beacon Press, 1992.

Brelis, Dean and Jill Krementz. *The Face of South Vietnam.* Boston: Houghton Mifflin Company, 1968.

Brinkley, Douglas. *Tour of Duty: John Kerry and the Vietnam War.* New York: William Morrow, 2004.

Browne, Malcolm W. *Muddy Boots and Red Socks: A Reporter's Life.* New York: Times Books, 1993.

Buckley, Gail. *American Patriots: The Story of Blacks in the Military from the Revolution to Desert Storm.* New York: Random House, 2001.

Buckley, William F. *God and the Man at Yale: The Superstitions of Academic Freedom.* Chicago: Regnery, 1951.

Butler, David. *The Fall of Saigon.* New York: Simon & Schuster, 1985.

Chafe, William H. *The Unfinished Journey: America Since World War II.* New York: Oxford University Press, 1986.

Chapelle, Dickey. *What's A Woman Doing Here?* New York: William Morrow and Company, 1962.

Currey, Cecil. *Edward Lansdale: The Unquiet American.* Boston: Houghton Mifflin Company, 1988.

Dallek, Robert. *Nixon and Kissinger: Partners in Power.* New York: HarperCollins, 2007.

Diamonstein, Barbaralee. *Open Secrets.* New York: Viking Press, 1970.

Dickerson, Nancy. *Among those Present: A Reporter's View of Twenty-five Years in Washington.* New York: Random House, 1976.

Dudman, Richard. *40 Days with the Enemy: The Story of a Journalist Held Captive by Guerrillas in Cambodia.* New York: Liveright, 1971.

Duiker, William J. *Ho Chi Minh: A Life.* New York: Hyperion, 2000.

Ebener, Charlotte. *No Facilities for Women.* New York: Alfred A. Knopf, 1955.

Edwards, Julia. *Women of the World: The Great Foreign Correspondents*. Boston: Houghton Mifflin Company, 1988.

Ellis, Frederick. "Dickey Chapelle: A Reporter and her Work." Master's Thesis, University of Wisconsin, 1972.

Ellsberg, Daniel. *Secrets: A Memoir of Vietnam and the Pentagon Papers*. New York: Viking, 2002.

Elwood Akers, Virginia. *Women War Correspondents in the Vietnam War, 1961–1975*. Metuchen, N.J.: Scarecrow, 1988.

Emerson, Gloria. *Gaza: A Year in the Intifada*. New York: Atlantic Monthly Press, 1991.

———. *Loving Graham Greene*. New York: Random House, 2000.

———. *Some American Men*. New York: Simon & Schuster, 1985.

———. *Winners & Losers: Battles, Retreats, Gains, Losses and Ruins From a Long War*. New York: Random House, 1976.

Emery, Edwin. *The Press and America: An Interpretive History of the Mass Media*. Englewood Cliffs, N.J.: Prentice-Hall, 1972.

Epstein, Edward J. *News From Nowhere*. New York: Random House, 1973.

Faas, Horst and Tim Page, eds. *Requiem: By the Photographers Who Died in Vietnam and Indochina*. New York: Random House, 1997.

Fall, Bernard. *Hell in a Very Small Place: The Siege of Dien Bien Phu*. New York: Vintage Books, 1968.

———. *The Street Without Joy: Indochina at War 1946 –1954*. Harrisburg, Pa.: Stackpole Press, 1961.

———. *Vietnam Witness 1953–1966*. New York: Praeger, 1966.

Fishel, Wesley, ed. *Problems of Freedom: South Vietnam Since Independence*. New York: Free Press of Glencoe, 1961.

FitzGerald, Frances. *Fire in the Lake: The Vietnamese and The American in Vietnam*. New York: Atlantic Monthly Press, 1972.

Frank, Reuven. *Out of Thin Air: The Brief Wonderful Life of Network News*. New York: Simon & Schuster, 1991.

Friedan, Betty. *The Feminine Mystique*. New York: W. W. Norton and Company, 1963.

Gellhorn, Martha. *The Face of War*. New York: Atlantic Monthly Press, 1988.

Gilbert, Marc Jason and William Head, eds. *The Tet Offensive*. Westport, Conn.: Praeger Publishers, 1996.

Gitlin, Todd. *The Sixties*. New York: Bantam Books, 1989.

Gray, J. Glenn. *The Warriors: Reflections on Men in Battle*. New York: Harper & Row, 1970.

Greene, Graham. *The Quiet American*. New York: Viking, 1956.

Halberstam, David. *The Best and the Brightest*. New York: Random House, 1972.

———. *The Coldest Winter: America and the Korean War*. New York: Hyperion, 2007.

———. *The Fifties*. New York: Villard Books, 1993.

———. *The Making of a Quagmire*. New York: Random House, 1965.

———. *The Powers That Be*. New York: Alfred A. Knopf, 1979.

Hammond, William, M. *Public Affairs: The Military and the Media, 1962–1968*. Washington D.C.: Center of Military History, U.S. Army, 1988.

———. *Public Affairs: The Military and the Media, 1968–1973*. Washington, D.C.: Center of Military History, U.S. Army, 1996.

Hallin, Daniel C. *The 'Uncensored' War: The Media and Vietnam*. New York: Oxford University Press, 1986.

Hearst, William Randolph Jr. and Jack Casserly. *The Hearsts: Father and Son*. Niwot, Colo.: Roberts Rinehart Publishers, 1991.

Herr, Michael. *Dispatches*. New York: Alfred A. Knopf, 1978.

Herring, George. *America's Longest War: The United States in Vietnam, 1950–1975*. Fourth Edition. New York: McGraw-Hill, 2000.

Hersh, Seymour. *The Dark Side of Camelot*. Boston: Little Brown & Company, 1997.

Hickey, Gerald. *The Village in Vietnam*. New Haven: Yale University Press, 1964.

Higgins, Marguerite. *Our Vietnam Nightmare*. New York: Harper and Row, 1963.

Hinckle, Warren and William Turner. *Deadly Secrets*. New York: Thunder's Mouth Press, 1989.

Hodgson, Godfrey. *America in Our Time*. New York: Vintage Books, 1976.

Howe, Peter. *Shooting Under Fire*. New York: Artisan, 2002.

Huston, John. *An Open Book*. New York: Alfred A. Knopf, 1980.

Isaacs, Arnold R. *Without Honor: Defeat in Vietnam & Cambodia*. New York: Vintage Books, 1984.

Kalb, Marvin and Bernard. *Kissinger*. New York: Little Brown & Company, 1974.

Karnow, Stanley. *Vietnam: A History*. New York: Viking Press, 1983.

Kluger, Richard. *Simple Justice: The History of Brown v. Board of Education and Black America's struggle for equality*. New York: Alfred A. Knopf, 1976.

———. *The Paper: The Life and Death of the New York Herald Tribune*. New York: Alfred A. Knopf, 1986.

Knightley, Philip. *The First Casualty: From the Crimea to Vietnam: The War Correspondent as Hero, Propagandist, and Myth Maker*. New York: Harcourt Brace Jovanovich, 1975.

Kolko, Gabriel. *Anatomy of a War: Vietnam, the United States, and the Modern Historical Experience*. New York: The New Press, 1985.

Landers, James. *The Weekly War, News Magazines and Vietnam*. Columbia: University of Missouri Press, 2004.

Lansdale, Edward G. *In The Midst of Wars*. New York: Harper & Row, 1972.

Laurence, John. *The Cat From Hue: A Vietnam War Story*. New York: PublicAffairs, 2002.

Leroy, Catherine. *Under Fire: Great Writers and Photographers in Vietnam*. New York: Random House, 2005.

Lubow, Arthur. *The Reporter Who Would Be King: A Biography of Richard Harding Davis*. New York: Charles Scribner's Sons, 1992.

Luce, Don and John Sommer. *Vietnam: The Unheard Voices*. Ithaca, N.Y.: Cornell University Press, 1969.

Martin, Christine. "The Women Correspondents in Vietnam: Historical Analysis and Oral Histories." Master's Thesis, University of Maryland, 1988.

Marzolf, Marian. *Up From the Footnote: A History of Women Journalists*. New York: Hastings House, 1977.

Maurer, Henry. *Strange Ground: An Oral History of Americans in Vietnam, 1945–1975*. New York: Avon Books, 1989

May, Antoinette. *Witness to War: A Biography of Marguerite Higgins*. New York: Beaufort Books, Inc., 1983.

McCoy, Alfred W. *The Politics of Heroin in Southeast Asia*. New York: Harper and Row, 1972.

Mecklin, John. *Mission in Torment: An Intimate Account of the U.S. Role in Vietnam*. New York: Doubleday, 1965.

Michener, James A. *The Bridge at Andau*. New York: Random House, 1957.

Mills, Kay. *A Place in the News: From the Women's Pages to the Front Page*. New York: Dodd, Mead & Company, 1988.

Moorehead, Caroline. *Gellhorn: A Twentieth Century Life*. New York: Henry Holt, 2003.

Myrdal, Gunnar. *An American Dilemma; the Negro Problem and Modern Democracy*. New York: Harper & Brothers, 1944.

Nolan, Keith William. *Battle for Hue: Tet, 1968*. Novato, Calif.: Presidio Press, 1983.

Oberdorfer, Don. *Tet!* New York: Doubleday and Company, 1971.

Ostroff, Roberta. *Fire in the Wind: The Life of Dickey Chapelle*. New York: Ballantine Books, 1992.

Palmer, Laura. *Shrapnel in the Heart: Letters and Remembrances from the Vietnam Veterans Memorial*. New York: Random House, 1987.

Pisor, Robert. *The End of the Line: The Siege of Khe Sanh*. New York: W. W. Norton & Company, 1982.

Porter, Gareth, ed. *Vietnam: A History in Documents*. New York: New American Library, 1979.

Pratt, John Clark, ed. *The Quiet American: Text and Criticism*. New York: Penguin Books, 1996.

Prochnau, William. *Once Upon A Distant War: David Halberstam, Neil Sheehan, Peter Arnett—Young Correspondents and Their Early Vietnam Battles*. New York: Times Books, 1995.

Pyle, Richard and Horst Faas. *Lost Over Laos: A True Story of Tragedy, Mystery, and Friendship*. Cambridge, Mass.: Da Capo Press, 2002.

Reuven, Frank. *Out of Thin Air: The Brief and Wonderful Life of Network News*. New York: Simon & Schuster, 1991.

Roberts, Gene and Hank Klibanoff. *The Race Beat: The Press, The Civil Rights Struggle and the Awakening of a Nation.* New York: Alfred A. Knopf, 2006.

Robertson, Nan. *The Girls in the Balcony: Women, Men, and The New York Times.* New York: Random House, 1992.

Rollyson, Carl. *Nothing Ever Happens to the Brave: The Story of Martha Gellhorn.* New York: St. Martin's Press, 1990.

Ross, Ishbel. *Ladies of The Press: The Story of Women in Journalism by an Insider.* New York: Harper and Brothers, 1936.

Rubin, Joan Shelley. *The Making of Middlebrow Culture.* Chapel Hill: University of North Carolina Press, 1992.

Safer, Morley. *Flashbacks: On Returning to Vietnam.* New York: Random House, 1990.

Sanders, Pamela. *Miranda.* New York: Little Brown & Company, 1978.

Seebohm, Caroline. *No Regrets: The Life of Marietta Tree.* New York: Simon & Schuster, 2003.

Shawcross, William. *Sideshow: Kissinger, Nixon and the Destruction of Cambodia.* New York: Simon & Schuster, 1979.

Sheehan, Neil. *A Bright Shining Lie: John Paul Vann and America in Vietnam.* New York: Random House, 1988.

Snepp, Frank. *A Decent Interval: An Insider's Account of Saigon's Indecent End.* New York: Random House, 1977.

Sorel, Nancy Caldwell, *The Women Who Wrote the War.* New York: Arcade Publishing, 1999.

Stein, M. L. *Under Fire: The Story of American War Correspondents.* Parsippany, N.J.: Silver Burdett Press, 1995.

Sterba, Jim. *Frankie's Place.* New York: Grove Press, 2003.

Streitmatter, Rodger. *Raising Her Voice: African-American Women Journalists Who Changed History.* Lexington: The University Press of Kentucky, 1994.

Swigart, Edmund K. *An Emerson-Benson Saga.* Baltimore: Gateway Press, Inc., 1994.

Talese, Gay. *The Kingdom and the Power.* New York: The World Publishing Company, 1969.

Tarbell, Ida M. *The History of Standard Oil Company.* New York: Harper & Row, 1955.

Thomas, Evan. *The Very Best Men: Four Who Dared: The Early Years of the CIA.* New York: Simon & Schuster, 1995.

Tifft, Susan and Alex Jones. *The Trust: The Private and Powerful Family Behind the New York Times.* New York: Little Brown & Company, 1999.

Tregaskis, Richard. *Vietnam Diary.* New York: Holt Rinehart and Winston, 1963.

Trotta, Liz. *Fighting for Air: In the Trenches with Television News.* Columbia: University of Missouri Press, 1994.

———. *Jude: A Pilgrimage to the Saint of Last Resort.* San Francisco: Harper San Francisco, 1998.

Utley, Garrick. *You Should Have Been Here Yesterday.* New York: PublicAffairs, 2000.

Volkert, Kurt and T. Jeff Williams. *A Cambodian Odyssey and The Deaths of 25 Journalists.* Lincoln, Neb.: Writer's Showcase, 2001.

Wade, Betsy, ed. *Forward Positions: The War Correspondence of Homer Bigart.* Fayetteville: University of Arkansas Press, 1992.

Wagner, Lilya. *Women War Correspondents of World War II.* New York: Greenwood Press, 1989.

Wambold, Carolyn. "Women of the Mosquito Press." PhD Diss., University of Texas, Austin, 1990.

Webb, Kate. *On the Other Side: 23 Days with the Viet Cong.* New York: Quadrangle Books, 1971.

West, Helen, ed. *Insight Guides: Vietnam.* Hong Kong: APA Publications, 1991.

Westmoreland, William C. *A Soldier Reports.* New York: Da Capo Press, 1989.

Wicker, Tom. *On Press.* New York: Viking, 1978.

Wolseley, Roland E. *The Black Press.* Ames: Iowa State University Press, 1971.

Yoder, Edwin Jr. *Joseph Alsop's Cold War: A Study of Journalistic Influence and Intrigue.* Chapel Hill: University of North Carolina Press, 1995.

Young, Marilyn. *The Vietnam Wars 1945–1990.* New York: Harper Perennial, 1991.

Interview List

Pham Xuan An
David Anrade
Dave Anderson
Arthur Arundel
Tad Bartimus
Elizabeth Beechner
Marylin Bender
Ralph Blumenthal
James Boylan
Benjamin Bradlee
Dean Brelis
Malcolm Browne
Fox Butterfield
Denis Cameron
John Carland
Gloria Clyne
Archie Clapp
Elyette Conein
Neale Copple
Les Crystal
Cecil B. Currey
Mary H. Dohmen
Richard Dudman
Richard Duncan
Daniel Ellsberg
Frederick Ellis
George Esper
Horst Faas
Denby Fawcett
Frances FitzGerald
Reuven Frank
Gerald Frasier
Wilber E. Garrett
John M. Gates Jr.
Peter Gates

Barbara Gluck
James Greenfield
Peter Grose
David Halberstam
William Hammond
Roger Hanson
Margaret Harrigan
Gerald Hickey
James Hudson
Richard Hughes
Victor Hugo
Ward Just
Stanley Karnow
Jurate Kazickas
Jill Krementz
Grace Lake
A. J. Langguth
Edie Lederer
Catherine Leroy
Phyllis Levin
Flora Lewis
Florence Vallencourt
    Lindsay
Don Luce
Robert McCabe
Marion Meyer
Rachel Miller
Nancy Moran
Laura Palmer
Iver Peterson
Rufus C. Phillips III
Elizabeth Pond
William Prochnau
Richard Pyle
Joseph Redick

Jack Reynolds
Nan Robertson
Roy Rowan
Zasha Z. Rogers
Pamela Sanders
Sydney Schanberg
John Sharkey
Jack Shepherd
Alvin Shuster
Allan Siegal
Terence Smith
Frank Snepp
Ron Steinman
James Sterba
Nancy Caldwell Sorel
Seymour Topping
Joseph Treaster
Jacqueline Trescott
Liz Trotta
Emma Valeriano
Richard Wald
Kate Webb
Bernard Weinraub
Anne Westerfield
Putney Westerfield
Craig Whitney
Marilyn Widler
Robert Wiener
Ogden Williams
Jackie Williamson
Frank Wisner Jr.
Christopher Wren
Ron Yates
Barry Zorthian

Acknowledgments

ANY BOOK THAT takes years to come to life owes a measure of its existence to the kindness and forbearance of advocates, believers, and cheerleaders. Family members and close friends who watched for a decade and wondered, "what's taking her so long," for the most part kept those thoughts to themselves. For that self-restraint, I am profoundly grateful.

My deepest appreciation goes to the women who are my subjects in this book—for the extraordinary lives they lived; for their courage, imagination, and abundant talents, all of which fused into the marvelous stories I've had the joy of telling here. Their experiences and accomplishments have given shape to my own life as a writer and elevated me to the ranks of those who call themselves historians.

I applaud the three graduate students who long ago recognized how little of the journalism produced by women in Vietnam had been woven into histories of the war. Too frequently, as these three studies demonstrated, the noteworthy achievements of so many women, if mentioned at all, were portrayed as a minor if amusing endnote in the larger telling of history. Often the women who reported on the war, far-ranging though their work was, were all lumped together in an undefinable mish-mash, as if gender delineated a particular type of journalism. The ground covered by Donna Jones Born in her 1987 doctoral dissertation, and Virginia Elwood-Akers in 1981 and Christine Martin in 1988, in their master's theses, created the foundation for this and any other exploration of the women who were journalists in Vietnam. It is they who toiled in what is left of the military accreditation files, had interviews, exchanged correspondence, and compiled oral histories of many women at a time when their recollections were far fresher than they are today.

This project was embraced by many individuals whose help I sought. The aid of Nan Robertson and Marylin Bender was especially valuable in providing an insight into the role of women in the structure of newspaper fashion pages in the 1950s and 1960s. My conversations with both women, along with Robertson's book, *The Girls in the Balcony*, gave me a sense of how circumscribed opportunities for women were during the years following World War II. Robertson's book provides a rich understanding of the Women's

Caucus and the battle royal its brave members waged at the *New York Times* for equal opportunity and equal pay. Marian Marzolf's *Up From the Footnote,* a sweeping overview of the role of women in journalism through three centuries of American history, was another helpful study. I am thankful also for her generosity in giving me her personal set of the invaluable resource, the Washington Press Club Foundation's "Women in Journalism" oral history project. I have made extensive use of that material, especially the transcripts of conversations with Ethel Payne, Flora Lewis, and Tad Bartimus.

Craig Whitney of the *New York Times* has my enduring gratitude, too. I turned to him again and again for information about the *Times*' Saigon bureau, about Gloria Emerson and Flora Lewis, and for countless other favors. Allan Siegal, a former assistant managing editor at the *Times*, shared with me pieces of his vast institutional memory to help me put together my portrait of the newspaper's Saigon bureau and assisted my efforts in tracking down an assortment of other information about New York City's great gray lady. I have also turned repeatedly to William Prochnau, in whose book, *Once Upon a Distant War,* I found inspiration, for advice and guidance in finding sources of information.

As is the case with any work of history, this book also owes its existence to the help of staffers in a dozen or more libraries. First among them is Karen Vaughan, who, in the assortment of official positions she has held in Old Dominion University's Perry Library, has for more than a decade remained my unofficial "go-to" person with all manner of research questions. I also owe a special thank you as well to J. C. Johnson of the Howard Gotlieb Archival Research Center at Boston University and Harold L. Miller at the State Historical Society of Wisconsin. Jackie Williamson of the Thayer County Historical Society gave me an immense understanding of life in the Nebraska plains in the 1940s and 1950s and Shirley Soenksen at the University of Northern Colorado Libraries searched the James A. Michener files to anwer my questions. I am also grateful to the staff of the Benson Memorial Library in Titusville, Pennsylvania.

The assistance of several graduate students at Old Dominion University cannot go unremarked. Rania Mahmoud, a Fulbright scholar from Egypt who was my graduate assistant for two years, ranks as the most tireless of them all. My gratitude goes as well to Dee Heart and Andrea Murphy, and Kyra Kaszynski, a graduate student at Columbia University who was my New York City "go-to" person. During one of my two trips to Vietnam, when Dao Thai Hai was my interpreter and driver, and all around helper. His able assistance gave me an understanding of the commitment so many Vietnamese made to Americans decades ago. Dick Hull, a retired Marine officer and former neighbor who became my de facto military researcher on all questions related to "the Few, the Proud."

At Da Capo Press I am grateful for the patience, understanding, and ever-sunny disposition of Bob Pigeon, whose faith in this project sustained both it and me. My able and generous editors, Erica Smith and Jennifer Blakebrough-Raeburn, have invested themselves in this work as if it were there own.

I will forego the temptation to recite a chorus of gratitude to the scores of people I interviewed, memorable though they most assuredly were. Two, however, deserve special mention for their novelty and larger significance. My six-hour conversation with Pham Xuan An in the rooftop dining room of Saigon's Majestic Hotel ranks as one of the most extraordinary interviews in my working lifetime as a scholar and journalist. An, who in the aftermath of the war was revealed to have been a North Vietnamese agent, was, it seemed, delighted to revisit these years of his life and his associations with so many of the women who are part of this book. A few of his revelations, particularly about his role in securing the release of Elizabeth Pond, were quite astonishing. Following David Halberstam's untimely death in April 2007, I reread my notes of our 1998 interview and realized, in ways that I had not before, how much his responses to my questions and the obvious thought he had given the subject in advance of our conversation served to validate my still-nascent undertaking.

It has taken a measure of fortitude to acknowledge, even to myself, just how long this project has been aborning. My work as a professor continued during most of those years, to be sure. Still, is was a long, long time, as I was forced to acknowledge when I reviewed my endnotes and confronted dates in the citations of my earliest interviews. Frances FitzGerald graciously sat down with me for the first of our interviews June of 1997. Our talk preceded by a few days a trip that took me first to Paris, where I spoke with Flora Lewis, later to Germany, for conversations with Elizabeth Pond and Pamela Sanders, and finally to Vietnam, where I visited places with names that echoed back to long ago headlines. A full decade elapsed between those first conversations and the fall of 2007 when I concluded a series of interviews with Laura Palmer, one of the later arrivals on the Saigon scene.

Many, many family members and friends have kept the faith during these years. My siblings Janet Hobbs, and Karl and Kurt Hoffmann, are an ongoing source of strength. Friends, too, have sustained me, chief among them Harriet Kesselman and Debora Meltz, who seem eternally interested in my adventures, as does my lifelong friend Louise VanderHaeghen. Enduring friendships with Walt Harrington and Beryl Basher, both of whom read the manuscript, have been no less fortifying. Thanks also to Anne Gray, my sister-in-law and cheerleader, whose faith in my abilities often exceeds my own.

It is my patient husband to whom I owe my greatest appreciation. My earliest work on this book predates our marriage, so he had little idea of how large—and occasionally unwelcome—a place it would take in our lives. He is an ever-supportive presence, helping me always to be the best that I can be.

Index